Lecture Notes in Computer Science 15663

Founding Editors

Gerhard Goos
Juris Hartmanis

AF172768

The series Lecture Notes in Computer Science (LNCS), including its subseries Lecture Notes in Artificial Intelligence (LNAI) and Lecture Notes in Bioinformatics (LNBI), has established itself as a medium for the publication of new developments in computer science and information technology research, teaching, and education.

LNCS enjoys close cooperation with the computer science R & D community, the series counts many renowned academics among its volume editors and paper authors, and collaborates with prestigious societies. Its mission is to serve this international community by providing an invaluable service, mainly focused on the publication of conference and workshop proceedings and postproceedings. LNCS commenced publication in 1973.

Piotr Didyk · Junhui Hou

Editors

Computational Visual Media

13th International Conference, CVM 2025
Hong Kong SAR, China, April 19–21, 2025
Proceedings, Part I

Editors
Piotr Didyk 🆔
Università della Svizzera italiana
Lugano-Viganello, Switzerland

Junhui Hou 🆔
Department of Computer Science
City University of Hong Kong
Kowloon, Hong Kong

ISSN 0302-9743   ISSN 1611-3349 (electronic)
Lecture Notes in Computer Science
ISBN 978-981-96-5808-4   ISBN 978-981-96-5809-1 (eBook)
https://doi.org/10.1007/978-981-96-5809-1

This Springer imprint is published by the registered company Springer Nature Singapore Pte Ltd.
The registered company address is: 152 Beach Road, #21-01/04 Gateway East, Singapore 189721, Singapore

If disposing of this product, please recycle the paper.

Preface

The 13th International Conference on Computational Visual Media (CVM 2025) was held on April 19–21, 2025, in Hong Kong, China. With the rapid development of Internet technology, large-scale visual data has become increasingly accessible, presenting significant opportunities for novel visual information processing and commercial applications. The Computational Visual Media Conference series provides a platform for researchers and practitioners to exchange cutting-edge research ideas and showcase practical advancements in various domains and applications of visual media.

The primary objective of this conference series is to foster cross-disciplinary research that integrates computer graphics, computer vision, machine learning, image processing, video processing, visualization, and geometric computing. We seek original research contributions in areas related to the classification, composition, retrieval, synthesis, and understanding of visual media.

CVM 2025 received 335 valid paper submissions. With the invaluable support of 193 international experts on our Program Committee, we conducted a rigorous review process to ensure the highest quality of accepted papers. Each submission was carefully evaluated by three reviewers, selected based on their expertise and research interests. The program co-chairs made final decisions on the submissions after considering reviewer feedback, categorizing papers as either conditionally accepted for the journal track, conditionally accepted as a poster paper, or rejected. Conditionally accepted poster papers underwent a shepherding process to ensure necessary revisions were incorporated. To maintain the integrity and fairness of the review process, submissions co-authored by a program chair or committee member were assigned to other program chairs or committee members for evaluation.

Out of 335 submissions, 33 papers were accepted as journal track papers, and 67 papers were published in the proceedings (acceptance rate: 29.8%). The journal track papers were conditionally accepted for publication in leading journals in the fields of computer graphics and visual media.

We extend our sincere gratitude to everyone who contributed their time and expertise to the review process and the success of CVM 2025. We thank all authors for their submissions, the members of the CVM 2025 Program Committee, and the external reviewers for their invaluable efforts. We are also grateful to Shi-Min Hu for his support in conference management and coordination with the journals, Taijiang Mu for managing the submission system, and Springer Nature for publishing the CVM 2025 proceedings in the Lecture Notes in Computer Science (LNCS) series. Finally, we deeply appreciate the unwavering support of the CVM Steering Committee.

March 2025

Piotr Didyk
Junhui Hou

Organization

Conference Co-chairs

Hongbo Fu   Hong Kong University of Science and Technology, China

Karan Singh   University of Toronto, Canada

Program Co-chairs

Piotr Didyk   Università della Svizzera italiana, Switzerland

Junhui Hou   City University of Hong Kong, China

Publication Chair

Shi-Min Hu   Tsinghua University, China

AMC AI Film Festival Chair

Anyi Rao   Hong Kong University of Science and Technology, China

Organization Co-chairs

Ping Li   Hong Kong Polytechnic University, China

Hui Ye   Hong Kong University of Science and Technology, China

Organizing Committee

Tai-Jiang Mu   Tsinghua University, China

Jiaye Leng   City University of Hong Kong, China

Chufeng Xiao   Hong Kong University of Science and Technology, China

Program Committee

Francesco Banterle	ISTI-CNR, Italy
Bedrich Benes	Purdue University, USA
Amit Bermano	Tel-Aviv University, Israel
Mikhail Bessmeltsev	University of Montreal, Canada
Jun-Xiong Cai	Huawei Technologies, China
Marcel Campen	Osnabrück University, Germany
Juan Cao	Xiamen University, China
Mingwei Cao	Anhui University, China
Yanpei Cao	VAST, USA
Haoxiang Chen	Tsinghua University, China
Jie Chen	Hong Kong Baptist University, China
Xuejin Chen	University of Science and Technology of China, China
Zhiwen Chen	City University of Hong Kong, China
Zhonggui Chen	Xiamen University, China
Mingming Cheng	Nankai University, China
Xianjing Cheng	Harbin Institute of Technology, China
Zhanglin Cheng	Shenzhen Institutes of Advanced Technology, China
Ming-Te Chi	National Chengchi University, Taiwan
Hung-Kuo Chu	National Tsing Hua University, Taiwan
Bailin Deng	Cardiff University, UK
Yoshinori Dobashi	Hokkaido University, Japan
Minjing Dong	City University of Hong Kong, China
Weiming Dong	Institute of Automation, CAS, China
Xiao Dong	BNU-HKBU United International College, China
Zhiyang Dou	University of Hong Kong, China
Zhengjun Du	Qinghai University, China
Hui Fang	Loughborough University, UK
Xiaonan Fang	Macau University of Science and Technology, China
Bin Feng	Huazhong University of Science and Technology, China
Lin Gao	Institute of Computing, CAS, China
Jie Guo	Nanjing University, China
Menghao Guo	Tsinghua University, China
Xiaohu Guo	University of Texas at Dallas, USA
Ruize Han	Shenzhen Institute of Advanced Technology, CAS, China
Ying He	Nanyang Technological University, Singapore

Zhibin He	Northwestern Polytechnical University, China
Kai Hormann	Università della Svizzera italiana, Switzerland
Fei Hou	Institute of Software, CAS, China
Jinhui Hou	City University of Hong Kong, China
Ruizhen Hu	Shenzhen University, China
Wei Hu	Peking University, China
Haibin Huang	ByteDance, USA
Shi-Sheng Huang	Beijing Normal University, China
Xiaolei Huang	Penn State University, USA
Xingchang Huang	Max Planck Institute for Informatics, Germany
Yuheng Jia	Southeast University, China
Luo Jiang	Nanjing University of Science and Technology, China
Yu Jiang	City University of Hong Kong, China
Xiaogang Jin	Zhejiang University, China
Petr Kellnhofer	TU Delft, The Netherlands
Jiri Kosinka	University of Groningen, The Netherlands
Manuel Lagunas	Google, USA
Yu-Kun Lai	Cardiff University, UK
Rushi Lan	Guilin University of Electronic Technology, China
Thomas Leimkühler	Max Planck Institute for Informatics, Germany
Chenhui Li	East China Normal University, China
Feng Li	Hefei University of Technology, China
Haodong Li	Shenzhen University, China
Hua Li	Hunan University, China
Jinjiang Li	Shandong Technology and Business University, China
Xin Li	Texas A&M University, USA
Zhouhui Lian	Peking University, China
Cheng Lin	University of Hong Kong, China
I-Chen Lin	National Chiao Tung University, Taiwan
Juncong Lin	Xiamen University, China
Yuji Lin	Xi'an Jiaotong University, China
Zheng Lin	Tsinghua University, China
Hanchao Liu	Tsinghua University, China
Libin Liu	Peking University, China
Ligang Liu	University of Science and Technology of China, China
Shixia Liu	Tsinghua University, China
Tiantian Liu	Taichi Graphics, China
Xialei Liu	Nankai University, China
Xinyu Liu	City University of Hong Kong, China

Yuan Liu	University of Hong Kong, China
Yue Liu	University of the Chinese Academy of Sciences, China
Ziquan Liu	Queen Mary University of London, UK
Xiaoxiao Long	University of Hong Kong, China
Xuequan Lu	University of Western Australia, Australia
Chongyang Ma	ByteDance, USA
Jiawei Ma	City University of Hong Kong, China
Kede Ma	City University of Hong Kong, China
Kwan-Liu Ma	University of California, Davis, USA
Lizhuang Ma	Shanghai Jiao Tong University, China
Rui Ma	Jilin University, China
Weiyin Ma	City University of Hong Kong, China
Zhan Ma	Nanjing University, China
Aihua Mao	South China University of Technology, China
Tai-Jiang Mu	Tsinghua University, China
Yongwei Nie	South China University of Technology, China
Fuzhao Ou	City University of Hong Kong, China
Fabio Pellacini	Sapienza University of Rome, Italy
Sida Peng	Zhejiang University, China
Yifan Peng	University of Hong Kong, China
Zhihao Peng	Chinese University of Hong Kong, China
Michal Piovarci	ETH Zurich, Switzerland
Yue Qian	Tencent AI Lab, China
Yipeng Qin	Cardiff University, UK
Weize Quan	Institute of Automation, CAS, China
Bo Ren	Nankai University, China
Jianfeng Ren	University of Nottingham Ningbo China, China
Siyu Ren	City University of Hong Kong, China
Tobias Ritschel	University College London, UK
Paul Rosin	Cardiff University, UK
Eston Schweickart	Weta Digital, New Zealand
Ana Serrano	Universidad de Zaragoza, Spain
Tianjia Shao	Zhejiang University, China
Bin Sheng	Shanghai Jiao Tong University, China
Ran Song	Shandong University, China
Wanchao Su	Monash University, Australia
Yuejiao Su	Hong Kong Polytechnic University, China
Shinjiro Sueda	Texas A&M University, USA
Guodao Sun	Zhejiang University of Technology, China
Mingjie Sun	Soochow University, China
Min Tang	Zhejiang University, China

Yingzhi Tang	City University of Hong Kong, China
Zhenhua Tang	Hefei University of Technology, China
Jing Tian	National University of Singapore, Singapore
Ruofeng Tong	Zhejiang University, China
Yu-Ting Tsai	Yuan Ze University, Taiwan
Cara Tursun	University of Groningen, The Netherlands
Renjie Wan	Hong Kong Baptist University, China
Beibei Wang	Nanjing University of Science and Technology, China
Charlie Wang	University of Manchester, UK
Jiepeng Wang	University of Hong Kong, China
Miao Wang	Beihang University, China
Ningna Wang	University of Texas at Dallas, USA
Peng-Shuai Wang	Peking University, China
Pengyu Wang	East China University of Science and Technology, China
Rui Wang	Zhejiang University, China
Xu Wang	Shenzhen University, China
Yunhai Wang	Shandong University, China
Yi Wang	Hong Kong Polytechnic University, China
Tien-Tsin Wong	Monash University, Australia
Joel Wretborn	Wētā FX, Sweden
Jun Wu	Delft University of Technology, The Netherlands
Lintai Wu	City University of Hong Kong, China
Qiangqiang Wu	City University of Hong Kong, China
Burkhard Wuensche	University of Auckland, New Zealand
Jiazhi Xia	Central South University, China
Chufeng Xiao	Hong Kong University of Science and Technology, China
Shi-Qing Xin	Shandong University, China
Guanyu Xing	Sichuan University, China
Gang Xu	Nankai University, China
Huaiyuan Xu	Hong Kong Polytechnic University, China
Kai Xu	National University of Defense Technology, China
Kun Xu	Tsinghua University, China
Pengfei Xu	Shenzhen University, China
Qunce Xu	Tsinghua University, China
Senzhe Xu	Tsinghua University, China
Wei-Wei Xu	Zhejiang University, China
Dongming Yan	Institute of Automation, CAS, China
Lingqi Yan	University of California, Santa Barbara, USA

Chen Yang	City University of Hong Kong, China
Jufeng Yang	Nankai University, China
Shuojin Yang	Tsinghua University, China
Wenhan Yang	Pengcheng National Lab, China
Yin Yang	Clemson University, USA
Bo Yang	Hong Kong Polytechnic University, China
Hantao Yao	Institute of Automation, CAS, China
Yuxin Yao	City University of Hong Kong, China
Hui Ye	Hong Kong University of Science and Technology, China
Tian Ye	Hong Kong University of Science and Technology (Guangzhou), China
Ran Yi	Shanghai Jiao Tong University, China
Renjiao Yi	National University of Defense Technology, China
Dongshuo Yin	Tsinghua University, China
Meng You	City University of Hong Kong, China
Deng Yu	Shandong University, China
Xin Yuan	Westlake University, China
Ming Zeng	Xiamen University, China
Wei Zeng	Hong Kong University of Science and Technology (Guangzhou), China
Yiming Zeng	City University of Hong Kong, China
Lei Zhang	Beijing Institute of Technology, China
Qi Zhang	Shenzhen University, China
Qijian Zhang	City University of Hong Kong, China
Songhai Zhang	Tsinghua University, China
Xiaoyan Zhang	Shenzhen University, China
Yifan Zhang	City University of Hong Kong, China
Yun Zhang	Communication University of Zhejiang, China
Juyong Zhang	University of Science and Technology of China, China
Junhong Zhao	Victoria University of Wellington, New Zealand
Xi Zhao	Xi'an Jiaotong University, China
Jianmin Zheng	Nanyang Technological University, Singapore
Wei-Shi Zheng	Sun Yat-sen University, China
Zichun Zhong	Wayne State University, China
Jingtao Zhou	City University of Hong Kong, China
Yang Zhou	Shenzhen University, China
Yu Zhou	Shenzhen University, China
Yuanfeng Zhou	Shandong University, China
Haoyu Zhu	Hong Kong Polytechnic University, China

Lei Zhu	Hong Kong University of Science and Technology (Guangzhou), China
Zhe Zhu	Purdue University, USA
Zhiyu Zhu	City University of Hong Kong, China
Huiping Zhuang	South China University of Technology, China

Organizers

Organized by

Hosted by

In Cooperation with

Sponsors

Contents – Part I

Image Enhancement and Generation

Vision Modeling in Complex Scenarios

Contents – Part II

Generation and Editing

Image Processing and Optimization

Contents – Part III

Geometrical Processing

Applications

Medical Image Analysis

AGTCNet: Hybrid Network Based on AGT and Curvature Information for Skin Lesion Detection

ZhiWei Dong⬤, Genji Yuan⬤, and Jinjiang Li(✉)⬤

School of Computer Science and Technology, Shandong Technology and
Business University, Yantai, China
lijinjiang@gmail.com

Abstract. Early detection and diagnosis of skin cancers is essential to improve patient survival. However, traditional diagnostic methods have limitations due to the complexity and diversity of skin lesions. Although deep learning-based skin disease detection methods are available, the ambiguity of the boundaries of skin lesion regions may lead to model neglect and misclassification, generating suboptimal results and affecting clinical decisions. To address this problem, this paper proposes a hybrid network based on Adaptive Grouped Transformer (AGT) and curvature information fusion for skin lesion detection, called AGTCNet. AGTC-Net enhances the network's adaptive multi-scale learning capability by introducing AGT. In addition, a curvature-based guidance enhancement module (CGEM) is proposed in this paper, which utilizes the curvature information to effectively guide the model in enhancing its capture of complex lesion edge information. To further optimize the model performance, the deep supervision mechanism is used to dynamically calculate the loss at each stage and adjust the learning strategy based on the loss feedback. Through comprehensive experimental validation on the ISIC2016, ISIC2017, and PH2 skin lesion segmentation datasets, the results show that AGTCNet significantly outperforms the existing mainstream methods on all datasets, and especially exhibits excellent performance in detailed feature processing and fuzzy region segmentation.

Keywords: Skin Lesion Segmentation · Adaptive Grouped Transformer · Curvature Information · Deep Supervision

1 Introduction

Medical image segmentation [1] aims to separate different anatomical structures and tissues from an image to help physicians accurately locate and measure lesions or abnormal regions, which plays a key role in disease diagnosis and treatment. In recent years, skin diseases are still a serious health threat, but they may mislead doctors' diagnosis due to the variability and similarity of their visual features. Therefore, clinicians need more detailed information to support their decisions.

Traditional medical image segmentation techniques help clinicians understand images more intuitively and make accurate diagnoses by extracting image

P. Didyk and J. Hou (Eds.): CVM 2025, LNCS 15663, pp. 3–15, 2025.
https://doi.org/10.1007/978-981-96-5809-1_1

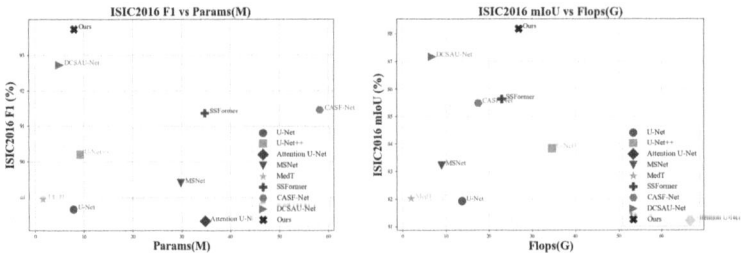

Fig. 1. Performance comparison of AGTCNet with other models.

features. However, these methods rely on hand-designed features, and their performance is affected by subjective factors and domain knowledge, leading to a decrease in the accuracy and consistency of segmentation results. In addition, when dealing with medical images with complex textures, traditional methods are difficult to effectively capture and abstract their complex features, exposing technical limitations.

To address the limitations, the application of deep learning methods in the medical field is rapidly expanding, especially in medical image segmentation showing higher accuracy and robustness. Deep learning methods are free from the limitation of hand-designed features and can automatically learn and extract complex textural and structural features from large amounts of data. Convolutional neural networks (CNNs) [2] perform particularly well in medical image segmentation tasks, where features are usually extracted through convolutional layers and further abstracted through fully connected layers. CNN architectures, represented by AlexNet [3], have achieved significant success in image classification. However, classification tasks only need to recognize image categories without involving object boundaries or pixel-level distinctions. Fully Convolutional Networks (FCNs) [4] extend image prediction to the pixel level for the first time, achieving a key breakthrough from image classification to image segmentation.

However, excessive attention to pixel-level information may lead to the loss of boundary details. U-Net [5] partially mitigates this problem by introducing jump connections in the encoder-decoder structure, which preserves more boundary information. Based on its simplicity and scalability, several improved models have been derived. U-Net++ [6] incorporates a Dense structure to fuse features of different resolutions and bridge the semantic differences in the convolutional layers; MALUNet [7] enhances feature interactions at different stages through a bridge attention module; and EGE-UNet [8] employs dilation convolution [9] to integrate multiscale features, realizing the combination of global and local information. However, CNNs are difficult to capture long-distance dependencies due to the sensory field limitation. Transformer [10], on the other hand, utilizes the self-attention mechanism [11,12] to effectively solve this problem by dynamically adjusting the attention weights, which significantly enhances the ability to capture global information. Taking TransUnet [13] as an example, the model combines the global modeling capability of Transformer and the local information recovery of U-Net and demonstrates superior performance in multi-organ and heart segmentation tasks.

However, the pure Transformer model [14,15] has limitations in capturing local details and lacks the translation invariance and local correlation of CNN, which leads to its underperformance in processing low-level information. To address this problem, hybrid models [16] combine the advantages of CNN and Transformer in vision tasks. TransFuse [17] significantly improves detail capture and overall characterization by parallel fusion of the local feature extraction capability of CNN with the global modeling capability of Transformer. Inspired by this, we propose a dual backbone network architecture, AGTCNet, which combines the detailed extraction of CNN and the global modeling of Transformer to achieve efficient feature representation and learning performance.

Furthermore, we note that some Transformer-based architectures use a fixed convolutional kernel for fine-grained feature extraction before operating on the attention mechanism, which limits the ability to capture multi-scale features. For this reason, we optimize this approach to better learn and characterize multi-scale features by dividing the input features into multiple channel groups and introducing depth-separable dynamic convolution, which allows the network to dynamically adjust the sensory fields according to the different scales of the image.

The contributions of this paper are as follows:

- We propose an Adaptive Grouped Transformer or AGT. This module efficiently combines adaptive grouped convolution and the Transformer architecture to achieve adaptive learning of multi-scale features.
- We propose the Curvature-based Guidance Enhancement Module or CGEM. This module directs the model to focus on the salient regions at the feature edges by capturing the curvature information of the feature maps.
- We construct a hybrid network based on AGT and curvature information for skin lesion detection, i.e., AGTCNet. Through extensive experimental validation on three publicly available skin lesion datasets, the results show that AGTCNet exhibits significant competitive advantages in several key performance metrics.

2   The Proposed Method

Patch Embedding Layer. For a layered representation, we apply a patch embedding layer to adjust the properties of intermediate features. This layer specifically consists of two key steps: a 2×2 stepwise convolution as well as a normalization layer composition. The patch embedding layer is used to tune the feature scales as well as the channel dimensions, enabling the network to generate multi-scale feature representations at different stages.

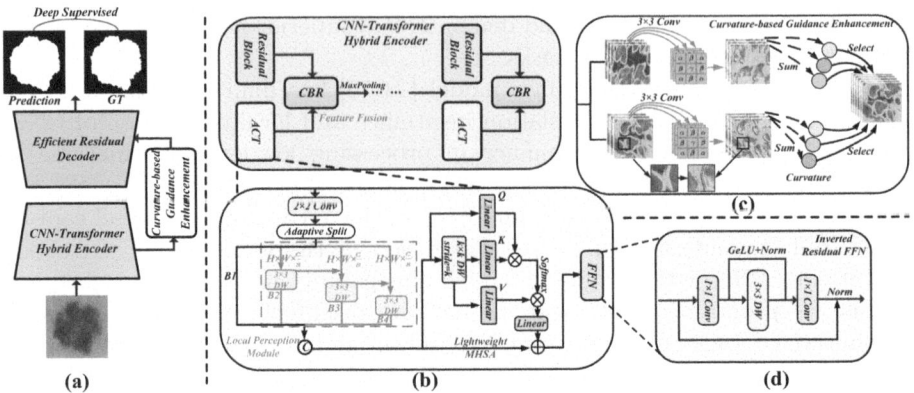

Fig. 2. Hybrid network based on AGT and curvature information for skin lesion detection. (a) shows the main framework architecture of AGTCNet. (b) shows the detailed architecture of the AGT module, where (d) shows the inverse residual feedforward network (IRFFN) structure in the ACT module. (c) The figure shows the specific design of the CGEM module.

Local Perception Module. In vision tasks, the absolute positional encoding used by the Transformer model introduces unique positional information for each image patch, thus potentially destroying translational invariance and increasing the instability of the model, making it difficult to generalize to new data with translational variations. To address this challenge, we introduce a local-awareness module. In this module, we borrow the idea of Res2Net [18], adopt a multi-scale processing approach, and develop the hierarchical representation into a single-block implementation. As shown in Fig. 2, we group the feature images along the channel axis at different stages, and the number of channels in each group is $\frac{C}{S}$, where C represents the number of input feature image channels, S represents the number of groups in the group, and S takes the value of $S \in \{1, 2, 3, 4\}$. The specific implementation scheme is to partition the input tensor along the channel axis into S subsets, each of which has the shape of $H \times W \times \frac{C}{S}$, and then apply a 3×3 deep convolutional process to each feature subset, and finally, through the Concatenation operation to integrate the feature subsets into one feature representation. This strategy significantly enhances the spatial awareness of the output feature representation, making it more flexible and adaptive, while significantly reducing the computational complexity. The adaptive grouped convolution module can be defined as:

$$ACT(X) = Cat(DW_3(X_1), \cdots, DW_3(X_s)), s\epsilon\{1,4\} \tag{1}$$

where X denotes the feature input from the previous stage, $X \in \mathbb{R}^{H \times W \times C}$, $H \times W$ is the resolution of the input in the current stage, and C denotes the dimensionality of the features. Cat stands for Concatenation, DW_3 denotes deep convolution with a convolution kernel of 3, e denotes the Sth subset of features, and $X_S \in \mathbb{R}^{H \times W \times \frac{C}{S}}$, depending on the stage S takes the value $\{1, 2, 3, 4\}$.

Lightweight Multihead Self-Attention Module. To improve the stability of the input distribution during forward propagation and the stability of the gradient in backpropagation, we first perform LayerNorm [19] on the output of the feature from the LPM, with the normalization operation performed on the hidden dimension. Subsequently, the normalized features are fed into the Lightweight Multi-Headed Self-Attention Module (LMHSA). Different from the traditional self-attention mechanism, we reduce the computational complexity effectively by processing the deep convolution of K × K convolution kernel to reduce the spatial dimensions of K and V before computing the attention weights. Next, the combination of Q and K is utilized to compute the attention weights, which are applied to V to generate the weighted feature output.

In addition, to enhance the model's ability to model the relative positional relationships between elements in sequence data, we introduce a relative positional bias for each self-attention module B. The core process of the lightweight multi-head self-attention module can be defined as follows:

$$K' = DW_{k \times k}(K) \in \mathbb{R}^{\frac{n}{k^2} \times d_k} \tag{2}$$

$$V' = DW_{k \times k}(V) \in \mathbb{R}^{\frac{n}{k^2} \times d_k} \tag{3}$$

$$LightAttn(Q, K, V) = Softmax\left(\frac{QK'^T}{\sqrt{d_k}} + B\right)V'. \tag{4}$$

After that, according to the number of input heads h, h sequences of size h × d are generated and these sequences are connected into a comprehensive sequence of n × d to integrate the information of each attention head to form a more comprehensive feature representation. Next, the generated sequence information is normalized through the LayerNorm layer, and the processed feature information is directed to the IRFFN.

Inverse Residual Feedforward Network. As shown in Fig. 2, the structure of IRFFN consists of two 1 × 1 convolutional layers for extending the feature dimensions and projecting to a lower dimensional feature space, respectively. To realize deeper feature transformations, we introduce a 3 × 3 deep convolutional layer between these two convolutional layers. The expanded features are processed by the GeLU [20] activation function and BatchNorm to further enhance the expressive power of the model. With the introduction of residual structure, IRFFN effectively improves the propagation efficiency of gradient between different layers. Finally, the output features of IRFFN are normalized by BatchNorm to ensure the stability of the output features in a statistical distribution. The mathematical expression of IRFFN is as follows:

$$IRFFN(X) = Conv_1(DW_3(Conv_1(X))) \tag{5}$$

where X represents the feature sequence output by LMHSA, $Conv_1$ represents the convolution with convolution kernel 1, and DW_3 represents the depth-separated convolution with convolution kernel 3.

The above four modules constitute our proposed ACT module, which is mathematically represented as:

$$P_i = PE\left(X_{i-1}\right) \tag{6}$$

$$L_i = LPM\left(P_i\right) \tag{7}$$

$$Y_i = LMHSA\left(L_i\right) + L_i \tag{8}$$

$$X_i = IRFFN\left(Y_i\right) + Y_i \tag{9}$$

where P_i, L_i, and Y_i denote the output characteristics of the PE, LPM, and LMHSA modules of the ith block, respectively.

2.1 Curvature-Based Guidance Enhancement Module

To effectively deal with the problem of edge ambiguity in skin lesion regions, we propose a curvature-based guidance enhancement module (CGEM), whose detailed architecture is shown in Fig. 2. In terms of curvature feature selection, we adopt the mean curvature as the main feature parameter because it can reflect the non-uniformity on the image surface more accurately, which helps to improve the model's ability in edge feature capture. By borrowing the simplified linear convolutional computation method proposed by Gong et al. [21]. we can efficiently approximate the mean curvature solution, which enhances the model's performance in recognizing and segmenting edge region features. The relevant formulas are as follows:

$$C = [C_1 \ C_2 \ C_3] \circledast X \tag{10}$$

where the values of $C_1 = [\alpha, \beta, \alpha]^T$, $C_2 = [\beta, \gamma, \beta]^T$, $C_3 = [\alpha, \beta, \alpha]^T$, α, β, and γ are -1/16, 5/16 and -1, respectively. $\circledast$ denotes convolution, X denotes the input image and C denotes the mean curvature.

2.2 AGTCNet

Medical images usually contain multimodal information, such as morphological and textual information. Convolutional neural networks excel at extracting both low-level and high-level visual features from images, while the Transformer model performs well in processing sequence data as well as linguistic information while being able to capture high-level semantic information in images. In this paper, we construct a hybrid network based on AGT and curvature information for skin lesion detection. The model significantly improves the segmentation accuracy while maintaining high efficiency. The specific model parameters (Params) and floating point operations (FLOPs) are shown in Fig. 1.

The specific structure of AGTCNet still utilizes a U-Net-like encoder-decoder architecture. In the encoder stage, we design a two-branch feature extraction backbone network fusing CNN and Transformer to obtain multimodal feature representations. The CNN branch employs simple residual blocks to focus on capturing local features. The Transformer branch generates multi-scale feature maps through a hierarchical cascade structure by stacking different numbers of ACT modules at each stage. In the first to fourth stages, 3, 3, 16, and 3 ACT modules are stacked, respectively, and the feature information extracted in each stage is retained and passed layer by layer to ensure multi-scale feature fusion.

To achieve the dual-branch interaction, we employ a simplified Convolution-Batch Normalization-Activation (CBR) with MaxPooling operation at each stage to facilitate the feature fusion between the CNN and Transformer branches. Meanwhile, a CGEM module is introduced between the encoder and decoder to strengthen the model's ability to learn and extract edge features. In addition, to supervise the feature reconstruction process, the network employs a deep supervision mechanism to compute the loss at different stages, which strengthens the training process by optimizing the loss. The mathematical representation of the loss function is as follows:

$$l_i = BCE\,(y, \hat{y}) + Dice\,(y, \hat{y}) \tag{11}$$

$$\mathbb{L} = \sum_{i=0}^{4} \lambda_i \times l_i \tag{12}$$

where BCE and Dice represent binary cross-entropy loss and Dice loss, respectively. λ_i denotes the weights of the different stages. In the network, the values of λ_i 's at each stage are 0.4, 0.3, 0.2, 0.1.

3   Experiments

3.1   Experimental Parameters

All experiments were conducted in the Ubuntu 18.04 operating system and completed in the PyTorch 1.7.1 environment. Computational resources are provided by NVIDIA TITAN RTX to support efficient computation during training. Through extensive experimental validation, we set the initial learning rate of the model to 5e-4, the maximum number of training rounds to 400, and saved the optimal model and the latest rounds of the model during the training process. To enhance the generalization ability of the model, we introduce a variety

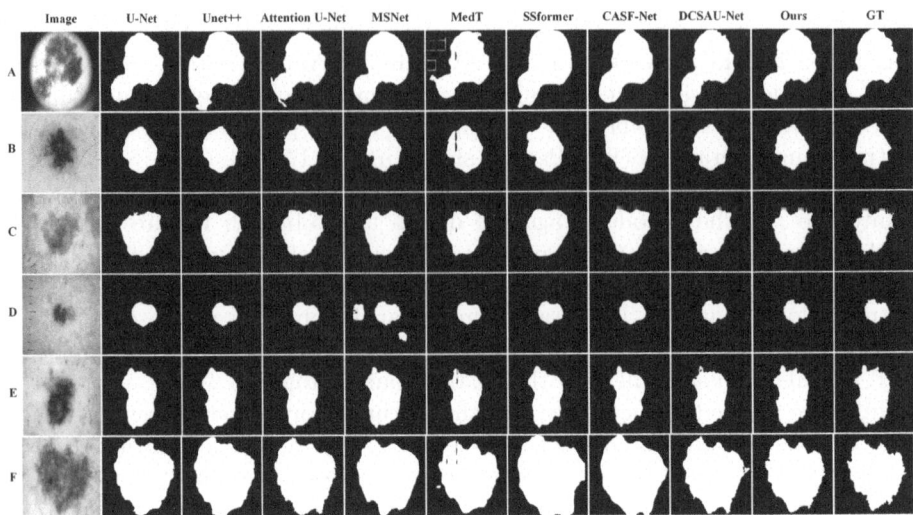

Fig. 3. Visual presentation of predictions for selected samples from ISIC2016.

of data enhancement techniques, including vertical flipping, horizontal flipping, and random rotation, to increase the diversity of samples and the robustness of the model.

3.2 Comparative Experiments

Figure 3 shows the segmentation results of representative samples in the ISIC2016 test set. It can be seen that the Ours method significantly outperforms the other methods in the segmentation of the overall lesion contour and

Table 1. Performance metrics results for the various comparison methods on the ISIC2016 dataset. The best results are marked in red and the second best results are marked in blue (%).

Method	F1	mIoU	Precision	Recall
U-Net	88.66	81.92	90.48	91.17
U-Net++	90.20	83.83	92.94	90.68
Attention U-Net	88.34	81.22	93.77	87.32
MSNet	89.40	83.22	91.54	91.52
MedT	88.95	82.03	90.11	91.78
SSformer	91.37	85.63	90.18	93.22
CASF-Net	91.46	85.50	92.26	88.22
DCSAU-Net	92.72	87.18	91.42	94.05
Ours	94.09	88.77	93.49	94.70

Table 2. Performance metrics of the different compared methods on the ISIC2017 dataset. The best results are marked in red and the second best results are marked in blue (%).

Method	F1	mIoU	Precision	Recall
U–Net	78.73	64.92	89.66	70.18
U–Net++	80.16	66.89	92.54	70.70
Attention U–Net	80.66	67.59	88.15	74.34
MSNet	83.31	71.41	**91.07**	76.79
MedT	73.99	58.72	88.15	68.13
SSformer	83.43	71.30	81.51	85.54
CASF-Net	84.20	72.71	85.14	84.51
DCSAU-Net	**85.93**	**75.71**	83.93	**88.01**
Ours	87.36	77.49	82.95	92.26

local detail capture, and especially exhibits stronger performance when dealing with blurred regions. For sample A, although U-Net, MSNet [22], and CASF-Net can separate lesion regions with similar colors to the environment, Ours performs more finely in capturing edge details. For samples B and C, due to their complex edge features, although DCSAU-Net [23] and Ours can accurately capture the overall contours, Ours exhibits higher edge detection accuracy and robustness when dealing with complex edges (e.g., the lower right of sample B and the upper right of sample C), which further proves its superiority in dealing with complex lesion edges. Figure 4 demonstrates the segmentation results of the Ours method with other methods on the ISIC2017 dataset. In sample A, the previous method misidentifies the lesion region as background, resulting in significant deviation from GT, which may stem from insufficient capture of complex features; Ours accurately identifies the lesion region by enhancing the capture of contextual information, with delicate edge processing, and the result is more closely aligned with GT. Sample C is subjected to the interference of hair, which generates obvious noise by methods such as U-Net. In contrast, Ours effectively reduces the noise by combining local and global features through the two-branch backbone network. Sample D, the other methods failed to accurately reduce the noise, and the result is highly consistent with GT. In sample D, other methods fail to accurately segment the fuzzy lesion area, while Ours is closer to GT by its stronger feature extraction ability. Figure 5 illustrates the segmentation prediction visualization of the different methods on some samples of the PH2 dataset. The local zoom analysis of samples A, B, and C reveals subtle differences between SSFormer, CASF-Net, DCSAU-Net, and Ours. In Sample D, U-Net++ and Attention U-Net misidentify the background as a lesion, while U-Net and DCSAU-Net avoid this problem but are insufficient in capturing the edge details; Ours, on the other hand, significantly improves the overlap with GT through accurate edge processing. In Sample E, the boundary processing of U-Net and MedT is confusing, while Ours achieves more accurate edge recogni-

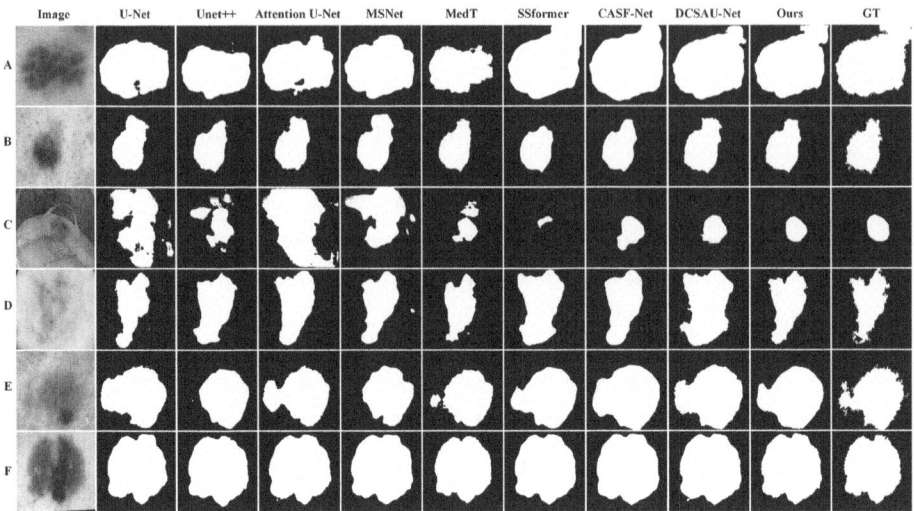

Fig. 4. Visual presentation of predictions for selected samples from ISIC2017.

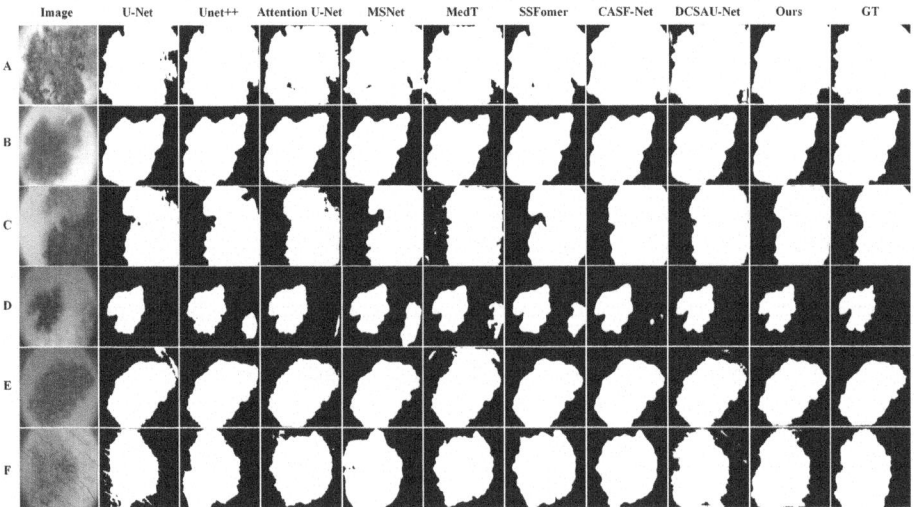

Fig. 5. Visual presentation of predictions for selected samples in PH2.

tion by introducing curvature information. The segmentation results of Sample F show that the other methods have irregular boundaries in fuzzy regions, while Ours excels in accuracy and consistency and is closer to GT. Table 1, Table 2, and Table 3 respectively summarize the performance of each method on the ISIC2016, ISIC2017, and PH2 datasets. AGTCNet achieved the best results in terms of F1 score, mIoU, precision, and recall, demonstrating its superior segmentation accuracy.

Table 3. Performance metrics of the different comparison methods on the PH2 dataset. The best results are marked in red and the second best results are marked in blue (%).

Method	F1	mIoU	Precision	Recall
U–Net	86.43	76.21	84.43	88.51
U–Net++	93.57	88.07	93.40	93.74
Attention U–Net	92.35	85.93	91.66	93.05
MSNet	94.55	89.82	94.93	**94.18**
MedT	92.18	85.65	92.70	91.67
SSformer	93.12	87.28	94.53	91.76
CASF-Net	**94.60**	**90.08**	**95.44**	93.78
DCSAU-Net	94.11	89.03	95.00	93.23
Ours	95.12	90.69	96.05	94.20

3.3 Ablation Experiments

In this section, we validate the effectiveness of the proposed module through ablation experiments, all of which are conducted based on the ISIC2016, ISIC2017 and PH2 datasets. Specifically, Table 4 shows the different model variants. AGTCNet-1 removes the ACT module and uses only the Residual Block as the backbone structure to evaluate the role of the ACT module in global feature capture.

According to Table 4, the three ablation variants have significant gaps with the AGTCNet model in terms of F1 and mIoU metrics, indicating that the ACT module, CGEM module, and the depth supervision mechanism play a key role in enhancing edge feature extraction, improving segmentation accuracy, and dealing with fuzzy regions robustly, verifying their effectiveness. In the second set of samples, the edge processing results reveal the degree of misclassification of the models, especially AGTCNet-1 incorrectly recognizes the surrounding environment as the lesion region, validating the importance of the ACT module in contextual understanding and separation of lesion and background. In addition, the performance metrics in Table 4 further support the effectiveness and robustness of AGTCNet in fuzzy region processing and edge detail recognition. This conclusion is further supported by the data in Table 4, which shows that the overall performance of the three ablation models is lower than that of AGTCNet, validating the effectiveness of the proposed module.

Table 4. Structural demonstration of different ablation variants.

Method	ACT	CGEM	Deep supervision	ISIC2016		ISIC2017		PH2	
				F1	IoU	F1	IoU	F1	IoU
AGTCNet-1	×	✓	✓	92.63	86.72	85.75	75.11	93.83	88.39
AGTCNet-2	✓	×	✓	93.39	87.65	86.55	76.17	94.58	89.72
AGTCNet-3	✓	✓	×	93.80	88.27	86.92	76.79	94.76	90.11
AGTCNet	✓	✓	✓	94.09	88.77	87.36	77.49	95.12	90.69

4   Conclusion

In this paper, a novel hybrid network named AGTCNet is proposed for skin lesion detection and targeted to solve the problem of incomplete extraction of the edge region of skin lesions. AGTCNet adopts a two-branch backbone network structure based on CNN and Transformer, which is able to capture both global features and local detail information, thus significantly enhancing the network's characterization ability. In order to improve the model's deficiency in edge detail processing, a CGEM module is designed to guide the model to accurately recognize lesion edges by collecting curvature information. In addition, AGTCNet introduces a deep supervision mechanism to dynamically supervise the feature loss and optimize the learning strategy in real time based on feedback. The effectiveness and superiority of the AGTCNet network architecture is verified through extensive experiments on three public datasets.

Acknowledgments. AThis research was supported by the National Natural Science Foundation of China (61772319, 62272281, 62002200, 62202268), Shandong Natural Science Foundation of China (ZR2023MF026, ZR2022MA076), Yantai science and technology innovation development plan(2022JCYJ031).

Disclosure of Interests. The authors declare that no potentail competing interests exist. There is no an undisclosed relationship thay may pose a competing interest. There is no an undisclosed funding source that may pose a competing interest.

References

1. Dong, Z., Yuan, G., Hua, Z., Li, J.: Diffusion model-based text-guided enhancement network for medical image segmentation. Expert Syst. Appl. **249**, 123549 (2024)
2. LeCun, Y., Bottou, L., Bengio, Y., Haffner, P.: Gradient-based learning applied to document recognition. Proc. IEEE **86**(11), 2278–2324 (1998)
3. Krizhevsky, A., Sutskever, I., Hinton, G.E.: Imagenet classification with deep convolutional neural networks. Adv. Neural Inf. Process. Syst. **25** (2012)
4. Long, J., Shelhamer, E., Darrell, T.: Fully convolutional networks for semantic segmentation. In: Proceedings of the IEEE Conference on Computer Vision and Pattern Recognition, pp. 3431–3440 (2015)

5. Ronneberger, O., Fischer, P., Brox, T.: U-Net: convolutional networks for biomedical image segmentation. In: Navab, N., Hornegger, J., Wells, W.M., Frangi, A.F. (eds.) MICCAI 2015. LNCS, vol. 9351, pp. 234–241. Springer, Cham (2015). https://doi.org/10.1007/978-3-319-24574-4_28

6. Zhou, Z., Rahman Siddiquee, M.M., Tajbakhsh, N., Liang, J.: UNet++: a nested U-Net architecture for medical image segmentation. In: Stoyanov, D., et al. (eds.) DLMIA/ML-CDS -2018. LNCS, vol. 11045, pp. 3–11. Springer, Cham (2018). https://doi.org/10.1007/978-3-030-00889-5_1

7. Ruan, J., Xiang, S., Xie, M., Liu, T., Fu, Y.: MALUNet: a multi-attention and lightweight unet for skin lesion segmentation. In: 2022 IEEE International Conference on Bioinformatics and Biomedicine (BIBM), pp. 1150–1156. IEEE (2022)

8. Zhou, Z., Rahman Siddiquee, M.M., Tajbakhsh, N., Liang, J.: UNet++: a nested U-Net architecture for medical image segmentation. In: Stoyanov, D., et al. (eds.) DLMIA/ML-CDS -2018. LNCS, vol. 11045, pp. 3–11. Springer, Cham (2018). https://doi.org/10.1007/978-3-030-00889-5_1

9. Yu, F., Koltun, V.: Multi-scale context aggregation by dilated convolutions. arXiv preprint arXiv:1511.07122 (2015)

10. Vaswani, A., et al.: Attention is all you need. Adv. Neural Inf. Process. Syst. **30** (2017)

11. Guo, M.H., Lu, C.Z., Liu, Z.N., Cheng, M.M., Hu, S.M.: Visual attention network. Comput. Vis. Media **9**(4), 733–752 (2023)

12. Guo, M.-H., et al.: Attention mechanisms in computer vision: a survey. Computational Visual Media, pp. 1–38 (2022). https://doi.org/10.1007/s41095-022-0271-y

13. Chen, J., et al.: TransUNet: transformers make strong encoders for medical image segmentation. arXiv preprint arXiv:2102.04306 (2021)

14. He, Y., Chen, L., Yuan, Y.J., Chen, S.Y., Gao, L.: Multi-level patch transformer for style transfer with single reference image. In: International Conference on Computational Visual Media, pp. 221–239. Springer (2024)

15. Wu, Z., Guo, J., Zhuang, C., Xiao, J., Yan, D.M., Zhang, X.: Joint specular highlight detection and removal in single images via UNet-transformer. Comput. Vis. Media **9**(1), 141–154 (2023)

16. Dong, Z., Li, J., Hua, Z.: Transformer-based multi-attention hybrid networks for skin lesion segmentation. Expert Syst. Appl. **244**, 123016 (2024)

17. Zhang, Y., Liu, H., Hu, Q.T.: Fusing transformers and CNNs for medical image segmentation. arxiv (2021). arXiv preprint arXiv:2102.08005

18. He, K., Zhang, X., Ren, S., Sun, J.: Identity mappings in deep residual networks. In: Leibe, B., Matas, J., Sebe, N., Welling, M. (eds.) ECCV 2016. LNCS, vol. 9908, pp. 630–645. Springer, Cham (2016). https://doi.org/10.1007/978-3-319-46493-0_38

19. Ba, J.L.: Layer normalization. arXiv preprint arXiv:1607.06450 (2016)

20. Hendrycks, D., Gimpel, K.: Gaussian error linear units (GELUs). arXiv preprint arXiv:1606.08415 (2016)

21. Gong, Y., Sbalzarini, I.F.: Curvature filters efficiently reduce certain variational energies. IEEE Trans. Image Process. **26**(4), 1786–1798 (2017)

22. Zhao, X., Zhang, L., Lu, H.: Automatic polyp segmentation via multi-scale subtraction network. In: de Bruijne, M., Cattin, P.C., Cotin, S., Padoy, N., Speidel, S., Zheng, Y., Essert, C. (eds.) MICCAI 2021. LNCS, vol. 12901, pp. 120–130. Springer, Cham (2021). https://doi.org/10.1007/978-3-030-87193-2_12

23. Xu, Q., Ma, Z., Na, H., Duan, W.: DCSAU-Net: a deeper and more compact split-attention u-net for medical image segmentation. Comput. Biol. Med. **154**, 106626 (2023)

Among General Spine Segmentation with Multi-scale and Discriminate Feature Fusion

Tingwei Wen[1], Yao Lu[1], Xiaosheng Chen[2], Xinhai Lu[2], and Guangming Lu[1(✉)]

[1] Harbin Institute of Technology, Shenzhen, China
luguangm@hit.edu.cn
[2] Shenzhen Second People's Hospital, Shenzhen, China

Abstract. Automatic spine segmentation from X-ray images is an important step for diagnosing spinal diseases like scoliosis. However, manual segmentation is time-consuming and prone to errors due to subjective judgments. Thesis proposes a supervised convolutional neural network for accurate and efficient spine segmentation based on X-ray images. The proposed network adopts DUCK-Net, a U-Net structure with six parallel convolution paths, as the backbone and introduces several improvements. To detect vertebrae with different sizes, we introduce Attention Gates between encoder-decoder layers to strengthen multi-scale feature fusion. Channel Interaction Attention block is proposed to enhanced feature fusion process for more discriminate feature representation. Additionally, a curvature loss is included as a regularization term during training to discourage connected vertebrae segmentation. We evaluate our method on a spine segmentation dataset and a polyp segmentation dataset, showing that it achieves reliable performance on Dice coefficient, Jaccard similarity, Precision and Recall. Our model have achieved state-of-the-art performance in spine segmentation from X-ray images and has been implemented in an automated scoliosis diagnosis system in hospital, which shows significant clinical application value and theoretical significance.

Keywords: Medical images · scoliosis · spine segmentation · semantic segmentation · convolutional neural networks

1 Introduction

The spine is one of the most vital structures in human body. It serves numerous essential functions, including bearing the weight of body and protecting the spinal cord and nerves within it. In both anterior and posterior views, the normal spine should be upright and located in the center of the pelvis, while scoliosis is a pathological condition where the spine is abnormally curved to the left or right side. Around 2% to 5% of adolescents worldwide suffer from scoliosis, which typically emerges during the rapid growth of the spine and can cause physical deformities in body appearance. In severe cases, it can even lead to paralysis. Therefore, giving an accurate diagnosis of whether adolescent patients suffer from scoliosis is particularly important to provide treatment plans for patients. Clinically, the general method for diagnosing scoliosis is to capture

© The Author(s), under exclusive license to Springer Nature Singapore Pte Ltd. 2025
P. Didyk and J. Hou (Eds.): CVM 2025, LNCS 15663, pp. 16–28, 2025.
https://doi.org/10.1007/978-981-96-5809-1_2

X-ray images of the patient's spine, manually measuring the scoliosis severity. However, clinicians need to rely on a great wealth of experience, leading to a significant risk of diagnostic errors due to subjective judgments. In addition, with the popularization of medical imaging equipment such as X-rays, CT, MRI, etc., the number of medical images rapidly increases, putting enormous pressure on clinicians, further affecting the efficiency and accuracy.

Therefore, it is an urgent requirement to develop an automated technology to precisely measure scoliosis. In this study, we present a supervised convolutional neural network architecture for spine segmentation. Our model uses DUCK-Net [4] as backbone, which is a model with U-Net architecture, using six variations of convolutional blocks in parallel for better feature extract. DUCK-Net is evaluated on several benchmark datasets for polyp segmentation and achieved state-of-the-art results, however, performed poorly in spine X-ray image segmentation. The segmentation results were prone to problems such as adjacent vertebrae being connected, incomplete segmentation of vertebrae or incorrect segmentation of spinal boundaries. Compared with images of polyps, spine X-ray images have lower brightness and contrast, blurred boundaries, smaller vertebrae near neck while larger vertebrae near pelvis, and issues with rib interference. We considered that DUCK-Net used addition as the feature fusion method, which caused the neglect of edge features that should be paid attention to after addition. Thus, we introduce the Channel Interaction Attention block, changing the way of feature fusion to concatenation without feature loss, and selecting task relevant channel in-formation from the feature maps and reducing the number of channels. Besides, we use Attention Gates [13] on each skip connection between encoders and decoders, exchanging the information among layers, enhancing the information extracted from features at different scales to adapt to different sizes of vertebrae. Applying such two modules, our model can utilize multi-scale information fusion to obtain more discriminate features. Lastly, we introduce curvature loss as a regularization term to punish the segmentation of connected vertebrae. Our main contributions are summarized as follows:

Our Attention Gates merge the relevant information from two encoders of adjacent layers to generate a fused feature map and send it to the decoder, effectively fusing the multi-scale information and alleviating the information gaps between layers, to make the model focus more on the vertebrae, even if the sizes are inconsistent.

Our CIA (Channel Interaction Attention) block can preserve important features such as edges during the feature fusion process, automatically learn the importance of channels and implicitly provide higher weights for these channels, driving the model to utilize these high weighted channels when reducing the number of channels, enabling a learnable feature fusion process.

Our curvature loss uses the curvature of discrete points in the segmentation results as a regularization loss, which produces the model looks to minimize curvature loss, aims to smooth the segmentation curvature, and makes the segmentation results closer to the real vertebrae.

Our model can accurately segment the spine in the X-ray images with low brightness and low contrast, which is conducive to the subsequent calculation of various spinal scoliosis parameters and the diagnosis of spinal scoliosis.

2 Related Work

Giannoglou and Stylianidis [5] published a review on scoliosis measurement for spinal scoliosis and spinal X-ray image processing. They mentioned that the processing order in spinal X-ray images is generally: segment image to extract regions of interest, recognize individual vertebra, and predict spinal curvature degree. Image segmentation is mentioned as the first step in spine X-ray image processing and the core of the entire process. The segmentation result directly affects the subsequent calculation of parameters. The correct segmentation of images is an essential step in medical image processing, with the main task being to remove unimportant parts of the image and extract parts containing special meaning or targets for further analysis. Currently, the mainstream medical image segmentation methods are based on deep learning method.

In recent years, deep convolutional neural networks have shown great potential in medical image segmentation. Unlike traditional machine learning, convolutional neural networks do not require manual feature extraction during training and can perform end-to-end target segmentation. U-Net [14], an encoder-decoder model developed initially for biomedical image segmentation, combines shallow features of compressed path and deep features of expanded path through skip connections to achieve the trade-off between local features and contextual information, reducing the loss of edge features caused by downsampling operations to a certain extent. U-Net and its variants Unet++ [20], V-net [12], etc., have simple structures, small numbers of parameters, and require less data for network training, making them suitable for medical image segmentation. Horng et al. [7] extracted a rectangular region of the spine in the X-ray image based on pixel intensity, and then fed it into U-Net for segmentation. Imran et al. [8] made some improvements to U-Net. They used a convolution operation at each layer of the U-Net decoder to extract the outputs of that layer and fused them together as the final outputs. These progressive lateral outputs ensured that the deep features in the image were not lost by the decoder. The model achieved better results in spine segmentation than U-Net. Shen et al. [16] replaced the fully connected layers of VGG-Net with the decoder of U-Net and incorporated a wavelet decomposition module to enhance the detail information of images. Shao et al. [15]established a semi-supervised training framework that utilized Stable Diffusion to generate a large number of spinal X-ray images. They employed ResNet50 as the backbone network and used a feature pyramid network to extract features, predicting the spinal contour and four corner points to calculate the Cobb angle.

In medical image segmentation task, polyp segmentation datasets are widely recognized, where many models have demonstrated their performance. Srivastava et al. [17] added a global multi-scale feature fusion mechanism based on

ResNet [6], combined with cross-scale attention and subsequent multi-scale feature selection modules, proposed GMSRF-Net to achieve accurate and generalized segmentation of polyps. Chen et al. [2] used Transformer to encode tokenized image patches from a convolution neural network (CNN) feature map as the input sequence for extracting global contexts, and then used decoder to upsample the encoded features which are then combined with the high-resolution CNN feature maps to enable precise localization. Tomar et al. [18] used residual blocks with ResNet-50 as the backbone and takes the advantage of transformer self-attention mechanism as well as dilated convolution, proposed TransResU-Net. Dumitru et al. [4] used their custom-built convolutional block, DUCK (Deep Understanding Convolutional Kernel), which allowed more in-depth feature selection, enabling the model to locate the polyp targets accurately and correctly to predict the borders, and residual downsampling, which allowed the model to use the initial image information at each resolution level in the encoder. DUCK-Net achieved the state-of-the-art in polyp segmentation task. We employed the DUCK-Net as the backbone and made some improvements and proposed our spine segmentation model.

3   Methodology

Figure 1 shows the architecture of our proposed model. Our enhancement involves employing Attention Gates to enhance the information exchange from adjacent layers with different scales for vertebrae of different sizes, introducing Channel Interaction Attention block to strengthen the feature fusion process also facilitate a learnable feature integration process, and taking curvature loss as a regularization loss to punish the segmentation of connected vertebrae.

3.1   Backbone: DUCK-Net

DUCK-Net uses the encoder-decoder architecture of the U-Net, with two significant improvements: a novel convolutional block called DUCK block and residual downsampling. DUCK block contains six variations of convolutional blocks in parallel to locate the target precisely and detect the border accurately. The Residual block, which is first introduced in ResUNet++ [11], is one of the DUCK block components, aiming to understand the small details. There are combinations of one, two and three Residual blocks in parallel. The other two components are Midscope and Widescope blocks using dilated convolutions to understand the higher-level features. The last one is the Seperated block, which uses a 1 × N kernel and an N × 1 kernel to simulate an N × N kernel, enabling the model to capture the spatial connections in both vertical and horizontal directions. DUCK-Net replaces the 3 × 3 convolutional blocks used by U-Net with the DUCK block and adds a secondary downscaling layer that does no convolutional operations as the residual downsampling to handle the issue caused by DUCK block such as losing details. DUCK-Net evaluated on several benchmark datasets for medical image segmentation and achieved state-of-the-art results in

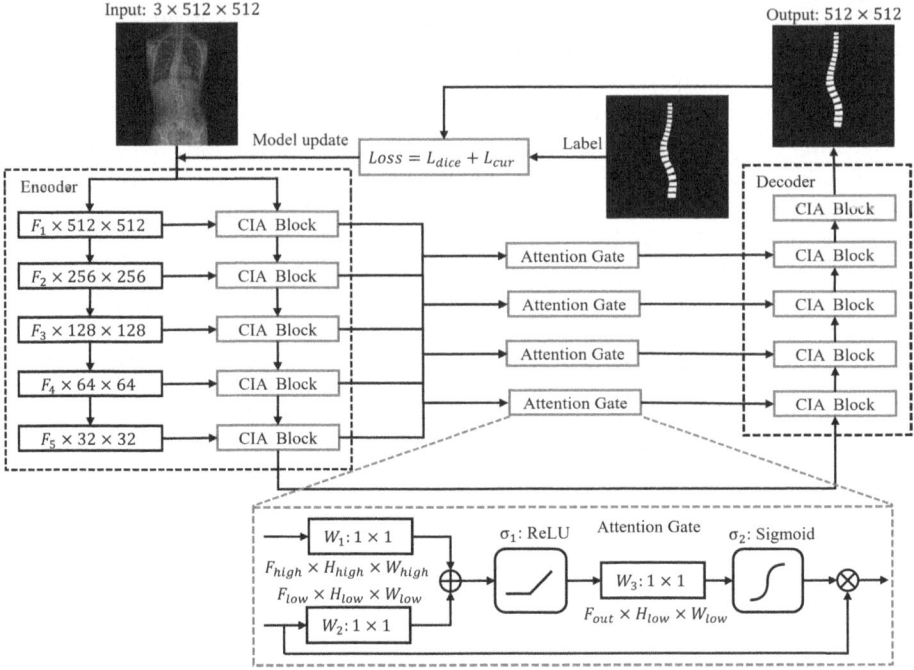

Fig. 1. The architecture of the proposed model. Input images are resized as $3 \times 512 \times 512$ and are downsampled for 5 times in the encoder. Attention Gates are integrated into the skip connections of each layer. CIA blocks are introduced in both encoder and decoder for feature extract. Curvature is introduced in loss function as a regularization loss.

terms of mean Dice coefficient, Jaccard index and other metrics, showing strong generalization abilities with limited training data. Therefore, we use DUCK-Net as the model backbone for spine X-ray image semantic segmentation.

3.2   Attention Gates

U-Net adopts an encode-decoder structure and directly sends the results of the encoders to the decoders through skip connections, alleviating the loss of features caused by downsampling to some extent. However, only connections between encoders and decoders within the same layer exist in U-Net, which may lead to ineffective utilization of features at different scales, while vertebrae are of different sizes that features from all scales matter. To address this issue, we introduce Attention Gates, which were originally used in natural image analysis, knowledge graphs, and natural language processing (NLP) for image captioning, machine translation, and classification tasks. Attention U-Net [13] proposed a novel self-attention gating module that can be utilized in U-Net for image segmentation tasks. The Attention Gate takes the output features of two adjacent encoder layers as inputs and generates attention coefficients. This allows the signals of the same region of interest in the two feature maps to be enhanced, while the different regions between them can also serve as auxiliary information, achieving the aggregation of information between two feature maps of different scales. As shown in Fig. 1, the Attention Gate performs a pixel-wise 1×1 convolution on the outputs of two adjacent encoder layers, adds them up as an attention coefficient map, to obtain more accurate results than multiplicative attention. After that, a ReLU activation function and a linear transformation through a 1×1 convolution are applied. Finally, we normalize the attention coefficients using sigmoid activation function. The Attention Gate is formulated as follows:

$$F_{out} = \sigma_2(W_3(\sigma_1(W_1F_1 + W_2F_2 + b_1)) + b_3) \tag{1}$$

where W_1, W_2 and W_3 represent the linear transformations, b_1 represents the sum of the bias terms corresponding to W_1 and W_2, b_3 represents the bias term corresponding to W_3, σ_1 corresponds to ReLU activation function and σ_2 corresponds to sigmoid activation function. The result attention map is a grid signal based on image spatial information, aggregating information from multiple imaging scales. After performing attention calculation with the encoder output, the result is superimposed on the decoder. Attention Gates are integrated into the skip connections of each layer, utilizing two feature maps from the current layer and the subsequent deeper layer. Through the Attention Gates, relevant information in the feature maps of two scales are merged to generate a fused feature map, which is then concatenated with the upsampled results, facilitating the exchange of information between layers within the U-Net structure.

3.3   Channel Interaction Attention Block

In the DUCK block [4], features extracted from six parallel paths are fused using the add operation, which is a simple and efficient way of feature fusion. Although the amount of computation is small, add operation has the disadvantage of losing features because after addition, the original features disappear directly and the number of features decreases, which cannot be learned or under controlled. Therefore, we changed the feature fusion method in the block to concatenation operation. Concatenation operation directly stacks the features of different paths on the channel dimension without causing feature loss, preserving important features like edges. However, after stacking, the number of features expands to 6 times than the original number, needed to be screened. Inspired by ECA-Net proposed by Wang et al. [19] and DACE framework proposed by Chen et al. [1], we propose a channel interaction attention mechanism that automatically learns the importance of channels, to assign different weights to each channel, and finally reduce the number of channels with 1×1 convolution. Figure 2 shows the architecture of the proposed Channel Interaction Attention block.

The main idea of Channel Interaction Attention block is to automatically select task relevant channel information in the feature map and provide higher weights for these channels. Specifically, given the output feature map F of each

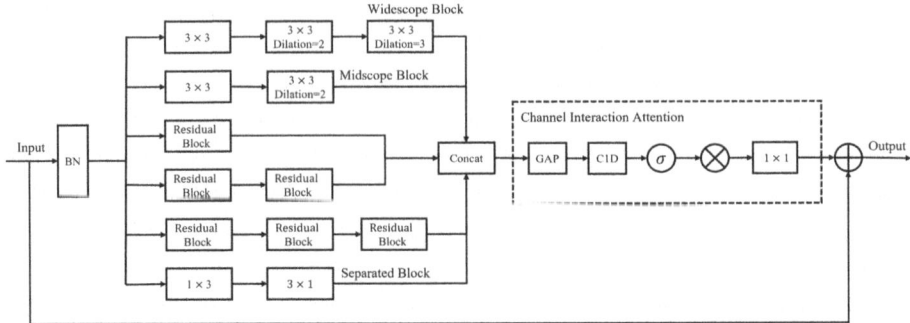

Fig. 2. The architecture of the Channel Interaction Attention block, which extracts features through six parallel paths and then fuses feature by concatenation operation to avoid information loss. We introduce channel interaction attention mechanism to learn the importance of channels and reduce channels according to channel weights.

convolutional block as an input, a Global Average Pooling is firstly performed, describing the global information as a channel descriptor, and generating defined statistical information for each channel, which can be defined as:

$$F' = GAP(F) = \frac{1}{h \times w} \sum_{i=1}^{h} \sum_{j=1}^{w} F(i,j) \tag{2}$$

where h and w denote the height and width of each feature map. The CIA block generates weights for each channel using one-dimensional convolution with a kernel size of α. Finally, the responses from each channel are re-calibrated using the corresponding weights, with the output defined as: which is formulated as follows:

$$\hat{F} = \sigma(C1D_\alpha(F')) \cdot F' \tag{3}$$

where $C1D(\cdot)$ denotes a one-dimensional convolution operation, α denotes the kernel size of one-dimensional convolution, σ represents the generation of normalized weights using a simple gating mechanism with sigmoid activation.

After obtaining the channels with their importance re-calibrated by attention weights, a 1×1 convolution is introduced to reduce the number of channels. During training, channels with high weight values contribute significantly to the results and have higher gradients. This drives the parameter updates of the 1×1 convolution to gradually favor preserving these channels, enabling a learnable feature fusion process. With the help of Interaction Attention block, the proposed model can better utilize features and achieve discriminate feature fusion.

3.4   Loss Function

Due to the relatively small gap between spinal blocks, it is easy for adjacent vertebrae to be connected on the left or right side in the segmentation result. The shapes of vertebrae are basically similar and can be approximated as rounded rectangles. However, in the segmentation result where the vertebrae are connected with each other, two vertebrae are connected on one side and there is a very obvious hollow on the other side. To address this phenomenon, we calculate the curvature of each piece of vertebra segmentation results and use the curvature as a regularization loss. The correct segmentation of the vertebrae can be approximated as many rounded rectangles, with small curvature at each point on edges, while the curvature of the concave parts in two connected vertebrae is very large. During the training process, the model seeks to minimize curvature loss, aiming to smooth the segmentation curvature, thereby penalizing the segmentation of vertebrae into a continuous entity. This can be interpreted as adding a prior knowledge to the model: the desired shape of the segmentation outcome is to achieve a more stable and smooth form. Given that pixel points are discrete, the curvature approximation of a discrete point is described in differential form. The curvature calculation formula is as follows:

$$curvature = \frac{d\theta}{ds} = \frac{arctan(y_{i+1} - y_i, x_{i+1} - x_i)}{\sqrt{(y_{i+1} - y_i)^2 + (x_{i+1} - x_i)^2}} \tag{4}$$

where (x_i, y_i) and (x_{i+1}, y_{i+1}) denote two neighboring points on a contour, θ represents the angle difference between two points to approximate the radian, s denotes the distance between two points to approximate the arc length. $d\theta/ds$ represents the rate of change of radians with respect to arc length, which is curvature. By representing the curvature using discrete values, the average curvature of the entire contour is taken as the regularization term loss L_{cur}.

The Dice loss is a loss function commonly used in medical image segmentation tasks. It uses the Dice coefficient, which measures the overlap between two sets. In image segmentation, the Dice loss can penalize the model for incorrect or incomplete segmentation of objects, and handle class imbalance, which is often a concern in medical image segmentation, where some classes may be much more prevalent than others. The whole loss function is defined as:

$$L = L_{dice} + \lambda \cdot L_{cur} \tag{5}$$

where λ is the coefficient for the curvature loss. Initially, we set it to a small value of 0.001, aiming for the Dice loss to dominate the overall loss function. As the number of training epochs increased, we gradually raised λ to 0.005, intending for the model to focus on the connected vertebrae in the segmentation results during the later stages of training.

4   Experiment

4.1   Settings

We used a dataset of 1367 high-resolution spine X-Ray images with evidence of scoliosis to various extents. We split the dataset into training (1147), testing (110), and validation (110) sets. To keep the original aspect ratio of images, the training images were zero-padded into square and then resized to 512 × 512. We trained the model for 200 epochs using Adam optimizer, with learning rate set to 1e-4. In addition to the spine X-ray image dataset, we also validated our model on a polyp segmentation dataset, Kvasir-SEG [10], to assess its performance on other medical imaging segmentation datasets. We evaluated the segmentation results generated by the model using four metrics to measure the extent of similarity between the predicted mask and the ground truth: the Dice coefficient (Dice), Jaccard similarity (JS), precision (PRE), and recall (REC).

4.2 Experiments on Spine Segmentation

From Table 1, we have the following observations: 1) Attention U-Net exhibits a significant performance improvement over U-Net, indicating that the Attention Gate structure can play a vital role in spine segmentation. 2) DUCK-Net outperforms both U-Net and ResUNet, demonstrating the feasibility of the DUCK block and residual downsampling. 3) Our model achieves the highest scores on all metrics and beats DUCK-Net, GMSRF-Net and TransResUnet, which were the state-of-the-arts on the Kvasir-SEG dataset, confirming the viability of our proposed CIA block and curvature loss. Especially in terms of the precision metric, the experimental results show a more significant improvement, which demonstrates the effectiveness of curvature loss. This is because the introduction of curvature loss inhibits the connection between spines, and the connected parts are false positives, which would reduce precision. Thus, these comparative results demonstrate the effectiveness of the proposed model for spine segmentation. Figure 3 shows an examples of spine segmentation results compared to other models, from which we can see that Unet++ and TransResU-Net are affected by ribs or other factors that segmentation results contain incorrect parts, incomplete vertebrae segmentation results exist in Attention U-Net, ResUNet and TransUNet, and there are connected vertebrae in UNet, nnU-Net, GMSRF-Net and DUCK-Net. The results of our model were not affected by interference, with a relatively complete spine segmentation, and there is no phenomenon of vertebrae that connect with each other, which proves the effectiveness of our improvement. Figure 4 shows the changes in loss function and Dice coefficient of the proposed model during the training process, from which we can see that as the number of training epochs increases, the Dice coefficient gradually rises while the loss consistently decreases, indicating an improvement in the model's performance. Furthermore, after the 160th training epoch, the trends of the Dice coefficient and the loss stabilize, signifying that the model has converged and reached a relatively stable level of performance.

4.3 Experiments on Kvasir-SEG Dataset

Table 2 shows the experiments conducted on the polyp segmentation dataset Kvasir-SEG, aiming to evaluate the performance of our model on other medical image segmentation datasets, compared with the other state-of-the-art methods. The experiment results indicate that our model outperforms other models such

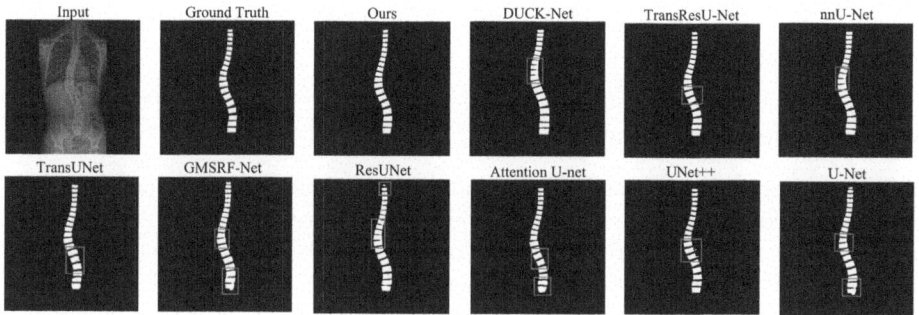

Fig. 3. Comparison of spine segmentation results predicted by different models.

Table 1. Segmentation results on the spine segmentation dataset. Best model results are in bold.

Method	Dice	JS	PRE	REC
U-Net [14]	0.7764	0.6345	0.7827	0.7703
ResUNet [3]	0.7835	0.6441	0.7898	0.7773
Unet++ [20]	0.7860	0.6474	0.7922	0.7799
Attention U-Net [13]	0.7961	0.6613	0.8026	0.7897
TransUNet [2]	0.8029	0.6707	0.8094	0.7965
GMSRF-Net [17]	0.8097	0.6802	0.8028	0.7988
TransResU-Net [18]	0.8279	0.7064	0.8540	0.8034
nnU-Net [9]	0.8293	0.7085	0.8360	0.8229
DUCK-Net [4]	0.8379	0.7211	0.8372	0.8387
Ours	**0.8725**	**0.7739**	**0.8801**	**0.8651**

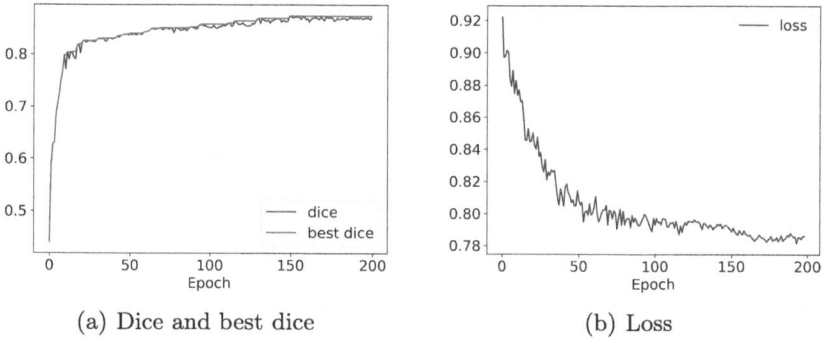

(a) Dice and best dice   (b) Loss

Fig. 4. Training process of the proposed model.

as U-Net, nnU-Net, TransResU-Net and GMSRF-Net, and is closely comparable to DUCK-Net, demonstrating a robust polyp segmentation capability. The empirical evidence indicates that the proposed model demonstrates robust generalization abilities, which not only excels in the domain of spine segmentation but also shows efficacy when applied to diverse datasets pertaining to medical image segmentation.

4.4 Ablation Experiments

To evaluate the effectiveness of each component added in the proposed model, we conduct comprehensive ablation experiments by removing each component. The experiment results are shown in Table 3, where CIA represents Channel Interaction Attention block, AGs represents Attention Gates, and DUCK-Net is the baseline of our work. All the w/o curvature loss model, w/o CIA model and w/o AGs model outperform the backbone DUCK-Net, verifying the effectiveness of the three improvements. When the curvature loss was removed, precision decreased even more significantly compared to dice coefficient, indicating an increase in the number of false positives in the segmentation results. Before the introduction of curvature loss, there was a phenomenon of vertebrae connected with each other in the segmentation results, where the connected parts correspond to false positives. These experiment results demonstrate the effectiveness of curvature loss in reducing the number of connected vertebrae. After removing

Table 2. Segmentation results on Kvasir-SEG dataset. Best model results are in bold.

Method	Dice	JS	PRE	REC
U-Net [14]	0.8125	0.6842	0.8126	0.8124
ResUNet [3]	0.8158	0.6890	0.8042	0.8278
Unet++ [20]	0.8320	0.7124	0.8125	0.8524
Attention U-Net [13]	0.8340	0.7153	0.8283	0.8398
TransUNet [2]	0.8706	0.7709	0.8769	0.8645
GMSRF-Net [17]	0.9286	0.8667	0.9321	0.9251
TransResU-Net [18]	0.8884	0.8214	0.9022	0.9106
nnU-Net [9]	0.9341	0.8763	0.9315	0.9367
DUCK-Net [4]	**0.9502**	**0.9501**	**0.9628**	0.9379
Ours	0.9483	0.9016	0.9555	**0.9412**

Table 3. Ablation studies results on spine segmentation dataset. Best model results are in bold.

Method	Dice	JS	PRE	REC
DUCK-Net [4]	0.8379	0.7211	0.8372	0.8387
w/o curvature loss	0.8492	0.7379	0.8487	0.8497
w/o CIA	0.8482	0.7364	0.8641	0.8328
w/o AGs	0.8519	0.7421	0.8678	0.8367
Ours	**0.8737**	**0.7757**	**0.8937**	**0.8545**

CIA model, the evaluation scores drop significantly, and the complete proposed model apparently outperform the w/o AGs model, indicating that under the guidance of the two modules, our proposed model can better detect boundaries and distinguish vertebrae of different sizes. The ablation experiments confirmed the effectiveness of the components, with no conflicts observed between them.

5   Conclusion

In thesis, we have proposed an effective model for X-ray images spine segmentation. Our key contributions include introducing Attention Gates to enhance the information extracted from features at different scales to detect different sizes of vertebrae, designing a Channel Interaction Attention block for better feature fusion to reduce the loss of important features such as edges, introducing curvature as a regularization term in loss function to punish segmentation with connected vertebrae. Extensive experiments on spine segmentation and polyp segmentation datasets demonstrate the superiority of our method over previous state-of-the-arts. The proposed network provides an effective solution for automated spine segmentation based on X-ray images, which can benefit scoliosis diagnosis.

Acknowledgments. This work was supported in part by the NSFC fund (NO. 62206073, 62176077), in part by the Shenzhen Key Technical Project (NO. JCYJ20241202123728037, JSGG20220831092805009, JSGG20220831105603006, JSGG20201103153802006), in part by the Guangdong International Science and Technology Cooperation Project (NO. 2023A0505050108), in part by the Guangdong Provincial Key Laboratory of Novel Security Intelligence Technologies (NO. 2022B1212010005), in part by the Guangdong Shenzhen joint Youth Fund under Grant 2021A151511074, and in part by the Natural Science Foundation of Guangdong Province under Grant 2023A1515010893.

References

1. Chen, B., et al.: Deep active context estimation for automated COVID-19 diagnosis. ACM Tran. Multimedia Comput. Commun. Appl. (TOMM) **17**(3s), 1–22 (2021)
2. Chen, J., et al.: TransUNet: transformers make strong encoders for medical image segmentation. arXiv preprint arXiv:2102.04306 (2021)
3. Diakogiannis, F.I., Waldner, F., Caccetta, P., Wu, C.: ResUNet-a: a deep learning framework for semantic segmentation of remotely sensed data. ISPRS J. Photogramm. Remote. Sens. **162**, 94–114 (2020)
4. Dumitru, R.G., Peteleaza, D., Craciun, C.: Using duck-net for polyp image segmentation. Sci. Rep. **13**(1), 9803 (2023)
5. Giannoglou, V., Stylianidis, E.: Review of advances in cobb angle calculation and image-based modelling techniques for spinal deformities. ISPRS Ann. Photogrammetry Remote Sens. Spat. Inf. Sci. **3**, 129–135 (2016)

6. He, K., Zhang, X., Ren, S., Sun, J.: Deep residual learning for image recognition. In: Proceedings of the IEEE Conference on Computer Vision and Pattern Recognition, pp. 770–778 (2016)
7. Horng, M.H., Kuok, C.P., Fu, M.J., Lin, C.J., Sun, Y.N.: Cobb angle measurement of spine from X-ray images using convolutional neural network. Comput. Math. Methods Med. **2019**(1), 6357171 (2019)
8. Imran, A.A.Z., et al.: Analysis of scoliosis from spinal X-ray images. arXiv preprint arXiv:2004.06887 (2020)
9. Isensee, F., Jaeger, P.F., Kohl, S.A., Petersen, J., Maier-Hein, K.H.: nnU-Net: a self-configuring method for deep learning-based biomedical image segmentation. Nat. Methods **18**(2), 203–211 (2021)
10. Jha, D., et al.: Kvasir-SEG: a segmented polyp dataset. In: MultiMedia modeling: 26th International Conference, MMM 2020, Daejeon, South Korea, January 5–8, 2020, proceedings, part II 26, pp. 451–462. Springer (2020). https://doi.org/10.1007/978-3-030-37734-2_37
11. Jha, D., et al.: ResUNet++: an advanced architecture for medical image segmentation. In: 2019 IEEE international symposium on multimedia (ISM). pp. 225–2255. IEEE (2019)
12. Milletari, F., Navab, N., Ahmadi, S.A.: V-Net: fully convolutional neural networks for volumetric medical image segmentation. In: 2016 Fourth International Conference on 3D vision (3DV), pp. 565–571. IEEE (2016)
13. Oktay, O., et al.: Attention U-Net: learning where to look for the pancreas. arXiv preprint arXiv:1804.03999 (2018)
14. Ronneberger, O., Fischer, P., Brox, T.: U-Net: convolutional networks for biomedical image segmentation. In: Medical Image Computing and Computer-Assisted Intervention–MICCAI 2015: 18th International Conference, Munich, Germany, October 5-9, 2015, proceedings, part III 18, pp. 234–241. Springer (2015). https://doi.org/10.1007/978-3-319-24574-4_28
15. Shao, Z., Yuan, Y., Ma, L., Yeung, D.Y., Zhu, X.: SG-LRA: self-generating automatic scoliosis cobb angle measurement with low-rank approximation. arXiv preprint arXiv:2411.12604 (2024)
16. Shen, X., Zhang, Y., Zhang, R., Shi, Q., Song, Y., Zhang, Q.: Segmentation method of X-ray whole spine coronal image based on VGG-Net. Foreign Electron. Measur. Technol. **43**(01), 135–140 (2024)
17. Srivastava, A., Chanda, S., Jha, D., Pal, U., Ali, S.: GMSRF-Net: an improved generalizability with global multi-scale residual fusion network for polyp segmentation. In: 2022 26th International Conference on Pattern Recognition (ICPR), pp. 4321–4327. IEEE (2022)
18. Tomar, N.K., Shergill, A., Rieders, B., Bagci, U., Jha, D.: TransResU-Net: transformer based ResU-Net for real-time colonoscopy polyp segmentation. arXiv preprint arXiv:2206.08985 (2022)
19. Wang, Q., Wu, B., Zhu, P., Li, P., Zuo, W., Hu, Q.: ECA-Net: efficient channel attention for deep convolutional neural networks. In: Proceedings of the IEEE/CVF Conference on Computer Vision and Pattern Recognition, pp. 11534–11542 (2020)
20. Zhou, Z., Rahman Siddiquee, M.M., Tajbakhsh, N., Liang, J.: UNet++: a nested U-Net architecture for medical image segmentation. In: Deep Learning in Medical Image Analysis and Multimodal Learning for Clinical Decision Support: 4th International Workshop, DLMIA 2018, and 8th International Workshop, ML-CDS 2018, Held in Conjunction with MICCAI 2018, Granada, Spain, September 20, 2018, Proceedings 4, pp. 3–11. Springer (2018). https://doi.org/10.1007/978-3-030-00889-5_1

SSCL: A Spatial-Spectral and Commonality Learning Network for Semi-supervised Medical Image Segmentation

Yujie Liu, Zhonghao Du$^{(\boxtimes)}$, Xuanting Li, Zongmin Li, Jiayue Fan, and Chaozhi Yang

Qingdao Institute of Software, College of Computer Science and Technology, China University of Petroleum (East China), QingDao, China
z22070066@s.upc.edu.cn

Abstract. The semi-supervised method has greatly promoted the development of medical image segmentation, as it alleviates the pressure of obtaining a large number of medical image annotations. In this article, we propose a new spatial-spectral and commonality learning network (SSCL) that better utilizes unlabeled data for semi-supervised medical image segmentation. The motivation of the SSCL model is to observe that, existing methods only focus on the features of the target area during segmentation, ignoring the features which can represent the total image, we call them common features. Because there is also feature information in the common features that can better assist the network in segmentation. In addition, due to the low contrast and high noise characteristics of medical images, only allowing the model to learn features in the spatial domain is not sufficient for the network to learn enough information. Due to insufficient feature information, the network will make more erroneous predictions when segmenting the edges of the target area than when segmenting the central area. Therefore, our proposed SSCL model consists of two new designs to address the above issues. First, we propose a reliable commonality learning module to learn the common features to help the network improve the segmentation performance. Second, we design a spectral convolution module to learn spectral feature information. Experimental results on three medical image datasets show that our framework outperforms previous state-of-the-art methods.

Keywords: Semi-supervised learning · Medical image segmentation · Spectral feature · Common feature · Commonality learning

1 Introduction

In the medical field, accurately segmenting internal structures from medical images plays an important role in many clinical applications [19], such as disease diagnosis and quantitative analysis. Due to the power of deep neural networks, many researchers have tried to use them to solve the task of medical image segmentation, and segmentation models based on a large amount of labeled data have achieved great results [7,10,24,37,40].

© The Author(s), under exclusive license to Springer Nature Singapore Pte Ltd. 2025
P. Didyk and J. Hou (Eds.): CVM 2025, LNCS 15663, pp. 29–48, 2025.
https://doi.org/10.1007/978-981-96-5809-1_3

However, since medical image labeling often requires specialized knowledge and clinical experience, the labeling work is only suitable to be done by doctors or professionals, which makes it very difficult and expensive to acquire large amounts of labeled data. But obtaining a large amount of unlabeled data is much easier than obtaining labeled data, so how to use a small portion of labeled data and a large amount of unlabeled data to train the network to be able to solve the task of medical image segmentation becomes very important, this is called semi-supervised. Semi-supervised medical image segmentation methods have arisen under such a need and become an important research direction in computerized medical vision tasks.

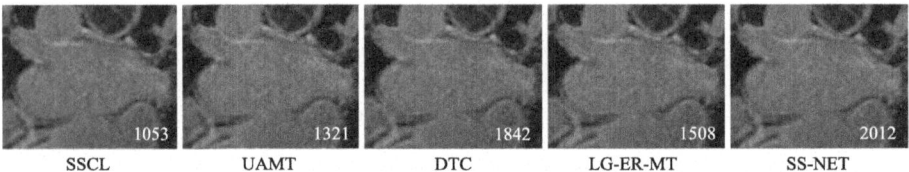

| SSCL | UAMT | DTC | LG-ER-MT | SS-NET |

Fig. 1. Visualization of the model's erroneous predictions and the number of incorrectly predicted pixels. The red masks represent the model's wrong predictions, and the white numbers represent the number of wrong pixels.

Semi-supervised learning can be subdivided into two categories of methods: pseudo-labeling and consistency learning. Pseudo-labeling [13] methods are based on previously labeled data, where unlabeled data is simply pseudo-labeled and used along with labeled data to train the network; this method aims to expand the training dataset and thus improve the performance of the model. Consistency learning [4,27,38] methods encourage agreement in predictions between different perturbations by introducing perturbations to the model structure or input images, an approach designed to further train the network to improve its performance. However, previous methods [4,9,14,16,17,25,30–32,34,38] further improve the accuracy of segmentation results, there are still two problems with current semi-supervised medical image segmentation methods: (1) The network only focuses on the features of the target area, neglecting the features that can represent the total image, we call them common features. In previous work, labels or pseudo labels were usually used to supervise the network learning of the features of the target area in the image, which made the network only focus on extracting the features of the target area and ignoring other feature information in the image. However when using pseudo labels, due to inaccurate supervised signals, it is difficult for the network to learn accurate target area features. There is some information in common features that can help the network better segment the target area. Therefore, learning only the features of the target area limits the network's ability to segment the target area; (2) Lack of sufficient feature information leads to more errors in edge segmentation. Due to the poor imaging quality of medical images, the edge information of medical images is very difficult to distinguish, they may contain very limited information in the spatial domain, so the networks only learn features in the spatial domain and cannot obtain sufficient feature information, leading to more erroneous predictions when segmenting the target area. As shown in Fig. 1, displayed the model's incorrect predictions and the number of pixels with incorrect predictions. It can be seen that the erroneous pixels are mainly located in the edge area of the target, which is caused by insufficient information obtained by the network from the image. Therefore, learning image features only in the spatial domain can not provide sufficient feature information for the segmentation network.

To alleviate the above existing problems, we propose a spatial-spectral and commonality learning network (SSCL) for semi-supervised medical image segmentation. Firstly, we propose a commonality learning module to learn common features, to solve the problem of networks only focusing on the features of the target region while ignoring common features. Specifically, outside of the segmentation network, we trained a reconstruction network as a commonality learning module. The commonality learning module does not require additional labeling to learn common features, because the label of the reconstruction network is the input image, and the common features learned by the reconstruction network are provided as compensation information to the segmentation network to help it better segment the target area. Furthermore, in the field of semi-supervised medical image segmentation, we have for the first time introduced the extraction and processing of spectral domain information, to solve the problem of insufficient feature information leading to more edge segmentation errors. Previous work [8] has shown that there are spectral features that existing methods may miss in medical images, and semi-supervised learning requires more information than fully supervised learning. Therefore, we combine spectral and spatial features to provide more information to the network. Specifically, we have added a new spectral encoder to the network. During the training process, the input image will be fed to the spatial encoder and spectral encoder to learn spatial and spectral features respectively. In this way, the network can learn more feature information.

In summary, the main contributions of this paper are as follows:

- We propose a commonality learning module to learn common features, which is used to help the segmentation network better grasp the features of the target area and train the module without adding additional labels, ensuring the accuracy of learning features (Sect. 3.2).
- We introduce spectral features that extract and process information from the spectral domain to provide more feature information for the network, to solve the problem of only learning features in the spatial domain without sufficient feature information (Sect. 3.3).
- We validate the proposed SSCL on three public benchmark datasets, and the experimental results show that the proposed SSCL outperforms other state-of-the-art methods in all three benchmarks, indicating that SSCL is a superior architecture for semi-supervised medical image segmentation. The ablation

experiments further demonstrate the effectiveness of each proposed module (Sect. 4).

2   Related Work

2.1   Medical Image Segmentation

Segmenting target organs or lesions from medical images plays a vital role in many clinical applications, as accurate segmentation information can help doctors better assess a patient's condition. The development of deep learning has greatly improved the accuracy and stability of medical image segmentation results. In the field of medical image segmentation, U-Net [6,21] and its encoder-decoder framework have been widely used due to their simplicity and accuracy. The main advantage of U-Net is its skip connection design. To improve performance, various methods have been proposed, such as redesigning skip connections [41], introducing residual/dense convolution blocks in the network [1,15], or optimizing feature maps by introducing attention mechanisms [20]. nnU-Net [12] proposed by Isensee et al. enables the segmentation network to adapt to training strategies and network frameworks automatically. In recent years, with the remarkable achievements of transformer in traditional computer vision tasks, transformer have also received widespread attention in the field of medical segmentation, and many transformer-based segmentation methods have been proposed. Chen et al. [3] improved the segmentation performance by replacing the encoder in U-Net with a transformer. Cao et al. [2] constructed a pure transformer segmentation network, Swin-Unet, by using transformer blocks to replace the convolution blocks in the U-Net framework. VNet [18] was proposed by Milletari et al. to address the challenges in medical image segmentation, especially when processing 3D volume data. Although these methods have achieved great results in the medical segmentation field, they are all based on supervised training mode, and obtaining medical image annotations is very complex and costly, which limits these methods to a small amount of labeled data.

2.2   Semi-supervised Learning

Semi-supervised learning trains a network by utilizing a combination of labeled and unlabeled data, allowing the network's performance to approach that of fully supervised learning. The theoretical basis of semi-supervised learning comes from three fundamental assumptions [28]: (1) smoothness assumption: for two adjacent input samples $x1$, $x2 \in X$ in the input space, the corresponding labels $y1$ and $y2$ should be the same, and vice versa. (2) low-density assumption: samples within a single class tend to form a cluster, so the decision boundary of the classifier should pass through low-density areas in the input space, and not high-density regions. (3) manifold assumption: samples located on the same low-dimensional manifold should belong to the same class, reflecting the local smoothness of the decision boundary.

As mentioned in the introduction section, semi-supervised learning methods can be divided into two categories:pseudo-labeling and consistency learning. The pseudo-labeling method attempts to generate pseudo-labels similar to ground truth labels to expand the training set for network training. Lee et al. [13] proposed using the predictions of a fully supervised network as pseudo-labels for unlabeled data, but this method introduces a lot of noise during the training process. To address this issue, Sohn et al. [26] reduced the number of erroneous predictions by setting a threshold for the predicted values and only retaining high-confidence annotations.

The core idea of consistency learning is that for an input, even if perturbed, the network can still produce an output that is consistent with the original. One typical representative is the mean teacher proposed by Tarvainen et al. [27], which applies two different augmentations to the same input to increase perturbation and uses the output of the teacher model to supervise the student model. After that, many works have extended the mean teacher framework differently. Because the teacher network in the mean teacher framework updates parameters through exponential moving average (EMA) [27], the performance of the teacher network is limited by the student network. Therefore, Chen et al. [4] proposed a cross-pseudo-supervision method where two networks with different parameter initialization supervise each other and independently update their parameters.

2.3 Semi-supervised Medical Image Segmentation

The difficulty in obtaining labeled medical image data and the success of semi-supervised learning have driven the development of semi-supervised medical image segmentation research. Variants of the mean teacher framework have been widely used in semi-supervised medical image segmentation. Yu et al. proposed a mean teacher framework UA-MT [38] that uses uncertainty information to guide the student network to learn more reliable targets from the teacher network and enhances network performance by introducing transformation perturbations. Wang et al. proposed a dual uncertainty-weighted method Double-UA [32] based on this uncertainty-aware teacher-student model, which simultaneously considers the uncertainty of predictions and features and refines the predictions of the teacher model during training. Afterward, Wang et al. proposed a triple uncertainty-guided mean teacher framework Triple-UA [31] by defining two auxiliary tasks on the mean teacher network to help the model learn different features and make better predictions. Hang et al. used the global-local structure-aware entropy minimization method LG-ER-MT [9] based on the mean teacher network. CoraNet [25] proposed a model that can generate both deterministic and uncertain regions, where the student network assigns different weights to the regions given by the teacher network. In addition, some other methods have also achieved good results. SASSNet [14] introduced a shape-aware semi-supervised segmentation strategy that integrates more flexible geometric representations into the network to improve performance. DTC [16] proposed a dual-task consistency framework by building task-level regularization training, which encourages consistent predictions of the same input under different tasks. Luo et al.

proposed a pyramid multi-scale architecture (URPC) [17], which encourages consistent regularization of predictions of unlabeled inputs at multiple scales. Wang et al. proposed a generative Bayesian deep learning model (GBDL) [30] to learn the joint distribution of data and labels. Wu et al. proposed a new competitive winning method (ComWin) [33] to improve the quality of pseudo labels. Xu et al. proposed a novel ambiguity-consensus mean-teacher(AC-MT) [23] model. Shen et al. proposed a multi-network collaborative training UCMT [36] with high-confidence pseudo labels. Although previous methods have improved the accuracy of segmentation results, they only learn the features in the spatial domain and cannot provide sufficient feature information for the segmentation network; And only learn the features of the target area, ignoring the information in the common features may also play a promoting role in network segmentation. This article proposes solutions to these problems.

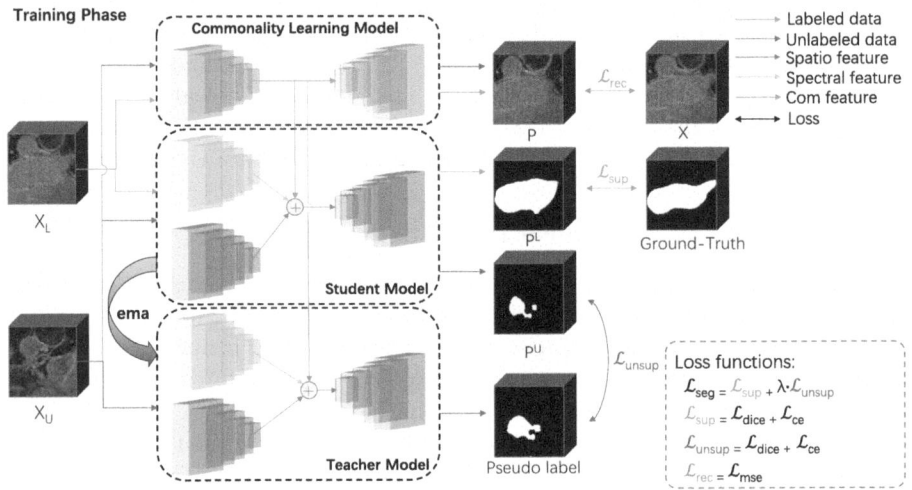

Fig. 2. The process of our proposed SSCL framework.

3   Method

3.1   Overview of the Framework

In the task of semi-supervised medical image segmentation, we assume a complete dataset that contains two types of data: labeled data and unlabeled data. The number of labeled data is N, and the number of unlabeled data is M, where $M \gg N$. For the sake of simplicity, we define the two types of data as two subsets of the dataset, denoted as $D = \{D_L, D_U\}$. The labeled subset is represented as $D_L = (X_i^L, Y_i^L)_{i=1}^N$, and the unlabeled subset is represented as $D_U = (X_i^U)_{i=1}^M$. Here, $X \in R^{W \times H \times D}$ represents the input image during the training phase, and

Y represents the corresponding labels (only for labeled data). The goal of semi-supervised medical image segmentation is to predict the label mapping $\hat{Y} \in \{0, 1, ..., C\}^{W \times H \times D}$ for each voxel $k \in X$, where 0 represents the background class, and the rest correspond to target classes.

The overall training process of the proposed SSCL is illustrated in Fig. 2. SSCL is based on the Mean Teacher framework, which consists of a teacher network $T(F_T(\cdot))$, a student network $S(F_S(\cdot))$, and commonality learning module $R\ (F_R(\cdot))$, where the commonality learning module is a reconstruction network. A batch of input data X contains an equal number of labeled data (X_L, Y_L) and unlabeled data X_U. The input data X is first passed through the reconstruction network to obtain the common features F_c and the reconstruction prediction $\hat{X}$ for the two types of data.

$$\hat{X}, F_c = F_R(X) \tag{1}$$

Note that the common features F_c are the output of the encoder in the reconstruction network. Then, the common features F_c, along with the input data X, are separately fed into the teacher and student networks to obtain the predicted values:

$$\hat{Y}_T = F_T(X^U, F_c) \tag{2}$$

$$\hat{Y}_S = F_S(X, F_c) \tag{3}$$

The overall network output includes the segmentation predictions $\hat{Y}_T$ and $\hat{Y}_S$ from the teacher and student networks, respectively, as well as the reconstruction predictions $\hat{X}$ for the two types of data. The student network is pseudo-supervised using the predictions from the teacher network. The loss function L_{seg} consists of both supervised and unsupervised losses, which are combined by cross-entropy loss and dice loss [18], this is a popular approach in medical image segmentation. The input for the reconstruction network, as well as the supervised labels, is the input image X. Therefore, this network does not differentiate between the two types of data. The loss function L_{rec} is composed of the MSE loss. The reconstruction network and the student network independently update their parameters based on the calculated losses, while the teacher network updates its parameters using exponential moving average (EMA) [27].

3.2   Commonality Learning Module

The purpose of the commonality learning module is to learn the common features of labeled and unlabeled data and help the segmentation network better capture the features of the target regions. In semi-supervised segmentation networks, the lack of reliable supervision signals prevents the segmentation network from accurately learning the features of the target regions in unlabeled data. The proposed commonality learning module, as shown in Fig. 2, consists of a VNet [18]. The input and supervised labels for this module are both the input image, and the output is the reconstructed input image. The entire network is trained by calculating the loss between the reconstructed and input images.

Therefore, we use the common features learned by the commonality learning module as compensatory information provided to the segmentation network.

When the input image X enters the commonality learning module, the network extracts the common features F_c. Here, we take the features outputted by the last layer of the encoder in the network as the common features F_c provided to the segmentation network. The common features F_c are added to the final features F_f (which will be discussed in the next section) outputted by the last layer of the encoder in the segmentation network. The combined features are then passed to the decoder for segmentation, resulting in the final segmentation result $\hat{Y}$:

$$\hat{Y} = D(F_c + F_f) \tag{4}$$

Since the commonality learning module is trained in a fully supervised manner, it can ensure the accuracy of the learned common features. By providing common features as supplementary information to the segmentation network, the segmentation network can improve the segmentation performance of the target area with the help of common features.

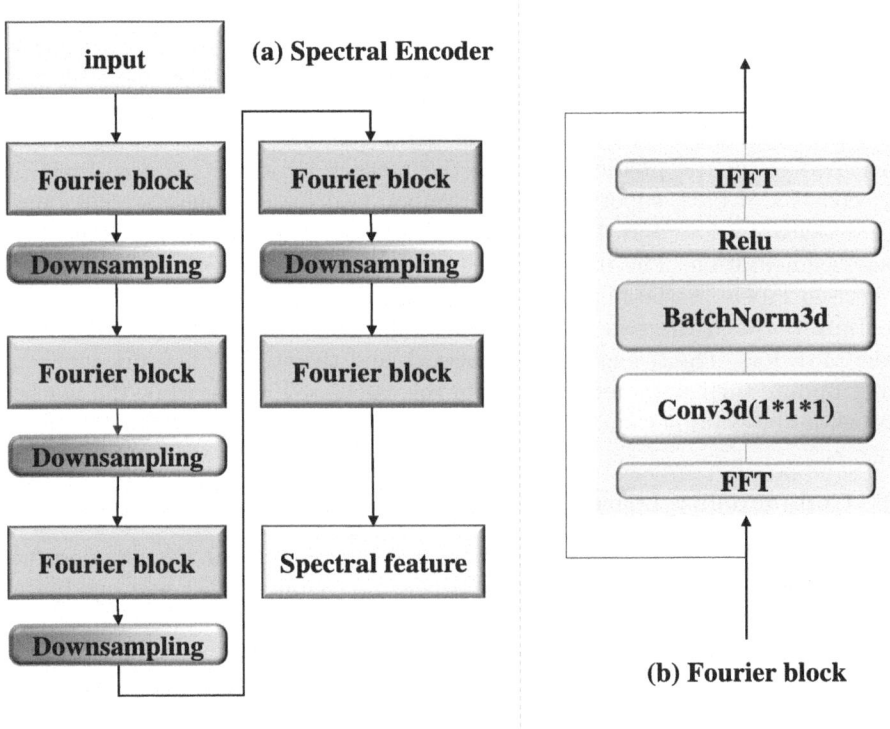

Fig. 3. The Spectral Encoder (a) and Fourier block (b).

3.3 Spectral Feature Extraction

As shown in Fig. 2, the student and teacher networks for image segmentation consist of two encoder branches, E_{spa} and E_{spe}, and a decoder D. E_{spa} is a spatial encoder (the blue part in Fig. 2) used to extract spatial features F_{spa} from the image, which has the same structure as the encoder in the VNet and is composed of five convolution blocks. On the other hand, E_{spe} is a spectral encoder (the yellow part in Fig. 2) used to extract spectral features F_{spe} from the image. Its structure, as shown in Fig. 3(a), consists of five Fast Fourier Convolution (FFC) [5] blocks, which have the same overall structure as the spatial encoder but with FFC blocks instead of convolution blocks. D is a VNet decoder that outputs the segmentation results. Since medical images have limited inherent information, using only a spatial encoder to learn image features may not be sufficient. Therefore, we introduce a spectral encoder to extract and process spectral features from the spectral domain, providing additional feature information to the segmentation network and helping improve segmentation accuracy.

The input of the spectral encoder E_{spe} is the same as that of the spatial encoder E_{spa}. When the input image enters the spectral encoder E_{spe}, its processing procedure is similar to the spatial encoder E_{spa}. FFC blocks are used to convolve and learn features, followed by downsampling operations. The features F_{spe} outputted by the spectral encoder E_{spe} are added to the features F_{spa} to get the final features F_f, complementing the network with spectral feature information.

$$F_f = F_{spa} + F_{spe} \tag{5}$$

The final features F_f, combined with the common features F_c obtained from the commonality learning module, then passed to the decoder D to obtain the final results.

The FFC block in the spectral encoder, as shown in Fig. 3(b), first performs a 3D Fast Fourier Transform (FFT) on the input to obtain the real and imaginary parts, $a + bi \in C$. The concatenated real and imaginary parts were then passed through a convolutional layer with a kernel size of 1 to learn spectral features. After that, the output of the convolutional layer goes through an activation layer and batch normalization layer. The output is then split into two parts, the real and imaginary parts, finally, a 3D inverse Fast Fourier Transform (IFFT) is performed to transform the spectral features back to the spatial domain, aligning the spectral features with the corresponding spatial domain features.

3.4 Loss Function

In the SSCL framework, two networks need to be updated through loss computation: the student network and the reconstruction network. Therefore, the loss function includes two parts: the segmentation loss L_{seg} for training the student network and the reconstruction loss L_{rec} for training the reconstruction network.

The segmentation loss L_{seg} for training the student network consists of two components: the supervised loss and the unsupervised loss. It can be represented as follows:

$$L_{seg} = L_{sup} + \lambda L_{unsup} \tag{6}$$

L_{sup} is the supervised loss, L_{unsup} is the unsupervised loss, and λ is a balancing parameter with a default value of 0.5. Both supervised and unsupervised losses are composed of a combination of dice loss [18] and cross-entropy loss. The difference is that the supervised loss is supervised by ground truth labels, while the unsupervised loss is pseudo-supervised using pseudo-labels generated by the teacher network. The representation is as follows:

$$L_{sup} = DICE(\hat{Y}^L, Y^L) + CE(\hat{Y}^L, Y^L) \tag{7}$$

$$L_{unsup} = DICE(\hat{Y}^U, Y^P) + CE(\hat{Y}^U, Y^P) \tag{8}$$

Y^P represents pseudo-labels, which are determined by applying a common threshold of 0.5 to the predicted values $\hat{Y}_T$ of the teacher network.

The reconstruction loss L_{rec} for the reconstruction network is relatively straightforward. It is trained by calculating the MSE loss between the reconstructed image outputted by the network and the input image. It can be represented as follows:

$$L_{rec} = MSE(\hat{X}, X) \tag{9}$$

$\hat{X}$ represents the reconstructed image, and X represents the input image.

The teacher network updates its parameters W_T^{k+1} at the (k+1)th iteration using an exponential moving average (EMA). The update of the teacher network parameters is represented as follows:

$$W_T^{k+1} = \alpha W_T^k + (1 - \alpha)W_S^k \tag{10}$$

Here, α is the weight parameter, default is 0.999, and W_S^k represents the parameters of the student network at the k-th iteration.

3.5   Testing Phase

The testing phase of SSCL is shown in Fig. 4. During testing, we use two networks: the trained student network and the reconstruction network. The reconstruction network is kept during testing because the common features learned by the reconstruction network can be added to the features of the segmentation network to improve the segmentation performance. For a test image X_t, it is sent to both networks separately. The reconstruction network provides the common features F_c of the test image X_t to the student network, and the final prediction Y_t can be obtained from the student network:

$$Y_t = F_S(X_t, F_c) \tag{11}$$

4   Experiments

4.1   Dataset and Implementation Details

Left Atrial Dataset (LA) [35]: The LA dataset is the benchmark dataset for the 2018 Atrial Segmentation Challenge, containing 100 3D gadolinium-enhanced

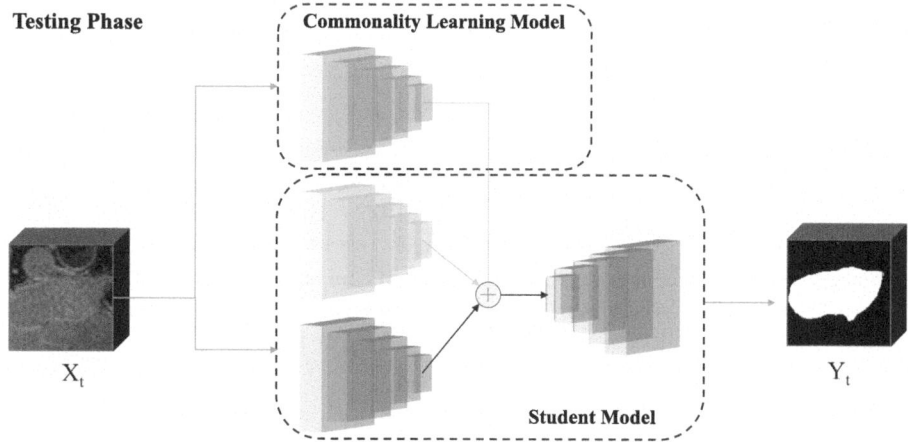

Fig. 4. The process of testing phase. Note that only the student model and the commonality learning model are needed in the testing phase.

magnetic resonance imaging (GE-MRI) scans with labels. Following the settings used in DTC [16] and UA-MT [38], we use 80 data for training and 20 data for testing. In our experiments, we conducted two typical semi-supervised settings, using 10% and 20% labeled data for training. NIH-pancreas dataset [22]: The Pancreas CT dataset is publicly available from the National Institutes of Health Clinical Center and includes 82 abdominal CT images manually annotated by experienced physicians. The size of CT scans ranges from $512 \times 512 \times 181$ to $512 \times 512 \times 466$ voxels, with interlayer spacing ranging from 1.5 to 2.5mm. During preprocessing, we used a soft tissue CT window range of [-125,275]HU and resampled all images to isotropic resolution of $1.0 \times 1.0 \times 1.0$mm. In the experiments, we used 62 samples for training and the remaining 20 samples for testing, following the setting in CoraNet [25]. Kits19 dataset [11]: It is a kidney tumor segmentation dataset containing 210 labeled 3D computed tomography (CT) scans for training and validation. Following previous work [30], we use 160 data for training and 50 data for testing.

Implementation details: We implemented our model in PyTorch and conducted all experiments on an NVIDIA 3090TI GPU with a fixed random seed. We use the SGD optimizer with an initial learning rate of 0.01, weight decay of 0.0001, and momentum of 0.9 to train the model. VNet is used as the backbone and sets the batch size to 4, including 2 labeled data and 2 unlabeled data. The iteration numbers for pre-training and formal training were set to 4k and 30k, respectively. To avoid overfitting, rotation, and flip operations are implemented to augment the data, following previous work. Since 3D data training requires a lot of computation, we cropped all training data into small patches during training. The training patch sizes for LA, Pancreas-CT, and Kits19 were $112 \times 112 \times 80$, $96 \times 96 \times 96$, and $128 \times 128 \times 64$, respectively. During the testing phase, we use the slide window strategy to obtain the final results, with a step size of $18 \times 18 \times 4$ for LA and Kits19, and a step size of $16 \times 16 \times 16$ for Pancreas-CT.

4.2 Evaluation Metrics

We use four metrics to evaluate the performance of the model, including Dice, Jaccard, average surface distance (ASD), and 95% Hausdorff distance (95HD). The Dice and Jaccard coefficients are primarily used to calculate the percentage of overlap between two object regions. The ASD measures the average distance between the boundaries of the two object regions, while the 95HD measures the distance between the closest points of the two object regions.

4.3 Results

LA dataset: We first evaluated our proposed method on the left atrial segmentation task. The compared methods included UA-MT [38], SASSNet [14], Double-UA [32], Tripled-UA [31], CoraNet [25], URPC [17], DTC [16], SS-Net [34], LG-ER-MT [9], GBDL [30], AC-MT [36], and UCMT [23]. We conducted semi-supervised experiments under different labeling ratios (10% and 20%). In addition, VNet is used as the baseline with 10% and 20% labeled data. As shown in Table 1, all methods benefited from the unlabeled data, and our method outperformed the state-of-the-art methods in terms of Dice and Jaccard coefficients in both cases, for example, compared with UA-MT and GBDL, the Dice coefficients of SSCL increased by 5% and 0.9%, respectively, on 10% of labeled data. It can also be seen that our segmentation results are significantly better than the compared methods from Fig. 5, whether in 2D or 3D results, our SSCL prediction is closest to the Ground Truth. Figure 1 also shows that our SSCL reduces more false predictions at the target edge compared to UAMT, DTC, LG-ER-MT, and SS-NET. Demonstrating the superiority of SSCL in semi-supervised medical image segmentation. On the two metrics of 95HD and ASD, it can be seen that our SSCL is better than most methods, but GBDL achieved the best results on both indicators in both cases. We consider that this is possibly due to GBDL extracting voxel data as slices for segmentation instead of directly segmenting the voxel data, as the heart is an irregularly shaped organ, therefore, slice segmentation may achieve better results on these two metrics than directly segmenting voxels.

NIH-Pancreas dataset: We further evaluated our proposed method on the pancreas dataset with 20% labeled data. Since the pancreas is located deep in the abdomen and has large variations in size, location, and shape, and the pancreas CT has a more complex background than left atrial MRI, pancreas segmentation is more challenging than left atrial segmentation. However, our proposed SSCL still showed good performance. We compared our method with DAN [39], ADVNET [29], VNet [18], UA-MT [38], SASSNet [14], DTC [16], and CoraNet [25], ComWin [33], as shown in Table 2. Compared with these methods, SSCL performed significantly better in terms of Dice, Jaccard, and 95HD, especially, on Dice, it improved by 0.9% compared to CoraNet, and on Jaccard,

Table 1. Comparison with state-of-the-art semi-supervised segmentation methods on the LA dataset.

Method	Volumes used		Metrics			
	Labeled	Unlabeled	Dice↑	Jaccard↑	95HD↓	ASD↓
VNet	8(10%)	0	0.786	0.670	21.20	6.07
VNet	16(20%)	0	0.870	0.773	11.85	3.22
VNet	80(100%)	0	0.914	0.844	5.48	1.51
UA-MT [38] (MICCAI 2019)	8(10%)	72(90%)	0.843	0.735	13.83	3.36
SASSNet [14] (MICCAI 2020)			0.873	0.777	9.62	2.55
Double-UA [32] (MICCAI 2020)			0.859	0.758	12.67	3.31
LG-ER-MT [9] (MICCAI 2020)			0.855	0.751	13.29	3.77
Tripled-UA [31] (MICCAI 2021)			0.868	0.768	10.42	2.98
URPC [17] (MICCAI 2021)			0.850	0.744	15.37	3.96
DTC [16] (AAAI 2021)			0.875	0.782	8.23	2.36
SS-Net [34] (MICCAI 2022)			0.886	0.796	7.49	1.90
CoraNet [25] (TMI 2022)			0.866	0.781	12.11	2.40
GBDL [30] (CVPR 2022)			0.884	0.792	**5.89**	**1.60**
UCMT [23] (IJCAI 2023)			0.881	0.791	9.14	3.06
AC-MT [36] (MedIA 2023)			0.891	0.805	11.05	2.19
SSCL (ours)			**0.893**	**0.807**	7.40	2.03
UA-MT [38] (MICCAI 2019)	16(20%)	64(80%)	0.889	0.802	7.32	2.26
SASSNet [14] (MICCAI 2020)			0.895	0.812	8.24	2.20
Double-UA [32] (MICCAI 2020)			0.897	0.814	7.04	2.03
LG-ER-MT [9] (MICCAI 2020)			0.896	0.813	7.16	2.06
Tripled-UA [31] (MICCAI 2021)			0.893	0.810	7.42	2.21
URPC [17] (MICCAI 2021)			0.887	0.799	12.73	3.66
DTC [16] (AAAI 2021)			0.894	0.810	7.32	2.10
SS-Net [34] (MICCAI 2022)			0.889	0.802	8.02	2.36
CoraNet [25] (TMI 2022)			0.887	0.811	7.55	2.45
GBDL [30] (CVPR 2022)			0.894	0.822	**4.03**	**1.48**
UCMT [23] (IJCAI 2023)			0.904	0.825	6.31	1.70
AC-MT [36] (MedIA 2023)			0.903	0.824	6.21	1.76
SSCL (ours)			**0.905**	**0.828**	6.39	1.94

it improved by 0.8% compared to ComWin, confirming that our proposed SSCL can better utilize unlabeled data and has stronger information extraction ability.

Kits19 dataset: The experimental results on the kidney segmentation dataset are shown in Table 3, where we experimented with 10% labeled data. We compared our method with UA-MT [38], SASSNet [14], Double-UA [32], Tripled-UA [31], CoraNet [25], and GBDL [30]. From the table, we can see that our method

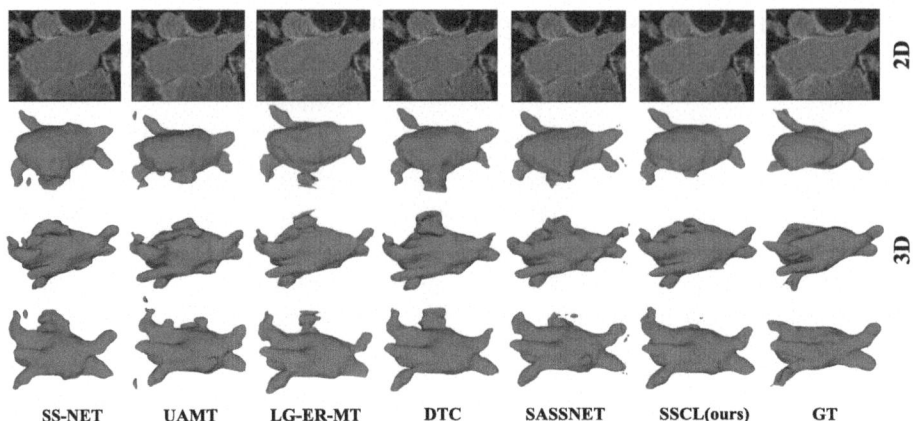

Fig. 5. Visualizations of several semi-supervised segmentation methods obtained by SS-NET [34], UAMT [38], LG-ER-MT [9], DTC [16], SASSNET [14], our SSCL model with 20% labeled data and ground truth on LA dataset.

Table 2. Comparison with state-of-the-art semi-supervised segmentation methods on the NIH-Pancreas dataset.

Method	Volumes used		Metrics			
	Labeled	Unlabeled	Dice↑	Jaccard↑	95HD↓	ASD↓
VNet	12(20%)	0	0.706	0.567	22.54	6.29
VNet	62(100%)	0	0.818	0.697	5.13	1.34
VNet [18](3DV 2016)	12(20%)	50(80%)	0.700	0.556	14.27	1.64
DAN [39](MICCAI 2017)			0.767	0.633	11.13	2.97
ADVNET [29](CVPR 2019)			0.753	0.617	11.72	3.88
UA-MT [38](MICCAI 2019)			0.773	0.638	11.90	3.06
SASSNet [14](MICCAI 2020)			0.777	0.641	10.93	3.05
DTC [16](AAAI 2021)			0.783	0.648	8.36	2.25
CoraNet [25](TMI 2022)			0.797	0.667	7.59	1.89
ComWin [33](TMI 2023)			0.796	0.670	6.95	**1.34**
SSCL (ours)			**0.806**	**0.678**	**5.83**	1.63

SSCL exhibited the best performance in all four evaluation metrics, outperforming all compared methods and further validating the effectiveness of SSCL in medical image segmentation. It is worth noting that our SSCL not only outperforms GBDL in Dice and Jaccard but also outperforms GBDL in 95HD and ASD metrics in this dataset, which was not achieved in the LA dataset. We think this may be because the kidney has a more regular shape compared to the heart, so the advantage of slicing for segmentation on these two metrics is lost.

Table 3. Comparison with state-of-the-art semi-supervised segmentation methods on the Kits19 dataset.

Method	Volumes used		Metrics			
	Labeled	Unlabeled	Dice↑	Jaccard↑	95HD↓	ASD↓
UA-MT [38](MICCAI 2019)	16(10%)	144(90%)	0.883	0.802	9.46	2.89
SASSNet [14](MICCAI 2020)			0.891	0.822	7.54	2.41
Double-UA [32](MICCAI 2020)			0.895	0.828	7.42	2.16
Tripled-UA [31](MICCAI 2021)			0.887	0.815	7.55	2.12
CoraNet [25](TMI 2022)			0.898	0.820	7.23	1.89
GBDL [30](CVPR 2022)			0.911	0.840	6.38	1.51
SSCL (ours)			**0.913**	**0.843**	**5.08**	**1.30**

Table 4. Ablation studies of different parts in SSCL on LA dataset.

Method	Volumes used		Metrics			
	Labeled	Unlabeled	Dice↑	Jaccard↑	95HD↓	ASD↓
Baseline	8(10%)	0	0.831	0.717	21.46	6.55
Upper-bound	80(100%)	0	0.911	0.836	10.09	2.67
Baseline + REC	8(10%)	72(90%)	0.867	0.768	14.86	4.50
Baseline + FFC			0.878	0.784	13.48	3.62
SSCL			**0.893**	**0.807**	**7.40**	**2.03**

4.4 Ablation Studies

Effectiveness of Each Component: To better understand and evaluate the components of our proposed SSCL method, we conducted ablation experiments on the LA dataset with 10% labeled data, and the results are shown in Table 4. We used VNet as the backbone and trained it using only 10% labeled data, with its performance as the baseline, and trained it using 100% labeled data, with its performance as the upper limit. We evaluated the effectiveness of each module by gradually adding the proposed modules to the baseline model and observing the changes in segmentation performance. REC refers to the commonality learning module, and FFC refers to the spectral feature learning module. From Table 4, we can see that after adding the two modules separately to the baseline method, all metrics improved significantly, with the Dice coefficient increasing by more than 3% for each module. Moreover, the performance obtained by combining the two modules was further improved based on the separate addition of the two modules, and the improvement was very significant. The experimental results indicate that the addition of these two modules contributes to the segmentation performance, and when the two modules are combined, the performance gain is maximized.

Weight λ in Loss Function: To balance the weights of supervised and unsupervised losses, we weighted the unsupervised loss and set the default value of λ

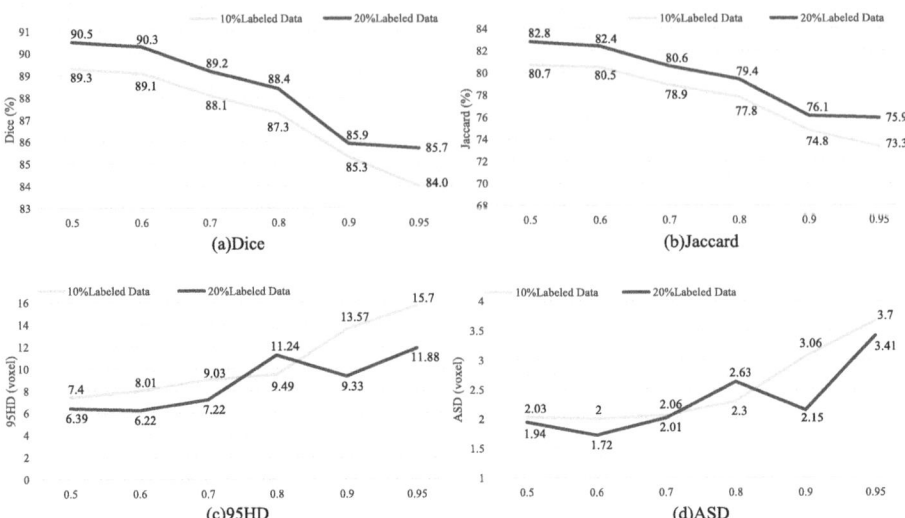

Fig. 6. The results of SSCL with different thresholds on the LA datasets.

Table 5. Ablation studies of weights λ in the loss function with 10% labeled data.

λ	Metrics			
	Dice↑	Jaccard↑	95HD↓	ASD↓
$\lambda = 0.5$	**0.893**	**0.807**	**7.40**	**2.03**
$\lambda = 1.0$	0.890	0.803	8.28	2.56
$\lambda = 1.5$	0.888	0.800	9.96	3.12
$\lambda = 2.0$	0.887	0.797	11.82	3.29
$\lambda = 2.5$	0.869	0.771	12.02	3.87
$\lambda = 3.0$	0.711	0.560	26.88	9.43

to 0.5. We conducted experiments on the LA dataset with 10% labeled data by changing $\lambda = \{0.5, 1, 1.5, 2, 2.5, 3\}$ to observe the effects of different weights on the network performance and the results are shown in Table 5. From the table, we can see that the best performance was achieved when $\lambda = 0.5$, and the performance of the model did not differ much when $\lambda \leq 2$. However, when $\lambda > 2$, the model performance decreased significantly.

Weight α in EMA: In the teacher-student network framework, the parameters of the teacher network are updated using the exponential moving average (EMA) based on the parameters of the student model. And the weight was set to 0.99 default. However as shown in Table 6, we found that changing the weight from 0.99 to 0.999 improved the performance of the model. This may be because as parameter updates became slower, the robustness of the teacher model was enhanced, allowing the student network to learn more stable information from the teacher network.

Effectiveness of Threshold: Fig. 6 shows the performance of the SSCL model trained with different pseudo-label thresholds on the LA dataset. The results indicate that as the pseudo-label threshold increases, the overall performance of the model on all four evaluation indicators shows a downward trend. This may be because as the pseudo-label threshold increases while filtering out erroneous information, effective information is also greatly filtered. Therefore, we ultimately used a pseudo-label threshold of 0.5 to generate pseudo-labels on all datasets.

Table 6. Ablation studies of weights α in EMA with 10% and 20% labeled data.

λ	Metrics			
	Dice↑	Jaccard↑	95HD↓	ASD↓
$\alpha = 0.99$	0.891	0.805	7.89	2.04
$\alpha = 0.999$	**0.893**	**0.807**	**7.40**	**2.03**
$\alpha = 0.99$	0.900	0.820	6.99	2.44
$\alpha = 0.999$	**0.905**	**0.828**	**6.39**	**1.94**

5   Discussion

Compared to other methods, SSCL performs better for two main reasons. Firstly, it provides common features that are missed during segmentation for the segmentation network. Other methods have ignored the common features of the image, while in our method, we successfully compensated the lost common features back to the segmentation network. The experimental results confirm that helping the segmentation network compensate for common features can better improve the segmentation effect. The second reason is to add a spectral encoder to the segmentation network to learn the spectral features of the image. The visualization of segmentation results also shows that due to the increase in feature information, our SSCL produces fewer erroneous predictions for edge segmentation compared to other methods. Due to these two reasons, our SSCL ultimately achieved very good segmentation results.

Although the proposed SSCL method has achieved success in semi-supervised medical image segmentation, the fusion strategy of the three features in the proposed model is a simple addition processing, and the three networks trained in the model result in high training time costs. Future work can attempt to find better feature fusion strategies to more effectively utilize feature information, and design a better network structure to reduce the training cost of SSCL.

6 Conclusion

In this paper, we propose a semi-supervised medical image segmentation framework called SSCL, which reconstructs input images to obtain common features and introduces spectral feature information to help the network better learn the features of the target region in the image and improve segmentation accuracy. The proposed commonality learning module in SSCL ensures the accuracy of common features without introducing additional labels in a fully supervised manner. The spectral feature extraction module helps the network obtain more feature information by learning the spectral features of the input image. We conducted experiments on three common benchmark datasets with two different modalities, including the left atrial dataset of MR scans, the pancreas dataset, and the kidney segmentation dataset of CT scans, the segmentation results outperformed the previous state-of-the-art methods, demonstrating the effectiveness, robustness, and generalization of SSCL, as well as its potential in semi-supervised medical image segmentation.

Acknowledgments and Disclosure of Funding. This work is partly supported by National key r&d program (Grant no. 2019YFF0301800), National Natural Science Foundation of China (Grant no. 61379106), the Shandong Provincial Natural Science Foundation (Grant nos. ZR2013FM036, ZR2015FM011).

References

1. Alom, M.Z., Yakopcic, C., Hasan, M., Taha, T.M., Asari, V.K.: Recurrent residual U-Net for medical image segmentation. J. Med. Imaging **6**, 014006 (2019)
2. Cao, H., et al.: Swin-Unet: Unet-like pure transformer for medical image segmentation. In: European Conference on Computer Vision, pp. 205–218 (2022). https://doi.org/10.1007/978-3-031-25066-8_9
3. Chen, J., et al.: TransUNet: transformers make strong encoders for medical image segmentation. arXiv preprint arXiv:2102.04306 (2021)
4. Chen, X., Yuan, Y., Zeng, G., Wang, J.: Semi-supervised semantic segmentation with cross pseudo supervision. In: Proceedings of the IEEE/CVF Conference on Computer Vision and Pattern Recognition, pp. 2613–2622 (2021)
5. Chi, L., Jiang, B., Mu, Y.: Fast Fourier convolution. Adv. Neural. Inf. Process. Syst. **33**, 4479–4488 (2020)
6. Çiçek, Ö., et al.: 3D U-Net: learning dense volumetric segmentation from sparse annotation. In: Medical Image Computing and Computer-Assisted Intervention – MICCAI 2016, pp. 424–432 (2016)
7. Dou, Q., Liu, Q., Heng, P.A., Glocker, B.: Unpaired multi-modal segmentation via knowledge distillation. IEEE Trans. Med. Imaging **39**, 2415–2425 (2020)
8. Farshad, A., Yeganeh, Y., Gehlbach, P., Navab, N.: Y-Net: a spatiospectral network for retinal oct segmentation. In: International Conference on Medical Image Computing and Computer-Assisted Intervention (2022)

9. Hang, W., et al.: Local and global structure-aware entropy regularized mean teacher model for 3D left atrium segmentation. In: Medical Image Computing and Computer Assisted Intervention– MICCAI 2020, pp. 562–571 (2020)

10. He, Q., Yang, Q., Su, H., Wang, Y.: Multi-task learning for segmentation and classification of breast tumors from ultrasound images. Comput. Biol. Med. **173**, 108319 (2024)

11. Heller, N., et al.: The state of the art in kidney and kidney tumor segmentation in contrast-enhanced CT imaging: results of the KiTS19 challenge. Med. Image Anal. **67**, 101821 (2021)

12. Isensee, F., Jaeger, P.F., Kohl, S.A., Petersen, J., Maier-Hein, K.H.: NNU-Net: a self-configuring method for deep learning-based biomedical image segmentation. Nat. Methods **18**, 203–211 (2021)

13. Lee, D.H.: Pseudo-label : the simple and efficient semi-supervised learning method for deep neural networks. In: ICML 2013 Workshop : Challenges in Representation Learning (WREPL) (2013)

14. Li, S., Zhang, C., He, X.: Shape-aware semi-supervised 3D semantic segmentation for medical images. In: Medical Image Computing and Computer Assisted Intervention–MICCAI 2020, pp. 552–561 (2020)

15. Li, X., Chen, H., Qi, X., Dou, Q., Fu, C.W., Heng, P.A.: H-DenseUNet: hybrid densely connected UNet for liver and tumor segmentation from CT volumes. IEEE Trans. Med. Imaging **37**, 2663–2674 (2018)

16. Luo, X., Chen, J., Song, T., Wang, G.: Semi-supervised medical image segmentation through dual-task consistency. In: Proceedings of the AAAI Conference on Artificial Intelligence, vol. 35, pp. 8801–8809 (2021)

17. Luo, X., et al.: Efficient semi-supervised gross target volume of nasopharyngeal carcinoma segmentation via uncertainty rectified pyramid consistency. In: Medical Image Computing and Computer Assisted Intervention – MICCAI 2021, pp. 318–329 (2021)

18. Milletari, F., Navab, N., Ahmadi, S.A.: V-Net: fully convolutional neural networks for volumetric medical image segmentation. In: 2016 Fourth International Conference on 3D Vision (3DV), pp. 565–571 (2016)

19. Newman, M., Girvan, M.: Abdominal multi-organ segmentation with organ-attention networks and statistical fusion. Med. Image Anal. **55**, 88–102 (2019)

20. Oktay, O., et al.: Attention U-Net: learning where to look for the pancreas. In: Medical Imaging with Deep Learning (2018)

21. Ronneberger, O., Fischer, P., Brox, Thomas", E.N., Hornegger, J., Wells, W.M., Frangi, A.F.: U-Net: convolutional networks for biomedical image segmentation. In: Medical Image Computing and Computer-Assisted Intervention – MICCAI 2015, pp. 234–241 (2015)

22. Roth, H.R., et al.: DeepOrgan: multi-level deep convolutional networks for automated pancreas segmentation. In: Medical Image Computing and Computer-Assisted Intervention– MICCAI 2015, pp. 556–564 (2015)

23. Shen, Z., Cao, P., Yang, H., Liu, X., Yang, J., Zaiane, O.R.: Co-training with high-confidence pseudo labels for semi-supervised medical image segmentation. In: Proceedings of the Thirty-Second International Joint Conference on Artificial Intelligence, "IJCAI-23", pp. 4199–4207 (2023)

24. Shi, T., Jiang, H., Zheng, B.: C2MA-Net: cross-modal cross-attention network for acute ischemic stroke lesion segmentation based on CT perfusion scans. IEEE Trans. Biomed. Eng. **69**(1), 108–118 (2022). https://doi.org/10.1109/TBME.2021.3087612

25. Shi, Y., et al.: Inconsistency-aware uncertainty estimation for semi-supervised medical image segmentation. IEEE Trans. Med. Imaging **3**, 41 (2022)
26. Sohn, K., et al.: FixMatch: simplifying semi-supervised learning with consistency and confidence. Adv. Neural. Inf. Process. Syst. **33**, 596–608 (2020)
27. Tarvainen, A., Valpola, H.: Mean teachers are better role models: weight-averaged consistency targets improve semi-supervised deep learning results. Adv. Neural Inf. Process. Syst. **30** (2017)
28. van Engelen, J.E., Hoos, H.H.: A survey on semi-supervised learning. Mach. Learn. **109**(2), 373–440 (2019). https://doi.org/10.1007/s10994-019-05855-6
29. Vu, T.H., Jain, H., Bucher, M., Cord, M., P"é"rez, P.: Advent: adversarial entropy minimization for domain adaptation in semantic segmentation. In: Proceedings of the IEEE/CVF Conference on Computer Vision and Pattern Recognition, pp. 2517–2526 (2019)
30. Wang, J., Lukasiewicz, T.: Rethinking Bayesian deep learning methods for semi-supervised volumetric medical image segmentation. In: Proceedings of the IEEE/CVF Conference on Computer Vision and Pattern Recognition, pp. 182–190 (2022)
31. Wang, K., et al.: Tripleduncertainty guided mean teacher model for semi-supervised medical image segmentation. In: Medical Image Computing and Computer Assisted Intervention– MICCAI 2021, pp. 450–460 (2021)
32. Wang, Y., et al.: Doubleuncertainty weighted method for semi-supervised learning. In: Medical Image Computing and Computer Assisted Intervention–MICCAI 2020, pp. 542–551 (2020)
33. Wu, H., Li, X., Lin, Y., Cheng, K.T.: Compete to win: enhancing pseudo labels for barely-supervised medical image segmentation. IEEE Trans. Med. Imaging **42**, 3244–3255 (2023)
34. Wu, Y., Wu, Z., Wu, Q., Ge, Z., Cai, J.: Exploring smoothness and class-separation for semi-supervised medical image segmentation. In: International Conference on Medical Image Computing and Computer-Assisted Intervention, pp. 34–43 (2022)
35. Xiong, Z., et al.: A global benchmark of algorithms for segmenting the left atrium from late gadolinium-enhanced cardiac magnetic resonance imaging. Med. Image Analy. **67**, 101832 (2021)
36. Xu, Z., et al.: Ambiguity-selective consistency regularization for mean-teacher semi-supervised medical image segmentation. Med. Image Anal. **88**, 102880 (2023)
37. Yi, X., Walia, E., Babyn., P.: Generative adversarial network in medical imaging: a review. Med. Image Anal. **58**, 101552 (2019)
38. Yu, L., Wang, S., Li, X., Fu, C.W., Heng, P.A.: Uncertainty-aware self-ensembling model for semi-supervised 3D left atrium segmentation. In: Medical Image Computing and Computer Assisted Intervention–MICCAI 2019, pp. 605–613 (2019)
39. Zhang, Y., Yang, L., Chen, J., Fredericksen, M., Hughes, D.P., Chen, D.Z.: Deep adversarial networks for biomedical image segmentation utilizing unannotated images. In: Medical Image Computing and Computer Assisted Intervention- MICCAI 2017, pp. 408–416 (2017)
40. Zhao, T., et al.: 3D graph anatomy geometry-integrated network for pancreatic mass segmentation, diagnosis, and quantitative patient management. In: Proceedings of the IEEE/CVF Conference on Computer Vision and Pattern Recognition, pp. 13743–13752 (2021)
41. Zhou, Z., Siddiquee, M.M.R., Tajbakhsh, N., Liang, J.: UNet++: redesigning skip connections to exploit multiscale features in image segmentation. IEEE Trans. Med. Imaging **39**, 1856–1867 (2019)

A Multiscale Edge-Guided Polynomial Approximation Network for Medical Image Segmentation

Fuxian Sui[1], Hua Wang[2], and Fan Zhang[1,3(✉)]

[1] School of Computer Science and Technology, Shandong Technology and Business University, Shandong Yantai, China
zhangfan51@sina.com
[2] School of Information and Electrical Engineering, Ludong University, Yantai, Shandong, China
[3] Shandong Future Intelligent Financial Engineering Laboratory, Shandong, Yantai, China

Abstract. As the core cornerstone of building an efficient medical care system, especially promoting accurate disease diagnosis and treatment, medical image segmentation is of great importance. However, medical segmentation faces many challenges, including complex background, shape and size changes, resulting in inaccurate or fuzzy segmentation boundaries. To meet these challenges, this paper proposes a multiscale edge-guided polynomial approximation network (AMEPANet). The well-designed edge guided bridge module in this paper uses the Laplacian operator to accurately capture and strengthen the edge information in the image, and realizes the robust preservation of edge information across multiple scales. At the same time, by building an information mixed attention mechanism, the network can further mine and use the subtle features of the boundary area to further improve the segmentation accuracy. In order to maximize the use of rich feature information at different scales and stages, this paper combines Kolmogorov-Arnold theorem to build an efficient decoder architecture, which can seamlessly integrate multi-source features to achieve comprehensive fusion and optimization of feature information. In addition, this paper also proposes an innovative C^1 continuous activation function, which shows significant advantages in reducing the fluctuation of model calculation and promoting the stable convergence of the model, and further enhances the comprehensive processing ability of the model for complex medical image features. Through extensive and in-depth experiments on multiple authoritative data sets such as Synapse, the excellent performance of AMEPANet has been verified.

Keywords: Segmentation · Boundary Detection · Piecewise Polynomial Curve · Medical Image · Polynomial Approximation

1 Introduction

In medical image segmentation, while traditional methods have established a strong foundation, their performance is often hindered by factors such as inconsistent image quality, complex anatomical structures, and the high variability of

P. Didyk and J. Hou (Eds.): CVM 2025, LNCS 15663, pp. 49–73, 2025.
https://doi.org/10.1007/978-981-96-5809-1_4

lesion areas, making accurate and robust segmentation challenging in dynamic clinical environments. In recent years, with the vigorous rise of deep learning technology, especially the extensive application of convolutional neural networks (CNN) [8,44,55], it has brought revolutionary progress for medical image segmentation. Among them, UNet, with its unique jumping connection mechanism, has shown outstanding performance in fusing multi-scale features to generate high-resolution segmentation images, which has inspired the emergence of many variants (such as CE-Net [18]), which have made remarkable achievements in further improving segmentation accuracy.

However, the inherent limitations of CNN are also gradually emerging, especially its convolution operation is limited by the local receptive field, and it is difficult to effectively capture the long-distance dependency between pixels in the image, which is particularly obvious when dealing with pathological areas with complex backgrounds, significant changes in shape and size. In addition, CNN is also insufficient in dealing with fuzzy boundaries, which limits its further application in complex medical image segmentation tasks. In order to overcome the above problems, researchers tried to expand the receptive field by introducing dilated convolutions (such as CPFNet [16], DenseASPP [51]), and to strengthen key feature mapping by integrating attention mechanisms (such as CA-Net [17], BCDU-Net [2], Ms-red [13]), but these methods failed to fundamentally solve the problems of remote dependency and local detail capture.

With the great success of Transformer [42] in the field of natural language processing, its powerful global modeling capability has attracted widespread attention [49,57]. The proposal of Vision Transformer (ViT) [14] marks a new chapter of Transformer in image recognition and analysis. Researchers began to explore its potential applications in image processing and medical image segmentation. In order to improve computing efficiency and meet the processing requirements of high resolution medical images, hierarchical transformer architectures such as Swin Transformer [28] based on window attention came into being. Parallel MERIT [35] and other models are designed with dual transformer encoders, which increases the accuracy and model complexity at the same time. In addition, Pyramid Vision Transformer (PVT) [47] based on space reduction attention and TransDeeplab [3] integrating Transformer and DeepLab further expand the application boundary of Transformer in medical image segmentation. MISS-Former [20], DAEformer [1], Swin-Unet [7] and TransUNet [8] use different transformer blocks to replace the convolution part in UNet, and enhance the remote capture capability of the model. These methods alleviate the remote dependency problem to a certain extent by combining the global view of Transformer and the local feature extraction ability of CNN. However, the pure Transformer architecture still has shortcomings in capturing local context information of images, and it is difficult to accurately process the complex details in medical images.

In order to remedy this defect, PVTv2 [48] and other models embed convolutional layers in the Transformer encoder, aiming to enhance the ability of local feature learning. At the same time, CASCADE and its variants (e.g., EMCAD

[36], G-CASCADE [34], PVT-CASCADE [33]) enhance the model's ability to detect multi-scale targets in complex medical images by integrating attention-driven decoders and multi-scale processing techniques. However, although these improvements have enhanced the local learning and global modeling capabilities of the model to a certain extent, they still fail to meet the challenges of complex background, shape and size changes, and fuzzy boundaries in medical images. At the same time, in recent years, the trend of revealing the black box behavior of neural networks has attracted extensive attention. The interpretability of neural networks is crucial [29].

In view of this, this paper aims to propose an innovative medical image segmentation method, which deeply mines the complementary advantages of Transformer and CNN, and introduces a new mechanism to better deal with the diversity and uncertainty in complex medical images. Specifically, we propose an edge guided bridge, which uses the Laplacian operator to retain the edge information, so that the model can emphasize the complete edge information on various scales. Mixed attention is used in the encoder and decoder, combining the advantages of channel attention and spatial attention to improve attention scores and obtain more boundary information. Based on Kolmogorov Arnold theorem, an efficient decoder architecture is designed to integrate multi-source features and achieve comprehensive fusion and optimization of feature information. At the same time, a new C^1 continuous activation function is designed. In general, the contributions of this paper are as follows:

1. We designed Edge Guided Bridge (EGB) module. The EGB module robustly maintains edge information on multiple scales, and retains initial high-frequency information, especially boundary information, through the Laplacian operator to better fill the semantic gap between low-level features extracted by the encoder and high-level features generated by the decoder.

2. This paper proposes an information mixed attention module (IMAM), which skillfully combines the internal Q, K and V of the two attention mechanisms for hybrid operations, so that it can focus on multiple levels and different parts of the input data at the same time. Furthermore, combining Kolmogorov Arnold representation theorem, a high-performance decoder architecture is carefully constructed. The multi-source feature information from the encoder is integrated to realize the deep fusion and optimization of feature information.

3. In this paper, we address issues such as the existence of non-differentiable points in commonly used activation functions like LeakyReLU. We propose a novel C^1 continuous activation function, which reduces fluctuations in the model's computational process, leading to more stable convergence and better integration of different features.

4. Our proposed AMEPANet has demonstrated superior performance on multiple different types of datasets.

2   Related Works

The UNet architecture is renowned for its effectiveness in medical segmentation and has been widely applied in fields such as organ segmentation and polyp segmentation. In this section, we will focus on introducing the relevant background of our proposed model, including boundary detection algorithms, Kolmogorov-Arnold and Vision Transformer.

2.1   Boundary Detection Algorithm

Boundary detection algorithms aim to precisely locate object boundaries or contours in the field of images, with widespread applications including image segmentation, edge enhancement, and various other computer vision tasks [52]. To improve boundary perception accuracy, research has focused on optimizing network training with novel loss functions, including advanced techniques like Boundary Loss [25] and HD Loss [24], which directly guide the network to enhance boundary discrimination. Additionally, some classical techniques continue to play important roles in capturing boundary information. The Sobel operator, as a classical gradient-based algorithm, relies on computing image pixel gradients to identify edges, estimating horizontal and vertical gradients through simple convolution and synthesizing an edge intensity map. However, its high sensitivity to image noise may lead to edge misjudgment. In contrast, the Canny edge detection algorithm follows a more complex multi-step process, including Gaussian smoothing, gradient computation, non-maximum suppression, and hysteresis thresholding, to achieve precise edge detection and connection, although this process is computationally intensive and highly parameter-dependent. The Prewitt operator, as a homologous technique to the Sobel operator, employs different convolution kernel configurations to estimate gradients and also faces the issue of false-positive edges. The Laplacian operator, by performing second-order derivative operations on the image, exhibits higher sensitivity to details and is adept at revealing subtle edges, but this may also increase sensitivity to image noise. As multi-task learning paradigms are increasingly applied in medical image segmentation, new approaches have been explored to integrate boundary detection as an auxiliary task, boosting the model's boundary perception abilities [31,46]. Furthermore, advanced network structures dynamically highlight key boundary features through the integration of spatial attention mechanisms [50], further enhancing the expressiveness of boundary regions and demonstrating fine-grained processing of boundary information. In this context, our research takes a novel approach, aiming to integrate the essence of traditional boundary detection with insights from modern deep learning, proposing an Edge-Guided Bridge mechanism that robustly maintains and enhances image boundary information across multiple scales.

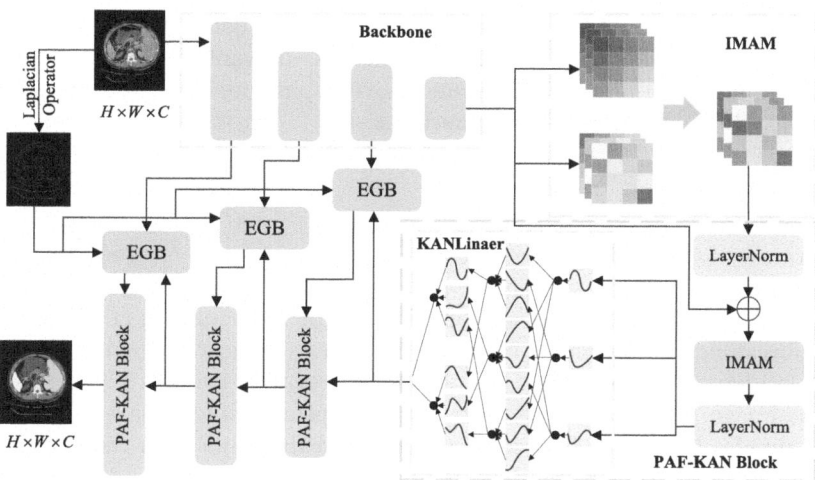

Fig. 1. The main architecture of AMEPANet is shown in the figure.

2.2 Kolmogorov-Arnold

Kolmogorov-Arnold theory [29] is based on multivariable continuous functions, and any multivariable continuous function f can be expressed as a combination of finite single variable continuous functions.

$$f(x) \ = \ f(x_1, x_2, ...x_n) = \sum_{q=1}^{2n+1} \psi_q(\sum_{p=1}^{n} \phi_{q,p}(x_p)) \tag{1}$$

where $\phi_{q,p} : [0,1] \rightarrow \mathbb{R}$, $\psi_q : \mathbb{R} \rightarrow \mathbb{R}$. This theorem has laid a solid theoretical foundation for the construction of Kolmogorov-Arnold Network (KAN). Unlike traditional neural networks, which use fixed activation functions, KANs introduce learnable activation functions at the edge of the network. This design allows each weight parameter in the network to be replaced by a highly flexible single variable function, which is usually parameterized in the form of a spline function. This feature not only significantly improves the flexibility of the model, but also effectively simulates complex functional relationships by reducing the number of parameters, thus enhancing the interpretability and generalization ability of the model. In the development process of KANs, Azam et al. [4] conducted in-depth research on their effectiveness in visual tasks such as image recognition, which promoted the application of KANs in this field. Vaca et al. [41] further expanded the application scope of KANs, introduced them into the time series prediction and control problem, and verified the strong learning ability and wide applicability of KANs. Although KANs have made significant progress in theoretical research and preliminary application, their deep integration and application in the general vision network architecture are still insufficient, especially in the complex real vision tasks, which lack extensive practice and verification. In view of this, this paper explores and designs a general vision network architecture integrating KANs, aiming to give full play to KANs' advantages in flexibility and interpretability, and promote their innovative applications in visual recognition, analysis and broader computer vision tasks.

2.3 Transformer

The Transformer architecture and its various variants have emerged prominently in the domain of medical imaging analysis, particularly in segmentation, demonstrating extraordinary potential applications. In particular, ViT represents a groundbreaking advancement in visual data processing, challenging the dominant paradigm of traditional Convolutional Neural Networks. ViT revolutionizes the image processing pipeline by fully adopting self-attention mechanisms: it first divides the image into small patches and then processes these sequences through the Transformer architecture for in-depth analysis. This innovation not only competes with CNNs on core visual tasks such as object detection but in some scenarios surpasses them, redefining the paradigm of visual information processing. Building upon this foundation, TransUnet ingeniously integrates Transformer and Unet structures to broaden the applicability and efficacy of image segmentation tasks, showcasing the advantages of cross-architecture integration. However, the inherent high computational complexity of the original Transformer, especially the resource consumption of quadratic computations, hinders its broader applications. Addressing this challenge, Swin Transformer emerges with a core focus on introducing a sliding window attention mechanism, significantly reducing computational overhead by confining self-attention calculations within non-overlapping windows. This simultaneously ensures effective capturing of long-range dependencies, achieving dual optimization of efficiency and performance. Furthermore, MaxViT takes an important step in exploring a new dimension of fusion between Transformer and convolution, innovatively integrating self-attention mechanisms with convolutional elements to create a novel architectural unit. By integrating a streamlined multi-scale architecture, this framework empowers MaxViT to dynamically adjust to diverse vision challenges, demonstrating the efficacy of combined computational strategies in advancing visual perception systems.

3 Proposed Method

3.1 Network Architecture

The Vision Transformer (ViT) architecture has emerged as a prominent research focus within computer vision studies, with various ViT-derived methodologies demonstrating exceptional performance across multiple visual recognition tasks. MaxViT [40] effectively combines attention with convolution on the basis of ViT to generate a new architectural element, enhancing segmentation performance.

Building upon MaxViT, we propose a multiscale edge-guided polynomial approximation network -AMEPANet to accurately segment medical images. The overall architecture of our model is illustrated in Fig. 1.

3.2   Edge Guided Bridge

Currently, most methods [1,8,32] employ pooling or convolution in the encoder to downsample feature maps, reducing the amount of information to be processed. While this operation offers significant advantages in constructing deep architectures, it often leads to information loss as downsampling layers accumulate at deeper levels. LOD-Net [11] refines boundary prediction by learning adjustable directional derivatives for each pixel, selecting large-derivative pixels as boundary candidates, and combining high-level semantic features. BAT-Former [27] generates boundary-aware windows through entropy-based adaptive windowing, applying local self-attention within these windows to preserve boundary details. CSAP-UNet [15] strengthens edge features by introducing a boundary enhancement module (BEM) in the shallow layers, integrating local and global features via an attention fusion module. These methods still have some limitations in preserving edge information and integrating boundary and background features. To better address this issue and robustly preserve edge information at multiple scales, we propose an Edge-Guided Bridge (EGB), as shown in the Fig. 2. At the ith layer, this module takes three inputs: the features X_i^e from the encoder, the high-frequency edge features X_i^α obtained through the Laplacian operator, and the more advanced features $X_{i+1}^d \in \mathbb{R}^{H_i \times W_i \times 1}$ from the decoder. To simplify calculations and reduce channel numbers, we apply a convolution to the feature maps at each layer, obtaining the final input $X_i^e \in \mathbb{R}^{H_i \times W_i \times C_i}$ for the EGB module.

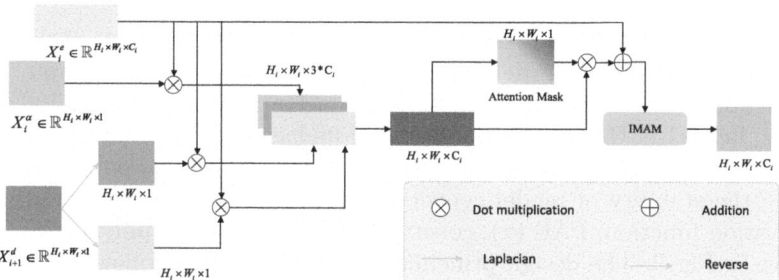

Fig. 2. Edge Guided Bridge takes feature X_i^e from the encoder, edge information X_i^α extracted by Laplacian operator and more advanced prediction feature X_{i+1}^d as input.

We utilize Laplacian pyramid, an effective technique for preserving image edge information. The Laplacian operator is a gradient-based second-order derivative operator that can detect finer edges and is more sensitive to details. In practical applications, we initially smooth the original image using a Gaussian filter, i.e., employing the Laplacian of Gaussian function. The Laplacian pyramid encompasses crucial low-level details at different scales:

$$P_k = P, \ if \ k = 0$$
$$P_k = d\left(g\left(P_{k-1}\right)\right), \ if \ k \geq 1 \tag{2}$$
$$G_k = P_k - \mu(P_{k+1})$$

where, P represents the input image, g represents the Gaussian filtering convolution operator, d represents downsampling by a factor of 2, G_k represents the k-th level of the Laplacian pyramid, and μ represents the corresponding upsampling operation. The Laplacian operator detects second-order variations in the image, such as edges, contours, and other high-frequency details, which are crucial for medical segmentation. Therefore, the feature $X_i^\alpha \in \mathbb{R}^{H_i \times W_i \times 1}$ from the i-th layer of the Laplacian pyramid is provided to the i-th layer of the EGB module. The calculation formula for X_i^α is as follows:

$$X_0^\alpha = G_1$$
$$X_i^\alpha = (d(X_0^\alpha))^i, \ if \ i \geq 1 \tag{3}$$

where $(d(X))^i$ represents downsampling X by a factor of 2 for i times. Inspired by [10], we decompose the advanced features generated by the decoder into two different attention maps, X_{i+1}^{d1} and X_{i+1}^{d2}. We then perform element-wise multiplication and concatenation of X_i^e and X_i^α with these two features as shown in Fig. 2. Finally, after passing through the attention module, we extract the feature relationships between the background and boundary regions.

3.3   Piecewise Activation Function

Activation functions play a crucial role in improving the accuracy of the model. In our model, LeakyReLU demonstrates a significant advantage over activation functions such as Sigmoid, Tanh, and ReLU in enhancing model accuracy. However, LeakyReLU is C^0 continuous, and its lack of C^1 continuity causes discontinuity during backpropagation, leading to fluctuations in computations and affecting the stability of model convergence. To address this issue, we propose an activation function, PAF (x), constructed from piecewise polynomial curves, as shown in Fig. 3. The design principles of PAF (x) are as follows: it is similar in shape to LeakyReLU, it is C^1 continuous, and it consists of four segments of curves. Specifically, in the intervals $(-\infty, -1)$ and $(1, +\infty)$, it consists of two segments of linear polynomial functions, while in the intervals $[-1, 0]$ and $(0, 1]$, it consists of two segments of cubic polynomial functions. First, let's discuss the construction in the intervals $[-1, 0]$ and $(0, 1]$. From this, we can construct Hermite interpolation functions $P_1(x)$ and $P_2(x)$ over the intervals $[x_i, x_{i+1}]$, where

i=1,2:

$$P_i(x) = m_0(x)F_i + d_0(x)\frac{dF_i}{dx} + m_1(x)F_{i+1} + d_1(x)\frac{dF_{i+1}}{dx}$$

$$m_0(x) = (x_{i+1} - x)^2 (2(x - x_i) + h) / h^3$$

$$m_1(x) = (x - x_i)^2 (2(x_{i+1} - x) + h) / h^3 \qquad (4)$$

$$d_0(x) = (x_{i+1} - x)^2 (x - x_i)/h^2$$

$$d_1(x) = -(x - x_i)^2 (x_{i+1} - x) / h^2$$

$$h = x_{i+1} - x_i$$

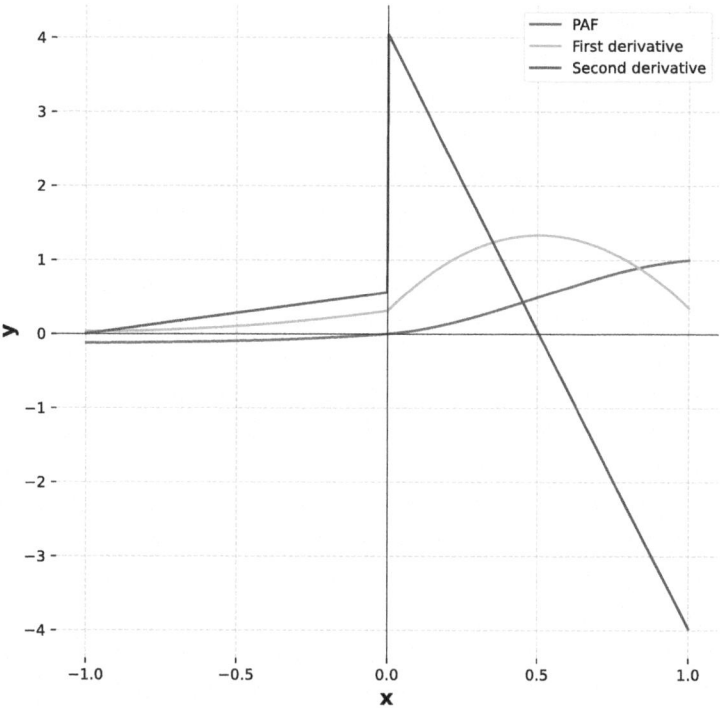

Fig. 3. We use curves of different colors to represent PAF and its first and second derivatives.

Based on the similarity with LeakyReLU, the function values of $P(x)$ at points $x_1 = -1$, $x_2 = 0$, and $x_3 = 1$ are $F_1 = -0.125$, $F_2 = 0$, and $F_3 = 1$, respectively. Then, based on the design by interaction, the first derivatives of PAF(x) at x_1, x_2 and x_3 are set to $\frac{F_1}{dx} = 0.0313$, $\frac{F_2}{dx} = 0.3125$, and $\frac{F_3}{dx} = 0.35$. From equations (4), $P_1(x)$ and $P_2(x)$ are uniquely determined. To reduce computational complexity, we express $P_1(x)$ and $P_2(x)$ in terms of power series:

$$P_1(x) = ((0.0938x + 0.2813)x + 0.3125)x$$
$$P_2(x) = ((-1.3375x + 2.025)x + 0.3125)x \tag{5}$$

Let's discuss the construction of the linear function $P_0(x)$ on the interval $(-\infty, -1)$. The function value and the first derivative of $P_1(x)$ at $x = -1$ are -0.125 and 0.0313, respectively. Since $P_0(x)$ and $P_1(x)$ are C^1 continuous at $x = -1$, we have $P_0(x) = 0.0313(x + 1) - 0.125$. Simplifying this, we get $P_0(x) = 0.0313x - 0.0937$. Similarly, by ensuring the C^1 continuity of $P_2(x)$ and $P_3(x)$ at $x = 1$, we can obtain:

$$P_3(x) = 0.35x + 0.65 \tag{6}$$

Therefore, PAF(x) can be defined as:

$$PAF(x) = \begin{cases} P_0(x), & x < -1, \\ P_1(x), & -1 \le x < 0, \\ P_2(x), & 0 \le x \le 1, \\ P_3(x), & x > 1. \end{cases} \tag{7}$$

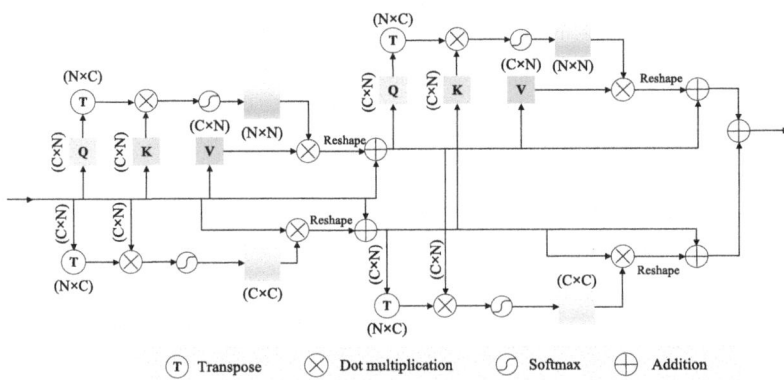

Fig. 4. The architecture of Information Mixed Attention Module.

3.4 PAF-KAN Block

A significant amount of research has found that both spatial attention and channel attention play important roles in the field of segmentation. However, we have observed that the current usage of these two attention mechanisms is limited to simple serial or parallel implementations [13,32], which may not fully exploit the advantages of both. Therefore, we propose an Information Mixed Attention

Module, as shown in Fig. 4. This module is based on the cross mixing of spatial attention and channel attention, which makes spatial attention and channel attention cross complement each other, and further excavates and utilizes the subtle features of boundary areas to further improve the accuracy of attention.

This module takes an input $Y \in \mathbb{R}^{H \times W \times C}$. First, spatial attention and channel attention are applied separately to the input data Y, resulting in $Y^s \in \mathbb{R}^{H \times W \times C}$ and $Y^c \in \mathbb{R}^{H \times W \times C}$. Y^s is chosen as the anchor data, and Y^c as the complementary data. The following formulas were used to calculate Q, K, and V:

$$
\begin{aligned}
Q^s &= Y^s \cdot P_1^Q \\
K^c &= Y^c \cdot P_1^K \\
V^s &= Y^s \cdot P_1^V
\end{aligned}
\tag{8}
$$

where P_1^Q, P_1^K, $P_1^V \in \mathbb{R}^{C \times D}$ represent the learned weight matrices, where D is the number of channels after the linear transformation. The mixed attention was calculated using the following formula:

$$
SA(Q^s, K^c, V^s) = SoftMax(Q^s \cdot (K^c)^T / \sqrt{D}) \cdot V^s
\tag{9}
$$

where SoftMax represents the row-wise SoftMax operation. Similarly, X^c as the anchor data and X^s were chosen as the complementary data, and another set of Q, K, and V was calculated:

$$
\begin{aligned}
Q^c &= X^c \cdot P_2^Q \\
K^s &= X^s \cdot P_2^K \\
V^c &= X^c \cdot P_2^V
\end{aligned}
\tag{10}
$$

The mixed attention for this instance can be calculated using the following formula:

$$
CA(Q^c, K^s, V^c) = SoftMax(Q^c \cdot (K^s)^T / \sqrt{D}) \cdot V^c
\tag{11}
$$

Therefore, the global-local cross-mix attention module can be represented as follows:

$$
IMAM = SA(Q^s, K^c, V^s) + CA(Q^c, K^s, V^c)
\tag{12}
$$

In the segmentation task, effective use of multi-source information is crucial to improve the recognition and segmentation performance of various size objects. Multi-scale information fusion strategy has been proved to be the key to improve performance [39,45,53,54]. For this reason, this paper uses the information mixed attention module to design an efficient decoder architecture, integrate multi-source features, achieve comprehensive fusion and optimization of feature information, and further enhance the model's ability to understand and represent complex scenes. Specifically, the decoding architecture accepts data $t1$ and $t2$ from different processing stages as inputs. Except for the first layer encoder, $t1$ in other layers is the edge information output from the edge guidance bridge, and $t2$ is the high-level semantic information from the upper layer decoder. First, the high-level semantic information $t2$ is normalized,

$$t2 = LayerNorm(t2) \tag{13}$$

Then it is spliced with the edge information t1, and IMAM is used to mine and utilize features in a deeper level, and normalization processing is carried out.

$$t = LayerNorm(IMAM(t1 + t2)) \tag{14}$$

When extracting key information, we innovatively use KAN to calculate, using the following formula definition.

$$\phi(t) = \omega(b(t) + spline(t)) \tag{15}$$

$$b(t) = PAF(t) \tag{16}$$

$$spline(t) = \sum_n c_n B_n(t) \tag{17}$$

where c_n is a trainable parameter, ω is a constant, $B_n(x)$ is a B-spline, and PAF is the activation function above. The flexibility of spline enables it to adaptively model complex relationships in data by adjusting the shape, make full use of spline to optimize the extracted features, and enhance the learning ability of subtle features.

3.5 Loss Function

We use a combination of binary cross-entropy (BCE) loss and Dice loss as the loss function for network training. The definitions of BCE loss and Dice loss are:

$$\begin{aligned} \mathcal{L}_{BCE} &= -\frac{1}{N} \sum_{i=1}^{N} y_i \cdot log\,(p_i) + (1 - y_i) \cdot log\,(1 - p_i) \\ Dice &= \frac{2 \sum_{i=1}^{N} y_i \cdot p_i + \epsilon}{\sum_{i=1}^{N} y_i + \sum_{i=1}^{N} p_i + \epsilon} \\ \mathcal{L}_{Dice} &= 1 - Dice \end{aligned} \tag{18}$$

where, $p_i \in 0, 1$ represents the predicted value of the model, $y_i \in 0, 1$ represents the true label, and $N = W * H$ represents the number of pixels.

4 Experiments

4.1 Datasets

Synapse Multi-organ Segmentation: First, we use the Synapse Multi-organ Dataset [26] to evaluate the performance of our method. This dataset comprises 30 abdominal CT scans consisting of a total of 3779 axial contrast-enhanced

Table 1. We compare AMEPANet with several competing models on the Synapse dataset, emphasizing the best-performing results in bold.

Methods	Spl	RK	LK	Gal	Liv	Sto	Aor	Pan	Average DSC	HD95
UNet [37]	81.48	62.64	72.41	56.70	86.98	67.96	84.00	48.73	70.11	44.69
TransUNet [8]	85.08	77.02	81.87	63.16	94.08	75.62	87.23	55.86	77.49	31.69
Swin-UNet [7]	90.66	79.61	83.28	66.53	94.29	76.60	85.47	56.58	79.13	21.55
TransDeeplab [3]	89.00	79.88	84.08	69.16	93.53	78.4	86.04	61.19	80.16	21.25
MISSFormer [21]	91.92	82.00	85.21	68.65	94.41	80.81	86.99	65.67	81.96	18.20
HiFormer [19]	90.99	79.77	85.23	65.23	94.61	81.08	86.21	59.52	80.39	14.70
DAEFormer [1]	91.82	82.39	87.66	71.65	95.08	80.77	87.84	63.93	82.63	16.39
PVT-CASCADE [33]	90.10	80.37	82.23	70.59	94.08	83.69	83.01	64.43	81.06	20.23
TransUnet [9]—	88.14	69.73	81.11	76.95	93.64	77.84	88.01	61.22	79.58	28.73
Parallel MERIT [35]	91.21	84.31	87.21	73.48	95.06	84.15	88.38	69.97	84.22	16.51
EMCAD [36]	**92.17**	84.10	88.08	68.87	95.26	83.92	88.14	68.51	83.63	15.68
G-CASCADE [34]	90.52	82.38	85.64	74.86	**95.33**	83.65	88.27	**71.99**	84.08	18.89
Ours	91.19	**85.61**	**89.29**	**77.13**	95.16	**85.99**	**88.52**	70.79	**85.55**	**14.39**

abdominal CT images. Each CT scan contains 85 to 198 slices with a size of 512×512 pixels. The voxel spacing is ([0:54-0:54]×[0:98-0:98]×[2:55:0]) mm^3. Our evaluation follows the settings outlined in [8], where we segment eight anatomical structures including the gallbladder (Gal), aorta (Aor), left kidney (LK), liver (Liv), right kidney (RK), stomach (Sto), pancreas (Pan) and spleen (Spl).

Automated Cardiac Diagnosis Challenge (ACDC): The ACDC dataset [6] is designed for automatic cardiac diagnosis and consists of 100 cardiac MRI scans, each containing three cardiac structures: the myocardium (Myo), right ventricle (RV) and left ventricle (LV). In line with the methodology presented in [36], we use 20 for testing, 20 samples for validation, and 70 for training.

Table 2. The comparison results between our method and other competitive methods on polyp segmentation dataset and skin lesion segmentation dataset.

Methods	ETIS DSC	IoU	MAE	CVC-300 DSC	IoU	MAE	ISIC2018 IOU	DICE	ACC	Recall	PH2 IOU	DICE	ACC	Recall
UNet [37]	39.80	33.50	3.60	71.00	62.70	2.20	81.69	88.81	95.68	88.58	87.07	92.62	95.57	92.86
BCDU-Net [2]	64.71	26.72	3.10	74.01	42.86	2.05	80.84	88.33	95.48	89.13	87.41	93.06	95.61	91.11
CE-Net [18]	65.65	32.62	13.16	85.10	61.57	2.79	82.82	89.59	95.97	90.54	89.62	94.36	96.68	94.51
CPF-Net [16]	77.75	50.82	4.32	88.08	69.41	1.55	82.92	89.63	96.02	90.62	89.91	94.52	96.72	93.74
Ms-Red [13]	73.95	44.17	4.72	90.45	73.83	1.77	82.13	89.05	95.71	90.82	90.14	94.65	96.80	94.73
PVT-CASCADE [33]	79.28	68.43	2.03	88.34	82.30	0.84	82.83	90.21	95.62	92.38	89.87	94.51	96.30	95.91
Parallel MERIT [35]	69.73	62.82	1.74	88.21	81.23	1.12	83.44	90.05	95.66	91.92	89.70	94.30	96.81	95.43
EMCAD [36]	80.68	68.53	1.72	88.71	81.33	0.83	82.81	89.46	95.55	**93.81**	90.25	94.69	96.69	96.11
G-CASCADE [34]	78.13	67.34	2.24	88.15	80.69	1.42	82.98	89.57	95.74	93.27	89.69	94.40	95.69	94.93
Ours	**81.51**	**68.82**	**1.70**	**90.92**	**83.34**	**0.61**	**83.82**	**90.37**	**96.05**	93.25	**90.41**	**94.82**	**96.91**	**96.24**

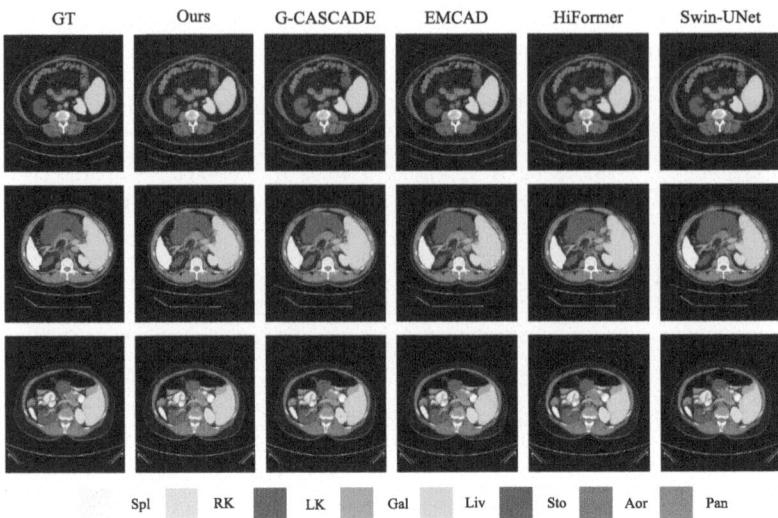

Fig. 5. A qualitative comparison of various visualization methods on the Synapse dataset is shown. Our approach demonstrates fewer false predictions and preserves more detailed information.

Polyp Segmentation: To better validate the generalization ability of our proposed model, we further evaluated it on a polyp segmentation dataset. For fair comparison, we followed the same experimental settings as [56],selecting 1450 images from the Kvasir [23] and CVC-ClinicDB [5] datasets as the training set, and testing on the EITS and CVC-300 datasets [38].

Skin Lesion Image Segmentation: The ISIC2018 dataset [12] is a public collection for skin lesion segmentation, consisting of 2594 skin lesion images with varying resolutions. The PH2 dataset [30] contains 200 color images of skin lesions. For fair model comparison, in line with previous work [13], both datasets are resampled to 224×320 pixels. PH2 is split into 80 training images, 100 test images, and 20 validation images, while The ISIC2018 dataset is divided into training, test sets, and validation in a 7:2:1 ratio.

4.2 Implementation Details

The network uses AdamW, with an initial learning rate of 0.001, momentum of 0.001, and weight attenuation of 0.0001. The batch size is set to 12. For CT datasets such as Synapse and ACDC, we train 400 epochs. For polyp segmentation datasets and skin lesion image segmentation datasets, we train 200 epochs to prevent network overfitting. All experiments were conducted on a single NVIDIA A100.

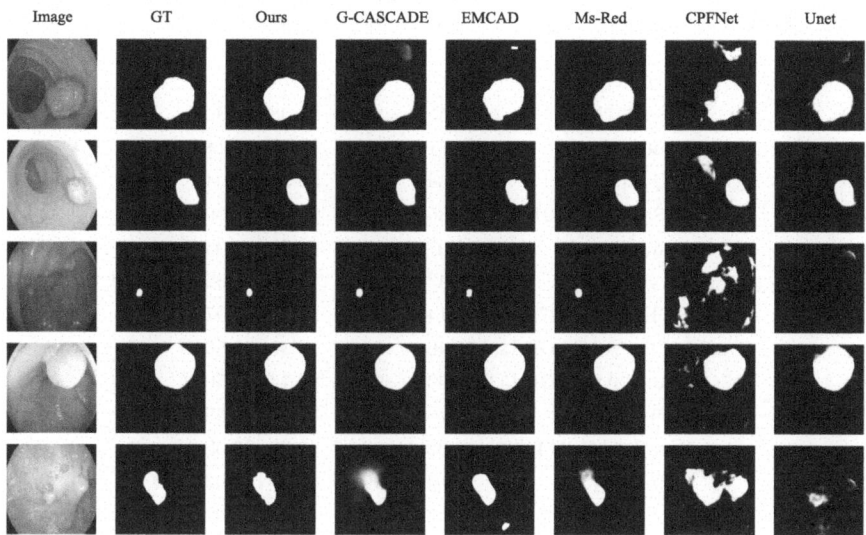

Fig. 6. Qualitative comparison of different visualization methods on polyp segmentation dataset. It can be seen that our method can accurately locate the lesion area and achieve more accurate segmentation.

4.3   Performance Comparisons

Synapse Dataset: Synapse Dataset: Table 1 presents a comprehensive comparison of the proposed method's performance with other SOTA approaches. The results show that our method significantly surpasses the previous SOTA method. Specifically, compared with the EMCAD method, our method achieves 1.92% performance improvement; Compared with G-CASCADE method, it shows an advantage of 1.47%. In the task of segmentation of specific regions such as kidney, aorta and stomach, our method has also achieved remarkable results. It is particularly worth mentioning that our method has achieved a performance leap of up to 2.27% compared with the second ranking method for small and difficult to accurately segment pancreatic regions, which marks a critical step in achieving more accurate segmentation results. The qualitative comparison results between different methods are shown in Fig. 5.

Polyp Segmentation: The comparison results of this method and other SOTA methods in polyp segmentation dataset are shown in Table 2. It is worth noting that our method is superior to the competitive method in all indicators of ETIS and CVC-300 data sets. This advantage observed on different data sets emphasizes the powerful generalization ability of this method. The qualitative comparison of results is shown in Fig. 6. It can be seen that our method has excellent performance in maintaining a low false positive rate, which accurately avoids mistakenly classifying healthy areas as tumors.

Table 3. Our Method compared with various competing models on the ACDC dataset.

Methods	Avg Dice	RV	Myo	LV
UNet [37]	87.55	87.10	80.63	94.92
TransUNet [8]	89.71	86.67	87.27	95.18
nnU-Net [22]	92.34	90.67	90.30	96.04
MISSFormer [21]	90.86	89.55	88.04	94.99
Swin-UNet [7]	88.07	85.77	84.42	94.03
MT-UNet [43]	90.43	86.64	89.04	95.62
BATFormer [27]	91.14	87.99	89.48	95.97
PVT-CASCADE [33]	91.46	89.97	88.90	95.50
TransCASCADE [33]	91.63	90.25	89.14	95.50
nnFormer [58]	91.78	90.22	89.53	95.59
Parallel MERIT [35]	92.32	90.87	90.00	96.08
EMCAD [36]	92.14	90.65	89.68	96.02
G-CASCADE [34]	92.23	90.64	89.96	96.08
Ours	**92.68**	**91.64**	**90.33**	**96.08**

ACDC Dataset: Table 3 shows the DICE scores of our method and other SOTA methods for heart organ segmentation on MRI images of ACDC dataset. Our method achieves the highest average DICE score of 92.68%, which is about 0.45% higher than that of G-CASCADE. At the same time, the segmentation of the left ventricle, the right ventricle and the myocardium achieves about the same result.

Skin Lesion Segmentation: The data presented in Table 2 highlights the excellent performance of our method in PH2 and ISIC2018 skin lesion segmentation data sets, especially in PH2 data sets. Our method outperforms other competitive methods in all evaluation indicators. Specifically, we achieved 90.37% of the DICE score on the ISIC2018 dataset, 0.8% higher than the nearest competitive method G-CASCADE; In another data set, the DICE score reached 94.82%, 0.42% ahead of G-CASCADE. In addition, in terms of accuracy, our method also showed significant advantages. Compared with G-CASCADE, it improved 0.31% on ISIC2018 dataset and achieved 1.22% growth on PH2 dataset. Figure 7 visualizes the results of our method alongside other competing approaches on both datasets. The figure clearly shows that our method exhibits superior generalization performance compared to the others on both datasets.

4.4 Ablation Study

To evaluate the effectiveness of each module in our proposed network, we conducted a large number of ablation experiments. We referred to the network without the EGB, IMAM, and PAF modules as the baseline model.

Qualitative Study: Figure 8 illustrates the advantages of the baseline model and the other three models mentioned by us on the Synapse dataset. It can be

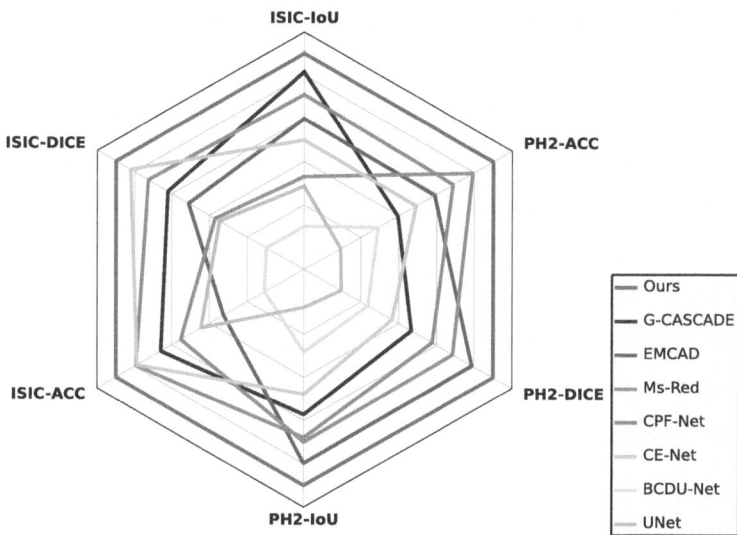

Fig. 7. Visual comparison of indicators between our method and other competitive methods on ISIC2018 and PH2.

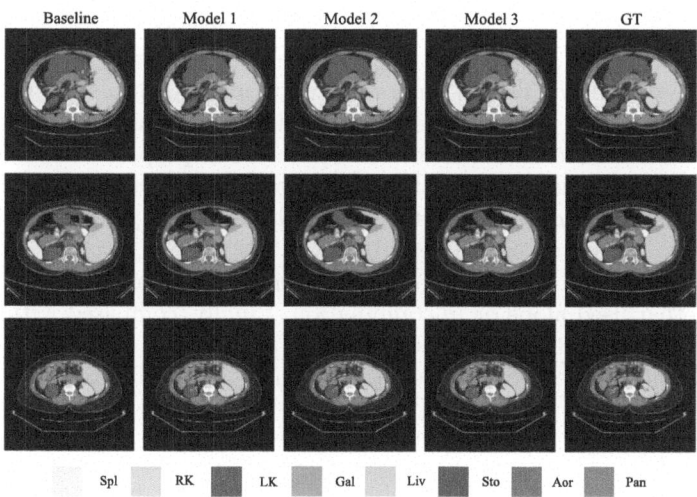

Fig. 8. Visual comparison of segmentation by different models on the Synapse dataset, where Model 1 represents Baseline + IMAM; Model 2 represents Baseline + IMAM + EGB; Model 3 represents Baseline + IMAM + EGB + PAF.

clearly seen from the figure that the organic combination of various modules effectively improves the segmentation performance, can more accurately locate the organ position, and make the segmentation boundary more accurate and clear.

Table 4. Research on ablation of each module on Synapse dataset.

Network			Dice	HD95
IMAM	EGB	PAF		
×	×	×	82.22	18.82
✓	×	×	82.59	17.98
×	✓	×	83.74	16.99
×	×	✓	83.22	17.87
✓	✓	×	84.27	15.71
✓	×	✓	84.17	16.83
×	✓	✓	84.36	16.91
✓	✓	✓	85.55	14.39

Table 5. Research on parameters and time efficiency.

Network		Params(M)	Flops(G)	Infer-Times(ms)
IMAM	EGB			
×	×	86.92	17.88	49.69
✓	×	87.95	18.17	51.64
✓	✓	93.21	20.95	57.30

Quantitative Study: Table 4 shows the experimental results of the detailed quantitative study of the baseline model and the three modules proposed by us. In order to ensure that the effectiveness of our proposed method is fully verified, we have implemented a thorough experimental strategy, including the independent application of these three modules and the pairwise combination between them. From the experimental data in the table, it can be seen that the proposed method can significantly improve the segmentation accuracy of the model, whether used alone or in combination. Finally, compared with Baseline, Dice increased by 3.33% and HD95 decreased by 4.43%, significantly improving the performance of the entire model. Table 5 shows the study on parameters and time efficiency.

Table 6. A comparative study of our proposed PAF and several commonly used activation functions on the Synapse dataset.

Activation Function				Dice	HD95
Relu	LeakyRelu	Gelu	PAF		
✓	×	×	×	83.57	16.33
×	✓	×	×	83.91	15.55
×	×	✓	×	81.81	31.23
×	×	×	✓	85.55	14.39

Significance Analysis: We conducted five experiments with two models: one using the method proposed in this paper and the other without it. The five sets of DSC data obtained were [85.53, 85.50, 85.48, 85.55, 85.52] for the model using the proposed method, and [82.10, 81.95, 82.00, 82.22, 82.15] for the model without it. We performed an analysis of variance (ANOVA) on these two groups of data, calculating an F-statistic of 4615.45 and a p-value of 2.45×10^{-12}. The p-value is far smaller than the significance level (0.05), which means we can reject the null hypothesis. The null hypothesis suggests there is no difference between the groups, but the results indicate that the performance of the model with the proposed method is significantly different from that of the model without it. The extremely small p-value further supports that the effectiveness of the proposed model is highly reliable and stable.

Activation Function: Our proposed PAF is a novel C^1 continuous activation function. To fully validate its performance, we compared it with activation functions like LeakyRelu, Relu, Gelu, etc. As shown in Table 6, it is evident that our PAF achieves better segmentation performance. As can be seen from Fig. 9, compared with these commonly used activation functions, PAF can better reduce the fluctuation of the model, make the training process more stable, and improve the segmentation performance better.

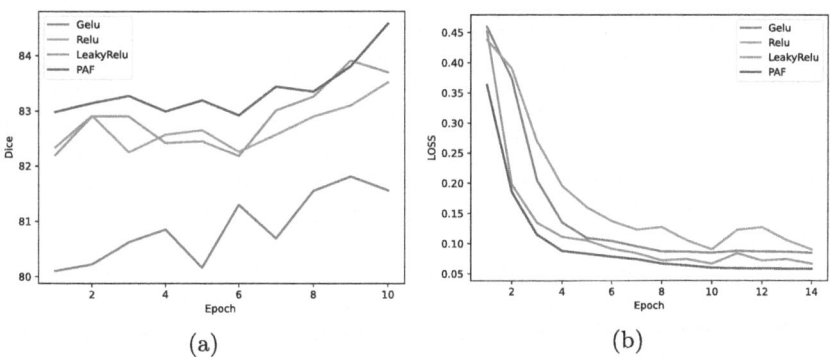

Fig. 9. The figure (a) shows the impact of our proposed PAF and several other commonly used activation functions on model training. Figure (b) shows the impact of several methods on the loss during the training process. It can be clearly seen that our PAF can better reduce the fluctuation in the model training process.

Research on Ablation within the IMAM: Research on ablation within the IMAM module: In the exploration of the internal mechanism of IMAM, we innovatively combined two different types of attention mechanisms for hybrid computing. In order to comprehensively evaluate the effectiveness of this design decision, we carefully designed a group of experiments to compare the performance of different attention combinations. The experimental results are shown in Table 7, from which we can intuitively see that the IMAM design proposed

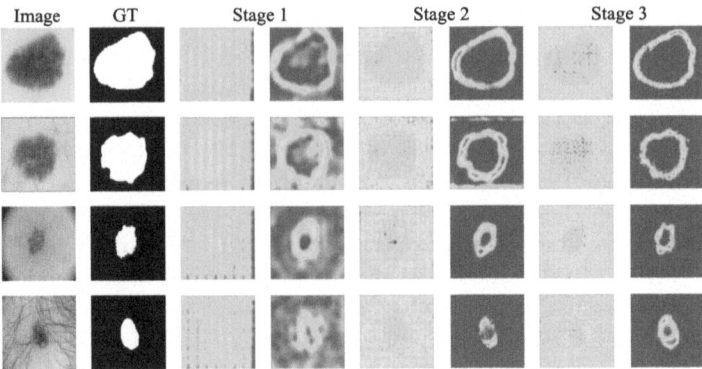

Fig. 10. Visualization of the EGB module's specific functions is presented. In every stage, the left side depicts the model's output without EGB, while the right side shows the result after applying EGB. Stages 1 to 3 correspond to the three EGBs in the deeper to shallower layers of the network.

in this paper shows the most outstanding performance compared with other architecture configurations, fully verifying the correctness and superiority of our design ideas.

Table 7. Research on ablation within the IMAM on the Synapse dataset.

Methods	Attention Parallel	Attention Serial	Ours
Dice	83.64	83.94	85.55
HD95	19.34	17.46	14.39

Comparison with Different Backbone Networks: To validate our choice, we expanded ResNet101 and ResNet50 networks to have a comparable number of parameters to MaxVit and applied the same pre-training regimen. We then replaced the backbone with these networks. The results in Table 8 demonstrate the soundness of our decision to use MaxVit.

Table 8. An analysis of the effect of different backbones on the network performance.

Backbone	ResNet50	ResNet101	Maxvit
Dice	77.39	82.89	85.55
HD95	20.87	20.06	14.39

Research on the EGB Module: This paper proposes an edge guided bridge module to capture edge information robustly on multiple scales. We show the specific function of this module in the form of thermodynamic diagram, as shown in Fig. 10. It can be clearly seen from the figure that EGB can make the model focus more on the boundary of the lesion area in each stage, and pay more attention to the edge information, so that the model can more accurately segment the boundary.

Sensitivity Analysis: In this study, we conducted a sensitivity analysis on the learning rate and batch size to evaluate the impact of different hyperparameter combinations on model performance. The experimental results are shown in Table 9. Overall, this sensitivity analysis confirms the appropriateness of the learning rate and batch size settings used in this study.

Table 9. Study on sensitivity analysis of super parameters.

lr	batch size			
	4	8	12	16
0.00001	94.08	92.24	92.07	91.76
0.0001	94.54	94.76	94.82	94.79
0.001	94.73	94.78	94.55	94.60
0.01	82.34	90.78	83.62	89.62

5   Conclusion

In this paper, we propose a multiscale edge guided polynomial approximation network (AMEPANet). The well-designed EGB module in the network uses the Laplacian operator to accurately capture and enhance the edge information in the image, and realizes the robust preservation of edge information across multiple scales. By building an information mixed attention mechanism, the network can further mine and use the subtle features of the boundary area, and combine it with Kolmogorov-Arnold theorem to build an efficient decoder architecture, seamlessly integrate multi-source features, and achieve comprehensive fusion and optimization of feature information. In addition, this paper also proposes a C^1 continuous activation function using polynomial approximation, which shows significant advantages in reducing model calculation fluctuations and promoting model stability and convergence. Through extensive and in-depth experiments on several authoritative data sets such as Synapse, the advanced performance of our proposed model is proved. However, our model also has some limitations. Our main concern is how to improve the segmentation performance, while ignoring whether it can be deployed in real life scenarios. Therefore, our future work will improve this aspect.

Acknowledgement. This work was supported in part by the following: the Joint Fund of the National Natural Science Foundation of China under Grant No. U24A20219, the National Natural Science Foundation of China under Grant No. 62272281, the Special Funds for Taishan Scholars Project(tsqn202306274), and the Youth Innovation Technology Project of Higher School in Shandong Province under Grant No. 2023KJ212.

References

1. Azad, R., Arimond, R., Aghdam, E.K., Kazerouni, A., Merhof, D.: DAE-Former: dual attention-guided efficient transformer for medical image segmentation. In: International Workshop on Predictive Intelligence In Medicine, pp. 83–95. Springer (2023)
2. Azad, R., Asadi-Aghbolaghi, M., Fathy, M., Escalera, S.: Bi-directional ConvLSTM U-Net with Densley connected convolutions. In: Proceedings of the IEEE/CVF International Conference on Computer Vision Workshops (2019)
3. Azad, R., et al.: TransDeepLab: convolution-free transformer-based DeepLab V3+ for medical image segmentation. In: International Workshop on Predictive Intelligence In Medicine, pp. 91–102. Springer (2022)
4. Azam, B., Akhtar, N.: Suitability of KANs for computer vision: a preliminary investigation. arXiv preprint arXiv:2406.09087 (2024)
5. Bernal, J., Sánchez, F.J., Fernández-Esparrach, G., Gil, D., Rodríguez, C., Vilariño, F.: WM-DOVA maps for accurate polyp highlighting in colonoscopy: validation vs. saliency maps from physicians. Comput. Med. Imag. Graph. **43**, 99–111 (2015)
6. Bernard, O., et al.: Deep learning techniques for automatic MRI cardiac multi-structures segmentation and diagnosis: is the problem solved? IEEE Trans. Med. Imag. **37**(11), 2514–2525 (2018)
7. Cao, H., et al.: Swin-Unet: Unet-like pure transformer for medical image segmentation. In: European Conference on Computer Vision, pp. 205–218. Springer (2022)
8. Chen, J., et al.: TransUnet: transformers make strong encoders for medical image segmentation. arXiv preprint arXiv:2102.04306 (2021)
9. Chen, J., et al.: TransUnet: rethinking the U-net architecture design for medical image segmentation through the lens of transformers. Med. Image Anal. **97**, 103280 (2024)
10. Chen, S., Tan, X., Wang, B., Hu, X.: Reverse attention for salient object detection. In: Proceedings of the European Conference on Computer Vision (ECCV), pp. 234–250 (2018)
11. Cheng, M., Kong, Z., Song, G., Tian, Y., Liang, Y., Chen, J.: Learnable oriented derivative network for polyp segmentation. In: Medical Image Computing and Computer Assisted Intervention–MICCAI 2021: 24th International Conference, Strasbourg, France, September 27–October 1, 2021, Proceedings, Part I 24, pp. 720–730. Springer (2021)
12. Codella, N., et al.: Skin lesion analysis toward melanoma detection 2018: a challenge hosted by the international skin imaging collaboration (ISIC). arXiv preprint arXiv:1902.03368 (2019)
13. Dai, D., et al.: Ms RED: a novel multi-scale residual encoding and decoding network for skin lesion segmentation. Med. Image Anal. **75**, 102293 (2022)
14. Dosovitskiy, A., et al.: An image is worth 16x16 words: transformers for image recognition at scale. arXiv preprint arXiv:2010.11929 (2020)

15. Fan, X., Zhou, J., Jiang, X., Xin, M., Hou, L.: CSAP-UNet: convolution and self-attention paralleling network for medical image segmentation with edge enhancement. Comput. Biol. Med. **172**, 108265 (2024)
16. Feng, S., et al.: CPFNet: context pyramid fusion network for medical image segmentation. IEEE Trans. Med. Imag. **39**(10), 3008–3018 (2020)
17. Gu, R., et al.: CA-Net: comprehensive attention convolutional neural networks for explainable medical image segmentation. IEEE Trans. Med. Imag. **40**(2), 699–711 (2020)
18. Gu, Z., et al.: CE-Net: context encoder network for 2D medical image segmentation. IEEE Trans. Med. Imag. **38**(10), 2281–2292 (2019)
19. Heidari, M., et al.: HiFormer: hierarchical multi-scale representations using transformers for medical image segmentation. In: Proceedings of the IEEE/CVF Winter Conference on Applications of Computer Vision, pp. 6202–6212 (2023)
20. Huang, X., Deng, Z., Li, D., Yuan, X.: MissFormer: an effective medical image segmentation transformer. arXiv preprint arXiv:2109.07162 (2021)
21. Huang, X., Deng, Z., Li, D., Yuan, X., Fu, Y.: MissFormer: an effective transformer for 2D medical image segmentation. IEEE Trans. Med. Imag. (2022)
22. Isensee, F., Jaeger, P.F., Kohl, S.A., Petersen, J., Maier-Hein, K.H.: NNU-Net: a self-configuring method for deep learning-based biomedical image segmentation. Nat. Methods **18**(2), 203–211 (2021)
23. Jha, D., et al.: Kvasir-SEG: a segmented polyp dataset. In: MultiMedia Modeling: 26th International Conference, MMM 2020, Daejeon, South Korea, January 5–8, 2020, Proceedings, Part II 26, pp. 451–462. Springer (2020)
24. Karimi, D., Salcudean, S.E.: Reducing the Hausdorff distance in medical image segmentation with convolutional neural networks. IEEE Trans. Med. Imag. **39**(2), 499–513 (2019)
25. Kervadec, H., Bouchtiba, J., Desrosiers, C., Granger, E., Dolz, J., Ayed, I.B.: Boundary loss for highly unbalanced segmentation. In: International Conference on Medical Imaging with Deep Learning, pp. 285–296. PMLR (2019)
26. Landman, B., Xu, Z., Igelsias, J., Styner, M., Langerak, T., Klein, A.: MICCAI multi-atlas labeling beyond the cranial vault–workshop and challenge. In: Proceedings of the MICCAI Multi-Atlas Labeling Beyond Cranial Vault-Workshop Challenge, vol. 5, p. 12 (2015)
27. Lin, X., Yu, L., Cheng, K.T., Yan, Z.: BATFormer: towards boundary-aware lightweight transformer for efficient medical image segmentation. IEEE J. Biomed. Health Inform. **27**(7), 3501–3512 (2023)
28. Liu, Z., et al.: Swin transformer: hierarchical vision transformer using shifted windows. In: Proceedings of the IEEE/CVF International Conference on Computer Vision, pp. 10012–10022 (2021)
29. Liu, Z., et al.: KAN: Kolmogorov-Arnold networks. arXiv preprint arXiv:2404.19756 (2024)
30. Mendonça, T., Ferreira, P.M., Marques, J.S., Marcal, A.R., Rozeira, J.: PH 2-a dermoscopic image database for research and benchmarking. In: 2013 35th Annual International Conference of the IEEE Engineering in Medicine and Biology Society (EMBC), pp. 5437–5440. IEEE (2013)
31. Meng, Y., et al.: Graph-based region and boundary aggregation for biomedical image segmentation. IEEE Trans. Med. Imag. **41**(3), 690–701 (2021)
32. Mou, L., et al.: CS2-Net: deep learning segmentation of curvilinear structures in medical imaging. Med. Image Anal. **67**, 101874 (2021)

33. Rahman, M.M., Marculescu, R.: Medical image segmentation via cascaded attention decoding. In: Proceedings of the IEEE/CVF Winter Conference on Applications of Computer Vision, pp. 6222–6231 (2023)
34. Rahman, M.M., Marculescu, R.: G-cascade: efficient cascaded graph convolutional decoding for 2D medical image segmentation. In: Proceedings of the IEEE/CVF Winter Conference on Applications of Computer Vision, pp. 7728–7737 (2024)
35. Rahman, M.M., Marculescu, R.: Multi scale hierarchical vision transformer with cascaded attention decoding for medical image segmentation. In: Medical Imaging with Deep Learning, pp. 1526–1544. PMLR (2024)
36. Rahman, M.M., Munir, M., Marculescu, R.: EMCAD: efficient multi-scale convolutional attention decoding for medical image segmentation. In: Proceedings of the IEEE/CVF Conference on Computer Vision and Pattern Recognition, pp. 11769–11779 (2024)
37. Ronneberger, O., Fischer, P., Brox, T.: U-net: convolutional networks for biomedical image segmentation. In: Medical Image Computing and Computer-Assisted Intervention–MICCAI 2015: 18th International Conference, Munich, Germany, October 5-9, 2015, Proceedings, Part III 18, pp. 234–241. Springer (2015)
38. Silva, J., Histace, A., Romain, O., Dray, X., Granado, B.: Toward embedded detection of polyps in WCE images for early diagnosis of colorectal cancer. Int. J. Comput. Assist. Radiol. Surg. **9**, 283–293 (2014)
39. Tao, H., Li, J., Hua, Z., Zhang, F.: DUDB: deep unfolding based dual-branch feature fusion network for pan-sharpening remote sensing images. IEEE Trans. Geosci. Remote Sens. (2023)
40. Tu, Z., et al.: MaxViT: multi-axis vision transformer. In: European Conference on Computer Vision, pp. 459–479. Springer (2022)
41. Vaca-Rubio, C.J., Blanco, L., Pereira, R., Caus, M.: Kolmogorov-Arnold networks (KANs) for time series analysis. arXiv preprint arXiv:2405.08790 (2024)
42. Vaswani, A., et al.: Attention is all you need. Adv. Neural Inf. Process. Syst. **30** (2017)
43. Wang, H., et al.: Mixed transformer u-net for medical image segmentation. In: ICASSP 2022-2022 IEEE International Conference on Acoustics, Speech and Signal Processing (ICASSP), pp. 2390–2394. IEEE (2022)
44. Wang, M., Wang, H., Zhang, F.: FAMC-Net: frequency domain parity correction attention and multi-scale dilated convolution for time series forecasting. In: Proceedings of the 32nd ACM International Conference on Information and Knowledge Management, pp. 2554–2563. CIKM '23, Association for Computing Machinery, New York, NY, USA (2023). https://doi.org/10.1145/3583780.3614876
45. Wang, M., Wang, H., Zhang, F.: FAMC-Net: frequency domain parity correction attention and multi-scale dilated convolution for time series forecasting. In: Proceedings of the 32nd ACM International Conference on Information and Knowledge Management, pp. 2554–2563 (2023)
46. Wang, S., He, K., Nie, D., Zhou, S., Gao, Y., Shen, D.: CT male pelvic organ segmentation using fully convolutional networks with boundary sensitive representation. Med. Image Anal. **54**, 168–178 (2019)
47. Wang, W., et al.: Pyramid vision transformer: a versatile backbone for dense prediction without convolutions. In: Proceedings of the IEEE/CVF International Conference on Computer Vision, pp. 568–578 (2021)
48. Wang, W., et al.: PVT v2: improved baselines with pyramid vision transformer. Comput. Vis. Media **8**(3), 415–424 (2022)

49. Wang, X., Wang, H., Zhang, M., Zhang, F.: Combining optical flow and Swin transformer for space-time video super-resolution. Eng. Appl. Artif. Intell. **137**, 109227 (2024)

50. Wu, H., Pan, J., Li, Z., Wen, Z., Qin, J.: Automated skin lesion segmentation via an adaptive dual attention module. IEEE Trans. Med. Imag. **40**(1), 357–370 (2020)

51. Yang, M., Yu, K., Zhang, C., Li, Z., Yang, K.: DenseASPP for semantic segmentation in street scenes. In: Proceedings of the IEEE Conference on Computer Vision and Pattern Recognition, pp. 3684–3692 (2018)

52. Zhang, F., Wang, H., Fan, H., Zhang, C.: Rational polynomial image magnification based on edge and distance constraints. Sci. Sin. Inform. **51**, 1270–1286 (2021)

53. Zhang, F., Chen, G., Wang, H., Li, J., Zhang, C.: Multi-scale video super-resolution transformer with polynomial approximation. IEEE Trans. Cir. Syst. Video Technol. (2023)

54. Zhang, F., Chen, G., Wang, H., Zhang, C.: CF-DAN: facial-expression recognition based on cross-fusion dual-attention network. Comput. Vis. Media, 1–16 (2024)

55. Zhang, F., Guo, T., Wang, H.: DFNet: decomposition fusion model for long sequence time-series forecasting. Knowl.-Based Syst. **277**, 110794 (2023)

56. Zhang, R., Li, G., Li, Z., Cui, S., Qian, D., Yu, Y.: Adaptive context selection for polyp segmentation. In: Medical Image Computing and Computer Assisted Intervention–MICCAI 2020: 23rd International Conference, Lima, Peru, October 4–8, 2020, Proceedings, Part VI 23, pp. 253–262. Springer (2020)

57. Zhang, W., Wang, H., Zhang, F.: Skip-Timeformer: skip-time interaction transformer for long sequence time-series forecasting

58. Zhou, H.Y., Guo, J., Zhang, Y., Yu, L., Wang, L., Yu, Y.: nnFormer: interleaved transformer for volumetric segmentation. arXiv preprint arXiv:2109.03201 (2021)

HIFNet: Medical Image Segmentation Network Utilizing Hierarchical Attention Feature Fusion

Zhou Yang[1], Hua Wang[2], and Fan Zhang[1,3(✉)]

[1] School of Computer Science and Technology, Shandong Technology and Business University, Shandong, Yantai, China
zhangfan51@sina.com
[2] School of Information and Electrical Engineering, Ludong University, Shandong, Yantai, China
[3] Shandong Future Intelligent Financial Engineering Laboratory, Shandong, Yantai, China

Abstract. The Transformer model has demonstrated immense potential and significant importance as an efficient tool in the field of medical image analysis, primarily due to its capability to capture global context. However, its limitation in capturing local information to some extent constrains the full performance of Transformer in this domain. To mitigate this issue, we propose a novel medical image segmentation network, HIFNet, based on hierarchical attention feature fusion. Specifically, we utilize a pre-trained MaxViT as the encoder. In our newly constructed decoder, spatial attention is applied to feature maps of different sizes to focus more on critical regions of the input images. Additionally, we incorporate multiple attention mechanisms, including criss-cross attention, to capture sensitive spatial relationships within medical images. Furthermore, we employ coordinate attention in skip connections to embed positional information in different directions, thereby generating feature maps containing sensitive positional information. Experiments conducted on relevant medical image datasets demonstrate the effectiveness and scalability of our proposed encoder.

Keywords: Medical image Segmentation · Transformer · Multi-scale network

1 Introduction

Medical image segmentation, as a component in image processing tasks, is not only crucial in the field of computer science but also serves as a key tool for computer-aided diagnosis in clinical applications. By classifying the pixels in medical images, it aids doctors in rapidly identifying organs, tumors, and other related lesion areas. Traditional medical image segmentation networks utilize U-Net [26] as the backbone to construct a symmetrical U-shaped network. Most of these networks are based on Convolutional Neural Networks (CNNs) and have introduced a series of related work on this foundation, such as U-Net++ [49], UNet3+ [12], nnunet [15], etc. [11,19,20]. These networks can generate relatively clear segmentation maps. However, the use of a single CNN model is limited by factors such as its restricted receptive field [10] and inherent inductive biases [2], which constrain the ultimate segmentation performance. Therefore, researchers have also introduced attention mechanisms [29,37] into related architectures, such as SCAU-net [48], DRAu-net [27]. To mitigate the limitations of CNNs in capturing long-distance dependencies. Attention enhances segmentation results by capturing salient features in the image [8,11]. Despite improvements in segmentation performance through the introduction of attention mechanisms, there is still room for enhancement in capturing important feature information in images.

Recently, Transformers have demonstrated excellent performance in natural language processing-related fields [29], attributed to their use of Self-Attention (SA) mechanisms within their structures. Researchers have subsequently introduced Vision Transformer [10] (ViT) into the image domain and achieved great success. By dividing the input image into small patches and leveraging the self-attention mechanism to capture the relationships among these patches, Vision Transformer (ViT) aims to extract global information features. Furthermore, researchers have developed and proposed various Transformer variants suitable for the image domain, such as Swin-Transformer [18], PVT [34,35], MaxViT [28], and MERIT [23]. In particular, the successful application of Transformers in medical images [9,19,21,23,30] further demonstrates their great potential. However, due to the limitations of the self-attention module in understanding local spatial information, some methods have incorporated convolutional attention modules to alleviate this issue [36,39]. But, because of the limitations of convolution, these methods struggle to capture the relationships between long-distance pixels.

To address the above issues, we consider improving the use of attention mechanisms to capture both global and local dependencies across all corresponding dimensions. Therefore, we have designed a new Transformer network for medical image segmentation, namely HIFNet. This network uses MaxViT as the encoder and incorporates a novel decoder designed by us. Additionally, we employ coordinate attention to embed information in the skip connections within the network. Our contributions are as follows:

- We propose a new decoder. Each decoder is composed of a mixed attention mechanism across different spatial directions and a multi-scale feature mixing module, allowing the decoder to obtain more comprehensive and detailed feature information. By mixing attention results in different directions, the decoder can capture correlations between different positions in the input data, extract more detailed contextual information, and facilitate the output of more refined segmentation results.
- To enhance the model's learning capability of latent features, we process skip connection information using a coordinate attention mechanism between multi-stage encoders and decoders for feature merging. This method enhances the model's acquisition of key location information and improves the final segmentation performance. By combining dilated convolutions of different

scales with related operations, the model expands its receptive field, enabling it to capture long-distance dependencies.

2 Related Work

2.1 Medical Image Segmentation with CNN

U-Net [26], as a cornerstone in medical image segmentation in recent years, has demonstrated tremendous potential and achievements in this field. As the first CNN-based medical image segmentation model, it has sparked numerous subsequent research efforts, including the development of a series of U-Net-based models such as U-Net++ [49], U-Net3+ [12], and Attention-Unet [20]. These U-shaped architecture models have shone brightly in various medical image segmentation tasks due to their simple and effective encoder-decoder structure, such as segmenting lesions, tumors, and organs [7,9,36,46]. These studies collectively indicate that U-Net and its related subsequent models have become the de facto benchmarks for medical image segmentation [11,19]. After introducing U-Net to medical image segmentation, researchers also encountered some challenges. Although CNN-based U-Net models excel in segmentation results, they still have issues capturing long-distance critical information. To overcome this problem, researchers proposed using attention-based U-Net models, such as MA-Unet [3], which employs an attention mechanism to manipulate multi-scale features, and APAUnet [16], which uses axial projection attention. These models demonstrate that attention can compensate for the long-distance modeling capabilities limited by using a single CNN. Therefore, in the encoder we designed, we further enhance the model's long-distance modeling capability by incorporating attention mechanisms in different directions.

2.2 Vision Transformers

Given the tremendous achievements of transformers in other fields [33,43–45], researchers first proposed Vision Transformer (ViT) [10], the first model to apply transformers to the field of vision. ViT learns global information between pixels using a self-attention mechanism. Subsequent models have improved upon ViT through various methods, including integrating CNN features into the architecture (MaxViT [28], PvTv2 [35]), using new attention mechanisms (Swin-Transformer [18]), and proposing new architectures (PVT [34], SegFormer [39]). The Swin-Transformer calculates local attention through sliding window attention shifts, SegFormer leverages MiXFFN to aggregate information from different levels, and MaxViT computes self-attention after decomposing the spatial axis. Although many transformer models [5,6,38] for computer vision have mitigated the long-distance modeling limitations of using CNNs, they still face challenges in capturing local information and feature relationships. In this paper, we address this limitation by introducing a decoder that integrates an attention mechanism with a multi-scale feature convolution module. This encoder models sensitive information in the image through coordinate attention and cruciform cross-attention, while simultaneously extracting features through a multi-scale attention feature mixing module with a pyramid-like structure. This enhances the model's ability to model key information.

2.3   Medical Image Segmentation with Transformers

Despite the tremendous achievements of CNN-based medical image segmentation networks, the limitation of their global information modeling poses constraints on model performance. In the research on medical image segmentation tasks, researchers prefer to use transformer-based networks, and proposed a series of models that utilize Transformer for medical image segmentation. [17, 40–42, 47] For example, Swin-Unet [4] proposes a U-shaped pure transformer architecture based on Swin-Transformer [18], while TransUnet [7] combines CNNs and transformers to capture low-level and high-level features. Additionally, some researchers use pre-trained models as encoders, benefiting from the rich features already learned by these models on large datasets, which reduces the need for new data. For instance, PVT-Polyp [9] achieves good results in polyp segmentation by using a pre-trained PVT as the encoder, and G-CASCADE [22] generates finer segmentation maps by combining MaxViT as the encoder with a decoder that includes graph convolution. EMCAD [24] also employs a pre-trained model as the encoder and captures complex spatial relationships by constructing a mechanism that includes spatial, channel, and grouped gating attention. Therefore, we have decided to adopt a similar approach, utilizing a pre-trained model as the encoder and constructing a complex architecture that integrates attention and convolution as the decoder to capture important contextual relationships in medical images (Fig. 1).

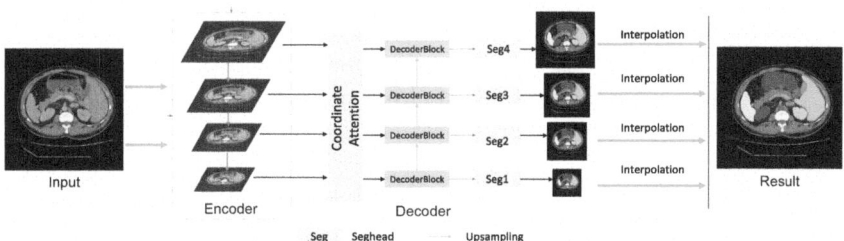

Fig. 1. As shown in the figure, this is the overall network architecture we proposed. On the left side of the network is the pre-trained MaxViT encoder we utilized, which performs attention operations using different window sizes.

3   Method

3.1   Overall Architecture

To further enhance the long and short-distance modeling capabilities of transformer models in medical image segmentation, we drew inspiration from the previous design of MaxViT [28]. MaxViT achieves information interaction between global and local scales by decomposing the traditional self-attention mechanism into two types of sparse attention: non-overlapping window attention and grid attention, along the spatial axis. In our proposed HIFNet, we inherited the essence of MaxViT by utilizing a pre-trained MaxViT model in the encoder stage. Simultaneously, we innovatively reconstructed the encoder stage. Specifically, we first constructed a top-down multi-scale information extraction path corresponding to the encoder in the decoder stage, ensuring that the image can fully utilize information features of different scales during the decoder stage. Subsequently, we processed the information in the encoder using skip connections with positional embeddings and fed it into the corresponding decoder sections. This pyramid-like structure design enhances the model's ability to utilize information of different scales and allows the model to more comprehensively capture the key location information of the image, thereby significantly improving the model's segmentation performance.

3.2   Multi-scale Attention Feature Extraction Decoder

Due to its inherent limitations in modeling local information, Transformer may lose critical details when processing medical images, thereby affecting the final segmentation performance of the model. To mitigate this issue, besides using a pre-trained MaxViT in the encoder, we have redesigned the decoder stage to include a Multi-Scale Attention Feature Extraction Decoder (MAFED), as illustrated in the figure. The decoder begins with layer normalization, followed by upsampling the input data to match the size of the encoder output. Then, we use convolution to ensure that the dimensions match those of the skip connection inputs before they enter the decoder, and normalization is applied. The specific formula is shown below:

$$x = concat((LN(Conv(Up(x_1)))), CDA(x_1)) \qquad (1)$$

Here, $concat$ denotes concatenation, x_1 represents the corresponding encoder output, CDA stands for Coordinate Attention [14], LN for Layer Normalization, $conv$ for applying convolution for dimension processing, and UP for upsampling. Subsequently, a depthwise convolution is used to reduce the channel dimension by half, and the result is input into the encoder for further processing. In the encoder, we introduce cross-shaped attention [14] to process the input data. The horizontal and vertical attention modules extract contextual information in the horizontal and vertical directions, respectively, as shown in Fig. 2(a). Given a feature map $H \in R^{H \times W \times C}$, The module first generates feature maps $Q, K,$ and V for attention calculation using 1×1 convolutions along the H dimension.

The size of the mappings for Q and K is $H \times W \times C_1$, The reason C_1 is smaller than C is to perform dimensionality reduction on the channels, thereby reducing computational load. Subsequently, through the Affinity operation, a feature map of size $P \in R^{(H+W-1) \times W \times C}$ is generated, capturing the relationships between each pixel and its horizontally and vertically adjacent pixels in the feature map. The calculation of Affinity is as follows:

$$d_{i,u} = Q_u \Omega_{i,u} \tag{2}$$

Here,$\Omega_{i,u}$ represents the feature vector at position iu in the feature map, with $\Omega_{i,u} \in R^c$, Q_u denotes the feature vector at position u in the feature map P After computation, a new feature map of size $(H + W - 1) \times W \times C$ is obtained. Subsequently, a softmax operation is applied to this feature map. Then, the same operation is performed for each position to reconstruct a feature map of size $H \times W \times C$ that once again contains information about the relationships between pixels. After applying the cross-shaped attention mechanism, we utilize a multi-scale feature extraction module to further extract and model key positional information. The structure of this module is illustrated in the figure. By applying spatial attention to features of different scales, the model can further focus on important regions. Specifically, the feature extraction module employs multiple dilated convolutional layers with different dilation rates in the extraction stage to capture features of various scales. Subsequently, in each output branch stage, an attention mechanism is used to further assess the importance of the extracted features. To avoid information loss when using a single dilated convolution, we incorporate 1×1 convolutions and pooling to ensure complete information preservation. The specific formula for the module is as follows:

$$P = softmax(R(Conv(x_{in}))^T \times R(Conv(x_{in}))) \tag{3}$$

Here R and R' represents the opposite operation, R denotes the reshaping of the original input feature vector to its original size $R^{C \times N}$, $N = H \times W$, Then, the obtained weights are combined with the input data to produce an enhanced feature map output, as shown below.

$$x_{out} = x_{in} + R'(R(Conv(x_{in})) \times P^T) \tag{4}$$

Subsequently, the model employs the Multi-Scale Attention Feature Extraction module to further extract features from the data, as specifically illustrated in Fig. 2.

After the computations are completed, each layer of the decoder will pass through a corresponding 1×1 segmentation head to generate output segmentation maps. There are a total of four layers, and these segmentation maps of different sizes will ultimately be upsampled using an interpolation function to produce the final segmentation result.

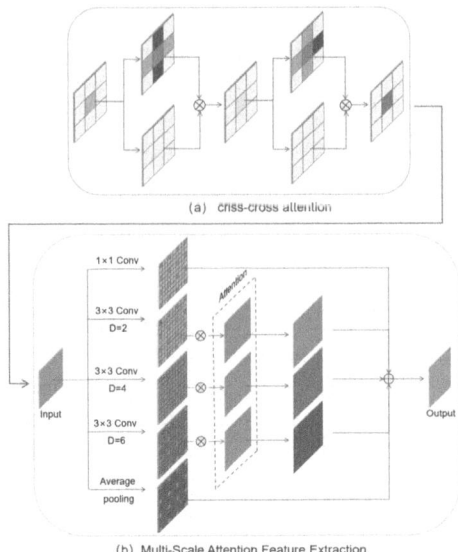

(a) criss-cross attention

(b) Multi-Scale Attention Feature Extraction

Fig. 2. As shown in the figure, the cross-shaped attention is depicted at the top (a), and the multi-scale feature extraction module is shown at the bottom (b). Together, these two components constitute the decoder.

3.3 Multi-axis Vision Transformer Encoder

Due to the recent tremendous potential demonstrated by Transformers in the field of medical image segmentation, MaxViT, as one of them, has achieved good results in the medical image domain due to its unique design. Networks such as G-CASCADE and EMCAD have utilized MaxViT pre-trained models as encoders and constructed networks for medical image segmentation. Building on previous successful experiences, in our network, we adopt MaxViT as the encoder. Specifically, we use a pre-trained model with an input size of 256×256, and in the four stages of downsampling, we embed feature vectors of sizes [96, 192, 384, 768]. Each layer employs [2, 2, 5, 2] MaxViT blocks, respectively. Additionally, in the four encoder layers, we use skip connections to pass the feature representations to the corresponding decoders, enabling the corresponding decoder segmentation heads to achieve precise segmentation of the results. The final segmentation results are as follows:

$$SegOut = p_1 + p_2 + p_3 + p_4 \tag{5}$$

Table 1. The segmentation results on Synapse. We labeled the segmentation results for each individual organ using DICE, and we also labeled the average value of the segmentation results with DICE. The results of the various comparison models are referenced from previous research. Among the various indicators, the bold font represents the best, and the underlined represents the second best, higher DICE indicates a better performance, while a lower HD95 indicates a better performance as well.

Methods	DICE↑	HD95↓	Aorta	GB	KL	KR	Liver	PC	SP	SM
UNet [26]	70.11	44.69	84.00	56.70	72.41	62.64	86.98	48.73	81.48	67.96
AttnUNet [20]	71.70	34.47	82.61	61.94	76.07	70.42	87.54	46.70	80.67	67.66
R50+UNet [7]	74.68	36.87	84.18	62.84	79.19	71.29	93.35	48.23	84.41	73.92
R50+AttnUNet [7]	75.57	36.97	55.92	63.91	79.20	72.71	93.56	49.37	87.19	74.95
SSFormer [32]	78.01	25.72	82.78	63.74	80.72	78.11	93.53	61.53	87.07	76.61
PolypPVT [9]	78.08	25.61	82.34	66.14	81.21	73.78	94.37	59.34	88.05	79.4
TransUNet [7]	77.61	26.9	86.56	60.43	80.54	78.53	94.33	58.47	87.06	75.00
SwinUNet [4]	77.58	27.32	81.76	65.95	82.32	79.22	93.73	53.81	88.04	75.79
MT-UNet [31]	78.59	26.59	87.92	64.99	81.47	77.29	93.06	59.46	87.75	76.81
MISSFormer [13]	81.96	18.20	86.99	68.65	85.21	82.00	94.41	65.67	91.92	80.81
PVT-CASCADE [21]	81.06	20.23	83.01	70.59	82.23	80.37	94.08	64.43	90.1	83.69
TransCASCADE [21]	82.68	<u>17.34</u>	86.63	68.48	**87.66**	<u>84.56</u>	84.43	65.33	**90.79**	83.52
PVT-EMCAD [24]	83.16	**15.68**	<u>88.20</u>	<u>73.34</u>	84.28	82.13	<u>94.76</u>	<u>68.52</u>	90.08	<u>83.96</u>
HIF-Net(our)	**83.81**	18.63	**88.38**	**74.17**	<u>86.12</u>	83.59	**95.25**	68.53	<u>90.43</u>	**84.06**

3.4 Loss Function

In our model, we follow previous research [25] by utilizing activation functions and training the model by mixing features from multiple stages. The advantage of this approach is that it enables the model to converge better and is also beneficial for medical image segmentation tasks. According to the loss function we use during the training phase, we generate $2^n - 1$ non-empty subsets containing n prediction maps, and aggregate all non-empty subsets to produce the final prediction maps used for calculating the loss value. We then compute both the DICE loss and the cross-entropy loss for these generated prediction maps. The final loss function equation is as follows:

$$Loss = 0.3L_{dice} + 0.7L_{ce} \tag{6}$$

Where 0.3 and 0.7 are the weights for the DICE and CE loss functions, respectively.

4 Experiments and Results

4.1 Datasets

ACDC Dataset: We used both the ACDC dataset and the Synapse dataset to train our model. The ACDC dataset contains 100 patient cases, each including

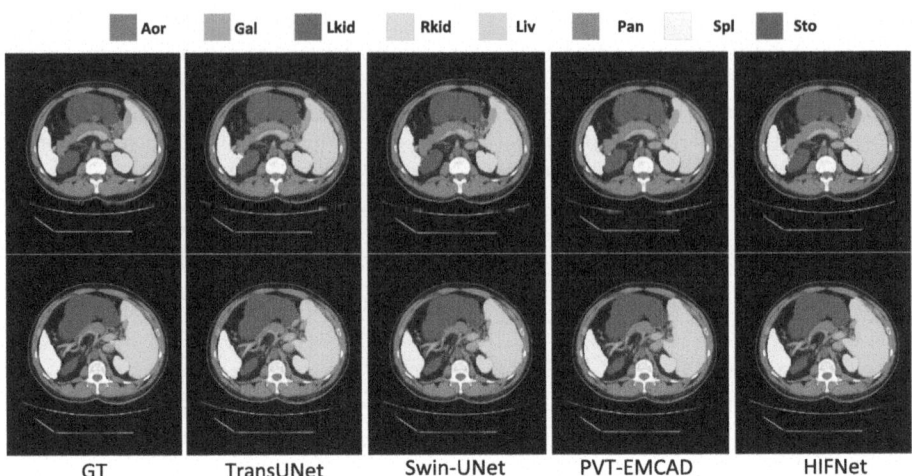

Fig. 3. As shown in the figure, we have visualized the results of the model on Synapse, displaying images from the same case but obtained from different models. GT represents the ground truth segmentation results. We used different colors to represent the organs, including the aorta, gallbladder, left kidney, right kidney, liver, pancreas, spleen, and stomach, from left to right.

annotations for the left ventricle (LV), right ventricle (RV), and myocardium (Myo). During model training, we split the dataset into a training set, validation set, and test set in a 7:1:2 ratio.

Synapse Dataset: The Synapse dataset comprises 30 abdominal CT scans, totaling 3779 abdominal CT axial contrast-enhanced slices. Our dataset setup follows a similar approach to previous work with TransUNet, where we randomly divided the dataset into 18 cases for training and 12 for validation. We segmented eight organs in the results: aorta, left kidney, right kidney, liver, pancreas, stomach, and spleen.

ISIC Dataset: We evaluated our model on the ISIC2017 and ISIC2018 datasets. During training, we randomly split the datasets into training, validation, and test sets in a 8:1:1 ratio. To ensure that our results are more realistic and accurate, we validated our results on the ISIC dataset using five-fold cross-validation (Fig. 4).

4.2 Experiments Details

We conducted our experiments on an NVIDIA A100 GPU, using PyTorch 1.11.0 to implement model training. We initialized the model's encoder with MaxViT weights pre-trained on the ImageNet dataset. For the Synapse dataset, we trained the model for a total of 800 epochs. During training, we used the AdamW optimizer with a learning rate set to 0.0001 and weight decay set to 0.0001. As the loss function during training, we used a weighted combination of the DICE and CrossEntropy functions. For all of the ACDC, ISIC and Synapse datasets, we resized the images to 256×256 for input and set the batch size to 12. Additionally, we applied various data augmentation techniques to the datasets, such as rotation, scaling, and translation.

4.3   Evaluation Metrics

For the ACDC dataset, we used DICE as the final evaluation metric. For the Synapse dataset, we assessed the model's final performance using both DICE and HD95 (95% percentile Hausdorff distance). On the ISIC dataset, we evaluated the model based on DICE, Specificity (SP), Sensitivity (SE), and Accuracy (ACC). The calculation formulas for DICE and HD95 are as follows:

$$DICE = \frac{2 \mid X \cap Y \mid}{\mid X \mid + \mid Y \mid} \tag{7}$$

$$HD\left(X, Y\right) = max\left\{d_{XY}, d_{YX}\right\}$$
$$= max\left\{\max_{x \in X} \min_{y \in Y} d(x, y), \max_{y \in Y} \min_{x \in X} d(x, y)\right\} \tag{8}$$

Here, X and Y represent the real image and the predicted segmentation result image respectively.

On the ISIC 2017 and 2018 datasets, we used DSC, ACC, SP, and SE. Among them, ACC stands for Accuracy, which is a commonly used indicator to measure

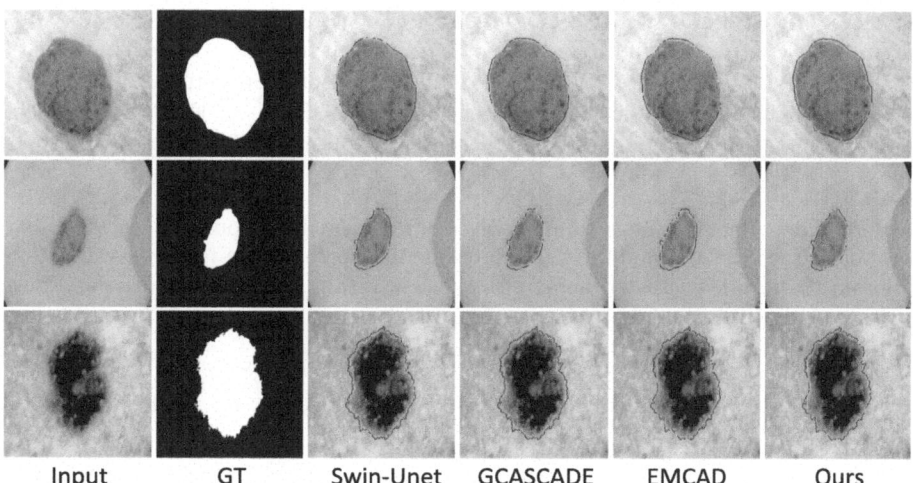

| Input | GT | Swin-Unet | GCASCADE | EMCAD | Ours |

Fig. 4. Qualitative comparison of our method on the ISIC2017 dataset, where blue represents the ground truth boundary and green indicates the predicted boundary. Compared to previous methods, our method is able to segment the boundary more accurately. (Color figure online)

the performance of a classifier. It represents the proportion of pixels that are correctly classified by the model out of all the pixels. The formula for calculating ACC is:

$$ACC = \frac{TP + TN}{TP + TN + FP + FN} \tag{9}$$

SP stands for Specificity, and its value range is also between 0 and 1. A higher value of SP indicates that the model has stronger ability to recognize background or non-target regions. The formula for calculating SP is as follows:

$$SP = \frac{TN}{TN + FP} \tag{10}$$

SE stands for Sensitivity, also known as Recall. It measures the completeness of the model's recognition of the target region. The formula for calculating SE is:

$$SE = \frac{TP}{TP + FN} \tag{11}$$

4.4   Comparative Analysis of Results

We compared our proposed network with other convolutional neural network-based methods and recent state-of-the-art (SOTA) methods on the Synapse, ACDC, and ISIC datasets. Table 1 presents the comparative results of our network against CNN-based and Transformer-related methods on the Synapse multi-organ segmentation dataset, our network achieved excellent results compared to the comparison methods, indicating that our method can clearly identify organs in the images and provide more refined segmentation maps. Additionally, we visualized the results on the Synapse dataset as shown in Fig. 3. In medical image segmentation, segmenting small organs is often challenging due to their

Table 2. This table presents a comparison of our proposed method with recent similar methods on the ISIC2017 and ISIC2018 datasets. We employed five-fold cross-validation to obtain the results presented here, with the best results bolded and the second best results underlined in the table.

Methods	ISIC2017				ISIC2018			
	DICE	SE	SP	ACC	DICE	SE	SP	ACC
U-Net [26]	0.8159	0.8172	0.9680	0.9164	0.8545	0.8800	0.9697	0.9404
AttU-Net [20]	0.8082	0.7998	0.9776	0.9145	0.8566	0.8674	0.9863	0.9376
TransNorm [1]	0.8933	0.8535	**0.9859**	0.9582	0.8951	0.8750	<u>0.9790</u>	0.9519
Swin-Unet [4]	0.8845	0.8893	<u>0.9778</u>	0.9476	0.8946	0.9056	**0.9798**	<u>0.9645</u>
PVT-GCASCADE [21]	<u>0.9089</u>	<u>0.9380</u>	0.9732	<u>0.9684</u>	<u>0.9007</u>	**0.9333**	0.9662	0.9609
PVT-EMCAD [24]	0.9006	0.9370	0.9682	0.9656	0.8974	0.9243	0.9675	<u>0.9617</u>
HIF-Net(our)	**0.9155**	**0.9396**	0.9759	**0.9706**	**0.9070**	<u>0.9300</u>	0.9709	**0.9683**

Table 3. The segmentation results on the ACDC dataset. RV stands for the right ventricle, Myo represents the myocardium, and LV represents the left ventricle. The bold font indicates the best performance, while the underlined indicates the second best.

Methods	DICE	RV	Myo	LV
R50+UNet [7]	87.55	87.10	80.63	94.92
R50+AttnUNet [7]	86.75	87.58	79.20	93.47
ViT+CUP [7]	81.45	81.46	90.71	92.18
R50+ViT+CUP [7]	87.57	86.07	81.88	94.75
TransUNet [7]	89.71	86.67	87.27	95.18
SwinUNet [4]	88.07	85.77	84.42	94.03
MT-UNet [31]	90.43	86.64	89.04	95.62
MISSFormer [13]	90.86	89.55	88.04	94.99
PVT-CASCADE [21]	91.46	89.97	88.90	95.50
Cascaded MERIT [21]	91.85	90.23	89.53	95.80
PVT-EMCAD [24]	<u>92.12</u>	<u>90.65</u>	<u>89.68</u>	**96.02**
HIF-Net(our)	**92.34**	**91.18**	**89.84**	<u>96.00</u>

complex structures and ambiguous boundaries with other organs. However, our proposed method can better understand and identify the shapes and boundaries of small organs, thereby improving the segmentation results.

Tables 2 and 3 respectively detail the segmentation performance of our model on the ISIC skin disease dataset and the ACDC dataset. From the results, it can be seen that our model has demonstrated excellent performance on both datasets. On the ACDC dataset, our method also performed exceptionally well, achieving remarkable performance. Specifically, our model achieved an improvement of 0.12 in the average DICE metric, significantly surpassing existing methods. Furthermore, our method also delivered significantly better results in the segmentation tasks of the left ventricle (LV), right ventricle (RV), and left ventricular myocardium (MYO), fully demonstrating the superior ability of our model in detailed processing.

Table 2 displays the outcomes of our method on the ISIC 2017 and ISIC 2018 datasets. We compared our method with recent approaches and classic medical image segmentation models from the past. The table highlights that our model has achieved satisfactory results. Specifically, the excellent outcomes of our model across different types of datasets demonstrate its robust generalization ability.

4.5   Ablation Studies

Table 4 presents the results of ablation experiments conducted on the components of our model. From the results, we observe that after incorporating Multi-Scale Feature Extraction (MSFE) into the baseline model, there is a slight improvement in the DICE and LV scores, indicating that MSFE aids in capturing more detailed features at different scales. Subsequently, the addition of Coordinate Attention (note: originally referred to as Cross-Domain Attention but corrected here for clarity, assuming it was a typographical error) led to an increase in the scores, suggesting that it enhances the model's sensitivity and capture ability for positional information. We then tested CDA alone, and the results validated the rationality of using CDA. When MSFE and CDA are used simultaneously, the segmentation metrics further improve, demonstrating that these two components are complementary during model training. Finally, we incorporated the Cross-Attention Mechanism, and the metrics were further enhanced. Meanwhile, the results for Myo and LV remained competitive, indicating that the Cross-Attention Mechanism further boosts the model's ability to perceive important information in the image. This demonstrates that all the components we proposed contribute to the final segmentation results.

Table 4. Ablation experiments on the model using the ACDC dataset. Bold numbers indicate the best results, and underlined numbers represent the second-best results.

Method	DICE	RV	Myo	LV
Baseline	92.19	90.82	89.76	95.99
MSFE	92.27	90.84	_89.91_	96.07
CDA	92.25	_91.00_	89.85	95.59
CDA+MSFE	_92.30_	90.81	**90.01**	**96.09**
CDA+MSFE+CCA	**92.34**	**91.18**	89.84	_96.00_

5   Conclusion

We introduce a medical image segmentation network named HIFNet, which leverages dilated convolutions with varying parameters to capture broader spatial context, thereby enhancing detail perception and segmentation accuracy. Additionally, to bolster the model's capacity for capturing local information, we utilize a pre-trained MaxViT as the encoder, effectively extracting local features from the data. To optimize the capture of sensitive information, we incorporate cross-shaped attention, which is pivotal for understanding complex anatomical structures. Coordinate attention further enables the model to focus on key regions, thereby improving the localization precision of lesions or organs. Our model exhibits outstanding performance on multiple datasets, surpassing other advanced methods in terms of accuracy and segmentation fineness.

Additionally, our model boasts excellent scalability. In the future, we plan to conduct further experiments by applying different pre-trained encoders to the decoder we proposed. We will also experiment with medical images of various modalities to further demonstrate its generalization capability.

Acknowledgements. This work was supported in part by the following: the Joint Fund of the National Natural Science Foundation of China under Grant No. U24A20219, the National Natural Science Foundation of China under Grant No. 62272281, the Special Funds for Taishan Scholars Project (tsqn202306274), and the Youth Innovation Technology Project of Higher School in Shandong Province under Grant No. 2023KJ212.

References

1. Azad, R., Al-Antary, M.T., Heidari, M., Merhof, D.: TransNorm: transformer provides a strong spatial normalization mechanism for a deep segmentation model. IEEE Access **10**, 108205–108215 (2022)
2. Azad, R., Fayjie, A.R., Kauffmann, C., Ben Ayed, I., Pedersoli, M., Dolz, J.: On the texture bias for few-shot CNN segmentation. In: Proceedings of the IEEE/CVF Winter Conference on Applications of Computer Vision, pp. 2674–2683 (2021)
3. Cai, Y., Wang, Y.: MA-Unet: an improved version of UNet based on multi-scale and attention mechanism for medical image segmentation. In: Third International Conference on Electronics and Communication; Network and Computer Technology, ECNCT 2021, vol. 12167, pp. 205–211. SPIE (2022)
4. Cao, H., Wang, Y., Chen, J., Jiang, D., Zhang, X., Tian, Q., Wang, M.: Swin-Unet: Unet-like pure transformer for medical image segmentation. In: European Conference on Computer Vision, pp. 205–218. Springer (2022)
5. Chen, B., Liu, Y., Zhang, Z., Lu, G., Kong, A.W.K.: TransAttUnet: multi-level attention-guided U-Net with transformer for medical image segmentation. IEEE Trans. Emerg. Top. Comput. Intell. (2023)
6. Chen, C.F.R., Fan, Q., Panda, R.: CrossViT: cross-attention multi-scale vision transformer for image classification. In: Proceedings of the IEEE/CVF International Conference on Computer Vision, pp. 357–366 (2021)
7. Chen, J., et al.: TransUNet: transformers make strong encoders for medical image segmentation. arXiv preprint arXiv:2102.04306 (2021)
8. Chen, S., Tan, X., Wang, B., Hu, X.: Reverse attention for salient object detection. In: Proceedings of the European Conference on Computer Vision (ECCV), pp. 234–250 (2018)
9. Dong, B., Wang, W., Fan, D.P., Li, J., Fu, H., Shao, L.: Polyp-PVT: polyp segmentation with pyramid vision transformers. arXiv preprint arXiv:2108.06932 (2021)
10. Dosovitskiy, A.: An image is worth 16x16 words: transformers for image recognition at scale. arXiv preprint arXiv:2010.11929 (2020)
11. Fan, D.P., et al.: PraNet: parallel reverse attention network for polyp segmentation. In: International Conference on Medical Image Computing and Computer-Assisted Intervention, pp. 263–273. Springer (2020)
12. Huang, H., et al.: UNet 3+: a full-scale connected UNet for medical image segmentation. In: 2020 IEEE International Conference on Acoustics, Speech and Signal Processing (ICASSP), ICASSP 2020, pp. 1055–1059. IEEE (2020)
13. Huang, X., Deng, Z., Li, D., Yuan, X.: MISSFormer: an effective medical image segmentation transformer. arXiv preprint arXiv:2109.07162 (2021)
14. Huang, Z., Wang, X., Huang, L., Huang, C., Wei, Y., Liu, W.: CCNet: criss-cross attention for semantic segmentation. In: Proceedings of the IEEE/CVF International Conference on Computer Vision, pp. 603–612 (2019)

15. Isensee, F., Jaeger, P.F., Kohl, S.A., Petersen, J., Maier-Hein, K.H.: nnU-Net: a self-configuring method for deep learning-based biomedical image segmentation. Nat. Meth. **18**(2), 203–211 (2021)
16. Jiang, Y., Zhang, Z., Qin, S., Guo, Y., Li, Z., Cui, S.: APAUNet: axis projection attention UNet for small target in 3D medical segmentation. In: Proceedings of the Asian Conference on Computer Vision, pp. 283–298 (2022)
17. Lin, A., Chen, B., Xu, J., Zhang, Z., Lu, G., Zhang, D.: DS-TransUNet: dual Swin transformer U-Net for medical image segmentation. IEEE Trans. Instrum. Meas. **71**, 1–15 (2022)
18. Liu, Z., et al.: Swin transformer: hierarchical vision transformer using shifted windows. In: Proceedings of the IEEE/CVF International Conference on Computer Vision, pp. 10012–10022 (2021)
19. Lou, A., Guan, S., Loew, M.: DC-UNet: rethinking the u-net architecture with dual channel efficient CNN for medical image segmentation. In: Medical Imaging 2021: Image Processing, vol. 11596, pp. 758–768. SPIE (2021)
20. Oktay, O., et al.: Attention U-Net: learning where to look for the pancreas. arXiv preprint arXiv:1804.03999 (2018)
21. Rahman, M.M., Marculescu, R.: Medical image segmentation via cascaded attention decoding. In: Proceedings of the IEEE/CVF Winter Conference on Applications of Computer Vision, pp. 6222–6231 (2023)
22. Rahman, M.M., Marculescu, R.: G-CASCADE: efficient cascaded graph convolutional decoding for 2D medical image segmentation. In: Proceedings of the IEEE/CVF Winter Conference on Applications of Computer Vision, pp. 7728–7737 (2024)
23. Rahman, M.M., Marculescu, R.: Multi-scale hierarchical vision transformer with cascaded attention decoding for medical image segmentation. In: Medical Imaging with Deep Learning, pp. 1526–1544. PMLR (2024)
24. Rahman, M.M., Munir, M., Marculescu, R.: EMCAD: efficient multi-scale convolutional attention decoding for medical image segmentation. In: Proceedings of the IEEE/CVF Conference on Computer Vision and Pattern Recognition, pp. 11769–11779 (2024)
25. Rahman, M.M., Shokouhmand, S., Bhatt, S., Faezipour, M.: MIST: medical image segmentation transformer with convolutional attention mixing (CAM) decoder. In: Proceedings of the IEEE/CVF Winter Conference on Applications of Computer Vision, pp. 404–413 (2024)
26. Ronneberger, O., Fischer, P., Brox, T.: U-Net: convolutional networks for biomedical image segmentation. In: Proceedings of the 18th International Conference on Medical Image Computing and Computer-Assisted Intervention, MICCAI 2015, Part III 18, Munich, Germany, 5–9 October 2015, pp. 234–241. Springer (2015)
27. Soltani-Gol, M., Fattahi, M., Soltanian-Zadeh, H., Sheikhaei, S.: DRAU-Net: double residual attention mechanism for automatic MRI brain tumor segmentation. In: 2022 30th International Conference on Electrical Engineering (ICEE), pp. 587–591. IEEE (2022)
28. Tu, Z., et al.: MaxViT: multi-axis vision transformer. In: European Conference on Computer Vision, pp. 459–479. Springer (2022)
29. Vaswani, A.: Attention is all you need. In: Advances in Neural Information Processing Systems (2017)
30. Wang, H., Cao, P., Wang, J., Zaiane, O.R.: UCTransNet: rethinking the skip connections in U-Net from a channel-wise perspective with transformer. In: Proceedings of the AAAI Conference on Artificial Intelligence, vol. 36, pp. 2441–2449 (2022)

31. Wang, H., et al.: Mixed transformer u-net for medical image segmentation. In: 2022 IEEE International Conference on Acoustics, Speech and Signal Processing (ICASSP), ICASSP 2022, pp. 2390–2394. IEEE (2022)

32. Wang, J., Huang, Q., Tang, F., Meng, J., Su, J., Song, S.: Stepwise feature fusion: local guides global. In: International Conference on Medical Image Computing and Computer-Assisted Intervention, pp. 110–120. Springer (2022)

33. Wang, M., Wang, H., Zhang, F.: FAMC-Net: frequency domain parity correction attention and multi-scale dilated convolution for time series forecasting. In: Proceedings of the 32nd ACM International Conference on Information and Knowledge Management, pp. 2554–2563 (2023)

34. Wang, W., et al.: Pyramid vision transformer: a versatile backbone for dense prediction without convolutions. In: Proceedings of the IEEE/CVF International Conference on Computer Vision, pp. 568–578 (2021)

35. Wang, W., et al.: PVT v2: improved baselines with pyramid vision transformer. Comput. Vis. Media 8(3), 415–424 (2022)

36. Wang, Z., Cun, X., Bao, J., Zhou, W., Liu, J., Li, H.: Uformer: a general U-shaped transformer for image restoration. In: Proceedings of the IEEE/CVF Conference on Computer Vision and Pattern Recognition, pp. 17683–17693 (2022)

37. Woo, S., Park, J., Lee, J.Y., Kweon, I.S.: CBAM: convolutional block attention module. In: Proceedings of the European Conference on Computer Vision (ECCV), pp. 3–19 (2018)

38. Wu, H., et al.: CVT: introducing convolutions to vision transformers. In: Proceedings of the IEEE/CVF International Conference on Computer Vision, pp. 22–31 (2021)

39. Xie, E., Wang, W., Yu, Z., Anandkumar, A., Alvarez, J.M., Luo, P.: SegFormer: simple and efficient design for semantic segmentation with transformers. Adv. Neural. Inf. Process. Syst. 34, 12077–12090 (2021)

40. Xu, G., Zhang, X., He, X., Wu, X.: LeViT-UNet: make faster encoders with transformer for medical image segmentation. In: Chinese Conference on Pattern Recognition and Computer Vision (PRCV), pp. 42–53. Springer (2023)

41. Yao, C., Hu, M., Li, Q., Zhai, G., Zhang, X.P.: TransClaw U-Net: claw U-Net with transformers for medical image segmentation. In: 2022 5th International Conference on Information Communication and Signal Processing (ICICSP), pp. 280–284. IEEE (2022)

42. You, C., et al.: Class-aware adversarial transformers for medical image segmentation. Adv. Neural. Inf. Process. Syst. 35, 29582–29596 (2022)

43. Zhang, F., Chen, G., Wang, H., Li, J., Zhang, C.: Multi-scale video super-resolution transformer with polynomial approximation. IEEE Trans. Circ. Syst. Video Technol. 33(9), 4496–4506 (2023)

44. Zhang, F., Chen, G., Wang, H., Zhang, C.: CF-DAN: facial-expression recognition based on cross-fusion dual-attention network. Comput. Vis. Media 10, 593–608 (2024)

45. Zhang, F., Guo, T., Wang, H.: DFNet: decomposition fusion model for long sequence time-series forecasting. Knowl. Based Syst. 277, 110794 (2023)

46. Zhang, X., et al.: DRA U-Net: an attention based U-Net framework for 2D medical image segmentation. In: 2021 IEEE International Conference on Big Data (Big Data), pp. 3936–3942. IEEE (2021)

47. Zhang, Y., Liu, H., Hu, Q.: TransFuse: Fusing transformers and CNNs for medical image segmentation. In: Proceedings of the 24th International Conference on Medical Image Computing and Computer Assisted Intervention, MICCAI 2021, Part I 24, Strasbourg, France, 27 September–1 October 2021, pp. 14–24. Springer (2021)

48. Zhao, P., Zhang, J., Fang, W., Deng, S.: SCAU-Net: spatial-channel attention u-net for gland segmentation. Front. Bioeng. Biotechnol. **8**, 670 (2020)
49. Zhou, Z., Rahman Siddiquee, M.M., Tajbakhsh, N., Liang, J.: UNet++: a nested U-Net architecture for medical image segmentation. In: Deep Learning in Medical Image Analysis and Multimodal Learning for Clinical Decision Support: Proceedings of the 4th International Workshop, DLMIA 2018, and 8th International Workshop, ML-CDS 2018, Held in Conjunction with MICCAI 2018, Granada, Spain, 20 September 2018, pp. 3–11. Springer (2018)

YNet: Medical Image Segmentation Model Based on Wavelet Transform Boundary Enhancement

Wenzhe Meng, Xiaoliang Zhu$^{(\boxtimes)}$, and Yanxiang Li

School of Software, Xinjiang University, Urumqi 830091, China
zhuxiaoliang3721@163.com

Abstract. Medical image segmentation is critical in understanding pathological changes and computer-aided diagnosis. Most of the existing medical segmentation models focus on the overall segmentation effect of the model and lack of thinking about the problems of boundary blurring and model generalization ability. Given this, a bipartite segmentation model YNet based on boundary enhancement is proposed, which is based on the encoder-decoder architecture and consists of two core components: boundary enhancement module (BEM) and feature fusion module (FFM). The BEM utilizes the wavelet transform to separate the frequency domain information from the original image, allowing the model to dynamically adjust the boundary details in the original image, thus enhancing the model's ability to perceive the boundary information and mitigating the effect of noise on the model. An attention mechanism is introduced in the FFM to enhance the model's generalization ability by dynamically adjusting the channel and spatial information weights to emphasize critical features and suppress redundant information. Experimental results comparing other methods on CVC-ClinicDB, Kvasir-SEG, DSB2018, and ISIC2018 datasets show that the model has more explicit boundaries and better segmentation generalization. The source code of our YNet will be made available at https://github.com/DeadlyCodeGod/YNet.

Keywords: Double-branch networks · Wavelet transform · Feature fusion · Attention mechanism · Boundary enhancement

1 Introduction

Medical image segmentation plays a vital role in medical image processing, where the main goal is to classify each pixel in an image and generate a masked image to identify lesion areas in medical images [24] accurately. This technique is crucial in assisting physicians to more accurately diagnose diseases, develop treatment plans, and track the health status of patients. Researchers have been developing convolutional neural network (CNN) based medical image segmentation methods to achieve this purpose and have made significant progress [9,17,28]. The most representative method is UNet [24], which improves the segmentation of edge details by combining the encoder's shallow features with the decoder's high-resolution features through hopping connections. Okatay [21] et al. proposed an

© The Author(s), under exclusive license to Springer Nature Singapore Pte Ltd. 2025
P. Didyk and J. Hou (Eds.): CVM 2025, LNCS 15663, pp. 91–108, 2025.
https://doi.org/10.1007/978-981-96-5809-1_6

attentional mechanism for the UNet-based segmentation model, which can better focus on the relevant regions of the pancreas. Zhou [35] et al. proposed a variant of UNet called UNet++, in which the decoder sub-network solves the sizeable semantic gap between the encoder and decoder in UNet through dense hopping connections. On this basis, Srivastava et al. [27] proposed a multi-scale feature extraction and fusion mechanism for the feature extraction and fusion problem in medical image segmentation, effectively utilising different levels of features to capture richer contextual information. ColonSegNet [10] employs multi-scale feature extraction to capture different scales of contextual information. At the same time, an attention mechanism is introduced to enhance the attention to critical regions. Although these research results have achieved significant improvements in segmentation performance, there are still two key issues that need to be addressed in medical image segmentation tasks: (1) Insufficient utilization of original image information: most models tend to focus on optimizing the design of the framework while ignoring the rich available information in the original image, such as texture and structure information. (2) Challenges of segmentation boundaries: Due to the varying sizes of lesions, their boundaries with surrounding tissues often need to be more explicit, resulting in segmentation models that are prone to under-segmentation or over-segmentation, which affects the reliability of the models in clinical applications.

Aiming at the above problems, this paper proposes a wavelet transform-based boundary information enhancement module, which can be enough to separate the high and low-frequency information of the original image without additional training data and which helps to help the model filter noise. In the frequency domain, low-frequency (LF) information expresses the abstract semantics of the image, while high-frequency (HF) information is rich in detailed features of the image boundary [29,32]. This enables YNet to learn tiny structures, abstract semantic content, and overlapping or low-light parts of an image, and these details and semantic features are crucial for medical image analysis and diagnosis [3,4,23]. However, single-branch convolutional neural networks have limitations in dealing with these details and need help thoroughly learning the information they contain [15,25,36]. So, inspired by the above studies and limitations, this paper proposes a double-branch segmentation model YNet driven by LF and HF information for medical image segmentation tasks. The dual-branch encoder in the model learns the image features enhanced by LF and HF, respectively, so that the YNet model can capture the correlation of potential inter-split features and enhance the ability of the network to link semantic and detailed features. In order to overcome the problem that the fusion of the frequency domain information of the dual-branch taps may lead to the weakening of the model's generalization ability, this paper fuses the LF and HF information with the original information separately in an adaptive manner and designs the attention feature fusion module.

The contributions of this article are described below:

(1) This paper uses the wavelet transform theory to design the BEM. This module separates the LF and HF information of an image and weighted fusion of

the separated information with the original image in a self-learning manner. This form of adaptive feature fusion enhances the model's generalisation ability and reduces the need for model parameter tuning.

(2) The double-branch model named YNet is proposed. It learns the original image information enhanced by global information on the LF encoder branch and learns to capture fine edge details from the original image on the HF encoder branch. This complementary learning approach enhances the model's ability to perceive boundary information.

(3) In order to better fuse the complementary information of the double-branch taps, this paper designs the FFM, which suppresses or enhances the feature maps in an attentional manner on the channel as well as spatially, to improve the module's ability to perceive and select important feature information.

2 Related Work

In recent years, thanks to the advancement of deep learning technology, the field of medical images has been developing rapidly, and numerous models with excellent performance have emerged [11, 21, 28]. However, when dealing with complex scenes, single-branch networks usually can only process features on one path and are prone to encounter bottlenecks in feature fusion at different scales and model generalization ability. In contrast, dual-branch networks perform well in this scenario [11]. The double-branch model architecture improves multi-scale feature learning. It enhances model generalization capability by designing independent branching paths that can process different kinds of features or learn different aspects of features separately [34]. In addition, this architecture allows the model to dynamically adapt to different feature requirements and effectively integrate multi-scale information when facing complex segmentation tasks, thus demonstrating enhanced performance capabilities when dealing with complex scenes. However, learning the complementary information between bipartition splits recognizes a vital issue in the design of bipartition-based models, which should be considered for the original feature processing in addition to considering the model coding layer.

An essential advantage of the wavelet transform is its ability to separate the high and low information and retain the frequency range and spatial location information effectively at the same time, which makes the wavelet transform uniquely valuable in image processing, especially in tasks that need to distinguish between image details and global structure [26, 28]. Therefore, the combination of wavelet transform and deep learning models can help the models to improve segmentation accuracy when processing complex images, especially in tasks that require precise boundary detection [8, 19]. Azimi et al. [1] proposed a symmetric CNN algorithm augmented by wavelet transform to effectively solve the problem of improving segmentation accuracy in semantic segmentation tasks. The algorithm better preserves boundary details and complex structures by introducing wavelet transform. However, the method needs more flexibility when dealing with different tasks. Its performance needs to be more robust for tasks with high complexity or significant differences in feature distribution, and its generalization ability needs to be improved. Duan et al. [6] used the wavelet transform constrained pooling layer to replace the traditional maximum pooling or average pooling operation to solve the problem of better retaining detailed information. However, it is more sensitive to HF noise, and the wavelet transform pooling operation is more significant in computational volume, which increases the network's computational complexity and training time. Li et al. [18] enhance the network's ability to capture and reconstruct detailed information by using the wavelet transform to extract the details in the downsampling stage and the wavelet inverse transforms to recover the details in the upsampling stage. However, this method imposes strong constraints on the network structure while enhancing image details, resulting in a less scalable model across tasks and datasets, exhibits instability, and is challenging to adapt to diverse application scenarios. In contrast, YNet has a more flexible operation by focusing on LF and HF information through a double-branch architecture without imposing constraints on the network.

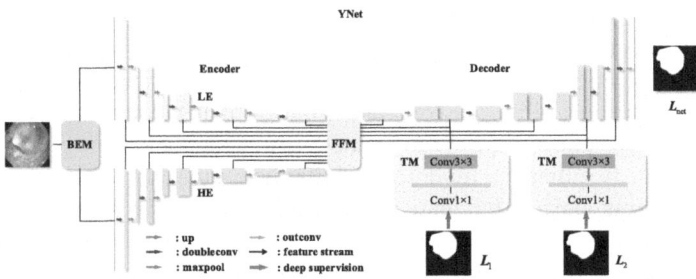

Fig. 1. The model framework diagram of YNet shows that BEM is a boundary enhancement module that separates images' LF and HF information. LE and HE are LF information encoders and HF information encoders, respectively. FFM is a Feature Fusion Module that fuses the features learned from the double-branch encoder. The TM Module is the Deep-Supervised Transformation Module.

3   Method

3.1   Overview

The YNet network proposed in this paper adopts the traditional encoder-decoder architecture, and the specific network architecture is illustrated in Fig. 1, which consists of five parts: (1) the HF and LF information separation module BEM, which helps the model to better learn the essential features in the subsequent processing steps; (2) two fully convolutional double-branch network encoders, which are able to extract different kinds of features at the same time, thus improving the multi-scale feature learning capability; (3) a feature fusion module FFM, which enhances the model's understanding of both detailed and global information and improves the accuracy of the segmentation results; (4) a profoundly supervised feature transformation module TM, which ensures that the model's learning is effectively guided at different levels, and improves the model's stability during the training process [16]; (5) a decoder for generating segmentation predictions, which partially ensures the meticulousness of the segmentation results by gradually restoring the spatial resolution of the image.

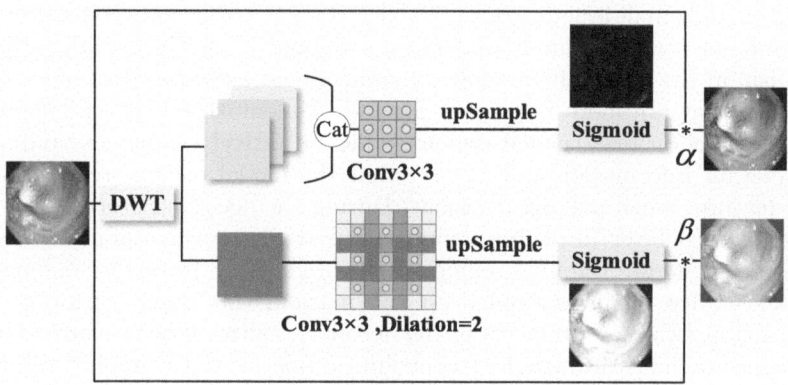

Fig. 2. Module framework diagram of BEM. BEM uses different convolution operations to extract HF and LF information selectively. In order to ensure effective fusion with the original features, the upSample operation is used to recover the feature dimension size. α and β represent the gating factors that fuse the HF and LF features with the original images.

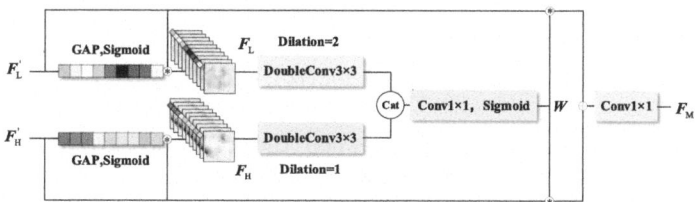

Fig. 3. The FFM's structural diagram shows the fusion process of HF and LF features.

Overall, the original image is first processed by BEM to extract the LF and HF feature information. Then, this feature information is adaptively fused with the original image to enhance the edge and semantic features of the original image, respectively, to form the feature maps LF and HF. The enhanced feature maps LF and HF are sent to the dual-branch encoder for encoding operations, as illustrated in Fig. 1, where the LF information is learned in the LF encoder (LE). In contrast, the HF information is learned in the HF encoder (IIE). The LE branch extracts features with larger sensory fields through the hollow convolution operation to extract features with larger receptive fields to better understand the overall layout of the image. HE, on the other hand, enhances the learning of details through small convolution kernels to more accurately capture the image's boundaries and small lesion regions. The FFM collects LE and HE feature maps containing rich semantic and boundary information. Then, through the attention mechanism in the FFM, the module dynamically adjusts these features to highlight those that are more important for the segmentation task, enhancing the decoder's focus on task-critical regions, which effectively suppresses redundant and irrelevant information and ensures that the model pays more attention to critical features when making decisions. During the decoding process, the fused features of each layer form jump connections with the corresponding decoder layer, which generate the final segmentation prediction. To further enhance the network's ability to understand deep information, this paper performs depth supervision at two random layers of the decoder, realizes feature conversion and dimension matching through 1×1 convolution operation to simplify the model complexity, and offsets the model decoding heavy burden to deeper layers to ensure that the coherence of information transfer is maintained in the multilevel feature maps, and enhances the model's performance in the segmentation task. In order to ensure that the decoding process has stronger feature representation ability at different scales, this paper designs a combined loss function, denoted as L_{total}, which combines the losses from three different feature layers, namely: the network output loss L_{net}, the loss at the fourth decoder layer L_1 and the loss at the second decoder layer L_2, and combines them to generate the final loss L_{total}. Its mathematical expressions are as in Eqs. (1) and (2):

$$L_{\text{total}} = L_{\text{net}} + \lambda(L_1 + L_2) \tag{1}$$

$$L_{\text{net}} = L_1 = L_2 = -\frac{1}{N} \sum_{i=1}^{N} [y_i \log(p_i) + (1 - y_i) \log(1 - p_i)] \tag{2}$$

where λ is the balance parameter between the network output loss and the middle layer loss. The cross-entropy loss is used for L_{net}, L_1 and L_2. N is the number of samples, y_i is the actual label (0 or 1) of the ith sample, and p_i is the probability that the model predicts a positive class for the ith sample.

3.2   Boundary Enhancement Module

Figure 2 demonstrates the basic framework of the BEM proposed in this paper. The wavelet transform usually decomposes the image into the following four

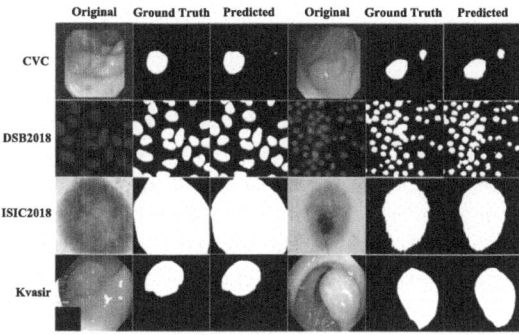

Fig. 4. Experimental predicted Kvasir, ISIC2018, DSB2018, and CVC maps against the actual values. Where original denotes the Original image, Ground Truth denotes the actual value, and Predicted denotes the prediction of YNet.

parts: the LF component LL retains the LF information of the original image; the vertical HF component LH retains the HF information of the image in the vertical direction; the horizontal HF component HL retains the HF information of the image in the horizontal direction; and the diagonal HF component HH retains the HF information of the image in the diagonal. In this paper, these three HF components are combined as the sum of all HF components. This treatment can simplify the model while still retaining enough HF detail information. This paper uses $\mathbf{L}$ to denote the LF component and $\mathbf{H}$ to denote the sum of the three HF components in different directions. Moreover, the upSample operation is utilized to recover the problem of space size reduction brought about by the wavelet transform. The specific $\mathbf{L}$ and $\mathbf{H}$ definitions are shown in Eqs. (3), (4) and (5):

$$\mathbf{F}_{LL}, \mathbf{F}_{LH}, \mathbf{F}_{HL}, \mathbf{F}_{HH} = \text{BEM}(\mathbf{F}_{\text{input}}) \tag{3}$$

$$\mathbf{L} = \text{upSample}(\mathbf{F}_{LL}) \tag{4}$$

$$\mathbf{H} = \text{upSample}(\mathbf{F}_{LH} + \mathbf{F}_{HL} + \mathbf{F}_{HH}) \tag{5}$$

where **upSample** denotes the upSampling operation that recovers the reduced spatial dimensions brought about by the wavelet transform.

From Fig. 2, it can be seen that L focuses on retaining the semantic information of the image, while H emphasizes the boundary detail information in the image. This paper applies the first-order wavelet transform and Haar wavelet basis to implement the discrete wavelet transform (DWT) algorithm. The first-order wavelet transform can adaptively adjust the decomposition according to the signal's local changes, making it more flexible than the traditional Fourier transform in processing images. The Haar wavelet, on the other hand, is characterized as a uniform square wave with rapidly changing jumps. It is particularly suitable for detecting edge and detail features in an image as it can be pinpointed in regions where the signal is changing rapidly [11]. The DWT algorithm preliminarily separates the high- and low-frequency information into LF and HF and then learns the LF features using a null convolution block, which makes the BEM module able to capture a more extensive range of contextual information; HF is learned using a small kernel convolution, which improves the module's ability in detail processing. In order to further improve the fusion ability of the model in the frequency and spatial domains, this paper introduces an adaptive mechanism, which is used to adjust the contribution of the frequency dynamic features to the original features so that the model can flexibly process the key details and semantic information in the image under different scenarios, thus improving the analysis ability and adaptability to complex medical images. The adaptive mechanism controls the regulation through two parameters, α and β., as shown in Eqs. (6) and (7):

$$\mathbf{H} = \alpha \mathbf{H'} + \mathbf{I} \tag{6}$$

$$\mathbf{L} = \beta \mathbf{L'} + \mathbf{I} \tag{7}$$

where $\mathbf{I}$ denotes the original image, and α and β both belong to the interval [0, 1], which are used to control the contribution of $\mathbf{L'}$ and $\mathbf{H'}$ to $\mathbf{I}$:

Table 1. Comparison of the four datasets

Dataset	Number of images	Image data format	Image size
CVC	612	.tif	512 * 512
Kvasir	1000	.jpg	528 * 622
DSB2018	670	.png	Variable resolution
ISIC2018	2595	.jpg	512 * 512

Table 2. Comparison of YNet in Kvasir-SEG and CVC-ClinicDB metrics

Dataset	Kvasir				CVC			
Metric	mDice	mIoU	mPrecision	mReccall	mDice	mIoU	mPrecision	mReccall
U-Net [24]	0.782	0.714	0.724	0.745	0.846	0.773	0.849	0.879
U-Net++ [35]	0.747	0.631	0.758	0.670	0.845	0.755	0.832	0.791
ResUNet [5]	0.512	0.379	0.593	0.597	0.522	0.416	0.563	0.589
ResUNet++ [13]	0.807	0.723	0.799	0.787	0.521	0.413	0.583	0.569
ColonSegNet [10]	0.841	0.754	0.849	0.854	0.879	0.804	0.884	0.860
MSRF-Net [27]	0.858	0.791	0.869	0.867	0.912	0.872	0.902	0.901
SAM [14]	0.862	0.805	0.872	0.870	0.915	0.875	0.908	0.895
YNet(Ours)	**0.875**	**0.822**	**0.888**	**0.900**	**0.925**	**0.885**	**0.910**	**0.932**

3.3   Feature Fusion Module

In order to effectively fuse the features of the double-branch tap, this paper designs the FFM module, whose architecture is illustrated in Fig. 3. The design concept of FFM is to enhance the model's ability to extract and utilize critical information through multi-level feature processing. Specifically, the features $\mathbf{F}'_L$ and $\mathbf{F}'_H$ of the double-branch taps are first aggregated using the global average pooling (GAP) operation, respectively, and their spatial channel information is captured. The captured information is used to generate the two-channel attention weights using the Sigmoid function $\mathbf{M}_L \in \mathbb{R}^{C \times 1 \times 1}$ and $\mathbf{M}_H \in \mathbb{R}^{C \times 1 \times 1}$, which dynamically adjust the feature maps of $\mathbf{F}'_L$ and $\mathbf{F}'_H$ through these two weights, highlighting the critical channel information and blocking out the irrelevant information to obtain more accurate $\mathbf{F}_L$ and $\mathbf{F}_H$ features, preparing them for fusion. The specific steps are shown in Eqs. (8), (9), (10), and (11):

$$\mathbf{M}_L = \text{Sigmoid}(\text{GAP}(\mathbf{F}'_L)) \tag{8}$$

$$\mathbf{M}_H = \text{Sigmoid}(\text{GAP}(\mathbf{F}'_H)) \tag{9}$$

$$\mathbf{F}_L = \mathbf{M}_L * \mathbf{F}'_L \tag{10}$$

$$\mathbf{F}_H = \mathbf{M}_H * \mathbf{F}'_H \tag{11}$$

In this paper, we utilize the 3×3 atrous double convolution operation to learn further the global features of $\mathbf{F}_L$ focus on learning the detailed boundary features of $\mathbf{F}_H$ with the 3×3 standard double convolution operation, further filter the features of the double-branching tunnels to be merged, and apply a 1×1 convolution operation to the merged feature map. Operation: this operation not only helps to improve the expression ability of the features but also can not generate the final attention weight to reduce the amount of computation. The Sigmoid function is applied to generate the final attention weights $\mathbf{W} \in R^{H \times W}$, as in Eqs. (12) and (13). to enhance the network's perception of essential features and to improve the network's representation. Finally, as in Eqs. (14), this fused feature map is further processed using 1×1 convolution to adjust the channel dimensions of the features and integrate the information to generate the final fused feature map $\mathbf{F}_M$:

$$\mathbf{T} = \text{Concat}(\text{DConv}_{3 \times 3}(\mathbf{F}_L), \text{Conv}_{3 \times 3}(\mathbf{F}_H)) \tag{12}$$

$$\mathbf{W} = \text{Sigmoid}(\text{Conv}_{1 \times 1}(\mathbf{T})) \tag{13}$$

$$\mathbf{F}_M = \text{Conv}_{1 \times 1}(\mathbf{W} * \mathbf{F}_L + \mathbf{W} * \mathbf{F}_H) \tag{14}$$

4   Experiments

4.1   Datasets

The performance evaluation of the YNet model is based on four different open medical image datasets, including CVC-ClinicDB [2], Kvasir-SEG [12], DSB2018

[31], and ISIC2018 [20]. CVC-ClinicDB (CVC) is an endoscopic image focused on diagnosing and analysing gastrointestinal diseases. Kvasir-SEG (Kvasir) is a dataset of endoscopic images containing various gastrointestinal diseases. DSB2018 is a chest X-ray image for lung cancer screening. ISIC2018 is a dataset focusing on dermatology image analysis. Specifically, as shown in Table 1, these datasets have essential applications in the fields of medical image processing, deep learning research, and data science, where they provide researchers and developers with a large amount of image and labelling data that can be used to train and test a variety of deep learning models to improve medical diagnosis and disease screening.

4.2   Implementation Details

In this paper, a series of steps are taken to ensure the data's consistency, quality and reliability when training YNet. In this paper, the original medical images are resized to a uniform H×W, where both H and W are 352, to maintain consistency [7,30,33]. To minimize the blending problems that may be introduced by image resizing, anti-aliasing techniques are introduced to improve the quality and reliability of image processing [22]. The original image and the segmentation maps are normalized to values in the range [0, 1] to facilitate loss computation and model training. According to [7,22,30], the dataset is divided into training, validation and test sets in the ratio of 8:1:1. A series of stochastic data enhancement operations including horizontal and vertical flips, affine transformations including angular rotations, horizontal and vertical translations, and angular shears were performed on the training set. The YNet model was trained on each dataset using a batch size of 8 and an Adam optimizer with weight decay. The learning rate is adaptively updated using an annealing algorithm, which is initially set to 1e−4 when the performance of the validation set improves by no more than 10% over ten cycles and decreases by a factor of 2 before reaching a minimum of 1e−6. These steps ensure that the data processing and model training of the YNet model during the training period are highly quality and reliable and provide consistency and comparability. The proposed model is implemented using PyTorch and trained on an NVIDIA GeForce RTX4090 GPU with 24 GB of memory.

4.3   Evaluation Metrics

In order to obtain a more comprehensive YNet performance evaluation for each dataset, this paper adopts several metrics commonly used in the field of image segmentation: mDice, mIoU, mPrecision, and mRecall, where m denotes the average value taken over the entire test set. By calculating the average value of each metric overall test sample, the comprehensive performance of the model over the entire test set can be evaluated, which helps to eliminate the chance brought by a single sample and provides a more stable and comprehensive performance evaluation. The specific defining Eqs. are shown in (15), (16), (17) and (18).

Table 3. Comparison of YNet's metrics in DSB2018 and ISIC2018

Dataset	DSB2018				ISIC2018			
Metric	mDice	mIoU	mPrecision	mRecall	mDice	mIoU	mPrecision	mRecall
U-Net [24]	0.887	0.808	0.872	0.920	0.868	0.782	0.879	0.849
U-Net++ [35]	0.886	0.814	0.874	0.918	0.809	0.720	0.881	0.786
ResUNet [5]	0.906	0.817	0.880	0.915	0.856	0.756	0.875	0.833
ResUNet++ [13]	0.894	0.822	0.900	0.903	0.857	0.813	0.864	0.881
ColonSegNet [10]	0.920	0.855	0.910	0.919	0.850	0.778	0.883	0.865
MSRF-Net [27]	0.924	0.853	0.902	0.930	0.882	0.837	0.915	0.889
SAM [14]	0.927	0.858	0.912	0.933	0.890	0.845	0.918	0.892
YNet(Ours)	**0.930**	**0.865**	**0.918**	**0.940**	**0.900**	**0.860**	**0.925**	**0.905**

$$mDice = \frac{\sum_{i=1}^{n} \frac{2|X_i \cap Y_i|}{|X_i|+|Y_i|}}{p} \tag{15}$$

$$mIoU = \frac{\sum_{i=1}^{n} \frac{|X_i \cap Y_i|}{|X_i \cup Y_i|}}{p} \tag{16}$$

$$mPrecision = \frac{\sum_{i=1}^{n} \frac{TP_i}{TP_i+FP_i}}{p} \tag{17}$$

$$mRecall = \frac{\sum_{i=1}^{n} \frac{TP_i}{TP_i+FN_i}}{p} \tag{18}$$

where TP_i, FP_i, FN_i represent true examples, false positive examples, and false negative examples, respectively, which are the basic elements in the confusion matrix used to evaluate the classification or segmentation performance of the model. X_i, Y_i represents the prediction results and true labels. m represents the average value of the test set, and p is the number of images in the test set.

4.4 Performance Comparisons

To evaluate the performance of the YNet model, this paper compares it to several previous models using the same experimental setup to ensure a fair comparison. Four different datasets are used for the experiments, and a series of quantitative metrics and prediction examples are used to compare the performance of YNet with other models. As illustrated in Fig. 4, some prediction examples of YNet on these datasets are shown in this paper. It can be seen from the figure that YNet's segmentation results in the edge part of the performance of the protection of stronger finesse and coherence to alleviate the common phenomenon of

Table 4. Ablation experiments. Includes ablation experiments for the BEM module, the FFM module, and the double-branch model.

BEM		×	×	✓	✓
FFM		×	✓	×	✓
Dataset	Metric				
CVC	mDice	0.890	0.892	0.861	**0.925**
	mIoU	0.794	0.792	0.802	**0.885**
	mPrecision	0.883	0.872	0.856	**0.910**
	mRecall	0.892	0.843	0.905	**0.932**
Kvasir	mDice	0.853	0.861	0.870	**0.875**
	mIoU	0.809	0.815	0.810	**0.822**
	mPrecision	0.869	0.871	0.873	**0.888**
	mRecall	0.889	0.876	0.895	**0.900**
DSB2018	mDice	0.910	0.915	0.917	**0.930**
	mIoU	0.845	0.844	0.847	**0.865**
	mPrecision	0.900	0.908	0.913	**0.918**
	mRecall	0.919	0.916	0.920	**0.940**
ISIC2018	mDice	0.867	0.870	0.866	**0.900**
	mIoU	0.806	0.800	0.802	**0.860**
	mPrecision	0.913	0.916	0.914	**0.925**
	mRecall	0.866	0.869	0.872	**0.905**

edge blurring and breakage, and this effect is due to the feature fusion module and the attention mechanism of the model to extract and enhance the edge information sufficiently, which makes the segmentation results of the contour lines more sharp. The result is sharper contour lines.

This paper evaluates the performance of YNet on multiple datasets using mDice, mIoU, mPrecision and mRecall metrics. The experiments compare multiple existing segmentation models, including:

(1) U-Net [24] proposed by Ronneberger et al. U-Net is a classical medical image segmentation network with an encoder-decoder structure that utilizes jump connections to preserve high-resolution features for enhanced recovery of detailed information.
(2) U-Net++ [35], proposed by Zhou et al. introduces nested jump paths on top of U-Net, enhancing the feature reuse capability and improving the segmentation performance, especially in segmentation tasks with complex structures.
(3) ResUNet [5], proposed by Zhang et al., combines the advantages of U-Net and residual learning. Referencing residual blocks enhances the network's expressive ability and reduces training difficulty.

(4) ResUNet++ [13], proposed by Zhang et al., is an improved version of ResUNet. It adopts a more complex jump-connection structure to improve the flexibility of feature fusion and thus enhance the segmentation effect.
(5) ColonSegNet [10], proposed by Jha et al., is designed for segmenting colon endoscopic images. It uses a deep convolutional neural network structure combined with a multiscale feature extraction technique to improve the recognition of colon adenomas.
(6) MSRF-Net [27], proposed by Huang et al., utilizes a multiscale residual learning architecture designed to improve the robustness and accuracy of image segmentation, especially excelling in processing medical images.
(7) Segment Anything Model (SAM) [14], proposed by Kirillov et al., is a general-purpose image segmentation model based on Vision Transformer (ViT). It performs excellently across various image scenarios, including medical image segmentation.

The experimental results on Kvasir and CVC datasets are shown in Table 2, from which it can be seen that the YNet model almost outperforms the existing models in four metrics and reaches the SOTA level. As illustrated in Fig. 4, YNet performs particularly well in the segmentation of complex structures and tiny lesions and can maintain stable performance in medical images with high noise and background complexity, showing good robustness and more explicit segmentation boundaries, thanks to the design of the BEM and the double-branch tap. Although mis-segmentation may still occur in some overlapping regions, overall, the effectiveness and robustness of YNet in dealing with complex medical image segmentation tasks are fully verified.

To further demonstrate the excellent generalization ability of the YNet model, this paper also conducts comparative experiments on the DSB2018 and ISIC2018 datasets, the results of which are shown in Table 3. The YNet model also outperforms the existing models on these two datasets, reaching the SOTA level. These excellent results are attributed to FFM, a module that effectively improves the model's performance during feature extraction and fusion. FFM adaptively adjusts the importance of different feature maps so that the model can better retain critical information and effectively suppress the influence of noise when processing complex images. This feature enables YNet to maintain a high-performance level on various datasets, showing good generalization ability and robustness. Therefore, the FFM module plays a vital role in improving the model's performance, further consolidating the competitiveness of YNet in medical image segmentation.

As can be illustrated in Fig. 5, YNet demonstrates excellent segmentation performance on datasets with different distributional characteristics. In most evaluation metrics, YNet achieves better scores than existing models, proving its strong generalization ability and adaptability. Especially when dealing with different types of medical images, YNet can effectively capture critical features and maintain high accuracy in the segmentation task. Figure 6 shows some sample prediction results of YNet on the four datasets with other models. The comparison shows that YNet exhibits excellent segmentation accuracy in images of

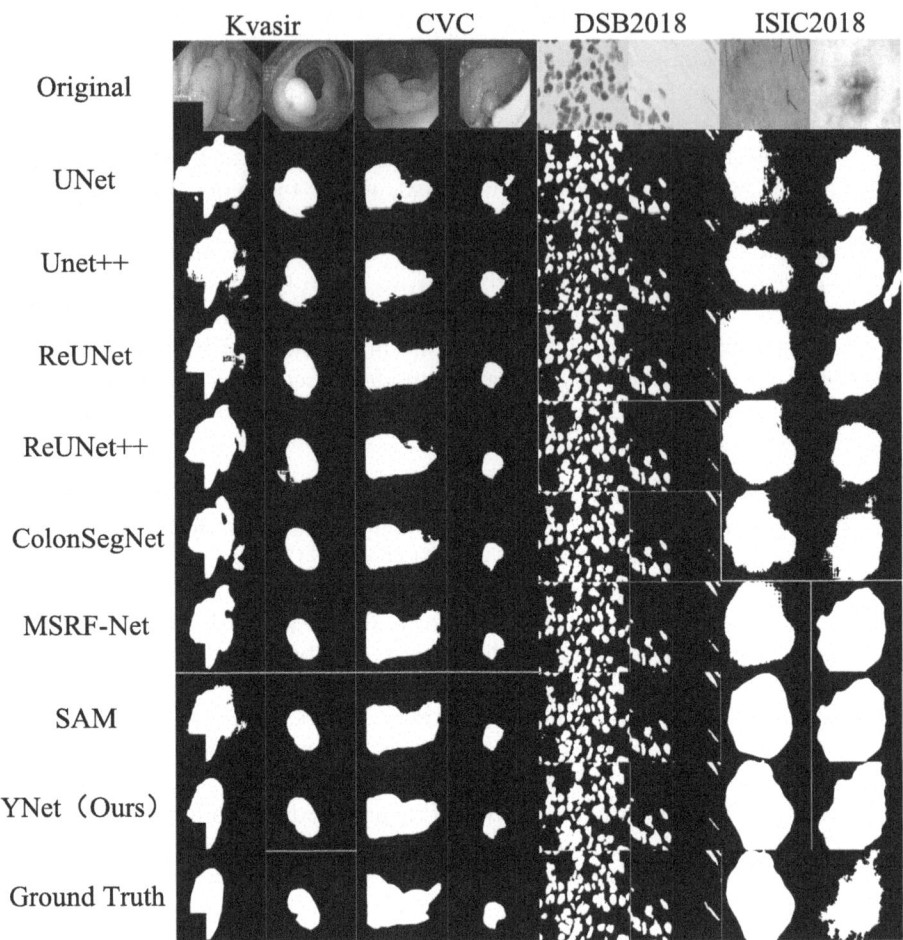

Fig. 5. It shows the comparison of the results of seven models on four datasets, and from the figure, the segmentation prediction results of the YNet model are superior.

various morphology and complexity, especially in processing fine structure and boundary information.

4.5 Ablation Studies

In order to verify the effectiveness of the designed BEM and FFM, ablation studies are conducted in this paper. The experimental results are shown in Table 4. In the absence of FFM, although BEM enhances the segmentation ability of boundary details, the global feature fusion and processing need to be improved. This quickly leads to the lack of global context information, thus affecting the overall segmentation performance. Moreover, when there is no BEM, although FFM can optimize the features globally, it does not process the details of the

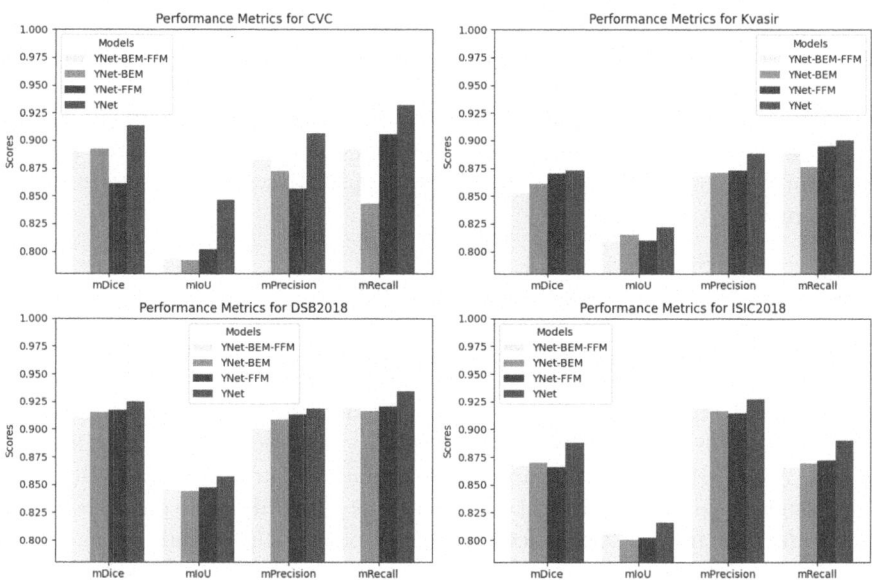

Fig. 6. Visualization of YNet model ablation experiments.

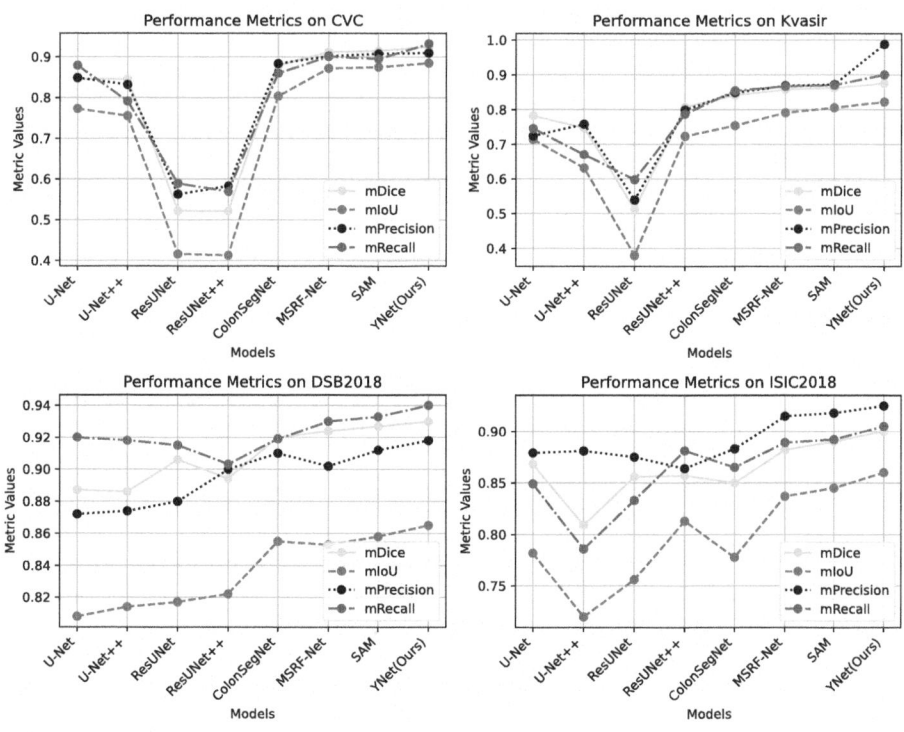

Fig. 7. Comparison of segmentation performance of different models on CVC, Kvasir, DSB2018, and ISIC2018 datasets.

boundary sufficiently, leading to the problem of blurred boundaries and unclear transitions. From Fig. 7, YNet can improve segmentation performance only when BEM and FFM are included. BEM needs FFM to fuse the information of different scales to avoid focusing only on local details. In contrast, FFM needs BEM to make up for its insufficiency in the boundary region to ensure the accurate capture of details. They are indispensable and must work together to achieve the best results.

5   Conclusions

This paper proposes a new medical image segmentation modelling framework, YNet, to achieve clear segmentation boundaries. YNet consists of two core modules, i.e., BEM and FFM. BEM combines the advantages of wavelet transform and convolution to generate enhanced information on boundaries, which in turn provides YNet with more learnable and detailed features. On the other hand, FFM provides a compelling fusion of the features of the bipartite encoder through adaptive feature fusion fused effectively. The experimental analysis shows that the YNet network architecture we constructed can effectively improve medical image segmentation performance, which provides essential technical support for doctors' decision-making in clinical diagnosis.

Acknowledgments. This work is sponsored by Natural Science Foundation of Xinjiang Uygur Autonomous Region (Grant no. 2022D01C425), the Postgraduate Education Scientific Research Projects of Xinjiang University (Grant nos. XJDX2024YJPK15, XJDX2022YALK11), Xinjiang Tianchi Talents Program (Grant no. E33B9401). The authors would like to express their heartfelt gratitude to those people who have helped with this manuscript and to the reviewers for their comments on the manuscript.

References

1. Azimi, S.M., Fischer, P., Körner, M., Reinartz, P.: Aerial LaneNet: lane-marking semantic segmentation in aerial imagery using wavelet-enhanced cost-sensitive symmetric fully convolutional neural networks. IEEE Trans. Geosci. Remote Sens. **57**(5), 2920–2938 (2018)
2. Bernal, J., Sánchez, F.J., Fernández-Esparrach, G., Gil, D., Rodríguez, C., Vilariño, F.: WM-DOVA maps for accurate polyp highlighting in colonoscopy: validation vs. saliency maps from physicians. Comput. Med. Imaging Graph. **43**, 99–111 (2015)
3. Chen, L., Gu, L., Fu, Y.: When semantic segmentation meets frequency aliasing. arXiv preprint arXiv:2403.09065 (2024)
4. Chen, L., Gu, L., Zheng, D., Fu, Y.: Frequency-adaptive dilated convolution for semantic segmentation. In: Proceedings of the IEEE/CVF Conference on Computer Vision and Pattern Recognition, pp. 3414–3425 (2024)
5. Diakogiannis, F.I., Waldner, F., Caccetta, P., Wu, C.: ResUNet-a: a deep learning framework for semantic segmentation of remotely sensed data. ISPRS J. Photogramm. Remote. Sens. **162**, 94–114 (2020)

6. Duan, Y., Liu, F., Jiao, L., Zhao, P., Zhang, L.: SAR image segmentation based on convolutional-wavelet neural network and Markov random field. Pattern Recogn. **64**, 255–267 (2017)

7. Fan, D.P., et al.: PraNet: parallel reverse attention network for polyp segmentation. In: International Conference on Medical Image Computing and Computer-Assisted Intervention, pp. 263–273. Springer (2020)

8. Gao, F., Wang, X., Gao, Y., Dong, J., Wang, S.: Sea ice change detection in SAR images based on convolutional-wavelet neural networks. IEEE Geosci. Remote Sens. Lett. **16**(8), 1240–1244 (2019)

9. Isensee, F., Jaeger, P.F., Kohl, S.A., Petersen, J., Maier-Hein, K.H.: nnU-Net: a self-configuring method for deep learning-based biomedical image segmentation. Nat. Meth. **18**(2), 203–211 (2021)

10. Jha, D., et al.: Real-time polyp detection, localization and segmentation in colonoscopy using deep learning. IEEE Access **9**, 40496–40510 (2021)

11. Jha, D., Riegler, M.A., Johansen, D., Halvorsen, P., Johansen, H.D.: DoubleU-Net: a deep convolutional neural network for medical image segmentation. In: 2020 IEEE 33rd International Symposium on Computer-Based Medical Systems (CBMS), pp. 558–564. IEEE (2020)

12. Jha, D., et al.: Kvasir-SEG: a segmented polyp dataset. In: Ro, Y.M., et al. (eds.) MMM 2020. LNCS, vol. 11962, pp. 451–462. Springer, Cham (2020). https://doi.org/10.1007/978-3-030-37734-2_37

13. Jha, D., et al.: ResUNet++: an advanced architecture for medical image segmentation. In: 2019 IEEE International Symposium on Multimedia (ISM), pp. 225–2255. IEEE (2019)

14. Kirillov, A., et al.: Segment anything. In: Proceedings of the IEEE/CVF International Conference on Computer Vision, pp. 4015–4026 (2023)

15. Le, M.Q., Tran, M.T., Le, T.N., Nguyen, T.V., Do, T.T.: Unveiling camouflage: a learnable Fourier-based augmentation for camouflaged object detection and instance segmentation. arXiv preprint arXiv:2308.15660 (2023)

16. Lee, C.Y., Xie, S., Gallagher, P., Zhang, Z., Tu, Z.: Deeply-supervised nets. In: Artificial Intelligence and Statistics, pp. 562–570. PMLR (2015)

17. Li, J., et al.: Automatic detection and classification system of domestic waste via multimodel cascaded convolutional neural network. IEEE Trans. Industr. Inf. **18**(1), 163–173 (2021)

18. Li, Q., Shen, L.: WaveSNet: wavelet integrated deep networks for image segmentation. In: Chinese Conference on Pattern Recognition and Computer Vision (PRCV), pp. 325–337. Springer (2022)

19. Liu, P., Zhang, H., Lian, W., Zuo, W.: Multi-level wavelet convolutional neural networks. IEEE Access **7**, 74973–74985 (2019)

20. Milton, M.A.A.: Automated skin lesion classification using ensemble of deep neural networks in ISIC 2018: skin lesion analysis towards melanoma detection challenge. arXiv preprint arXiv:1901.10802 (2019)

21. Oktay, O., et al.: Attention U-Net: learning where to look for the pancreas. arXiv preprint arXiv:1804.03999 (2018)

22. Parmar, G., Zhang, R., Zhu, J.Y.: On aliased resizing and surprising subtleties in GAN evaluation. In: Proceedings of the IEEE/CVF Conference on Computer Vision and Pattern Recognition, pp. 11410–11420 (2022)

23. Patro, B., Agneeswaran, V.: Scattering vision transformer: spectral mixing matters. In: Advances in Neural Information Processing Systems, vol. 36 (2024)

24. Ronneberger, O., Fischer, P., Brox, T.: U-Net: convolutional networks for biomedical image segmentation. In: Navab, N., Hornegger, J., Wells, W.M., Frangi, A.F. (eds.) MICCAI 2015. LNCS, vol. 9351, pp. 234–241. Springer, Cham (2015). https://doi.org/10.1007/978-3-319-24574-4_28

25. Sigillo, L., Grassucci, E., Uncini, A., Comminiello, D.: Generalizing medical image representations via quaternion wavelet networks. arXiv preprint arXiv:2310.10224 (2023)

26. Sinha, P., Wu, Y., Psaromiligkos, I., Zilic, Z.: Lumen & media segmentation of IVUS images via ellipse fitting using a wavelet-decomposed subband CNN. In: 2020 IEEE 30th International Workshop on Machine Learning for Signal Processing (MLSP), pp. 1–6. IEEE (2020)

27. Srivastava, A., et al.: MSRF-Net: a multi-scale residual fusion network for biomedical image segmentation. IEEE J. Biomed. Health Inform. **26**(5), 2252–2263 (2021)

28. Sun, K., Xiao, B., Liu, D., Wang, J.: Deep high-resolution representation learning for human pose estimation. In: Proceedings of the IEEE/CVF Conference on Computer Vision and Pattern Recognition, pp. 5693–5703 (2019)

29. Upadhyay, K., Agrawal, M., Vashist, P.: Wavelet based fine-to-coarse retinal blood vessel extraction using U-Net model. In: 2020 International Conference on Signal Processing and Communications (SPCOM), pp. 1–5. IEEE (2020)

30. Wang, J., Huang, Q., Tang, F., Meng, J., Su, J., Song, S.: Stepwise feature fusion: local guides global. In: International Conference on Medical Image Computing and Computer-Assisted Intervention, pp. 110–120. Springer (2022)

31. Yang, J., Sheng, Y., Zhang, Y., Jiang, W., Yang, L.: On-device unsupervised image segmentation. In: 2023 60th ACM/IEEE Design Automation Conference (DAC), pp. 1–6. IEEE (2023)

32. Yin, X., Xu, X.: A method for improving accuracy of DeepLabv3+ semantic segmentation model based on wavelet transform. In: International Conference in Communications, Signal Processing, and Systems, pp. 315–320. Springer (2021)

33. Zhang, Y., Liu, H., Hu, Q.: TransFuse: fusing transformers and CNNs for medical image segmentation. In: de Bruijne, M., et al. (eds.) MICCAI 2021. LNCS, vol. 12901, pp. 14–24. Springer, Cham (2021). https://doi.org/10.1007/978-3-030-87193-2_2

34. Zhou, Y., Huang, J., Wang, C., Song, L., Yang, G.: XNet: wavelet-based low and high frequency fusion networks for fully-and semi-supervised semantic segmentation of biomedical images. In: Proceedings of the IEEE/CVF International Conference on Computer Vision, pp. 21085–21096 (2023)

35. Zhou, Z., Rahman Siddiquee, M.M., Tajbakhsh, N., Liang, J.: UNet++: a nested U-Net architecture for medical image segmentation. In: Deep Learning in Medical Image Analysis and Multimodal Learning for Clinical Decision Support: 4th International Workshop, DLMIA 2018, and 8th International Workshop, ML-CDS 2018, Held in Conjunction with MICCAI 2018, Granada, Spain, 20 September 2018, Proceedings 4, pp. 3–11. Springer (2018)

36. Zhou, Z., Siddiquee, M., Tajbakhsh, N., Liang, J.: UNet++: redesigning skip connections to exploit multiscale features in image segmentation. IEEE Trans. Med. Imaging **39**(6), 1856–1867 (2019)

An Effective Algorithm for Skin Disease Segmentation Combining Inter-channel Features and Spatial Feature Enhancement

ZunWang Ke[1], YinFeng Wang[1], Run Guo[2], Minghua Du[3], Ji-Sheng Zhou[4], Gang Wang[5], and Yugui Zhang[6(✉)]

[1] School of Software, Xinjiang University, Urumqi 830091, China
kzwang@xju.edu.cn
[2] Department of Dermatology, Guang'anmen Hospital China Academy of Chinese Medical Sciences, No. 5 Beixiange, Xicheng District, Beijing 100053, China
[3] Department of Emergency, The First Medical Center, Chinese PLA General Hospital, Beijing, China
[4] Peking University Third Hospital, No. 49 Beihuayuan Road, Haidian District, Beijing 100191, China
[5] School of Computing and Data Engineering, NingboTech University, Ningbo 315100, China
wanggangnit@nit.zju.edu.cn
[6] Institute of Semiconductors, Chinese Academy of Sciences, Beijing 100083, China
zhangyugui@semi.ac.cn

Abstract. Skin lesion segmentation is essential for early disease detection and treatment planning in computer-aided diagnostic systems. However, U-Net faces challenges in handling long-distance dependencies and fully utilizing semantic information. Additionally, feature redundancy in channels and asymmetric supervised learning can lead to irrelevant features, resulting in suboptimal segmentation accuracy. To tackle these challenges, this paper presents a dermatological segmentation method that improves inter-channel and spatial features. The method introduces a compression excitation module and a channel mixing network, boosting both feature extraction capabilities and channel information exchange. Furthermore, the integration of a cross-region attention mechanism enhances the modeling of long-distance dependencies and spatial feature perception. The proposed approach also integrates a feature distillation loss function, which facilitates a balanced supervision mechanism between the encoder and decoder. This effectively minimizes redundant information within the U-Net architecture. Experiments conducted on the publicly available skin lesion datasets ISIC2016, ISIC2017, and ISIC2018 demonstrate that the proposed approach attains substantial performance enhancements in skin lesion image segmentation, showcasing its strong competitiveness.

© The Author(s), under exclusive license to Springer Nature Singapore Pte Ltd. 2025
P. Didyk and J. Hou (Eds.): CVM 2025, LNCS 15663, pp. 109–128, 2025.
https://doi.org/10.1007/978-981-96-5809-1_7

Keywords: skin lesion segmentation · inter-channel feature enhancement · spatial feature enhancement · feature distillation loss function

1   Introduction

Skin diseases, such as skin cancer, psoriasis, and eczema, are prevalent health issues globally, significantly affecting patients' quality of life. According to statistics, millions of new cases are diagnosed each year, and this number continues to rise [47]. Early identification and treatment of skin disorders is critical to optimizing patient outcomes, yet the process presents numerous challenges. Traditional diagnostic methods rely on physicians' experience and subjective judgment, which may lead to misdiagnosis or missed diagnosis. Advancements in medical imaging technology have made image analysis a key tool in aiding skin disease diagnosis. Especially in images of skin lesions, accurate segmentation of the lesion area is important for quantifying lesion characteristics, evaluating treatment effects and formulating personalized treatment plans. However, due to the diversity of morphology and texture of skin lesions, traditional image segmentation methods are often difficult to achieve satisfactory accuracy [7,8].

Recently, deep learning methods, particularly convolutional neural networks (CNNs), have accomplished significant advancements and demonstrated impressive results in medical image segmentation [11,32,44]. U-Net [35] is a notable instance of the CNN-based model, renowned for its uncomplicated architecture and scalability. A multitude of subsequent enhancements have been derived based on this U-shaped framework [9,37–39,51]. TransUnet [6], a pioneer in Transformer-based modeling, was the first to use a visual Transformer (ViT) in the encoding phase [12] to extract features and utilized CNNs in the decoding stage, showing its significant advantage in capturing global information. Subsequently, TransFuse [50] utilized a parallel architecture combining ViT and CNN to simultaneously capture both local and global features. In addition, SWin-UNet [4] integrates Swin Transformer [27] and U-shape architecture and proposes a U-shape model completely based on Transformer for the first time.

Models based on CNNs often confront issues in capturing long-range dependencies within images effectively, largely because their receptive fields are limited to local regions. This constrains their capacity to handle spatial features and inter-channel information. Moreover, while the U-Net structure excels in applications like medical image segmentation, it can suffer from issues such as feature redundancy and unbalanced supervision, which may negatively impact segmentation accuracy.

To solve these problems, this paper presents a dermatological segmentation strategy that combines inter-channel and spatial feature enhancement, incorporating various techniques optimized for medical image segmentation to showcase its potential in such tasks. Specifically, the method proposes an inter-channel feature enhancement module(CM-SSM) that combines compressive excitation and channel mixing, and a spatial feature enhancement module (CRA) based on cross-regional attention. The CM-SSM strengthens the network's feature extraction, channel information exchange, and local feature capture by learning the channel weights of the input feature map; CRA effectively combines regional information with channel attention, enhancing the network's capability to model long-range dependencies. Furthermore, this paper integrates Binary Cross-Entropy and Dice loss functions by incorporating cross-feature and internal feature distillation losses [43]. This approach aids in balancing supervision between the U-Net's encoder and decoder, while also reducing redundant information within the model.

In this study, a series of comprehensive experiments were carried out on segmentation tasks involving skin lesions, aiming to demonstrate the effectiveness of the proposed method in the field of medical image segmentation. Specifically, this study performed thorough evaluations on the standard datasets ISIC2016 [20], ISIC2017 [3], and ISIC2018 [10]. The experimental results highlight the method's capability to achieve outstanding results.

The remainder of the paper is structured as follows: Sect. 2 summarizes the relevant research. Section 3 outlines the detailed implementation of the proposed method. Section 4 describes the setup and results of the experiment in detail. Section 5 summarizes the main findings of this study and explores possible paths for future research.

2 Related Work

2.1 U-Net

Medical image segmentation has consistently posed challenges. In recent years, the application of deep learning technology in this area has been expanded significantly, leading to notable advancements. U-Net [35], as a benchmark network architecture in the field, is known for its encoder-decoder structure, which can efficiently extract and process image features. CE-Net [18] further integrates the contextual information encoding module to enhance the sensory field and semantic representation of the model. UNet++ [51] introduces a nested U-Net architecture that enhances segmentation accuracy by integrating multi-scale feature fusion. Besides convolution-based methods, Transformer-based models have also gained significant attention. Vision Transformer [12] demonstrated the effectiveness of Transformer in image recognition tasks. Medical Transformer [42] and TransUNet [6] incorporated the Transformer architecture into the field, resulting in impressive performance. In addition, the attention mechanism [40] and multi-scale feature fusion [22] and other techniques have also been extensively applied in tasks of the field. 3D segmentation models like multi-gated loop units [1] and efficient multi-scale 3D CNN [25] have also demonstrated notable success. Recently, Mamba [15] achieved a significant breakthrough by incorporating selection mechanisms and hardware-aware algorithms into previous work [16,19,31], enabling linear-time inference and an efficient training process. Building on the accomplishments of Mamba for vision applications, Vision Mamba [26] and VMamba [52] utilize bi-directional Vim blocks and cross-scan modules, each serving to capture global visual contexts that depend on data. Meanwhile,

VM-UNet [36] and U-Mamba [30] demonstrate excellent performance in medical image segmentation.

2.2 State Space Modeling

The State Space Model (SSM) is a mathematical framework commonly employed in control theory and signal processing to represent the dynamic behavior of a system's state as it evolves. By defining a set of state variables and their alteration rules, SSM is capable of capturing the dynamic behavior of the system. Its computational complexity increases linearly in proportion to the extent of the input sequence, and it is globally perceptive, which renders SSM particularly efficacious in processing sequence data. Mamba Modeling [26] is an application of SSM to natural language processing and vision tasks, which provides a new solution to visual perception tasks by combining the global information capture capability of SSM with the advantages of deep learning. In 2024, Liu et al. applied SSM to the field of vision and introduced Visual Mamba [26], a model that not only captures global information in images but also manages computational resources and time effectively. The application of SSM in vision tasks has been extended to several domains, including image classification [2,5], video processing [48], event camera data processing [45,53], etc. In the domain of medical image analysis, the use of SSM has resulted in substantial breakthroughs. An example is the U-Mamba model [30], which integrates the high efficiency of CNN in local feature extraction and the advantages of SSM in global information capture, thus improving the accuracy of segmentation. To reduce the computational resource consumption of SSM models, researchers have performed a series of optimizations. For example, the S4 model [17] implemented a diagonal architecture and a low-rank approach, while the S5 [41] and H3 models [13] enhanced efficiency by utilizing parallel scanning techniques and optimizing hardware use. The S6 version of Mamba [26], on the other hand, optimizes the linear time-invariant features of the model by combining data-dependent parameters and demonstrates superior performance on large-scale datasets. ViM [52] and VMamba [26] and other models further integrated SSM into the visual backbone design and achieved results comparable to ViT and CNN by adapting the characteristics of image data through multiple scanning directions. These research results not only promote the development of SSM-based vision models but also demonstrate the potential of SSM for various applications within the domain of computer vision, creating new avenues for future research and applications.

3 Methods

3.1 Model Structure

The overall architecture of the framework is illustrated in Fig. 1. More specifically, it concludes with a patch embedding layer, encoders, decoders, a final projection layer, and skip connections.

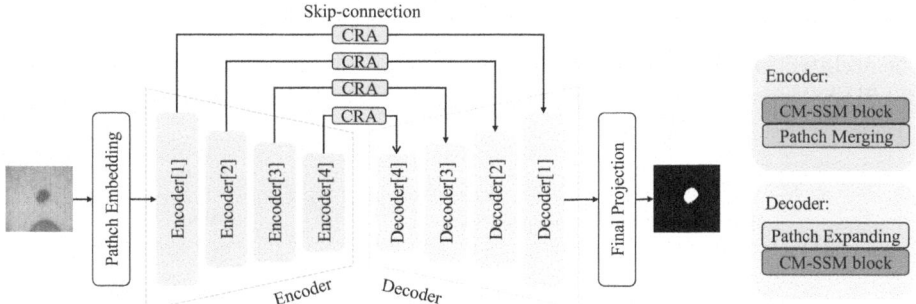

Fig. 1. General Framework Diagram.

In this paper, the last up-sampling block in the model is defined as the last decoder block, and in the symbolic representation, this paper uses $E_m^{(l)}/D_m^{(l)}$ to denote the mth encoder/decoder block in the mth l layer. Accordingly, in the order from encoder to decoder, the corresponding feature map is denoted as F_m^l ($E_1^{(1)}$, $E_1^{(2)}$,..., $D_3^{(2)}$, $D_2^{(1)}$, $D_2^{(2)}$).

The Patch Embedding layer segments the input image $x \in R^{H \times W \times 3}$ into small blocks of size $r \times r$ and then maps the dimensions of the image to the number of channels C of default size 96 to generate the embedded output $x' \in R^{\frac{H}{r} \times \frac{W}{r} \times C}$. Then, this paper uses layer normalization [35] to normalize x' and input it into the encoder for extracting features. The framework consists of four encoder blocks, in which patch merging operations are applied in the first three encoder blocks to reduce the input feature height and width while increasing the number of channels. In this paper, CM-SSM blocks [2, 2, 2, 2] are used in four encoder blocks respectively, and the number of channels of each encoder block is [C, 2C, 4C, 8C].

Similarly, the framework contains four decoder blocks. In the final three stages of the decoder, a patch extension strategy is applied to decrease the density of the feature channels while enhancing the vertical and horizontal dimensions of the feature map. In this paper, CM-SSM blocks [2, 2, 2, 1] are used in four decoder blocks respectively, and the channel count for each decoder block is [8C, 4C, 2C, C]. The decoder module is followed by a final mapping layer, whose role is to adjust the feature dimensions back to the dimensions corresponding to the original image.

For the jump connection part, this paper uses the cross-region attention to obtain the location information of regions within the feature map., and then fuses this region information with the feature map, after fusing the region location information, the feature map can better capture the spatial structure of the image as a way to improve the segmentation accuracy.

3.2 Interchannel Feature Enhancement Combining SE and CMN

The architectural framework of the CM-SSM block is shown in Fig. 2 and consists of a 2D-Selective-Scan Vision Space State (2D-SSVS) component and a Channel Mixing Network (CMN).

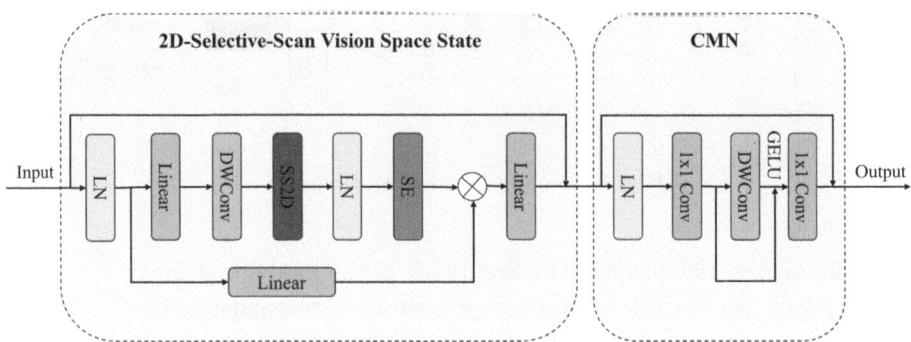

Fig. 2. CM-SSM Block Framework Diagram.

Among them, The SS2D module serves as the central component of the CM-SSM block and consists of three main components: scan expansion, S6 block, and scan merging. The scan expansion technique divides the input image into individual sequences by four-way decomposition, a step that ensures extensive spatial information coverage and enables multi-directional feature capture. The S6 block then selects the parameters of the state-space model using a selectivity mechanism to accurately identify and extract useful information while filtering out irrelevant parts. Specifically, the block receives inputs in feature format [B, L, D], where B represents the batch size, L indicates the sequence length, and D represents the feature dimension. The features are first transformed through a linear layer, followed by the application of update and output equations from the state-space model to generate the final output features. Finally, scanning and merging operations reconfigure these transformed sequences to generate an output image that matches the dimensions of the original input image. Through this series of fine-grained operations, the SS2D module provides the CM-SSM block with powerful feature extraction and processing capabilities, which are particularly important for medical image segmentation.

According to the relevant literature [23,34], this paper integrates a Squeeze-Excitation (SE) after a 2D scanning [21] block. The restructured features are processed using the Squeeze-Excitation block to capture the inter-channel relationships through global pooling and activation operations, and then use this information to re-weight the channels, enhancing important features and suppressing unimportant ones.

A departure from the traditional focus on token mixing in previous visual Mamba architectures [26,52], the design in this paper introduces a channel mixing network that consists of a deep convolution and two fully connected layers.

The layers enable the model to exchange information between different channels by extending and recovering the channels, thus increasing exchange between different channels and enhancing the representation of features. Deep convolution helps to capture local dependencies of different features in the channel dimension by applying convolution independently on each channel and then mixing these channel features by convolution, while capturing more complex local features since it operates on the channel after extension.

3.3   Spatial Feature Enhancement Based on CRA

Through the aforementioned method, this paper enhances inter-channel features. Nevertheless, spatial features play a vital role in the realm of segmentation, given that they enable the model to better grasp the contextual information within the image, thereby improving segmentation accuracy. Skip connections are also an important part of the model, and they bridge the information between the encoder and decoder. Therefore, in the present research, we choose to augment the spatial features at the skip connections using the cross-region attention mechanism.

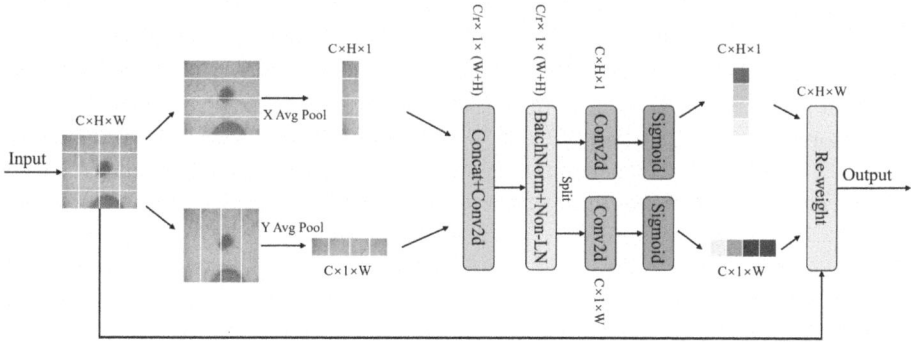

Fig. 3. Framework Diagram of the cross-region Attention Mechanism.

The Cross-region Attention mechanism (CRA) enhances the feature representation capability of deep neural networks by combining spatial region location information. As depicted in Fig. 3, the cross-region attention mechanism first generates two feature maps with height-oriented and width-oriented input feature maps through two global pooling operations,

$$z_c = \frac{1}{H \times W} \sum_{i=1}^{H} \sum_{j=1}^{W} x_c(i, j) \tag{1}$$

Specifically, for any input x, we initially apply a pooled filter with dimensions (H, 1) or (1, W) to extract features from the height and width regions of each channel, respectively. Thus, the height of h of the first c channel's output can be formulated as:

$$z_c^h(h) = \frac{1}{W} \sum_{0 \le i < W} x_c(h, i) \tag{2}$$

Likewise, the output of channel c with width w can be described as:

$$z_c^w(w) = \frac{1}{H} \sum_{0 \le j < H} x_c(j, w) \tag{3}$$

The two transformations mentioned above apply distinct spatial operations to the input x: one targeting the height direction and the other focusing on the width direction, thereby aggregating feature information. These transformations yield two separate feature maps, each designed to capture features in a single dimension. We then convert the feature map into two weight maps with long distance dependent coding along the width and height directions, respectively.

$$f = \delta(F_1([z^h, z^w])) \tag{4}$$

In the equation, the symbol $[\cdot, \cdot]$ indicates the concatenation of features across spatial dimensions. The symbol δ represents a nonlinear activation function, while f is an intermediate feature map with dimensions $R^{C/r \times (H+W)}$, which encodes spatial information in both height and width directions. Here, r is the reduction ratio. Next, we split f throughout the height and width dimension into two tensors: f^h and f^w where $f^h \in R^{C/r \times H}$ and $f^w \in R^{C/r \times W}$. We then apply two 1×1 convolution transformations, T_h and T_w, to convert f^h and f^w into tensors that match the channels of the input x, we get:

$$g^h = \sigma(T_h(f^h)) \tag{5}$$

$$g^w = \sigma(T_w(f^w)) \tag{6}$$

δ is the sigmoid function, we then extend the output g^h and g^w to enable their use as attention weights. Finally, the response from the cross-region attention layer of this paper can be expressed as:

$$y_c(i, j) = x_c(i, j) \times g_c^h(i) \times g_c^w(j) \tag{7}$$

In summary, the cross-region attention mechanism effectively merges region information with channel attention to boost the network's capacity to model long-range dependencies while keeping resource usage minimal.

3.4   Loss Function Complementary Optimization

In U-Net, the strength of the supervised signals differs between the encoder and decoder, resulting in certain encoder blocks learning information relevant to the segmentation task, while the decoder blocks in the last layer can more accurately understand the real segmentation region (the decoder can receive directly supervised signals from the outputs due to its closer proximity to the final segmentation result). Simultaneously, due to the over-parameterization of U-Net, there is a large amount of redundancy between the deeper feature channels, learning similar features, which can lead to performance degradation and unnecessary computational overhead.

To solve the above two problems, two loss functions, cross-feature distillation and internal feature distillation, are introduced in this paper. Among them, cross-feature distillation is used to solve the supervision asymmetry problem between encoder and decoder in U-Net. Since the D1 layer in the decoder has an accurate understanding of the ground is really segmented region, which contains the most semantic information, The feature maps from this layer serve to offer supplementary supervision for the other blocks within the U-Net, with the following formula:

$$\mathrm{T} = \frac{1}{|M-1||\mathcal{J}|}$$

$$\mathcal{L}_{CFD} = \mathrm{T} \sum_{m=1}^{M-1} \sum_{I \sim \mathcal{J}} \| \mathrm{RCS}(F_m^i) - \mathrm{AvgPool}(F_{final}) \|^2 \tag{8}$$

Where M denotes the count of blocks, and J represents the quantity of images, and F_{final} is the feature mapping located in the last decoded block (D_1) of the feature mapping, and F_m^i is all the feature mappings of layer i located in the Mth block ($\mathbf{E}_1^{(1)}$, $\mathbf{E}_1^{(2)}$, ..., $\mathbf{D}_3^{(2)}$, $\mathbf{D}_2^{(1)}$, $\mathbf{D}_2^{(2)}$) except for D_1. To align the features in both channel and spatial dimensions, this paper employs average pooling along with a random channel selection (RCS) operation.

Internal feature distillation addresses redundancy in deep feature channels by transferring information from shallow features to deeper ones. This is achieved using the L2 paradigm [6,20,40] penalty to encourage deeper features to acquire valuable contextual information, ultimately enhancing their sensitivity to context and improving the model's overall performance and accuracy. Specifically, it can be formulated as:

$$\mathcal{L}_{IFD} = \frac{1}{|M||\mathcal{J}|} \sum_{m=1}^{M} \sum_{I \sim \mathcal{J}} \| \widetilde{F_m^i} - \overline{F_m^i} \|^2 \tag{9}$$

Where M denotes the count of blocks, and J indicates the amount of images, and F_i^k denotes all feature pictures located in layer i of the mth block ($\mathrm{E}_1^{(1)}$, $\mathrm{E}_1^{(2)}$, ..., $\mathrm{D}_2^{(1)}$, $\mathrm{D}_2^{(2)}$). $\tilde{F}$ represents the channel feature from deep-level layers, and $\bar{F}$ refers to the channel feature from shallow-level layers. In this paper, the channels are divided into upper and lower halves and are bounded by this to ensure that the shallow and deep channels have the same number of features.

By the preceding explanation, the study integrates the cross-feature distillation loss with the intrinsic feature distillation loss to formulate the composite distillation loss, termed FDLoss (Feature Distillation Loss). The FDLoss is formulated as follows:

$$\mathcal{L}_{fd} = \lambda_1 \mathcal{L}_{CFD} + \lambda_2 \mathcal{L}_{IFD} \tag{10}$$

of which $\mathcal{L}_{CFD}$ and $\mathcal{L}_{IFD}$ are cross-characteristic distillation and internal characteristic distillation loss functions, respectively. λ_1 and λ_2 are the equilibrium parameters, and $(0.015, 0.015)$ is usually chosen as the default parameter.

Finally, the characteristic distillation loss (FDLoss), binary cross entropy and Dice coefficient loss are fused. This function is used to evaluate the difference between the estimated results and the true values. The detailed formulation is presented below:

$$
\begin{aligned}
L_{Bce} &= -\frac{1}{N} \sum_1 [y_i \log(\hat{y}_i) + (1 - y_i)\log(1 - \hat{y}_i)] \\
L_{Dice} &= 1 - \frac{2|X \cap Y|}{|X| + |Y|} \\
L_{BceDice} &= \lambda_1 L_{Bce} + \lambda_2 L_{Dice} \\
L_{total} &= L_{fd} + L_{BceDice}
\end{aligned}
\tag{11}
$$

Where N signifies the total sample size. y_i and $\hat{y}_i$ denote the true values and the estimated results, respectively. $|X|$ and $|Y|$ represent the ground truth and estimated values. λ_1 and λ_2 are the weights of the loss function with default values of 0.3 and 0.7, respectively.

4   Experiments

In this section, the paper conducts extensive experiments to assess the proposed approach's effectiveness. Specifically, the performance of the proposed methods is evaluated on the ISIC2016, ISIC2017, and ISIC2018 datasets.

4.1   Datasets

ISIC2016. ISIC2016 is a dataset of dermoscopic images from the International Symposium on Biomedical Imaging (ISBI) focusing on skin lesion analysis to tackle challenges in melanoma detection. The dataset comprises 1,279 dermoscopy images, each accompanied by corresponding segmentation mask labels. Adhering to the methodology of prior research, this manuscript partitions the dataset, allocating 70% for model training and reserving 30% for validation. The detailed allocation is detailed as: For the ISIC2016 dataset, 900 instances are allocated for training, while 379 are earmarked for the validation phase.

ISIC2017. ISIC2017 is a dermoscopy image dataset designed for skin lesion analysis at the ISBI, focusing on three types of disease challenges: melanoma, seborrheic keratosis, and benign nevi. It contains 2,150 dermoscopy images with corresponding segmentation mask labels. Similarly, the research applies a 7:3 split for the ISIC2017 dataset, creating separate subsets for training and evaluation. To be precise, the training subset encompasses 1,500 images, and the evaluation subset consists of 650 images.

ISIC2018. ISIC2018 is a dermoscopy image dataset for skin lesion analysis at the ISBI for seven types of skin disease challenges such as actinic keratoses, basal cell carcinomas, and benign keratoses. For the segmentation task, the ISIC2018 dataset encompasses 2694 dermatoscopic images paired with their segmentation masks. Adhering to the prior dataset division approach, this research similarly apportioned the data into a 7:3 training-to-testing ratio. In detail, the training subset encompasses 1,886 images, while the test subset comprises 808 images.

4.2 Evaluation Indicators

In order to evaluate the efficacy of the suggested approach, this study employs three key performance indicators for semantic segmentation: the Mean Intersection over Union (mIoU), the Dice Similarity Coefficient (DSC), and accuracy (Acc). The mIoU and DSC are measures of consistency between the predicted mask and the true annotation, while Acc is used to assess the overall accuracy of the model. The mathematical representations of mIoU, DSC, and Acc are summarized below:

$$mIoU = \frac{TP}{TP + FP + FN} \tag{12}$$

$$DSC = \frac{2 \cdot TP}{2 \cdot TP + FP + FN} \tag{13}$$

$$Acc = \frac{TN + TP}{N} \tag{14}$$

Here, TP denotes true positives, FP denotes false positives, TN denotes true negatives, and FN denotes false negatives. The variable N represents the aggregate number of instances.

4.3 Main Results

In line with prior research [4,37], the images from the ISIC2016, ISIC2017, and ISIC2018 datasets have been adjusted to a dimension of 256 by 256 pixels. To mitigate the possibility of overfitting, this analysis incorporated data augmentation techniques such as random horizontal flipping and rotational adjustments. The loss function delineated in Sect. 3.4 serves as the criterion for this dataset. For this analysis, batches of 32 examples were processed, and the AdamW [28] optimizer was chosen for the training phase, initiating the learning rate at 0.001. A Cosine Annealing Learning Rate Scheduler [29] was implemented to modulate the learning rate, with a cap at 50 cycles and a gradual reduction to a nadir of 1e−5. The training regimen spanned 300 epochs, and the computational experiments were executed on a solitary NVIDIA RTX 4090 GPU.

In order to assess the efficacy of the suggested approach, this research conducted empirical tests across the ISIC2016, ISIC2017, and ISIC2018 datasets, and juxtaposed the findings against those of contemporary leading techniques.

ISIC2016. This paper addresses the ISIC2016 dataset in U-Net [35], Attention-UNet [33], LV-UNet [24], VM-UNet [36] Exhaustive experiments were performed on these methods. The qualitative visualization results are shown in Fig. 4.

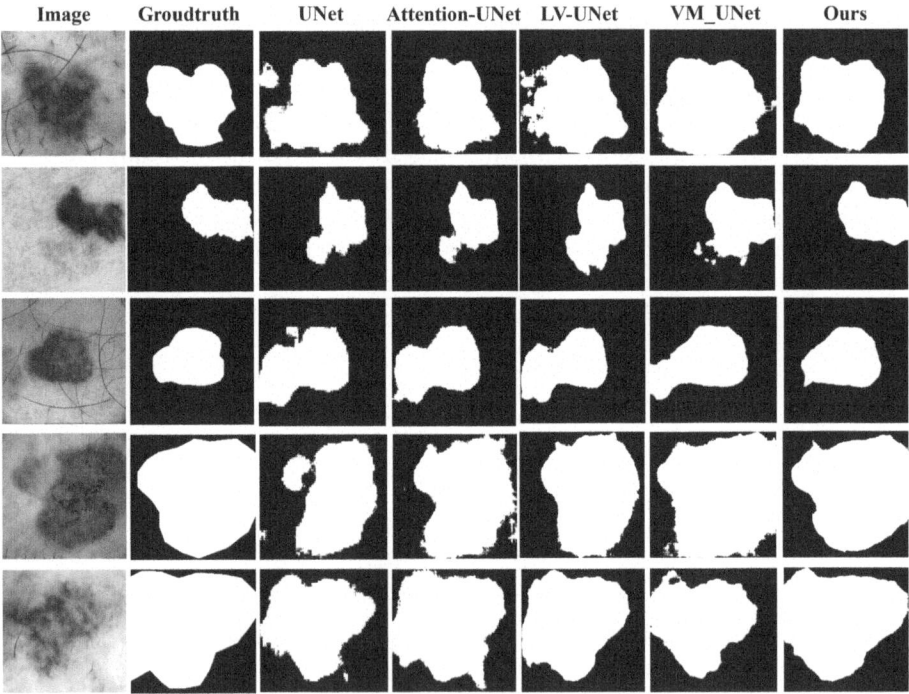

Fig. 4. Examples of segmentation results for different methods on ISIC2016 Dataset.

The visualization results show that the method proposed in this study has significant advantages in the image segmentation task of ISIC2016 dataset. This approach effectively extracts and utilizes both channel and spatial features by incorporating a channel mixing network and a cross-region attention mechanism. Additionally, feature redundancy and supervision imbalance are addressed through the integration of the feature distillation loss function. The method's performance is compared with other advanced techniques, and the results of the experiments are summarized in Table 1.

Table 1. Comparative experimental results of different methods (bold represents the best) on ISIC2016 Dataset.

Model	mIoU (%) ↑	DSC (%)↑	ACC (%)↑
U-Net	84.01	91.16	95.06
Attention-UNet	84.30	91.37	95.26
LV-UNet	85.95	92.35	95.25
VM-UNet	86.41	92.71	95.28
Ours	**88.16**	**93.71**	**95.52**

The data indicate that the proposed method demonstrates a significant performance enhancement compared to other existing techniques. Specifically, when compared to VM-UNet, this method achieves improvements of 1.75% in mIoU and 1% in the DSC on the ISIC2016 dataset. This improvement is mainly owing to the efficient extraction and effective use of channel and spatial features, as well as the resolution of feature redundancy and supervision imbalance within the model.

ISIC2017. For the ISIC2017 dataset, this paper is presented in U-Net [35], UTNetV2 [14], TransFuse [50], MALUNet [37], MedMamba [49], HC-Mamba [46] and VM-UNet [36] Exhaustive experiments were performed on these methods. The qualitative visualization results are shown in Fig. 5.

Figure 5 illustrates that the proposed approach achieves excellent image segmentation performance on the ISIC2017 dataset. The introduction of the channel mixing network and cross-region attention mechanism optimizes the extraction and utilization of both channel and spatial features, effectively addressing feature redundancy and supervision imbalance through the integration of the feature distillation loss function. The performance of this method is further compared with other advanced techniques, with the experimental results detailed in Table 2.

The results indicate that this method demonstrates significant advantages across all evaluation metrics. Specifically, on the ISIC2017 dataset, the proposed method achieves mIoU and Dice scores that are 1.94% and 1.19% higher than those of VM-UNet, respectively. This further confirms the superiority and reliability of the proposed approach for image segmentation tasks. These improvements stem from the optimized extraction of channel and spatial features, as well as the effective resolution of feature redundancy and supervision imbalance within the model.

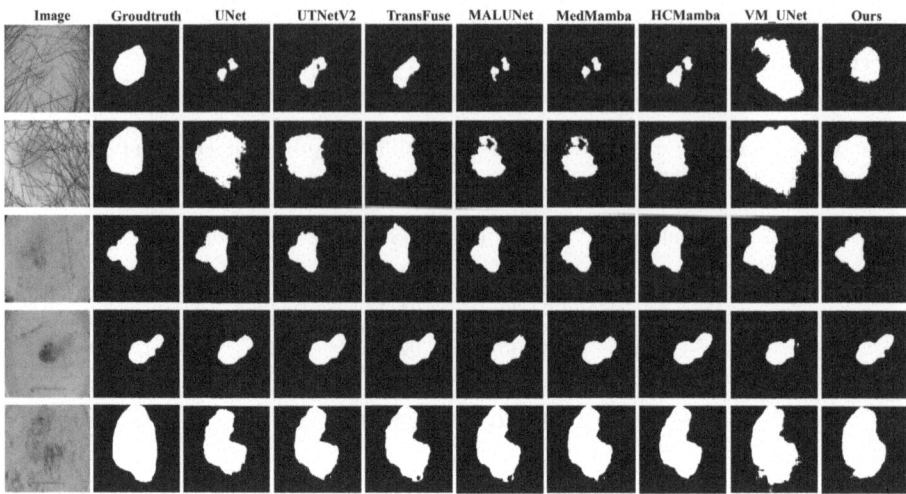

Fig. 5. Examples of segmentation results for different methods on ISIC2017 Dataset.

Table 2. Comparative experimental results of different methods (bold represents the best) on ISIC2017 Dataset.

Model	mIoU (%)↑	DSC (%)↑	ACC (%)↑
U-Net	76.98	86.99	95.65
UTNetV2	77.35	87.23	95.84
TransFuse	79.21	88.40	96.17
MALUNet	78.78	88.13	96.18
MedMamba	78.82	88.15	95.01
HC-Mamba	79.27	88.18	95.17
VM-UNet	79.54	88.60	96.29
Ours	**81.48**	**89.79**	**96.61**

ISIC2018. For the ISIC2018 dataset, the methods compared in this paper are U-Net [35], Unet++ [51], UTNetV2 [14], MALUNet [37], MedMamba [49], HC-Mamba [46] and VM-UNet [36]. The results of the qualitative visualization of the proposed method in this paper at ISIC2018 are shown in Fig. 6.

As illustrated in Fig. 6, on the ISIC2018 dataset, the method proposed in this study also shows excellent segmentation results. The success is attributed to the use of channel mixing networks and cross-zone attention mechanisms, which enhance the extraction and utilization of both channel and spatial features. Additionally, the application of the feature distillation loss function effectively mitigates feature redundancy and supervision imbalance within the model. In order to further verify the efficiency of this method, we compare it with many advanced methods. The relevant experimental data are shown in Table 3.

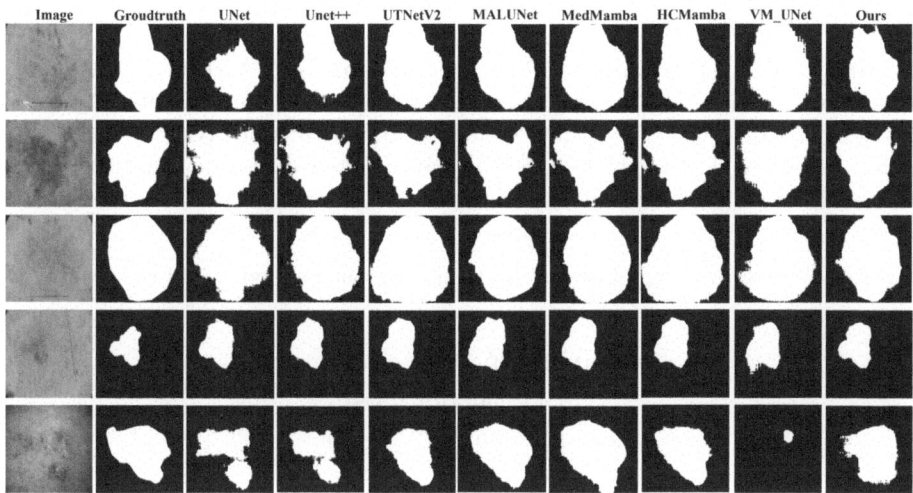

Fig. 6. Examples of segmentation results for different methods on ISIC2018 Dataset.

Table 3. Comparative experimental results of different methods (bold represents the best) on ISIC2018 Dataset.

Model	mIoU (%)↑	DSC (%)↑	ACC (%)↑
U-Net	77.86	87.55	94.05
Unet++	78.31	87.83	94.02
UTNetV2	78.97	88.25	94.32
MedMamba	79.13	88.35	94.23
MALUNet	80.25	89.04	94.62
HC-Mamba	80.60	89.25	94.84
VM-UNet	80.28	89.06	94.57
Ours	**81.25**	**89.65**	**94.94**

As shown above, our proposed method achieves optimal performance on all major evaluation indicators. Specifically, in the evaluation of the ISIC2018 dataset, our approach showed a significant performance advantage by improving mIoU and DSC by 0.97% and 0.59%, respectively, compared to the VM-UNet approach. These results are primarily due to enhancements in optimizing the extraction of channel and spatial features, as well as effectively addressing feature redundancy and supervision imbalance within the model. Such findings not only underscore the method's high efficiency and accuracy in dermatological image segmentation but also reinforce its leading position in the field of medical image segmentation.

4.4   Ablation Experiments

Results Under Different Module Combinations. Within this segment, we conduct dismantling studies focusing on the three components: Squeeze-and-Excitation Networks (SE) and Channel Mixing Network (CMN) and Cross Region Attention (CRA) proposed in this paper. These experiments aim to verify the contributions of these modules to the overall effectiveness of the method.

Table 4. Comparative experimental results of different methods (bold represents the best).

SE	CMN	CRA	Evaluation	
			mIoU(%)↑	DSC(%)↑
✗	✗	✗	79.54	88.60
✓	✗	✗	80.44	89.16
✗	✓	✗	79.98	88.88
✗	✗	✓	80.97	89.45
✓	✓	✗	81.31	89.69
✓	✗	✓	80.13	88.97
✗	✓	✓	80.39	89.13
✓	✓	✓	81.48	89.79

As shown in Table 4, compared to the baseline metrics, SE improved the mIoU and Dice coefficients by 0.9% and 0.56% on the ISIC2017 dataset, indicating that the SE module could effectively enhance the important features and suppress the unimportant features; the Channel Mixing Network (CMN) enhances the mIoU and Dice coefficients on the ISIC2017 dataset by 1.77% and 1.09% respectively. This indicates that CMN effectively boosts the exchange of channel information and the capture of channel features. Meanwhile, the Cross Region Attention (CRA) module improves the mIoU and DSCby 1.43% and 0.85%, respectively, demonstrating its ability to enhance the network's modeling of long-range dependencies, thereby improving segmentation accuracy. When the three modules are enabled at the same time, the proposed method achieves the highest performance on the ISIC2017 dataset, with mIoU and Dice coefficients increasing to 81.48% and 89.79%, respectively. This result fully proves the importance of the synergistic effect of the three modules to improve the model performance. The combination of the three modules not only optimizes the feature representation of the image, but also enhances the recognition ability of the model to the key areas, so as to achieve more accurate image segmentation.

Results Under Different Combinations of Loss Functions. In order to further verify the effectiveness of the optimization of loss function in this paper, ablation experiments were carried out on the introduced cross characteristic distillation loss function ($\mathcal{L}_{CFD}$) and internal characteristic distillation loss function ($\mathcal{L}_{IFD}$), and the results were shown in Table 5. The results show that $\mathcal{L}_{CFD}$ and $\mathcal{L}_{IFD}$ can effectively enhance the feature extraction capability of the model and improve the segmentation accuracy of the model.

Table 5. Ablation results of different loss functions on ISIC2017 dataset.

$\mathcal{L}_{CFD}$	$\mathcal{L}_{IFD}$	Evaluation	
		mIoU(%)↑	DSC(%)↑
×	×	80.66	89.26
✓	×	81.35	89.57
×	✓	81.24	89.44
✓	✓	81.48	89.79

5   Conclusion

This study introduces an innovative technique for dermatological medical image segmentation that improves the delineation of skin lesions by utilizing compressed excitation modules and cross-area attention mechanisms to enhance both channel and spatial features. Additionally, the model's feature extraction efficiency is further boosted by incorporating a channel mixing network and a feature distillation loss function. When compared to current state-of-the-art methods and recent Mamba-based algorithms, this approach demonstrates a significant enhancement in performance. Moving forward, we intend to thoroughly investigate the full potential of the method presented here, aiming to increase its segmentation accuracy in skin imaging. Simultaneously, we will explore the applicability of this technique on datasets acquired through other medical imaging methods.

Acknowledgments. This work was partially supported by Xinjiang Autonomous Region Natural Science Foundation General Program under Grant 2024D01C53, Finance Science and Technology Project of Xinjiang Uyghur Autonomous Region under Grant 2023B01029-1, Xinjiang Uygur Autonomous Region Key Research and Development Task Special Project under Grant 2022B02052-3, Ningbo Key R&D Program under Grant No. 2023Z231, the China Postdoctoral Science Foundation under Grant No. 2022M723863 and the Researchers Supporting Project number (RSPD2024R968), King Saud University Riyadh. The authors would like to express their heartfelt gratitude to those people who have helped with this manuscript and to the reviewers for their comments on the manuscript.

References

1. Andermatt, S., Pezold, S., Cattin, P.: Multi-dimensional gated recurrent units for the segmentation of biomedical 3D-data. In: Deep Learning and Data Labeling for Medical Applications: First International Workshop, LABELS 2016, and Second International Workshop, DLMIA 2016, Held in Conjunction with MICCAI 2016, Athens, Greece, 21 October 2016, Proceedings 1, pp. 142–151. Springer (2016)
2. Behrouz, A., Santacatterina, M., Zabih, R.: MambaMixer: efficient selective state space models with dual token and channel selection. arXiv preprint arXiv:2403.19888 (2024)
3. Berseth, M.: ISIC 2017-skin lesion analysis towards melanoma detection. arXiv preprint arXiv:1703.00523 (2017)
4. Cao, H., et al.: Swin-Unet: Unet-like pure transformer for medical image segmentation. In: European Conference on Computer Vision, pp. 205–218. Springer (2022)
5. Chen, C.S., Chen, G.Y., Zhou, D., Jiang, D., Chen, D.S.: Res-VMamba: fine-grained food category visual classification using selective state space models with deep residual learning. arXiv preprint arXiv:2402.15761 (2024)
6. Chen, J., et al.: TransUNet: transformers make strong encoders for medical image segmentation. arXiv preprint arXiv:2102.04306 (2021)
7. Chen, X., et al.: Recent advances and clinical applications of deep learning in medical image analysis. Med. Image Anal. **79**, 102444 (2022)
8. Choy, S.P., et al.: Systematic review of deep learning image analyses for the diagnosis and monitoring of skin disease. NPJ Digit. Med. **6**(1), 180 (2023)
9. Çiçek, Ö., Abdulkadir, A., Lienkamp, S.S., Brox, T., Ronneberger, O.: 3D U-Net: learning dense volumetric segmentation from sparse annotation. In: Ourselin, S., Joskowicz, L., Sabuncu, M.R., Unal, G., Wells, W. (eds.) MICCAI 2016. LNCS, vol. 9901, pp. 424–432. Springer, Cham (2016). https://doi.org/10.1007/978-3-319-46723-8_49
10. Codella, N., et al.: Skin lesion analysis toward melanoma detection 2018: a challenge hosted by the international skin imaging collaboration (ISIC). arXiv preprint arXiv:1902.03368 (2019)
11. Doi, K.: Computer-aided diagnosis in medical imaging: historical review, current status and future potential. Comput. Med. Imaging Graph. **31**(4–5), 198–211 (2007)
12. Dosovitskiy, A.: An image is worth 16x16 words: transformers for image recognition at scale. arXiv preprint arXiv:2010.11929 (2020)
13. Fu, D.Y., Dao, T., Saab, K.K., Thomas, A.W., Rudra, A., Ré, C.: Hungry hungry hippos: towards language modeling with state space models. arXiv preprint arXiv:2212.14052 (2022)
14. Gao, Y., Zhou, M., Liu, D., Metaxas, D.: A multi-scale transformer for medical image segmentation: architectures, model efficiency, and benchmarks. arXiv preprint arXiv:2203.00131 (2022)
15. Gu, A., Dao, T.: Mamba: linear-time sequence modeling with selective state spaces. arXiv preprint arXiv:2312.00752 (2023)
16. Gu, A., Goel, K., Gupta, A., Ré, C.: On the parameterization and initialization of diagonal state space models. Adv. Neural. Inf. Process. Syst. **35**, 35971–35983 (2022)
17. Gu, A., Goel, K., Ré, C.: Efficiently modeling long sequences with structured state spaces. arXiv preprint arXiv:2111.00396 (2021)

18. Gu, Z., et al.: CE-Net: context encoder network for 2D medical image segmentation. IEEE Trans. Med. Imaging **38**(10), 2281–2292 (2019)
19. Gupta, A., Gu, A., Berant, J.: Diagonal state spaces are as effective as structured state spaces. Adv. Neural. Inf. Process. Syst. **35**, 22982–22994 (2022)
20. Gutman, D., et al.: Skin lesion analysis toward melanoma detection: a challenge at the International Symposium on Biomedical Imaging (ISBI) 2016, hosted by the International Skin Imaging Collaboration (ISIC). arXiv preprint arXiv:1605.01397 (2016)
21. Hu, J., Shen, L., Sun, G.: Squeeze-and-excitation networks. In: Proceedings of the IEEE Conference on Computer Vision and Pattern Recognition, pp. 7132–7141 (2018)
22. Huang, H., et al.: UNet 3+: a full-scale connected UNet for medical image segmentation. In: 2020 IEEE International Conference on Acoustics, Speech and Signal Processing (ICASSP), ICASSP 2020, pp. 1055–1059. IEEE (2020)
23. Huang, T., Pei, X., You, S., Wang, F., Qian, C., Xu, C.: LocalMamba: visual state space model with windowed selective scan. arXiv preprint arXiv:2403.09338 (2024)
24. Jiang, J., Wang, M., Tian, H., Cheng, L., Liu, Y.: LV-UNet: a lightweight and vanilla model for medical image segmentation. arXiv preprint arXiv:2408.16886 (2024)
25. Kamnitsas, K., et al.: Efficient multi-scale 3D CNN with fully connected CRF for accurate brain lesion segmentation. Med. Image Anal. **36**, 61–78 (2017)
26. Liu, Y., et al.: VMamba: visual state space model (2024). https://arxiv.org/abs/2401.10166
27. Liu, Z., et al.: Swin transformer: hierarchical vision transformer using shifted windows. In: Proceedings of the IEEE/CVF International Conference on Computer Vision, pp. 10012–10022 (2021)
28. Loshchilov, I.: Decoupled weight decay regularization. arXiv preprint arXiv:1711.05101 (2017)
29. Loshchilov, I., Hutter, F.: SGDR: stochastic gradient descent with warm restarts. arXiv preprint arXiv:1608.03983 (2016)
30. Ma, J., Li, F., Wang, B.: U-Mamba: enhancing long-range dependency for biomedical image segmentation. arXiv preprint arXiv:2401.04722 (2024)
31. Mehta, H., Gupta, A., Cutkosky, A., Neyshabur, B.: Long range language modeling via gated state spaces. arXiv preprint arXiv:2206.13947 (2022)
32. Muhammad, G., Hossain, M.S., Kumar, N.: EEG-based pathology detection for home health monitoring. IEEE J. Sel. Areas Commun. **39**(2), 603–610 (2020)
33. Oktay, O., et al.: Attention U-Net: learning where to look for the pancreas. arXiv preprint arXiv:1804.03999 (2018)
34. Pei, X., Huang, T., Xu, C.: EfficientVMamba: atrous selective scan for light weight visual mamba. arXiv preprint arXiv:2403.09977 (2024)
35. Ronneberger, O., Fischer, P., Brox, T.: U-Net: convolutional networks for biomedical image segmentation. In: Navab, N., Hornegger, J., Wells, W.M., Frangi, A.F. (eds.) MICCAI 2015. LNCS, vol. 9351, pp. 234–241. Springer, Cham (2015). https://doi.org/10.1007/978-3-319-24574-4_28
36. Ruan, J., Xiang, S.: VM-UNet: vision mamba UNet for medical image segmentation. arXiv preprint arXiv:2402.02491 (2024)
37. Ruan, J., Xiang, S., Xie, M., Liu, T., Fu, Y.: MALUNet: a multi-attention and lightweight UNet for skin lesion segmentation. In: 2022 IEEE International Conference on Bioinformatics and Biomedicine (BIBM), pp. 1150–1156. IEEE (2022)

38. Ruan, J., Xie, M., Gao, J., Liu, T., Fu, Y.: EGE-UNet: an efficient group enhanced UNet for skin lesion segmentation. In: International Conference on Medical Image Computing and Computer-Assisted Intervention, pp. 481–490. Springer (2023)

39. Ruan, J., Xie, M., Xiang, S., Liu, T., Fu, Y.: MEW-UNet: multi-axis representation learning in frequency domain for medical image segmentation. arXiv preprint arXiv:2210.14007 (2022)

40. Schlemper, J., et al.: Attention gated networks: learning to leverage salient regions in medical images. Med. Image Anal. **53**, 197–207 (2019)

41. Smith, J.T., Warrington, A., Linderman, S.W.: Simplified state space layers for sequence modeling. arXiv preprint arXiv:2208.04933 (2022)

42. Valanarasu, J., Oza, P., Hacihaliloglu, I., Patel, V.M.: Medical transformer: gated axial-attention for medical image segmentation. In: de Bruijne, M., et al. (eds.) MICCAI 2021. LNCS, vol. 12901, pp. 36–46. Springer, Cham (2021). https://doi.org/10.1007/978-3-030-87193-2_4

43. Wang, H., Cao, P., Wang, J., Zaiane, O.R.: UCTransNet: rethinking the skip connections in U-Net from a channel-wise perspective with transformer. In: Proceedings of the AAAI Conference on Artificial Intelligence, vol. 36, pp. 2441–2449 (2022)

44. Wang, S., Zhao, Z., Ouyang, X., Wang, Q., Shen, D.: ChatCAD: interactive computer-aided diagnosis on medical image using large language models. arXiv preprint arXiv:2302.07257 (2023)

45. Wang, Z., et al.: MambaPupil: bidirectional selective recurrent model for event-based eye tracking. In: Proceedings of the IEEE/CVF Conference on Computer Vision and Pattern Recognition, pp. 5762–5770 (2024)

46. Xu, J.: HC-Mamba: vision MAMBA with hybrid convolutional techniques for medical image segmentation. arXiv preprint arXiv:2405.05007 (2024)

47. Yakupu, A., et al.: The burden of skin and subcutaneous diseases: findings from the global burden of disease study 2019. Front. Public Health **11**, 1145513 (2023)

48. Yang, J.X., Zhou, J., Wang, J., Tian, H., Liew, A.W.C.: HSIMamba: hyperpsectral imaging efficient feature learning with bidirectional state space for classification. arXiv preprint arXiv:2404.00272 (2024)

49. Yue, Y., Li, Z.: MedMamba: vision mamba for medical image classification. arXiv preprint arXiv:2403.03849 (2024)

50. Zhang, Y., Liu, H., Hu, Q.: TransFuse: fusing transformers and CNNs for medical image segmentation. In: de Bruijne, M., et al. (eds.) MICCAI 2021. LNCS, vol. 12901, pp. 14–24. Springer, Cham (2021). https://doi.org/10.1007/978-3-030-87193-2_2

51. Zhou, Z., Rahman Siddiquee, M.M., Tajbakhsh, N., Liang, J.: UNet++: a nested U-Net architecture for medical image segmentation. In: Deep Learning in Medical Image Analysis and Multimodal Learning for Clinical Decision Support: 4th International Workshop, DLMIA 2018, and 8th International Workshop, ML-CDS 2018, Held in Conjunction with MICCAI 2018, Granada, Spain, 20 September 2018, Proceedings 4, pp. 3–11. Springer (2018)

52. Zhu, L., Liao, B., Zhang, Q., Wang, X., Liu, W., Wang, X.: Vision mamba: efficient visual representation learning with bidirectional state space model. arXiv preprint arXiv:2401.09417 (2024)

53. Zubic, N., Gehrig, M., Scaramuzza, D.: State space models for event cameras. In: Proceedings of the IEEE/CVF Conference on Computer Vision and Pattern Recognition, pp. 5819–5828 (2024)

Detection and Recognition

A Comprehensive Framework
for Fine-Grained Object Recognition
in Remote Sensing

Xin Chi[1,2], Yu Sun[1,2]($\boxtimes$), Yingjun Zhao[1,2], Donghua Lu[1,2], Jun Yang[1,2],
and Yiting Zhang[1,2]

[1] Beijing Research Institute of Uranium Geology, Beijing, China
HD9818@briug.cn, 13664284913@163.com
[2] National Key Laboratory of Uranium Resources Exploration-Mining and Nuclear
Remote Sensing, Beijing, China

Abstract. Fine-grained object recognition represents a practical
requirement for intelligent interpretation of high-resolution remote sensing imagery. Existing research primarily concentrates on the detection of
stumpy targets. Nevertheless, slender objects characterized by a height
significantly exceeding their length or width are also common in practical applications. Current research is inadequate to tackle the challenges
presented by slender targets, and there is an urgent need for effective
methodologies to address this issue. To this end, this paper proposes
a model, named Generalized Adaptive Rotation Faster R-CNN (GA-
RFRCNN). The GA-RFRCNN optimizes feature representation across
multiple scales by integrating selective enhancement feature pyramid
network (SE-FPN). Besides, it introduces an enhanced rotation region
proposal network (ERRPN) to enhance the object localization. Furthermore, a dynamically adjusted training process is used to handle difficult-
to-detect samples by introducing the adaptive slide loss (ASLoss). We
conduct extensive experiments on the transmission tower custom dataset
(TT-OBB) and the HRSC2016 dataset, and the results show that our
model achieves significant improvements in recognition accuracy and oriented bounding box detection.

Keywords: Fine-grained object recognition · High-resolution remote
sensing imagery · Oriented bounding box detection · Varied object
structures

1 Introduction

With advancements in remote sensing technology and the widespread adoption of
deep learning, high-resolution remote sensing images have significantly enhanced
the accuracy of earth observation and information extraction. Accurate recognition of targets in remote sensing imagery not only improves our understanding
of terrestrial phenomena but also has important applications in areas such as
disaster prevention [1–5], infrastructure management [6,7], and smart city development [8–10].

© The Author(s), under exclusive license to Springer Nature Singapore Pte Ltd. 2025
P. Didyk and J. Hou (Eds.): CVM 2025, LNCS 15663, pp. 131–150, 2025.
https://doi.org/10.1007/978-981-96-5809-1_8

However, as application requirements evolve, traditional detection models exhibit limitations in addressing fine-grained recognition [11]. These constraints stem from substantial intra-class variation and minimal inter-class differences [12]. Targets within the same category may exhibit considerable differences in appearance due to factors such as viewing angles, lighting conditions, occlusion, and background clutter. Conversely, targets from different categories often share structural similarities that complicate differentiation. This complexity hinders the model's ability to extract stable features necessary for distinguishing fine-grained categories. Moreover, targets in remote sensing images are often embedded in complex backgrounds and exhibit significant scale variations, further increasing the difficulty of detection and classification. Some progress has been made in addressing challenges related to complex backgrounds and angular rotations [15, 17, 43–45].

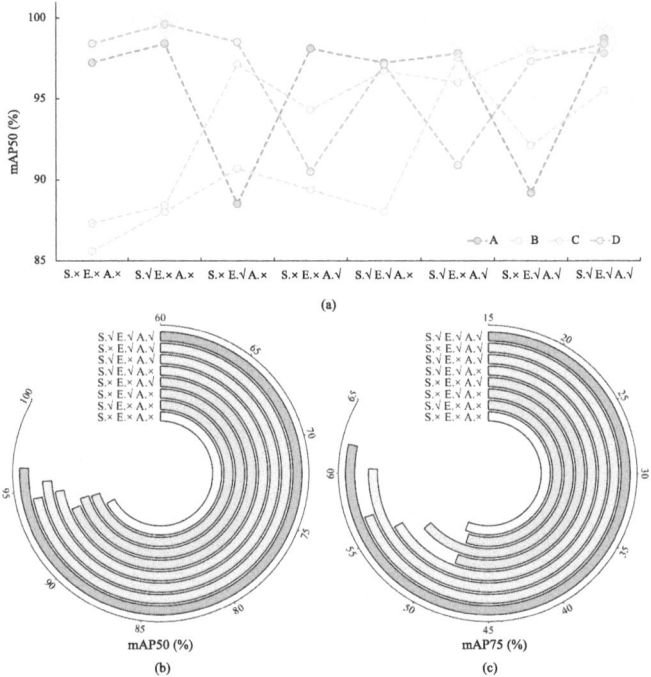

Fig. 1. Detection performance of different network configurations on the TT-OBB dataset, with ablation analysis for (b) mAP50 and (c) mAP75. The highlighted section in (a) shows the scenario with the highest category accuracy. S. represents SE-FPN, E. represents ERRPN, and A. represents ASLoss.

Despite this progress, most current research focuses on fine-grained recognition challenges associated with stumpy targets such as ship and aircraft [12–18]. In contrast, slender targets like high-voltage transmission towers, wind power towers, and industrial chimneys receive less attention, despite their practical significance. Their slender morphology, with a height significantly exceeding their length and width, makes them difficult to detect. In satellite remote sensing imagery, the perspective often compresses these vertical objects, resulting in a smaller pixel representation. Additionally, the imaging process is influenced by various factors such as lighting conditions, atmospheric interference, and satellite viewing angles, leading to substantial differences in imaging quality [21,22,46–48]. These factors, combined with the frequent appearance of slender targets in complex backgrounds at varying angles, further challenge traditional detection methods, often resulting in failure to capture their complete structure and essential features.

Environmental factors and geographical variations can alter the structure, scale, and orientation of slender targets in imagery. Traditional horizontal bounding box (HBB) detection techniques often include excessive background information, complicating the accurate representation of an object's orientation and shape. Therefore, the introduction of oriented bounding boxes (OBBs), aligned with the actual orientation of the object, has become a critical strategy for improving detection and classification performance of slender targets.

To address these challenges and expand the application scope of fine-grained recognition in remote sensing, this paper proposes the Generalized Adaptive Rotation Faster R-CNN (GA-RFRCNN) model. This model is specifically designed to accommodate a broader range of fine-grained recognition tasks by integrating several key innovations aimed at improving accuracy and robustness.

- Transmission Tower Oriented Bounding Box (TT-OBB) Datasets: To enable a fine-grained analysis of slender targets in remote sensing imagery, this study presents a specialized dataset for transmission tower detection. The dataset validates model performance on slender targets, complementing public datasets that primarily focus on stumpy targets. This approach ensures a comprehensive evaluation of the model across various target types.
- Network Architecture Optimization: Modifications to GA-RFRCNN include optimized feature extraction techniques, enhanced region proposal mechanisms, and dynamically adjusted loss functions. These enhancements aim to improve both accuracy and recall in complex environments. The model is particularly effective for objects with varying sizes and orientations, especially slender targets.
- Comprehensive Validation: Extensive evaluations were conducted on both custom datasets and the publicly available HRSC2016 dataset. These experiments demonstrate the model's effectiveness in fine-grained recognition and high-precision oriented bounding box detection.

The rest of this article is organized as follows: Sect. 2 surveys related work, Sect. 3 elaborates on network architecture and its enhancements, Sect. 4 details the experimental setup and outcomes, and Sect. 5 synthesizes the main findings and proposes future research directions.

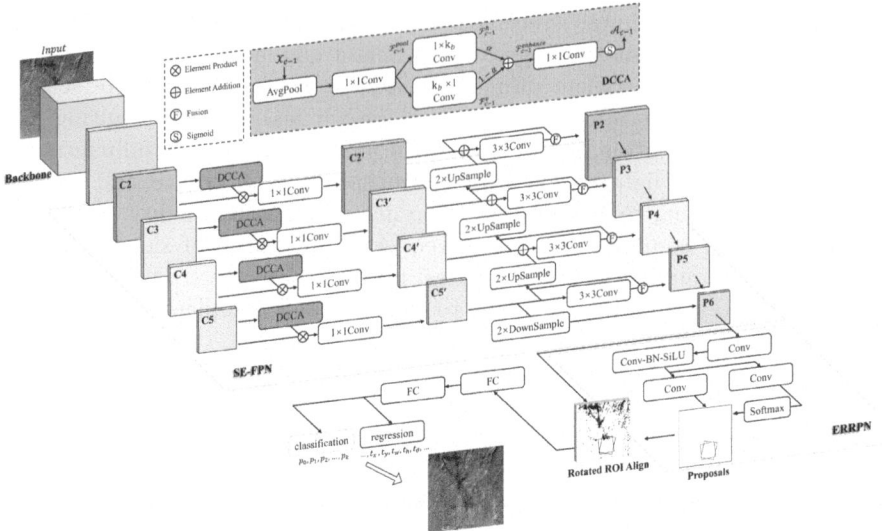

Fig. 2. Overview of GA-RFRCNN. The SE-FPN integrates the innovative DCCA module along with enhanced feature fusion mechanisms. ERRPN and ASLoss are also essential components, with detailed descriptions provided in later sections.

2   Related Work

2.1   Fine-Grained Object Recognition in Remote Sensing Imagery

Fine-grained recognition in remote sensing imagery is a critical research area. It focuses on distinguishing targets with highly similar structures and appearances, which pose challenges for traditional detection methods. The diversity of objects and subtle visual differences complicate accurate recognition. The detailed capture of ground features by high-resolution optical satellite imagery enables precise detection and monitoring of infrastructure. In this context, deep learning methodologies play a key role in enhancing recognition accuracy. These methods help distinguish objects with minimal inter-class variation and significant intra-class differences, which are often influenced by environmental and observational factors.

Several studies have addressed the challenges of fine-grained object recognition, particularly for diverse and complex targets. For instance, Osswald-Cankaya and Mayer [19] proposed a method for fine-grained recognition in satellite images based on task separation and orientation normalization. Their approach separates detection and classification tasks and normalizes object orientations, leading to improved accuracy on the FAIR1M dataset. Guo et al. [13] introduced MSRIP-Net, a multi-scale rotation-invariant network, which excels at fine-grained aircraft identification without additional annotations. Zhao et al. [20] developed a two-stage CNN architecture using Sentinel-2 imagery for detecting and localizing reservoirs across China, addressing the crucial challenge of accurate identification for water management and flood control.

To further improve detection accuracy across various fine-grained targets, researchers have focused on techniques specifically designed for slender objects. These techniques leverage auxiliary information, such as shadows and imaging parameters, to improve localization. Huang et al. proposed SI-STD [21] and IPC-Det [22], which use shadow information and imaging parameters to improve the localization of slender targets, like transmission towers. However, these methods not only rely heavily on image-specific parameters, such as solar altitude and satellite viewing angles, but also increase the need for labor-intensive manual labeling, limiting their scalability for large-scale fine-grained recognition tasks.

2.2   Dataset Limitations and Challenges

The constraints of publicly available datasets have significantly impacted the development of robust fine-grained recognition models in remote sensing. Many widely used datasets rely on HBBs for object annotation. While HBBs are effective for conventional detection, they struggle to represent objects with arbitrary orientations. This limitation hampers the model's ability to fully utilize spatial and angular information, which is critical for detecting and classifying complex objects with rotational variance.

Moreover, existing fine-grained recognition datasets, though beneficial, have notable scope limitations. Datasets like HRSC2016 [23], RarePlanes [24], FGSC-23 [25], and FGSCR-42 [12] mainly focus on stumpy object types such as ships, aircraft, and vehicles. However, less attention has been given to objects with distinct slender features. Expanding the diversity of objects in fine-grained recognition datasets could significantly enhance model performance across a broader range of remote sensing detection tasks.

3   Methodology

The GA-RFRCNN model, as shown in Fig. 2, includes three main innovations designed to enhance fine-grained recognition in complex remote sensing images. SE-FPN boost the model's object recognition capabilities by using a channel attention mechanis m and an adaptive fusion strategy. This approach facilitates more effective handling of intricate geometric shapes against complex backgrounds. ERRPN improves target localization by incorporating high-level convolutional layers and multi-layer feature fusion, which accurately captures the rotational characteristics of objects, especially those appearing in various orientations. ASLoss fine-tunes training by dynamically adjusting loss weights, focusing more on hard-to-classify targets. This targeted optimization improves the model's detection accuracy for slender objects commonly missed in complex backgrounds.

In summary, these innovations in GA-RFRCNN strengthen its ability to classify and detect a broader range of objects, with an emphasis on improving performance for the slender targets that traditional methods often overlook.

3.1   Selective Enhancement Feature Pyramid Network (SE-FPN)

Fine-grained recognition in remote sensing imagery presents significant challenges due to the structural and appearance variations of multi-scale objects. To address this issue, this paper introduces the SE-FPN, which integrates channel attention mechanisms and adaptive feature fusion to improve object detection accuracy. SE-FPN selectively enhances key features and integrates multi-scale information, more effectively, overcoming the limitations of traditional Feature Pyramid Networks (FPNs).

SE-FPN extracts multi-scale feature maps C2, C3, C4, C5 from the backbone network. Its core innovation is the Dual-Channel Convolutional Attention (DCCA) module, enhancing feature expressiveness by capturing spatial dependencies and emphasizing critical features. This approach is inspired by prior research [26–28]. For a given feature map, the DCCA applies average pooling and 1×1 convolutions to extract local features:

$$\mathcal{F}_{c-1}^{pool} = \text{Conv}_{1\times1}(\mathcal{P}_{\text{avg}}(\mathcal{X}_{c-1})) \tag{1}$$

where $\mathcal{P}_{\text{avg}}$ represents the average pooling operation. Horizontal and vertical convolutions are then applied to capture directional context:

$$\mathcal{F}_{c-1}^{h} = \text{Conv}_{1\times k_b}(\mathcal{F}_{c-1}^{pool}) \tag{2}$$

$$\mathcal{F}_{c-1}^{v} = \text{Conv}_{k_b\times1}(\mathcal{F}_{c-1}^{pool}) \tag{3}$$

where k_b represents the kernel size. A learnable parameter α balances these features, and the combined representation is:

$$\mathcal{F}_{c-1}^{\text{enhance}} = \alpha \times \mathcal{F}_{c-1}^{h} + (1 - \alpha) \times \mathcal{F}_{c-1}^{v} \tag{4}$$

where σ is the Sigmoid activation function. The attention weight is computed as:

$$\mathcal{A}_{c-1} = \sigma\left(\text{Conv}_{1\times1}\left(\mathcal{F}_{c-1}^{\text{enhance}}\right)\right) \tag{5}$$

The DCCA module also utilizes adaptive padding to maintain consistent feature map dimensions. Afterward, the feature fusion module of SE-FPN aggregates multi-scale features through both up-sampling and down-sampling techniques. This fusion process is guided by a weighted combination [29] of aligned features:

$$\mathcal{X}_{c-1}' = \text{Conv}_{1\times1}\left(\mathcal{A}_{c-1} \times \mathcal{X}_{c-1}\right) \tag{6}$$

$$\mathcal{X}_{p-1}^{\text{td}} = \text{Conv}_{3\times3}\left(X_{c-1}' + \text{Resize}(X_c')\right) \tag{7}$$

$$\mathcal{X}_{p-1} = \text{Conv}_{1\times1}\left(\frac{\omega_1 \cdot \mathcal{X}_{c-1}' + \omega_2 \cdot \mathcal{X}_{p-1}^{\text{td}}}{\omega_1 + \omega_2 + \epsilon}\right) \tag{8}$$

where $\mathcal{X}_{c-1}'$ represents the enhanced feature map obtained after combining the feature map $\mathcal{X}_{c-1}$ with its corresponding attention weight $\mathcal{A}_{c-1}$. $\mathcal{X}_{p-1}^{\text{td}}$ denotes the intermediate feature at the p-th level in the top-down pathway. The learnable weights ω_i balance each input feature, and ϵ prevents division by zero.

SE-FPN overcomes the limitations of traditional FPNs, improving the detection of multi-scale and complex objects. Its ability to capture subtle structural variations makes it highly effective for fine-grained recognition tasks.

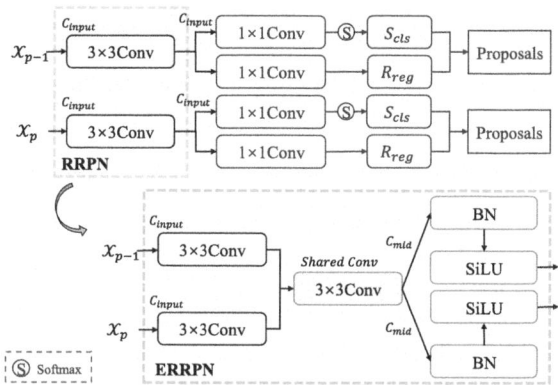

Fig. 3. Structure comparison between RRPN and ERRPN.

3.2 Enhanced Rotation Region Proposal Network (ERRPN)

Accurate localization of rotated objects is essential for fine-grained recognition in optical remote sensing. ERRPN enhances this process by reengineering the traditional Rotated Region Proposal Network (RRPN) [30] through advanced convolutional layers. These enhancements significantly improve its ability to detect objects with arbitrary orientations, a prevalent challenge in remote sensing imagery.

As illustrated in Fig. 3, ERRPN's proposal generation is centered around a series of convolutional layers. It commences with a shared 3×3 convolutional block (padding = 1). This step augments feature representation by transforming the input channels into intermediate channels, which is critical for accurate proposal generation.

Subsequently, a Batch Normalization (BN) layer combined with SiLU activation functions to smooth gradients, stabilizing training and enhancing convergence. The network then diverges into two branches: one for classification and one for regression.

Classification Head: Generates a score map S_{cls}, which estimates the probability of each anchor containing an object:

$$S_{\text{cls}} = \text{Conv}_{1 \times 1}(C_{\text{mid}}, N \times C_{\text{cls}}) \tag{9}$$

where C_{mid} is the transformed middle channel, N is the number of anchors per location, and C_{cls} represents the classification output (object vs. background).

Regression Head: Outputs five parameters-x, y, w, h, and θ-for each anchor, predicting rotated bounding boxes:

$$R_{\text{reg}} = \text{Conv}_{1\times 1}(C_{\text{mid}}, N \times 5) \tag{10}$$

These parameters are decoded to recover final bounding box coordinates in the original image space. Non-Maximum Suppression (NMS), adapted for rotation angles, is then applied to refine proposal selection.

3.3   Adaptive Slide Loss (ASLoss)

ASLoss enhances fine-grained recognition by dynamically adjusting classification loss based on the Intersection over Union (IoU) between predicted and ground truth bounding boxes. In contrast to Slide Loss [31], which rely solely on IoU, ASLoss incorporates a confidence factor that allows for more precise and adaptable loss adjustments. This innovation helps the model better handle challenging samples, particularly complex targets, by refining predictions that are nearly accurate but lack confident classification.

The key innovation of ASLoss lies in its use of a modulation weight ω, which is determined by the IoU, $confidence$, and a threshold τ. This combination allows ASLoss to dynamically adjust the classification loss, placing more emphasis on difficult or ambiguous predictions. The IoU between a ground truth box A and a predicted box B is defined as:

$$\text{IoU} = \frac{A \cap B}{A \cup B} \tag{11}$$

The modulation weight ω is computed as:

$$\omega = \begin{cases} 1 & \text{IoU} \leq \tau - 0.1 \\ e^{(1-\tau)} & \tau - 0.1 < \text{IoU} < \tau \\ e^{(2-\text{confidence})} & \text{IoU} \geq \tau \end{cases} \tag{12}$$

where $confidence$ refers to the predicted confidence score of the bounding box, typically ranging between 0 and 1. This formulation ensures that predictions near the threshold τ, which are often more challenging, receive greater emphasis.

The total loss for GA-RFRCNN is composed of two components: the classification loss L_{cls} and the regression loss L_{reg}. These components jointly optimize the model for both accurate class prediction and precise bounding box localization.

The classification loss is defined as:

$$L_{\text{cls}} = \frac{1}{N} \sum_{i=1}^{N} \left[\omega \cdot \left(\log\left(1 + e^{-p_i}\right) - y_i \cdot p_i \right) \right] \tag{13}$$

where N is the number of samples, y_i is the ground truth label, p_i is the predicted probability and ω is the modulation weight.

The regression loss measures the difference between predicted and ground truth bounding boxes:

$$L_{\text{reg}} = \frac{1}{N} \sum_{i=1}^{N} F_{\text{reg}}(t_i, t_i^*) \tag{14}$$

where t_i is the predicted bounding box parameter (coordinates, width, height, and angle) and t_i^* is the ground truth. F_{reg} is the Smooth L1 loss.

The total loss function is a weighted sum of the classification and regression losses:

$$L = L_{\text{cls}} + \lambda \cdot L_{\text{reg}} \tag{15}$$

where λ balances the importance of classification and regression components, ensuring optimal model performance across various tasks.

Fig. 4. Example transmission tower categories (A, B, C, D) in natural scene images and remote sensing images.

4 Experiments

4.1 Datasets

In this study, we developed the TT-OBB dataset, specifically for detecting transmission towers in optical satellite remote sensing imagery. Transmission towers were chosen because of their diverse designs and complex structures, making them ideal slender targets for fine-grained recognition studies. The dataset contains 1804 high-resolution satellite images, primarily sourced from Google Earth and SuperView satellites. These images were partitioned into training, validation, and test sets in an 8:1:1 ratio. Each image has a resolution of 1024×1024 pixels, with a spatial resolution ranging from approximately 0.3 to 0.6 m per pixel. Focusing on the northwestern region of China, which is characterized by extensive transmission infrastructure, the dataset provides a diverse array of examples essential for the development and evaluation of detection algorithms.

Notably, the TT-OBB dataset employs the OBB annotation method. This approach accommodates the varied orientations and perspectives of transmission towers in satellite imagery, substantially enhancing the accuracy and robustness of detection. Moreover, the dataset meticulously categorizes transmission towers into four common types, as shown in Fig. 4. These categories encompass the most prevalent transmission tower designs, laying a robust foundation for advancing fine-grained recognition research.

To further evaluate the effectiveness and generalizability of the models, the publicly available HRSC2016 dataset was incorporated into the experiments. This dataset is widely utilized for ship detection in remote sensing applications and comprises 1,061 aerial images with dimensions ranging from 300 × 300 to 1500×900 pixels. Although HRSC2016 includes 29 fine-grained categories, we followed the methodology in [17], testing on 19 categories including Nimitz (Nim.), Enterprise (Ent.), Arleigh Burke (Arl.), WhidbeyIsland (Whi.), Perry (Per.), Sanantonio (San.), Ticonderoga (Tic.), Admiral (Adm.), Austen (Aus.), Tarawa (Tar.), Container (Con.), Command ship (Com.), Car carrier A (CarA.), Container ship A (ConA.), Submarine (Sub.), Lute-shaped warship (War.), Medical ship (Med.), Car carrier B (CarB.) and Midway (Mid). Combining this evaluation with the TT-OBB dataset provided a comprehensive framework, significantly enhancing the reliability of the findings.

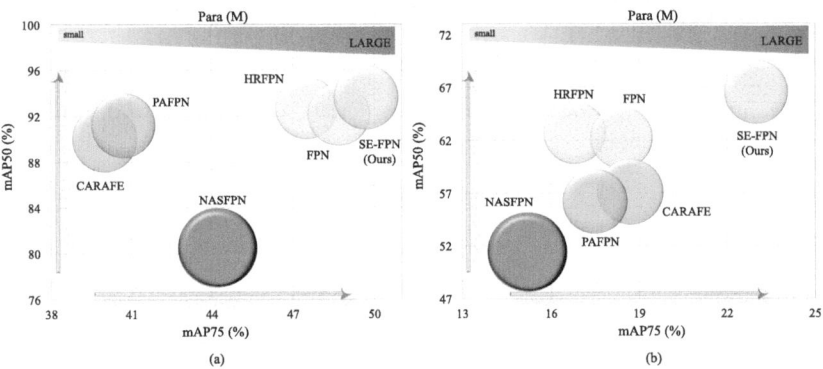

Fig. 5. Performance comparison of multi-level feature fusion methods on (a) TT-OBB and (b) HRSC2016 datasets. The size and color of the circles represent the number of parameters (Para) in each method, with larger and darker circles indicating higher parameter counts. The position of each circle indicates the trade-off between model accuracy (mAP) and complexity.

4.2 Implementation Details

For the training of remote sensing object detectors, experiments were conducted using the MMRotate [32] framework. Models were trained on both training and validation sets before testing on the testing set. The models were trained for 36 epochs on HRSC2016 and 20 epochs on TT-OBB, utilizing the AdamW [33] optimizer with an initial learning rate of 0.0001 and weight decay of 0.0005. Training was performed on eight RTX3090 GPUs with a batch size of eight.

Model performance was primarily evaluated using mean average precision at IoU thresholds of 50% (mAP50) and 75% (mAP75). While mAP50 provides a general measure of detection accuracy, it may not be stringent enough for tasks requiring precise angle estimation. In contrast, mAP75 demands tighter alignment between predicted bounding boxes and ground truth boxes, including accurate angle predictions, making it a more reliable performance indicator for oriented object detection tasks [34]. Additionally, we considered model parameters to evaluate detection efficiency and complexity.

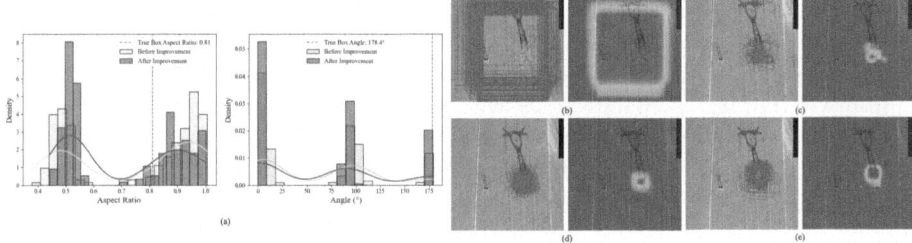

Fig. 6. (a) Aspect ratio and angle distribution before and after ERRPN improvement on a sample from the TT-OBB dataset; Region proposal visualizations of different RPN variants on the same sample: (b) RPN, (c) RRPN, (d) Oriented RPN [35], and (e) ERRPN.

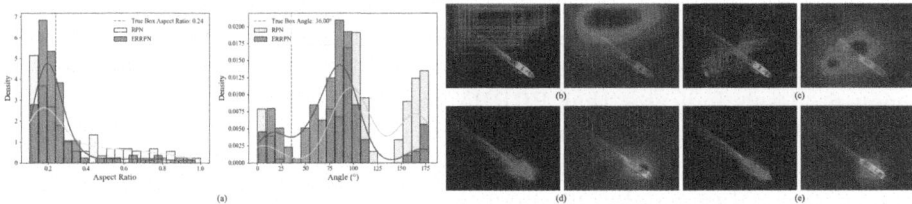

Fig. 7. (a) Aspect ratio and angle distribution before and after ERRPN improvement on a sample from the HRSC2016 dataset; Region proposal visualizations of different RPN variants on the same sample: (b) RPN, (c) RRPN, (d) Oriented RPN, and (e) ERRPN.

Table 1. Ablation study results on the HRSC2016 dataset. S. represents SE-FPN, E. represents ERRPN, and A. represents ASLoss.

S.	E.	A.	Nim.	Ent.	Arl.	Whi.	Per.	San.	Tic.	Adm.	Aus.	Tar.	Con.	Com.	CarA.	ConA.	Sub.	War.	Med.	CarB.	Mid.	mAP50 (%)	mAP75 (%)
✗	✗	✗	90.4	97.4	55.4	51.2	68.4	58.7	37.7	69.2	55.8	69.5	50.0	72.9	52.7	32.3	30.7	65.2	86.5	58.2	81.8	62.2	20.4
✓	✗	✗	51.6	80.5	68.9	74.1	66.9	**81.5**	**57.0**	47.2	52.1	78.8	64.5	66.7	97.7	55.3	44.4	41.5	72.5	80.8	82.6	66.5	23.0
✗	✓	✗	82.3	64.7	62.2	87.3	65.7	70.3	50.1	82.3	58.2	50.4	53.4	79.6	55.6	**70.7**	31.9	57.7	**92.0**	55.6	80.5	65.8	22.5
✗	✗	✓	57.8	89.6	61.1	73.5	60.0	69.7	45.8	57.4	50.6	70.9	49.4	65.9	86.8	68.7	55.6	44.2	81.3	53.5	73.4	64.0	20.0
✓	✓	✗	87.7	63.6	69.9	78.2	78.4	81.1	51.6	76.8	54.5	68.7	65.4	71.3	54.5	49.8	38.4	67.5	90.9	**81.8**	71.5	67.3	27.7
✓	✗	✓	68.4	81.6	72.6	**91.6**	**79.8**	75.6	42.1	74.8	62.7	53.5	**70.0**	72.5	56.6	64.9	**61.6**	51.4	91.4	56.6	75.5	68.6	24.2
✗	✓	✓	91.3	75.7	70.9	89.1	64.9	74.8	42.5	**87.5**	**67.4**	**82.3**	66.3	**81.2**	61.7	65.5	49.7	43.8	80.9	71.7	82.7	69.5	25.6
✓	✓	✓	**96.4**	**98.6**	**76.5**	86.7	76.2	61.7	49.1	79.1	44.1	67.1	61.2	67.7	**98.6**	57.5	38.8	**70.3**	74.7	59.2	**89.5**	**71.2**	**33.5**

4.3 Ablation Study

Comparison of Multi-level Feature Fusion Strategies. To assess the effectiveness of SE-FPN in multi-scale feature fusion for fine-grained object recognition, we have compared it with advanced methods such as FPN, HRFPN, PAFPN, NASFPN, and CARAFE across two challenging datasets. As illustrated in Fig. 5(a), SE-FPN enhances the mAP50 by 1.5% and mAP75 by 1.0% on the TT-OBB dataset compared to FPN. This demonstrates its capability for cross-scale feature integration.

SE-FPN shows significant advantages over other methods, achieving a maximum mAP50 of 93.6% in categories with substantial structural variation. While there is a slight increase in computational cost, SE-FPN effectively balances performance and efficiency, making it suitable for high-precision remote sensing applications. Despite the inherent challenges of transmission tower detection, SE-FPN continues to exhibit robust performance improvements.

On the HRSC2016 dataset, as shown in Fig. 5(b), SE-FPN achieves 66.5% mAP50 and 23.0% mAP75, surpassing FPN within complex categories. Its consistent performance across various object types highlights its ability to manage diverse scales and complexities. Results from both datasets confirm SE-FPN's high flexibility in fine-grained recognition tasks, especially when detecting objects with varying shapes and complexities.

Comparison of Different Region Proposal Networks. Experiments on the TT-OBB and HRSC2016 datasets demonstrate significant improvements in region proposal accuracy with ERRPN. An analysis of 200 randomly selected region proposals indicates that ERRPN markedly enhances both aspect ratio and angle prediction, as illustrated in Fig. 6 and Fig. 7.

In aspect ratio prediction, ERRPN produces results closely aligned with true object aspect ratios, exhibiting minimal deviation. This contrasts with RRPN, which displays a broader and less accurate distribution of predictions. In angle prediction, ERRPN also shows clear advancements, aligning predicted angles more closely with actual object orientations.

The impact of ERRPN is particularly evident in visualizations of region proposals. Before the improvement, RRPN generated scattered and overlapping proposals, which led to lower localization precision. After the improvement, the proposals become more focused and better aligned with object locations, reducing noise and improving accuracy-critical for detecting complex shapes and orientations. Furthermore, the heat map shows that ERRPN exhibits higher response values in central areas compared to the more dispersed responses of Oriented RPN.

Table 2. Results of different threshold τ.

τ	mAP50 (%)	mAP75 (%)
0.3	92.6	47.3
0.5	93.1	**48.4**
0.7	**93.5**	48.1

Performance Evaluation of ASLoss. Results from the TT-OBB dataset validate ASLoss's efficacy in enhancing classification accuracy, especially for objects with arbitrary orientations in remote sensing imagery. As shown in Table 2, mAP50 consistently increases as the threshold τ is raised from 0.3 to 0.7, while mAP75 reaches its peak at 48.4% when τ is set to 0.5. This indicates that a threshold of 0.5 may enable the model to more effectively manage lower IoU samples, thereby improving its performance in complex scenarios characterized by imprecise object boundaries.

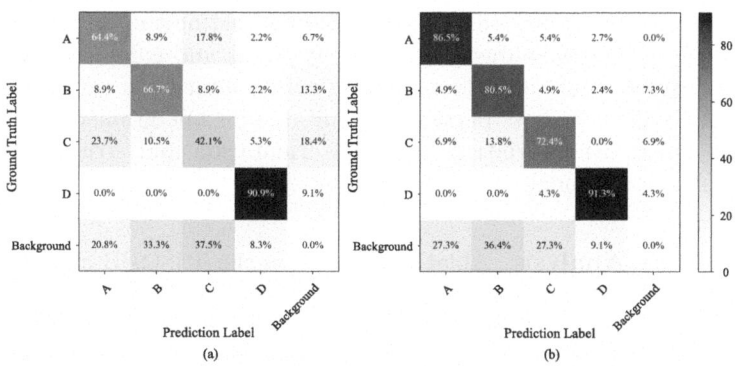

Fig. 8. Comparison of normalized confusion matrices: before improvement - CrossEntropy Loss (a) and after improvement - ASLoss (b) on the TT-OBB dataset.

The confusion matrix analysis (Fig. 8 and Fig. 9) for both the TT-OBB and HRSC2016 datasets demonstrates significant performance enhancements with ASLoss. On the TT-OBB dataset, accuracy for category A increases from 64.4% to 86.5%, while category C rises from 42.1% to 72.4%. Notably, there is a marked

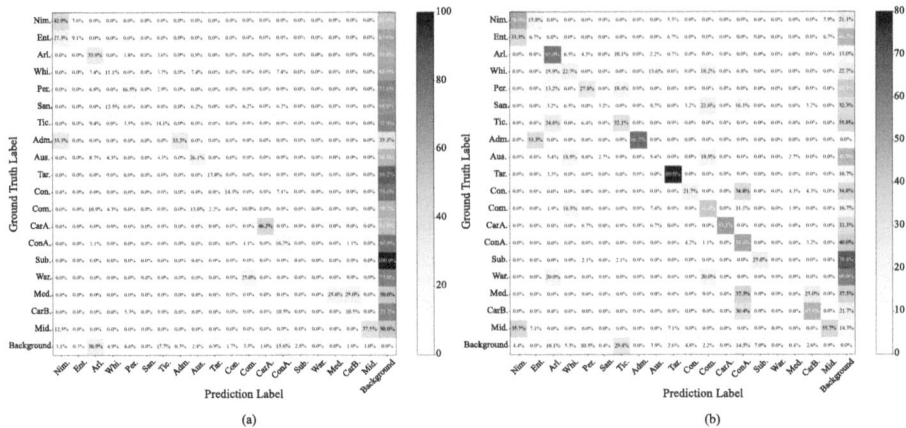

Fig. 9. Comparison of normalized confusion matrices: before improvement - CrossEntropy Loss (a) and after improvement - ASLoss (b) on the HRSC2016 dataset.

reduction in misclassifications between similar categories, particularly between A and C. Similarly, on the HRSC2016 dataset, ASLoss contributes to enhanced accuracy in categories such as ConA. and Tar., achieving accuracies of 51.6% and 80.0%, respectively. Moreover, the reduced occurrence of missed detections, particularly in the background category, highlights ASLoss's ability to better capture and classify previously overlooked objects. This significantly decreases the rate of false negatives.

Overall, across both datasets, ASLoss consistently outperforms the previously used CrossEntropy loss method by dynamically adjusting the classification loss. This approach mitigates confusion among categories and enhances the model's capability to differentiate objects exhibiting subtle inter-class variations. These advancements render ASLoss particularly suitable for fine-grained classification tasks where substantial variation in object orientation and structure presents challenges for conventional methods.

Ablation Study Analysis. Ablation studies on the TT-OBB and HRSC2016 datasets reveal significant performance enhancements due to the integration of SE-FPN, ERRPN, and ASLoss, as depicted in the Fig. 1 and Table 1. These improvements are particularly pronounced in fine-grained recognition tasks, with Rotated Faster R-CNN serving as the baseline model.

On the TT-OBB dataset, the comprehensive model that incorporates SE-FPN, ERRPN, and ASLoss attains an impressive mAP50 of 96.3% and an mAP75 of 62.0%. In contrast, the baseline Rotated Faster R-CNN records an mAP50 of 92.1% and an mAP75 of 48.7%. The advancements are especially notable in challenging categories such as B and C.

On the HRSC2016 dataset, the full model achieves an mAP50 of 71.2% and an mAP75 of 33.5%, significantly surpassing the performance of the baseline

Rotated Faster R-CNN (mAP50 of 62.2% and mAP75 of 20.4%). The improvements are most evident in fine-grained categories including CarA., Whi., ConA., and Arl.

These enhancements enable the model to more effectively capture subtle variations in object appearance, orientation, and scale, ultimately leading to improved performance and robustness across both datasets.

Table 3. Experimental results on TT-OBB dataset.

Model	A	B	C	D	mAP50 (%)	mAP75 (%)
DETR-based						
AO2-DETR [36]	87.4	89.4	87.1	87.7	86.9	45.6
ARS-DETR [37]	**99.8**	90.0	97.4	97.2	95.0	52.4
One-stage						
R3Det [38]	97.5	94.0	87.2	86.1	92.9	45.9
S2ANet [39]	98.7	**97.5**	86.9	87.4	94.5	45.1
YOLOv8x [40]	54.4	97.4	95.7	80.2	82.1	40.3
Two-stage						
G.V. [41]	93.3	80.8	88.9	93.5	89.1	44.3
RoI Trans [42]	98.5	95.9	93.6	98.8	95.2	47.1
O-RCNN [35]	88.1	84.7	93.3	94.1	90.1	53.8
GA-RFRCNN	98.7	95.5	**97.8**	**98.4**	**96.3**	**62.0**

Table 4. Experimental results on HRSC2016 dataset.

Model	Nim.	Ent.	Arl.	Whi.	Per.	San.	Tic.	Adm.	Aus.	Tar.	Con.	Com.	CarA.	ConA.	Sub.	War.	Med.	CarB.	Mid.	mAP50 (%)	mAP75 (%)
DETR-based																					
AO2-DETR	74.6	89.7	66.1	81.3	79.9	67.4	51.2	82.5	48.3	79.1	55.3	71.6	70.1	54.3	51.6	77.1	61.2	40.1	84.8	51.3	23.1
ARS-DETR	76.3	93.7	68.4	84.2	**82.1**	69.7	53.1	**91.5**	55.7	**81.7**	56.8	78.4	72.5	56.1	**53.1**	**79.9**	63.4	41.8	87.1	58.9	**40.7**
One-stage																					
R3Det	66.3	86.0	53.3	74.5	73.1	58.5	41.1	70.9	38.1	69.6	45.4	62.5	61.4	39.5	41.6	71.0	52.4	30.4	76.9	57.6	21.7
S2ANet	73.3	91.2	69.3	80.5	78.4	63.0	50.9	82.7	44.0	75.8	53.0	70.1	69.4	56.1	51.2	77.4	60.3	38.9	83.1	55.5	27.2
YOLOv8x	64.9	70.4	60.2	71.3	68.3	55.2	40.8	70.5	35.7	65.8	42.5	62.7	58.3	45.0	38.1	69.1	50.1	30.0	72.9	49.7	18.9
Two-stage																					
G.V.	63.8	53.9	33.2	79.4	49.8	73.2	**59.7**	50.4	45.4	59.1	**74.1**	67.8	68.2	52.9	27.7	65.0	65.9	74.2	66.9	61.1	24.5
RoI Trans	79.4	74.9	76.9	45.3	74.2	65.2	55.6	77.0	**76.4**	39.8	39.4	**86.6**	61.2	**67.9**	33.1	31.5	68.1	40.0	87.6	62.2	32.6
O-RCNN	76.4	59.4	**86.7**	41.6	39.3	**76.2**	57.9	73.8	39.5	73.2	32.3	74.7	60.9	66.5	51.5	34.9	39.7	**74.2**	87.2	62.8	30.5
GA-RFRCNN	**96.4**	**98.6**	76.5	**86.7**	76.2	61.7	49.1	79.1	44.1	67.1	61.2	67.7	**98.6**	57.5	38.8	70.3	**74.7**	59.2	**89.5**	**71.2**	33.5

4.4 Comparison With Other Methods

Among the compared detectors, GA-RFRCNN achieves the highest mAP75, as shown in Tables 3 and 4. It shows significant improvements over traditional models, particularly for objects with complex geometries and diverse forms. While two-stage methods such as RoI Transformer and O-RCNN exhibit commendable performance, they still fall short of GA-RFRCNN's efficacy. This underscores the effectiveness of the enhancements introduced, including SE-FPN, ERRPN, and ASLoss, in fine-grained recognition tasks. These improvements are especially evident when detecting slender structures and objects with intricate shapes and orientations. GA-RFRCNN also proves highly competitive with popular detectors like DETR, showing strong performance on both the custom TT-OBB dataset and publicly available datasets.

In visual comparisons on the TT-OBB and HRSC2016 datasets, the baseline Rotated Faster R-CNN frequently misclassifies and mislocalizes objects, particularly within cluttered environments. In contrast, GA-RFRCNN significantly enhances both classification accuracy and bounding box alignment. It reduces missed detections and errors in challenging scenarios when detecting transmission towers and ships, as shown in Fig. 10 and Fig. 11. These results confirm GA-RFRCNN's superior performance in remote sensing applications.

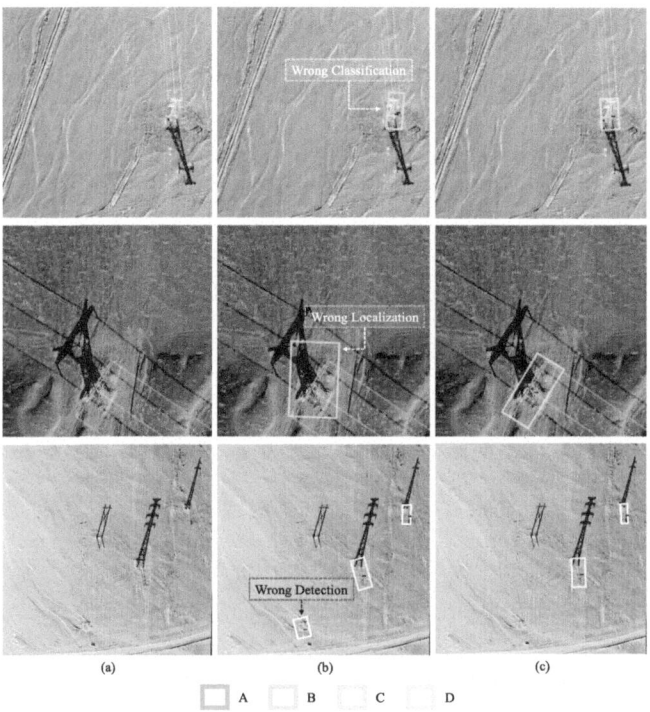

Fig. 10. Visual results on TT-OBB dataset: (a) input image; (b) baseline; (c) GA-RFRCNN.

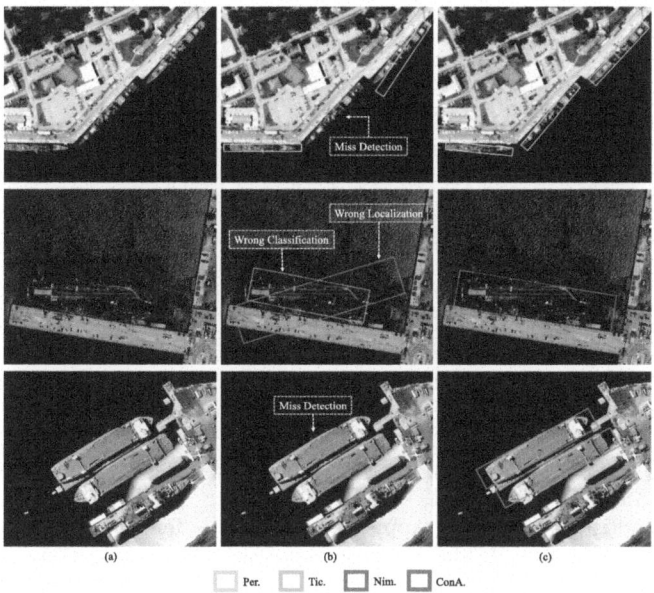

Fig. 11. Visual results on HRSC2016 dataset: (a) input image; (b) baseline; (c) GA-RFRCNN.

5   Conclusion

In this study, we investigated the challenges associated with fine-grained object recognition in remote sensing imagery, emphasizing the intricate geometric structures, diverse forms, and challenging environments inherent to these tasks. To tackle these challenges, we propose GA-RFRCNN, which incorporates SE-FPN, ERRPN, and ASLoss to enhance detection accuracy and robustness across various datasets. These innovations not only demonstrate their efficacy in managing complex details and various object types within fine-grained recognition tasks but also underscore significant advancements in detecting vertically structured objects.

Although our methods were tested on satellite imagery with large viewing angles, which introduced certain detection constraints, future work will aim to incorporate additional contextual information, such as shadow features. This could further enhance object localization and category predictions, especially in environments with complex lighting conditions and subtle visual cues.

Acknowledgments. This study was funded by National Key Laboratory of Uranium Resources Exploration-Mining and Nuclear Remote Sensing (6142A012301).

References

1. Ahmad, R.: Smart remote sensing network for disaster management: an overview. Telecommun. Syst. **87**, 213–237 (2024)
2. Panda, S., Yadav, V.-S., Tripathi, V.-K.: Application of remote sensing in natural resource management. Sustain. Dev. Geospat. Technol. **2**, 173–180 (2024)
3. Casagli, N., Intrierl, E., Tofani, V., Gigli, G., Raspini, F · Landslide detection, monitoring and prediction with remote-sensing techniques. Nat. Rev. Earth Environ. **4**(1), 51–64 (2023)
4. Kucharczyk, M., Hugenholtz, C.-H.: Remote sensing of natural hazard-related disasters with small drones: global trends, biases, and research opportunities. Remote Sens. Environ. **264**, 112577 (2021)
5. Kaku, K.: Satellite remote sensing for disaster management support: a holistic and staged approach based on case studies in Sentinel Asia. Int. J. Disaster Risk Reduction **33**, 417–432 (2019)
6. Ejaz, N., Choudhury, S.: Computer vision in drone imagery for infrastructure management. Autom. Constr. **163**, 105418 (2024)
7. Fan, J., Saadeghvaziri, M.-A.: Applications of drones in infrastructures: challenges and opportunities. Int. J. Mech. Mechatron. Eng. **13**(10), 649–655 (2019)
8. Zhu, S., Yang, K.: Deep remote sensing object detection for smart city applications. In: 2024 2nd International Conference on Mechatronics, IoT and Industrial Informatics (ICMIII), pp. 167–171 (2024). https://doi.org/10.1109/ICMIII62623.2024.00039
9. Liu, Y.: Application of remote sensing technology in smart city construction and planning. J. Phys: Conf. Ser. **2608**(1), 012052 (2023)
10. Xi, Y., et al.: A satellite imagery dataset for long-term sustainable development in united states cities. Sci. Data **10**(1), 866 (2023)
11. Sun, X., et al.: FAIR1M: a benchmark dataset for fine-grained object recognition in high-resolution remote sensing imagery. ISPRS J. Photogramm. Remote. Sens. **184**, 116–130 (2022)
12. Di, Y., Jiang, Z., Zhang, H.: A public dataset for fine-grained ship classification in optical remote sensing images. Remote Sens. **13**(4), 747 (2021)
13. Guo, Z., et al.: MSRIP-Net: addressing interpretability and accuracy challenges in aircraft fine-grained recognition of remote sensing images. IEEE Trans. Geosci. Remote Sens. **62**, 1–17 (2024)
14. Song, S., Zhang, R., Hu, M., Huang, F.: Fine-grained ship recognition based on visible and near-infrared multimodal remote sensing images: dataset, methodology and evaluation. Comput. Mater. Continua **79**(3), 5243–5271 (2024)
15. Cheng, G., Li, Q., Wang, G., Xie, X., Min, L., Han, J.: SFRNet: fine-grained oriented object recognition via separate feature refinement. IEEE Trans. Geosci. Remote Sens. **61**, 1–10 (2023)
16. Guan, Q., Liu, Y., Chen, L., Zhao, S., Li, G.: Aircraft detection and fine-grained recognition based on high-resolution remote sensing images. Electronics **12**(14), 3146 (2023)
17. Han, Y., Yang, X., Pu, T., Peng, Z.: Fine-grained recognition for oriented ship against complex scenes in optical remote sensing images. IEEE Trans. Geosci. Remote Sens. **60**, 1–18 (2021)
18. Liang, W., Li, J., Diao, W., Sun, X., Fu, K., Wu, Y.: FGATR-Net: automatic network architecture design for fine-grained aircraft type recognition in remote sensing images. Remote Sens. **12**(24), 4187 (2020)

19. Osswald-Cankaya, M., Mayer, H.: Fine-grained airplane recognition in satellite images based on task separation and orientation normalization. In: 2023 IEEE International Geoscience and Remote Sensing Symposium (IGARSS), pp. 6545–6548 (2023). https://doi.org/10.1109/IGARSS52108.2023.10283156
20. Zhao, G., Yao, P., Fu, L., Zhang, Z., Lu, S., Long, T.: A deep learning method based on two-stage CNN framework for recognition of Chinese reservoirs with Sentinel-2 images. Water **14**(22), 3755 (2022)
21. Huang, Z., Wang, F., You, H., Hu, Y.: Shadow information-based slender targets detection method in optical satellite images. IEEE Geosci. Remote Sens. Lett. **19**, 1–5 (2021)
22. Huang, Z., Wang, F., You, H., Hu, Y.: Imaging parameters-considered slender target detection in optical satellite images. Remote Sens. **14**(6), 1385 (2022)
23. Liu, Z., Yuan, L., Weng, L., Yang, Y.: A high resolution optical satellite image dataset for ship recognition and some new baselines. In: 6th International Conference on Pattern Recognition Applications and Methods (ICPRAM), pp. 324–331 (2017). https://doi.org/10.5220/0006120603240331
24. Shermeyer, J., Hossler, T., Van-Etten, A., Hogan, D., Lewis, R., Kim, D.: RarePlanes: synthetic data takes flight. In: 2021 IEEE Winter Conference on Applications of Computer Vision (WACV), pp. 207–217 (2021). https://doi.org/10.1109/WACV48630.2021.00025
25. Zhang, X., Lv, Y., Yao, L., Xiong, W., Fu, C.: A new benchmark and an attribute-guided multilevel feature representation network for fine-grained ship classification in optical remote sensing images. IEEE J. Sel. Top. Appl. Earth Observ. Remote Sens. **13**, 1271–1285 (2020)
26. Cai, X., Lai, Q., Wang, Y., Wang, W., Sun, Z., Yao, Y.: Poly kernel inception network for remote sensing detection. In: 2024 IEEE/CVF Conference on Computer Vision and Pattern Recognition (CVPR), pp. 27706–27716 (2024). https://doi.org/10.1109/CVPR52733.2024.02617
27. Li, Y., Hou, Q., Zheng, Z., Cheng, M. M., Yang, J., Li, X.: Large selective kernel network for remote sensing object detection. In: 2023 IEEE/CVF International Conference on Computer Vision (ICCV), pp. 16794–16805 (2023). https://doi.org/10.1109/ICCV51070.2023.01540
28. Tang, Y., Han, K., Guo, J., Xu, C., Xu, C., Wang, Y.: GhostNetv2: enhance cheap operation with long-range attention. Adv. Neural. Inf. Process. Syst. **35**, 9969–9982 (2022)
29. Tan, M., Pang, R., Le, Q. V.: EfficientDet: scalable and efficient object detection. In: 2020 IEEE/CVF Conference on Computer Vision and Pattern Recognition (CVPR), pp. 10781–10790 (2020). https://doi.org/10.1109/CVPR42600.2020.01079
30. Ma, J., et al.: Arbitrary-oriented scene text detection via rotation proposals. IEEE Trans. Multimedia **20**(11), 3111–3122 (2018)
31. Ma, J., et al.: YOLO-FaceV2: a scale and occlusion aware face detector. arXiv arXiv:2208.02019 (2022). https://doi.org/10.48550/arXiv.2208.02019
32. Zhou, Y., et al.: MMRotate: a rotated object detection benchmark using PyTorch. In: 30th ACM International Conference on Multimedia, pp. 7331–7334 (2022). https://doi.org/10.1145/3503161.3548541
33. Loshchilov, I.: Decoupled weight decay regularization. arXiv arXiv:1711.05101 (2017). https://doi.org/10.48550/arXiv.1711.05101
34. Zeng, Y., Guo, Y., Li, J.: Recognition and extraction of high-resolution satellite remote sensing image buildings based on deep learning. Neural Comput. Appl. **34**(4), 2691–2706 (2022)

35. Xie, X., Cheng, G., Wang, J., Yao, X., Han, J.: Oriented R-CNN for object detection. In: 2021 IEEE/CVF International Conference on Computer Vision (ICCV), pp. 3520–3529 (2021). https://doi.org/10.1109/ICCV48922.2021.00350

36. Dai, L., Liu, H., Tang, H., Wu, Z., Song, P.: AO2-DETR: arbitrary-oriented object detection transformer. IEEE Trans. Circ. Syst. Video Technol. **33**(5), 2342–2356 (2022)

37. Zeng, Y., Chen, Y., Yang, X., Li, Q., Yan, J.: ARS-DETR: aspect ratio-sensitive detection transformer for aerial oriented object detection. IEEE Trans. Geosci. Remote Sens. **62**, 1–15 (2024)

38. Yang, X., Yan, J., Feng, Z., He, T.: R3Det: refined single-stage detector with feature refinement for rotating object. In: 35th AAAI Conference on Artificial Intelligence, pp. 3163–3171 (2021). https://doi.org/10.1609/aaai.v35i4.16426

39. Han, J., Ding, J., Li, J., Xia, G.-S.: Align deep features for oriented object detection. IEEE Trans. Geosci. Remote Sens. **60**, 1–11 (2021)

40. YOLOv8. https://github.com/ultralytics/ultralytics/tree/main. Accessed 12 Nov 2023

41. Xu, Y., et al.: Gliding vertex on the horizontal bounding box for multi-oriented object detection. IEEE Trans. Pattern Anal. Mach. Intell. **43**(4), 1452–1459 (2020)

42. Ding, J., Xue, N., Long, Y., Xia, G.-S., Lu, Q.: Learning RoI transformer for oriented object detection in aerial images. In: 2019 IEEE/CVF Conference on Computer Vision and Pattern Recognition (CVPR), pp. 2849–2858 (2019). https://doi.org/10.1109/CVPR.2019.00296

43. Sun, P., Zheng, Y., Wu, W., Xu, W., Bai, S., Lu, X.: Learning critical features for arbitrary-oriented object detection in remote sensing optical images. IEEE Trans. Instrum. Meas. **73**, 1–12 (2024)

44. Yu, Y., Yang, X., Li, Q., Zhou, Y., Da, F., Yan, J.: H2RBox-v2: incorporating symmetry for boosting horizontal box supervised oriented object detection. Adv. Neural. Inf. Process. Syst. **36**, 1–14 (2024)

45. Sun, P., Zheng, Y., Wu, W., Xu, W., Bai, S.: Metric-aligned sample selection and critical feature sampling for oriented object detection. arXiv arXiv:2306.16718 (2023). https://doi.org/10.48550/arXiv.2306.16718

46. Zha, W., Hu, L., Sun, Y., Li, Y.: ENGD-BiFPN: a remote sensing object detection model based on grouped deformable convolution for power transmission towers. Multimedia Tools Appl. **82**(29), 45585–45604 (2023)

47. Zha, W., Hu, L., Duan, C., Li, Y.: Semi-supervised learning-based satellite remote sensing object detection method for power transmission towers. Energy Rep. **9**, 15–27 (2023)

48. Huang, Z., Wang, F., You, H., Hu, Y.: STC-Det: a slender target detector combining shadow and target information in optical satellite images. Remote Sens. **13**(20), 4183 (2021)

Towards Reflected Object Detection: A Benchmark

Yiquan Wu[1], Zhongtian Wang[1], You Wu[2], Ling Huang[2], Hui Zhou[2], and Shuiwang Li[2(✉)]

[1] Nanjing University of Aeronautics and Astronautics, Nanjing, China
[2] Guilin University of Technology, Guilin, China
`lishuiwang0721@163.com`

Abstract. Object detection has greatly improved over the past decade, thanks to advances in deep learning and large-scale datasets. However, detecting objects reflected on surfaces remains an underexplored area. Reflective surfaces are ubiquitous in daily life, appearing in homes, offices, public spaces, and natural environments. Accurate detection and interpretation of reflected objects are essential for various applications. This paper addresses this gap by introducing an extensive benchmark specifically designed for Reflected Object Detection. Our Reflected Object Detection (ROD) dataset features a diverse collection of images showcasing reflected objects in various contexts, providing standard annotations for both real and reflected objects. This distinguishes it from traditional object detection benchmarks. The ROD dataset encompasses 10 categories and 6 reflective surfaces, including 23,520 images of real and reflected objects on different backgrounds, complete with standard bounding-box annotations and the classification of objects as real or reflected. In addition, we present baseline results by adapting five state-of-the-art object detection models to address this challenging task. The experimental results underscore the limitations of existing methods when applied to reflected object detection, highlighting the need for specialized approaches. By releasing the ROD dataset, we aim to support and advance future research on detecting reflected objects. The dataset and code are available at: https://github.com/jirouvan/ROD.

Keywords: Reflected object detection · Benchmark · Object detection · ROD dataset

1 Introduction

The field of object detection has seen remarkable advancements over the past decade, driven by the development of deep learning techniques and the availability of large-scale datasets [2,51,54]. These advancements have significantly improved the accuracy and robustness of object detection systems in various applications [29]. However, one area that remains underexplored is the detection of objects reflected in surfaces, such as glass, metal, water, plastic, polishing and tile. See Fig. 1 for an illustration of the difference between conventional object detection and reflected object detection.

P. Didyk and J. Hou (Eds.): CVM 2025, LNCS 15663, pp. 151–172, 2025.
https://doi.org/10.1007/978-981-96-5809-1_9

Reflective surfaces are ubiquitous in our daily lives, appearing in a wide array of environments and applications [24,35,49]. Mirrors, glass windows, water surfaces, and polished metals are just a few examples of materials that produce reflections. These reflective surfaces are prevalent in various settings, including homes, offices, public spaces, and natural environments, making the ability to detect and interpret reflected objects a crucial aspect of many technological applications [19,25,28,35]. For instance, in surveillance, security systems can more effectively identify real intrusions or threats by differentiating reflections from genuine objects [38,40,41]. For autonomous driving, accurate identification of real objects versus reflections enables vehicles to navigate more safely and avoid accidents caused by misinterpretation [9,21,34,50]. For service robots, robots can perform tasks with greater accuracy, such as picking and placing items, by correctly identifying real objects instead of their reflections [24,36]. This improved object detection also facilitates better navigation in environments with reflective surfaces, such as warehouses [7,31]. In smart homes, systems can provide more tailored responses by recognizing when a person is truly present rather than reacting to their reflection [6,33,42]. In medical applications, imaging and diagnostic tools yield more accurate results when they accurately interpret reflections, leading to better patient outcomes and more precise medical interventions.

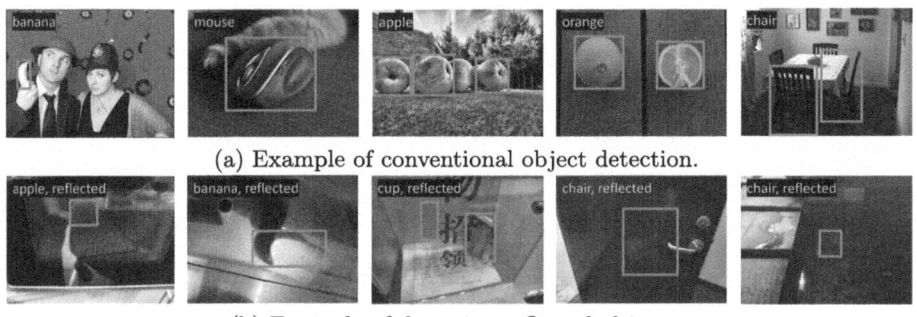

(a) Example of conventional object detection.

(b) Example of detecting reflected objects.

Fig. 1. While previous object detection focused on the identification and localization of objects, this work focuses on information beyond that and concerns about the nature of objects in addition, as shown in (a) and (b), respectively. Note the nature of the objects (i.e., real or reflected) are marked in (b) additionally.

Given the widespread presence of reflective surfaces in daily life, developing technologies that can effectively detect and interpret reflected objects is essential. This capability can enhance the performance and reliability of various applications, including smart home systems, surveillance, autonomous driving, and medical devices. However, to the best of our knowledge, there is currently no public benchmark for reflected object detection. This paper aims to address this gap by introducing a benchmark specifically designed for this purpose. We propose a comprehensive benchmark that includes a diverse set of images featuring reflected objects in various contexts. Our benchmark is designed to test the limits of current object detection methods and provide a standardized evaluation framework for developing and comparing new algorithms tailored to reflected object detection. The benchmark provides standard annotations used in object detection for identifying both actual (real) objects and their reflections. Additionally, it offers extra details that indicate whether an object is real or a reflection. This feature distinguishes it from traditional object detection benchmarks, which typically do not provide information about whether an object is a reflection. In addition to introducing the benchmark, this paper also presents baseline results by adapting several state-of-the-art object detection models. These results highlight the limitations of existing methods when applied to reflected object detection and underscore the need for specialized approaches. We analyze the performance of these models across different reflection scenarios and provide insights into the specific challenges posed by reflections.

The deployment of reflective object detection (ROD) systems in surveillance scenarios raises critical privacy concerns. Security systems utilizing ROD may inadvertently capture individuals' private activities behind reflective surfaces (e.g., windows, mirrors). Improper handling or leakage of such data could compromise individual privacy rights and entail legal liabilities. To mitigate these risks, developing ROD technologies necessitates the establishment of comprehensive ethical guidelines and regulatory frameworks to ensure lawful, transparent, and privacy-preserving implementations. Concurrent technical safeguards—such as encrypted data transmission protocols, role-based access controls, and edge-computing architectures for localized data processing—should be prioritized to enhance security while maintaining functional efficacy.

1.1 Contribution

In this work, we make the first attempt to explore reflected object detection by introducing the ROD benchmark, which is specifically designed for detecting reflected objects. This benchmark provides a well-annotated dataset and robust evaluation metrics to facilitate research in this challenging area. The ROD benchmark fills a crucial gap in current object detection methods by focusing on reflected objects. It aims to provide researchers with a valuable resource to develop and test algorithms that handle the complexities of reflected objects. ROD dataset comprises a diverse set of 10 classes and 6 reflective surfaces of generic objects, totaling 23,520 images annotated with axis-aligned bounding boxes, category labels, and object nature (real or reflected). Sample images from the ROD dataset are illustrated in Fig. 2. In addition, we developed five baseline detectors based on five state-of-the-art algorithms, namely RO-YOLOv8, RO-YOLOv10, RO-RTMDet, RO-YOLOX, and RO-PPYOLOE. These baselines serve to evaluate detectors' performance and provide benchmarks for future research on ROD dataset. In summary, our contributions include:

- We make the first attempt to explore detecting reflected objects, a previously underexplored area in object detection. By focusing on this unique challenge, we hope to inspire further research and innovation in the detecting reflected objects.

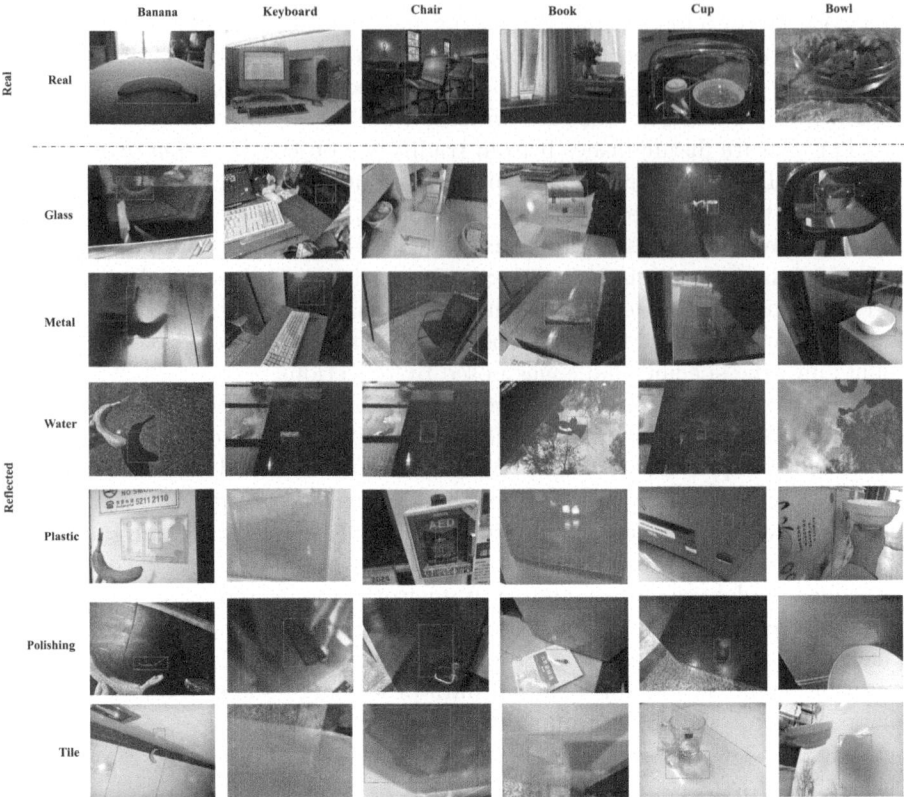

Fig. 2. Samples from six categories (i.e., 'banana', 'keyboard', 'chair', 'book', 'cup', and 'bowl', from left to right) and their corresponding natures (i.e., 'real' and 'reflected' from top to bottom) in the ROD dataset. Note that the objects have been marked with green bounding boxes. (Color figure online)

- We introduce ROD dataset, the first benchmark dedicated to detecting reflected objects, consists of 10 classes and 6 reflective surfaces of generic objects, with 23,520 images annotated with bounding boxes, object categories, and the characteristics of the objects. This dataset will enable detailed analysis and evaluation of algorithms developed for detecting reflected objects.
- To support further research on ROD dataset, we develop five baseline detectors based on state-of-the-art models: RO-YOLOv8, RO-YOLOv10, RO-RTMDet, RO-YOLOX, and RO-PPYOLOE. These baseline models will provide initial performance metrics and serve as reference points for future studies.

2   Related Work

2.1   Object Detection Algorithms

Object detection has been a critical area of research in computer vision, significantly advancing over the past few decades. Traditional object detection methods relied heavily on handcrafted features and shallow learning techniques. The advent of deep learning has revolutionized this field, leading to the development of more robust and accurate algorithms. Modern object detection methods are categorized into two types: two-stage detectors and one-stage detectors. Two-stage detectors, such as R-CNN [16], Fast R-CNN [15], Faster R-CNN [39], and Mask R-CNN [18], initially generate region proposals and then refine them through classification and bounding box regression, achieving high precision and efficiency. Variants like Cascade R-CNN [5] further enhance detection performance through multi-stage detection and regression. One-stage detectors, including SSD [30], YOLO, RetinaNet [26], and EfficientDet [43], predict object locations and categories in a single step, providing faster performance suitable for real-time applications. The YOLO series has evolved to YOLOv8 [44] and YOLOv10 [45], further optimizing speed and accuracy.

Despite these advancements, identifying objects reflected in surfaces like mirrors and glass remains a particularly challenging and underexplored problem. Reflections can severely distort object appearance, introducing ambiguous visual cues that complicate the detection process. Most current object detection algorithms are not designed to distinguish between real objects and their reflections, which can lead to frequent misclassifications. These algorithms often struggle to differentiate between an actual object and its mirror image, resulting in false positives and reduced accuracy, especially in environments rich in reflective surfaces, such as bathrooms, retail stores, or even city streets with glass-fronted buildings. Our work aims to address this gap by introducing a benchmark and developing specialized approaches for reflected object detection.

2.2   Object Detection Benchmarks

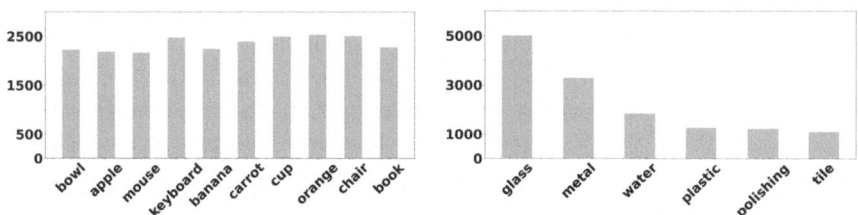

(a) Number of images per category in ROD dataset.

(b) Number of images per reflected in ROD dataset.

Fig. 3. Statistics for each object category and reflection nature in the dataset.

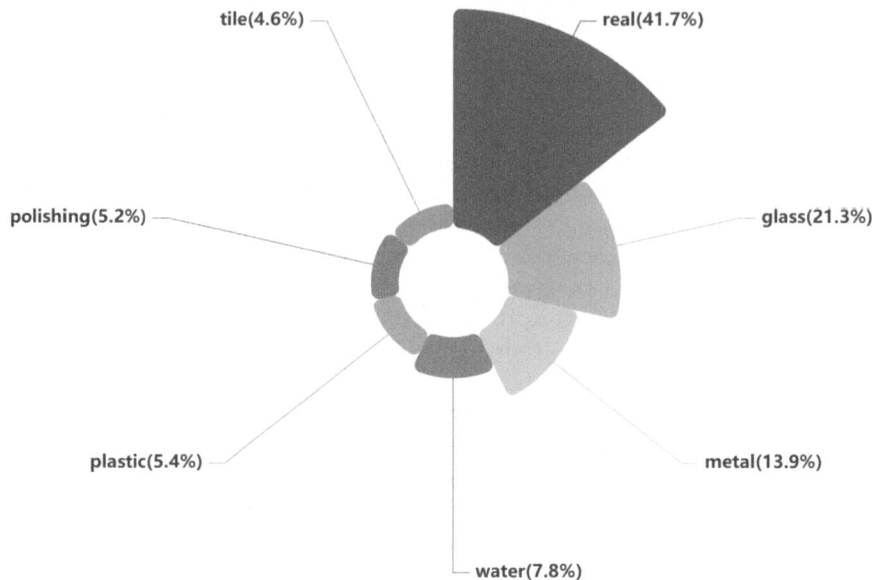

Fig. 4. Number of images containing real or reflected objects in the ROD dataset.

Object detection benchmarks play a crucial role in the development and evaluation of detection algorithms by providing standardized datasets and evaluation metrics that facilitate consistent and fair comparisons among different approaches. Over the years, several prominent benchmarks have emerged, each contributing uniquely to the field, such as PASCAL VOC [11], MS COCO [27], and ImageNet [20]. These benchmarks provide large-scale images and standardized evaluation metrics. For instance, PASCAL VOC comprises 20 categories with 11,530 images and 27,450 annotated bounding boxes. ImageNet covers 200 categories with approximately 500,000 annotated bounding boxes. MS COCO includes 91 categories, over 300,000 images, and 2.5 million annotated instances. These datasets have been instrumental in pushing the boundaries of object detection research, promoting the development of more accurate and robust models. In addition to these established benchmarks, several domain-specific benchmarks have emerged to address particular challenges in object detection. For instance, KITTI [14] focuses on autonomous driving scenarios, providing annotated data for detecting objects such as cars, pedestrians, and cyclists in street scenes. UAVDT (UAV Detection and Tracking) [10] provides benchmarks for aerial object detection, emphasizing challenges unique to unmanned aerial vehicle (UAV) imagery, such as varying altitudes and viewpoints.

Despite significant advancements in object detection, no public benchmark specifically targets reflected object detection. This gap hinders the development and evaluation of algorithms for handling reflections. Reflective surfaces are common in real-world scenarios such as surveillance, autonomous driving, and smart homes. Accurate detection of reflected objects is crucial for enhancing performance and safety in these applications. This paper addresses this gap by introducing a benchmark specifically tailored for reflected object detection. This benchmark includes a variety of scenes with reflective surfaces, such as mirrors, windows, and glossy floors, providing a diverse set of scenarios where reflections are prominent. The benchmark not only serves as a tool for evaluating the performance of detection algorithms in these challenging conditions but also encourages the development of more sophisticated methods capable of distinguishing between real objects and their reflections.

2.3 Dealing With Mirrors and Reflections in Vision

Mirrors or other reflective surfaces are common in natural images, and can cause false positive results in the tasks of detection, segmentation, counting, robotic navigation, scene reconstruction, and etc. [4,8,19,25,28,35]. Reflection detection focuses on identifying regions in an image that contain reflections. When we take a picture through glass windows, the photographs are often degraded by undesired reflections. One of the primary approaches to dealing with reflections involves removing or suppressing the reflections in images. For instance, Abiko et al. employed generative adversarial networks (GANs) to enhance the quality of reflection removal, yielding more natural and clear images [1]. Arvanitopoulos et al. propose a single image reflection suppression method based on a Laplacian data fidelity and an l-zero gradient sparsity regularization term [3]. Particularly, mirror surface detection aims to identify and segment mirror surfaces within a scene. For instance, Yang et al. proposed to address the mirror segmentation problem with a computational approach [49]. Since then, numerous methods have been developed to address mirror detection and segmentation [19,25,28,35]. As these methods have progressed, several specialized datasets have been created to assess their performance. Notably, both the MSD and Progressive Mirror Detection datasets share the goal of advancing mirror detection by providing images and annotations for training and evaluation. However, the MSD dataset [49] is smaller in scale and focuses primarily on indoor scenes, offering limited scene diversity. In contrast, the Progressive Mirror Detection dataset [25] is larger, encompassing both indoor and outdoor scenes with more diverse data and higher-quality annotations. These advancements in datasets, alongside the progression of algorithms, continue to drive innovation in dealing with mirrors and reflections.

Despite extensive research efforts dedicated to dealing with mirrors and reflections in vision, most of these works focus primarily on identifying, localizing, segmenting, and suppressing reflective regions in images. In this work, we make the first attempt to differentiate reflected objects from real ones, a critical capability for various applications, including surveillance, autonomous driving, service robots, and smart homes.

3   Benchmark for Reflected Object Detection

We construct a dedicated dataset for Reflected Object Detection (ROD) dataset, which is a dataset that contains labels of both class and object nature, with prediction bounding-box labeled for each image.

3.1   Image Collection

For image collection, We selected 10 objects with 6 common reflective surfaces in daily life, guided by the selection principles of PASCAL VOC [12] and COCO [27]. The chosen objects for ROD dataset are bowl, apple, mouse, keyboard, banana, carrot, cup, orange, chair, and book, all of which are categories included in the COCO dataset. However, gathering varied images of these objects or their reflected ones in different scenes can be challenging. To address this, we initially sourced images using web crawlers and online repositories that focus on real-world scenarios with reflective surfaces. Additionally, we conducted field photography sessions in various environments such as homes, offices, and public spaces to capture images that include mirrors and other reflective surfaces. To ensure that the dataset was representative of real-world conditions, we made sure to capture images under various lighting conditions and from different angles. The final collection comprises 23,520 images, encompassing 10 distinct objects (bowl, apple, mouse, keyboard, banana, carrot, cup, orange, chair, and book) and 2 attributes that indicate the nature of the objects (i.e., real or reflected). These objects are represented across 6 types of reflective surfaces (i.e., glass, metal, water, plastic, and tile). The shooting location is Guilin, Nanjing and Bengbu City of China. The vivo x100 pro is used to screen the pictures while ensuring the natural and clear objects in the pictures. The resolution will be reduced to 1600×1200 and 1200×900 in the later stage, and the coding method is H.265. Figure 2 presents some sample images from ROD dataset, demonstrating that each object category is captured in multiple scenes.

3.2   Annotation

This section provides a detailed introduction to the image annotation process, covering three aspects: category, bounding box, and the nature of the object, as follows:

– **Category:** one of: bowl, apple, mouse, keyboard, banana, carrot, cup, orange, chair, and book.
– **Bounding box:** an axis-aligned bounding box that encloses the visible part of the object in the image.
– **Nature of the object:** a real or reflected object.

We follow three steps, i.e., manual annotation, visual inspection, and box refinement, to complete the annotation of images, guided by the annotation guidelines proposed in [12,27]. Specifically, all the images are first annotated by

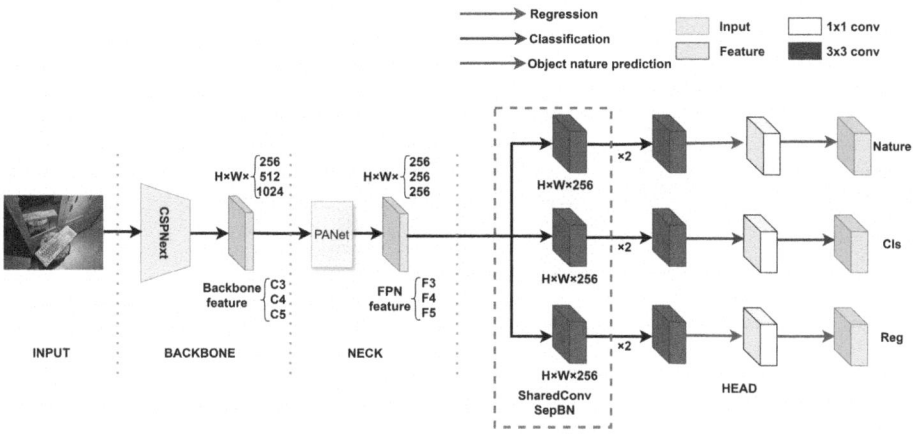

Fig. 5. The network structure of the RO-RTMDet detector, inherited from RTMDet, is different from the addition of an additional branch head for the object nature.

an expert, i.e., a student engaged in object detection, during the initial stage. Manual annotation can lead to occasional errors or inconsistencies, prompting the verification team to carefully review the annotated files in the second step. Annotation errors identified by the validation team in the third stage will be sent back to the initial annotation stage for refinement. By employing this three-stage strategy, the dataset ensures its contained objects have high-quality annotation. We imported all the images into the label-studio tool and annotated each image carefully, exported them into COCO and VOC data set formats, and provided three formats of annotated files: json, xml and excel. Figure 2 displays five examples of box annotations from ROD dataset.

3.3   Dataset Statistics

The statistics of the ROD dataset are summarized in Fig. 3. Figure 3 (a) presents a histogram showing the number of images in the dataset for each category. Observations indicate that the number of objects in each category is relatively balanced, with the 'chair' category being the most prevalent, comprising 2,512 images. Figure 3 (b) presents a histogram that illustrates the dataset is dominated by the 'glass' category, which contains 5,005 images. The 'metal' category follows with 3,278 images, while 'water' has 1,839. The 'plastic', 'polishing', and 'tile' categories contain 1,264, 1,226, and 1,093 images, respectively. This distribution underscores the prominence of 'glass' and 'metal' as the most frequent reflective surfaces. The glass and metal materials are smooth, the reflection is more obvious, and the detailed texture of the reflected object is more, while the reflective surface such as the polishing of the plastic box is more fuzzy, the surface is more rough, and the detailed characteristics of the reflective surface are less.

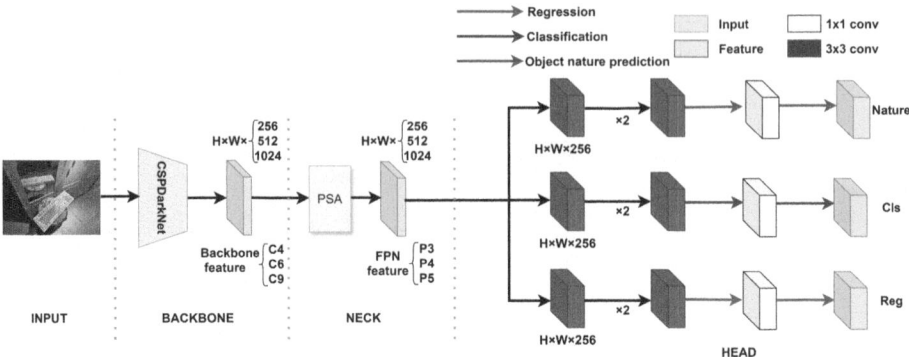

Fig. 6. The network structure of the RO-YOLOv8 detector is inherited from YOLOv8, except for the addition of an additional reflected nature branch head.

Figure 4 further illustrates the number of images containing real or reflected objects. This detailed breakdown highlights the distribution and prevalence of each object category within the dataset, offering insights into its composition and the representation of reflections. The dataset contains 9,815 real images and 13,705 images of reflected objects. A total of 15,112 images were captured using the Vivo X100 Pro camera, which includes 6,695 images at a resolution of 1600×1200 and 8,417 images at a resolution of 1200×900. Additionally, 8,407 images were sourced from open-source image sites, web crawlers, and public image portfolios. To facilitate training and evaluation, the ROD dataset is divided into two primary subsets: the training set and the test set, with a ratio of 7:3.

4   Baseline Detectors for Detecting Reflected Objects

We develop five baseline detectors based on five state-of-the-art object detection algorithms, i.e., RTMDet [32], YOLOv10 [45], YOLOv8 [44], YOLOX [13], and PPYOLOE [48], to facilitate the development of detecting reflected objects. For each model, we add an additional head or branch to predict the nature of the objects without altering the overall framework. The resulting baseline detectors are named RO-RTMDet, RO-YOLOv10, RO-YOLOv8, RO-YOLOX, and RO-PPYOLOE, respectively. Given space constraints and the fact that YOLOv10, YOLOv8, YOLOX, and PPYOLOE are all YOLO variants, we detail only RO-RTMDet, YOLOv8 and RO-YOLOv10 in the following sections. The extension to YOLOX and PPYOLOE is straightforward and will not be elaborated upon here (Fig. 6).

4.1   RO-RTMDet

The network architecture of the proposed RO-RTMDet is shown in Fig. 5. CSP-Net [46] serves as the backbone, generating output features C3, C4, and C5 with

128, 256, and 512 channels, respectively. These features are fused into CSP-PAFPN [32], the neck of RO-RTMDet, which employs the same block as the backbone. The classification head and the regression head are two parallel components used for classification and regression, respectively, forming the head of the original RTMDet. Building upon the original RTMDet model, we introduce a new classification head to predict the nature of objects (i.e., real or reflected). During RO-RTMDet training, the overall loss of the model is defined as follows:

$$L = L_{cls} + L_{reg} + \lambda L_{nat}, \tag{1}$$

where L_{cls}, L_{reg}, and L_{nat} represent the losses for classification, regression, and object nature prediction, respectively. λ is a constant that weights the loss for the reflected objects prediction head. Below are their specific definitions:

$$L_{cls} = \frac{1}{N_{pos}} \sum_{n=1}^{N_{pos}} \sum_{cls \in classes} -|y_n^{cls} - p_n^{cls}|^\beta$$
$$((1 - y_n^{cls})log(1 - p_n^{cls}) + y_n^{cls}log(p_n^{cls})),$$

$$L_{reg} = \frac{1}{N_{pos}} \sum_{n=1}^{N_{pos}} \left[1 - (\text{IOU}(b_n^t, b_n^p) - \frac{|C - b_n^t \bigcup b_n^p|}{|C|}) \right], \tag{2}$$

$$L_{nat} = \frac{1}{N_{pos}} \sum_{n=1}^{N_{pos}} \sum_{nat \in natures} -|y_n^{nat} - p_n^{nat}|^\beta$$
$$((1 - y_n^{nat})log(1 - p_n^{nat}) + y_n^{nat}log(p_n^{nat})),$$

where y_n^{cls} and y_n^{nat} are the labeled value of classification and the object nature, p_n^{cls} and p_n^{nat} are the corresponding predictions, N_{pos} is the number of positive anchor, β is the hyperparameter for the dynamic scale factor, which is set to 2, b_n^t and b_n^p represent the ground truth bounding boxes and the prediction, respectively; IOU and C are the IOU loss function and the smallest enclosing convex box of these two bounding boxes. We utilize the same training pipeline as RTMDet for training RO-RTMDet.

4.2   RO-YOLOv10

The network architecture of the proposed RO-YOLOv10 detector is shown in Fig. 7. RO-YOLOv10 uses a modified CSPDarknet as backbone. It replaces the C2f module used in YOLOv8 [44] with a compact inverted block (CIB) module and introduces an efficient partial self-attention (PSA) module [45]. These features are input into the neck to enhance feature representation, which is made up of the PAN (Path Aggregation Network). The original YOLOv10 model has two types of heads: (1) a one-to-many (o2m) head for regression and classification tasks, and (2) a one-to-one (o2o) head for precise localization. In RO-YOLOv10, we add object nature prediction branch into both of these two heads. During RO-YOLOv10 training, the overall loss of the model is defined as follows:

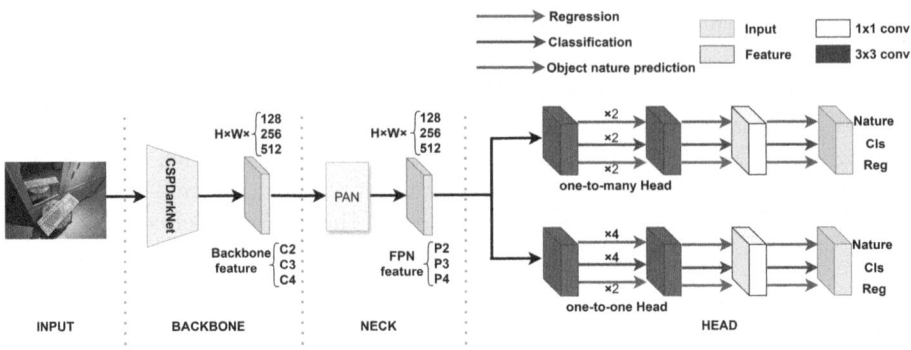

Fig. 7. The network structure of the RO-YOLOv10 detector is inherited from YOLOv10, except for the addition of an additional reflected nature branch head.

$$L = L_{o2m-head} + L_{o2o-head},$$
$$L_{o2m-head} = L_{o2m-cls} + \lambda L_{o2m-nat} + L_{o2m-reg} + L_{o2m-dfl}, \qquad (3)$$
$$L_{o2o-head} = L_{o2o-cls} + \lambda L_{o2o-nat} + L_{o2o-reg} + L_{o2o-dfl}.$$

In the o2m head, $L_{o2m-cls}$ and $L_{o2m-nat}$ represent the losses for classification and object nature prediction, respectively, while L_{reg} and L_{dfl} indicate the Complete Intersection over Union (CIoU) Loss [52] and the Distribution Focal loss (DFL) [22]. Similarly, each loss function in the o2o head carries the same meaning as in the the o2m head. λ is a constant that weights the loss for the object nature prediction branch. Below, the L_{cls} and L_{nat} in the o2m head are used as examples to provide their specific definitions. The specific definition of L_{reg} and L_{dfl} are omitted, as it is too intricate to elaborate on here and may divert from the main focus of our discussion. For a comprehensive understanding of L_{reg} and L_{dfl}, we recommend referring to the detailed explanations provided in the original documentation by Zheng et al. [52] and Li et al. [22].

$$L_{cls} = \frac{1}{N_{pos}} \sum_{n=1}^{N_{pos}} \sum_{cls \in classes} y_n^{cls} log(p_n^{cls}) + (1 - y_n^{cls}) log(1 - p_n^{cls}),$$
$$(4)$$
$$L_{nat} = \frac{1}{N_{pos}} \sum_{n=1}^{N_{pos}} \sum_{nat \in natures} y_n^{nat} log(p_n^{nat}) + (1 - y_n^{nat}) log(1 - p_n^{nat}),$$

where y_n^{cls} and y_n^{nat} are the labeled value of classification and the object nature, p_n^{cls} and p_n^{nat} are the corresponding predictions, N_{pos} is the number of positive anchor. We utilize the same training pipeline as YOLOv10 for training RO-YOLOv10.

Table 1. The evaluation results of the five proposed baseline detectors, i.e., RO-YOLOv8, RO-YOLOv10, RO-RTMDet, RO-YOLOX, and RO-PPYOLOE, on the ROD dataset. It is important to note that APc, APn, and APcn represent the precision metrics for predicting the object's category, the object's nature, and the combination of both.

Method	{APc, APn, APcn}@0.5	{APc, APn, APcn}@0.75	{mAPc, mAPn, mAPcn}
RO-YOLOv8	(0.795,0.729,**0.571**)	(0.741,0.684,0.541)	(**0.683**,0.637,**0.522**)
RO-YOLOv10	(**0.812**,**0.790**,0.570)	(**0.744**,**0.731**,**0.542**)	(0.679,**0.677**,0.515)
RO-RTMDet	(0.720,0.474,0.537)	(0.656,0.438,0.511)	(0.601,0.406,0.480)
RO-YOLOX	(0.754,0.735,0.490)	(0.654,0.638,0.445)	(0.574,0.558,0.378)
RO-PPYOLOE	(0.713,0.565,0.538)	(0.649,0.514,0.512)	(0.598,0.476,0.481)

5 Evaluation

5.1 Evaluation Metrics

In the experiment, the proposed baseline detectors are evaluated for the performance by using two common metrics, i.e., average precision (AP) and mean average precision (mAP). IOU (Intersection over Union) measures the overlap between the predicted bounding box (bbox) and the ground truth bbox. In object detection tasks, a complete prediction comprises two main components: first, the model must identify specific objects within a given image, and second, it needs to accurately determine their respective locations. Specifically, precision is the proportion of objects predicted by the model that match the real objects, whereas recall measures the proportion of real objects detected by the model. These two measures are combined in mAP, which highlights the significance of properly balancing each during the evaluation process.

Guided by the COCO evaluation [27], three IoU thresholds are used: fixed thresholds at 0.5 and 0.75 and a range threshold from 0.5 to 0.95 with a step size of 0.05. The corresponding average precisions (APs) are evaluated under these IoU thresholds, denoted as AP@0.5, AP@0.75, and AP@[.50:.05:.95], respectively. In the experiment, COCO mAP is employed to evaluate the performance of detectors in detecting reflected objects. Following [17,23,37,47,53], we use APc, APn, and APcn to represent the precision metrics for predicting the object's category, the object's nature, and their combination, respectively. Additionally, an extra prefix 'm' is added to represent mean AP, i.e., mAP.

APcn represents an evaluation metric that integrates both category and nature characteristics. The output of a standard object detection task consists of three components: bounding box (bbox), identifier (id), and confidence scores. The fusion strategy for these components is as follows:

- **Bounding-box:** Reusing bounding boxes for both category and nature attributes.
- **ID:** Since the model must infer both class and reflected nature, two decoupled heads, for cls and nature, are employed. To ensure consistency, a unified encoding method is required. In the dataset annotation, we assigned

the category to the least significant bit and the reflected nature to the next significant bit. Given that there are 10 categories in the ROD dataset, our encoding should be in decimal format. Consequently, the merged identifier can be expressed as $ID_c + 10ID_n$. For instance, if the identified category is 'cup', with ID_c marked as 6, and it is in the reflected nature with ID_n marked as 1, the fused ID_{cn} would be calculated as $6+10\text{x}1=16$. This indicates that the fused ID_{cn} will only yield the correct value if both the category and reflected nature identifiers are accurate.

– **Scores:** Calculate the geometric mean of the APc and APn scores.

$$
\begin{aligned}
Bbox_{cn} &= Bbox_c = Bbox_n, \\
ID_{cn} &= ID_c + 10ID_n, \\
Scores_{cn} &= \sqrt{Scores_c \times Scores_n}.
\end{aligned}
\tag{5}
$$

Since the value of ID_{cn} must satisfy the condition that both the category and reflected nature are correct simultaneously, the value of APcn should be lower than that of APc and APn. This relationship is also demonstrated in the subsequent experiments.

5.2   Evaluation Results

Overall Performance. We conducted a comprehensive evaluation of the five baseline detectors proposed in this paper—RO-YOLOv8, RO-YOLOv10, RO-RTMDet, RO-YOLOX, and RO-PPYOLOE—on the ROD dataset. All models were trained on Nvidia Tesla P40 GPUs with a batch size of 32 over 300 epochs, ensuring that each model achieved convergence. For instance, RO-PPYOLOE converges at the 30th epoch, while RO-YOLOv10 converges at the 90th epoch. This trend indicates that the average precision (AP) values for each model gradually increase, followed by a slow decline after reaching the convergence epoch, ultimately attaining optimal performance at the point of convergence. Table 1 presents the evaluation results using the three accuracy metrics defined in Sect. 5.1, namely APc, APn, and APcn. It can be seen that RO-YOLOv10 is the best-performing detector, significantly outperforming the other detectors in all AP metrics.

Additionally, the evaluation results of the five baseline detectors on target categories show that the AP under fixed IoU thresholds (especially 0.5 and 0.75 IoU) and the average AP for categories are both lower than those for target attributes. For all these detectors, the difference between category AP and attribute AP exceeds 2%. Notably, the RO-YOLOX detector demonstrates the largest gap, reaching 20%. This indicates that in the ROD dataset, identifying and locating the objects themselves is more challenging than recognizing their attributes.

It is also worth noting that when traditional object detection is combined with target attribute prediction to form a compound task, known as reflective object detection, the performance of the detectors is lower than when handling each task individually. This suggests that the reflective object detection task proposed in this paper is more challenging than traditional object detection. This performance drop highlights the importance of developing more specialized algorithms and training strategies to better address the complexity of this compound task.

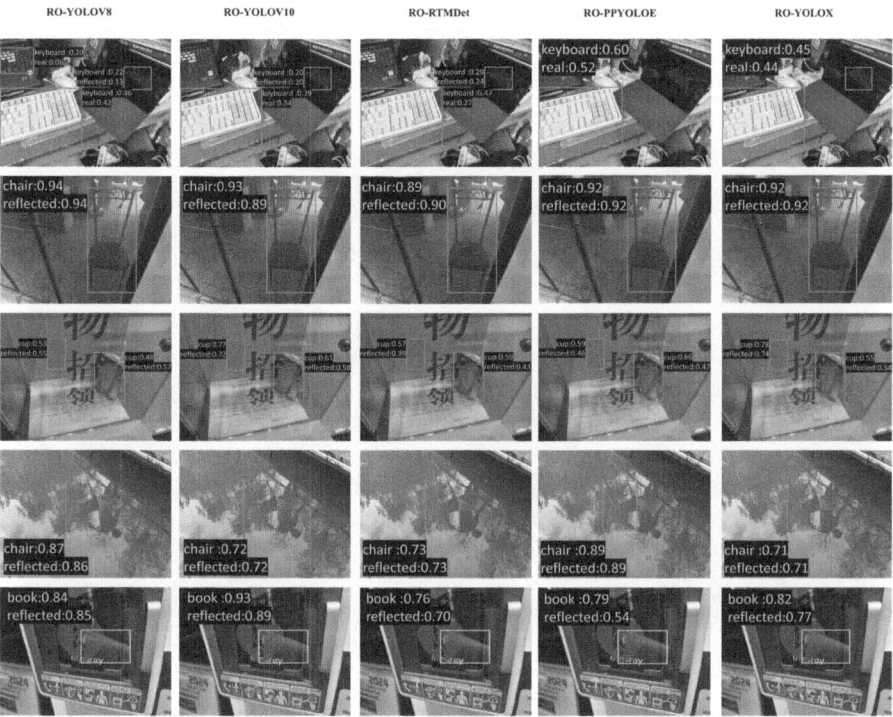

Fig. 8. A qualitative comparison of the five detectors on 5 samples from the keyboard, chair, cup, and the book category, respectively. Note that all these detectors successfully detect the object but fail to detect the keyboard correctly. The predicted bounding box, object category, object nature, and the corresponding scores have been marked in the images.

Performance on per Category. To get a deeper analysis and understanding of the performance in detecting the nature of objects using our proposed baseline detectors, we further conduct performance evaluations on each category. Table 2 presents the mAP_{cn} of the five detectors evaluated on ROD dataset.

As observed, these five detectors perform best on the chair category, while they perform worst on the carrot category. For the chair category, the mAP_{cn} values all exceed 90%, except for the RO-YOLOX detector. For the banana category, the mAP_{cn} values are all below 80%, as for the carrot category with RO-RTMDet, and RO-PPYOLOE even scoring below 50%. This disparity can be explained by the fact that images typically contain only one chair object,

Table 2. Comparison of the mAP_{cn} of the five baseline detectors on the ROD dataset. It is important to note that mAP_{cn} is the mAP for prediction of the composite of the object's category and its nature.

	bowl	apple	mouse	keyboard	banana	carrot	cup	orange	chair	book
mAP_{cn}(RO-YOLOv8)	**0.766**	0.672	0.874	0.883	**0.794**	0.673	0.847	0.721	**0.924**	0.792
mAP_{cn}(RO-YOLOv10)	0.764	**0.731**	0.849	0.858	**0.794**	0.811	**0.881**	0.782	0.915	**0.801**
mAP_{cn}(RO-RTMDet)	0.755	0.637	0.891	**0.889**	0.770	0.457	0.821	0.499	0.922	0.557
mAP_{cn}(RO-YOLOX)	0.713	0.556	0.797	0.838	0.729	0.742	0.787	0.763	0.875	0.744
mAP_{cn}(RO-PPYOLOE)	0.755	0.608	0.885	0.879	0.768	0.463	0.832	0.489	0.923	0.827

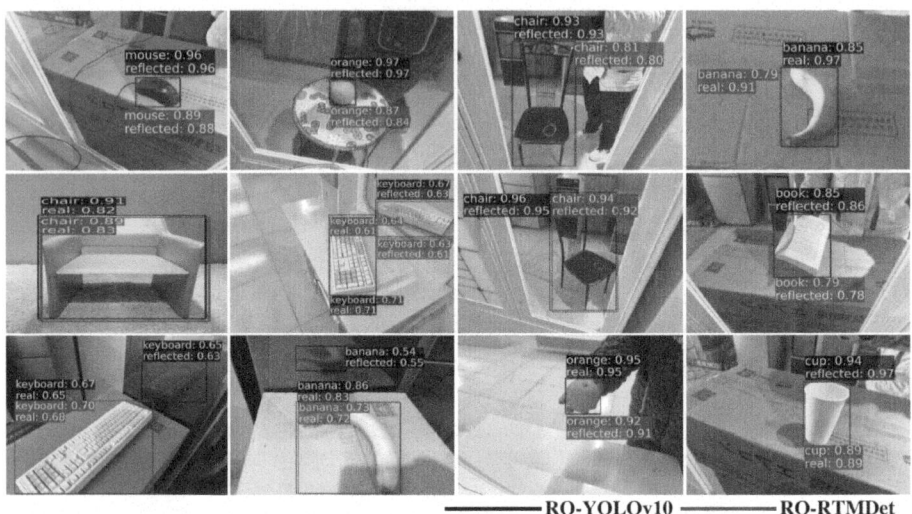

─────── **RO-YOLOv10** ─────── **RO-RTMDet**

Fig. 9. A qualitative evaluation was conducted on 12 samples from ROD dataset. The first two rows display examples accurately predicting the nature of objects using RO-YOLOv10 and RO-RTMDet detectors, while the last row shows error detection results generated by these two detectors. Note that the predicted bounding box, object category, object nature, and the corresponding scores have been marked in the images.

Table 3. The ablation study of the RO-YOLOv10 model is conducted on ROD dataset using various weighting coefficients.

λ	{APc, APn, APcn}@0.5	{APc, APn, APcn}@0.75	{mAPc, mAPn, mAPcn}
0.2	(**0.821**, 0.778, 0.565)	(**0.760**, 0.729, 0.536)	(**0.694**, 0.678, 0.515)
0.4	(0.815, 0.786, 0.569)	(0.754, 0.732, 0.537)	(0.688, 0.680, 0.518)
0.6	(0.819, **0.796**, 0.579)	(0.754, **0.742**, 0.548)	(0.689, **0.692**, 0.525)
0.8	(0.819, 0.791, **0.584**)	(0.754, 0.739, **0.554**)	(0.690, 0.687, **0.528**)
1.0	(0.812, 0.790, 0.570)	(0.744, 0.731, 0.541)	(0.679, 0.677, 0.515)
1.2	(0.793, 0.776, 0.552)	(0.729, 0.720, 0.519)	(0.666, 0.666, 0.493)
1.4	(0.808, 0.782, 0.559)	(0.744, 0.723, 0.529)	(0.678, 0.670, 0.501)
1.6	(0.800, 0.774, 0.556)	(0.737, 0.715, 0.525)	(0.670, 0.659, 0.498)
1.8	(0.797, 0.774, 0.545)	(0.732, 0.715, 0.516)	(0.665, 0.660, 0.487)
2.0	(0.791, 0.770, 0.549)	(0.725, 0.714, 0.517)	(0.662, 0.658, 0.489)

often presented at a standard size. In contrast, images frequently contain a large number of carrot objects, leading to crowding and occlusion. Please refer to Fig. 8 for a visual comparison of examples from these five categories. The first row shows qualitative results for the keyboard category from the five detectors. The challenges of detecting keyboards on the screen are exacerbated by their size and the reflective properties of the screen itself. Compared to a mirror, the screen has a lower reflectance coefficient, which complicates the recognition of keyboards in reflections. This reduced reflectance hampers detectors such as RO-YOLOX and RO-PPYOLOE in accurately identifying the reflective features of keyboards. Additionally, the similar color and appearance between carrots and oranges further confuse detectors like RO-PPYOLOE, leading to misclassification in object categorization. In contrast, these detectors excel in detecting chairs due to the high reflectance of mirrors and the absence of cluttered backgrounds. Furthermore, the experimental results in Table 2 also indicate that the performance of the same detector varies across different categories. This disparity may be attributed to the inherent differences in object characteristics, such as size, shape, texture, and background environment in the images, as well as the imbalance in category distribution. These results underscore the importance of considering object-specific challenges when detecting reflective objects.

Qualitative Evaluation. Given the potential for overwhelming viewers with too many methods in a single image, Fig. 9 presents qualitative detection results from just the RO-YOLOv10 and RO-RTMDet detectors. The first two rows display eight correctly predicted samples, while the third row shows examples where the detectors inaccurately predicted the object's nature. In these cases, reflected objects might blend into low-light backgrounds or lack distinct texture features (i.e., the first and second samples), or their mirrored background may resemble the real background (i.e., the third and fourth samples), leading to missed or inaccurate detections. This evaluation highlights that in complex scenes, the detectors are prone to struggle with accurately identifying the nature of objects.

In view of the shortcomings of the model itself in processing complex reflective surface information, more powerful feature extraction modules, such as the module based on attention mechanism, can be considered to make the model more focused on the key features of the reflected object and ignore the interference information brought by the reflected surface. For object occlusion, we can learn from some advanced algorithms in the field of object detection, such as multi-view information fusion or occlusion reasoning mechanism based on deep learning, to improve the detection performance of the model in occlusion scenes. At the same time, how to improve the training strategy of the model is discussed, such as adding more adversarial training samples, simulating various complex reflection and occlusion scenes, so that the model can learn more robust feature representation.

5.3 Ablation Study

Since RO-YOLOv10 obtained the best mAP value in the comparison experiment and the model converged at the 90th epoch, the ablation experiment would keep the batch size and other hyperparameters consistent and take the 90th epoch in each experiment. We train the RO-YOLOv10 model on ROD dataset using different weighting coefficients, i.e., λ in Eq. (3), which varies from 0.2 to 2.0 in steps of 0.2, in order to study the impact of the coefficient for weighting the loss of predicting the nature of objects. This experiment aims to determine how different weightings influence the model's ability to balance the two tasks: detecting the objects and predicting their nature. By adjusting λ, we can observe how the model prioritizes the nature prediction task relative to the conventional object detection task. Table 3 presents the experimental results for the mAP and the AP at fixed IoUs (0.5 and 0.75). RO-YOLOv10 achieves some of the best AP values when λ is set to 0.6 or 0.8. Although APc reaches its maximum value at λ = 0.2, its corresponding APcn is significantly low, resulting in poor performance. A notable discrepancy between APc and APn is evident.

Overall, as λ varies from 0.2 to 1.6, APc initially increases before decreasing, while APn consistently rises, reaching optimal values at 0.6 and 0.8, respectively. A compromise is achieved at λ =0.8, which serves as the default setting, where APcn attains its highest value. Specifically, the maximum mAPc of 0.694 occurs at λ = 0.2, the maximum mAPn of 0.692 occurs at λ = 0.6, and the maximum mAPcn of 0.528 occurs at λ = 0.8. The results suggest that there may be a counteracting impact between object localization and prediction of objects' nature when these two tasks are done concurrently as a composite task. More effective methods for mitigating this counteracting effect are needed.

6   Conclusions

In this paper, we investigated the underexplored challenge of reflective object detection and introduced the Reflective Object Detection (ROD) dataset, an extensive benchmark specifically designed for this task. ROD dataset includes 10 categories, 6 reflective surfaces and 23,520 images of real or reflected objects in various backgrounds, accompanied by standard annotations of bounding boxes and the nature of the objects (real or reflected), distinguishing it from traditional object detection benchmarks. In addition to introducing ROD dataset, we adapted five state-of-the-art object detection models to this challenging task and presented baseline results. The experimental findings reveal the limitations of current methods when applied to reflected object detection, underscoring the necessity for specialized approaches. By releasing ROD dataset, we aim to foster and advance future research in detecting reflected objects. This dataset provides a valuable resource for developing and evaluating new methods, ultimately contributing to improved performance in applications such as surveillance, autonomous driving, service robots, smart homes, and medical imaging. While the current ROD dataset encompasses diverse reflective surfaces and object categories, it lacks scene complexity and environmental variety. Baseline models exhibit suboptimal performance in handling intricate reflections. Future research should prioritize dataset expansion through multi-environment image collection under varying illumination, coupled with advanced deep learning frameworks integrating reflection-aware mechanisms with complementary techniques (e.g., semantic segmentation, object tracking) to address complex vision tasks.

References

1. Abiko, R., Ikehara, M.: Single image reflection removal based on GAN with gradient constraint. IEEE Access **7**, 148790–148799 (2019). https://api.semanticscholar. org/CorpusID:204820165
2. Amjoud, A.B., Amrouch, M.: Object detection using deep learning, CNNs and vision transformers: a review. IEEE Access **11**, 35479–35516 (2023). https://api. semanticscholar.org/CorpusID:258077107
3. Arvanitopoulos, N., Achanta, R., Süsstrunk, S.: Single image reflection suppression. In: 2017 IEEE Conference on Computer Vision and Pattern Recognition (CVPR), pp. 1752–1760 (2017). https://api.semanticscholar.org/CorpusID:13095034
4. Bajcsy, R., Lee, S.W., Leonardis, A.: Detection of diffuse and specular interface reflections and inter-reflections by color image segmentation. Int. J. Comput. Vis. **17**, 241–272 (1996). https://api.semanticscholar.org/CorpusID:6799933
5. Cai, Z., Vasconcelos, N.: Cascade r-CNN: delving into high quality object detection. In: Proceedings of the IEEE Conference on Computer Vision and Pattern Recognition, pp. 6154–6162 (2018)
6. Chakraborty, A., Islam, M., Shahriyar, F., Islam, S., Zaman, H.U., Hasan, M.: Smart home system: a comprehensive review. J. Electr. Comput. Eng. **2023**(1), 7616683 (2023)
7. Damodaran, D., Mozaffari, S., Alirezaee, S., Ahamed, M.J.: Experimental analysis of the behavior of mirror-like objects in lidar-based robot navigation. Appl. Sci. (2023). https://api.semanticscholar.org/CorpusID:257188940
8. DelPozo, A., Savarese, S.: Detecting specular surfaces on natural images. In: 2007 IEEE Conference on Computer Vision and Pattern Recognition, pp. 1–8 (2007). https://api.semanticscholar.org/CorpusID:16144262
9. Díaz, J., Ros, E., Mota, S., Botella, G., Cañas, A., Sabatini, S.: Optical flow for cars overtaking monitor: the rear mirror blind spot problem. Ecovision (European Research Project) (2003)
10. Du, D., et al.: The unmanned aerial vehicle benchmark: object detection and tracking. In: Proceedings of the European Conference on Computer Vision (ECCV), pp. 370–386 (2018)
11. Everingham, M., Gool, L.V., Williams, C., Winn, J., Zisserman, A.: The Pascal visual object classes (VOC) challenge (2012). http://host.robots.ox.ac.uk/pascal/ VOC/
12. Everingham, M., Van Gool, L., Williams, C.K., Winn, J., Zisserman, A.: The Pascal visual object classes (VOC) challenge. Int. J. Comput. Vis. **88**, 303–338 (2010)
13. Ge, Z., Liu, S., Wang, F., Li, Z., Sun, J.: YOLOX: exceeding YOLO series in 2021. arXiv preprint arXiv:2107.08430 (2021)
14. Geiger, A., Lenz, P., Urtasun, R.: Are we ready for autonomous driving? The Kitti vision benchmark suite. In: Conference on Computer Vision and Pattern Recognition (CVPR) (2012)
15. Girshick, R.: Fast r-CNN. In: Proceedings of the IEEE International Conference on Computer Vision, pp. 1440–1448 (2015)
16. Girshick, R., Donahue, J., Darrell, T., Malik, J.: Rich feature hierarchies for accurate object detection and semantic segmentation. In: Proceedings of the IEEE Conference on Computer Vision and Pattern Recognition, pp. 580–587 (2014)

17. Guo, Y., Chen, Y., Deng, J., Li, S., Zhou, H.: Identity-preserved human posture detection in infrared thermal images: a benchmark. Sensors **23**(1), 92 (2022)

18. He, K., Gkioxari, G., Dollár, P., Girshick, R.: Mask r-CNN. In: Proceedings of the IEEE International Conference on Computer Vision, pp. 2961–2969 (2017)

19. Ji, G.P., Fu, K., Wu, Z., Fan, D.P., Shen, J., Shao, L.: Full-duplex strategy for video object segmentation. Comput. Vis. Media **9**, 155–175 (2021). https://api.semanticscholar.org/CorpusID:236950747

20. Krizhevsky, A., Sutskever, I., Hinton, G.E.: ImageNet classification with deep convolutional neural networks. Adv. Neural Inf. Process. Syst. **25** (2012)

21. Li, D., Hagura, H., Miyabashira, T., Kawai, Y., Ono, S.: Traffic mirror detection and annotation methods from street images of open data for preventing accidents at intersections by alert. In: 2023 IEEE/CVF International Conference on Computer Vision Workshops (ICCVW), pp. 3256–3262. IEEE (2023)

22. Li, X., et al.: Generalized focal loss: learning qualified and distributed bounding boxes for dense object detection. arXiv preprint arXiv:2006.04388 (2020)

23. Li, Y., et al.: Beyond human detection: a benchmark for detecting common human posture. Sensors **23**(19), 8061 (2023)

24. Lin, J., Tan, X.Y., Lau, R.W.H.: Learning to detect mirrors from videos via dual correspondences. In: 2023 IEEE/CVF Conference on Computer Vision and Pattern Recognition (CVPR), pp. 9109–9118 (2023). https://api.semanticscholar.org/CorpusID:261081000

25. Lin, J., Wang, G., Lau, R.W.H.: Progressive mirror detection. In: 2020 IEEE/CVF Conference on Computer Vision and Pattern Recognition (CVPR), pp. 3694–3702 (2020). https://api.semanticscholar.org/CorpusID:219964489

26. Lin, T.Y., Goyal, P., Girshick, R., He, K., Dollár, P.: Focal loss for dense object detection. In: Proceedings of the IEEE International Conference on Computer Vision, pp. 2980–2988 (2017)

27. Lin, T.-Y., et al.: Microsoft COCO: common objects in context. In: Fleet, D., Pajdla, T., Schiele, B., Tuytelaars, T. (eds.) ECCV 2014. LNCS, vol. 8693, pp. 740–755. Springer, Cham (2014). https://doi.org/10.1007/978-3-319-10602-1_48

28. Liu, F., Liu, Y., Lin, J., Xu, K., Lau, R.W.H.: Multi-view dynamic reflection prior for video glass surface detection. In: AAAI Conference on Artificial Intelligence (2024). https://api.semanticscholar.org/CorpusID:268678293

29. Liu, L., et al.: Deep learning for generic object detection: a survey. Int. J. Comput. Vis. **128**, 261 – 318 (2018). https://api.semanticscholar.org/CorpusID:52177403

30. Liu, W., et al.: SSD: single shot multibox detector. In: Leibe, B., Matas, J., Sebe, N., Welling, M. (eds.) ECCV 2016. LNCS, vol. 9905, pp. 21–37. Springer, Cham (2016). https://doi.org/10.1007/978-3-319-46448-0_2

31. Lu, V.N., et al.: Service robots, customers and service employees: what can we learn from the academic literature and where are the gaps? J. Serv. Theory Pract. (2020). https://api.semanticscholar.org/CorpusID:212964611

32. Lyu, C., et al.: RTMDet: an empirical study of designing real-time object detectors. arXiv preprint arXiv:2212.07784 (2022)

33. Marikyan, D., Papagiannidis, S., Alamanos, E.: A systematic review of the smart home literature: a user perspective. Technol. Forecast. Soc. Chang. **138**, 139–154 (2019)

34. Noriaki, I., Shintaro, O., Yoshihiro, S., Kazuya, O., Grewe, R.: Collision risk prediction utilizing road safety mirrors at blind intersections. In: 27th International Technical Conference on the Enhanced Safety of Vehicles (ESV) National Highway Traffic Safety Administration, No. 23-0164 (2023)

35. Owen, D., Chang, P.L.: Detecting reflections by combining semantic and instance segmentation. arXiv preprint arXiv:1904.13273 (2019)
36. Park, D., Park, Y.H.: Identifying reflected images from object detector in indoor environment utilizing depth information. IEEE Rob. Autom. Lett. **6**, 635–642 (2021). https://api.semanticscholar.org/CorpusID:231714728
37. Qin, L., Zhou, H., Wang, Z., Deng, J., Liao, Y., Li, S.: Detection beyond what and where: a benchmark for detecting occlusion state. In: Chinese Conference on Pattern Recognition and Computer Vision (PRCV), pp. 464–476. Springer (2022)
38. Ray, B.R., Aalsma, M., Zaller, N.D., Comartin, E.B., Sightes, E.: The perpetual blind spot in public health surveillance. J. Correctional Health Care Official J. Nat. Comm. Correctional Health Care (2022)
39. Ren, S., He, K., Girshick, R., Sun, J.: Faster r-CNN: towards real-time object detection with region proposal networks. Adv. Neural Inf. Process. Syst. **28** (2015)
40. Shen, Y., Yan, W.Q.: Blind spot monitoring using deep learning. In: 2018 International Conference on Image and Vision Computing New Zealand (IVCNZ), pp. 1–5 (2018)
41. Singhal, C., Barick, S.: ECMS: energy-efficient collaborative multi-UAV surveillance system for inaccessible regions. IEEE Access **10**, 95876–95891 (2022)
42. Sovacool, B.K., Del Rio, D.: Smart home technologies in Europe: a critical review of concepts, benefits, risks and policies. Renew. Sustain. Energy Rev. **120**, 109663 (2020)
43. Tan, M., Pang, R., Le, Q.V.: EfficientDet: scalable and efficient object detection. In: Proceedings of the IEEE/CVF Conference on Computer Vision and Pattern Recognition, pp. 10781–10790 (2020)
44. Ultralytics: YOLOV8: real-time object detection and image segmentation (2023). https://github.com/ultralytics/ultralytics
45. Wang, A., et al.: YOLOV10: real-time end-to-end object detection. arXiv preprint arXiv:2405.14458 (2024)
46. Wang, C.Y., Liao, H.Y.M., Wu, Y.H., Chen, P.Y., Hsieh, J.W., Yeh, I.H.: CSPNet: a new backbone that can enhance learning capability of CNN. In: Proceedings of the IEEE/CVF Conference on Computer Vision and Pattern Recognition Workshops, pp. 390–391 (2020)
47. Wu, Y., Ye, H., Yang, Y., Wang, Z., Li, S.: Liquid content detection in transparent containers: a benchmark. Sensors **23**(15), 6656 (2023)
48. Xu, S., et al.: PP-YOLOE: an evolved version of YOLO. arXiv preprint arXiv:2203.16250 (2022)
49. Yang, X., Mei, H., Xu, K., Wei, X., Yin, B., Lau, R.W.H.: Where is my mirror? In: 2019 IEEE/CVF International Conference on Computer Vision (ICCV), pp. 8808–8817 (2019). https://api.semanticscholar.org/CorpusID:201666156
50. Zhang, C., Steinhauser, F., Hinz, G., Knoll, A.: Traffic mirror-aware POMDP behavior planning for autonomous urban driving. In: 2022 IEEE Intelligent Vehicles Symposium (IV), pp. 323–330. IEEE (2022)
51. Zhao, Z.Q., Zheng, P., tao Xu, S., Wu, X.: Object detection with deep learning: a review. IEEE Trans. Neural Netw. Learn. Syst. **30**, 3212–3232 (2018). https://api.semanticscholar.org/CorpusID:49862415
52. Zheng, Z., et al.: Enhancing geometric factors in model learning and inference for object detection and instance segmentation. IEEE Trans. Cybern. **52**, 8574–8586 (2020). https://api.semanticscholar.org/CorpusID:218538057

53. Zhou, H., Wu, Y., Li, J., Pan, L., Ye, H., Li, S.: Beyond animal detection: a benchmark for detecting animal age group. In: Fifth International Conference on Artificial Intelligence and Computer Science (AICS 2023), vol. 12803, pp. 506–515. SPIE (2023)
54. Zou, Z., Shi, Z., Guo, Y., Ye, J.: Object detection in 20 years: a survey. Proc. IEEE **111**, 257–276 (2019). https://api.semanticscholar.org/CorpusID:152282225

Consensus-Aware Balance Learning for Sexually Suggestive Video Classification

Di Zhou[1,2], Jiahui Li[1], Haiying Wang[2], Matthew Burns[2], and Meng Liu[1(✉)]

[1] Shan Dong Jian Zhu University, Jinan, China
mengliu.sd@gmail.com
[2] Ulster University, Belfast, UK
{HY.WANG,M.BURNS2}@ulster.ac.uk

Abstract. In recent years, discussions surrounding sex education have gained considerable attention, as the lack of comprehensive sex education has been linked to various societal issues. While micro-video platforms offer new opportunities for disseminating sex education content, they have also contributed to the proliferation of sexually suggestive videos. Existing video classification methods face significant challenges in this context, such as the difficulty of abstract concepts, cross-domain variation, and training bias due to class imbalance. To address these challenges, we propose a method for classifying sexually suggestive videos. Our approach introduces a consensus-aware visual encoder to assist the model in focusing on the common features of videos within the same category at both the distribution and feature levels, while effectively filtering out irrelevant visual distractions. This improves the model's ability to capture abstract and complex features. Additionally, we employ a label distribution-aware training strategy that allocates more learning capacity to tail classes, ensuring balanced learning across all categories. Experimental results on the SexTok dataset demonstrate that our method excels in classifying sexually suggestive videos, offering improved handling of abstract and imbalanced video content.

Keywords: Sexually suggestive videos · Video classification · Imbalanced learning · Consensus-aware learning

1 Introduction

In recent years, the discourse surrounding sexual education has gained significant attention as a pressing societal issue. The lack of comprehensive sex education has been linked to both psychological and physical health concerns, alongside the emergence of various social challenges. Addressing these gaps through the promotion of sexual knowledge and reducing the stigma around sexuality is critical for improving individual well-being and fostering societal progress [4].

With the advent of the digital era, micro-video platforms such as Snapchat, TikTok, and Instagram have emerged as pivotal ways of disseminating sexual

© The Author(s), under exclusive license to Springer Nature Singapore Pte Ltd. 2025
P. Didyk and J. Hou (Eds.): CVM 2025, LNCS 15663, pp. 173–191, 2025.
https://doi.org/10.1007/978-981-96-5809-1_10

(a) Abstract Concept

(b) Cross-domain Variation

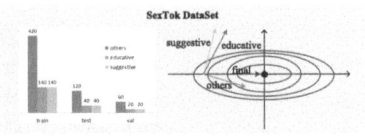

(c) Class Imbalance

Fig. 1. Examples from the SexTok dataset illustrate the challenges of sexually suggestive video classification from three key aspects: abstract concepts, cross-domain variation, and class imbalance.

education. These platforms, known for their concise content, diverse formats, and global reach, offer unique opportunities to deliver educational materials across geographical, cultural, and contextual boundaries, capturing the attention of diverse audiences worldwide [12]. However, the accessibility and open nature of these platforms, coupled with minimal oversight in content creation, have also led to the proliferation of sexually suggestive material. The lack of stringent regulations around video context, production, and presentation presents a significant challenge in controlling the spread of sexually suggestive content. However, in current video context understanding tasks, such as action recognition [5,28,37,38], video classification [25,26,33], video anomaly detection [39–41], and sentiment analysis [20,43], there is limited focus on distinguishing between suggestive and sex education content. As a result, researchers are increasingly focusing on developing robust strategies to mitigate the spread of such material while maintaining the educational potential of these platforms.

Existing video classification methods typically focus on extracting intra-modal differences to distinguish between video categories. However, these methods face substantial challenges when applied to the classification of sexually suggestive content due to several key factors:

1. **Abstract Concept**: Traditional video datasets [2,6,9,18,24], such as Kinetics-400 [3] in Fig. 1 (a), allow for straightforward classification based on clear, observable actions and scenes. In contrast, the SexTok dataset [16] presents videos where the depicted objects and scenes often lack direct semantic connections to the labels. As illustrated in Fig. 1(a), videos with distinct labels may feature creators in similar revealing clothing and similar indoor settings, devoid of distinguishing background features. This highlights a fundamental difficulty: sexually suggestive content, sex education, and general

videos often rely on abstract concepts without concrete actions or clear visual distinctions, leading to significant overlap in their visual characteristics.

2. **Cross-domain Variation:** The "others" category in the SexTok dataset encompasses a wide range of content, including daily activities, virtual effects, and animal behavior. As illustrated in Fig. 1(b), this category exhibits significant visual diversity, which makes it challenging to extract consistent and discriminative features. The broad scope of content within this category complicates the classification process by increasing the variability of features that the model must handle, thereby making accurate categorization more difficult.

3. **Class Imbalance:** The number of general videos significantly outweighs that of sexually suggestive and sex education videos, leading to class imbalance during training, as illustrated in Fig. 1(c). This imbalance causes the model to overfit on the common categories, while underrepresenting rare categories, which hinders the model's ability to capture distinguishing features of minority classes. As a result, classification accuracy and generalization performance deteriorate, posing a persistent challenge for effective video classification in highly imbalanced datasets.

To address these challenges, we propose a novel method for sexually suggestive video classification, built on two key components: 1) **Consensus-aware Visual Encoder**: To overcome the challenges posed by abstract visual expressions in suggestive and educative videos, as well as the wide cross-domain diversity of "others" category videos, we design a consensus-aware visual encoder. It leverages the audio modality as an auxiliary source of information to complement the visual modality. It introduces two sub-modules: multimodal distribution consistency learning and multimodal feature consistency learning. These sub-modules work at both the distribution and feature levels to minimize interference from irrelevant abstract features in the visual modality, thereby improving the extraction of consistent features within category and discriminative features across categories. 2) **Label Distribution-aware Training Strategy**: To tackle class imbalance, we devise a training strategy that dynamically adjusts the learning process based on label distribution. This strategy allocates additional learning capacity to tail classes (i.e., categories with fewer examples) by modifying class boundaries, allowing the model to learn distinguishing features from underrepresented categories. By optimizing learning across all classes, this approach reduces overfitting to dominant categories and ensures more balanced model performance across the dataset. We conduct experiments on datasets containing sexually suggestive videos, and the experimental results demonstrate that our method significantly outperforms existing approaches in classifying such content. The results highlight the exceptional effectiveness of our approach in overcoming challenges related to abstract concepts, cross-domain variation, and class imbalance, thereby showcasing its robustness and improved performance in this complex classification task.

The key contributions of this paper are as follows:

- We introduce a consensus-aware visual encoder, which enhances the representation of the visual modality to effectively tackle the unique challenges posed by sexually suggestive video classification.
- We propose a label distribution-aware training strategy that addresses class imbalance by allocating additional learning capacity to tail classes, promoting balanced learning across all categories during training.
- Our method outperforms baseline approaches on the SexToK dataset, demonstrating its robustness and effectiveness in classifying sexually suggestive videos.

2   Related Work

With the rapid expansion of internet technology and the increasing openness of social platforms, preventing the dissemination of pornographic and obscene content in online environments has become a critical research focus.

Early work primarily centered on explicit content detection, with an emphasis on nudity detection approaches. Many models [11,13,14,22,29,36] rely on segmenting skin-colored regions to identify nudity. However, while these methods can detect overt explicit behaviors, they struggle with more nuanced forms of suggestive content. Another prevalent approach is the bag of visual words model [7,27,35,42], which addresses the semantic gap between low-level visual features and high-level concepts related to explicit content. These models use a collection of image features (visual "words") to capture the visual structure of explicit imagery and achieve more accurate detection. Motion-based analysis techniques have also been explored, capturing movement features in videos to determine inappropriate content. For example, Rea et al. [31] used motion periodicity to identify inappropriate content, while Zuo et al. [44] developed a multimodal detection framework using a Gaussian mixture model to analyze pornographic sounds, combined with contour-based image recognition for visual detection. The final decision is made by integrating both visual and audio inputs. Despite the progress made by these methods, most focus on overtly explicit behaviors characterized by significant skin exposure or large, noticeable movements.

Current detection approaches tend to overlook more subtle, suggestive behaviors, where individuals may be fully clothed or exhibit minimal movement. Moreover, reliance on skin exposure as a criterion for sexual suggestiveness can lead to high false positive rates, especially in contexts such as beachwear or bikinis. The challenge becomes even more complex when suggestive behaviors coexist with educational content, such as sexual health education videos. Existing methods struggle to differentiate between suggestive and educative material, underscoring the need for more sophisticated techniques to detect subtle suggestive behaviors without conflating them with educational content.

3   Methodology

As illustrated in Fig. 2, our model architecture is composed of two primary components: consensus-aware visual encoder and label distribution-aware training.

The following sections will provide a detailed explanation of the design and functionality of each component.

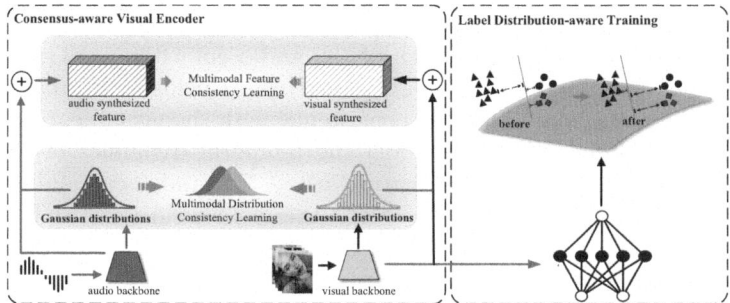

Fig. 2. Overview of the proposed Commonalities-Aware Learning Video Classification Network.

3.1 Consensus-Aware Visual Encoder

To mitigate the interference caused by abstract visual representations in suggestive and educative videos, as well as the diverse visual expressions resulting from the broad cross-domain nature of "others" videos, we introduce the naturally occurring audio modality as additional supervisory information. To leverage this, we design a consensus-aware visual encoder that incorporates two key components: multimodal distribution consistency learning and multimodal feature consistency learning. These components operate at both the distribution and feature levels, enhancing the model's ability to extract informative and robust visual representations by aligning audio and visual features. This approach helps the model focus on meaningful patterns while reducing the impact of irrelevant visual cues.

Multimodal Feature Extraction. Let the untrimmed video be denoted as $\mathcal{V} = \{f_1, \ldots, f_t, \ldots, f_T\}$, where f_t represents the t-th frame and T denotes the total number of frames. We utilize a visual feature extractor (CLIP) [30], pre-trained on a large-scale image dataset (ImageNet) [6], to derive the visual embeddings $\mathbf{V} = [\mathbf{v}_1, \ldots, \mathbf{v}_t, \ldots, \mathbf{v}_T]$. These embeddings are projected into a D-dimensional space using a fully connected (FC) layer with a ReLU activation function. To enhance the model's capability to capture temporal dynamics, we employ a Long Short-Term Memory (LSTM) [19] to obtain both the global visual feature $\mathbf{v}^g \in \mathbb{R}^D$ and local visual features $\bar{\mathbf{V}} = [\bar{\mathbf{v}}_1, \ldots, \bar{\mathbf{v}}_t, \ldots, \bar{\mathbf{v}}_T] \in \mathbb{R}^{T \times D}$. Finally, we fuse the global and local visual features to generate the combined visual feature $\widehat{\mathbf{v}}$:

$$\widehat{\mathbf{v}} = \mathbf{v}^g + \mathcal{F}_{avg\_pooling}(\bar{\mathbf{V}}), \tag{1}$$

where $\mathcal{F}_{avg\_pooling}(\cdot)$ represents the average pooling function, which aggregates the local features across all frames to contribute to the final representation.

The separated audio signal from the untrimmed video $\mathcal{V}$, and then we utilize the audio feature processor AST [17], pre-trained on AudioSet [15], it would be to extract the audio embeddings $\mathbf{A} = [\mathbf{a}_1, \ldots, \mathbf{a}_t, \ldots, \mathbf{a}_T]$, where $\mathbf{a}_t \in \mathbb{R}^D$ and T represents the sequence length of the audio embeddings. These embeddings are then projected into D-dimensional space using a FC layer with a ReLU activation function. To ensure consistency with the visual feature extracting, we apply another LSTM to model the temporal dynamics of the audio, extracting both the global audio feature $\mathbf{a}^g \in \mathbb{R}^D$ and local audio features $\bar{\mathbf{A}} = [\bar{\mathbf{a}}_1, \ldots, \bar{\mathbf{a}}_t, \ldots, \bar{\mathbf{a}}_T^s] \in \mathbb{R}^{T \times D}$. Ultimately, the global and local audio features are fused to form the combined audio feature representation $\widehat{\mathbf{a}}$, providing robust support for subsequent multimodal information fusion:

$$\widehat{\mathbf{a}} = \mathbf{a}^g + \mathcal{F}_{avg\_pooling}(\bar{\mathbf{A}}), \tag{2}$$

where $\mathcal{F}_{avg\_pooling}(\cdot)$ represents the average pooling function, which aggregates the local features across all frames to contribute to the final representation.

Multimodal Distribution Consistency Learning. The goal of the multimodal distribution consistency learning module is to reduce the macro-level differences between the visual and audio modalities. Specifically, both modalities are modeled as Gaussian distributions. To represent these distributions, we define two statistical functions, $\mathcal{G}_v(\cdot)$ and $\mathcal{G}_a(\cdot)$. These functions are implemented using one FC layer followed by ReLU activation functions to compute the parameters of the Gaussian distributions for the visual and audio modalities, denoted as $\mathcal{N}(\boldsymbol{\mu}_v, \boldsymbol{\sigma}_v^2)$ and $\mathcal{N}(\boldsymbol{\mu}_a,$ respectively. The parameters $\boldsymbol{\mu}_*$ and $\boldsymbol{\sigma}_*^2 \in \mathbb{R}^K$ represent the mean and variance of each modality, where K denotes the dimensionality of the latent space. The relationships are formulated as follows:

$$\begin{cases} \mathcal{N}(\boldsymbol{\mu}_v, \boldsymbol{\sigma}_v^2) = \mathcal{G}_v(\widehat{\mathbf{v}}), \\ \mathcal{N}(\boldsymbol{\mu}_a, \boldsymbol{\sigma}_a^2) = \mathcal{G}_a(\widehat{\mathbf{a}}). \end{cases} \tag{3}$$

To align the Gaussian distributions of the visual and audio modalities, we minimize the divergence between them by optimizing the Kullback-Leibler (KL) divergence. Specifically, we aim to reduce the KL divergence between $\mathcal{N}(\boldsymbol{\mu}_v, \boldsymbol{\sigma}_v^2)$ and $\mathcal{N}(\boldsymbol{\mu}_a, \boldsymbol{\sigma}_a^2)$, effectively minimizing the differences between the distributions. The objective function for this optimization is defined as follows:

$$\mathcal{L}_{KL} = -\frac{1}{2} \sum_{k=1}^{K} [log(g_k) - g_k - \gamma_k + 1], \tag{4}$$

where $\mathbf{g} = \dfrac{\boldsymbol{\sigma}_v^2}{\boldsymbol{\sigma}_a^2}$ and $\boldsymbol{\gamma} = \dfrac{(\boldsymbol{\mu}_v - \boldsymbol{\mu}_a)^2}{\boldsymbol{\sigma}_v^2}$, K is the dimension of the latent space, and $*_k$ denotes the k-th element of the corresponding vector. This optimization ensures that the visual and audio feature distributions are statistically aligned, enabling better multimodal consistency.

Multimodal Feature Consistency Learning. The goal of multimodal feature consistency learning is to further align the visual and audio modalities at the feature level by reducing their discrepancies. This module ensures the alignment of internal similarities between the visual and audio feature distributions, facilitating a precise alignment in feature representation.

We begin by employing a reparameterization technique to generate synthesized features $\mathbf{v}^r \in \mathbb{R}^D$ for the visual modality and $\mathbf{a}^r \in \mathbb{R}^D$ for the audio modality:

$$\begin{cases} \mathbf{v}^r = \mathcal{F}_{map_v}(\boldsymbol{\mu}_v + \boldsymbol{\sigma}_v^2 \delta_I), \\ \mathbf{a}^r = \mathcal{F}_{map_a}(\boldsymbol{\mu}_a + \boldsymbol{\sigma}_a^2 \delta_I), \end{cases} \tag{5}$$

where $\delta_I \sim \mathcal{N}(0, \mathbf{1})$ follows a normal distribution, and $\mathcal{F}_{map_a}(\cdot)$ and $\mathcal{F}_{map_v}(\cdot)$ are mapping functions that project the synthesized features from $\mathbb{R}^K$ to $\mathbb{R}^D$. These mapping functions consist of an FC layer followed by a ReLU activation function for both visual and audio modalities.

Next, we compute the intra-modal feature similarity matrices for the visual and audio modalities by calculating the cosine similarity between each pair of videos. For the visual modality, the similarity score $s_{i,j}^v$ between the i-th and j-th videos is given by:

$$s_{i,j}^v = \left(\frac{\mathbf{v}_i^r + \widehat{\mathbf{v}}_i}{||\mathbf{v}_i^r + \widehat{\mathbf{v}}_i||_2}\right)^T \left(\frac{\mathbf{v}_j^r + \widehat{\mathbf{v}}_j}{||\mathbf{v}_j^r + \widehat{\mathbf{v}}_j||_2}\right), \tag{6}$$

and for the audio modality, the similarity score $s_{i,j}^a$ is:

$$s_{i,j}^a = \left(\frac{\mathbf{a}_i^r + \widehat{\mathbf{a}}_i}{||\mathbf{a}_i^r + \widehat{\mathbf{a}}_i||_2}\right)^T \left(\frac{\mathbf{a}_j^r + \widehat{\mathbf{a}}_j}{||\mathbf{a}_j^r + \widehat{\mathbf{a}}_j||_2}\right). \tag{7}$$

Finally, to achieve precise feature-level alignment between the visual and audio modalities, we minimize the distance between the visual modality similarity matrix $\mathbf{s}^v = [s_{1,1}^v, \ldots, s_{1,j}^v, \ldots, s_{i,j}^v, \ldots, s_{B,B}^v]$ and the audio modality similarity matrix $\mathbf{s}^a = [s_{1,1}^a, \ldots, s_{1,j}^a, \ldots, s_{i,j}^a, \ldots, s_{B,B}^a]$. This optimization ensures that the feature representations of the two modalities are consistent:

$$\mathcal{L}_{sim} = \frac{1}{B^2} \sum_{i=1}^{B} \sum_{j=1}^{B} (s_{i,j}^v - s_{i,j}^a)^2, \tag{8}$$

where B represents the size of the minibatch. This approach ensures that visual and audio features are closely aligned at the feature representation level, improving multimodal consistency and enhancing the model's ability to extract meaningful cross-modal information.

3.2   Label Distribution-Aware Training

After passing through multimodal distribution consistency learning and multimodal feature consistency learning, the visual feature $\widehat{\mathbf{v}}$ has absorbed the semantic information from the audio modality and exhibits enhanced discriminative ability. Therefore, in the final prediction stage, we design a simple yet effective classification network to process these visual features. The visual feature $\hat{\mathbf{v}}$ is passed through the classification network, $\mathcal{F}_{MLP}(\cdot)$, which consists of two FC layers and a ReLU activation function. This network analyzes the visual features comprehensively and computes the class probabilities $\mathbf{p} = [p_1, ..., p_c, ..., p_C]$, where C represents the number of categories in the dataset. The final probability for the c-th class is calculated as follows:

$$\mathbf{p} = \mathcal{F}_{MLP}(\hat{\mathbf{v}}). \tag{9}$$

To improve the generalization ability for tail classes and mitigate the adverse effects of class imbalance during model training, In other words, by increasing the minimum distance between long-tail class samples and the decision boundary, the classification margin is expanded, effectively reducing the generalization error for long-tail classes First, the total number of samples for each class in the dataset is computed and represented as $\mathcal{C}_{class} = \{Num_c\}_{c=1}^{C}$, where Num_c represents the total number of samples in the c-th class. We then define a hyperparameter θ as the maximum boundary value, and the boundary value $\overline{\theta}_c$ for each class is calculated as follows:

$$\begin{cases} \theta_c = \dfrac{1}{\sqrt[4]{Num_c}}, & c \in \{1, \ldots, C\} \\ \overline{\theta}_c = \dfrac{\theta * \theta_c}{max\{\theta_1, \theta_2, ..., \theta_C\}}, & c \in \{1, \ldots, C\}. \end{cases} \tag{10}$$

Finally, we incorporate the margin coefficient into the standard cross-entropy loss function, resulting in a label distribution-aware balanced cross-entropy loss that is formulated as:

$$\mathcal{L}_{balance} = -log\left[\dfrac{e^{\beta \cdot (p_c - \overline{\theta}_c)}}{e^{\beta \cdot (p_c - \overline{\theta}_c)} + \sum_{\hat{c} \neq c} e^{p_{\hat{c}}}}\right], \tag{11}$$

where β is an adjustable hyperparameter, and $p_*, * \in \{1, ..., c, ..., C\}$ represents the class score assigned to the sample by the model, are learned through the classification network. This strategy expands the decision boundary for tail class samples by increasing the minimum distance between the decision boundary and tail class samples, thus providing a larger margin for these classes. This approach enhances classification performance on tail classes while improving overall generalization.

The overall loss function $\mathcal{L}$ is defined as:

$$\mathcal{L} = \mathcal{L}_{balance} + \lambda_1 \mathcal{L}_{KL} + \lambda_2 \mathcal{L}_{sim}, \tag{12}$$

where λ_1 and λ_2 are hyperparameters to weigh the contributions of different loss functions.

4 Experiment

4.1 Datesets

The SexTok dataset, introduced by George et al. [16], is currently the only publicly available dataset for the task of sexually suggestive video classification.

Specifically curated from the TikTok platform, the dataset categorizes videos into three distinct classes: suggestive, educative, and others, with the latter covering a wide range of content. The dataset consists of 1,000 videos with durations ranging from 1 s to 7 min. The video content is diverse, spanning everyday life, educational, and entertainment contexts. This dataset provides a valuable resource for exploring this emerging task.

For evaluating the performance of classification models, the SexTok dataset is divided into training, validation, and test sets. Notably, the dataset exhibits a significant class imbalance, as sexually suggestive and sex education content are substantially outnumbered by other videos. Specifically, sexually suggestive videos make up around 20%, sex education videos account for another 20%, and the remaining 60% fall under the others video category. This imbalance poses challenges for model training and optimization, making the dataset a suitable benchmark for testing the effectiveness of multimodal alignment and class balancing strategies.

Table 1. Performance comparison with several state-of-the-art baselines on the SexTok dataset. The best performance is highlighted in **bold**.

Methods	Accuracy	Micro			Macro		
		Precision	Recall	F1	Precision	Recall	F1
All-text Bert [16]	68%	76%	50%	60%	71%	63%	64%
Non-empty Text Bert [16]	75%	78%	54%	64%	74%	65%	68%
Visual-VideoMAE [16]	70%	61%	51%	55%	68%	57%	61%
Slowfast [10]	80%	95%	63%	76%	81%	73%	76%
Timesformer [1]	75%	93%	52%	66%	75%	65%	68%
ResNet [21]	77%	90%	75%	63%	77%	64%	67%
Uniformer [23]	74%	93%	55%	69%	73%	66%	68%
Ours	**86%**	**97%**	**81%**	**88%**	**85%**	**84%**	**84%**

4.2   Evaluation Metrics

We performed a comprehensive evaluation of our model and baseline methods using a variety of assessment metrics on the SexTok dataset. The evaluation metrics include accuracy, precision, recall, and F1 score to provide a standard comparison of classification performance. We further refined the evaluation by calculating micro-precision, micro-recall, and micro-F1 scores, where we treated the "other" category as the negative class and excluded it from the final score. This approach allows for a more focused evaluation of the model's performance on the inappropriate content classes. Additionally, we computed macro-precision, macro-recall, and macro-F1 scores, which offer a better understanding of the model's effectiveness across all categories, regardless of class size, thus addressing the challenges posed by the imbalanced data distribution.

Table 2. Performance comparison with several state-of-the-art baseline models for overall F1 performance across each category label. The best performance for each category is highlighted in **bold**.

Methods	Suggestive	Educative	Others
All-text Bert	30%	83%	80%
Non-empty Text Bert	38%	84%	81%
Visual-VideoMAE	55%	63%	72%
Slowfast	74%	68%	86%
Timesformer	67%	55%	83%
ResNet	64%	54%	84%
Uniformer	71%	55%	80%
Ours	**81%**	82%	**90%**

4.3 Implementation Details

Our model was optimized using a single GeForce RTX 2080 Ti GPU and implemented with the PyTorch library. Frame-wise visual features were extracted using a CLIP model [30] pre-trained on the ImageNet [6] dataset, while audio features were obtained from an AST model [17] pre-trained on the AudioSet [15] dataset.

Given the variation in video lengths within the SexTok [16] dataset, we standardized the sequence length to 800 frames, which represents the median value across the dataset. For videos containing more than 800 frames, we applied a uniform sampling strategy to select 800 frames. For videos with fewer than 800 frames, we used interpolation to expand the sequence to 800 frames. To avoid excessive redundancy in videos that are significantly shorter than 800 frames, which could lead to increased computational overhead, we implemented a sliding window approach. Specifically, we used a window size of 16 frames with a stride of 8, followed by average pooling within each window. This process standardizes all videos to 100 frames.

For model optimization, we used the AdamW optimizer with a mini-batch size of 16 and a learning rate of $6e - 5$. The balance parameters λ_1 and λ_2 were set to 0.01 and 0.9, respectively, while the hyperparameter s was fixed at 30. During the experiments, the model with the best test performance was selected as the final model for evaluation.

4.4 Baselines

To demonstrate the effectiveness of our proposed model, we conducted a comprehensive benchmarking against several state-of-the-art models. This comparison included BERT [8,16], configured for both All-text and Non-empty text scenarios, Visual-VideoMAE [16,34], SlowFast [10], TimeSformer [1], ResNet [21], and UniFormer [23]. The benchmarking was carried out on the SexTok dataset.

With the exception of BERT and Visual-VideoMAE, the other baseline methods were constructed by freezing the model parameters, utilizing them as powerful visual feature extractors, and attaching a classifier on top. Below is a detailed explanation of these baseline methods:

- **All-text Bert** and **Non-empty Text Bert:** We followed the model configuration used by George et al. [16] to fine-tune the BERT-base-multilingual-cased model [8] for classifying text transcripts from videos. These transcripts were generated by converting audio information into text using OpenAI's Whisper (medium) [32]. Since some videos consist solely of music or lack audio, resulting in empty transcripts, we implemented two distinct setups: the All-text BERT model, which includes all video transcriptions, and the Non-empty Text BERT model, which excludes videos without text.
- **Visual-VideoMAE:** In line with George et al. [16], we fine-tuned the MCG-NJU/videomae-base model (Tong et al., 2022), which is designed for video classification tasks. The video data was preprocessed and sampled using the same strategies as George et al. to ensure consistency in evaluation.
- **Slowfaster:** SlowFast [10] is a dual-pathway model that processes video by integrating both temporal and spatial information. It uses a Slow pathway for capturing spatial details and a Fast pathway for temporal dynamics. We used the SlowFast model pre-trained on the Kinetics-400 (K400) dataset as a baseline, to assess its performance on the SexTok dataset.
- **Timesformer:** TimeSformer [1] is a Transformer-based model designed for video content, employing a "Divided Space-Time Attention" mechanism to handle spatio-temporal information efficiently. Pre-trained on the Kinetics-400 dataset, TimeSformer served as a baseline model for evaluating performance on the SexTok dataset.
- **ResNet:** ResNet [21] uses a residual learning framework that helps mitigate the vanishing gradient problem, enabling deep networks to remain trainable. A ResNet model pre-trained on ImageNet was used as a baseline to evaluate its generalization in classifying videos within the SexTok dataset.
- **Uniformer:** UniFormer [23] is a hybrid Transformer architecture that combines the strengths of convolutional and self-attention mechanisms for learning spatiotemporal features from video data. Pre-trained on Kinetics-400, the UniFormer model was used as a baseline to evaluate its effectiveness in handling poor-quality video classification and its performance on the SexTok dataset.

4.5   Performance Comparison

The analysis of Tables 1 and 2 reveals several key observations. Models based on a single visual modality generally outperform those based on a single text modality. Except for Visual-VideoMAE, most visual modality models outperform text-based models across all evaluation metrics, suggesting that the visual modality provides more comprehensive information for sexually suggestive classification tasks. However, in the task of sexually suggestive video classification, despite their strong performance in other tasks, visual modality models fall short compared to our proposed model. This can be attributed to the complexity of abstract labels, the similarity in visual features, and the wide diversity of cross-domain video content, which challenge models relying solely on visual information. Specifically, our model achieves an accuracy of 86%, which is 6% points higher than the next-best model. In the micro evaluation group, our model's precision is 2% points higher than the second-best, with an increase in recall of 6% points, and a 12%-point improvement in F1-score. In the macro group, our model surpassed others by 4% in precision, 11% in recall, and 8% in the F1-score. These results demonstrate our model's superior ability to understand abstract concepts and extract critical information from videos with similar visual representations and diverse cross-domain categories.

4.6 Ablation Study

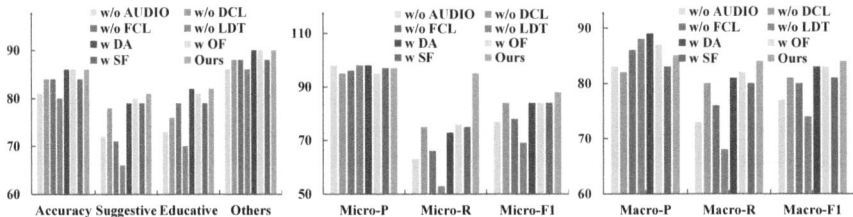

Fig. 3. Ablation study results on the SexTok dataset.

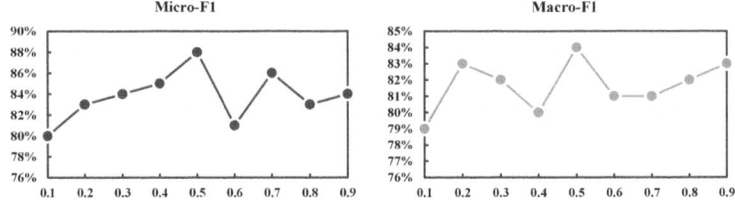

Fig. 4. Influence of θ on the classification performance.

In this section, we present the results of the ablation study to evaluate the contribution of each module in our proposed model to the overall performance. Specifically, we examined the impact of the consensus-aware visual encoder, label distribution-aware training strategy, and feature selection on sexually suggestive video classification.

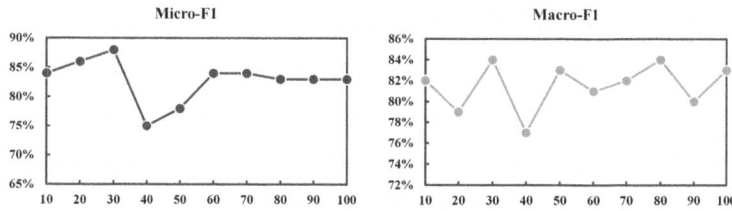

Fig. 5. Influence of β on the classification performance.

On Consensus-Aware Visual Encoder. To assess the effectiveness of the consensus-aware visual encoder in understanding abstract labels, addressing the similarity of visual representations, and managing the broad scope of cross-domain videos, we introduced three variations of the model:

- **w/o AUDIO:** In this variation, we removed the audio modality information from the commonalities-aware learning, retaining only the operations on the visual modality. This allows us to verify the effectiveness of using only visual information in the classification task and understand the contribution of the audio modality to performance.
- **w/o DCL:** We eliminated the multimodal distribution consistency learning to assess the importance of aligning the Gaussian distributions of the visual and audio modalities at a macro level. This variation helps quantify the impact of distribution-level alignment on overall classification accuracy and performance.
- **w/o FCL:** In this model variation, we removed the multimodal feature consistency learning to evaluate the necessity of aligning the visual and audio modalities at the feature level. This analysis highlights the contribution of feature-level consistency to the model's ability to generalize across different modalities and video categories.

From Fig. 3, we can see that our model consistently outperforms the other variants across various metrics. Specifically, when compared to the w/o AUDIO model, we observed improvements of 6% in Accuracy, 6% in Micro-Recall, 4% in Micro-F1, 3% in Macro-Precision, 4% in Macro-Recall, 3% in Macro-F1, and further gains of 2% in the classification accuracy for the "Suggestive", "Educative", and "Others" categories. Similarly, when compared to the w/o DCL model, we saw improvements of 2% in Accuracy, 1% in Micro-Recall, 3% in Micro-F1, 3% in Macro-Precision, 3% in Macro-Recall, 2% in Macro-F1, 3% in the "Suggestive" category, 3% in the "Educative" category, and 2% in the "Others" category. The same pattern emerged when comparing our model to the w/o FCL variant, with improvements of 2% in Accuracy, 2% in Micro-Recall, 3% in Micro-F1, 3% in Macro-Precision, 3% in Macro-Recall, 2% in Macro-F1, 3% in the "Suggestive" category, 3% in the "Educative" category, and 2% in the "Others" category, respectively.

These results demonstrate that our proposed consensus-aware visual encoder significantly boosts the model's capacity to comprehend abstract concepts, effectively addressing challenges related to visual similarity and the wide diversity of cross-domain video content.

On Label Distribution-Aware Training. To further emphasize the importance of the label distribution-aware training strategy introduced in our model, we designed two variants of our model:

- **w/o LDT:** In this variant, we removed the label distribution-aware training strategy, thus disregarding the impact of data imbalance on the model. This baseline variant uses standard binary cross-entropy loss without accounting for class imbalance.
- **w DA:** This variant addresses the imbalance by replicating videos from the "suggestive" and "educative" categories to match the data size of the "others" category, thus artificially balancing the dataset through data augmentation.

As illustrated in Fig. 3, our model consistently achieves superior performance across multiple metrics. Compared to the w/o LDT model, we observed improvements of 6% in Accuracy, 25% in Suggestive, 17% in Educative, 5% in Others, 4% in Micro-Precision, 9% in Micro-Recall, 4% in Micro-F1, 3% in Macro-Precision, 4% in Macro-Recall, and 3% in Macro-F1. Similarly, when compared to the w DA model, the same metrics exhibited improvements of 2% in Suggestive, 2% in Micro-Recall, 4% in Micro-F1, 4% in Macro-Precision, 3% in Macro-Recall, and 1% in Macro-F1. Notably, the w/o LDT model performs the worst, consistently underperforming across nearly all metrics. This clearly demonstrates that applying a class balancing strategy is critical for enhancing the model's performance in the task of sexually suggestive video classification, particularly in the face of class imbalance. This strategy significantly contributes to improved classification accuracy and generalization across all video categories.

On Feature Selection. To investigate which feature is more beneficial for training the multimodal feature consistency learning module (in Eq. (6) and Eq. (7)), we designed two model variants:

- **w OF:** This variant uses only the original visual features for training the model, without incorporating any synthetic features.
- **w SF:** This variant relies solely on synthetic features, generated through Gaussian distribution calculations, for training.

As illustrated in Fig. 3, our model demonstrates a clear advantage by combining both synthetic and original features instead of using only one type of feature. Compared to the w OF variant, our model shows improvements of 1% in Suggestive, 1% in Educative, 1% in Others, 1% in Micro-Precision, 9% in Micro-Recall, 4% in Micro-F1, 3% in Macro-Precision, 9% in Macro-Recall, and 11% in Macro-F1, respectively. Similarly, when compared to the w SF variant, our model achieves increases of 2% in Accuracy, 2% in Suggestive, 3% in Educative, 2% in Others, 13% in Micro-Recall, 5% in Micro-F1, 2% in Macro-Precision,

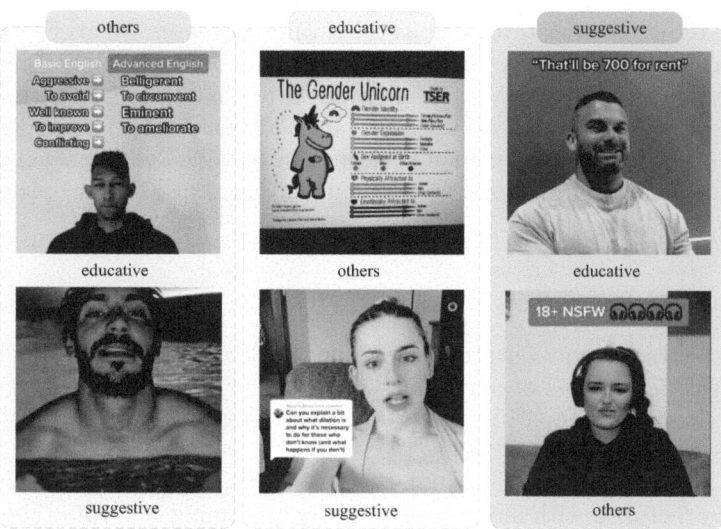

Fig. 6. Qualitative comparison of our model with the suboptimal model, SlowFast, on the SexTok dataset. The figure highlights cases where the SlowFast model made incorrect classifications: in the first column, the true label is "others"; in the second column, the true label is "educative"; and in the third column, the true label is "suggestive".

6% in Macro-Recall, and 4% in Macro-F1. These results strongly suggest that combining synthetic and original features within the multimodal feature consistency learning module significantly enhances the model's overall performance, allowing it to better capture and align features across modalities. This combined approach proves to be more effective than relying on either type of feature alone.

4.7 Parameter Analysis

The Maximum Boundary θ. To explore the impact of the maximum boundary θ in Eq. (10), we conducted a parameter analysis experiment on the SexTok dataset under different θ values (ranging from 0.1 to 0.9, with an increment of 0.1), evaluated using Micro-F1 and Macro-F1. The experimental results are shown in Fig. 4. The results demonstrate that as the θ value increases, both Micro-F1 and Macro-F1 follow a general trend of rising initially and then declining, reaching their peak at $\theta = 0.5$. Although additional fluctuations occur as θ increases, none of these surpass the optimal performance achieved at $\theta = 0.5$. Therefore, through this parameter analysis, we determined that $\theta = 0.5$ is the optimal value for our proposed model.

The Hyperparamete β. To explore the impact of the hyperparameter β in Eq. (11), we conducted a parameter analysis experiment on the SexTok dataset under different β values (ranging from 10 to 100, with an increment of 10), measured by Micro-F1 and Macro-F1. The experimental results are shown in

Fig. 5. The results demonstrate that as the β value increases, Micro-F1 follows an overall trend of rising initially, then declining, and finally stabilizing, achieving its best performance at $\beta = 30$. Macro-F1, on the other hand, fluctuates throughout but also reaches its peak at $\beta = 30$. Despite additional fluctuations as $\beta = 30$ increases, none surpass the optimal performance obtained at $\beta = 30$. Therefore, through this parameter analysis, we determined that $\beta = 30$ is the optimal value for our proposed model.

4.8   Qualitative Analysis

In Fig. 6, we present representative cases from the SexTok dataset to qualitatively evaluate the effectiveness of our proposed method. Each column corresponds to a specific category, comparing the classification results of our model with the second-best model, SlowFast [10].

In the first row of the first and third columns, the videos exhibit strong explanatory features, with individuals verbally explaining concepts. The second-best model, influenced by these "explanatory" characteristics, incorrectly classified these videos as "educative". In contrast, our model effectively distinguished between surface-level explanatory features and the actual content, resulting in correct classifications.

In the second row of the first and second columns, the videos contain prominent visual cues, such as significant exposure of body parts. The second-best model heavily relied on these obvious visual features, leading to incorrect classifications as "suggestive". However, our model avoided making decisions based solely on visual exposure and correctly identified the underlying content, demonstrating a deeper understanding of the video context.

Furthermore, the first row of the second column and the second row of the third column showcase videos that were accurately classified as "others" by both models. These videos have minimal visual complexity, limited movement, and rely primarily on audio cues for context. Our model was able to correctly capture the audio-dominant nature of these videos, preventing misclassification caused by oversimplified visual cues.

These qualitative analyses highlight the superior performance of our proposed method in handling complex and abstract concepts. Compared to the second-best model, our approach demonstrates greater precision in filtering out irrelevant features, focusing on key information, and enhancing both the accuracy and robustness of sexually suggestive video classification.

5   Conclusion

In this work, we address the challenge of classifying sexual education and sexually suggestive videos by proposing a novel video classification approach. Our method enhances the model's capacity to identify shared features across video content through the introduction of a consensus-aware visual encoder. Additionally, we implement a label distribution-aware training strategy that dynamically adjusts the learning process to provide additional support for underrepresented categories, ensuring balanced learning across all classes. Experimental results on the SexTok dataset demonstrate the effectiveness of our approach.

Acknowledgments. This work was supported in part by the National Natural Science Foundation of China, No.: 62376140 and No.: U23A20315; the Science and Technology Innovation Program for Distinguished Young Scholars of Shandong Province Higher Education Institutions, No.: 2023KJ128; the Special Fund for Taishan Scholar Project of Shandong Province; and the Special Fund for Distinguished Professors of Shandong Jianzhu University.

References

1. Bertasius, G., Wang, H., Torresani, L.: Is space-time attention all you need for video understanding? In: Proceeding of International Conference on Machine Learning, vol. 2, pp. 813–824 (2021)
2. Carreira, J., Noland, E., Banki-Horvath, A., Hillier, C., Zisserman, A.: A short note about kinetics-600. arXiv: Computer Vision and Pattern Recognition (2018)
3. Carreira, J., Zisserman, A.: Quo vadis, action recognition? A new model and the kinetics dataset. In: 2017 IEEE Conference on Computer Vision and Pattern Recognition, pp. 6299–6308 (2017)
4. Collins, R.L., Strasburger, V.C., Brown, J.D., Donnerstein, E., Lenhart, A., Ward, L.M.: Sexual media and childhood well-being and health. Pediatrics **140**(Supplement_2), S162–S166 (2017)
5. Dastbaravardeh, E., Askarpour, S., Saberi Anari, M., Rezaee, K.: Channel attention-based approach with autoencoder network for human action recognition in low-resolution frames. Int. J. Intell. Syst. **2024**(1), 1052344 (2024)
6. Deng, J., Dong, W., Socher, R., Li, L.J., Li, K., Fei-Fei, L.: Imagenet: a large-scale hierarchical image database. In: 2009 IEEE Conference on Computer Vision and Pattern Recognition, pp. 248–255 (2009)
7. Deselaers, T., Pimenidis, L., Ney, H.: Bag-of-visual-words models for adult image classification and filtering. In: 2008 19th International Conference on Pattern Recognition, pp. 1–4 (2008)
8. Devlin, J., Chang, M.W., Lee, K., Toutanova, K.: Bert: pre-training of deep bidirectional transformers for language understanding. In: Proceedings of the 2019 Conference of the North, pp. 4171–4186 (2019)
9. Dosovitskiy, A., et al.: An image is worth 16x16 words: Transformers for image recognition at scale. arXiv: Computer Vision and Pattern Recognition, pp. 1–22 (2020)
10. Feichtenhofer, C., Fan, H., Malik, J., He, K.: Slowfast networks for video recognition. In: Proceedings of the IEEE/CVF International Conference on Computer Vision, pp. 6202–6211 (2019)
11. Fleck, M.M., Forsyth, D.A., Bregler, C.: Finding naked people. In: The European Conference on Computer Vision, pp. 593–602 (1996)
12. Fowler, L.R., Schoen, L., Smith, H.S., Morain, S.R.: Sex education on tiktok: a content analysis of themes. Health Promot. Pract. **23**(5), 739–742 (2022)
13. Ganguly, D., Mofrad, M.H., Kovashka, A.: Detecting sexually provocative images. In: 2017 IEEE Winter Conference on Applications of Computer Vision, vol. 3, pp. 660–668 (2017)

14. Garcia, M.B., Revano, T.F., Habal, B.G.M., Contreras, J.O., Enriquez, J.B.R.: A pornographic image and video filtering application using optimized nudity recognition and detection algorithm. In: 2018 IEEE 10th International Conference on Humanoid, Nanotechnology, Information Technology, Communication and Control, Environment and Management, vol. 521, pp. 1–5 (2018)

15. Gemmeke, J.F., et al.: Audio set: an ontology and human-labeled dataset for audio events. In: 2017 IEEE International Conference on Acoustics, Speech and Signal Processing, pp. 776–780. IEEE (2017)

16. George, E., Surdeanu, M.: It's not sexually suggestive; it's educative| separating sex education from suggestive content on tiktok videos. In: Findings of the Association for Computational Linguistics: ACL 2023, pp. 5904–5915 (2023)

17. Gong, Y., Chung, Y.A., Glass, J.: AST: audio spectrogram transformer. arXiv preprint arXiv:2104.01778 (2021)

18. Goyal, R., et al.: The "something something" video database for learning and evaluating visual common sense. In: International Conference on Computer Vision (2017)

19. Graves, A., Graves, A.: Long short-term memory. Supervised sequence labelling with recurrent neural networks, pp. 37–45 (2012)

20. Hasan, F., Raza, D.M., Moon, H., Nahid, M.A.H.: Sentiment analysis from YouTube video using bi-LSTM-GRU classification check for updates. In: Proceedings of the 2nd International Conference on Big Data, IoT and Machine Learning: BIM 2023. vol. 867, p. 303. Springer (2024)

21. He, K., Zhang, X., Ren, S., Sun, J.: Deep residual learning for image recognition. In: Proceedings of the IEEE Conference on Computer Vision and Pattern Recognition, pp. 770–778 (2016)

22. Lee, H., Lee, S., Nam, T.: Implementation of high performance objectionable video classification system. In: 2006 8th International Conference Advanced Communication Technology, vol. 4, p. 4 pp. - 962 (2006)

23. Li, K., et al.: Uniformer: unified transformer for efficient spatial-temporal representation learning. In: International Conference on Learning Representations, pp. 1–19

24. Li, Y., Li, Y., Vasconcelos, N.: RESOUND: Towards Action Recognition Without Representation Bias. In: The European Conference on Computer Vision, pp. 520–535 (2018)

25. Liu, M., Nie, L., Wang, M., Chen, B.: Towards micro-video understanding by joint sequential-sparse modeling. In: Proceedings of the 25th ACM International Conference on Multimedia, pp. 970–978 (2017)

26. Liu, M., Nie, L., Wang, X., Tian, Q., Chen, B.: Online data organizer: microvideo categorization by structure-guided multimodal dictionary learning. IEEE Trans. Image Process. **28**(3), 1235–1247 (2019). https://doi.org/10.1109/TIP.2018.2875363

27. Lopes, A., Avila, S., Peixoto, A., Oliveira, R., Araújo, A.: A bag-of-features approach based on hue-sift descriptor for nude detection. European Signal Processing Conference, European Signal Processing Conference, pp. 1552–1556 (2009)

28. Ma, Y., Wang, R.: Relative-position embedding based spatially and temporally decoupled transformer for action recognition. Pattern Recogn. **145**, 109905 (2024)

29. Platzer, C., Stuetz, M., Lindorfer, M.: Skin sheriff. In: Proceedings of the 2nd International Workshop on Security and Forensics in Communication Systems, pp. 45–56 (2014)

30. Radford, A., et al.: Learning transferable visual models from natural language supervision. In: International Conference on Machine Learning, pp. 8748–8763 (2021)
31. Rea, R., Lacey, L., Dahyotit, D., Dahyot, D.: Multimodal periodicity analysis for illicit content detection in videos. In: Conference on Visual Media Production,Conference on Visual Media Production, pp. 106–116 (2006)
32. Summers, R.W.: Social Psychology: How Other People Influence Our Thoughts and Actions [2 volumes]. Bloomsbury Publishing USA (2016)
33. Tan, W., Yao, Q., Liu, J.: Overlooked video classification in weakly supervised video anomaly detection. In: Winter Conference on Applications of Computer Vision, pp. 202–210
34. Tong, Z., Song, Y., Wang, J., Wang, L.: Videomae: Masked autoencoders are data-efficient learners for self-supervised video pre-training. Adv. Neural. Inf. Process. Syst. **35**, 10078–10093 (2022)
35. Ulges, A., Stahl, A.: Automatic detection of child pornography using color visual words. In: 2011 IEEE International Conference on Multimedia and Expo. vol. 4, pp. 1–6 (2011)
36. Wang, D., Zhu, M., Yuan, X., Qian, H.: Identification and annotation of erotic film based on content analysis. In: SPIE Proceedings,Electronic Imaging and Multimedia Technology IV. vol. 5637, p. 88 (2005)
37. Wang, X., et al.: Clip-guided prototype modulating for few-shot action recognition. Int. J. Comput. Vision **132**(6), 1899–1912 (2024)
38. Wang, X.: HyRSM++: hybrid relation guided temporal set matching for few-shot action recognition. Pattern Recogn. **147**, 110110 (2024)
39. Wu, P., et al.: Open-vocabulary video anomaly detection. In: Proceedings of the IEEE/CVF Conference on Computer Vision and Pattern Recognition, pp. 18297–18307 (2024)
40. Wu, P., et al.: VadCLIP: adapting vision-language models for weakly supervised video anomaly detection. In: Proceedings of the AAAI Conference on Artificial Intelligence, vol. 38, pp. 6074–6082 (2024)
41. Yang, Z., Radke, R.J.: Context-aware video anomaly detection in long-term datasets. In: Proceedings of the IEEE/CVF Conference on Computer Vision and Pattern Recognition, pp. 4002–4011 (2024)
42. Zhang, J., Sui, L., Zhuo, L., Li, Z., Yang, Y.: An approach of bag-of-words based on visual attention model for pornographic images recognition in compressed domain. Neurocomputing **110**, 145–152 (2013)
43. Zhao, J., et al.: Sentiment analysis of video danmakus based on MIBE-RoBERTa-FF-BiLSTM. Sci. Rep. **14**(1), 5827 (2024)
44. Zuo, H., Wu, O., Hu, W., Xu, B.: Recognition of blue movies by fusion of audio and video. In: 2008 IEEE International Conference on Multimedia and Expo, pp. 37–40 (2008)

LightStar-Net: A Pseudo-Raw Space Enhancement for Efficient Low-Light Object Detection

Xin Feng[1] , Jie Wang[1] , Siping Wang[1], and Jiehui Zhang[2](✉)

[1] Chongqing University of Technology, Chongqing, China
xfeng@cqut.edu.cn
[2] Xi'an University of Science and Technology, Xi'an, China
jiehui_zhang@hotmail.com

Abstract. In low-light conditions, detectors trained on normal-light data often experience significant performance degradation. To address this issue, low-light image enhancement methods are commonly employed to improve detection performance. However, existing human vision-oriented enhancement techniques have shown limited effectiveness, while most machine vision-oriented methods rely on standard RGB image processing or RAW space conversion, often neglecting the preservation of key object features and incurring high computational costs. To overcome these limitations, we propose an efficient low-light object detection method based on Pseudo-RAW space enhancement-LightStar-Net. This method combines a Pseudo-RAW space Enhancement module (PRE) with a lightweight network, enhancing detection capabilities for machine vision in low-light environments. Using inverse mapping to convert RGB images into Pseudo-RAW feature space, the model dynamically adjusts image enhancement parameters to optimize detection performance. On benchmark datasets such as ExDark and DARK FACE, LightStar-Net achieves outstanding accuracy and inference speed. With a simple structure requiring only 3K parameters, it significantly improves detector performance in low-light environments.

Keywords: Low-Light Detection · Pseudo-RAW · Machine Vision · LightStar-Net

1 Introduction

Object detection is a fundamental task in computer vision, aiming to recognize and locate objects within an image. Despite significant advancements in object detection algorithms [5,8,14,21,22,24], real-world applications in low-light environments continue to face various challenges. Recently, many works have been proposed to enhance low-light image visual perception for downstream tasks such as object detection, semantic segmentation, and depth estimation.

Low-light object detection typically employs two main frameworks: a two-stage framework oriented towards human vision and a single-stage framework

P. Didyk and J. Hou (Eds.): CVM 2025, LNCS 15663, pp. 192–211, 2025.
https://doi.org/10.1007/978-981-96-5809-1_11

oriented towards machine vision. In the human vision-oriented framework, the enhancement network [9,17,35] and the detector operate as independent modules. The enhancement network is pre-trained on paired low-light and standard-light image datasets [2,28], transforming images into well-lit versions before training the detector. However, while this processing improves image brightness, it can reduce color saturation and increase noise (as shown in Fig. 1 left part), negatively impacting detection performance.

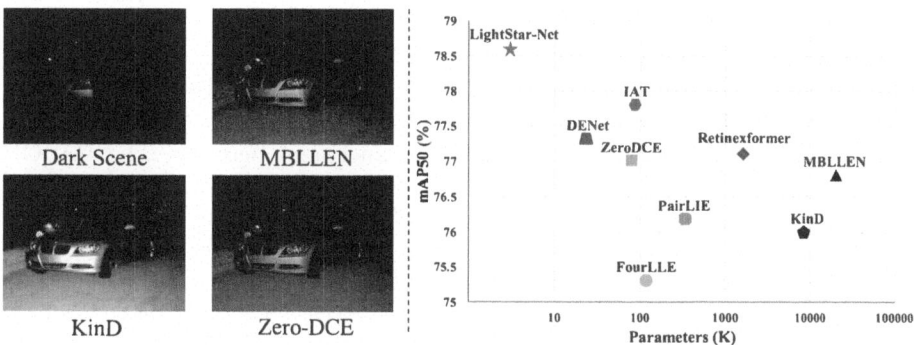

Fig. 1. The left part: results of enhancing night-time images using three different methods-MBLLEN [17], Kind [35], and Zero-DCE [9]. The right part: results of our method compared to other methods on the ExDark [15] dataset.

In contrast, the machine vision-oriented framework focuses on enhancing image attributes critical for detection tasks, such as contrast and target clarity, by end-to-end connecting the enhancement network [3,4,20,33] and the detector, optimizing them together. This approach directly boosts detection performance, reduces false positives, and enhances the algorithm's generalization ability under varying lighting conditions.

However, machine vision enhancement methods predominantly rely on standard RGB image processing, which can overlook the preservation and enhancement of critical target features during processing. Recently, some studies have proposed inverse mapping networks that restore RGB images to corresponding RAW space through processes such as decolorization, inverse transformation, and denoising, allowing the retrieval of more feature information [12,34]. Nonetheless, in low-light environments, RAW images may not fully utilize this information due to fixed processing workflows, potentially leading to detail loss or increased noise in certain cases.

Additionally, some enhancement methods overlook inference speed, causing the detection model to wait for enhancement during application. Typically, most enhancement methods [32,36] employ a down-sampling followed by an up-sampling approach to enhance images, such as the Laplacian pyramid structure to boost low-frequency information and restore high-frequency details. However, this makes the enhancement model overly complex.

To address these issues, this paper proposes an efficient low-light object detection network enhanced in the **Pseudo-RAW** space-LightStar-Net. This network is based on the concept of Pseudo-RAW space enhancement and dynamically generates optimized parameters according to the features and scenes of input images. This mechanism enables adaptive adjustment of image processing under various lighting conditions and environments, optimizing enhancement effects while avoiding detail loss caused by fixed workflows in traditional RAW image processing methods.

Specifically, LightStar-Net consists of two main components: the Pseudo-RAW space Enhancement module (PRE) and a Lightweight Enhancement Network. In the PRE, we introduce an inverse mapping network (IMRGB) and a pseudo-image signal processing (DOISP) enhancement network. The IMRGB module inversely maps RGB images to the Pseudo-RAW image feature space, enabling in-depth analysis of image features. Subsequently, the DOISP network directly operates in this Pseudo-RAW image feature space to generate adaptive optimization parameters. This design effectively avoids reduced contrast between objects and the background caused by excessive enhancement, thereby minimizing interference with the subsequent detection process.

Meanwhile, the lightweight enhancement network accelerates inference speed by reducing model parameters and computational complexity. It employs fewer convolutional layers or smaller convolutional kernels and utilizes structures like depthwise separable convolutions to significantly lower computational loads. This enables rapid inference in resource-constrained environments, making it particularly well-suited for low-light image processing tasks.

Building on this foundation, we introduce an auxiliary training strategy to expedite the extraction and learning of latent features from the PRE. To achieve this, we designed the feature stimulation network (FS-Net), which effectively integrates deep features from the PRE, optimizing the lightweight network's training process and reducing computational burdens. This collaborative mechanism ensures the lightweight enhancement network can quickly adapt to low-light environments, improving inference efficiency while maintaining high detection accuracy and responsiveness in practical applications. During the inference stage, the PRE module and FS-Net are omitted. In this way, LightStar-Net not only addresses detail loss but also significantly enhances the overall performance and practicality of low-light object detection.

We combined the proposed LightStar-Net with the classic detector YOLOv3 [21] to create an end-to-end efficient low-light object detection algorithm framework, named LightStar-YOLO. Extensive experiments were conducted on two low-light detection datasets, EXDark [15] and DarkFace [31]. The results demonstrate that LightStar-YOLO achieves state-of-the-art performance in low-light detection tasks. Notably, our model has only **3K** parameters (as shown in Fig. 1 right part), significantly fewer than previous state-of-the-art low-light detection models. Additionally, the average inference speed is **0.0004 s** per image, which is ten times faster than current leading methods [3, 4, 20]. Our contributions can be summarized as follows:

- We propose a novel enhancement network, LightStar-Net, for efficient low-light object detection. This network dynamically generates optimized parameters and adaptively adjusts based on the features and scenes of input images, ensuring optimal image processing results under varying lighting conditions. By avoiding detail loss caused by fixed workflows in traditional techniques when processing RAW images, this approach significantly enhances overall object detection performance.
- To accelerate the inference speed of LightStar-Net, we design FS-Net as an auxiliary training strategy that effectively integrates deep features from the PRE. This collaborative mechanism optimizes the lightweight enhancement network's training process while reducing computational burdens, enabling rapid adaptation to low-light environments. During the inference stage, omitting the PRE and FS-Net further improves inference efficiency, enhancing both the performance and practicality of low-light object detection.
- Extensive experimental results on two low-light detection datasets demonstrate that LightStar-YOLO outperforms current leading methods. Notably, LightStar-Net has only **3K** parameters and achieves a processing time of just **0.0004 s** per image.

2   Related Work

Object Detection. Mainstream object detectors are generally categorized into two types: single-stage and two-stage detectors. Single-stage detectors, such as SSD [14], YOLO [21], and FCOS [24], directly predict object bounding boxes and class labels in one step. In contrast, two-stage detectors, like RCNN [8], Faster R-CNN [22], and R-FCN [5], first generate candidate regions and then classify these regions while performing bounding box regression for refinement. The rapid advancement of object detection technologies has been largely driven by the availability of large-scale datasets, such as COCO [13] and Open Images [11], which provide extensive annotated examples for training and evaluation.

Low-Light Image Enhancement. The progress of deep learning has spurred significant advancements in low-light image enhancement techniques. Lore et al. [16] pioneered the use of deep autoencoders for dark-light image enhancement networks, establishing this field. Guo et al. [9] introduced Zero-DCE, which estimates light enhancement curves for no-reference images. Wei et al. [28] utilized the Retinex decomposition model for simultaneous light enhancement and denoising, further improving image quality. Cai et al. [1] incorporated a Transformer structure to model both reflectance and illumination damage, achieving remarkable results. While these methods aim to restore low-light images to well-lit scenes, the enhanced images often suffer from reduced color saturation and noise due to increased brightness.

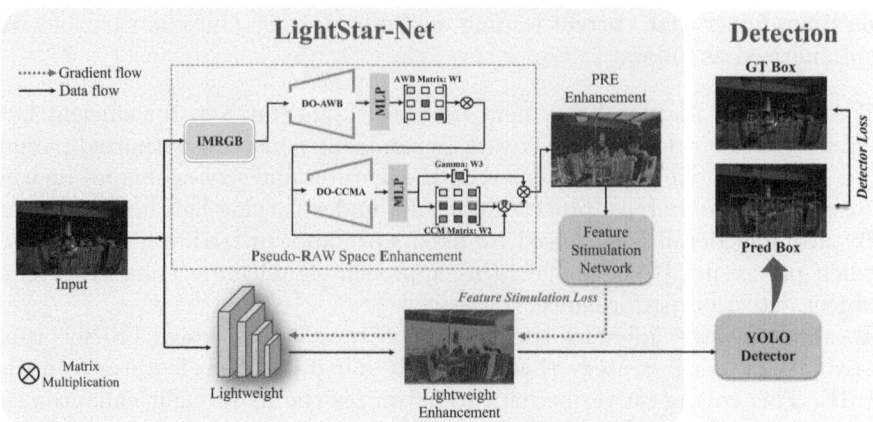

Fig. 2. The overall structure of LightStar-YOLO. This framework includes a Pseudo-RAW space enhancement module (PRE), a lightweight machine vision enhancement network, a feature stimulation network (FS-Net), and the YOLO detector. During training, FS-Net extracts image features enhanced by PRE and the lightweight network. In the inference phase, the PRE module and FS-Net are omitted.

The superior imaging quality of RAW images has prompted researchers to explore their use in low-light enhancement. Chen et al. [2] developed the first low-light enhancement network based on RAW images, demonstrating significant improvements in noise suppression and color saturation over traditional RGB methods. Xing et al. [30] introduced an inverse mapping network that restores RGB images to RAW space, enabling feature extraction. Zamir et al. [34] proposed the CycleISP network, which cyclically maps RGB images to RAW, adds noise, and then converts them back to RGB, facilitating the synthesis of realistic noise datasets for denoising RAW images. Although RAW images retain more details in low-light environments, they also introduce challenges such as increased noise, color distortion, and higher computational costs, which can affect model adaptability.

Low-Light Object Detection. In the field of low-light object detection, a common approach is to enhance images before detection to produce brighter images [7,18,29], known as the human vision-oriented two-stage enhancement detection framework. Another method combines image enhancement with detection in a machine vision-oriented single-stage approach. Related research [10,23] proposes image restoration training pipelines to improve detection robustness. Cui et al. [3] introduced the Illumination Adaptive Transformer (IAT), which dynamically adjusts image brightness by converting sRGB images to RAW-RGB space using inverse mapping. Du et al. [6] presented DAI-Net, which enhances low-light object detection through day-night domain adaptation, integrating Retinex theory and incorporating an interchange-redecomposition-coherence procedure to improve image decomposition. These methods primarily rely on RGB images and face challenges in effectively capturing complex lighting variations, often resulting in suboptimal performance in specific scenarios.

3   Method

In this section, we first introduce the PRE, the core component of LightStar-Net, providing a detailed description of its structure and composition. Next, we discuss the overall architecture of the efficient low-light detection framework, LightStar-YOLO, and explain the concept of auxiliary training, focusing on how FS-Net enhances the lightweight enhancement network's ability to extract and learn potential features from the PRE during pre-training.

3.1   Pseudo-RAW Space Enhancement

The PRE is responsible for enhancing discriminative features and contrast in dark regions for machine vision while adjusting the image color balance to suit machine vision requirements. As shown in Fig. 2, the PRE comprises the Inverse Mapping Network (IMRGB) and the Pseudo-image Signal Processing (DOISP) Enhancement Network. The IMRGB module maps RGB image space to a feature space referred to as the Pseudo-RAW image feature space, which does not contain actual RAW data. This feature space is not designed to restore the RGB image to its corresponding RAW image but rather provides a simulated imaging approach optimized for machine vision during end-to-end training.

The DOISP module processes the Pseudo-RAW image feature space further. Unlike the encoder-decoder structures typically used in two-stage enhancement detection algorithms, the DOISP module directly acts on the Pseudo-RAW image feature space to perform feature optimization, similar to Image Signal Processing (ISP). This approach avoids the loss of image detail and texture caused by upsampling and downsampling in encoder-decoder structures. It also mitigates the problem of reduced contrast between the target and background caused by excessive enhancement, which can interfere with subsequent detection. Additionally, the DOISP module employs an adaptive parameter optimization approach. The enhanced features are ultimately transmitted to the detector. By leveraging the strengths of ISP-based enhancement methods, the DOISP module adaptively optimizes the Pseudo-RAW image feature space under the constraints of the object detection loss function, enabling end-to-end low-light object detection.

Inverse Mapping Network. As shown in Fig. 3, the IMRGB module uses stacked Adaptive Enhancement Blocks (AEB) to process low-light images and extract mapping information. Initially, the module generates two independent feature maps and adjusts their channel numbers using convolution operations and a Tanh activation function.

$$[K_1, K_2] = f_{\text{AEB}}(X) \tag{1}$$

Here, K_1 and K_2 represent two independent feature maps, and X denotes the RGB image matrix under low-light conditions, and $\mathbf{X}_i$ signifies the Pseudo-RAW image feature space. The parameters α and β are adjustable and learned during training.

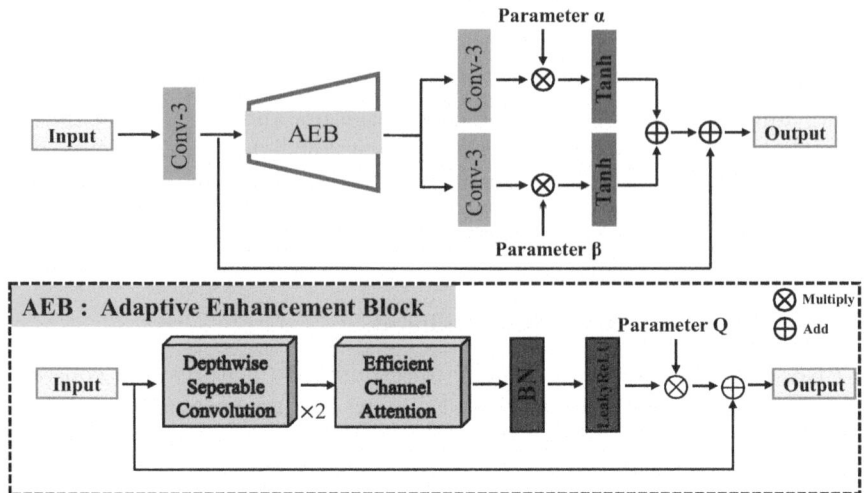

Fig. 3. IMRGB Network Structure

The AEB module primarily consists of depthwise separable convolution and the Efficient Channel Attention (ECA) mechanism [27]. Depthwise separable convolution effectively extracts image features while reducing both parameters and computational costs. The ECA mechanism uses one-dimensional convolution to adaptively adjust channel weights, enabling the extraction of key structural information from low-light images.

The ECA attention mechanism begins by compressing each channel of the feature map from a two-dimensional feature to a single value through a global average pooling layer (GAP), forming the basis for subsequent steps:

$$z_c = \frac{1}{H \times W} \sum_{i=1}^{H} \sum_{j=1}^{W} \mathbf{F}_c(i,j) \tag{2}$$

where F_c represents the feature map of the c_{th} channel.

Next, the kernel size of the adaptive one-dimensional convolution is determined and applied to the feature map to generate the weight vector for each channel:

$$\mathbf{w} = \sigma(\mathrm{Conv1D}(\mathbf{z})) \tag{3}$$

where Conv1D represents the one-dimensional convolution operation, $\mathbf{z}$ represents the global average pooling values of all channels, and σ represents the Sigmoid function.

Then, the output of the one-dimensional convolution is converted into the attention weights of the channels using the Sigmoid function:

$$\mathbf{w} = \sigma(\mathbf{w}) \tag{4}$$

Finally, these learned channel weights are applied to each channel of the original feature map to achieve adaptive feature attention:

$$\mathbf{F}'_c = \mathbf{w}_c \cdot \mathbf{F}_c \tag{5}$$

where $\mathbf{F}'_c$ represents the c_{th} channel feature map after processing by the ECA attention mechanism, and $\mathbf{w}_c$ represents the attention weight of the c_{th} channel.

Pseudo-image Signal Processing. RGB images are converted into corresponding Pseudo-RAW image feature space through the IMRGB module. In the real RAW imaging and ISP algorithm enhancement mechanism, RAW images undergo ISP processing, including image compression, white balance correction, black level correction, color correction, sharpening, and other steps, which finally convert the images to RGB images. Based on this enhancement idea, we designed a pseudo-ISP enhancement network called DOISP, which directly estimates various ISP correction parameters from Pseudo-RAW images for enhancing the Pseudo-RAW image feature space.

In DOISP, we propose two enhancement sub-modules: DO-AWB (Detection-Optimized Auto White Balance, As shown in Fig. 4) and DO-CCMA (Detection-Optimized Color Correction Matrix and Gamma) to simulate the enhancement process in ISP.

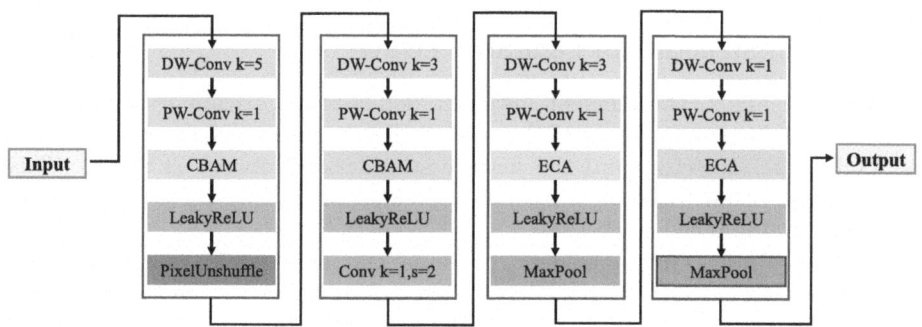

Fig. 4. DO-AWB Network Structure

In ISP processing, the purpose of auto white balance processing is to compensate for color deviations caused by the color temperature environment and inherent color channel gain deviations of the shooting instrument by changing the gain of color channels in the image, thus allowing the obtained image to correctly reflect the true colors of objects. Inspired by AWB, DO-AWB uses neural networks to dynamically simulate the gain values of the three color channels:

$$W_{\mathbf{1}} = f_{\mathrm{MLP}}(f_{DO-AWB}(X_i)) = \begin{pmatrix} t_1 & 0 & 0 \\ 0 & t_2 & 0 \\ 0 & 0 & t_3 \end{pmatrix} \tag{6}$$

$$X_e = W_{\mathbf{1}} \otimes X_i \tag{7}$$

In Eq. 6, X_i represents the simulated RAW image, $t_i, i \in (1,3)$ represents the gain value of each color channel optimized, and W_1 represents the generated optimization parameters. Equation 7 represents the simulated RAW image enhanced by the generated optimization parameters, where $\otimes$ represents matrix multiplication, and X_e represents the image enhanced by DO-AWB.

The DO-CCMA module simulates the process of the color correction matrix and gamma adjustment by learning the color correction matrix and gamma values through a multi-layer perceptron (MLP):

$$W_2 = f_{\mathrm{MLP}_1}(f_{DO-CCMA}(X_e)) = \begin{pmatrix} t_1 \ t_2 \ t_3 \\ t_4 \ t_5 \ t_6 \\ t_5 \ t_8 \ t_9 \end{pmatrix} \tag{8}$$

$$W_3 = f_{\mathrm{MLP}_2}(f_{DO-CCMA}(X_e)) = (t_{10}) \tag{9}$$

$$X_t = (W_2 \otimes X_e)^{W_3} \tag{10}$$

where Eq. 8 W_2 represents the generated color correction matrix parameter values, $t_i, i \in (1,9)$ represents the color correction values for each channel. In DO-CCMA, the Gamma coefficient W_3 is responsible for adjusting the global brightness of the image under machine vision. The entire optimization process of DO-CCMA is shown in Eq. 10, and X_e represents the final enhanced image.

3.2   Overall Structure of LightStar-YOLO

As shown in Fig. 2, the efficient low-light detection algorithm framework for auxiliary training consists of a PRE module, a lightweight enhancement network, the YOLO [21] detector, and the feature stimulation network (FS-Net). This detection algorithm framework is mainly divided into two stages: the training stage and the inference stage.

In the training stage, we first combine the lightweight machine vision enhancement network with the YOLO detector to form the end-to-end joint detection framework LightStar-YOLO. Next, we freeze the pre-trained weights of PRE and use FS-Net to extract the image features enhanced by PRE and the lightweight enhancement network. By further enhancing the learning capability of the lightweight network through the feature excitation loss function, we aim to better capture the potential features of PRE, thus improving the overall detection performance of the network. In the inference stage, to maintain efficient inference speed, we discard the PRE and feature stimulation modules, retaining only the detection network LightStar-YOLO, composed of the lightweight network and YOLO. This design reduces network complexity while still ensuring the efficiency and accuracy of the detection task. Through this structural design, the entire detection algorithm framework achieves superior performance and rapid response in practical applications.

Lightweight Enhancement Network. Figure 5 illustrates that the design of the lightweight enhancement network mainly consists of CBL convolution blocks and depthwise separable convolution blocks, which draws on the design principles

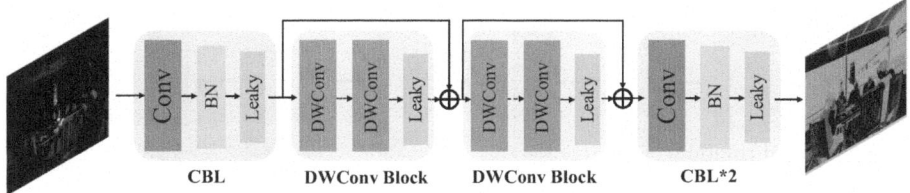

Fig. 5. Lightweight Network Structure

of residual networks. In visual enhancement tasks, downsampling feature maps can lead to a loss of spatial resolution, which diminishes the model's ability to capture fine structural information in images, making it prone to losing detail during the subsequent image reconstruction phase. To preserve as many original input features as possible throughout the enhancement process, the size of the feature maps is kept consistent with the input size, allowing for more accurate depiction and enhancement of details in the image, thus improving image quality and processing results.

Feature Stimulation Network. Based on the idea of auxiliary training, we propose a feature simulation network (FS-Net, as shown in Fig. 6). The primary goal of this network is to motivate the lightweight enhancement network to better extract and learn the potential features from the pre-trained PRE network, thereby addressing the issue of poor machine vision enhancement results due to the simple structure and weak feature extraction capability of the lightweight network when processing low-light images. The input data for FS-Net comes from the results of image enhancement processed by the PRE module and the lightweight network. In the construction of FS-Net, we primarily rely on a series of stacked Down modules. Whenever an enhanced image passes through a Down module, the size of the feature map is pooled to half the size of the previous feature map. To strengthen the excitation effect, FS-Net introduces an EMA [19] attention mechanism at the ends of the upper and lower parallel branches.

3.3   Loss Function

Tung et al. [25] suggested that in knowledge distillation, preserving knowledge by computing feature map similarity enables the teacher and student networks to produce similar activations for the same samples, thereby improving the distillation effect. Based on this idea, we propose the Channel Similarity Matrix Loss Function. This loss function measures the difference in high-level feature representations by comparing the inner products of corresponding channels in two feature maps, thereby enhancing LightStar-Net's performance in machine vision imaging. The formula for defining the Channel Similarity Matrix Loss Function is as follows:

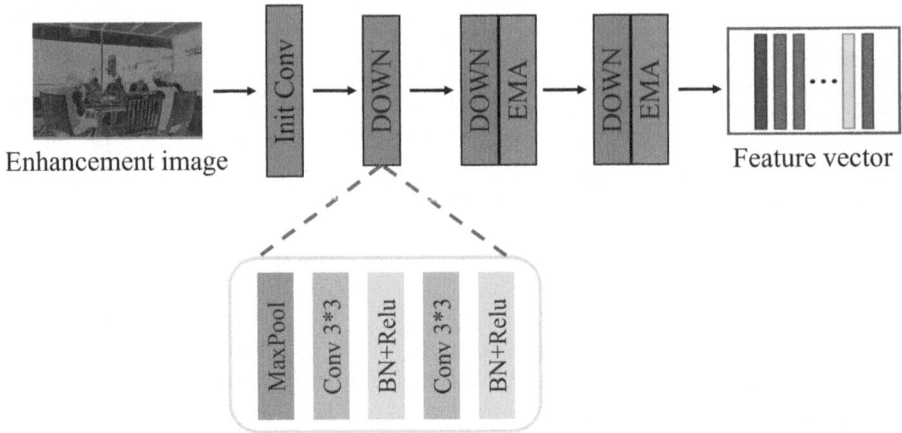

Fig. 6. Feature Stimulation Network Structure

$$D_c = \sum_i^w \sum_j^h A_{b,c,i,j} \cdot B_{b,c,i,j} \tag{11}$$

$$L_{CS} = \frac{1}{N_c} \sum_c^{N_c} \left(\frac{D_{i,j}}{W^2} - \frac{\hat{D}_{ij}}{W^2} \right)^2 \tag{12}$$

where D_c denotes the inner product of corresponding feature map tensors A and B for each channel C. b represents the batch size, N_c represents the number of channels, and w and h denote the width and height of the feature maps, respectively. i and j represent indices for width and height, respectively. W^2 denotes the square of the width. The overall definition of the Feature Stimulation Loss Function is expressed as follows:

$$L_k = L_{\text{smooth}_{L_1}} + L_{CS} \tag{13}$$

In the overall algorithm framework for training the machine vision enhancement module, we define the total loss function as the sum of the detector loss function and the feature excitation loss function. The specific formula for definition is as follows:

$$L_{total} = \lambda_1 L_{\text{smooth}_{L_1}} + \lambda_2 L_{CS} + \lambda_3 L_{\text{dec}} \tag{14}$$

where λ_1, λ_2, and λ_3 are balancing coefficients. Based on the performance comparison of the LCS and L1 loss functions in the ablation experiments, we set $\lambda_1 = 0.5$, $\lambda_2 = 0.3$, $\lambda_3 = 1.0$. These λ values were determined by comparing the effects of different loss functions.

4   Experiments

4.1   Training Details

We implemented our work using the open-source object detection toolbox MMDetection and employed data augmentation strategies (such as random cropping and random flipping) to assist in training the machine vision enhancement module. All images were resized to 608×608 pixels before enhancement. We chose stochastic gradient descent (SGD) as the optimizer, with an initial learning rate set to 0.001 and a step-based learning rate decay mechanism. To ensure fairness in the experiments, we used the SGD optimizer, as the comparison methods also employed this optimizer, avoiding the impact of optimizer differences on the results. The training process lasted for 25 epochs, with a learning rate warm-up strategy introduced to ensure stable convergence. All experiments were conducted on an Intel Core i7-12700F processor, 128GB of memory, and an NVIDIA RTX 3090 GPU.

4.2   Object Detection in Darkness

ExDark [15] and DARK FACE [31] are two well-known low-light detection datasets. We trained the models independently on these datasets and validated their performance using their respective test sets. The dataset splitting strategy was consistent with other methods, with 80% used for training and 20% for testing. The results were then compared with several state-of-the-art low-light scene enhancement detection models. Among them, MBLLEN [17], KinD [35], ZeroDCE [9], FourLLE [26], PairLIE [7], and Retinexformer [1] emphasize low-light image enhancement methods, where images are preprocessed before applying the YOLO detector. On the other hand, MAET [4], IAT [3], DENet [20], PE-YOLO [33] and DAI-Net [6] are single-stage low-light detection models aimed at machine vision. In the evaluation, we primarily focused on the mean Average Precision (mAP) at an IOU threshold of 0.5 and performed a visual analysis of the results on the ExDark [15] dataset.

The detection accuracy performance on the ExDark [15] dataset is shown in Table 1. The analysis results indicate that: 1) In low-light image enhancement models based on human visual recovery, simply adding the YOLO detector did not significantly improve detection performance in low-light scenes. In fact, this approach may even lead to a decline in the original method's detection performance. For example, the detection performance of KinD-YOLO and PairLIE-YOLO slightly decreased compared to the YOLO baseline model. ZeroDCE-YOLO's mAP50 (%) accuracy improved by only 0.7% over the YOLO baseline model, showing no significant enhancement in detection performance. 2) In integrated enhancement methods and domain generalization, the YOLO detector's detection performance in low-light scenes showed improvement. For example, PE-YOLO's mAP50 (%) accuracy improved by 1.7% over the YOLO baseline model, demonstrating some competitiveness. Our proposed LightStar-Net does not require pretraining on other dark datasets. LightStar-YOLO's mAP50 (%)

Table 1. Comparison of detection accuracy of different methods on ExDark. Red indicates the best result, and blue indicates the second best result.

Method	Bicycle	Boat	Bottle	Bus	Car	Cat	Chair	Cup	Dog	Motorbike	People	Table	mAP50(%)↑
YOLO [21] Baseline	80.7	73.9	77.5	92.1	83.1	66.5	71.5	78.6	76.4	76.7	81.5	57.0	76.3
MBLLEN [17] -YOLO	82.2	76.7	76.5	92.5	83.1	72.4	71.5	77.3	78.5	74.5	80.8	55.6	76.8
KinD [35] -YOLO	80.8	77.2	74.7	92.0	84.5	67.2	70.7	78.9	77.7	74.7	80.0	54.0	76.0
ZeroDCE [9] -YOLO	79.1	79.1	76.5	91.5	85.2	68.8	71.7	76.7	78.9	77.1	82.0	57.2	77.0
Retinexformer [1] -YOLO	82.0	80.5	80.9	91.3	83.1	70.8	70.3	76.9	75.8	75.4	80.8	57.8	77.1
PairLIE [7] -YOLO	82.5	76.7	76.4	91.6	82.9	71.0	70.0	76.9	78.9	72.6	79.9	55.3	76.2
FourLLE [26] -YOLO	81.8	78.1	74.2	91.3	82.6	67.7	69.1	73.0	76.1	74.8	79.5	55.3	75.3
MAET [4]	83.1	78.5	75.6	92.9	83.1	73.4	71.3	79.0	79.8	77.2	81.1	57.0	77.7
IAT-YOLO [3]	79.8	76.9	78.6	92.5	83.8	73.6	72.4	78.6	79.0	79.0	81.1	57.7	77.8
DENet [20]	80.4	79.7	77.9	91.2	82.7	72.8	69.9	80.1	77.2	76.7	82.0	57.2	77.3
PE-YOLO [33]	84.7	79.2	79.3	92.5	83.9	71.5	71.7	79.7	79.7	77.3	81.8	55.3	78.0
DAI-Net [6]	83.8	75.8	75.1	94.2	84.1	74.9	73.1	79.2	82.2	76.4	80.7	59.8	78.3
LightStar-YOLO (ours)	83.6	80.5	77.0	91.4	84.8	73.9	73.9	80.6	78.1	78.6	82.1	58.4	78.6

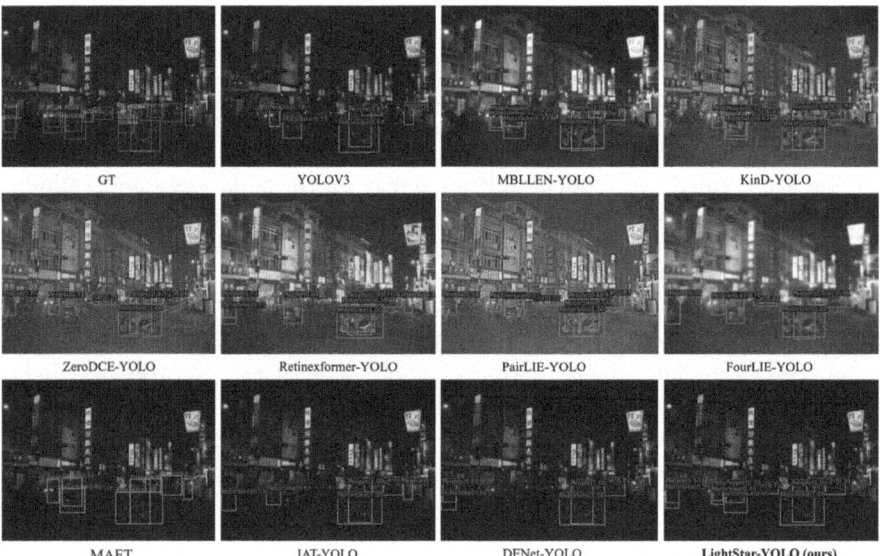

Fig. 7. Visualization of detection results in night-time street environments using different methods

accuracy improved by 2.3% over the YOLO baseline model. Compared to the state-of-the-art DAI-Net, the mAP50 (%) accuracy metric improved by 0.3%.

Figure 7 shows the detection performance of LightStar-YOLO in a night-time street scene, where it outperforms DENet-YOLO and IAT-YOLO in detection results. Table 1 and Fig. 7 show that the FS-Net Feature Stimulation function enables LightStar-YOLO to learn latent features from the PRE module, enhancing its machine vision capability in low-light environments. Furthermore, it outperforms other models used for low-light scene enhancement detection. These results demonstrate the effectiveness of the proposed detection algorithm

Table 2. Comparison of detection accuracy of different methods on DarkFace. Red indicates the best result, and blue indicates the second best result.

Method	Face	mAP50(%)↑
YOLO [21] Baseline	48.3	48.3
MBLLEN [17] -YOLO	51.6	51.6
KinD [35] -YOLO	51.6	51.6
ZeroDCE [9] -YOLO	54.2	54.2
Retinexformer [1] -YOLO	57.8	57.8
PairLIE [7] -YOLO	56.8	56.8
FourLLE [26] -YOLO	51.2	51.2
MAET [4]	55.8	55.8
IAT-YOLO [3]	53.1	53.1
DENet [20]	51.2	51.2
PE-YOLO [33]	51.1	51.1
DAI-Net [6]	57.0	57.0
LightStar-YOLO (ours)	58.5	58.5

framework, particularly in improving detection accuracy through the auxiliary training strategy based on the Pseudo-RAW image enhancement method.

Similar comparative experiments were conducted on the DARK FACE [31] dataset to verify the generalization capability and detection accuracy of the detection algorithm that combines Pseudo-RAW space Enhancement methods with auxiliary training strategies across different datasets. As shown in Table 2, the detection accuracy of LightStar-YOLO is 1.5% higher than that of the current state-of-the-art algorithm, with a mAP50 (%) detection accuracy of 58.5%. Additionally, LightStar-YOLO's detection accuracy also surpasses traditional two-stage enhancement detection framework methods, such as MBLLEN-YOLO, Retinexformer-YOLO, and FourLIE-YOLO. This further validates the effectiveness of the detection algorithm that combines Pseudo-RAW image enhancement methods with auxiliary training strategies in maintaining detection accuracy and demonstrates its strong generalization capability across various datasets.

4.3   Inference Efficiency Analysis

Table 3 lists the performance of different models in terms of the number of parameters and inference time. The MAET [4] method is excluded because it does not require additional parameters and computations. Since all methods are based on the unmodified YOLO model, we only compare the image enhancement network parts of each model to analyze and compare their inference efficiency. The image size used in this experiment is 256 × 256. Notably, LightStar-Net performs best in terms of model parameters and FLOPs (floating-point operations), with the shortest inference time. This result demonstrates the significant advantage of our proposed detection algorithm that combines Pseudo-RAW image enhancement

Table 3. Comparison of inference efficiency of different models. Red indicates the best result, and blue indicates the second best result.

Method	FLOPs(G)↓	Parameters(K)↓	Times(s)↓
MBLLEN [17]	19.95	20470	1.98121
KinD [35]	356.72	8160	0.03802
ZeroDCE [9]	2.53	80	0.00201
Retinexformer [1]	17.01	1605	0.01301
PairLIE [7]	22.34	341	0.00370
FourLLE [26]	2.54	119	0.00475
IAT [3]	1.44	90	0.00332
DENet [20]	0.31	24	0.00123
LightStar-Net (ours)	0.17	3	0.00037

methods with auxiliary training strategies in inference speed. Combining the data from Table 1 and Table 3, it can be observed that LightStar-Net exhibits excellent inference speed while maintaining detection accuracy, with an inference speed that is three times that of DENet [20]. Therefore, LightStar-Net has a notable efficiency advantage without significantly sacrificing machine vision enhancement capability. This lightweight and fast model is suitable for applications requiring strict real-time performance, such as smart driving, intelligent surveillance, and edge computing devices with limited memory resources.

4.4 Ablation Study

To evaluate the impact of each component on overall performance, a series of ablation experiments were conducted on the ExDark [15] dataset. These experiments involved removing or modifying specific parts of the model one by one to observe the effects on performance.

IMRGB and DOISP. The PRE consists of the IMRGB and DOISP modules. We conducted ablation experiments to evaluate their impact. Table 4 shows that adding only the IMRGB module increased the mAP50 (%) detection accuracy of LightStar-YOLO to 78.1%, an improvement of 1.8% over the base YOLO detector, indicating its positive impact. The accuracy achieved by adding only the DOISP module was 77.5%. Although DOISP improved performance, its impact was relatively weaker. However, when both IMRGB and DOISP modules were used together, the detection accuracy increased to 78.6%. This demonstrates their combined effect on model performance, effectively optimizing the detection results. The IMRGB module primarily adapts low-light RGB images to a Pseudo-RAW feature space. Even without the optimization of DOISP, the detector's loss function can still optimize the Pseudo-RAW feature space, enhancing the alignment of images with its perspective, thus improving detection performance to some extent. The DOISP module further enhances the Pseudo-RAW

Table 4. Comparison of ablation experiments for IMRGB module and DOISP module.

Method	IMRGB	DOISP	mAP50(%)↑
YOLO [21]	×	×	76.3
LightStar-YOLO	√	×	78.1
LightStar-YOLO	×	√	77.5
LightStar-YOLO	√	√	78.6

Table 5. Comparison of lesion experiments using DO-CCMA and DO-AWB modules.

	IMRGB	DOISP		mAP50(%)↑
		DO-AWB	DO-CCMA	
LightStar-YOLO	√	×	×	78.1
LightStar-YOLO	√	√	×	78.3
LightStar-YOLO	√	×	√	78.5
LightStar-YOLO	√	√	√	78.6

feature space for machine vision. Directly enhancing RGB images provides limited improvement to the detector. Therefore, PRE first maps the RGB image to the machine vision feature space and then enhances the features to achieve optimal performance.

DO-CCMA and DO-AWB. The DOISP module consists of two enhancement sub-modules: DO-CCMA and DO-AWB. To investigate the effects of these two modules on enhancing the feature space of Pseudo-RAW images, we conducted a series of ablation experiments. The comparison results in Table 5 show that LightStar-YOLO with the DO-AWB enhancement sub-module improved detection accuracy by 0.2%compared to the version using only the IMRGB module. Similarly, LightStar-YOLO with the DO-CCMA enhancement sub-module improved detection accuracy by 0.4% compared to the version using only the IMRGB module. This indicates that both DO-CCMA and DO-AWB have a positive impact on enhancing the feature space of Pseudo-RAW images. The DO-CCMA module introduces a Color Correction Matrix (CCM) capable of correcting color parameters and includes gamma parameters. Through gamma brightness adjustment, this module effectively enhances the global brightness of the image in machine vision. Therefore, compared to the DO-AWB module, the DO-CCMA module has a more significant effect on enhancing the feature space of Pseudo-RAW images.

Feature Stimulation Loss. Similarly, we validated the effectiveness of the Channel Similarity Matrix Loss. As shown in Table 6, we first added the $smooth_{L_1}$ loss function independently. The results indicated that this feature excitation module significantly enhanced overall performance, increasing mAP50

Table 6. Comparison of ablation experiments for feature stimulation loss functions.

Method	L_{CS}	$smooth_{L_1}$	mAP50(%)↑
YOLO	×	×	76.3
LightStar-YOLO	√	×	77.6
LightStar-YOLO	×	√	77.9
LightStar-YOLO	√	√	78.6

Table 7. EMA attention ablation experiment comparison.

Method	EMA	mAP50(%)↑
LightStar-YOLO	×	78.1
LightStar-YOLO	√	78.6

(%) detection accuracy by 1.6% percentage points compared to the YOLO baseline, thereby demonstrating the effectiveness of the $smooth_{L_1}$ loss function as a feature excitation mechanism. This loss function combines the characteristics of both L_1 and L_2, allowing LightStar-Net to converge quickly while remaining robust during optimization. Next, we independently added the Channel Similarity Matrix loss function, which showed that LightStar-YOLO's detection accuracy improved by 1.3% percentage points compared to the YOLO baseline. Although its contribution to LightStar-Net was lower, when combined with the $smooth_{L_1}$ loss function, LightStar-YOLO's detection accuracy reached 78.6%, achieving the best results. This indicates a synergistic effect between the two loss functions. The Channel Similarity Matrix loss function, unlike $smooth_{L_1}$, measures differences between two feature maps. This enables the network to capture low-light visual information more accurately, enhancing machine vision performance in complex environments.

Additionally, we conducted modular ablation experiments on FS-Net using the ExDark [15] dataset to validate the effectiveness of the EMA [19] attention mechanism. As shown in Table 7, the EMA attention mechanism effectively aligns the high-level features of the two enhancement networks. After adding this mechanism, the detection accuracy of LightStar-YOLO increased by 0.5%, indicating that the EMA attention mechanism effectively guides FS-Net in extracting key feature information. Through a cross-space learning strategy, the EMA attention mechanism successfully integrates the feature maps output by the two parallel sub-networks, enhancing the attention network's ability to extract features.

5   Conclusion

In this paper, we propose an efficient low-light object detection network enhanced in the Pseudo-RAW space, named LightStar-Net. To enhance the efficiency of machine vision-oriented low-light object detection, we introduce FS-Net with an auxiliary training strategy, enabling the lightweight network in LightStar-Net to rapidly extract deep latent features from the PRE module. LightStar-Net is embedded within an end-to-end object detection framework and optimized for performance. Extensive experiments on low-light object and face detection tasks demonstrate that the proposed LightStar-YOLO surpasses existing state-of-the-art methods in both detection accuracy and model complexity.

Acknowledgement. This work was supported by the Natural Science Foundation of Chongqing (Grant No. CSTB2022NSCQ-MSX0493), National Natural Science Foundation of China (Grant No. 62102309).

References

1. Cai, Y., Bian, H., Lin, J., Wang, H., Timofte, R., Zhang, Y.: Retinexformer: one-stage retinex-based transformer for low-light image enhancement. In: Proceedings of the IEEE/CVF International Conference on Computer Vision, pp. 12504–12513 (2023)
2. Chen, C., Chen, Q., Xu, J., Koltun, V.: Learning to see in the dark. In: Proceedings of the IEEE Conference on Computer Vision and Pattern Recognition, pp. 3291–3300 (2018)
3. Cui, Z., et al.: You only need 90k parameters to adapt light: a light weight transformer for image enhancement and exposure correction. arXiv preprint arXiv:2205.14871 (2022)
4. Cui, Z., Qi, G.J., Gu, L., You, S., Zhang, Z., Harada, T.: Multitask AET with orthogonal tangent regularity for dark object detection. In: Proceedings of the IEEE/CVF International Conference on Computer Vision, pp. 2553–2562 (2021)
5. Dai, J., Li, Y., He, K., Sun, J.: R-FCN: object detection via region-based fully convolutional networks. In: Advances in Neural Information Processing Systems, vol. 29 (2016)
6. Du, Z., Shi, M., Deng, J.: Boosting object detection with zero-shot day-night domain adaptation. In: Proceedings of the IEEE/CVF Conference on Computer Vision and Pattern Recognition, pp. 12666–12676 (2024)
7. Fu, Z., Yang, Y., Tu, X., Huang, Y., Ding, X., Ma, K.K.: Learning a simple low-light image enhancer from paired low-light instances. In: Proceedings of the IEEE/CVF Conference on Computer Vision and Pattern Recognition, pp. 22252–22261 (2023)
8. Girshick, R., Donahue, J., Darrell, T., Malik, J.: Rich feature hierarchies for accurate object detection and semantic segmentation. In: Proceedings of the IEEE Conference on Computer Vision and Pattern Recognition, pp. 580–587 (2014)
9. Guo, C., et al.: Zero-reference deep curve estimation for low-light image enhancement. In: Proceedings of the IEEE/CVF Conference on Computer Vision and Pattern Recognition, pp. 1780–1789 (2020)

10. Hashmi, K.A., Kallempudi, G., Stricker, D., Afzal, M.Z.: Featenhancer: enhancing hierarchical features for object detection and beyond under low-light vision. In: Proceedings of the IEEE/CVF International Conference on Computer Vision, pp. 6725–6735 (2023)
11. Kuznetsova, A., et al.: The open images dataset v4: unified image classification, object detection, and visual relationship detection at scale. Int. J. Comput. Vision **128**(7), 1956–1981 (2020)
12. Li, Z., Yi, S., Ma, Z.: Rendering nighttime image via cascaded color and brightness compensation. In: Proceedings of the IEEE/CVF Conference on Computer Vision and Pattern Recognition, pp. 897–905 (2022)
13. Lin, T.-Y., et al.: Microsoft COCO: common objects in context. In: Fleet, D., Pajdla, T., Schiele, B., Tuytelaars, T. (eds.) ECCV 2014. LNCS, vol. 8693, pp. 740–755. Springer, Cham (2014). https://doi.org/10.1007/978-3-319-10602-1_48
14. Liu, W., et al.: SSD: single shot multibox detector. In: Leibe, B., Matas, J., Sebe, N., Welling, M. (eds.) ECCV 2016. LNCS, vol. 9905, pp. 21–37. Springer, Cham (2016). https://doi.org/10.1007/978-3-319-46448-0_2
15. Loh, Y.P., Chan, C.S.: Getting to know low-light images with the exclusively dark dataset. Comput. Vis. Image Underst. **178**, 30–42 (2019)
16. Lore, K.G., Akintayo, A., Sarkar, S.: LlNet: a deep autoencoder approach to natural low-light image enhancement. Pattern Recogn. **61**, 650–662 (2017)
17. Lv, F., Lu, F., Wu, J., Lim, C.: MBLLEN: low-light image/video enhancement using CNNs. In: BMVC, vol. 220, p. 4. Northumbria University (2018)
18. Ma, L., Ma, T., Liu, R., Fan, X., Luo, Z.: Toward fast, flexible, and robust low-light image enhancement. In: Proceedings of the IEEE/CVF Conference on Computer Vision and Pattern Recognition, pp. 5637–5646 (2022)
19. Ouyang, D., et al.: Efficient multi-scale attention module with cross-spatial learning. In: ICASSP 2023-2023 IEEE International Conference on Acoustics, Speech and Signal Processing (ICASSP), pp. 1–5. IEEE (2023)
20. Qin, Q., Chang, K., Huang, M., Li, G.: DeNet: detection-driven enhancement network for object detection under adverse weather conditions. In: Proceedings of the Asian Conference on Computer Vision, pp. 2813–2829 (2022)
21. Redmon, J., Farhadi, A.: Yolov3: an incremental improvement. arXiv preprint arXiv:1804.02767 (2018)
22. Ren, S., He, K., Girshick, R., Sun, J.: Faster R-CNN: towards real-time object detection with region proposal networks. In: Advances in Neural Information Processing Systems, vol. 28 (2015)
23. Sun, S., Ren, W., Wang, T., Cao, X.: Rethinking image restoration for object detection. Adv. Neural. Inf. Process. Syst. **35**, 4461–4474 (2022)
24. Tian, Z., Shen, C., Chen, H., He, T.: FCOS: fully convolutional one-stage object detection. arxiv 2019. arXiv preprint arXiv:1904.01355 (1904)
25. Tung, F., Mori, G.: Similarity-preserving knowledge distillation. In: Proceedings of the IEEE/CVF International Conference on Computer Vision, pp. 1365–1374 (2019)
26. Wang, C., Wu, H., Jin, Z.: FourLLIE: boosting low-light image enhancement by Fourier frequency information. In: Proceedings of the 31st ACM International Conference on Multimedia, pp. 7459–7469 (2023)
27. Wang, Q., Wu, B., Zhu, P., Li, P., Zuo, W., Hu, Q.: ECA-net: efficient channel attention for deep convolutional neural networks. In: Proceedings of the IEEE/CVF Conference on Computer Vision and Pattern Recognition, pp. 11534–11542 (2020)
28. Wei, C., Wang, W., Yang, W., Liu, J.: Deep Retinex decomposition for low-light enhancement. arXiv preprint arXiv:1808.04560 (2018)

29. Wu, Y., et al.: Learning semantic-aware knowledge guidance for low-light image enhancement. In: Proceedings of the IEEE/CVF Conference on Computer Vision and Pattern Recognition, pp. 1662–1671 (2023)
30. Xing, Y., Qian, Z., Chen, Q.: Invertible image signal processing. In: Proceedings of the IEEE/CVF Conference on Computer Vision and Pattern Recognition, pp. 6287–6296 (2021)
31. Yang, W., et al.: Advancing image understanding in poor visibility environments: a collective benchmark study. IEEE Trans. Image Process. **29**, 5737–5752 (2020)
32. Yi, X., Xu, H., Zhang, H., Tang, L., Ma, J.: Diff-Retinex: rethinking low-light image enhancement with a generative diffusion model. In: Proceedings of the IEEE/CVF International Conference on Computer Vision, pp. 12302–12311 (2023)
33. Yin, X., Yu, Z., Fei, Z., Lv, W., Gao, X.: PE-YOLO: pyramid enhancement network for dark object detection. In: International Conference on Artificial Neural Networks, pp. 163–174. Springer (2023)
34. Zamir, S.W., et al.: CycleISP: real image restoration via improved data synthesis. In: Proceedings of the IEEE/CVF Conference on Computer Vision and Pattern Recognition, pp. 2696–2705 (2020)
35. Zhang, Y., Zhang, J., Guo, X.: Kindling the darkness: a practical low-light image enhancer. In: Proceedings of the 27th ACM International Conference on Multimedia, pp. 1632–1640 (2019)
36. Zhou, D., Yang, Z., Yang, Y.: Pyramid diffusion models for low-light image enhancement. arXiv preprint arXiv:2305.10028 (2023)

DASSF: Dynamic-Attention Scale-Sequence Fusion for Aerial Object Detection

Haodong Li[ID] and Haicheng Qu[(✉)][ID]

Liaoning Technical University, School of Software, Huludao 125105, China
472321734@stu.lntu.edu.cn, quhaicheng@lntu.edu.cn

Abstract. The detection of small objects in aerial images is a fundamental task in the field of computer vision. Moving objects in aerial photography have problems such as different shapes and sizes, dense overlap, occlusion by the background, and object blur, however, the original YOLO method has low overall detection accuracy due to its weak ability to perceive targets of different scales. In order to improve the detection accuracy of densely overlapping small targets and fuzzy targets, this paper proposes a dynamic-attention scale-sequence fusion method (DASSF) for small target detection in aerial images. First, we propose a dynamic scale sequence feature fusion (DSSFF) module that improves the upsampling mechanism and reduces computational load. Secondly, a x-small object detection head is specially added to enhance the detection capability of small targets. Finally, in order to improve the expressive ability of targets of different types and sizes, we use the dynamic head (DyHead). The model we proposed solves the problem of small target detection in aerial images and can be applied to multiple different versions of the YOLO method, which is universal. Experimental results demonstrate that when the DASSF method is applied to YOLOv8, it achieves a 10.2% and 4.2% improvement in mean Average Precision (mAP) on the VisDrone-2019 and DIOR datasets, respectively, compared to YOLOv8n. This performance surpasses that of current mainstream methods. Additionally, when the DASSF method is integrated into different versions of the YOLO model, the detection performance for aerial images significantly improves compared to the baseline models.

Keywords: Aerial images · Small target detection · Feature fusion · Upsampling method

1 Introduction

Object detection is now widely applied in fields such as intelligent transportation [6], medical diagnosis [20], industrial manufacturing [35], and re-identification [23]. With the ongoing advancements in drone technology and the growing maturity of remote sensing technology, aerial image object detection has emerged as a significant research area due to its immense potential. However, compared to traditional object detection in natural scenes, aerial images present unique challenges. These include a wide range of target scales, small

P. Didyk and J. Hou (Eds.): CVM 2025, LNCS 15663, pp. 212–227, 2025.
https://doi.org/10.1007/978-981-96-5809-1_12

Fig. 1. The primary challenges and obstacles encountered in aerial image object detection.

object sizes, diverse angle variations, complex backgrounds, and vulnerability to solar radiation and atmospheric conditions, as illustrated in Fig. 1. These factors greatly complicate the accurate detection and recognition of small targets in aerial images. The YOLO series networks, while popular, lack effective feature fusion and scale perception capabilities for objects of varying sizes and complex shapes in aerial images. In contrast, two-stage convolutional neural network (CNN) detection methods or Transformer-based DETR series methods consume excessive computational resources. Therefore, further research and innovation are essential to improve both the accuracy and efficiency of object detection in aerial images under these conditions.

According to the definition in the MS COCO dataset [14] for object detection, small targets refer to objects with a size of less than 32 × 32 pixels. Detecting small targets is crucial in many real-world applications. For instance, in agricultural pest control, small target detection technology can be used to identify pests in crops. By accurately detecting these tiny targets, it enables farmers to take timely prevention and control measures, ensuring the healthy growth of crops. In medical image analysis, small target detection is widely applied in cell detection and lesion identification. This is especially important in the early diagnosis of tumors, where accurate identification of tiny lesions is critical for improving treatment outcomes and increasing patient survival rates. Similarly, in marine biological monitoring, small target detection technology is employed to identify microorganisms and plankton communities in the ocean, providing valuable insights for ecological research and environmental protection. While existing object detection methods have made progress in these fields, small targets often occupy very small pixel areas in images and can easily blend into complex backgrounds, making it difficult for traditional methods to effectively extract fine features. This results in low detection accuracy. Additionally, factors such as object overlap and image blur further complicate small target detection, limiting the performance of current methods when dealing with multi-scale targets.

In this paper, to enhance the detection performance of the YOLO series network model in aerial images, particularly for small targets, we propose a YOLO model integrated with Dynamic-Attention Scale-Sequence Fusion (DASSF). The main contributions of this paper can be summarized as follows:

- We propose a new and effective method, DASSF, for aerial image object detection tasks, which combines multiple modules to effectively improve the detection of objects across different scales and categories, especially small objects.
- We design a dynamic scale sequence feature fusion (DSSFF) module to accurately and efficiently extract global high-level semantic information in images of different scales, which not only reduces the model complexity but also can accurately detect small objects through point sampling.
- We conduct detailed and comprehensive comparison and ablation experiments on the proposed DASSF method, which demonstrates its effectiveness. Additionally, we combine it flexibly with multiple YOLO series methods to showcase the versatility of the approach.

2   Related Work

2.1   Aerial Image Object Detection

In recent years, research on aerial image target detection has mainly focused on improving model performance by improving feature extraction and context learning. For example, CFIL [29] introduces a frequency domain feature extraction module [30] and a frequency domain feature interaction mechanism to enhance the ability to extract significant features and better distinguish targets in complex backgrounds. MFC [21] proposes a frequency domain filtering module to further enhance the feature expression ability of dense targets, thereby performing well in processing complex scenes. LR-FPN [12] improves remote sensing target detection by strengthening low-level position information and fine-grained context interaction, especially in application scenarios such as agriculture and urban planning. In addition, PBSL [22] can highlight relevant target features in aerial images and suppress irrelevant information by introducing a multimodal alignment method, thereby improving the robustness of overall detection.

Although these methods have achieved good results in aerial image target detection tasks, especially in the detection of dense targets and overlapping targets, they still have some limitations. First, most methods mainly improve the average detection accuracy of the overall target, but the detection effect of small targets is limited, especially under complex backgrounds and blurred conditions, the detection accuracy is still not ideal. Secondly, many existing methods are often optimized for specific model structures, lack versatility, and are difficult to flexibly apply under different detection tasks or model frameworks, which limits their widespread promotion in practical applications.

2.2   Small Object Detection

As a major challenge in the field of target detection, small target detection has received extensive attention in recent years. Existing research mainly improves the detection performance of small targets by integrating attention mechanisms, optimizing loss functions, and extracting features in stages. For example, the InsDist [11] method combines feature-based and relationship-based knowledge distillation to improve the detection effect of small objects in remote sensing images; in the field of agricultural control, GA-SGD [32] guides the model to focus on the detection of small pests by designing selection, crossover, and mutation operations, thereby improving the detection effect in complex environments; in addition, LESPS [33] uses a point supervision method for the detection of infrared small targets, which greatly reduces the cost of manual annotation and improves detection efficiency; UBDDM [17] achieves multi-scale recognition of significant areas in the image by constructing a small target perception module, and achieves good results in the two-stage bolt defect detection task.

Although these methods have made significant progress in small target detection tasks in different application fields, they still have some shortcomings. First, although the two-stage detection method improves the detection accuracy, its complex architecture greatly increases the computational overhead and inference time of the model, making it difficult to achieve efficient operation in application scenarios with limited resources or high real-time requirements. Secondly, the knowledge distillation method enhances the model's perception of small targets through a large amount of training, but the distillation process usually consumes a lot of computing resources, and the training process is complex and time-consuming, which is difficult to meet the needs of large-scale practical applications. Finally, many existing methods still have the problem of insufficient accuracy when dealing with dense and overlapping small targets, especially when the background is complex or the target is blurred, the detection performance is relatively limited. These problems limit the performance of existing small target detection methods in efficient and accurate detection.

3   Method

3.1   The Overall Architecture of DASSF-YOLO

Figure 2 shows the overall architecture of the dynamic-attention scale-sequence fusion method (DASSF) network model we designed. We use CSPDarknet53 as the backbone network. We utilize ASF-YOLO [9]'s neck network to enhance the detection of small, dense, and blurry targets in aerial images. The neck of the network utilizes the TFE in ASF-YOLO twice for fusing feature maps of different dimensions to obtain rich global channel information. Then apply the DSSFF to obtain accurate local location information. Then, the processed information is effectively interacted through the CPAM. Finally, by adding the x-small detection head and applying the dynamic head (DyHead). The model can detect objects of various scales in aerial images.

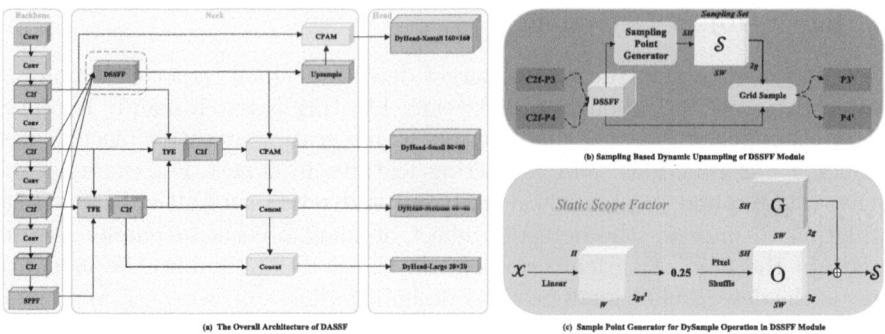

Fig. 2. (a) The overall architecture of our proposed DASSF. DSSFF refers to the dynamic scale sequence feature fusion module we propose. (b) and (c) show schematic diagrams of the DSSFF module, DySample. S represents the upsampling ratio, G denotes the grid sampling point coordinates, and O indicates the point position offset generated by the dynamic sampling point generator. SH and SW represent the sampling height and width, respectively. gs^2 refers to the number of channels in the feature map after the linear layer. The remaining components are: TFE, the triple feature encoding module; CPAM, the channel and position attention mechanism; and DyHead, the dynamic detection head.

3.2   Improvements to the Neck

Triple Feature Encoding Module. The TFE module is a feature fusion mechanism. First, adjust the number of channels of the large, medium and small feature layers to make them equal through CBS operation. Then, the large-scale feature map is subjected to a down-sampling operation of maximum pooling + average pooling, which helps to retain the high-resolution features and the diversity of semantic information of different objects in aerial images; for small-scale feature maps, the nearest neighbor interpolation method is used for upsampling, which can maintain the richness of local features of low-resolution images and prevent the loss of small target location feature information. Finally, feature maps of different scales are fused through concat operations.

Dynamic Scale Sequence Feature Fusion Module. The original SSFF module was designed for the P3 layer and is a key component used to process multiscale information and has the ability to extract features of different scales. Scale means detail in the image. A blurry image may lose details, but the structural features of the image can be preserved, helping to solve the image blur problem in satellite remote sensing images. The input image of SSFF is in formula 1.

$$F_o(w, h) = G_o(w, h) \times f(w, h). \tag{1}$$

where f(w, h) represents a 2D input image with width w and height h. $G_o(w, h)$ is the filter used for smooth convolution. This module contains two upsampling operations for the P4 and P5 layers. The nearest upsampling method in the original module will lead to the loss of key image details and requires a lot of calcu-

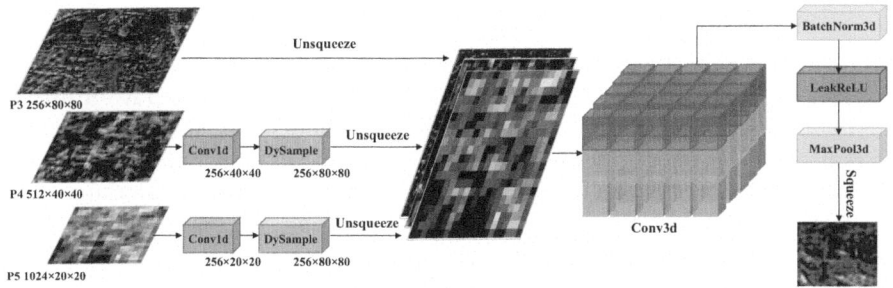

Fig. 3. The structure of the DSSFF. The features are extracted efficiently and accurately through dynamic upsampling, feature map stacking, and 3D convolution normalization activation operations. The detailed process of dynamic upsampling is shown in Algorithm 1.

Algorithm 1. The process of dynamic upsampling
___

   Input: The feature map x of size C H W, upsampling multiple scale and groups default to 4.

   Output: The feature map X' of size C scale H scale W.

1: Generate a 2D convolutional layer for offset and perform normal distribution initialization, and get out_1.
2: Generate the initial position for offset calculation, and get out_2.
3: Apply out_1 to the input x and adjust the range by 0.25, then append the offset of out_2, and then transform it into 2 -1 H W, and get out_3.
4: Create a normalized target coordinate grid, and get out_4.
5: Add out_3 and out_4 and normalize them to the [-1,1] interval, and get out_5.
6: Use pixel_shuffle to upsample coordinates for out_5 and adjust the output size, then use grid_sample for bilinear interpolation sampling, and get out.
7: **return** out.
___

lation and parameter overhead. Therefore, we introduce DySample [16], an ultra-lightweight and effective dynamic upsampler to replace the nearest upsampling method in the original module. The structure is shown in (b) and (c) of Fig. 2.

We adopt a static factor sampling method, based on the theory of adjusting point sampling position offset, to dynamically create a sampling set of point positions through the sample point generator in the feature map. If the input feature map is X (with size C × H × W), the offset O is obtained by the network through projection and multiplication by the static factor g.

$$O = g \times \text{Linear}(X). \tag{2}$$

Among them, Linear is a linear layer used to generate the offset O based on the input feature X, and g is a constant that controls the size of the offset.

$$S = G + O. \tag{3}$$

$$X' = \text{Grid\_sample}(X, S). \tag{4}$$

The generated offset O is added to the original sampling grid G and then passed into the grid sampling function along with the original feature map X for upsampling. This sampling point offset upsampling mechanism helps feature maps of different scales better distinguish boundary areas and extract object information at varying scales. Moreover, by controlling the offset position, the overlap of sampling points is reduced, the positions of sampling points are optimized, and thus the computational complexity is minimized. The structure of the DSSFF module is shown in Fig. 3. The pseudocode for dynamic upsampling with a static sampling factor of 0.25 is shown in Algorithm 1.

Channel and Position Attention Mechanism. The CPAM integrates the DSSFF and TFE modules, which focus on information-rich channels and small object features related to spatial location. This allows the model to more accurately identify and locate small targets in images, thereby improving the detection capabilities of detailed small objects. Input 1 is the detailed features after TFE processing as channel attention network, which is used to effectively capture cross-channel interactions. This is an attention mechanism that does not require dimensionality reduction. The capture of local cross-channel interactions is achieved using 1D convolutions of size k, where the kernel size k represents the coverage of local cross-channel interactions. Using the output of the channel attention mechanism and the feature map processed by DSSFF as the input of the position attention network, the position information of different targets can be extracted.

3.3   Improvements to the Head

Dynamic Head. The aerial imagery targets used in this study presented complex backgrounds. Because the target in the drone image is blocked by houses and trees and the target in the remote sensing image is affected by light and clouds. The scale of the target is easy to change, and the image is easy to become blurred and distorted. Therefore, it is crucial that the detection method has a full range of perception capabilities. DyHead [3] was proposed by Dai et al., which simultaneously combines scale-aware attention (π_L) in formula 5, spatial-aware attention (π_S) in formula 6, and task-aware attention (π_C) in formula 7, enhances the model's adaptability to various target sizes, understanding of object placement, and context understanding.

$$\pi_L(F) \cdot F = \sigma \left(f \left(\frac{1}{S \cdot C} \sum_{S,C} F \right) \right) \cdot F. \tag{5}$$

Scale-aware attention (π_L) performs average pooling on the input feature map, then uses a 1×1 convolution layer and ReLU activation function for feature extraction, then uses the hard-sigmoid function to balance model accuracy and speed, finally the elements are multiplied with the input feature map.

$$\pi_S(F) \cdot F = \frac{1}{L} \sum_{l=1}^{L} \sum_{j=1}^{K} w_{l,j} \cdot F \left(l; p_j + \Delta p_j; c \right) \cdot \Delta m_j. \tag{6}$$

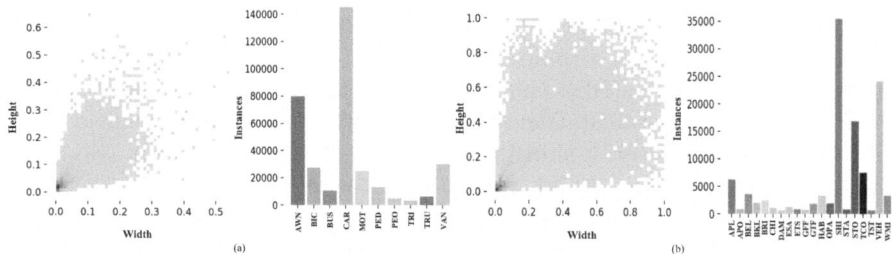

Fig. 4. (a) Size distribution and object count of the VisDrone-2019 dataset; (b) Size distribution and object count of the DIOR dataset.

Spatial-aware attention (π_S) first processes the input tensor using a 3×3 convolutional layer to obtain the offset value of the feature map and the weight term of the feature map offset, and then weights and sums all features.

$$\pi_C(F) \cdot F = \max \left(\alpha^1(F) \cdot F_C + \beta^1(F), \alpha^2(F) \cdot F_C + \beta^2(F) \right). \tag{7}$$

Task-aware attention (π_C) is first average pooling in the L × S dimension to reduce the number of channels. Subsequently, two fully connected layers are adopted and activated using the ReLU function and then passed through a normalization layer. Finally, different channel values are output according to different tasks to complete the task perception of the feature map.

4   Experiment and Analysis

In order to validate the superiority of the proposed DASSF method, we combine it with YOLOv8n and conduct comparison, ablation and general experiments on two datasets. Throughout the experiments, we maintain consistency in hyperparameters and other experimental details. The comparison results show that our proposed method significantly improves the accuracy of small targets in aerial images. The comparison results show that our proposed method significantly improves the accuracy of small targets in aerial images.

4.1   Datasets

In our experiments, we use two datasets. The first is the Tianjin University AISKYEYE team publicly released the VisDrone-2019 [4] dataset. This dataset is designed for target detection in UAV images of remote sensing scenes with high diversity. The images are annotated with labels for ten categories, including awning-tricycle (Awn), bicycle (Bic), bus (Bus), car (Car), motorcycle (Mot), pedestrian (Ped), person (Peo), tricycle (Tri), truck (Tru) and van (Van). The dataset is divided into three distinct subsets: 6471 images for training, 548 images for validation, and 1610 images for testing. The second is the DIOR [13] remote sensing dataset was released by Northwestern Polytechnical University in 2018. This benchmark dataset contains 23,463 images and 192,472 instances for object detection in optical remote sensing images. It covers 20 common places and object categories, including airplane (AE), airport (AT), baseballfield (BD), basketballcourt (BT), bridge (BE), chimney (CY), dam (DM), Expressway-Service-area (EA), Expressway-toll-station (EN), golffield (GO), groundtrackfield (GR), harbor (HR), overpass (OS), ship (SP), stadium (SM), storagetank (SK), tenniscourt (TT), trainstation (TN), vehicle (VE), windmill (WL). The dataset is divided into three different subsets: 14077 images for training, 4694 images for validation, and 4692 images for testing. The size and category distributions of the two datasets are shown in Fig. 4.

4.2   Implementation Details and Evaluation Metrics

The hardware configuration of this experiment includ-es: CPU: AMD EPYC 7551P 32-Core Processor, GPU: NVIDIA RTX A4000, Memory: 16G. The software environment includes: Ubuntu 20.04.1, python 3.8.10, Torch 1.13.1.

The hyperparameter settings are as follows: training is conducted for 200 epochs, the batch size is set to 8, parameters are updated using stochastic gradient descent (SGD), the learning rate is set to 0.0001, the weight decay rate is 0.0005, and the intersection over union (IOU) threshold is set to 0.7.

The data augmentation settings are as follows: the image hue is set to 0.015, the image saturation is set to 0.7, the image brightness is set to 0.4, and the image flip probability is set to 0.5.

In order to evaluate the model's performance, this experiment uses precision (Pre), recall (Rec), mean average precision (mAP), and frames per second (FPS) as indicators.

4.3   Comparison with State-of-the-Art Methods

Table 1. Comparison of detection results of mainstream methods on the VisDrone-2019 dataset.

Method	Year	Awn	Bic	Bus	Car	Mot	Ped	Peo	Tri	Tru	Van	mAP50	mAP50:95
ATSS [34]	2020	10.8	14.1	41.3	74.2	36.3	37.9	18.5	20.5	32.6	36.2	32.2	19.8
Deformable-DETR [36]	2020	13.1	12.0	56.6	69.2	28.1	27.8	16.4	16.1	40.1	36.5	31.6	17.3
Conditional-DETR [19]	2021	8.2	11.3	33.5	62.8	36.5	30.4	25.6	20.2	30.5	30.2	28.9	15.0
DDOD [2]	2021	14.2	18.2	58.5	78.8	47.5	47.4	34.9	27.5	**41.0**	45.4	40.7	24.8
TOOD [5]	2021	14.2	**19.8**	56.4	79.3	49.2	46.8	35.4	27.2	40.9	45.6	38.8	24.3
Dab-DETR [15]	2022	15.3	12.7	57.5	66.7	26.2	21.4	14.3	19.7	39.3	38.2	31.1	15.5
YOLOv6n [10]	2022	11.1	5.0	42.9	73.5	31.1	30.0	24.6	18.0	24.2	35.3	29.6	17.1
DAMO-YOLO [31]	2022	11.8	7.2	42.6	75.1	35.6	34.2	27.4	21.2	27.3	36.9	31.9	18.3
RTMDET [18]	2022	14.6	12.1	56.1	75.2	40.4	34.2	28.3	25.1	36.3	41.4	36.4	21.5
YOLO-MS [1]	2023	10.9	7.4	44.7	74.5	34.1	32.8	26.2	19.7	24.3	36.9	31.1	17.6
Gold-YOLO [25]	2023	12.1	8.5	48.8	75.7	37.0	33.9	27.4	22.1	28.2	38.8	33.2	19.3
ASF-YOLO [9]	2023	11.0	7.2	43.8	74.4	33.4	32.8	25.8	19.1	26.6	37.2	31.1	17.9
Baseline [8]	2023	11.0	7.0	44.8	75.1	35.1	33.6	26.9	20.4	27.4	37.5	31.9	18.2
Ours	-	**17.5**	15.2	**57.6**	**82.9**	**49.7**	**47.6**	**39.3**	**27.8**	36.0	**47.2**	42.1	**25.2**

Table 2. Statistics of all objects in the VisDrone-2019 dataset that are less than 32 × 32 pixels in size.

Category	Awn	Bic	Bus	Car	Mot	Ped	Peo	Tri	Tru	Van
Proportion (%)	58.5	82.8	47.4	51.0	83.2	89.0	92.0	61.4	40.5	49.3

Comparisons on VisDrone-2019. We use the VisDrone-2019 dataset to conduct comparative experiments with mainstream target detection methods, including ATSS, Defor-mable-DETR, Conditional-DETR, DDOD, TOOD, Dab-DETR, YOLOv6n, DAMO-YOLO, RTMDET, YOLO-MS, Gold-YOLO, ASF-YOLO. The comparative experimental results in Table 1 show that our proposed method surpasses the selected target detection method YOLOv8n and improves the detection accuracy by 10.2%. And it surpassed other mainstream target detection methods in the table, achieving new SOTA results of 42.1% and 25.2% in mAP50 and mAP50:95 respectively. The best detection accuracy was achieved in 8 out of 10 categories. Due to the addition of a small target detection head and the application of the DSSFF module, the model's ability to detect small targets and extract and fuse features of objects of different scales are enhanced. Excellent detection results can be achieved for large-sized targets such as buses and garbage trucks, as well as small-sized targets such as pedestrians and motorcycles.

Additionally, to more intuitively demonstrate the impact of our proposed DASSF method on small target detection in aerial images, we calculate the proportion of all objects in the VisDrone-2019 dataset that are smaller than 32 × 32 pixels. The statistical results are presented in Table 2. Combined with our comparative experimental results in Table 1, it is evident that the DASSF method excels in small target detection. With the exception of the 4th (Bic) and 10th (Tru) categories in the statistics for objects smaller than 32 × 32 pixels, all other object categories achieved the highest detection accuracy.

Comparisons on DIOR. Furthermore, we also compare the proposed method with mainstream methods on the DIOR dataset. As shown in Table 3, the proposed method outperforms other mainstream target detection methods in terms of overall accuracy, achieving the best results in 12 out of 20 categories in the DIOR dataset, with an overall accuracy of 87.1%. Exceeding Conditional-DETR, TOOD, and RTMDET by 7.9%, 3.1%, and 1.8% respectively on mAP50. Due to the use of DyHead with self-attention, the model's ability to perceive objects of different scales in remote sensing images is enhanced. Moreover, the DSSFF module solves the problem of misdetection and leakage of targets such as chimneys and windmills that are affected by light, clouds and other factors. And due to the improved upsampling mechanism in the scale sequence feature fusion module, which reduces the amount of calculation, the FPS exceeds the ten target detection methods in the table, ensuring the real-time performance of the proposed method.

Table 3. Comparison of detection results of mainstream methods on the DIOR dataset.

Method	AE GR	AT HR	BD OS	BT SP	BE SM	CY SK	DM TT	EA TN	EN VE	GO WL	mAP50	mAP50:95
ATSS	94.8	88.1	93.9	90.7	50.5	90.9	70.5	90.8	76.6	86.7	80.4	56.6
	87.7	65.3	67.1	75.0	94.4	75.1	95.2	64.8	57.6	91.6		
Deformable-DETR	90.8	85.3	92.2	85.7	55.2	92.0	70.4	90.5	82.0	85.4	78.0	50.6
	88.1	39.0	72.1	68.9	93.8	67.4	92.4	60.5	59.7	89.7		
Conditional-DETR	89.6	89.9	91.0	86.7	55.7	**94.2**	85.9	92.9	78.8	88.2	79.2	52.9
	89.8	39.8	73.9	59.8	96.3	60.6	92.3	69.5	57.6	90.4		
DDOD	94.7	91.8	94.5	91.0	55.7	90.8	77.8	94.1	81.5	88.8	82.9	59.2
	88.8	69.0	70.5	75.7	95.8	78.4	95.8	68.1	62.4	93.6		
TOOD	93.3	90.0	92.4	87.3	**62.1**	94.6	80.5	94.7	82.0	87.7	84.0	60.7
	90.0	64.4	**75.8**	81.3	94.9	83.6	94.3	72.7	67.1	92.0		
Dab-DETR	95.0	91.0	94.1	90.2	55.3	91.7	76.7	93.7	82.4	87.8	82.7	59.3
	89.6	69.1	71.0	76.1	94.6	77.7	95.4	66.9	62.2	93.3		
YOLOv6n	95.2	91.3	93.6	91.6	51.7	86.3	75.5	95.1	77.3	86.0	82.9	60.2
	88.2	73.8	67.3	92.8	96.5	82.6	96.4	71.2	56.3	89.9		
DAMO-YOLO	95.9	92.6	95.1	92.7	54.8	89.5	80.3	96.6	87.3	90.1	85.5	62.7
	90.8	75.7	70.1	94.0	95.5	85.9	97.2	72.9	61.2	92.6		
RTMDET	96.2	**94.2**	94.4	**94.3**	56.7	93.6	78.4	96.3	86.0	**90.8**	85.3	63.1
	90.8	**77.8**	71.9	77.7	96.5	79.2	96.9	**78.1**	65.0	92.0		
YOLO-MS	95.2	90.9	95.2	90.9	52.4	88.1	76.3	95.1	80.2	86.8	83.9	60.3
	89.4	74.3	68.2	93.7	96.1	85.2	96.8	70.5	60.3	92.6		
Gold-YOLO	96.2	93.2	95.8	92.9	57.2	89.9	79.8	96.8	85.9	88.5	85.6	62.7
	90.9	74.7	72.2	94.2	97.0	86.5	97.4	76.2	61.5	94.2		
ASF-YOLO	95.2	91.5	94.3	91.8	53.3	87.4	76.7	94.5	80.6	86.4	83.6	60.0
	88.4	73.6	68.6	93.2	96.3	85.4	96.4	68.0	58.2	92.2		
Baseline	94.6	89.6	94.1	90.5	51.6	87.1	75.0	93.4	77.8	83.5	82.4	58.6
	88.4	72.9	67.1	92.4	96.3	83.8	95.8	68.5	56.1	89.9		
Ours	**97.0**	92.8	**96.6**	91.7	56.6	90.0	**80.7**	**96.7**	**87.9**	89.9	**87.1**	**63.8**
	91.0	76.0	69.9	**95.3**	**97.3**	**90.6**	**97.9**	70.7	**69.7**	**95.0**		

4.4 Ablation Studies and Analysis

Ablation Experiments on Different Modules of DASSF Method. We conduct ablation experiments on the proposed method on two datasets, and the experimental results are shown in Table 4. Baseline is YOLOv8n. The detection accuracy index of the baseline model is at the lowest position. The mAP50 and mAP50:95 of the finally proposed improved model on the two datasets increased by 10.2%, 7.0%, 4.2% and 5.2% respectively compared with the baseline model. This shows that the improved model has a slight increase in calculation volume and inference time due to the addition of attention and x-small target detection heads, but can significantly improve detection performance. With the improvements to DSSFF, mAP50 and mAP50:95 increase by 0.9% and 0.4% on the VisDrone-2019 dataset, respectively. On the DIOR dataset, mAP50 and mAP50:95 increase by 2.1% and 2.9%, respectively, indicating that the feature

Table 4. Ablation study on VisDrone-2019 and DIOR datasets.

Dataset	VisDrone-2019				DIOR			
Method	Pre	Rec	mAP50	mAP50:95	Pre	Rec	mAP50	mAP50:95
Baseline	43.4	31.8	31.9	18.2	87.8	75.9	82.4	58.6
DSSFF	45.4	32.8	33.3	19.3	87.0	77.3	84.5	61.5
X-small	44.1	34.1	33.7	19.6	87.9	79.1	85.5	62.7
DyHead	43.9	33.2	32.6	18.5	87.2	78.1	84.5	59.8
DSSFF+X-small	47.4	36.4	37.2	22.0	**89.0**	78.5	85.7	62.3
DSSFF+DyHead	48.7	35.3	36.6	21.6	88.3	78.7	85.0	62.2
X-small+DyHead	47.8	35.8	37.0	21.7	88.4	79.5	86.2	63.0
Ours	**52.6**	**40.0**	**42.1**	**25.2**	88.8	**80.7**	**86.6**	**63.8**

fusion mechanism of DSSFF not only aids in identifying dense small objects but also refines the detection of objects at different scales, as reflected in the high-threshold mAP50:95 metric. For the enhancement of the X-small object detection head, mAP50 and mAP50:95 rise by 1.8% and 1.4% on the VisDrone-2019 dataset, and by 3.1% and 4.1% on the DIOR dataset, respectively. This demonstrates that introducing the X-small detection head boosts the model's ability to detect objects of various scales, especially small-sized ones, thus comprehensively improving both mAP50 and mAP50:95 on the two aerial image datasets. Regarding the improvements to DyHead, mAP50 and mAP50:95 on the two datasets increase by 0.7%, 0.3%, 2.1%, and 1.2%, respectively, while the FPS decreases. This indicates that DyHead, which combines size, spatial, and task attention, enhances the overall expressiveness of the model but also increases the computational load and inference time. When considering the pairwise combination of these three improvements, further accuracy gains can be achieved beyond what each single improvement provides. On the DIOR dataset, adding DSSFF and the X-small detection head surpasses the final proposed DASSF method in terms of the precision metric. However, this does not change the overall trend of improved detection accuracy.

Ablation Experiments on Different Upsampling Methods of DSSFF Module. We conduct variant experiments on the proposed DSS-FF module using different upsampling methods on the VisDrone-2019 dataset. As can be seen from the experimental results in Table 5, the upsampling method using DySample is optimal in all four accuracy indicators and has the highest FPS. Compared with the original nearest sampling method, precision, recall, mAP50 and mAP50:95 increase by 2.4%, 1.2%, 0.7% and 0.4% respectively. FPS reaches 46.7. This demonstrates that the DSSFF module we implement in the model not only enhances detection performance but also decreases computational overhead.

4.5 Universal Experiment of DASSF Method

We also experiment with the proposed DASSF method on two datasets using the YOLOv5n, YOLOv7tiny, YOLOv8n, YOLOv9t, and YOLOv10n models. Table 6

Table 5. Experimental results of DSSFF module and different upsampling methods on VisDrone-2019 dataset.

Method	Pre	Rec	mAP50	mAP50:95	FPS
Bilinear	49.9	38.5	40.6	23.6	34.1
CARAFE [28]	50.0	38.2	40.2	23.5	35.3
Nearest	50.2	38.8	41.4	24.8	45.8
DySample (Ours)	**52.6**	**40.0**	**42.1**	**25.2**	**46.7**

Table 6. General experiments on different versions of YOLO for the DASSF method on the VisDrone-2019 and DIOR datasets.

Dataset	VisDrone-2019				DIOR			
Method	Pre	Rec	mAP50	mAP50:95	Pre	Rec	mAP50	mAP50:95
YOLOv5n [7]	40.8	31.0	30.4	17.4	86.5	74.8	81.4	57.2
YOLOv5n+DASSF	50.8	39.6	40.9	24.3	88.2	78.2	85.2	61.5
YOLOv7tiny [26]	46.4	37.3	34.4	17.6	84.5	79.3	83.7	56.4
YOLOv7tiny+DASSF	52.1	42.0	41.0	22.8	85.6	75.8	82.4	58.5
YOLOv8n [8]	45.4	32.8	33.3	19.3	87.8	75.9	82.4	58.6
YOLOv8n+DASSF	52.6	40.0	42.1	25.2	88.8	80.7	86.6	63.8
YOLOv9t [27]	43.1	31.8	32.2	18.7	81.6	72.2	78.3	53.9
YOLOv9t+DASSF	46.8	33.9	35.3	20.4	88.8	78.0	84.6	62.9
YOLOv10n [24]	42.9	33.5	33.1	18.8	88.3	77.3	84.8	61.1
YOLOv10n+DASSF	52.9	40.9	42.5	25.4	87.4	79.4	85.8	62.2

presents the experimental results. Compared with YOLOv5n, YOLOv7tiny, YOLOv8n, YOLOv9t, and YOLOv10n, although the Precision of DASSF on the DIOR dataset is slightly lower than that of YOLOv10n, our proposed DASSF method surpasses the original YOLO models in terms of Precision, Recall, mAP50, and mAP50:95. This demonstrates that the proposed DASSF method can be flexibly applied to various mainstream YOLO models, showing universality while achieving better results in aerial image target detection compared to the original YOLO models.

4.6   Visualization

Figure 5 presents a comparative visualization of two dat-asets using DASSF-YOLOv8 and YOLOv8n. In the figure, red circles highlight missed detections, while yellow circles indicate false detections. The analysis demonstrates that the DASSF-YOLOv8 model not only enhances accuracy in detecting densely overlapping objects, such as motorcyclists and port areas, but also excels at identifying small targets obstructed by houses and trees, as well as those in blurred images. This leads to a reduction in missed detection rates. Furthermore, the model accurately distinguishes between positive and negative samples, resulting in fewer false detections.

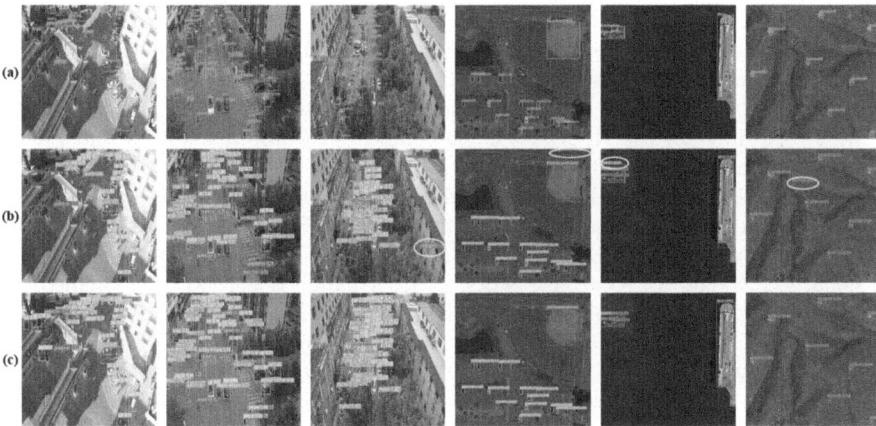

Fig. 5. Comparison of detection results on VisDrone-2019 and DIOR datasets. The (a) row shows the ground truth result of the image, the (b) row shows the visualization result of the baseline model, and the (c) row shows the visualization result of our model.

5   Conclusion

This study proposed an effective aerial image detection method based on dynamic-attention scale- sequence fusion, which improves the problem of low detection accuracy of small targets in aerial images and can be flexibly applied to different YOLO models. We proposed DSSFF module to reduce the amount of calculation. By incorporating additional x-small detection heads, the detection capability of small targets can be improved. Enhanced expression capabilities for various types of targets through the use of DyHead. Compared with the baseline method and other mainstream detection methods, this approach improved detection accuracy across various challenging scenarios in aerial object detection. However, our method still has the drawback of not being fast enough during inference. In the future, we will continue to explore further lightweighting our method to ensure effective model deployment and operation even in resource-constrained environments.

Acknowledgments. This paper was supported by the National Natural Science Foundation of China (GrantNo. 42271409) and the Scientific Research Foundation of the Higher Education Institutions of Liaoning Province (GrantNo. LJKMZ20220699).

Disclosure of Interests. The authors have no competing interests to declare that are relevant to the content of this article.

References

1. Chen, Y., Yuan, X., Wu, R., Wang, J., Hou, Q., Cheng, M.M.: Yolo-MS: rethinking multi-scale representation learning for real-time object detection. arXiv preprint arXiv:2308.05480 (2023)

2. Chen, Z., Yang, C., Li, Q., Zhao, F., Zha, Z.J., Wu, F.: Disentangle your dense object detector. In: Proceedings of the 29th ACM International Conference on Multimedia, pp. 4939–4948 (2021)

3. Dai, X., et al.: Dynamic head: unifying object detection heads with attentions. In: Proceedings of the IEEE/CVF Conference on Computer Vision and Pattern Recognition, pp. 7373–7382 (2021)

4. Du, D., et al.: Visdrone-det2019: the vision meets drone object detection in image challenge results. In: Proceedings of the IEEE/CVF International Conference on Computer Vision Workshops, pp. 0–0 (2019)

5. Feng, C., Zhong, Y., Gao, Y., Scott, M.R., Huang, W.: Tood: task-aligned one-stage object detection. In: 2021 IEEE/CVF International Conference on Computer Vision (ICCV), pp. 3490–3499. IEEE Computer Society (2021)

6. Jiao, Y., Qiu, S., Chen, M., Han, D., Li, Q., Lu, Y.: DSAM-GN: graph network based on dynamic similarity adjacency matrices for vehicle re-identification. In: Pacific Rim International Conference on Artificial Intelligence, pp. 353–364. Springer (2023)

7. Jocher, G.: YOLOv5 by Ultralytics (2020). https://doi.org/10.5281/zenodo.3908559, https://github.com/ultralytics/yolov5

8. Jocher, G., Chaurasia, A., Qiu, J.: Ultralytics YOLO (2023). https://github.com/ultralytics/ultralytics

9. Kang, M., Ting, C.M., Ting, F.F., Phan, R.C.W.: ASF-yolo: a novel yolo model with attentional scale sequence fusion for cell instance segmentation. arXiv preprint arXiv:2312.06458 (2023)

10. Li, C., et al.: Yolov6 v3. 0: a full-scale reloading. arXiv preprint arXiv:2301.05586 (2023)

11. Li, C., Cheng, G., Wang, G., Zhou, P., Han, J.: Instance-aware distillation for efficient object detection in remote sensing images. IEEE Trans. Geosci. Remote Sens. **61**, 1–11 (2023)

12. Li, H., Zhang, R., Pan, Y., Ren, J., Shen, F.: LR-FPN: enhancing remote sensing object detection with location refined feature pyramid network. arXiv preprint arXiv:2404.01614 (2024)

13. Li, K., Wan, G., Cheng, G., Meng, L., Han, J.: Object detection in optical remote sensing images: a survey and a new benchmark. ISPRS J. Photogramm. Remote. Sens. **159**, 296–307 (2020)

14. Lin, T.-Y., et al.: Microsoft COCO: common objects in context. In: Fleet, D., Pajdla, T., Schiele, B., Tuytelaars, T. (eds.) ECCV 2014. LNCS, vol. 8693, pp. 740–755. Springer, Cham (2014). https://doi.org/10.1007/978-3-319-10602-1_48

15. Liu, S., et al.: Dab-DETR: dynamic anchor boxes are better queries for DETR. arXiv preprint arXiv:2201.12329 (2022)

16. Liu, W., Lu, H., Fu, H., Cao, Z.: Learning to upsample by learning to sample. In: Proceedings of the IEEE/CVF International Conference on Computer Vision, pp. 6027–6037 (2023)

17. Luo, P., Wang, B., Wang, H., Ma, F., Ma, H., Wang, L.: An ultrasmall bolt defect detection method for transmission line inspection. IEEE Trans. Instrum. Meas. **72**, 1–12 (2023)

18. Lyu, C., et al.: RTMDET: an empirical study of designing real-time object detectors. arXiv preprint arXiv:2212.07784 (2022)

19. Meng, D., et al.: Conditional DETR for fast training convergence. In: Proceedings of the IEEE/CVF International Conference on Computer Vision, pp. 3651–3660 (2021)

20. Ni, H., et al.: Multiple visual fields cascaded convolutional neural network for breast cancer detection. In: Geng, X., Kang, B.-H. (eds.) PRICAI 2018. LNCS (LNAI), vol. 11012, pp. 531–544. Springer, Cham (2018). https://doi.org/10.1007/978-3-319-97304-3_41

21. Qiao, C., et al.: A novel multi-frequency coordinated module for SAR ship detection. In: 2022 IEEE 34th International Conference on Tools with Artificial Intelligence (ICTAI), pp. 804–811. IEEE (2022)

22. Shen, F., Shu, X., Du, X., Tang, J.: Pedestrian-specific bipartite-aware similarity learning for text-based person retrieval. In: Proceedings of the 31th ACM International Conference on Multimedia (2023)

23. Shen, F., Xie, Y., Zhu, J., Zhu, X., Zeng, H.: GIT: graph interactive transformer for vehicle re-identification. IEEE Trans. Image Process. (2023)

24. Wang, A., et al.: Yolov10: real-time end-to-end object detection. arXiv preprint arXiv:2405.14458 (2024)

25. Wang, C., et al.: Gold-yolo: efficient object detector via gather-and-distribute mechanism. In: Advances in Neural Information Processing Systems, vol. 36 (2024)

26. Wang, C.Y., Bochkovskiy, A., Liao, H.Y.M.: Yolov7: trainable bag-of-freebies sets new state-of-the-art for real-time object detectors. In: Proceedings of the IEEE/CVF Conference on Computer Vision and Pattern Recognition, pp. 7464–7475 (2023)

27. Wang, C.Y., Yeh, I.H., Liao, H.Y.M.: Yolov9: learning what you want to learn using programmable gradient information. arXiv preprint arXiv:2402.13616 (2024)

28. Wang, J., Chen, K., Xu, R., Liu, Z., Loy, C.C., Lin, D.: Carafe: content-aware reassembly of features. In: Proceedings of the IEEE/CVF International Conference on Computer Vision, pp. 3007–3016 (2019)

29. Weng, W., Ling, W., Lin, F., Ren, J., Shen, F.: A novel cross frequency-domain interaction learning for aerial oriented object detection. In: Chinese Conference on Pattern Recognition and Computer Vision (PRCV). Springer (2023)

30. Weng, W., Wei, M., Ren, J., Shen, F.: Enhancing aerial object detection with selective frequency interaction network. IEEE Trans. Artif. Intell. **1**(01), 1–12 (2024)

31. Xu, X., Jiang, Y., Chen, W., Huang, Y., Zhang, Y., Sun, X.: Damo-yolo: a report on real-time object detection design. arXiv preprint arXiv:2211.15444 (2022)

32. Ye, Y., et al.: Field detection of small pests through stochastic gradient descent with genetic algorithm. Comput. Electron. Agric. **206**, 107694 (2023)

33. Ying, X., et al.: Mapping degeneration meets label evolution: learning infrared small target detection with single point supervision. In: Proceedings of the IEEE/CVF Conference on Computer Vision and Pattern Recognition, pp. 15528–15538 (2023)

34. Zhang, S., Chi, C., Yao, Y., Lei, Z., Li, S.Z.: Bridging the gap between anchor-based and anchor-free detection via adaptive training sample selection. In: Proceedings of the IEEE/CVF Conference on Computer Vision and Pattern Recognition, pp. 9759–9768 (2020)

35. Zhao, Z., Li, B., Dong, R., Zhao, P.: A surface defect detection method based on positive samples. In: Geng, X., Kang, B.-H. (eds.) PRICAI 2018. LNCS (LNAI), vol. 11013, pp. 473–481. Springer, Cham (2018). https://doi.org/10.1007/978-3-319-97310-4_54

36. Zhu, X., Su, W., Lu, L., Li, B., Wang, X., Dai, J.: Deformable DETR: deformable transformers for end-to-end object detection. arXiv preprint arXiv:2010.04159 (2020)

Image Enhancement and Generation

Degradation-Aware Frequency-Separated Transformer for Blind Super-Resolution

Hanli Zhao[1], Binhao Wang[1], Wanglong Lu[1(✉)], and Juncong Lin[2]

[1] College of Computer Science and Artificial Intelligence,
Wenzhou University, Wenzhou, China
lwlxhl@gmail.com
[2] School of Informatics, Xiamen University, Xiamen, China

Abstract. Blind image super-resolution involves reconstructing high-resolution images from low-resolution inputs with various unknown degradations. It is a challenging task due to the limited information available from the degraded images. While existing methods have achieved impressive results, they often overlook high-frequency or low-frequency features, reducing their effectiveness. To solve this problem, we propose a frequency-separated Transformer framework with degradation-aware learning for blind super-resolution. We first introduce a multi-patch contrastive learning approach to implicitly learn discriminative degradation representations. To fully utilize degradation representations as guidance information, a frequency-separated self-attention mechanism is introduced to extract global structural and local detail features separately. Our degradation-aware frequency-separated Transformer progressively restores high-quality images using successive frequency-separated self-attention blocks. Extensive experiments demonstrate that our approach outperforms state-of-the-art methods on four benchmark blind super-resolution datasets, while also achieving lower GPU memory usage during training and faster inference speed.

Keywords: Image super-resolution · Blind super-resolution · Contrastive learning · Degradation representation · Transformers

1 Introduction

Blind image super-resolution (BSR) aims to reconstruct high-resolution (HR) images from low-resolution (LR) input images with unknown degradation. This challenging task is a crucial subset of the broader field of image restoration [24] in computer vision, including image denoising [42], dehazing [37], and various forms of super-resolution [3], all sharing the common goal of reconstructing high-quality images from degraded inputs.

In the realm of super-resolution, numerous outstanding approaches have been developed, leveraging both convolutional neural networks (CNN) [6,53] and Transformer architectures [4,20]. However, these methods are primarily non-blind and operate under the assumption of a specific, predefined degradation type, such as bicubic downsampling. When confronted with degradations that deviate from this assumption, models trained on fixed degradation conditions, often struggle to deliver satisfactory outcomes.

© The Author(s), under exclusive license to Springer Nature Singapore Pte Ltd. 2025
P. Didyk and J. Hou (Eds.): CVM 2025, LNCS 15663, pp. 231–252, 2025.
https://doi.org/10.1007/978-981-96-5809-1_13

To achieve high-quality BSR, two widely recognized challenges dominate recent literature. The first one is accurately predicting the degradation type from a given image, which is crucial for providing more effective guidance during the subsequent super-resolution process. However, existing methods typically rely on limited perspectives to learn implicit degradation representation, potentially restricting their ability to capture the degradation representations [17,36]. The exploration of multi-patch approaches for BSR remains relatively underexplored in current research. The second challenge is efficiently utilizing the predicted degradation representations to extract deep-level features. While the goal is to fully leverage the obtained representations to handle complex degradations, CNN-based methods [17,36] often lack the large receptive field necessary for capturing long-range dependencies in features. On the other hand, Transformer-based methods [22,31] are better at modeling global context but often compromise by using moderately sized windows to balance the computational demands. Some methods further utilize high- and low-frequency features [29] to boost the extraction of global and local information. However, research for the modeling of high- and low-frequency features based on degradation guidance remains limited.

In this paper, we explore the ways to address these challenges. We first leverage multiple patches from a single image, to gain diverse perspectives, leading to more robust representations and reducing overfitting risks [2,52]. Second, recognizing that image features include high frequencies for fine details and low frequencies for global structures [29], we propose a conditional dual-path self-attention mechanism guided by degradation representations. The high-frequency path captures local details with small windows, while the low-frequency path models global interactions on compact feature maps. This approach boosts efficiency and both local and global feature modeling.

To this end, we propose a novel degradation-aware frequency-separated Transformer (DAFST) for blind super-resolution. First, we introduce a multi-patch contrastive learning approach to learn discriminative degradation representations implicitly. These representations serve as degradation information to guide the super-resolution process in our proposed frequency-separated attention blocks. Each block utilizes a frequency-separated self-attention mechanism to extract global structural and local detail features separately. The frequency-specific features are then fused in each block, progressively restoring high-quality images through successive blocks. We have extensively compared our method against the SOTA models and conducted comprehensive experiments to demonstrate its superiority. The contributions of this paper are as follows:

- We introduce a novel degradation-aware frequency-separated Transformer (DAFST) that effectively leverages implicit degradation representations to enhance feature extraction for high-quality blind super-resolution.
- We propose a degradation-guided frequency-separated attention mechanism that decouples global and local detail modeling, enhancing both modeling capabilities and inference efficiency.
- We design a multi-patch contrastive learning approach to capture degradation representations from diverse perspectives, leading to more robust features.
- Our method achieves state-of-the-art performance across multiple datasets and degradation types while maintaining faster inference speeds.

2   Related Work

2.1   Non-blind Image Super-Resolution

Image super-resolution is a fundamental problem in computer vision, aiming to reconstruct an HR image from an LR image. Early methods for image super-resolution predominantly relied on CNN, extensively discussed in the literature [45]. CNN-based SR methods, such as studies like [7,10,18,48], gained prominence due to their excellent local inductive bias. SRCNN [8], a seminal work in image super-resolution, employed a simple three-layer CNN to learn the LR-HR mapping for image super-resolution, catalyzing numerous subsequent advancements in the field.

Typically, super-resolution methods comprise three primary modules: shallow feature extraction, deep feature extraction, and super-resolution reconstruction modules. In recent years, significant enhancements have been made to the deep feature extraction and super-resolution reconstruction modules, with network processing strategies such as upsampling [9], residual learning [15], and sub-pixel convolutional upsampling [32] becoming standard paradigms for constructing super-resolution networks. With advancements in methods such as RCAN [53], SAN [6], and SwinIR [20], the performance of non-blind image super-resolution on fixed degradation types, like bicubic downsampling, has reached a plateau. Recent works, such as CAMixer [39], propose sampling convolution or visual attention based on the complexity of image regions, and MambaIR [12] utilizes 2D-selective-scan to replace traditional attention mechanisms. While these methods have achieved remarkable results, non-blind approaches often struggle to generalize effectively to unknown degradations beyond their predefined scope.

2.2   Blind Image Super-Resolution

Networks designed for fixed bicubic downsampling often suffer significant performance drops when faced with real-world degradations. Several blind super-resolution methods were proposed to tackle this challenge. Currently, three primary methods are employed for obtaining degradation: (1) Adapted non-blind super-resolution, which assumes known degradation and uses it as a prior. (2) Blind super-resolution based on explicit kernel estimation. (3) Blind super-resolution based on implicit degradation representation.

Adapted Non-blind Super-Resolution Methods. These methods explicitly incorporate blur kernels as additional inputs to guide the SR process. For instance, SRMD [50] and UDVD [43] introduced degradation kernels as inputs to handle varying degradation conditions, while DPSR [51] and USRNet [47] leveraged variable splitting techniques to optimize energy functions, treating blur kernels as independently optimized terms. However, these methods are highly dependent on the accurate input from the blur kernel, limiting their generalization to a broader degradation space. When faced with unseen degradations or without precise kernel information, their performance significantly degrades.

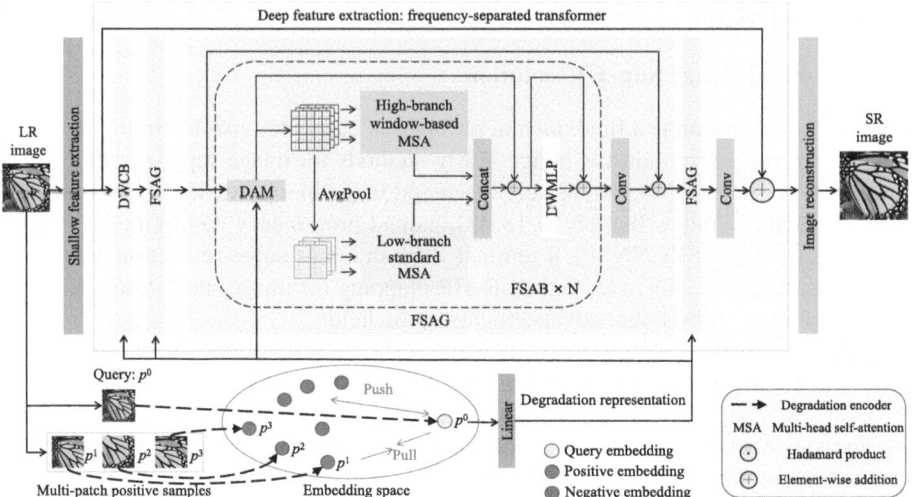

(a) The architecture of our degradation-aware frequency-separated Transformer (DAFST).

Fig. 1. Our DAFST integrates degradation representations with image features through multi-patch contrastive learning, the images are encoded into embeddings with the degradation encoder, aiming to maximize the similarity between query embeddings and positive embeddings while minimizing the similarity with negative embeddings. Guided by these representations, the frequency-separated self-attention blocks extract global and local features, which are then merged using depthwise convolutions and reconstructed via the image reconstruction module.

Explicit Kernel Estimation Methods. Other methods aim to guide the network by estimating blur kernels directly from the LR image. For example, Liang et al. [19] proposed using multiple mini super-resolution network experts to estimate diverse degradations. Gu [11] introduced an iterative kernel correction (IKC) method that refines the estimated degradation based on intermediate SR results. ZSSR [33] leverages internal image recurrence, utilizing repetitive structures within the LR image for iterative optimization. However, these methods often incur high computational costs due to multiple iterations of kernel estimation and correction during testing. To address this, DCLS [26] and MZSR [34] build upon IKC and ZSSR, respectively, reducing the number of iterative optimizations. Similarly, Luo et al. [25] developed a deep alternating network (DAN) to iteratively estimate degradation and restore SR images. Despite these advancements, these methods remain highly sensitive to the accuracy of kernel estimation, and inaccurate estimations can lead to suboptimal results, limiting their robustness in real-world scenarios.

Implicit Degradation Representation Methods. Recently, some studies have shown that implicit degradation representation is better suited to handle complex degradation scenarios. DASR [36] pioneered the integration of contrastive learning to guide deep feature extraction. Wei et al. proposed [40] unsupervised domain gap-aware training networks. Additionally, DSSR [17] introduced a detail structure modulation module to enhance details cyclically. KDSR [41] introduced knowledge distillation to enable

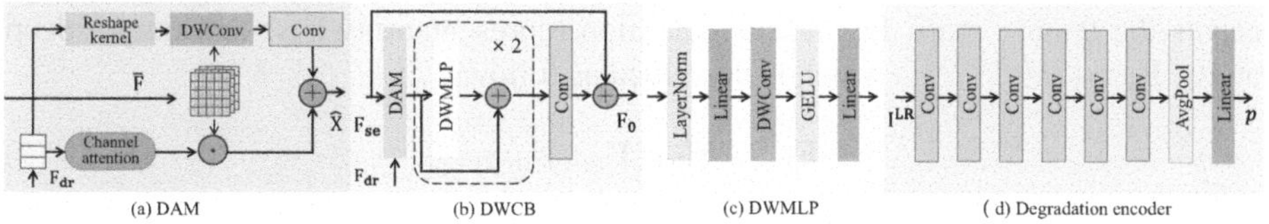

(a) DAM   (b) DWCB   (c) DWMLP   (d) Degradation encoder

Fig. 2. The details of our degradation-aware modulation (DAM), depthwise convolution block (DWCB), DWMLP, and degradation encoder. The DWConv means depthwise convolution.

a student model to learn degradation representations from another teacher model. DSAT [22] introduced residual Swin-Transformer blocks [23] to address the limited receptive field issue of CNN, setting a new benchmark in BSR. This paper proposes a novel degradation-aware frequency-separated Transformer with multi-patch contrastive learning to improve implicit degradation representation learning.

3   Methods

3.1   Overview

Figure 1 (a) shows the overall pipeline of our degradation-aware frequency-separated Transformer (DAFST) for blind super-resolution. Our DAFST takes a low-resolution image $\mathbf{I}^{LR}$ as input and produces a super-resolution image $\mathbf{I}^{SR}$, which is obtained as $\mathbf{I}^{SR} = \text{DAFST}(\mathbf{I}^{LR})$. The DAFST network consists of four key components: degradation encoder, shallow feature extraction, deep feature extraction, and image reconstruction modules.

Degradation Encoder. We apply a degradation encoder and a linear projection to learn distinctive degradation representations. The learned degradation representations guide the subsequent modules in extracting deep features. It can be represented as:

$$\mathbf{F}_{dr} = \text{Linear}(\text{Encoder}(\mathbf{I}^{LR})), \tag{1}$$

where $\mathbf{F}_{dr} \in \mathbb{R}^{256}$ signifies the degradation representations; $\text{Encoder}(\cdot)$ denotes the degradation encoder. We employ multi-patch contrastive learning to train our degradation encoder.

Shallow Feature Extraction Module. To extract shallow features, a simple 3×3 convolution layer is used as the shallow feature extraction module $\text{H}_{SE}(\cdot)$. It can be represented as:

$$\mathbf{F}_{se} = \text{H}_{SE}(\mathbf{I}^{LR}), \tag{2}$$

where $\mathbf{I}^{LR} \in \mathbb{R}^{H \times W \times 3}$; $\mathbf{F}_{se} \in \mathbb{R}^{H \times W \times C}$ denotes the extracted shallow features.

Frequency-Separated Transformer. The deep feature extraction involves a novel frequency-separated Transformer for BSR. It consists of a depthwise convolution block (DWCB) and groups of frequency-separated self-attention blocks (FSAB). Each block aims to extract deep features for reconstruction. The deep feature extraction module receives the feature maps $\mathbf{F}_{se}$ and degradation representations $\mathbf{F}_{dr}$, and output deep features $\mathbf{F}_{de} \in \mathbb{R}^{H \times W \times C}$, which is described as follows:

$$\mathbf{F}_{de} = \mathrm{H}_{\mathrm{DE}}(\mathbf{F}_{se}, \mathbf{F}_{dr}), \tag{3}$$

where $\mathrm{H}_{\mathrm{DE}}(\cdot)$ represents the deep extraction module.

Image Reconstruction Module. The image reconstruction module $\mathrm{H}_{\mathrm{REC}}(\cdot)$ consists of a convolutional layer and a sub-pixel convolutional upsampling layer [9]. We reconstruct high-quality images $\mathbf{I}^{\mathrm{SR}}$ by fusing shallow features and deep features as illustrated below:

$$\mathbf{I}^{\mathrm{SR}} = \mathrm{H}_{\mathrm{REC}}(\mathbf{F}_{se} + \mathbf{F}_{de}). \tag{4}$$

3.2 Frequency-Separated Transformer

Given the shallow feature maps $\mathbf{F}_{se}$, our frequency-separated Transformer $\mathrm{H}_{\mathrm{DE}}(\cdot)$ consists of two stages. The input features first go through a depthwise convolution block: $\mathbf{F}_0 = \mathrm{DWCB}(\mathbf{F}_{se}, \mathbf{F}_{dr})$. Then the intermediate features are continuously extracted through frequency-separated self-attention groups, which are expressed as:

$$\mathbf{F}_s = \mathrm{H}_{\mathrm{FSAG}_s}(\mathbf{F}_{s-1}, \mathbf{F}_{dr}), \quad s = 1, 2, \ldots, S, \tag{5}$$

where $\mathrm{DWCB}(\cdot)$ is the depthwise convolution block to extract shallow features; The $\mathrm{H}_{\mathrm{FSAG}_s}(\cdot)$ represents s-th frequency-separated self-attention group. Our frequency-separated Transformer contains S FSAG groups. After S groups feature extraction, we use a 3×3 convolution to get the output deep features $\mathbf{F}_{de} = \mathrm{Conv}_{3 \times 3}(\mathbf{F}_S)$.

Degradation-Aware Modulation (DAM). As shown in Fig. 2 (a), the degradation-aware modulation (DAM) mechanism is designed to integrate degradation representations during the super-resolution process. We use channel attention to obtain channel weights $\mathbf{F}_{co}$ from the degradation representations $\mathbf{F}_{dr}$ and to modulate convolutional layers for guidance-based feature extraction. Given the $\mathbf{F}_{dr}$, the generation of channel coefficients $\mathbf{F}_{co} \in \mathbb{R}^{H \times W \times C}$ can be expressed as:

$$\begin{aligned}
\mathbf{F}_{co} &= \mathrm{ChannelAttention}(\mathbf{F}_{dr}) \\
&= \mathrm{Sigmoid}\left(\mathrm{Conv}_{1 \times 1}\left(\mathrm{ReLU}\left(\mathrm{Conv}_{1 \times 1}(\mathbf{F}_{dr})\right)\right)\right),
\end{aligned} \tag{6}$$

where $\mathrm{Sigmoid}(\cdot)$ is the sigmoid activation; $\mathrm{Conv}_{1 \times 1}(\cdot)$ is the 1×1 convolution layer; $\mathrm{ReLU}(\cdot)$ is the LeakyReLU activation function with the 0.1 negative slope. Then we can get the degradation modulated depthwise convolution kernel:

$$\mathrm{DWConv}_{\mathbf{F}_{dr}} = \mathrm{GeneratedKernel}(\mathbf{F}_{dr}) = \mathrm{Reshape}(\mathbf{F}_{dr}), \tag{7}$$

We reshape $\mathbf{F}_{dr}$ as a convolution kernel $\in \mathbb{R}^{C \times 1 \times 3 \times 3}$ denoted as $\mathrm{DWConv}_{\mathbf{F}_{dr}}(\cdot)$ and get $\hat{\mathbf{X}} \in \mathbb{R}^{H \times W \times C}$ from the input feature tensor $\bar{\mathbf{F}}$. As shown in Fig. 2 (a), we ultimately obtain $\hat{\mathbf{X}}$ through the following operations:

$$\hat{\mathbf{X}} = \mathrm{Conv}_{1 \times 1}\left(\mathrm{DWConv}_{\mathbf{F}_{dr}}(\mathrm{ReLU}(\bar{\mathbf{F}}))\right) + (\bar{\mathbf{F}} \odot \mathbf{F}_{co}), \tag{8}$$

where $\hat{\mathbf{X}}$ is the intermediate feature obtained by fusing the input and degradation representations and $\odot$ denotes Hadamard product with broad-casting technique.

Depthwise Convolution Block (DWCB). As shown in Fig. 2 (b), our depthwise convolution block (DWCB) consists of a DAM and two depthwise multilayer perception (DWMLP) blocks. As shown in Fig. 2 (c), each DWMLP block contains two linear projections and a 3×3 depthwise convolution (DWConv) layer. It extracts shallow features and implicitly learns position encoding for the subsequent feature extraction.

Frequency-Separated Self-attention Group (FSAG). Each FSAG takes degradation representations $\mathbf{F}_{dr}$ and aggregates input image features to extract deeper features. Each FSAG consists of N FSAB blocks; each FSAB also leverages $\mathbf{F}_{dr}$ to enhance feature aggregation from the input images. Given the input features $\mathbf{Y}_0 = \mathbf{F}_{s-1}$, for the s-th group $\mathrm{H}_{\mathrm{FSAG}_s}(\cdot)$ with N frequency-separated attention blocks, the deep features $\mathbf{Y}_1, \mathbf{Y}_2, \ldots, \mathbf{Y}_N$ are extracted sequentially. This process in each group, defined as $\mathbf{F}_s = \mathrm{H}_{\mathrm{FSAG}_s}(\mathbf{F}_{s-1}, \mathbf{F}_{dr})$, and $\mathbf{F}_s = \mathbf{Y}_N$. It can be described as follows:

$$\mathbf{Y}_n = \mathrm{H}_{\mathrm{FSAB}_n}(\mathbf{Y}_{n-1}, \mathbf{F}_{dr}), \quad n = 1, 2, \ldots, N-1,$$
$$\mathbf{Y}_N = \mathrm{Conv}_{3 \times 3}(\mathrm{H}_{\mathrm{FSAB}_N}(\mathbf{Y}_{N-1}, \mathbf{F}_{dr})) + \mathbf{Y}_0, \tag{9}$$

where $\mathrm{H}_{\mathrm{FSAB}_n}(\cdot)$ denotes the n-th frequency-separated self-attention block within the s-th FSAB group.

Frequency-Separated Self-attention Block (FSAB). The FSAB primarily comprises two key components, the DAM and a frequency-separated self-attention mechanism. This design enables the block to effectively process and integrate degradation information and image features across different frequency bands. More details are shown in Algorithm 1.

Algorithm 1. Frequency-eparated self-attention block

1: **Input:** Input feature tensor $\bar{\mathbf{F}}$, degradation representations $\mathbf{F}_{dr}$
2: **Parameters:** Number of total attention heads O, number of high-frequency branch attention heads O_1, number of low-frequency branch attention heads O_2, and channel dimension per head C_o
3: # Degradation-aware modulation
4: $\mathbf{F}_{co} = \mathrm{ChannelAttention}(\mathbf{F}_{dr})$
5: $\mathrm{DWConv}_{\mathbf{F}_{dr}} = \mathrm{GeneratedKernel}(\mathbf{F}_{dr})$
6: $\hat{\mathbf{X}} = \mathrm{Conv}_{1 \times 1}(\mathrm{DWConv}_{\mathbf{F}_{dr}}(\mathrm{ReLU}(\bar{\mathbf{F}}))) + (\bar{\mathbf{F}} \odot \mathbf{F}_{co})$
7: # Frequency-separated self-attention
8: $\bar{\mathbf{X}} = \mathrm{Flatten}(\hat{\mathbf{X}})$ # $\bar{\mathbf{X}} \in \mathbb{R}^{L \times C}$
9: $\mathbf{X}^h, \mathbf{X}^l = \mathrm{Divide}(\bar{\mathbf{X}})$ # $\mathbf{X}^h \in \mathbb{R}^{O_1 \times L \times C_o}, \mathbf{X}^l \in \mathbb{R}^{O_2 \times L \times C_o}$
10: # Combine high and low frequency attention
11: $\mathbf{Y}' = \mathrm{Cat}[\mathrm{H\text{-}MSA}(\mathrm{LN}(\mathbf{X}^h)); \mathrm{L\text{-}MSA}(\mathrm{LN}(\mathrm{AvgPool}(\mathbf{X}^l)))] + \bar{\mathbf{X}}$
12: $\mathbf{Y}'' = \mathrm{DWMLP}(\mathbf{Y}') + \mathbf{Y}'$
13: **return** $\mathbf{Y}''$

Frequency-Separated Self-attention. Our frequency-separated self-attention mechanism consists of high-frequency and low-frequency multi-head self-attention (MSA) modules. The high-frequency attention focuses on capturing fine details, while the low-frequency attention extracts global information, such as structural elements, to enhance super-resolution performance. The input tensor $\hat{\mathbf{X}} \in \mathbb{R}^{H \times W \times C}$ is initially flattened into $\bar{\mathbf{X}} \in \mathbb{R}^{L \times C}$, where $L = H \times W$, which is denoted as $\bar{\mathbf{X}} = \text{Flatten}(\hat{\mathbf{X}})$. Then, the tensor $\bar{\mathbf{X}}$ is divided along with the channel dimension into high-frequency $\mathbf{X}^h \in \mathbb{R}^{O_1 \times L \times C_o}$ and low-frequency $\mathbf{X}^l \in \mathbb{R}^{O_2 \times L \times C_o}$ tensors, respectively. $O = O_1 + O_2$ represents the total number of attention heads, comprising O_1 high-frequency and O_2 low-frequency attention heads. $C_o = C/O$ corresponds to the channel number for each head. For the each frequency-separated self-attention feature extraction, denoted as $\mathbf{Y}_n = \text{HFSAB}_n(\mathbf{Y}_{n-1}, \mathbf{F}_{dr})$, we have $\mathbf{Y}_n = \mathbf{Y}''$. Our frequency-separated self-attention can be expressed as:

$$\mathbf{Y}' = \text{Cat}[\text{H-MSA}(\text{LN}(\mathbf{X}^h)); \text{L-MSA}(\text{LN}(\text{AvgPool}(\mathbf{X}^l)))] + \bar{\mathbf{X}}, \qquad (10)$$

$$\mathbf{Y}'' = \text{DWMLP}(\mathbf{Y}') + \mathbf{Y}', \qquad (11)$$

where H-MSA$(\cdot)$ and L-MSA$(\cdot)$ are features extracted from our high-frequency and low-frequency multi-head attention modules. The Cat$[\cdot]$ denotes the concatenation operation. AvgPool$(\cdot)$ is the average pooling operation. We concatenate the outputs from the dual branches, and the final multi-head attention can be calculated. A Layer-Norm (LN) layer is added before the multi-head self-attention, and residual connections are utilized in each block.

Here, we design a high-frequency self-attention module to extract high-frequency features, by adopting a window-based attention mechanism. The input $\mathbf{X}^h$ is partitioned into non-overlapping windows and reshaped to $O_1 \times \frac{L}{M^2} \times M^2 \times C_o$, where M represents the local window size. We set $M = 4$, using small local windows of 4×4 for self-attention to capture high-frequency fine-grained features instead of larger window sizes such as 8×8 or 16×16. Moreover, we do not use techniques like shift window [20] or multi-scale windows [44], which saves considerable computational complexity and makes our approach hardware-friendly. The high-frequency MSA branch can be described as: H-MSA$(\mathbf{X}^h) = \text{Cat}[\text{SA}_1(\mathbf{X}_1^h), \ldots, \text{SA}_o(\mathbf{X}_o^h), \ldots, \text{SA}_{O_1}(\mathbf{X}_{O_1}^h)]\mathbf{W}_{O_1}$. The o indicates the head index and $\mathbf{X}_o^h \in \mathbb{R}^{\frac{L}{M^2} \times M^2 \times C_o}$ is each single head. The projection matrix $\mathbf{W}_{O_1} \in \mathbb{R}^{(O_1 \times C_o) \times (O_1 \times C_o)}$ and Cat$(\cdot)$ concatenates the outputs from the O_1 attention heads. The SA$_o(\cdot)$ is the self-attention module.

Here, we design a low-frequency self-attention to capture global low-frequency features. Since it is unfeasible to perform global attention directly in the entire pixel space due to the high computational cost, we employ an average pooling to downsample the $\mathbf{X}^l$ into $\mathbf{X}' \in \mathbb{R}^{O_2 \times (L/D^2) \times C_o}$, which can be defined as: $\mathbf{X}' = \text{AvgPool}(\mathbf{X}^l)$, where D means the pooling kernel size and we set $D = 4$ in this paper. AvgPool$(\cdot)$ is used to encode inputs into a lower-dimensional latent space for extracting low-frequency global information. Then, we use a standard multi-head self-attention mechanism in the latent space to capture rich low-frequency information from the feature maps. We then have L-MSA$(\mathbf{X}') = \text{Cat}[\text{SA}_1(\mathbf{X}'_1), \ldots, \text{SA}_o(\mathbf{X}'_o), \ldots, \text{SA}_{O_2}(\mathbf{X}'_{O_2})]\mathbf{W}_{O_2}$ for the low-frequency MSA branch. $\mathbf{W}_{O_2} \in \mathbb{R}^{(O_2 \times C_o) \times (D^2 \times O_2 \times C_o)}$ is a projection matrix.

Now, we describe the details of the self-attention for o-th head SA$_o(\mathbf{X})$. Given the input feature maps $\mathbf{X} \in \mathbb{R}^{L \times C_o}$, $\mathbf{X}$ is used to compute the query $\mathbf{Q}$, key $\mathbf{K}$, and value

$\mathbf{V}$ matrices, each with dimensions $L \times C_o$. These matrices are derived through distinct linear transformations applied to $\mathbf{X}$, which can be expressed as:

$$\mathbf{Q} = \mathbf{X}\mathbf{W}_q, \mathbf{K} = \mathbf{X}\mathbf{W}_k, \mathbf{V} = \mathbf{X}\mathbf{W}_v, \tag{12}$$

where $\mathbf{W}_q, \mathbf{W}_k, \mathbf{W}_v \in \mathbb{R}^{C_o \times C_o}$ are learnable parameters, and C_o is the number of hidden dimensions per head. Next, the output of a self-attention head is obtained by the Softmax activation function applied to the scaled dot product of the query and key:

$$\mathrm{SA}_o(\mathbf{X}) = \mathrm{Softmax}\left(\frac{\mathbf{Q}\mathbf{K}^\top}{\sqrt{C_o}}\right)\mathbf{V}. \tag{13}$$

As depicted in Fig. 1 (a), the FSAB utilizes a low-frequency attention branch to capture the global dependencies inherent in the input image. This branch focuses on global attention and does not necessitate high-resolution feature maps. Conversely, the high-frequency attention branch is tailored to detect finely detailed local dependencies, utilizing a local attention mechanism on high-resolution feature maps to achieve this objective.

3.3 Loss Functions

Multi-patch Degradation Representation Learning. Contrastive learning has been used in unsupervised representation learning widely, such as MoCo [13], which aims to maximize mutual information within the representation embedding space by encouraging similar samples to be closer and dissimilar ones to be farther apart. To learn more robust features and reduce the risk of overfitting for single-view-based constructive learning, we propose to design a multiview scheme for contrastive learning approach to capture degradation representations from diverse perspectives.

Our degradation representation learning module consists of a contrastive learning encoder and an additional linear projection, which aims to capture degradation representations from LR images unsupervised implicitly. Specifically, a random image patch is cropped from an LR image as a query patch, other patches belonging to the same LR image are considered positive samples, and patches from different LR images are considered negative samples. Our encoder embeds the input into $p \in \mathbb{R}^{256}$ following the main structure of MoCo [13], as shown in Fig. 2 (d).

To learn discriminative degradation representations, a large set of negative samples is essential [16]. Instead of relying on large batch sizes, our model maintains a queue of diverse samples to achieve content-invariant degradation representations while enabling concurrent training of degradation learning and feature extraction modules.

As shown in Fig. 1, we randomly select batch-size LR images to represent different degradations. For i-th sampled LR image $\mathbf{I}_i^{\mathrm{LR}}$, it can be expressed as:

$$\boldsymbol{p}_i^t = \mathrm{Encoder}(\hat{\mathbf{I}}_{i,t}^{\mathrm{LR}}), t \in [0, 1, 2, \dots, T], \tag{14}$$

where $\hat{\mathbf{I}}_{i,t}^{\mathrm{LR}}$ is a randomly cropped image patch with different sizes (e.g., 32×32, 48×48, and 64×64) from the i-th image. For each image, we set $\boldsymbol{p}_i^0$ as a query embedding $\boldsymbol{q}_i \in \mathbb{R}^{256}$ and the others as T positive embeddings $\boldsymbol{p}_i^t \in \mathbb{R}^{256}, t \in [1, 2, \dots, T]$.

Conversely, any $p_j, j \neq i$ belonging to other LR images is treated as a negative sample embedding.

Multi-patch Contrastive Loss. We employ multi-patch contrastive loss as the degradation loss to optimize our contrastive learning encoder, incorporating a temperature coefficient τ, which is defined by the following equation:

$$\mathcal{L}_{\text{degrade}} = -\frac{1}{T} \sum_{t=1}^{T} \log \frac{\exp(q_i \cdot p_i^t / \tau)}{\sum_{j=1}^{U} [\exp(q_i \cdot q_j / \tau) + \sum_{t=1}^{T} \exp(q_i \cdot p_j^t / \tau)]}, \tag{15}$$

where U represents the number of samples in the negative sample queue. q_j and p_j^t denote the negative embeddings from j-th sample in the queue. We set temperature coefficient $\tau = 0.07$ to control the sharpness of the Softmax function used in the computation of the loss function. The queue size U is set to 1024.

L1 Loss. Like most image super-resolution works, we optimize our super-resolution network parameters by minimizing the L_1 pixel loss.

$$\mathcal{L}_{\text{SR}} = \left\| \mathbf{I}^{\text{HR}} - \mathbf{I}^{\text{SR}} \right\|_1. \tag{16}$$

Total Loss. The total loss function is defined as:

$$\mathcal{L}_{\text{Total}} = \mathcal{L}_{\text{SR}} + \mathcal{L}_{\text{degrade}}. \tag{17}$$

We optimize the network parameters of our degradation-aware frequency-separated Transformer by minimizing the total loss function. Our training strategy consists of two phases. We only train the degradation encoder for the first stage using $\mathcal{L}_{\text{degrade}}$ and then train the entire network using the $\mathcal{L}_{\text{Total}}$ in the second stage. This approach allows for focused optimization of degradation representations before integrating them into the whole model.

4 Experiments

4.1 Experimental Setup

Dataset. Unless otherwise specified, all the compared methods were trained on a dataset combining the DIV2K [35] training set and the Flickr2K [21] dataset. We evaluated using benchmark super-resolution datasets, including Set5 [1], Set14 [46], BSD100 [28], and Urban100 [14].

Degradation Settings. The degradation model of the LR image can be described as $\mathbf{I}^{\text{LR}} = (\mathbf{I}^{\text{HR}} \otimes \mathbf{k}_{(\lambda_1, \lambda_2, \Theta)}) \downarrow_r + \mathbf{n}_\epsilon$. According to the equation, LR images were synthesized for training and testing. The $\otimes$ denotes the convolution operation, the $\mathbf{k}_{(\lambda_1, \lambda_2, \Theta)}$ denotes the blur kernel controlled by $(\lambda_1, \lambda_2, \Theta)$; the noise $\mathbf{n}_\epsilon$ signifies additional random Gaussian noise with intensity ϵ; and $(\cdot) \downarrow_r$ indicates the downsampling operation with a scaling factor of r. The Gaussian kernel size is consistently set at 21×21. As the blur and noise intensities are unknown, the degree of degradation was adjusted by randomly sampling their hyperparameters, resulting in a diverse range of image degradations.

Table 1. Quantitative comparison on noise-free degradation and isotropic Gaussian kernels. The kernel widths (σ) are given for each column. The best and second-best results are marked in **bold** and <u>underlined</u>, respectively.

Method	Source	Scale	Set5			Set14			BSD100			Urban100		
			0.6	1.2	1.8	0.6	1.2	1.8	0.6	1.2	1.8	0.6	1.2	1.8
Bicubic		×2	32.30	29.28	27.07	29.21	27.13	25.47	28.76	26.93	25.51	26.13	24.46	23.06
RCAN [53]	ECCV 2018		35.91	32.31	28.50	32.31	28.48	26.33	31.16	28.04	26.26	29.80	25.38	23.44
SRMD [50]	CVPR 2018		34.77	34.13	33.80	31.35	30.78	30.18	30.33	29.89	29.20	28.42	27.43	27.12
IKC [11]	CVPR 2019		37.35	37.26	33.94	33.36	32.97	30.31	31.97	31.79	29.57	31.37	30.53	27.15
SwinIR [20]	ICCV 2021		35.96	31.21	28.51	32.38	28.49	26.33	31.19	28.04	26.26	29.92	25.39	23.45
DASR [36]	CVPR 2021		37.47	37.19	35.43	32.96	32.78	31.60	31.78	31.71	30.54	30.71	30.36	28.95
DAN [25]	Arxiv 2021		37.83	37.46	<u>35.76</u>	33.33	33.20	31.81	32.06	31.88	30.51	31.14	30.71	29.04
DSSR [17]	TMM 2022		37.94	<u>37.60</u>	**35.86**	33.40	33.29	**32.03**	32.15	32.06	30.88	31.42	<u>31.15</u>	**29.67**
HAT [5]	CVPR 2023		36.04	31.22	28.52	32.56	28.51	26.34	31.29	28.06	26.27	30.17	25.40	23.45
DSAT [22]	TMM 2024		<u>38.06</u>	37.59	35.65	<u>33.55</u>	<u>33.34</u>	31.88	<u>32.21</u>	<u>32.10</u>	<u>30.88</u>	<u>31.50</u>	31.03	<u>29.40</u>
DAFST (ours)			**38.09**	**37.65**	35.75	**33.78**	**33.57**	<u>31.94</u>	**32.25**	**32.11**	**30.89**	**31.76**	**31.18**	29.38

Method	Source	Scale	Set5			Set14			BSD100			Urban100		
			0.8	1.6	2.4	0.8	1.6	2.4	0.8	1.6	2.4	0.8	1.6	2.4
Bicubic		×3	29.42	27.24	25.39	26.84	25.42	24.09	26.72	25.52	24.41	24.02	22.95	21.89
RCAN [53]	ECCV 2018		32.90	29.12	26.75	29.49	26.75	24.99	28.56	26.55	25.18	26.89	24.89	22.30
SRMD [50]	CVPR 2018		32.63	32.27	28.62	29.25	28.01	26.90	28.25	28.11	26.56	26.61	26.35	24.06
SwinIR [20]	ICCV 2021		32.98	29.12	26.76	29.59	26.77	25.00	28.62	26.56	25.18	27.05	23.86	22.30
DASR [36]	CVPR 2021		34.08	33.57	31.15	29.99	28.66	28.42	28.90	28.62	28.13	27.36	26.86	25.95
HAT [5]	CVPR 2023		33.04	29.13	26.76	29.36	26.79	25.00	28.69	26.57	25.18	27.21	23.88	22.30
DSAT [22]	TMM 2024		<u>34.56</u>	<u>33.77</u>	<u>31.96</u>	**30.48**	**30.17**	<u>28.98</u>	<u>29.22</u>	<u>29.10</u>	<u>28.24</u>	**28.38**	**27.88**	**26.67**
DAFST (ours)			**34.57**	**34.01**	**32.27**	<u>30.39</u>	<u>30.12</u>	**29.06**	**29.25**	**29.18**	**28.30**	<u>28.27</u>	<u>27.89</u>	<u>26.65</u>

Method	Source	Scale	Set5			Set14			BSD100			Urban100		
			1.2	2.4	3.6	1.2	2.4	3.6	1.2	2.4	3.6	1.2	2.4	3.6
Bicubic		×4	27.30	25.12	23.40	25.24	23.83	22.57	25.42	24.20	23.15	22.68	21.62	20.65
RCAN [53]	ECCV 2018		30.26	26.72	24.66	27.48	24.93	23.41	26.89	25.09	23.93	24.71	22.25	20.99
SRMD [50]	CVPR 2018		29.35	29.27	28.65	26.15	26.20	26.17	26.15	26.33	25.63	25.00	24.10	24.08
IKC [11]	CVPR 2019		31.77	30.56	29.23	28.45	28.16	26.81	27.43	27.27	26.33	25.63	25.00	24.06
SwinIR [20]	ICCV 2021		30.35	26.73	24.67	27.54	24.94	23.42	26.92	25.10	23.94	24.82	22.27	20.99
DASR [36]	CVPR 2021		31.92	31.75	30.59	28.45	28.28	27.45	27.51	27.43	26.83	25.69	25.44	24.66
DAN [25]	Arxiv 2021		32.22	31.98	**30.94**	28.65	**28.54**	**27.69**	27.66	27.58	26.95	26.21	<u>25.97</u>	**25.08**
DSSR [17]	TMM 2022		32.26	<u>32.09</u>	<u>30.89</u>	<u>26.68</u>	**28.54**	**27.69**	27.65	27.58	26.95	26.09	25.83	<u>24.97</u>
HAT [5]	CVPR 2023		30.39	26.72	24.67	27.57	24.94	23.42	26.96	25.10	23.94	24.90	22.26	20.99
DSAT [22]	TMM 2024		**32.51**	32.00	30.31	<u>28.67</u>	<u>28.50</u>	<u>27.51</u>	**27.77**	**27.66**	<u>26.98</u>	**26.43**	**25.95**	24.89
DAFST (ours)			<u>32.44</u>	**32.25**	30.43	**28.78**	<u>28.53</u>	<u>27.53</u>	<u>27.70</u>	<u>27.61</u>	**27.02**	<u>26.21</u>	25.77	24.86

We conducted experiments under various degradation settings. In Subsect. 4.2, we evaluated ours and the existing state-of-the-art (SOTA) methods under the condition of isotropic Gaussian kernel degradation with kernel widths σ (it is equivalent to $(\lambda_1 = \sigma, \lambda_2 = \sigma, \Theta = 0)$) within the range of [0.2, 2.0] for ×2, [0.2, 3.0] for ×3 and [0.2, 4.0] for ×4 super-resolution training, respectively.

In Subsect. 4.3 and Subsect. 4.4, we further evaluated compared methods under more diverse conditions employing anisotropic Gaussian kernels and random noise to induce image degradation for ×4 super-resolution. These anisotropic kernels are described by eigenvalues $\lambda_1, \lambda_2 \sim U(0.2, 4.0)$ and a randomly determined rotation angle $\Theta \sim U(0, \pi)$. Noise intensity ϵ is varied within the range of [0, 25]. If not specified otherwise, the rotation angle Θ and noise intensity ϵ of the blur kernel is 0 during testing.

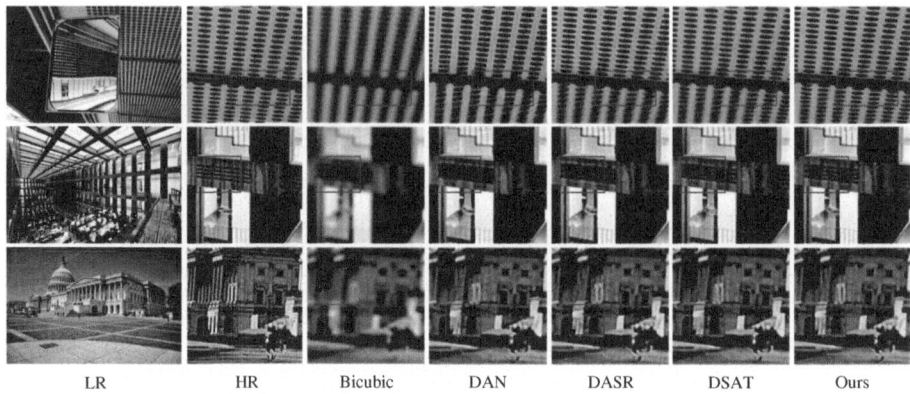

LR   HR   Bicubic   DAN   DASR   DSAT   Ours

Fig. 3. Visual results of compared methods and our DAFST on Urban100 dataset at a ×2 SR setting using isotropic Gaussian kernel degradation with $\sigma = 1.2$. Our results show clearer details.

Implementation. Our DAFST network consists of two depthwise convolution blocks (DWCB) and two frequency-separated self-attention groups (FSAG). The first group has six frequency-separated self-attention blocks (FSAB), and the second group has two. The hidden layer dimensionality is set to 180, with six attention heads per FSAB. Each FSAB is configured with five high-frequency ($O_1 = 5$) and one low-frequency ($O_2 = 1$) attention heads.

Additionally, for each image, we extracted one 48×48 sized query patch and three positive patches with different sizes (i.e., 32×32, 48×48, and 64×64, respectively) to improve the diversity of multi-patch.

During training, we used a batch size of 32 and applied data augmentation techniques, including 50% random vertical and horizontal flipping, as well as 50% random 90° rotations. We employed the Adam optimizer with $\beta_1 = 0.9$ and $\beta_2 = 0.999$. The training began with an initial learning rate of 10^{-4}, halved every 250 epochs. Our training has two phases: first, we trained the degradation encoder in isolation for 200 epochs with a learning rate of 10^{-3}, then trained the entire network using an additional 1000 epochs. All experiments were conducted on an NVIDIA GeForce RTX 4090 GPU.

4.2   Comparison on Noise-Free Degradation

We compared our model under noise-free conditions using isotropic Gaussian kernels of different widths with bicubic interpolation, CNN-based methods (RCAN [53], SRMD [50], IKC [11], DASR [36], DAN [25], and DSSR [17]), and Transformer-based methods (SwinIR [20], HAT [5], and DSAT [22]), on Set5, Set14, BSD100, and Urban100 datasets.

Table 1 provides a quantitative comparison of our method against SOTA approaches across various kernel widths on four benchmark datasets. While all methods recover details well, performance notably drops for ×4 SR compared to ×2 SR, highlighting the greater challenge of ×4 SR due to reduced contextual information. CNN-based methods, such as DSSR, have limited receptive fields, which hinders their ability to capture global features, resulting in a lack of competitiveness in ×2 SR compared to

Table 2. Quantitative comparison of ×4 super-resolution on the Set14 dataset. The eigenvalues and rotation values ($\lambda_1, \lambda_2, \Theta$) of anisotropic Gaussian kernels as well as the noise intensity (ϵ) are given for each column. **Bold** and <u>underline</u> represent the best and second-best performance, respectively.

Method	ϵ	(2.0, 0.2, 0)	(2.0, 1.0, 10)	(3.5, 1.5, 30)	(3.5, 2.0, 45)	(3.5, 2.0, 90)	(4.0, 1.5, 120)	(4.0, 2.0, 135)	(4.0, 3.0, 160)	(4.0, 4.0, 180)
DnCNN + RCAN [53]	0	26.44	26.22	24.48	24.23	24.29	24.19	23.9	23.42	23.01
	5	26.10	25.90	24.29	24.07	24.14	24.02	23.74	23.31	22.92
	10	25.65	25.47	24.05	23.84	23.92	23.8	23.54	23.14	22.77
DnCNN + IKC [11]	0	27.71	27.78	27.11	27.02	26.93	26.65	26.5	26.01	25.33
	5	26.91	26.80	24.87	24.53	24.56	24.40	24.06	23.53	23.06
	10	26.16	26.09	24.55	24.33	24.35	24.17	23.92	23.43	23.01
DnCNN + DCLS [26]	0	27.56	27.49	26.32	25.99	25.88	26.03	25.70	24.65	23.95
	5	26.20	26.02	24.44	24.21	24.28	24.14	23.88	23.40	22.98
	10	25.47	25.33	24.06	23.87	23.91	23.79	23.58	23.16	22.78
DASR [36]	0	27.99	27.97	27.53	27.45	27.43	<u>27.22</u>	27.19	26.83	26.21
	5	27.25	27.18	26.37	26.16	26.09	25.96	25.85	25.52	25.04
	10	26.57	26.51	25.64	25.47	25.43	25.31	25.16	24.80	24.43
HAT-Real [5]	0	25.82	25.86	25.44	24.95	24.92	24.57	24.61	24.54	24.38
	5	25.74	25.80	25.21	24.81	24.78	24.49	24.46	24.20	23.93
	10	25.33	25.30	24.57	24.35	24.44	24.24	24.12	23.76	23.51
DSAT [22]	0	**28.34**	**28.34**	**27.78**	**27.68**	<u>27.68</u>	**27.37**	<u>27.25</u>	26.98	26.47
	5	<u>27.55</u>	<u>27.47</u>	<u>26.59</u>	<u>26.43</u>	<u>26.43</u>	<u>26.31</u>	<u>26.14</u>	<u>25.80</u>	<u>25.36</u>
	10	<u>26.83</u>	<u>26.74</u>	25.87	25.71	25.71	25.60	25.44	25.10	24.70
DAFST (ours)	0	28.29	28.31	27.76	27.66	**27.78**	27.37	**27.28**	**27.10**	**26.57**
	5	**27.68**	**27.65**	**26.68**	**26.51**	**26.52**	**26.40**	**26.29**	**25.92**	**25.46**
	10	**26.94**	**26.85**	**25.94**	**25.75**	**25.72**	**25.63**	**25.49**	**25.17**	**24.77**

×4 SR. Transformer-based methods, like DSAT, excel at extracting global features but may neglect finer details critical for super-resolution. Methods like HAT, using hybrid attention mechanisms and larger attention windows, achieved significant performance in non-blind SR tasks. However, this enhancement did not improve the model's performance when faced with images of unknown degradation. In contrast, our low-frequency branch effectively captures global features with a larger receptive field, while the high-frequency branch enhances the generation of fine details. Our method demonstrates superior performance across all datasets for the SR tasks ×2 and ×3 and competitive results for ×4 SR. The relatively modest performance in ×4 SR is because the input image size is significantly small in ×4 SR, which reduces the amount of useful information available for inference. This limitation is a common challenge shared by the compared methods as well.

Figure 3 presents a visual comparison of the methods on the Urban100 dataset for the ×2 SR task. The DSAT, guided by learned degradation representations, delivers impressive results. Constrained by multi-patch contrastive learning, our DAFST produces clearer textures and sharper edges than other methods. This multi-patch contrastive learning allows for extracting more discriminative degradation features, and the combination of low and high-frequency feature extraction captures both global and local visual details at larger kernel widths.

4.3 Comparison on General Degradation

We conducted comparisons under general degradation conditions using anisotropic Gaussian kernels with added noise. We employed nine different anisotropic blur kernels and tested them under different noise intensities ϵ of 0, 5, and 10, respectively.

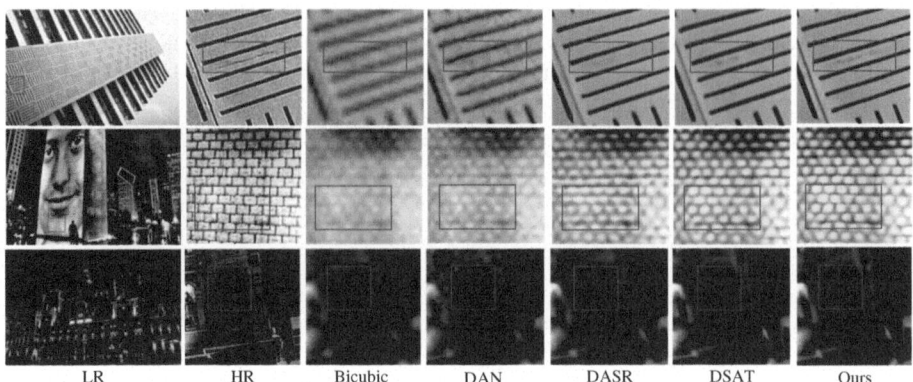

| LR | HR | Bicubic | DAN | DASR | DSAT | Ours |

Fig. 4. Visual results on the Urban100 dataset at a $\times 4$ SR setting using isotropic Gaussian kernel degradation with $\sigma = 1.8$ and $\epsilon = 5$. Our model outperforms others in preserving details in noisy images.

Table 3. Quantitative comparisons at $\times 4$ SR under varying noise intensities (ϵ) and kernel widths (σ).

Method	ϵ	Urban100 (PSNR/SSIM)			BSD100 (PSNR/SSIM)		
		$\sigma = 1$	$\sigma = 2$	$\sigma = 4$	$\sigma = 1$	$\sigma = 2$	$\sigma = 4$
DASR [36]	0	25.189/0.7527	24.777/0.7334	23.480/0.6667	27.315/0.7228	27.016/0.7094	26.060/0.6549
	5	24.823/0.7323	24.069/0.6952	22.456/0.6096	26.827/0.6932	26.209/0.6590	24.849/0.5920
	10	24.395/0.7123	23.595/0.6715	21.994/0.5857	26.269/0.6660	25.623/0.6313	24.335/0.5702
DSAT [22]	0	**25.684/0.7727**	**25.428/0.7606**	23.764/0.6720	**27.494/0.7318**	27.389/0.7244	26.229/0.6625
	5	25.364/0.7555	24.735/0.7267	22.931/0.6344	26.992/0.7031	26.458/0.6737	25.010/0.5991
	10	24.755/0.7326	24.070/0.6911	22.348/0.6063	26.380/0.6734	24.744/0.6413	24.505/0.5776
DAFST (ours)	0	25.663/0.7715	25.415/0.7593	**23.806/0.6809**	27.473/0.7300	**27.407/0.7242**	**26.288/0.6631**
	5	**25.398/0.7551**	**24.828/0.7264**	**23.023/0.6385**	**27.070/0.7066**	**26.591/0.6787**	**25.192/0.6094**
	10	**24.856/0.7302**	**24.121/0.6958**	**22.425/0.6080**	**26.452/0.6757**	**25.868/0.6439**	**24.611/0.5833**

Since RCAN [53], IKC [11], and DCLS [26] are not specifically designed to handle noise degradation, we incorporated a DnCNN [49] model as the pre-processing for fair comparisons.

Table 2 presents the quantitative results of the compared methods on the Set14 dataset. CNN-based approaches like RCAN and IKC demonstrate limited performance under complex degradation conditions. While IKC performs better, it relies on iterative estimation, making it time-consuming. HAT-Real is a version of HAT [5] trained according to ESRGAN's training settings [38] under multi-level degradation and noise conditions. Unlike our degradation-aware approach, it uses a generative adversarial network for training, which does not effectively distinguish between different levels of degradation. As a result, its performance on images with lower levels of degradation is limited. Implicit degradation representation-based methods, like DSAT, leverage contrastive learning to automatically learn degradation factors and demonstrate impressive performance. However, their reliance on a single view of the image during degradation learning may limit the learning effectiveness of degradation representations. In con-

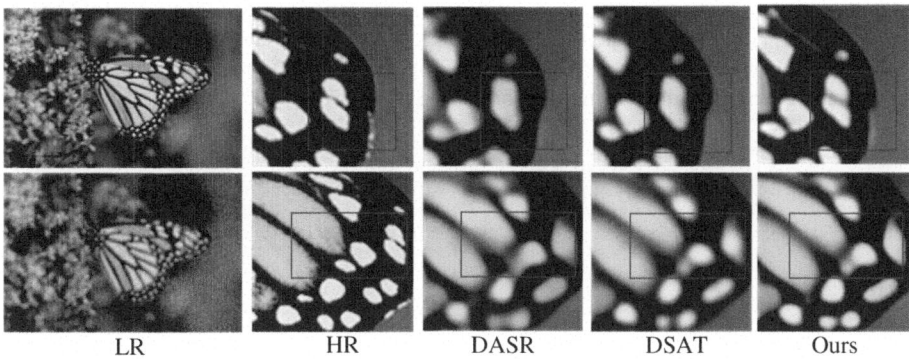

LR   HR   DASR   DSAT   Ours

Fig. 5. Visual comparison on the Set14 dataset. The settings of the anisotropic Gaussian blur kernel of the first row are $(\lambda_1 = 2.0, \lambda_2 = 0.2, \Theta = 0)$ and with $\epsilon = 0$; the settings of the blur kernel of the second are $(\lambda_1 = 4.0, \lambda_2 = 4.0, \Theta = 180)$ and with $\epsilon = 10$.

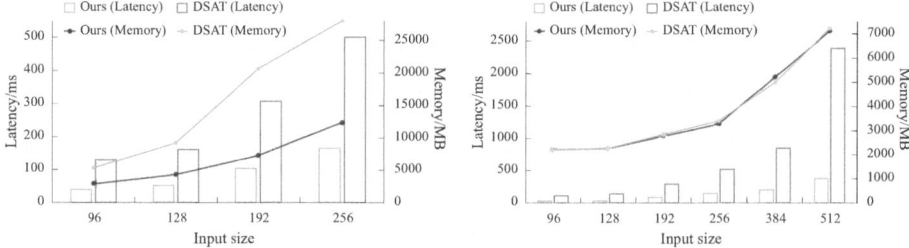

Fig. 6. Inference speeds and memory usages of DSAT and our method under various image sizes in training (left) and testing (right) phases. When training at a resolution of 256×256, DSAT encountered an out-of-memory issue, while our method supports higher resolutions.

trast, our DAFST employs multi-patch contrastive learning, allowing the model to learn more robust and discriminative degradation representations. This approach outperforms DCLS by over 1.0 dB across all degradation scenarios. Our method outperforms DSAT across most degradation scenarios. The multi-patch degradation learning provides clear guidance information to guide the subsequent super-resolution, and our high-frequency and low-frequency branches and smaller attention windows help capture global and local details with high efficiency.

Figure 4 illustrates the visual results of compared methods on the images from the Urban100 dataset with anisotropic Gaussian kernels and noise. The results reveal that DAN, which excelled under noise-free conditions, significantly deteriorates under noisy conditions. In contrast, our model adapts to more complex degradation scenarios, exhibiting clearer reconstruction results.

Figure 5 presents qualitative comparisons with methods using implicit degradation representations, such as DASR and DSAT, on the Set14 dataset. Our method demonstrates advantages in the accuracy and clarity of detailed textures, further demonstrating its robust adaptability.

Table 4. Ablation study of proposed components on the Set14 dataset. The kernel widths of isotropic Gaussian kernels (σ) and noise intensities (ϵ) are given for each column. The ratio means the numbers of high-to-low frequency attention heads. The DR represents the degradation representations learning, and the DWMLP means the DWMLP block.

Method	Ratio	DR	DWMLP	(1.2, 0) PSNR/SSIM	(1.2, 5) PSNR/SSIM	(1.2, 10) PSNR/SSIM	(2.4, 0) PSNR/SSIM	(2.4, 5) PSNR/SSIM	(2.4, 10) PSNR/SSIM	(3.6, 0) PSNR/SSIM	(3.6, 5) PSNR/SSIM	(3.6, 10) PSNR/SSIM
Model-I	6:0	✓	✓	28.332/0.7714	27.844/0.7490	27.129/0.7205	28.043/**0.7574**	26.960/0.7101	26.122/0.6777	26.880/0.7049	25.869/0.6674	25.087/0.6386
Model-II	3:3	✓	✓	28.315/0.7714	27.834/0.7487	27.097/0.7193	27.978/0.7540	26.943/0.7101	26.095/0.6770	26.843/0.7015	25.890/0.6668	25.096/0.6383
Model-III	1:5	✓	✓	28.304/0.7694	27.829/0.7488	27.084/0.7199	27.952/0.7513	26.966/0.7108	26.109/0.6767	26.860/0.7036	25.880/0.6670	25.100/0.6382
Model-IV	5:1	×	✓	28.265/0.7704	27.766/0.7477	27.043/0.7190	27.889/0.7437	26.869/0.7068	26.012/0.6755	26.764/0.6959	25.810/0.6635	25.041/0.6362
Model-V	5:1	✓	×	28.344/0.7702	27.838/0.7479	27.092/0.7196	28.041/0.7555	26.947/0.7099	26.115/0.6774	26.972/**0.7070**	25.891/0.6658	25.130/0.6384
Model-VI	5:1	×	×	28.221/0.7701	27.738/0.7455	27.029/0.7170	27.836/0.7432	26.861/0.7077	26.002/0.6727	26.809/0.6978	25.618/0.6549	24.990/0.6326
Model-VII (ours)	5:1	✓	✓	**28.423/0.7728**	**27.904/0.7505**	**27.144/0.7215**	**28.101**/0.7531	**27.035/0.7118**	**26.168/0.6795**	**27.022**/0.7040	**25.916/0.6684**	**25.155/0.6405**

4.4 More Comparisons

To further validate the effectiveness of our model, we compared it with methods using implicit degradation representations, like DASR and DSAT, on the Urban100 and BSD100 datasets. Since DSAT did not provide pre-trained weights, we retrained it according to the method described by the authors. Quantitative results shown in Table 3 indicate that our method also performs better on the Urban100 and BSD100 datasets.

Moreover, we show the memory consumption and inference speed, compared with the SOTA Transformer-based approach, DSAT. We specified the image size and input images to the model for $\times 4$ super-resolution. The time is averaged over 1000 samples. As shown in Fig. 6, our model consumes significantly less memory and higher speed during training than DSAT. Our model can be trained on datasets with large sizes to tap into the model's potential further. In detail, the network of DSAT has 15.64 million (M) of parameters, while our proposed method has a significantly reduced parameter number of 10.15M. Our degradation-aware frequency-separated attention mechanism utilizes smaller attention windows for high-frequency branches and compact visual embeddings for low-frequency branches to capture finer details and global structures for efficient BSR.

4.5 Ablation Study

We conducted ablation studies to evaluate the effectiveness of our proposed components. Specifically, the number ratio of high-to-low frequency attention heads in Model-I is 6:0 ($O = 6$ and $\hat{O} = 0$), which is equivalent to standard window-based attention; Model-II and Model-III have ratios of 3:3 ($O = 3$ and $\hat{O} = 3$) and 1:5 ($O = 1$ and $\hat{O} = 5$), respectively; Model-IV removes the degradation representations learning (DR); Model-V removes the DWConv within DWMLP and Model-VI remove both DR and DWConv; Model-VII (our full model) utilizes a high-to-low frequency ratio of 5:1 ($O = 5$ and $\hat{O} = 1$) and incorporates both DR and DWMLP.

As shown in Table 4, the results indicate that Model-VII outperformed all other models across all evaluation metrics. Model-IV, which lacks implicit representation guidance, significantly decreases SR performance. Model-V, which does not utilize depthwise convolution to aggregate high and low-frequency attention branches, exhibits a slight decrease in quantitative scores. Experimental results show that the best results

Table 5. Ablation study of different position encoding learning schemes on the Set14 dataset. The kernel widths (σ) of isotropic Gaussian kernels and noise levels (ϵ) are given for each column. The latency values are averaged over 1000 samples, each with an input resolution of 512×512.

Method	(1.2, 0) PSNR/SSIM	(1.2, 5) PSNR/SSIM	(1.2, 10) PSNR/SSIM	(2.4, 0) PSNR/SSIM	(2.4, 5) PSNR/SSIM	(2.4, 10) PSNR/SSIM	(3.6, 0) PSNR/SSIM	(3.6, 5) PSNR/SSIM	(3.6, 10) PSNR/SSIM	Latency
Model-VIII	28.314/0.7702	27.824/0.7485	27.097/0.7200	28.003/0.7540	26.953/0.7097	26.115/0.6775	26.975/**0.7084**	25.884/0.6660	25.130/0.6386	442ms
Model-IX	28.370/0.7717	27.822/0.7480	27.126/0.7200	28.014/0.7530	26.983/0.7093	**26.175**/0.6785	26.976/0.7082	**25.923**/0.6665	25.153/0.6393	467ms
Model-VII (ours)	**28.423 0.7728**	**27.904/0.7505**	**27.144/0.7215**	**28.101/0.7531**	**27.035/0.7117**	26.168/**0.6795**	**27.022**/0.7040	25.916/**0.6684**	**25.155/0.6405**	**375ms**

Table 6. Ablation study for different positive sample numbers on Set5 and Urban100 datasets (using PSNR). The scaling factor of super-resolution is $\times 2$; the kernel widths (σ) of isotropic Gaussian kernels are given for each column.

Positive samples	Set5				Urban100			
	0.0	0.5	1.0	1.5	0.0	0.5	1.0	1.5
1	38.082	38.111	37.946	36.897	32.225	**31.820**	**31.501**	30.367
3 (ours)	**38.130**	**38.141**	**37.968**	**36.931**	**32.325**	31.805	31.494	**30.417**
5	38.103	38.091	37.840	36.900	32.242	31.666	31.408	30.314
7	38.099	38.058	37.888	36.909	32.202	31.695	31.330	30.225

are achieved when the ratio of attention heads of high-to-low frequency branches is 5:1, indicating that more high-frequency information may be crucial in blind super-resolution tasks.

As shown in Table 5, we validated the effectiveness of the DWCB for shallow feature extraction. For a fair comparison, we created three variants with nearly identical parameters: one replaces the DWCB with two frequency-separated self-attention blocks (Model-VIII), another replaces the DWCB with two frequency-separated self-attention blocks incorporating convolutional position encoding Model-IX, and Model-VII (our full model). Our method with the DWCB demonstrates the best quantitative performance while maintaining faster inference speed.

4.6   Analysis

Analysis on the Number of Positive Samples. In our blind super-resolution task, contrastive learning efficacy exhibits a non-linear trend as the number of positive samples varies. As shown in Table 6, the optimal PSNR performance is achieved with three positive samples, followed by using one positive sample, while performance declines with five and seven samples. This phenomenon likely stems from the unique demands of capturing image degradation features in blind super-resolution. Three positive samples appear to achieve a good balance, maintaining sufficient feature variability while avoiding overfitting specific visual features. Thus, it enables the model to learn rich degradation representations while preserving sensitivity to specific patterns. Conversely, with five or seven samples, the model may overfit on over-averaged representations from the whole dataset, overlooking subtle yet crucial differences that play a pivotal role in high-quality image reconstruction.

Table 7. Ablation study of different window sizes for high-frequency attention branch ($\times 4$ BSR). The kernel width of isotropic Gaussian is $\sigma = 1.2$.

Window size	Set5	Set14	BSD100	Urban100
	PSNR/SSIM	PSNR/SSIM	PSNR/SSIM	PSNR/SSIM
2×2	31.864/**0.8907**	28.403/0.7711	27.455/**0.7294**	25.620/0.7690
4×4 (ours)	**31.948**/ 0.8903	**28.423/0.7728**	**27.460**/0.7272	**25.649**/0.7692
8×8	31.857/0.8893	28.377/0.7707	27.443/0.7264	25.627/**0.7696**

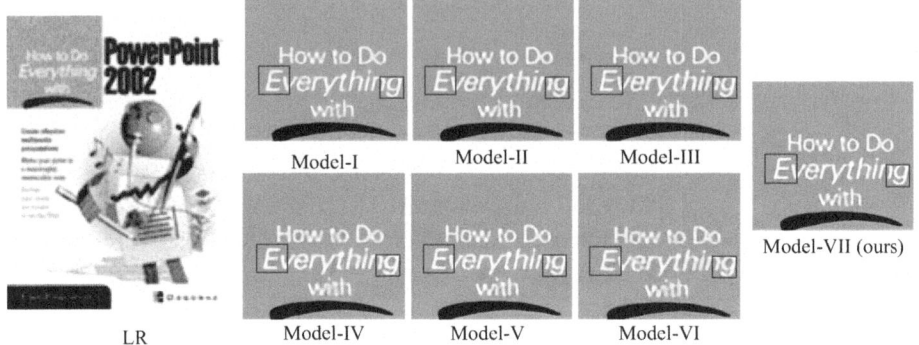

Fig. 7. Visualization of $\times 4$ super-resolution ablation study under the conditions of $\sigma = 2.4$ and $\epsilon = 5$. The SR image generated by Model-VII is visually more appealing, with clearer edge details in letters.

Analysis on the Window Size of High-frequency Attention Branch. We further conducted an ablation on different sizes of local attention windows based on Model-VII. The results in Table 7 indicate that appropriately sized local attention windows are more beneficial for feature extraction modeling. Excessively small or large windows do not necessarily facilitate extracting high-frequency local features.

As shown in Fig. 7, we visualized the qualitative performance of the models on Set14. The results demonstrate that our method (Model-VII) exhibits high-fidelity visual results, with the reconstructed high-resolution images containing rich textural details.

Analysis on Degradation Representation Learning. Here, we further analyze the effectiveness of the degradation representation learning by visualizing the projected degradation representations using degradation encoders in Model-IV and Model-VII (our full model), respectively. Note that the Model-IV was trained without the multi-patch contrastive learning. We used the BSD100 dataset to create LR images with different degradation degrees and input them into Model-IV and Model-VII to obtain embeddings from the degradation encoder. We then visualized these representations using the T-SNE [27].

Figure 8 shows that embeddings using our Model-VII with degradation learning can be distinctively clustered when faced with different kernel widths or varying levels of

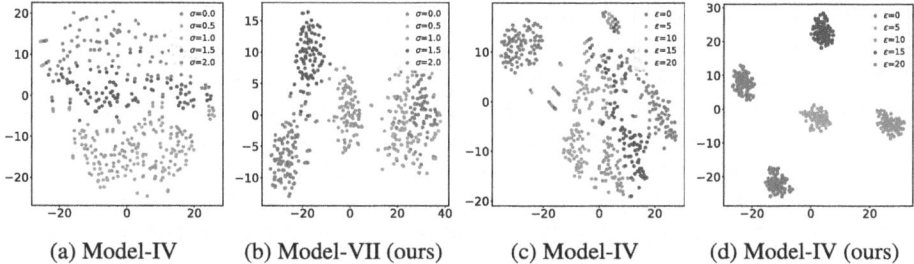

(a) Model-IV   (b) Model-VII (ours)   (c) Model-IV   (d) Model-IV (ours)

Fig. 8. Visualization of degradation representations under different kernel widths (σ) and noise levels (ϵ) using degradation encoder. (a) and (c) are without degradation learning. (b) and (d) are with our degradation learning.

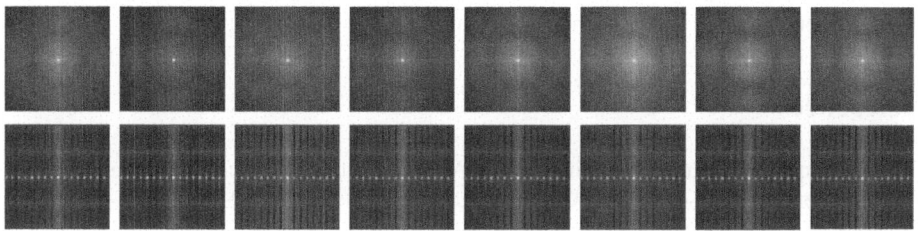

Fig. 9. The frequency amplitude (48×48) of the first eight output channels of the high branch (upper) and low branch (lower), in the last FSAB. The amplitude is averaged over 32 samples. The lighter the color, the higher the amplitude. Pixels closer to the center represent lower frequencies, and vice versa.

noise degradation. The performance of Model-IV and Model-VII on images degraded under different kernel widths and noise intensities. Table 4 also proves that the learning of degradation representations indeed helps our encoder learn discriminative representations to provide useful guidance for better blind super-resolution.

Visualization of Frequency Branches. In Fig. 9, we visualize the amplitude of frequency components by applying the Fast Fourier Transform (FFT) [30] to feature maps of the high and low-frequency self-attention branches separately. Some periodic spectral changes might be caused by the applied degrading blur kernel. Our visualization results indicate that the high-frequency branch captures more high-frequency information. In Fig. 3 first row, our model correctly restores the shape of the holes. In contrast, the low-frequency branch primarily focuses on low-frequency information. In Fig. 4 first and third rows, our method successfully recovers the structure of buildings. These results demonstrate the effectiveness of our proposed degradation-aware frequency-separated Transformer for high-quality blind super-resolution.

5   Conclusion

In this paper, we have presented a novel degradation-aware frequency-separated Transformer for blind super-resolution. Our approach effectively captures discriminative degradation representations through multi-patch contrastive learning. The proposed frequency-separated Transformer leverages degradation representations to efficiently extract both local details and global structural features via high- and low-frequency branches, combining fine-grained details with global context. Extensive comparisons, ablation studies, and analyses demonstrated the superior performance of our method and the effectiveness of the proposed components for blind super-resolution.

Our method has some limitations. First, like most Transformer-based methods, it faces significant memory and computational overhead when performing ultra-high-resolution images. Second, for extremely low-resolution images, performance is affected due to limited available information. Expanding the range of frequency representations would enhance the model's learning capacity. In the future, we aim to address these challenges by incorporating a broader range of frequencies. We would like to explore the application of our degradation-aware frequency-separated Transformer in other computer vision tasks, such as image recognition and detection.

References

1. Bevilacqua, M., Roumy, A., Guillemot, C., Alberi-Morel, M.: Low-complexity single-image super-resolution based on nonnegative neighbor embedding. In: BMVC, pp. 1–10. BMVA (2012)
2. Caron, M., Misra, I., Mairal, J., Goyal, P., Bojanowski, P., Joulin, A.: Unsupervised learning of visual features by contrasting cluster assignments. NeurIPS **33**, 9912–9924 (2020)
3. Chadha, A., Britto, J., Roja, M.M.: iSeeBetter: Spatio-temporal video super-resolution using recurrent generative back-projection networks. CVMJ **6**, 307–317 (2020)
4. Chen, H., et al.: Pre-trained image processing transformer. In: CVPR, pp. 12299–12310. IEEE (2021)
5. Chen, X., Wang, X., Zhou, J., Qiao, Y., Dong, C.: Activating more pixels in image super-resolution transformer. In: CVPR, pp. 22367–22377. IEEE (2023)
6. Dai, T., Cai, J., Zhang, Y., Xia, S., Zhang, L.: Second-order attention network for single image super-resolution. In: CVPR, pp. 11065–11074. IEEE (2019)
7. Dong, C., Loy, C.C., He, K., Tang, X.: Learning a deep convolutional network for image super-resolution. In: Fleet, D., Pajdla, T., Schiele, B., Tuytelaars, T. (eds.) ECCV 2014. LNCS, vol. 8692, pp. 184–199. Springer, Cham (2014). https://doi.org/10.1007/978-3-319-10593-2_13
8. Dong, C., Loy, C.C., He, K., Tang, X.: Image super-resolution using deep convolutional networks. IEEE TPAMI **38**(2), 295–307 (2015)
9. Dong, C., Loy, C.C., Tang, X.: Accelerating the super-resolution convolutional neural network. In: Leibe, B., Matas, J., Sebe, N., Welling, M. (eds.) ECCV 2016. LNCS, vol. 9906, pp. 391–407. Springer, Cham (2016). https://doi.org/10.1007/978-3-319-46475-6_25
10. Fritsche, M., Gu, S., Timofte, R.: Frequency separation for real-world super-resolution. In: ICCVW, pp. 3599–3608. IEEE (2019)
11. Gu, J., Lu, H., Zuo, W., Dong, C.: Blind super-resolution with iterative kernel correction. In: CVPR, pp. 1604–1613. IEEE (2019)
12. Guo, H., Li, J., Dai, T., Ouyang, Z., Ren, X., Xia, S.T.: MambaIR: a simple baseline for image restoration with state-space model. In: ECCV, vol. 15076, pp. 222–241. Springer (2024)
13. He, K., Fan, H., Wu, Y., Xie, S., Girshick, R.B.: Momentum contrast for unsupervised visual representation learning. In: CVPR, pp. 9726–9735. IEEE (2020)

14. Huang, J., Singh, A., Ahuja, N.: Single image super-resolution from transformed self-exemplars. In: CVPR, pp. 5197–5206. IEEE (2015)
15. Kim, J., Lee, J.K., Lee, K.M.: Accurate image super-resolution using very deep convolutional networks. In: CVPR, pp. 1646–1654. IEEE (2016)
16. Le-Khac, P.H., Healy, G., Smeaton, A.F.: Contrastive representation learning: a framework and review. IEEE Access **8**, 193907–193934 (2020)
17. Li, F., Wu, Y., Bai, H., Lin, W., Cong, R., Zhao, Y.: Learning detail-structure alternative optimization for blind super-resolution. IEEE TMM **25**, 2825–2838 (2023)
18. Li, Z., Yang, J., Liu, Z., Yang, X., Jeon, G., Wu, W.: Feedback network for image super-resolution. In: CVPR, pp. 3867–3876. IEEE (2019)
19. Liang, J., Zeng, H., Zhang, L.: Efficient and degradation-adaptive network for real-world image super-resolution. In: ECCV, vol. 13678, pp. 574–591. Springer (2022)
20. Liang, J., Cao, J., Sun, G., Zhang, K., Gool, L.V., Timofte, R.: SwinIR: image restoration using Swin transformer. In: ICCVW, pp. 1833–1844. IEEE (2021)
21. Lim, B., Son, S., Kim, H., Nah, S., Lee, K.M.: Enhanced deep residual networks for single image super-resolution. In: CVPR, pp. 1132–1140. IEEE (2017)
22. Liu, Q., Gao, P., Han, K., Liu, N., Xiang, W.: Degradation-aware self-attention based transformer for blind image super-resolution. IEEE TMM **26**, 7516–7528 (2024)
23. Liu, Z., et al.: Swin transformer: hierarchical vision transformer using shifted windows. In: CVPR, pp. 10012–10022. IEEE (2021)
24. Lu, W., Wang, J., Wang, T., Zhang, K., Jiang, X., Zhao, H.: Visual style prompt learning using diffusion models for blind face restoration. PR **161**, 111312 (2025)
25. Luo, Z., Huang, Y., Li, S., Wang, L., Tan, T.: End-to-end alternating optimization for blind super resolution. arXiv preprint arXiv:2105.06878 (2021)
26. Luo, Z., Huang, H., Yu, L., Li, Y., Fan, H., Liu, S.: Deep constrained least squares for blind image super-resolution. In: CVPR, pp. 17621–17631. IEEE (2022)
27. Van der Maaten, L., Hinton, G.: Visualizing data using t-SNE. JMLR **9**(11) (2008)
28. Martin, D.R., Fowlkes, C.C., Tal, D., Malik, J.: A database of human segmented natural images and its application to evaluating segmentation algorithms and measuring ecological statistics. In: ICCV, pp. 416–425. IEEE (2001)
29. Pan, Z., Cai, J., Zhuang, B.: Fast vision transformers with Hilo attention. NeurIPS **35**, 14541–14554 (2022)
30. Rao, Y., Zhao, W., Zhu, Z., Lu, J., Zhou, J.: Global filter networks for image classification. NeurIPS **34**, 980–993 (2021)
31. She, M., Mao, W., Shi, H., Wang, Z.: S2R: exploring a double-win transformer-based framework for ideal and blind super-resolution. In: ICANN, pp. 522–537. Springer (2023)
32. Shi, W., et al.: Real-time single image and video super-resolution using an efficient sub-pixel convolutional neural network. In: CVPR, pp. 1874–1883. IEEE (2016)
33. Shocher, A., Cohen, N., Irani, M.: Zero-shot super-resolution using deep internal learning. In: CVPR, pp. 3118–3126. IEEE (2018)
34. Soh, J.W., Cho, S., Cho, N.I.: Meta-transfer learning for zero-shot super-resolution. In: CVPR, pp. 3513–3522. IEEE (2020)
35. Timofte, R., Agustsson, E., Van Gool, L., Yang, M.H., Zhang, L.: NTIRE 2017 challenge on single image super-resolution: methods and results. In: CVPR, pp. 1110–1121. IEEE (2017)
36. Wang, L., et al.: Unsupervised degradation representation learning for blind super-resolution. In: CVPR, pp. 10581–10590. IEEE (2021)
37. Wang, T., et al.: Restoring vision in hazy weather with hierarchical contrastive learning. PR **145**, 109956 (2024)
38. Wang, X., et al.: ESRGAN: enhanced super-resolution generative adversarial networks. In: ECCV, vol. 11133, pp. 63–79. Springer (2018)

39. Wang, Y., Liu, Y., Zhao, S., Li, J., Zhang, L.: CAMixerSR: only details need more attention. arXiv preprint arXiv:2402.19289 (2024)
40. Wei, Y., Gu, S., Li, Y., Timofte, R., Jin, L., Song, H.: Unsupervised real-world image super resolution via domain-distance aware training. In: CVPR, pp. 13385–13394. IEEE (2021)
41. Xia, B., et al.: Knowledge distillation based degradation estimation for blind super-resolution. In: ICLR, OpenReview.net (2023)
42. Xu, J., Yuan, M., Yan, D.M., Wu, T.: Deep unfolding multi-scale regularizer network for image denoising. CVMJ **9**, 335–350 (2023)
43. Xu, Y., Tseng, S.R., Tseng, Y., Kuo, H., Tsai, Y.: Unified dynamic convolutional network for super-resolution with variational degradations. In: CVPR, pp. 12493–12502. IEEE (2020)
44. Yang, J., et al.: Focal self-attention for local-global interactions in vision transformers. arXiv preprint arXiv:2107.00641 (2021)
45. Yang, W., Zhang, X., Tian, Y., Wang, W., Xue, J.H., Liao, Q.: Deep learning for single image super-resolution: a brief review. IEEE TMM **21**(12), 3106–3121 (2019)
46. Zeyde, R., Elad, M., Protter, M.: On single image scale-up using sparse-representations. In: Curves and Surfaces, pp. 711–730. Springer (2012)
47. Zhang, K., Gool, L.V., Timofte, R.: Deep unfolding network for image super-resolution. In: CVPR, pp. 3214–3223. IEEE (2020)
48. Zhang, K., Li, Y., Zuo, W., Zhang, L., Van Gool, L., Timofte, R.: Plug-and-play image restoration with deep denoiser prior. IEEE TPAMI **44**(10), 6360–6376 (2021)
49. Zhang, K., Zuo, W., Chen, Y., Meng, D., Zhang, L.: Beyond a Gaussian denoiser: residual learning of deep CNN for image denoising. IEEE TIP **26**(7), 3142–3155 (2017)
50. Zhang, K., Zuo, W., Zhang, L.: Learning a single convolutional super-resolution network for multiple degradations. In: CVPR, pp. 3262–3271. IEEE (2018)
51. Zhang, K., Zuo, W., Zhang, L.: Deep plug-and-play super-resolution for arbitrary blur kernels. In: CVPR, pp. 1671–1681. IEEE (2019)
52. Zhang, Y., Tan, Z., Yang, J., Huang, W., Yuan, Y.: Matrix information theory for self-supervised learning. arXiv preprint arXiv:2305.17326 (2023)
53. Zhang, Y., Li, K., Li, K., Wang, L., Zhong, B., Fu, Y.: Image super-resolution using very deep residual channel attention networks. In: Ferrari, V., Hebert, M., Sminchisescu, C., Weiss, Y. (eds.) ECCV 2018. LNCS, vol. 11211, pp. 294–310. Springer, Cham (2018). https://doi.org/10.1007/978-3-030-01234-2_18

MAAU-UIE: Multiple Attention Aggregation U-Net for Underwater Image Enhancement

Junsheng Chang[1], Qin Shi[1], Yijun Zhang[1]($\boxtimes$), Zongtang Hu[1], and Xunlun Ye[2]

[1] China Mobile (Suzhou) Software Technology Co., Ltd., Suzhou, Jiangsu, China
[2] Faculty of Electrical Engineering and Computer Science, Ningbo University, Ningbo, Zhejiang, China
yexulun@nbu.edu.cn

Abstract. To address issues such as color distortion, blurriness, and low contrast in underwater images, a Multiple Attention Aggregation U-Net for Underwater Image Enhancement (MAAU-UIE) is proposed. The network is constructed using an encoder-decoder structure, with a multiple attention block designed to enhance the ability to extract features from low-quality underwater images. First, axial rectangular window attention and shifted axial rectangular window attention are alternately applied to learn local context and establish global dependencies, respectively. Additionally, channel convolution and spatial convolution are incorporated into the process of window attention calculation to further supplement local information. A channel enhancement module is then added to improve the modeling capability in the channel dimension. Finally, gradient loss and multi-scale structural similarity loss are used to enhance the network's ability to extract edge detail information and multi-scale structural features. Ablation experiments demonstrate the significant role of each proposed module plays in improving network performance. Quantitative experiments show that this method surpasses existing methods on various objective metrics. The peak signal-to-noise ratio (PSNR) and structural similarity (SSIM) on the benchmark dataset UIEB test set reach 24.467 and 0.920, respectively. The underwater image quality measurement (UIQM) and underwater color image quality evaluation (UCIQE) on the UIEB challenge set and in three color-bias environments of UCCS outperform cutting-edge methods. Qualitative experiments indicate a clear advantage in subjective visual effects, effectively restoring underwater images with natural colors and clear texture structures.

Keywords: Underwater Image Enhancement · Attention Aggregation · Rectangular Window Attention · Channel Feature Enhancement · Multi-Scale

P. Didyk and J. Hou (Eds.): CVM 2025, LNCS 15663, pp. 253–274, 2025.
https://doi.org/10.1007/978-981-96-5809-1_14

1   Introduction

With the continuous advancements in ocean exploration and underwater activities, the acquisition of underwater images has become increasingly important in fields such as marine science, archaeology, ocean engineering, and underwater robot navigation [1,2]. However, due to the complexity of the underwater environment, underwater images are often affected by factors such as light scattering and absorption [3], which lead to poor image quality. These issues mainly manifest as color distortion, reduced contrast, blurring, and increased noise [4,5], significantly lowering the usability and visual quality of underwater images. As a result, underwater image enhancement technologies have emerged, aiming to improve the visual quality of underwater images through algorithms and technical approaches, making them more suitable for human perception and computer vision applications.

Traditional methods [4–6] rely on statistical information and assumptions about the image. These methods attempt to improve visual quality by correcting color distortions and enhancing contrast through manually designed features. However, these methods are unable to adapt to dynamic scenes and perform poorly in terms of image quality restoration.

Convolutional neural networks (CNNs) perform excellently in feature extraction for images and are therefore widely used in image restoration and related fields. CNN-based methods [7–9] can automatically extract image features and achieve end-to-end image representation. However, the receptive field and fixed convolutional kernels of CNN-based methods limit their development in the field of image restoration. Due to the limitations of the receptive field, CNN-based methods cannot capture relationships between pixels over a larger range. Furthermore, the fixed convolutional kernels prevent CNN-based methods from adapting to the diversity of underwater images.

The transformer model, based on self-attention, was initially applied in natural language processing (NLP) [10]. In recent years, due to its outstanding performance in visual tasks, many transformer-based methods [11,12] have been applied to image restoration. However, due to its quadratic computational complexity, it faces challenges when dealing with high-resolution images, as the computational load becomes enormous and needs to be optimized.

The main contributions are summarized as follows:

1) The network is built upon the U-Net architecture, which leverages hierarchical up-sampling and down-sampling operations to effectively extract information from feature maps of different scales. This enhances the model's ability to handle various complex underwater environments.
2) Standard U-Net networks, relying purely on convolutional operations, have limited ability to capture global information. To address this, the base module of the U-Net is designed using a window attention mechanism. To mitigate the high computational cost of standard Transformer models, the feature map is divided into a series of rectangular windows, and attention is calculated within each window to effectively extract information in both horizontal and vertical

directions. Further, by shifting the axial rectangular window partitioning, connections between windows are strengthened.

3) To further enhance the feature extraction capabilities, convolution operations are integrated into the window attention computation to capture richer local detail information. Additionally, a channel enhancement module is added, which assigns different weight coefficients to each channel, improving modeling capacity.

4) In addition to pixel-based reconstruction loss, gradient loss and multi-scale structural similarity loss are incorporated to enhance the robustness of the model in recovering texture details.

5) Extensive experiments conducted on the UIEB benchmark dataset [13] show that our method significantly improves performance across various objective metrics and demonstrates superior subjective visual results. Furthermore, validation on the UCCS dataset [14] confirms that the proposed method achieves superior performance in underwater environments with three different color casts.

2   Related Work

In recent years, significant progress has been made in the field of underwater image enhancement. Traditional methods [5,6]continue to be optimized and applied, but more attention is being given to deep learning-based enhancement methods, which have gradually become a research hotspot. For instance, Islam et al. [15] designed a multi-scale convolutional neural network that improves the contrast and clarity of underwater images through multi-layer feature extraction and fusion.

Moreover, Generative Adversarial Networks (GANs) have demonstrated great potential in underwater image enhancement. Ye et al. [16] utilized GANs to achieve efficient image denoising and dehazing, significantly enhancing the visual quality of underwater images. Zhang et al. [17] proposed an enhanced GAN architecture that incorporates a self-attention mechanism in both the generator and discriminator, further improving color balance and detail representation. Cong et al. [18] introduced a GAN-based physical model for underwater image enhancement, which performed well in terms of visual aesthetics. However, GAN-based methods rely on large amounts of training data, and the training process may encounter mode collapse issues, leading to instability in the quality of the generated images.

In recent years, attention mechanisms and Transformer structures have also been introduced into the field of underwater image enhancement. Huang et al. [19] introduced a Transformer-based method for underwater image enhancement, which effectively integrates global and local information in the image through self-attention mechanisms, enabling more precise correction of color and contrast issues. Ren et al. [12,20] employed Transformers and self-attention mechanisms for underwater image enhancement, which can capture a broader range of pixel features from the input images, although these methods tend to have higher computational demands. The underwater image enhancement method based on Mamba [21] is another promising research direction. Lin et al. [22] proposed Pix-Mamba, applying Mamba to underwater image enhancement. Mamba offers efficient sequence modeling capabilities, its primary limitation lies in the increased difficulty of model tuning due to its complexity. Furthermore, its application in the image domain remains in the exploratory phase, requiring more experimental evidence to verify its effectiveness in underwater image enhancement.

Although significant progress has been made, current underwater image enhancement methods still face several challenges. First, the diversity and complexity of underwater environments lead to inconsistent performance of existing models across different settings, lacking generalizability. Second, deep learning-based methods require substantial computational resources and depend on large amounts of annotated data, which poses challenges for real-world applications. Additionally, most existing research focuses on a single image enhancement task, and there is still no unified framework that can simultaneously handle multiple tasks such as color correction, contrast enhancement, denoising, and dehazing. Therefore, further research is necessary to develop more general, efficient, and resource-light underwater image enhancement methods.

To address the above challenges, This paper proposes a Multiple Attention Aggregation U-Net [23] for Underwater Image Enhancement (MAAU-UIE) based on multiple attention mechanisms combined with effective loss functions, which achieves promising performance in underwater image enhancement.

3   Methodology

3.1   Network Architecture

This paper presents a Multiple Attention Aggregation U-Net network (MAAU-UIE) for underwater image enhancement. The network structure, as shown in Fig. 1, primarily consists of an encoder, a bottleneck layer, and a decoder. A novel Multiple Attention Block (MAB) is designed as the foundational module of the network. The original underwater image is first resized to a predefined dimension, denoted as $I_{in} \in R^{H \times W \times 3}$. The image is then passed through a 3×3 convolutional layer to map the number of channels to C. After that, a PatchEmbed layer is applied to divide the image into a series of patches of size $P \times P$, generating shallow encoded features, denoted as $X_0 \in R^{\frac{H}{P} \times \frac{W}{P} \times C}$.

The encoder consists of three Multiple Attention Blocks (MABs), each followed by a PatchMerging module used as a down-sampling (DS) operation. The PatchMerging reduces the width and height of the feature maps by half while doubling the number of channels. Taking the input X_0, the outputs of the three DS modules in the encoder are denoted as $E_1 \in R^{\frac{H}{2P} \times \frac{W}{2P} \times 2C}$, $E_2 \in R^{\frac{H}{4P} \times \frac{W}{4P} \times 4C}$ and $E_3 \in R^{\frac{H}{8P} \times \frac{W}{8P} \times 8C}$ respectively. The bottleneck layer includes one MAB that further enhances the features, producing the output $E_3^{'} \in R^{\frac{H}{8P} \times \frac{W}{8P} \times 8C}$.

The decoder has a symmetric structure to the encoder, also comprising three MABs. Each MAB in the decoder is followed by an up-sampling (UP) module,

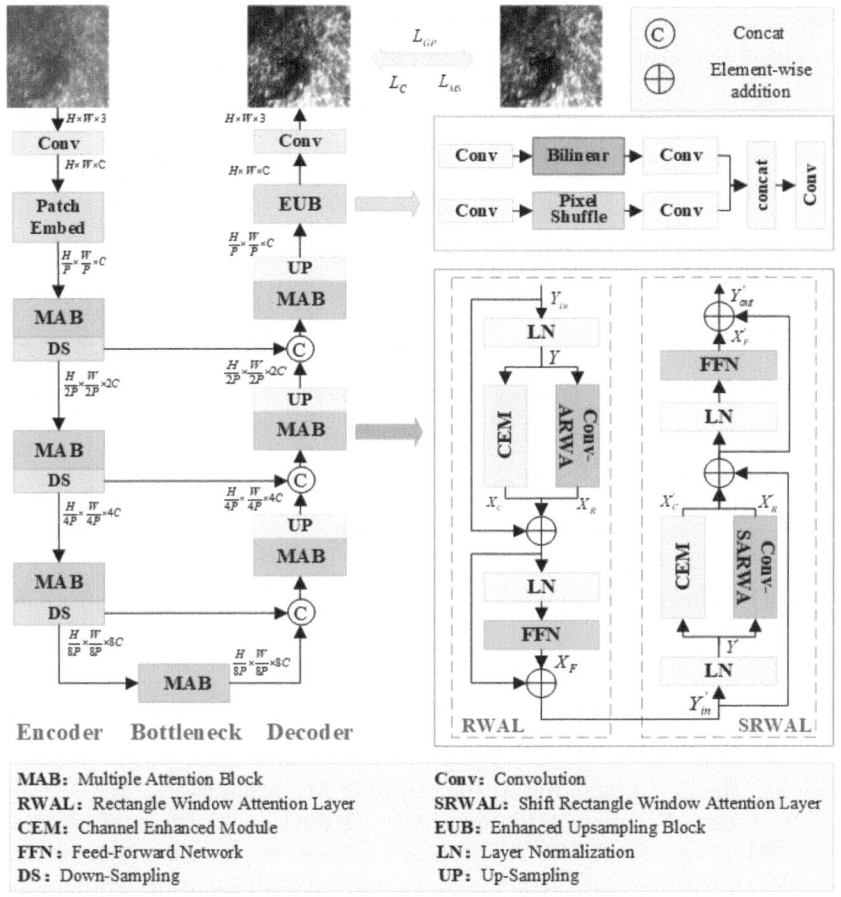

Fig. 1. The network structure of MAAU-UIE (Colour figure online)

which uses bicubic interpolation to double the width and height of the feature maps while halving the number of channels. The outputs of the three UP modules in the decoder are denoted as $D_1 \in R^{\frac{H}{4P} \times \frac{W}{4P} \times 4C}$, $D_2 \in R^{\frac{H}{2P} \times \frac{W}{2P} \times 2C}$ and $D_3 \in R^{\frac{H}{P} \times \frac{W}{P} \times C}$ respectively. Simultaneously, the feature maps from the encoder and decoder at corresponding positions are concatenated along the channel dimension. A fully connected (Linear) layer is then applied to reduce the number of channels by half, improving the information flow across the network.

To retain more image details and enhance the visual quality of the reconstructed image, an Enhanced Upsampling Block (EUB) is used after the decoder. This block employs parallel sub-pixel convolution (PixelShuffle) and bilinear interpolation to double the width and height of the feature map, followed by channel concatenation. The resulting feature map is then processed through a 1×1 convolutional layer to extract spatial features and restore the number of channels to C, resulting in output features $I_F \in R^{H \times W \times C}$. At the end of the network, a 3×3 convolutional layer is applied to map the channel dimension of I_F to 3, producing the enhanced underwater image, denoted as $I_{out} \in R^{H \times W \times C}$.

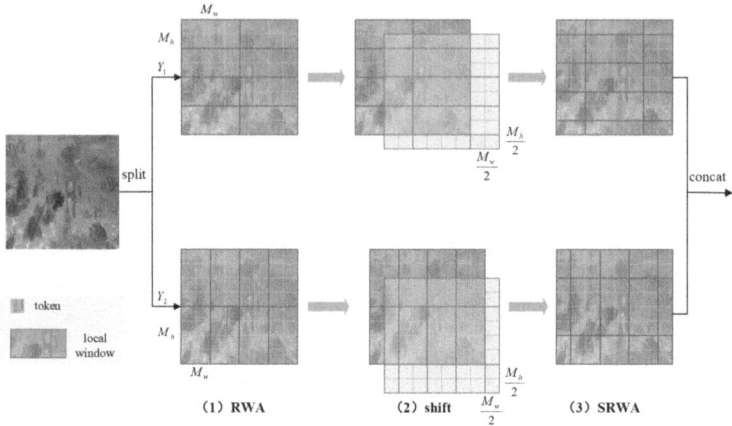

Fig. 2. The window partition method of RWA and SRWA (Colour figure online)

3.2　Multiple Attention Block

As shown in the blue box in Fig. 1, the Multiple Attention Block (MAB) consists of the Rectangle Window Attention Layer (RWAL) and the Shift Rectangle Window Attention Layer (SRWAL). These two window attention layers alternate to learn local features and extract global contextual information. For simplicity, let the input features of MAB be denoted as $Y_{in} \in R^{H \times W \times C}$, which are parallelly input into the Convolution-Axial Rectangle Window Attention (Conv-ARWA) and the Channel Enhanced Module (CEM).

The Conv-ARWA focuses on computing correlations within rectangular windows, extracting information in both horizontal and vertical directions, while utilizing convolution layers to enhance the learning of local features. The CEM establishes correlations between feature channels, and its output is combined with the results from Conv-ARWA through a weighted summation, controlling the weights of spatial and channel features during fusion. The overall process of RWAL is described by Eqs. (1) to (4):

$$X_R = Conv - ARWA(LN(Y_{in}) \tag{1}$$

$$X_C = CEM(LN(Y_{in})) \tag{2}$$

$$X_F = FFN(LN(\alpha \cdot X_C + X_R + Y_{in})) \tag{3}$$

$$Y_{in}^{'} = \alpha \cdot X_C + X_R + X_F \tag{4}$$

where LN represents Layer Normalization, FFN represents the Feed-Forward Network, and α represents the channel feature weights. The Shift Rectangle Window Attention Layer (SRWAL) replaces the Conv-ARWA in RWAL with Convolution-Shift Axial Rectangle Window Attention (Conv-SARWA), while the remaining steps are identical to RWAL.

3.3   Rectangle Window Partitioning

In the standard Transformer model [10], self-attention is computed across all pixels in the entire feature map, which results in high computational costs and limited capability in extracting local features. To ensure effective feature extraction while reducing computational load, the feature map is divided into a series of non-overlapping rectangular windows as described in [24]. Let the width and height of each rectangular window be denoted as M_w and M_h, respectively. Based on the relationship between M_w and M_h, the rectangular windows are categorized into two types. If $M_w > M_h$, the window is defined as a horizontal window, and if $M_w < M_h$, it is defined as a vertical window.

As illustrated in Fig. 2, Rectangle Window Attention (RWA) divides the feature map $Y \in R^{H \times W \times C}$ along the channel dimension into two parts, $Y_1 \in R^{H \times W \times \frac{C}{2}}$ and $Y_2 \in R^{H \times W \times \frac{C}{2}}$, and further partitions Y_1 and Y_2 into a series of horizontal and vertical windows, respectively. Let Y_1 and Y_2 be considered as consisting of $1 \times 1 \times \frac{c}{2}$ tokens, each with a dimension of $H \times W$; hence, each window can be viewed as containing $M_w \times M_h$ tokens. In Fig. 2, the green boxes represent tokens, and the blue rectangular boxes represent the partitioned windows used for subsequent attention calculation. Compared to square windows [11], rectangular windows capture more information along the horizontal and vertical directions for each pixel, which helps enhance the model's feature extraction capabilities.

Considering that Rectangle Window Attention (RWA) focuses on information interaction within each window and lacks connections between different windows, Shift Rectangle Window Attention (SRWA) is added to further expand the receptive field. As shown in Fig. 2, a cyclic shifting operation is applied: the windows partitioned in RWA are shifted downward by $\frac{M_h}{2}$ pixels and rightward by $\frac{M_w}{2}$ pixels, resulting in newly partitioned windows. Finally, the results from horizontal SRWA and vertical SRWA are concatenated along the channel dimension to obtain the final output of the window attention mechanism.

Furthermore, one side of the rectangular window is extended to match the full length of the input feature map (either H or W), while the other side takes a smaller value, denoted as M_l. As illustrated in Fig. 3, the orange pixel can now interact with all the pixels along its horizontal and vertical axes, within the orange-shaded region. This type of attention calculation is referred to as Axial Rectangle Window Attention (ARWA). Similarly, a Shift Axial Rectangle Window Attention (SARWA) is added after ARWA, and they alternate.

In terms of computational cost, the standard Transformer computes the similarity between pixels over the entire feature map of size $H \times W \times C$, which results in a computational complexity proportional to the square of the feature

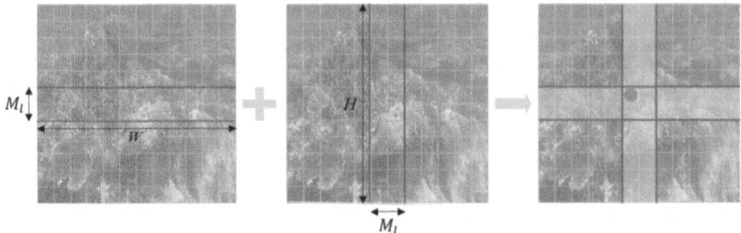

Fig. 3. The attention area of the pixel in ARWA

map size, as shown in Eq. (5). The Rectangle Window Attention (RWA) computes self-attention within a series of rectangular windows of size $M_h \times M_w \times C$, and the number of such windows is $\frac{H}{M_h} \times \frac{W}{M_w}$, leading to the computational complexity as given by Eq. (6).

$$\Omega(MSA) = 2(HW)^2C + 4HWC^2 \quad = HWC \times (2HW + 4C) \quad (5)$$

$$\Omega(RWA) = (2(M_hM_w)^2 + 4M_hM_wC^2) \times \frac{H}{M_h} \times \frac{W}{M_w}$$
$$= HWC \times (2M_hM_w + 4C) \quad (6)$$

Similarly, the computational complexity for Axial Rectangle Window Attention (ARWA) is provided in Eq. (7):

$$\Omega(ARWA) = HWC \times (HM_l + WM_l + 4C) \quad (7)$$

Although the computational cost of ARWA is higher than that of RWA, it is significantly reduced compared to the standard Transformer. Moreover, ARWA's window size changes flexibly with the feature map, making it more adaptable. Additionally, ARWA has a larger attention region, capable of capturing all information in both horizontal and vertical directions. Therefore, in the Multiple Attention Block (MAB), ARWA and SARWA are employed alternately.

3.4 Convolution-Enhanced Window Attention Calculation

Transformers are known for effectively capturing global dependencies, while Convolutional Neural Networks (CNNs) excel at local feature extraction and translation invariance, making them effective in capturing the two-dimensional local structure of images. Therefore, convolution operations are integrated into the calculation of rectangular window attention, resulting in Convolution-Axial Rectangle Window Attention (Conv-ARWA) and Convolution-Shift Axial Rectangle Window Attention (Conv-SARWA) to enhance local information within the windows and improve the model's ability to reconstruct image details.

In conventional window attention calculations [25], a fully connected layer is used to generate the Query, Key, and Value matrices from the input window feature map. In the proposed method, two convolutional layers are applied within

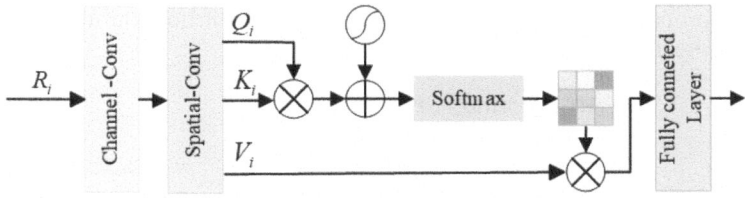

Fig. 4. The algorithm of the window attention combined with the convolution

the divided windows-one along the channel dimension and the other along the spatial dimension-to extract local features and generate the corresponding Query, Key, and Value matrices for each window. Figure 4 illustrates the workflow of convolution-enhanced window attention calculation.

By incorporating convolution operations, the Conv-ARWA and Conv-SARWA modules can extract richer local details, thereby enhancing the ability of the model to effectively reconstruct detailed features in underwater images. This fusion helps in retaining essential information that might be overlooked by purely attention-based mechanisms, ultimately leading to improved image enhancement results.

After dividing the feature map into a series of rectangular windows according to the approach in Sect. 2.3, denote the horizontal rectangular windows obtained from the first $\frac{C}{2}$ channels of the feature map as $R_i \in R^{M_h \times M_w \times \frac{C}{2}}[i = 1, 2, ..., \frac{H \times W}{M_h \times M_w}, M_h < M_w]$.

For window R_i, a 1×1 convolution is first applied along the channel dimension to facilitate information interaction, and the number of channels is expanded by three times. Then, a 3×3 convolution is used to enhance the extraction of local spatial features, resulting in features $G_i \in R^{M_h \times M_w \times \frac{3C}{2}}$, as shown in Eq. (8):

$$G_i = Conv_{3 \times 3}(Conv_{1 \times 1}(R_i)) \tag{8}$$

The dimensions of G_i are then reshaped to $M_h \times M_w \times \frac{3C}{2}$, and it is split evenly along the channel dimension to obtain the Query, Key, and Value matrices for the window, denoted as $Q_i \in R^{M_h \times M_w \times \frac{C}{2}}$, $K_i \in R^{M_h \times M_w \times \frac{C}{2}}$ and $V_i \in R^{M_h \times M_w \times \frac{C}{2}}$, respectively. The matrices Q_i, K_i and V_i are further divided into d heads along the channel dimension, with each head having a channel dimension of $D = C/2d$. The attention is computed for each head of the window in parallel, as shown in Eq. (9):

$$\begin{aligned} Q_i &= [Q^1, Q^2, ..., Q^d], \\ K_i &= [K^1, K^2, ..., K^d], \\ V_i &= [V^1, V^2, ..., V^d] \end{aligned} \tag{9}$$

The attention calculation process for the m-th head of horizontal window R_i is represented by Eq. (10):

$$
\begin{aligned}
X_i^m &= Attention(Q_i^m, K_i^m, V_i^m) \\
&= Softmax[\frac{Q_i^m(K_i^m)^T}{\sqrt{D}} + B]V_i^m, m = 1, 2, ..., d
\end{aligned}
\tag{10}
$$

where B represents the learnable positional encoding, and T represents matrix transpose. The attention results from all d heads for the horizontal window are concatenated along the channel dimension to obtain the attention output for the i-th horizontal window, denoted as $F_i \in R^{M_h \times M_w \times \frac{C}{2}} (M_h < M_w)$:

$$
F_i = Concat(X_i^m), m = 1, 2, ..., d
\tag{11}
$$

Finally, the attention outputs from all $\frac{H \times W}{M_h \times M_w}$ horizontal windows are recombined in the original partitioned order to restore the size of the original feature map, obtaining the horizontal window attention output $F \in R^{H \times W \times \frac{C}{2}}$:

$$
F = WindowReverse(F_i), i = 1, 2, ..., \frac{H \times W}{M_h \times M_w}
\tag{12}
$$

This process effectively extracts both local and global dependencies within each window and integrates them back to enhance the feature representation of the entire feature map.

For the vertical windows obtained from the remaining $\frac{C}{2}$ channels, attention is computed following the same steps as described above. Let the attention output for the i-th vertical window be denoted as $V - i \in R^{M_h \times M_w \times \frac{C}{2}} (M_h > M_w)$. The final attention output for all vertical windows, denoted as $V \in R^{H \times W \times \frac{C}{2}}$, is computed as follows:

$$
V = WindowsReverse(Vi), i = 1, 2, ..., \frac{H \times W}{M_h \times M_w}
\tag{13}
$$

Next, the outputs F and V are concatenated along the channel dimension, and a fully connected layer is applied to obtain the final output of the rectangular window attention, denoted as $X_R \in R^{H \times W \times C}$:

$$
X_R = Concat(F, V)W^o
\tag{14}
$$

where $W^o \in R^{C \times C}$ represents the linear mapping matrix. This step ensures that the information from both horizontal and vertical windows is fully integrated, capturing comprehensive spatial features and enriching the final feature representation.

3.5 Channel Enhanced Module

The channel dimension of an image contains rich color information, and enhancing the inter-channel associations can help in learning the color and intensity variations specific to underwater environments. In this work, a Channel

Enhanced Module (CEM) is added in parallel with the rectangular window attention mechanism. The structure of CEM is shown in Fig. 5. The input feature Y is
processed through two 3×3 convolutional layers with GELU activation functions
to extract features $U \in R^{H \times W \times C}$, as represented by Eq. (15):

$$U = Conv_{3\times3}(GELU(Conv_{3\times3}(Y))) \qquad (15)$$

This operation aims to strengthen the correlation between different channels,
capturing subtle variations in color that are critical for enhancing underwater
images. By using pointwise convolutions, the module focuses solely on channel-
wise interactions, without altering the spatial relationships, which effectively
boosts the model's ability to reconstruct color and texture details.

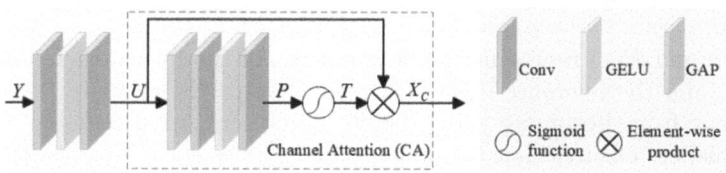

Fig. 5. The structure of CEM

Next, channel attention [26] is used to establish associations among different
channels of the feature map, adaptively assigning channel weights. Specifically,
the feature U is treated as consisting of C feature maps, each of size $H \times W$,
denoted as $U = [v_1, v_2, ..., v_C]$. Global Average Pooling (GAP) is applied to
capture the global information of each channel, as shown in Eq. (16):

$$U'_k = \frac{1}{H \times W} \sum_{i=1}^{H} \sum_{j=1}^{W} U(i,j,k), k = 1, 2, ..., C \qquad (16)$$

A 1×1 convolutional layer is used to reduce the number of channels to $\frac{C}{\gamma}$, where γ
is the channel compression ratio, set to 4. Then, the GELU activation function is
applied to enhance the nonlinearity of the features, followed by another $1 times 1$
convolutional layer to restore the number of channels back to C, as shown in Eq.
(17):

$$P = Conv_{1\times1}(GELU(Conv_{1\times1}(U'))) \qquad (17)$$

Subsequently, a gated activation function $Sigmoid = \frac{1}{1+e^{-x}}$ is applied to normalize the values of the feature map P between 0 and 1. Finally, element-wise
multiplication is performed with the input feature U, resulting in the output
feature of the Channel Enhanced Module X_C, as described in Eq. (18):

$$X_C = U \cdot Sigmoid(P) = U \cdot T \qquad (18)$$

3.6   Loss Function

A multi-task loss function is employed in this work, consisting of Charbonnier loss, gradient loss, and multi-scale structural similarity (MS-SSIM) loss. The weighted combination of these three loss components is given by Eq. (19):

$$L = L_C + \lambda_1 \cdot L_{GP} + \lambda_2 \cdot L_{MS} \tag{19}$$

where λ_1 and λ_2 are the balancing coefficients for the loss terms, with values set to 2 and 1, respectively. The Charbonnier loss aims to reduce the pixel-wise difference between the enhanced output image I_{out} and the reference image I_{gt}, as shown in Eq. (20):

$$L_C = E_{I_{out} \sim P(g), I_{gt} \sim P(o)} \sqrt{(I_{gt} - I_{out})^2 + \epsilon^2} \tag{20}$$

where $P(o)$ and $P(g)$ represent the distributions of the reconstructed enhanced image I_{out} and the reference image I_{gt}, respectively. ϵ is set to $1e^{-3}$ to prevent the gradient from becoming zero, thereby improving robustness to a certain extent. This loss ensures that the enhanced output is as close as possible to the reference, providing a strong foundation for pixel-level similarity and helping the model to effectively reduce artifacts and retain important details. Considering that Charbonnier loss lacks attention to the high-frequency information of the image, gradient loss [27] is used to emphasize the reconstruction of high-frequency details by constraining the difference between the enhanced image I_{out} and the reference image I_{gt} in terms of spatial gradients. The calculation is as follows:

$$I_{GP} = E_{\nabla I_{gt} \sim Q(g), \nabla I_{out} \sim Q(o)} (\nabla I_{gt} - \nabla I_{out}) \tag{21}$$

where ∇I_{gt} and ∇I_{out} represent the gradient fields of the reference image I_{gt} and the enhanced output image I_{out}, respectively. $Q(g)$ and $Q(o)$ represent the distributions of the gradients in the x and y directions for both ∇I_{gt} and ∇I_{out}
.

To further improve the perceptual quality of I_{out} for human viewers, multi-scale structural similarity (MS-SSIM) loss [25] is used to reduce the differences between I_{gt} and I_{out} in terms of luminance, contrast, and structure at multiple scales.

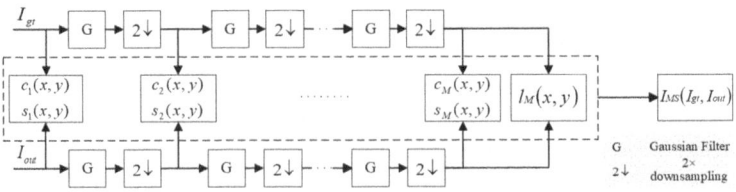

Fig. 6. The algorithm of MS-SSIM

As shown in Fig. 6, multiple scales of the image are obtained by repeatedly applying Gaussian filtering and 2x down-sampling to the original image. The original image is labeled as scale 1, and the image generated after $M - 1$ iterations is labeled as scale M. The multi-scale structural similarity (MS-SSIM) is calculated as follows:

$$I_{MS}(I_{gt}, I_{out}) = [l_M(I_{gt}, I_{out})]^{\alpha_M} \cdot \prod_{j=1}^{M} [c_j(I_{gt}, I_{out})]^{\beta_j} [s_j(I_{gt}, I_{out})]^{\gamma_j} \qquad (22)$$

where α^M, β_j and γ_j are the coefficients that adjust the importance of luminance, contrast, and structural components, respectively. $c_j(I_{gt}, I_{out})$ and $s_j(I_{gt}, I_{out})$ represent the contrast and structure differences at the j-th scale, and $l_M(I_{gt}, I_{out})$ represents the luminance difference at the M-th scale. The multi-scale structural similarity loss is computed as follows:

$$L_{MS} = 1 - I_{MS}(I_{gt}, I_{out}) \qquad (23)$$

4   Experimental Results and Analysis

4.1   Experimental Setup

The experiments in this study were conducted using the Pytorch 1.11 framework on an NVIDIA V100 GPU with 24GB memory. The batch size for training was set to 8, and the number of training epochs was 800. The learning rate was set to 5×10^{-4}, and the Adam optimizer was used to train the model, with parameters $\beta_1 = 0.9$ and $\beta_2 = 0.99$. The size of the underwater images used for both training and testing was uniformly adjusted to 256×256. The channel dimension C in the network was set to 64. In the PatchEmbed layer, the value of P was set to 2. In the Multiple Attention Block (MAB), six Rectangle Window Attention Layers (RWAL) and Shift Axial Rectangle Window Attention Layers (SRWAL) were used alternately, i.e., $N = 6$. The number of heads for multi-head self-attention in both horizontal and vertical rectangular windows was set to 4, i.e., $d = 4$.

4.2   Dataset

The experiments were conducted on the benchmark underwater image enhancement datasets UIEB [13] and UCCS [14]. The UIEB dataset contains 890 paired reference underwater images, with 800 pairs used as the training set, referred to as Train-800, and 90 pairs used as the testing set, referred to as Test-90. Additionally, UIEB includes 60 unpaired original underwater images, referred to as the Challenge Set (C60). The UCCS dataset contains 300 original underwater images without ground truth labels, consisting of 100 images each from three different color cast environments: blue, green, and blue-green. These datasets provide a diverse range of underwater conditions, allowing comprehensive evaluation of the model's ability to handle various underwater image enhancement challenges, including different lighting conditions and color distortions.

4.3 Evaluation Metrics

The evaluation metrics for underwater image enhancement in this study are divided into two categories: reference-based and non-reference. For underwater images with ground truth labels, reference-based metrics are used: Peak Signal-to-Noise Ratio (PSNR) [28] and Structural Similarity (SSIM) [29]. PSNR measures the pixel wise difference between the enhanced image and the reference image, indicating the overall reconstruction accuracy. SSIM measures the contrast, luminance, and structural similarity between images, which aligns better with human visual perception. Higher values of PSNR and SSIM indicate a higher similarity between the enhanced image and the reference image in terms of content. For underwater images without ground truth labels, non-reference metrics are used: Underwater Image Quality Measure (UIQM) [30] and Underwater Color Image Quality Evaluation (UCIQE) [31]. UIQM is defined as a linear combination of Underwater Image Colorfulness Measure (UICM), Underwater Image Sharpness Measure (UISM), and Underwater Image Contrast Measure (UIConM). UCIQE considers chroma, saturation, and contrast in underwater images. Higher values of UIQM and UCIQE indicate better balance in terms of colorfulness, contrast, and overall visual quality of the enhanced image. These metrics provide a comprehensive assessment of the model's performance in both objective accuracy and perceptual quality, allowing for a detailed evaluation of the enhancement results under different conditions and datasets.

Table 1. Comparison of different obfuscations in terms of their transformation capabilities

Model	U-Net(ResBlock)	ARWA & SARWA	Conv-ARWA & Conv-SARWA	CEM	Test-90	
					PSNR	SSIM
Base Model	✓				18.472	0.832
Model 1		✓			24.101	0.916
Model 2			✓		24.351	0.917
Model 3			✓	✓	24.467	0.920

4.4 Ablation Study

An ablation study was conducted on the UIEB dataset, with the model trained on Train-800 and tested on Test-90. To validate the contribution of the proposed modules to underwater image enhancement, the performance of three different network structures was evaluated.

- Model 1 integrates Axial Rectangle Window Attention (ARWA) and Shift Axial Rectangle Window Attention (SARWA) into the U-Net architecture.
- Model 2 adds convolution operations to the rectangular window attention mechanism, replacing ARWA and SARWA in Model 1 with Conv-ARWA and Conv-SARWA.

- Model 3 builds upon Model 2 by incorporating the Channel Enhanced Module (CEM), forming the final network, MAAU-UIE.

The experimental results are shown in Table 1. Compared to the baseline U-Net model, Model 1 achieved significant improvements in PSNR and SSIM, with increases of 5.629 and 0.084, respectively. This improvement is due to the limited global information modeling capability of the ResBlock, whereas Model 1 alternates between ARWA and SARWA, effectively combining local context extraction with global feature representation. Model 2, compared to Model 1, further increased PSNR by 0.250 and SSIM by 0.001, demonstrating that adding convolutional layers enhances the window attention mechanism's ability to learn spatial local information, thereby improving the model's detail enhancement capability. Model 3 achieved the best performance, indicating that integrating the Channel Enhanced Module allows for better utilization of global information, leading to improved reconstruction of color, brightness, and other variations. The combination of attention and channel enhancement contributed to a comprehensive enhancement of the underwater image quality.

Table 2. The effects of different widths and heights of the rectangle window

	(M_h, M_w)		Test-90	
	First $C/2$ channel	Last $C/2$ channel	PSNR	SSIM
Square Window	(4,4)	(4,4)	22.120	0.899
	(8,8)	(8,8)	22.866	0.903
Rectangle Window	(2,4)	(4,2)	23.029	0.907
	(4,16)	(16,4)	23.154	0.909
	(8,16)	(16,8)	23.226	0.915
Axial Window	(2,W)	(H,2)	24.037	0.914
	(4,W)	(H,4)	24.101	0.916
	(8,W)	(H,8)	24.102	0.916

Table 2 discusses the impact of different height (M_h) and width (M_w) combinations of the rectangular windows on the network performance. Based on Model 1, the height and width of the rectangular windows were varied. Compared to the first two rows with square window attention, Rectangle Window Attention (RWA) demonstrated significant performance advantages. Using Axial Rectangle Window Attention (ARWA) further improved the metrics, indicating that extending the longer side of the rectangular window to match the feature map's length better aggregates information along that direction. Additionally, increasing the shorter side of the axial rectangular window (M_l) allows each token to interact with more tokens, enhancing the extraction of global information. By comparing the last two rows of Table 2, it is observed that when M_l increases from 4 to 8, there is no significant performance improvement. Moreover, as indicated by Eq. (7), increasing $M - l$ leads to higher computational cost. Therefore, considering the balance between image reconstruction performance and computational efficiency, M_l was set to 4.

Table 3. Effects of the fusion factor α in CEM

α	Test-90	
	PSNR	SSIM
0	24.351	0.917
0.001	24.354	0.917
0.01	24.412	0.918
0.1	**24.467**	**0.920**
1	24.361	0.919

Table 4. Effects of different loss functions

Loss	Test-90	
	PSNR	SSIM
L_C	23.894	0.898
L_C, L_{MS}	24.210	0.911
L_C, L_{GP}	24.415	0.916
L_C, L_{GP}, L_{MS}	**24.467**	**0.920**

Table 3 compares the effect of different values of α in the Channel Enhanced Module (CEM) on the performance of the MAAU-UIE network. Setting $\alpha = 0$ indicates that the channel enhancement module is not used. Adding the channel enhancement module ($\alpha > 0$) slightly improved PSNR and SSIM. When $\alpha = 0.1$, the model achieved optimal performance, indicating that adjusting the balance between channel information and spatial information fusion can further optimize the model's performance. The results highlight the importance of carefully choosing hyperparameters for the attention mechanisms and channel enhancement module to achieve a good balance between enhancement effectiveness and computational efficiency.

Table 4 compares the results of training the MAAU-UIE network using different combinations of the three loss components. When gradient loss (L_{GP}) or multi-scale structural similarity loss (L_{MS}) was added individually on top of the Charbonnier loss (L_C), both PSNR and SSIM showed significant improvements. When all three loss components were used together, both metrics reached their optimal values. This indicates that reducing the difference between the enhanced image and the reference image in the high-frequency gradient domain, as well as enhancing their structural consistency, contributes significantly to improving the visual quality of the output image. The combination of these losses effectively ensures that the enhanced images not only closely match the reference in pixel values but also retain important textural and structural information, ultimately leading to a more visually appealing enhancement result (Table 5).

4.5   Quantitative Comparison

To validate the superiority of proposed method, various objective metrics were compared between the proposed approach and state-of-the-art underwater image enhancement methods. The models were trained on the UIEB training set (Train-800), and performance was compared on its testing set (Test-90) using PSNR

Table 5. The performance indicators of different methods on the test set Test-90 of UIEB

Method	Venue	Test-90	
		PSNR	SSIM
Ucolor [8]	TIP 21	21.093	0.872
URSCT [20]	TGRS 22	22.720	0.910
FiveA+ [32]	BMVC 23	23.061	0.911
U-shape [12]	TIP 23	22.910	0.910
PuGAN [18]	TIP 23	21.670	-
Semi-UIR [34]	CVPR 23	23.590	0.901
X-CAUNET [3]	ICASSP 24	24.121	0.871
PixMamba [22]	arXiv 24	23.587	**0.921**
Ours	-	**24.467**	0.920

and SSIM metrics. Additionally, for non-reference test sets (C60 from UIEB and UCCS), UIQM and UCIQE metrics were used for comparison.

Table 6 compares the UIQM and UCIQE metrics of various methods on C60 and UCCS datasets, respectively. According to Tables 6, the proposed method outperformed other methods on the UIQM metric for C60 and the UCIQE metric for UCCS, surpassing the second-best method by 0.004 and 0.003, respectively. These results indicate that the proposed method achieves superior sharpness and contrast, and exhibits strong robustness when processing underwater images with three different color casts in the UCCS dataset. This highlights the method's effectiveness in enhancing diverse underwater images and providing high visual quality, especially in challenging color-biased conditions.

Table 6 also compares the performance differences between our model and the current state-of-the-art models. From the metrics of parameters and FLOPs, it can be seen that our model outperforms most of the current state-of-the-art models.

4.6 Qualitative Comparison

To further verify the superiority of the proposed method, the visual enhancement effects on Test-90, C60, and UCCS were compared against mainstream underwater image enhancement algorithms, including URSCT [20], U-shape [12], PuGAN [18], X-CAUNET [3], and Pixmaba [22].

Figure 7 illustrates the enhancement results of different methods on Test-90. For example, URSCT shows issues of insufficient contrast and blurry details in the enhancement results of rows 1, 2, and 3. X-CAUNET produces an image with an overall reddish color cast in row 1, while the result in row 4 has a greenish tint and lacks clarity. Pixmaba produces dark images in row 4 and introduces yellow artifacts in the enhanced image in row 6.

Table 6. The performance indicators of different methods on the challenge set C60 of UIEB and UCCS

Method	Venue	C60		UCCS		1Params	FLOPs
		UIQM	UCIQE	UIQM	UCIQE		
Ucolor [8]	TIP 21	2.482	0.553	3.019	0.55	157.4M	34.68G
URSCT [20]	TGRS 22	2.642	0.543	2.947	0.544	11.41M	18.11G
MFEF [33]	EAAI 23	2.652	0.566	2.977	0.55	61.86M	26.52G
PuGAN [18]	TIP 23	2.652	0.566	2.977	0.53	95.66M	72.05G
Semi-UIR [34]	CVPR 23	2.667	0.574	**3.079**	0.55	**1.65M**	36.44G
X-CAUNET [3]	ICASSP 24	2.683	0.564	2.922	0.541	31.78M	261.48G
PixMamba [22]	arXiv 24	2.868	**0.586**	3.053	0.561	8.68M	**7.60G**
Ours	-	**2.872**	0.572	3.066	**0.564**	8.52M	9.84G

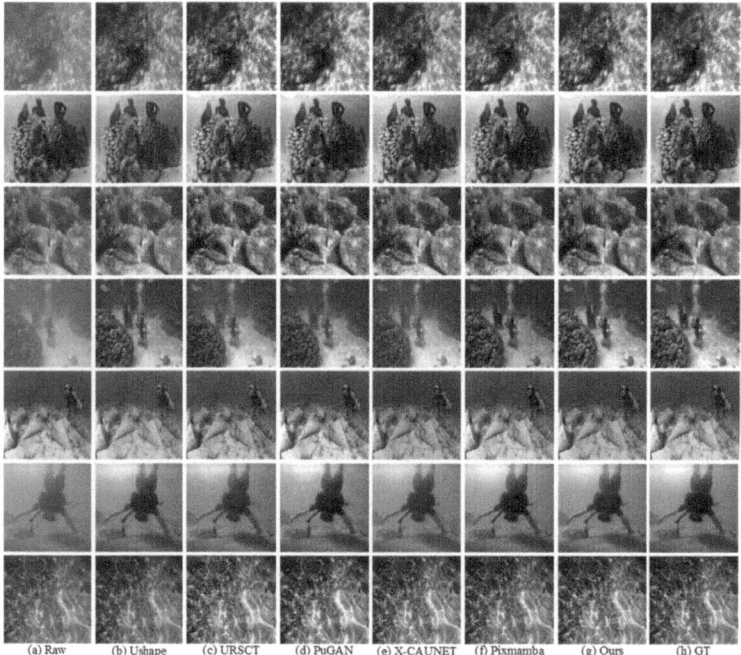

(a) Raw (b) Ushape (c) URSCT (d) PuGAN (e) X-CAUNET (f) Pixmamba (g) Ours (h) GT

Fig. 7. Visual comparison of different methods on the test set of UIEB named Test-90

The proposed method effectively avoids these issues, achieving higher contrast while enhancing detail information and improving color realism. This demonstrates the robustness and effectiveness of the method in providing visually superior enhancement results compared to existing approaches, especially in challenging underwater environments.

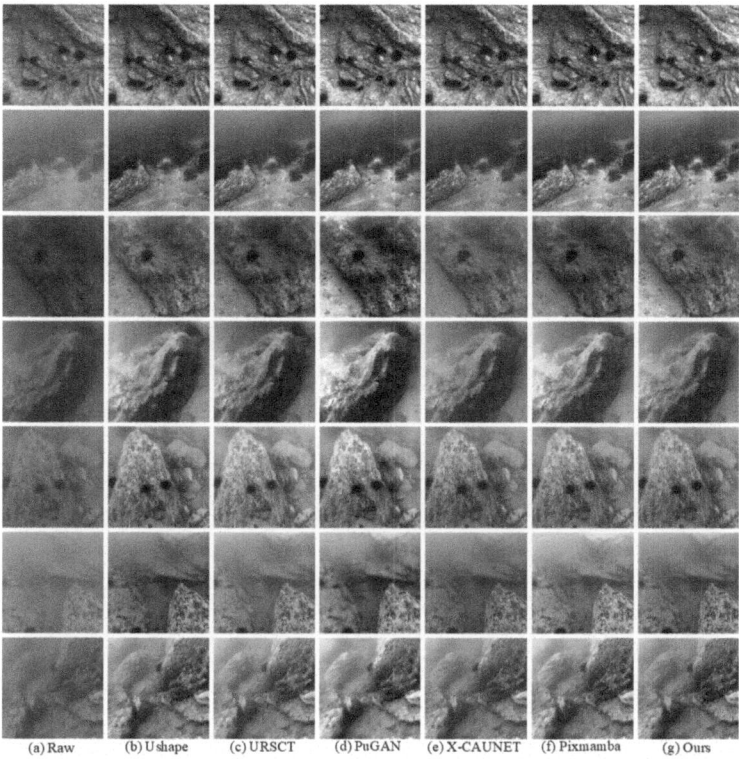

(a) Raw   (b) Ushape   (c) URSCT   (d) PuGAN   (e) X-CAUNET   (f) Pixmamba   (g) Ours

Fig. 8. Visual comparison of different methods on the challenge set of UIEB named C60

Figure 8 visualizes the output results of different methods on the C60 dataset. PuGAN shows issues of local over-enhancement and poor color balance in rows 1 and 2. X-CAUNET results in darkened areas in the enhanced images of rows 1 and 3. Pixmamba produces images with low contrast in rows 3 and 5. In contrast, the proposed method improves image contrast while avoiding issues of over-bright or overly dark regions.

Figure 9 shows the enhancement results of different methods on the UCCS dataset. The first two rows, the middle two rows, and the last three rows respectively show visual results from underwater environments with blue, green, and blue-green color casts in the UCCS dataset. It can be observed that the proposed method effectively removes the blue-green background and reduces color bias, resulting in images that are more consistent with human visual perception. These visual comparisons demonstrate the capability of the proposed method to handle different color cast environments effectively, ensuring balanced color distribution, improved contrast, and enhanced overall visual quality, thereby making the enhanced images more natural and appealing to the human eye.

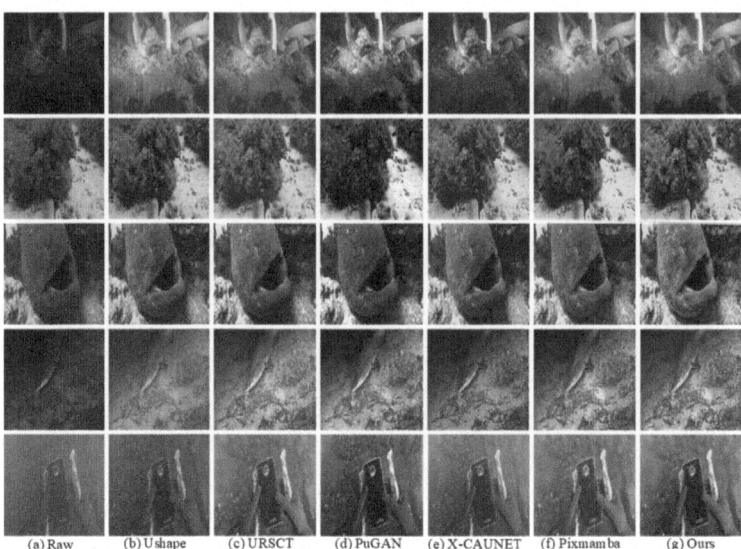

Fig. 9. Visual comparison of different methods on the UCCS

5   Conclusion

To address issues of color distortion, low contrast, and blurred details in underwater images, this paper proposed a Multiple Attention Aggregation U-Net for Underwater Image Enhancement (MAAU-UIE). The model combines Axial Rectangle Window Attention (ARWA) and Shift Axial Rectangle Window Attention (SARWA), leveraging their respective advantages in extracting local features and enhancing global information. The convolutional operations further enhance the ability of window attention to learn local details, while the Channel Enhanced Module (CEM) allows the network to focus more on important channel information. Additionally, gradient loss and multi-scale structural similarity loss are used to optimize the network's ability to recover edges and structures. Experimental results demonstrate that the proposed improvements effectively enhance the performance of underwater image enhancement. Compared to state-of-the-art methods, the proposed approach achieves superior results in PSNR, SSIM, UIQM, and UCIQE metrics, while also providing reconstructed images with realistic colors, high sharpness, and good contrast. Currently, the network's foundational modules are designed based on the Transformer architecture. Future work will focus on exploring more advanced Mamba architectures to further improve performance metrics and inference efficiency.

Acknowledgments. This study was funded by the National Key R & D Plan(grant number 2021YFB2801800).

References

1. Yu, F., He, B., Liu, J.X.: Underwater targets recognition based on multiple AUVs cooperative via recurrent transfer-adaptive learning (RTAL). IEEE Trans. Veh. Technol. **72**(2), 1574–1585 (2022)

2. Wang, R., Wang, S., Wang, Y., et al.: Development and motion control of biomimetic underwater robots: a survey. IEEE Trans. Syst. Man. Cybern. Syst. **52**(2), 833–844 (2020)

3. Pramanick, A., Sarma, S., Sur, A.: X-CAUNET: cross-color channel attention with underwater image-enhancing transformer. In: ICASSP 2024-2024 IEEE International Conference on Acoustics, Speech and Signal Processing (ICASSP), pp. 3550–3554. IEEE (2024)

4. Ancuti, C.O., Ancuti, C., De Vleeschouwer, C., et al.: Color balance and fusion for underwater image enhancement. IEEE Trans. Image Process. **27**(1), 379–393 (2017)

5. Berman, D., Levy, D., Avidan, S., et al.: Underwater single image color restoration using haze-lines and a new quantitative dataset. IEEE Trans. Pattern Anal. Mach. Intell. **43**(8), 2822–2837 (2020)

6. Zhuang, P., Wu, J., Porikli, F., et al.: Underwater image enhancement with hyper-Laplacian reflectance priors. IEEE Trans. Image Process. **31**, 5442–5455 (2022)

7. Fu, Z., Wang, W., Huang, Y., et al.: Uncertainty inspired underwater image enhancement. In: European Conference on Computer Vision, pp. 465–482. Springer, Cham (2022)

8. Li, C., Anwar, S., Hou, J., et al.: Underwater image enhancement via medium transmission-guided multi-color space embedding. IEEE Trans. Image Process. **30**, 4985–5000 (2021)

9. Li, C., Guo, C., Ren, W., et al.: An underwater image enhancement benchmark dataset and beyond. IEEE Trans. Image Process. **29**, 4376–4389 (2019)

10. Vaswani, A.: Attention is all you need. Adv. Neural Inf. Process. Syst. (2017)

11. Liu, Z., Lin, Y., Cao, Y., et al.: Swin transformer: hierarchical vision transformer using shifted windows. In: Proceedings of the IEEE/CVF International Conference on Computer Vision, pp. 10012–10022 (2021)

12. Peng, L., Zhu, C., Bian, L.: U-shape transformer for underwater image enhancement. IEEE Trans. Image Process. **32**, 3066–3079 (2023)

13. Li, C., Guo, C., Ren, W., et al.: An underwater image enhancement benchmark dataset and beyond. IEEE Trans. Image Process. **29**, 4376–4389 (2019)

14. Liu, R., Fan, X., Zhu, M., et al.: Real-world underwater enhancement: challenges, benchmarks, and solutions under natural light. IEEE Trans. Cir. Syst. Video Technol. **30**(12), 4861–4875 (2020)

15. Islam, M.J., Xia, Y., Sattar, J.: Fast underwater image enhancement for improved visual perception. IEEE Rob. Autom. Lett. **5**(2), 3227–3234 (2020)

16. Ye, X., Xu, H., Ji, X., et al.: Underwater image enhancement using stacked generative adversarial networks. In: Pacific Rim Conference on Multimedia, pp. 514–524. Springer, Cham (2018)

17. Zhang, D., Wu, C., Zhou, J., et al.: Hierarchical attention aggregation with multi-resolution feature learning for GAN-based underwater image enhancement. Eng. Appl. Artif. Intell. **125**, 106743 (2023)

18. Cong, R., Yang, W., Zhang, W., et al.: PUGAN: physical model-guided underwater image enhancement using GAN with dual-discriminators. IEEE Trans. Image Process. **32**, 4472–4485 (2023)

19. Huang, Z., Li, J., Hua, Z., et al.: Underwater image enhancement via adaptive group attention-based multiscale cascade transformer. IEEE Trans. Instrum. Meas. **71**, 1–18 (2022)
20. Ren, T., Xu, H., Jiang, G., et al.: Reinforced Swin-Convs transformer for simultaneous underwater sensing scene image enhancement and super-resolution. IEEE Trans. Geosci. Remote Sens. **60**, 1–16 (2022)
21. Gu, A., Dao, T.: Mamba: linear-time sequence modeling with selective state spaces. arXiv preprint arXiv:2312.00752 (2023)
22. Lin, W.T., Lin, Y.X., Chen, J.W., et al.: PixMamba: leveraging state space models in a dual-level architecture for underwater image enhancement. arXiv preprint arXiv:2406.08444 (2024)
23. Ronneberger, O., Fischer, P., Brox, T.: U-net: convolutional networks for biomedical image segmentation. In: Medical Image Computing and Computer-assisted Intervention–MICCAI 2015: 18th International Conference, Munich, Germany, October 5-9, 2015, Proceedings, part III 18, pp. 234–241. Springer (2015)
24. Chen, Z., Zhang, Y., Gu, J., et al.: Cross aggregation transformer for image restoration. Adv. Neural. Inf. Process. Syst. **35**, 25478–25490 (2022)
25. Wang, Z., Simoncelli, E.P., Bovik, A.C.: Multiscale structural similarity for image quality assessment. In: The Thrity-Seventh Asilomar Conference on Signals, Systems & Computers, 2003, vol. 2, pp. 1398–1402. IEEE (2003)
26. Zhang, Y., Li, K., Li, K., et al.: Image super-resolution using very deep residual channel attention networks. In: Proceedings of the European Conference on Computer Vision (ECCV), pp. 286–301 (2018)
27. Sun, J., Xu, Z., Shum, H.Y.: Gradient profile prior and its applications in image super-resolution and enhancement. IEEE Trans. Image Process. **20**(6), 1529–1542 (2010)
28. Korhonen, J., You, J.: Peak signal-to-noise ratio revisited: is simple beautiful?. In: 2012 Fourth International Workshop on Quality of Multimedia Experience, pp. 37–38. IEEE (2012)
29. Wang, Z., Bovik, A.C., Sheikh, H.R., et al.: Image quality assessment: from error visibility to structural similarity. IEEE Trans. Image Process. **13**(4), 600–612 (2004)
30. Panetta, K., Gao, C., Agaian, S.: Human-visual-system-inspired underwater image quality measures. IEEE J. Oceanic Eng. **41**(3), 541–551 (2015)
31. Yang, M., Sowmya, A.: An underwater color image quality evaluation metric. IEEE Trans. Image Process. **24**(12), 6062–6071 (2015)
32. Jiang, J., Ye, T., Bai, J., et al.: Five A $^+$ network: you only need 9K parameters for underwater image enhancement. arXiv preprint arXiv:2305.08824 (2023)
33. Zhou, J., Sun, J., Zhang, W., et al.: Multi-view underwater image enhancement method via embedded fusion mechanism. Eng. Appl. Artif. Intell. **121**, 105946 (2023)
34. Huang, S., Wang, K., Liu, H., et al.: Contrastive semi-supervised learning for underwater image restoration via reliable bank. In: Proceedings of the IEEE/CVF Conference on Computer Vision and Pattern Recognition, pp. 18145–18155 (2023)

MANet-CycleGAN: An Unsupervised LDCT Image Denoising Method Based on Channel Attention and Multi-scale Features

Jinglong Tian[1], Tianze Zhao[1], Zhijun Fan[2], Linlin Shen[1], Jieyao Wei[1], and Qiumei Pu[1(✉)]

[1] Minzu University of China, Beijing 100081, China
puqiumei@muc.edu.cn
[2] East China Jiaotong University, Jiangxi 330013, China

Abstract. Low-dose CT (LDCT) can significantly reduce health risks associated with radiation exposure compared to normal-dose CT (NDCT). However, the lower radiation dose may result in projection data being contaminated by noise, which can hinder the accurate identification of lesion details. Currently, most LDCT image denoising techniques employ supervised learning methods that rely on paired noisy and noise-free datasets for model training. In practical applications, however, obtaining such paired data is often challenging. To address this issue, we propose an unsupervised low-dose CT denoising method called MANet-CycleGAN, which can train a high-quality denoising model via unpaired data. Our design approach is as follows: 1. Eliminate the dependency of the denoising model training on paired data through a cyclic generative adversarial network architecture; 2. Apply the UNet architecture to generator for feature extraction and NDCT image generation, while using a PatchGAN discriminator to enhance the details of the generated images; 3. Introduce channel attention and multi-scale feature extraction capabilities through the Squeeze-and-Excitation (SE) module, Efficient Channel Attention (ECA), and Atrous Spatial Pyramid Pooling (ASPP) to improve image generation quality; 4. Utilize perceptual loss in training process to better preserve the structural features of the image while denoising. We conducted comparative experiments on the Mayo Clinic LDCT Grand Challenge dataset. The results demonstrate that the proposed method outperforms existing methods in both qualitative and quantitative aspects.

Keywords: Image Denoising · Cycle GAN · Low-dose CT

1 Introduction

Computed Tomography (CT) plays a crucial role in identifying subtle tissue abnormalities. In recent years, the application of CT technology has surged dramatically, particularly during the COVID-19 pandemic, when CT provided essential imaging assessments for the diagnosis and treatment of the disease [18]. Scanning the human body with high-dose X-ray beams can yield clear CT

P. Didyk and J. Hou (Eds.): CVM 2025, LNCS 15663, pp. 275–294, 2025.
https://doi.org/10.1007/978-981-96-5809-1_15

images, however, this radiation poses a risk of cellular and tissue damage, potentially adversely affecting human health [14]. Low-Dose CT (LDCT) significantly reduces harm compared to Normal-Dose CT (NDCT) [16], but it typically results in lower image quality. The reconstructed images often contain substantial noise and artifacts, which can obscure lesion details and ultimately affect diagnostic accuracy [21]. Suppressing noise in LDCT images while preserving texture and pathological information is a highly challenging task, highlighting the significant research value of denoising methods for LDCT images.

Compared to normal-dose CT, low-dose CT scans have a reduced radiation dose, resulting in a relatively lower number of photons detected by the detectors [12]. This decrease in photon count increases the likelihood of noise being introduced during the data acquisition process, leading to the appearance of white noise spots and blocky or waxy artifacts in the reconstructed images, which can adversely affect subsequent diagnoses. Traditional denoising methods used to enhance the clarity of low-dose CT images primarily fall into three categories: sine wave filtering, model-based statistical iterative reconstruction, and image domain denoising algorithms [17]. These denoising methods typically treat the noisy image as a simple superposition of a clean image and noise. These methods require a detailed estimation of the prior knowledge regarding the image and the noise distribution, resulting in a strong dependency on the noise model. Consequently, such denoising algorithms often incur high computational costs and are prone to losing important image details.

Deep learning-based low-dose CT (LDCT) denoising algorithms do not require explicit modeling of noise, instead they can directly learn the mapping relationships between images through neural networks. These algorithms generate corresponding NDCT images from input LDCT images, offering stronger generalization capabilities compared to traditional methods. However, most current deep learning based image denoising approaches rely heavily on supervised learning, which requires the use of manually labeled data along with appropriate training tasks to optimize the parameters of the deep neural network. This necessitates a substantial amount of paired data consisting of noisy and noise-free images for model training. The primary challenge of applying supervised deep learning algorithms to LDCT image denoising is the high cost of acquiring medical images such as LDCT. Typically, only a single NDCT or LDCT image can be obtained for the same patient, making it difficult to gather sufficient paired image data for model training. To address this issue, recent studies often employ methods to artificially add noise to NDCT images in order to generate simulated LDCT images, thereby constructing paired datasets for model training.

In this study, we approach the image denoising problem from a novel perspective by utilizing an unsupervised learning method to eliminate the dependence on paired datasets for LDCT image denoising. We conceptualize the task of LDCT image denoising as an image translation problem, where the objective is to transfer images from one domain, A (the noisy image domain), to another domain, B (the noise-free image domain), without altering the primary content, such as the anatomical structures present in the CT images.

To implement this approach, we designed a denoising framework based on CycleGAN. We enhanced the UNet architecture, which serves as the generator, by integrating channel attention mechanisms and multi-scale feature extraction to improve the quality of the generated noise-free images. Additionally, we employed a patch-based discriminator to enhance image details. Throughout the training process, we utilized a perceptual loss mixed with other loss functions to better preserve the structural integrity of the images. As a result, we achieved precise LDCT denoising without the need for paired datasets. Our main contributions are summarized as follows:

- We propose a CycleGAN-based image denoising framework that facilitates the mutual transformation of LDCT images between the noisy image domain and the noise-free image domain through two cycles, while preserving the integrity of the image content to achieve effective denoising.
- UNet is employed as the image generator, utilizing its U-shaped architecture and skip connections to effectively preserve structural information in the images, thereby generating high-quality noise-free images.
- Based on the characteristics of convolutional neural networks, we introduce a channel attention mechanism into the backbone network to quantify the importance of different channels in the feature maps. This mechanism assigns appropriate weights to enhance significant features while suppressing redundant or ineffective ones.
- In the spatial dimension, we integrate features with different receptive fields to obtain more comprehensive multi-scale information, which is beneficial for addressing the various scales of anatomical structures present in CT images.
- Perceptual loss is applied during the training process of CycleGAN, combined with the pixel-wise L1 loss as hybrid loss function. This approach assesses the differences between the generated images and the real images at the patch scale, thereby enhancing the effectiveness of model training.

2   Related Works

With the advancement of deep learning in recent years, numerous studies have demonstrated that many deep learning-based denoising methods significantly outperform traditional approaches. The image denoising problem can be represented by the degradation model $X = Y - N$, where X denotes the noise-free clean image, Y and N represent the noisy image and additive Gaussian white noise with a standard deviation of σ respectively. Image denoising methods without deep learning often rely on prior knowledge to estimate the noise in the images, which typically requires manual parameter selection for noise modeling and complex optimization algorithms to achieve satisfactory denoising results [3,7,19,25,34]. The key point of these methods lies in obtaining a detailed estimate of the noise distribution, however, in most real-world scenarios, the noise distribution is unknown, and significant variations often exist between the noise distributions of different datasets, greatly limiting the denoising performance and generalization ability of the models.

Deep learning-based denoising framework have gained widespread application in the field of image denoising due to their exceptional performance. Unlike traditional methods, deep learning algorithms do not rely on manual noise modeling, instead, they directly utilize data and specific training tasks to optimize the parameters of neural networks for end-to-end image denoising [22], These algorithms can effectively learn the mapping from noisy images to noise-free images, resulting in high generalization capabilities.

The process of deep learning-based image denoising can be summarized as follows: it first involves dimensionality reduction and feature extraction from the noisy images, followed by the generation of noise-free images using the extracted features. Both feature extraction and image generation are accomplished through neural networks, and a loss function is designed to minimize the difference between the generated noise-free images and the real noise-free images, with network parameters optimized using gradient descent.

Convolutional Neural Networks (CNNS) have been widely used in various image processing tasks due to their simple and efficient network structure. The inherent inductive biases of CNNs enable them to effectively extract image features, many studies have attempted to use CNNs for image denoising with success. RED-CNN [2] proposed a convolutional neural network that integrates an autoencoder network with a residual structure to map LDCT images to their corresponding NDCT images in an end-to-end manner, the network is composed entirely of convolutional layers, allowing it to theoretically handle images of any size. It optimizes network parameters using a mean squared error loss function to achieve image denoising. Subsequent research introduced batch normalization techniques and dilated convolutions to enhance denoising capabilities while reducing model parameters [36]. In addition to 2D images, a denoising algorithm based on 3D ResNet [9] models the spatial distribution of noise through 3D convolutions, thereby achieving denoising of 3D CT images. In recent years, new CNN based architectures have continuously been proposed and applied in the field of image denoising, aiming to improve denoising performance through improve the network structures [6,8,35].

Despite the success of CNN-based methods in various image denoising tasks, using convolutional neural networks to generate noise-free images often leads to over-smoothing, presenting significant challenges in preserving image edges and texture details. The UNet architecture was originally applied to image segmentation tasks [20], where an encoder encodes and reduces the dimensionality of the input image, followed by a decoder that generates the mask image. The encoder and decoder form a U-shaped structure, with skip connections that concatenate feature maps at the same depth, facilitating information transfer. The presence of skip connections allows the network to leverage the feature maps from shallow encoders to recover structural features that may have been degraded by down-sampling, thus producing higher-quality generated images.

Inspired by this, some studies have attempted to use UNet to convert noisy images into noise-free images while utilizing skip connections to preserve structural details. RatUNet [31] replaces the UNet convolutional blocks with residual blocks to avoid performance saturation, while also improving the upsampling method in the decoder and the skip connection structure to better recover image details, significantly enhancing image clarity in denoising tasks. FEUNet [27] employs UNet as an image generator, reducing network performance loss and accelerating training by generating a residual map between noisy and noise-free images. Many related studies utilize UNet as a generator to produce high-quality noise-free images, exploring improvements to the network's encoder, decoder, and skip connection structure to enhance overall performance. [4,15,32,33].

Optimizing network parameters through supervised learning can yield good image denoising results, however, this process often requires a large amount of paired data, which is challenging to obtain for medical images like LDCT images. An alternative approach is to use unsupervised learning methods for network training, thereby eliminating the dependence on paired data. Generative Adversarial Networks (GANs) do not directly compute the difference between generated images and real images, instead, they rely on a discriminator to assess the authenticity of the images. This provides a solution for unsupervised image denoising. GAN [5] employs a generator and a discriminator that learn the distribution of the image domain through adversarial training to achieve image generation. Subsequently, WGAN [1] improved GANs by utilizing Wasserstein distance, enhancing the stability of the learning process and addressing the issue of mode collapse. A WGAN-based deep learning method enforced cycle consistency using Wasserstein distance to establish a nonlinear end-to-end mapping from noisy input images to noise-free output images, achieving semi-supervised image denoising [30].

CycleGAN [38] offers a method for image transformation that does not rely on paired data for model training, enabling images to be converted between two different domains without altering their content. Some studies have already applied CycleGAN in the image denoising field [23,26,29,37]. However, issues such as training instability, model collapse, and poor image generation quality still persist. To address these problems, we propose a CycleGAN-based image denoising framework that aims to improve the denoising performance by improve the generator network and loss function, while also incorporating a patch-based discriminator for unsupervised image denoising.

3 Proposed Method

3.1 CycleGAN Based Denoising Model

To achieve unsupervised LDCT image denoising, we designed an image denoising framework based on CycleGAN, as shown in Fig. 1. Figure 1-A illustrates the training process of CycleGAN, where LDCT and NDCT refer to low-dose CT images and normal-dose CT images, respectively, images generated by the model are indicated with an asterisk superscript. We treat image denoising as an image translation task, where the goal is to convert images from the noisy image domain A to the noise-free image domain B without altering the content of the images. To achieve this goal, we simultaneously trained two image generators G_{AB} and G_{BA} as the mapping functions from domain A to domain B and from domain B to domain A respectively. We set up two adversarial discriminators, D_A and D_B, to train these two generators. The discriminators are used to differentiate between real images and generated images in domains A and B respectively. In addition, to strengthen the constraints on the mapping functions, we introduced two cycle consistency losses. These losses ensure that images, after being transformed from one domain to another, can be mapped back to the original domain while remaining as consistent as possible with their initial states. The training process consists of two parts: the forward cycle and the backward cycle, The forward cycle is illustrated by the blue arrows in Fig. 1-A, A randomly selected LDCT image A is processed through the generator G_{AB} to produce a synthetic NDCT image B^*, adversarial loss L_{GAN} is calculated through discriminator, and simultaneously employ the identity mapping loss $L_{Identity}$ to constrain the content difference between the generated synthetic image and the original image. This ensures that the content of the image remains undistorted after the domain transformation. Finally, we use the generator G_{BA} to map the synthetic image B^* back to image domain A and get the cycle consistency loss L_{Cycle}. The backward cycle, illustrated by the yellow arrows in Fig. 1-A, is the inverse process of the forward cycle. A randomly selected NDCT image B is used as input to generate a synthetic image and calculate the aforementioned three losses. Finally, all the losses are summed to perform backpropagation and optimize the network parameters. The three losses, along with the final overall loss computed, are shown in Eq. 1 to Eq. 4, In this context, we set two hyperparameters λ_{GAN} and $\lambda_{Identity}$ to adjust the proportions of the adversarial loss and the identity mapping loss, respectively. Through experiments, we found that set $\lambda_{GAN} = 10$ and $\lambda_{Identity} = 5$ yields better results. The function $Err(x, y)$ measures the difference between images x and y, and we chose to use the L1 loss function for this purpose.

$$L_{GAN} = E_{a \sim p(A)}[(D_B(G(a)) - 1)^2] + E_{b \sim p(B)}[(D_A(G(b)) - 1)^2] \qquad (1)$$

$$L_{Identity} = E_{a \sim p(A)} Err(G_{AB}(a), a) + E_{b \sim p(B)} Err(G_{BA}(b), b) \qquad (2)$$

$$L_{Cycle} = E_{a \sim p(A)} Err(G_{BA}(G_{AB}(a)), a) + E_{b \sim p(B)} Err(G_{AB}(G_{BA}(b)), b) \qquad (3)$$

$$Loss = \lambda_{GAN} L_{GAN} + \lambda_{Identity} L_{Identity} + L_{Cycle} \qquad (4)$$

To balance image generation quality and computational complexity, we adopted a classic UNet architecture as the backbone generator, which consists of both an encoder and a decoder. The encoder reduces the dimensionality of the

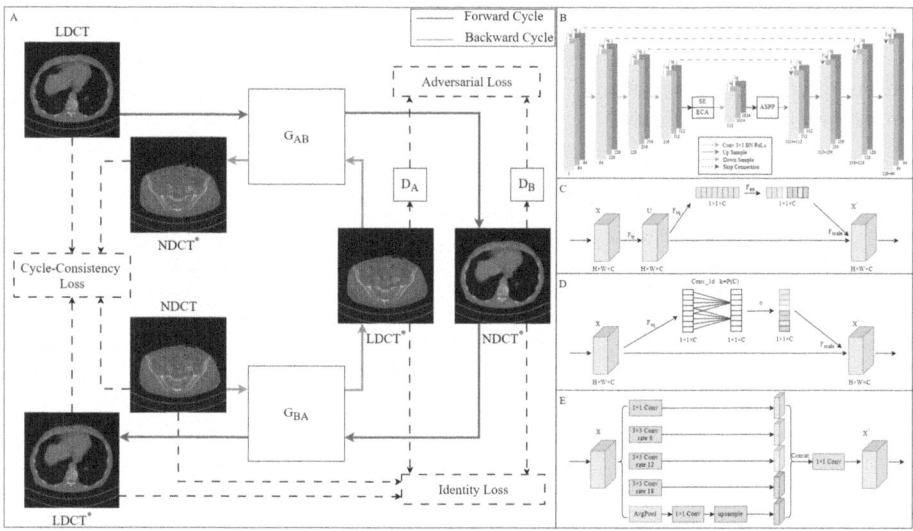

Fig. 1. The overall structure of MANet-CycleGAN. A: CycleGAN based image denoising framework; B: The proposed MANet generator network structure, which uses a UNet as the backbone. SE, ECA, and ASPP modules are added at the end of the encoder and the beginning of the decoder to enhance image generation performance; C: Structure of the SE module; D: Structure of the ECA module; E: Structure of the ASPP module.

image and extracts features through multiple convolutional layers and down-sampling operations. The decoder transforms the extracted low-dimensional high-level semantic information through upsampling and convolution, gradually restoring it to the original size to generate the target image. During the upsampling process in the decoder, skip connections are used to integrate feature maps from the corresponding depths of the encoder, recovering information lost during downsampling and ensuring that the output image maintains complete structural content. We improved the UNet architecture by incorporating channel attention and multi-scale feature extraction to enhance network performance. The network structure and details are illustrated in Fig. 1-B to Fig. 1-E.

For the discriminator, we adopted the PatchGAN design approach, where the discriminator assesses image authenticity at the scale of image patches rather than the entire image. This allows the discriminator to capture finer textures and local details, thereby guiding the generator to produce higher-quality images. We employed a 70×70 PatchGAN discriminator, as shown in Fig. 2. The discriminator network is entirely composed of convolutional layers, allowing it to theoretically process images of any size and produce corresponding output at that size. By adjusting the convolutional kernel size and stride, we control the receptive field of the final output feature map to be 70×70 pixels. This is equivalent to using a sliding window of 70 pixels in width across the original image, generating a judgment result for each position. Compared to producing a single judgment result for the entire image, this approach effectively captures the content of different regions in the spatial dimensions, thereby obtaining more comprehensive information.

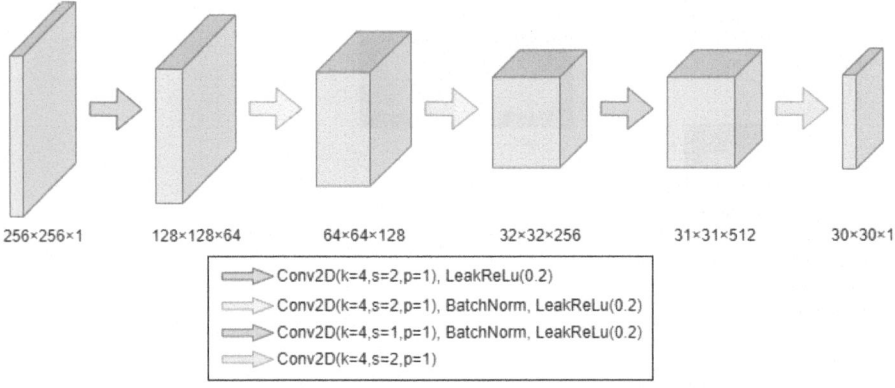

256×256×1   128×128×64   64×64×128   32×32×256   31×31×512   30×30×1

Conv2D(k=4,s=2,p=1), LeakReLu(0.2)
Conv2D(k=4,s=2,p=1), BatchNorm, LeakReLu(0.2)
Conv2D(k=4,s=1,p=1), BatchNorm, LeakReLu(0.2)
Conv2D(k=4,s=2,p=1)

Fig. 2. The structure of the PatchGAN discriminator.

3.2 Channel Attention in Convnet

Traditional convolution and pooling processes struggle to effectively recognize the importance differences among various feature channels. The Squeeze-and-Excitation (SE) module enhances the network's expressive power by modeling the interdependencies between the feature channels produced by the convolutional layers. The fundamental principle of the SE module is to explicitly weight the different channels in the network's feature maps to distinguish their importance. This is achieved by adding an attention mechanism along the channel dimension, as shown in Fig. 1-C, F_{tr} represents a standard convolution operation. The key components of the SE module lie in the two steps: Squeeze and Excitation, F_{sq} represents the Squeeze step, which essentially performs a global average pooling operation (Eq. 5), By calculating the mean across the spatial dimensions of the feature map, each channel is compressed from the original feature map into a single scalar, resulting in a compact feature representation. F_{ex} represents the Excitation step, which is used to accurately model the dependencies between feature channels. This is accomplished by concatenating two fully connected layers along with an activation function, as shown in Eq. 6, First, the first fully connected layer g transforms and reduces the dimensionality, followed by applying the activation function δ to introduce non-linearity, The activation function the ReLU is selected as δ, the output is then passed through a second fully connected layer f to restore the original dimensionality. This bottleneck structure design effectively reduces computational complexity. Finally, a Sigmoid activation function (denoted as σ in the figure) compresses the output values into the range $[0, 1]$ to serve as the channel attention scores. These scores are then applied to each channel through element-wise multiplication F_{scale} assigning the corresponding attention weights.

$$F_{sq}(X) = \frac{1}{HW} \sum_{i=1}^{H} \sum_{j=1}^{W} X_{ij} \tag{5}$$

$$F_{ex}(X) = \sigma(f(\delta(g(X)))) \tag{6}$$

The SE module adds attention weights along the channel dimension of the feature map, which enhances the model's response to important information in the input features. However, an analysis of its computation reveals two key issues. First, while the bottleneck structure of the two consecutive fully connected layers reduces computational complexity, it may lead to information loss, adversely affecting the precise prediction of channel attention. Second, using fully connected layers only captures global information along the channel dimension, resulting in a limited receptive field that can create redundant features. To address these issues, the ECA module replaces the fully connected layers of the SE module with a one-dimensional convolution of adaptive kernel size, as shown in Fig. 1-D, F_{sq} and F_{scale} remain the same as in the SE module, representing global average pooling and element-wise multiplication respectively. The function σ denotes the Softmax function, The channel attention weights are computed using a one-dimensional convolution, with the kernel size determined by the number of input feature map channels C. The calculation method is detailed in Eq. 7, the parameters γ and b are used to adjust the kernel size, where we set $\gamma = 2$, $b = 1$ in this study, $|\cdot|_{odd}$ indicates rounding up while ensuring that the kernel size k is an odd number.

$$P(C) = \left| \frac{log_2(C)}{\gamma} + \frac{b}{\gamma} \right|_{odd} \tag{7}$$

3.3 Multi Scale Feature Extraction

In the process of image feature extraction using convolutional layers, different sizes of convolutional kernels can capture information at various scales in the spatial dimensions of the image. Larger convolutional kernels have a greater receptive field, allowing them to capture the macro structure of the image content, while smaller kernels have a relatively smaller receptive field, making them more effective for extracting fine details. The ASPP module integrates multi-scale information from the image, enabling the network to obtain a more comprehensive view for noise identification and removal while preserving the integrity of image details and structure. The structure of the ASPP module is shown in Fig. 1-E, It first employs multiple dilated convolutions with different dilation rates to obtain feature maps with varying receptive fields. Then, pointwise convolutions are used for feature fusion while adjusting the output channel count.

The use of dilated convolutions allows the ASPP module to capture multi-scale information without introducing additional computational complexity, resulting in a more comprehensive feature representation.

3.4 Perceptual Loss

In the training phase of image translation tasks based on deep learning (such as image denoising, style transfer, and image super-resolution), the Mean Squared Error (L1) loss is often used to minimize the pixel-wise error between the input image and the target image. However, L1 loss can lead to blurry images and result in detail distortion or loss. Unlike L1 loss, which compares images on a pixel-by-pixel basis, perceptual loss first extracts high-level semantic information from images using a pre-trained convolutional neural network before calculating the error between the output vectors. Perceptual loss aligns more closely with human perception of image quality, placing greater emphasis on semantic information and being less sensitive to minor differences in pixel values. The calculation formulas for L1 loss and perceptual loss are given in Eq. 8 and Eq. 9, where N is the number of pixels in the image; $|| \cdot ||_F$ denotes the Frobenius norm; G represents the denoising network; ϕ is the pre-trained network used to extract image features, and dim is the dimension of the image feature vector encoded by ϕ.

During the training process of CycleGAN, we replaced the identity mapping loss $L_{Identity}$ with a mixed loss function that combines perceptual loss and L1 loss, ϕ in the perceptual loss refers to the pre-trained VGG16 network. The mixed loss function is formed by encoding images with the VGG network to obtain semantic features, which are then combined with pixel-wise L1 loss.

$$L_{L1}(G) = E_{(x,z)} \left[\frac{1}{N} ||G(z) - x||_1^2 \right] \tag{8}$$

$$L_{Perceptual}(G) = E_{(x,z)} \left[\frac{1}{dim} ||\phi(G(z)) - \phi(x)||_F^2 \right] \tag{9}$$

4 Experiments and Results

4.1 Data and Details of Implementation

Dataset for Experiments

This study evaluates the performance of the proposed low-dose CT image denoising method using the clinical CT dataset released by the Mayo Clinic for the "2016 NIH-AAPM-Mayo Clinic Low-Dose CT Grand Challenge" [13]. This dataset serves as a standard reference for assessing CT reconstruction and denoising techniques, covering X-ray projection images and reconstructed images of the head, chest, and abdomen from 10 anonymized patients. Each case includes paired normal-dose CT images (NDCT) and simulated low-dose CT images (LDCT) at 25% of the normal dose. The images have a thickness of 3 mm and a resolution of 512×512 pixels.

Comparison Metric

For quantitative analysis, this study employs four evaluation metrics to assess the image denoising performance: Peak Signal-to-Noise Ratio (PSNR), Structural Similarity Index Measure (SSIM), Gradient Magnitude Similarity Deviation (GMSD), and Root Mean Square Error (RMSE).

RMSE quantifies the difference between images by calculating the root mean square error on a pixel-by-pixel basis, making it the most direct method for comparing pixel value differences between two images. The calculation formula is shown in Eq. 10, where A and B represent the original noisy image and the denoised image, respectively, and M and N denote the height and width of the images. PSNR is commonly used to compare the differences between the denoised image and the original image to assess denoising effectiveness. A higher PSNR value indicates a greater ratio of retained information to suppressed noise in the denoised image, suggesting better denoising performance [24], as shown in Eq. 11.

$$RMSE = \sqrt{\frac{1}{MN} \sum_{i=1}^{M} \sum_{j=1}^{N} (A_{ij} - B_{ij})^2} \tag{10}$$

$$PSNR = 10 \times lg \left(\frac{(2^n - 1)^2}{RMSE^2} \right) \tag{11}$$

SSIM is an important metric for assessing image similarity, with the calculation formula provided in Eq. 12. In this formula, μ_x and μ_y represent the mean values of the images, serving as estimates of image brightness, σ_x and σ_y denote the standard deviations of the images, providing estimates of image contrast, and σ_{xy} indicates the covariance between the two images, also related to their contrast. By considering the three factors of brightness, contrast, and structure, SSIM compares the differences between two images. A value closer to 1 indicates greater similarity between the images.

$$SSIM(x, y) = \frac{(2\mu_x\mu_y + c_1)(2\sigma_{xy} + c_2)}{(\mu_x^2 + \mu_y^2 + c_1)(\sigma_x^2 + \sigma_y^2 + c_2)} \tag{12}$$

The gradient magnitude of an image reflects the structural information of its content. GMSD (Gradient Magnitude Similarity Deviation) quantifies the perceptual quality of an image by analyzing the variations in pixel-level gradient magnitude similarity between the reference image and the denoised CT image, using standard deviation as a measure. This approach effectively captures changes in local image quality. The calculation formulas are provided in Eq. 13 and Eq. 14, where N represents the total number of pixels in the image, GMS denotes the gradient magnitude of the image (which can be computed using the Sobel operator), and $GMSM$ is the mean of the gradient magnitudes. The value of GMSD reflects the range of distortion severity in the image. The higher the GMSD score, the greater the distortion range, and the lower the perceived image quality. For more detailed information about this evaluation metric, refer to [28].

$$GMSM = \frac{1}{N} \sum_{i=1}^{N} GMS(i) \qquad (13)$$

$$GMSD = \sqrt{\frac{1}{N} \sum_{i=1}^{N} (GMS(i) - GMSM)^2} \qquad (14)$$

Experimental Setup

We randomly selected 1,000 pairs of data from the Mayo abdominal CY dataset as the training set and 200 pairs as the validation set. The training data, consisting of NDCT and LDCT images, was shuffled to create unpaired dataset. To enhance training speed, we randomly cropped 256 × 256 pixel regions as input images during the network training phase, with a batch size set to 4, using the Adam optimizer. The validation set consists of paired NDCT and LDCT images, each with a resolution of 512 × 512 pixels.

Due to the inconsistency between the loss function and image generation quality in GAN-based image generation methods, this study computes the RMSE between the network output and the NDCT images using the validation set after each training epoch. This serves as an evaluation metric to quantify the network's denoising performance. During the training phase, we employed an early stopping strategy to prevent overfitting, setting the patience of the early stopping mechanism to 5. This means that training will stop if the validation set RMSE does not decrease for 5 consecutive epochs, and the parameters with the minimum error will be retained as the optimal parameters.

4.2   Results

First, we validated the effectiveness of the improvements made to the generator network through ablation experiments. Using the same dataset, denoising framework, and experimental configuration, we tested different generator networks, all composed of UNet along with SE, ECA, and ASPP modules. We quantitatively assessed and compared the performance of each network using four evaluation metrics: PSNR, SSIM, GMSD, and RMSE. The experimental results are presented in Table 1. Ours indicates training MANet using a perceptual loss function to replace $L_{Identity}$, while the other methods employed L1 loss. From the table, it is evident that the generator using our improved network, MANet, performs better in denoising compared to the original UNet. Additionally, training with perceptual loss leads to further improvements across multiple evaluation metrics, with the most significant enhancement observed in PSNR. While RMSE directly reflects the differences between the generated denoised image and the true noise-free image by comparing them pixel-by-pixel, providing the most straightforward indication of their disparity, the other three metrics focus on the structural content of the images and the distribution characteristics of the noise. Our proposed MANet achieves the best performance in PSNR, SSIM and RMSE, indicating its effectiveness in preserving the structural integrity and details of the image content.

Through the visual results shown in Fig. 3, rows 1, 3, 5, and 7 clearly demonstrate that the images generated by MANet exhibit sharper edges and more detailed structures. Rows 2, 4, 6, and 8 present the residual heatmaps between the generated noise-free images and the true noise-free images, these heatmaps are obtained by taking the absolute difference between each image and its corresponding label image, followed by normalization. Pixels in the images that appear more red indicate greater differences from the label image at those locations, while pixels that are more blue signify smaller differences. It is important to note that due to normalization, the pixel values in the heatmaps only reflect relative differences within the images and do not indicate absolute differences in values between different residual maps. By comparing the residual heatmaps in columns D, E, and F, it is evident that using both the SE and ECA modules together yields better results. It is worth noting that when the SE module is used alone in the original UNet network, there is a slight improvement in the PSNR metric but a higher GMSD score. However, when both the SE module and ECA module are used together, it is possible to achieve a higher PSNR while reducing the score of GMSD. This demonstrates the effectiveness of adding channel attention mechanisms to the network. Furthermore, the results after adding the ECA module show that performance can be further improved by optimizing the channel attention mechanism.

The ASPP module utilizes convolutional kernels of different sizes for feature extraction, allowing it to effectively handle structures of various scales within the image. Experimental results indicate that adding the ASPP module significantly enhances performance, resulting in clearer edges and detailed structures in the generated images. However, when the ASPP module is used alone, noticeable noise appears in the edge regions of the images. This issue is effectively mitigated when the ASPP module is paired with the other two channel attention modules, as shown in columns G and H of row 8 in Fig. 3.

Table 1. Comparison Study of the Generator

Generator	PSNR	SSIM	GMSD	RMSE
LDCT	26.932	0.967	0.026	12.169
U-Net	30.486	0.968	0.028	7.751
U-Net+SE	31.137	0.974	0.037	7.150
U-Net+ECA	31.612	0.979	0.027	6.951
U-Net+SE_ECA	31.734	0.985	**0.022**	6.939
U-Net+ASPP	32.076	0.980	0.023	6.506
MANet	32.990	0.985	0.026	5.875
Ours	**34.239**	**0.988**	0.023	**5.137**

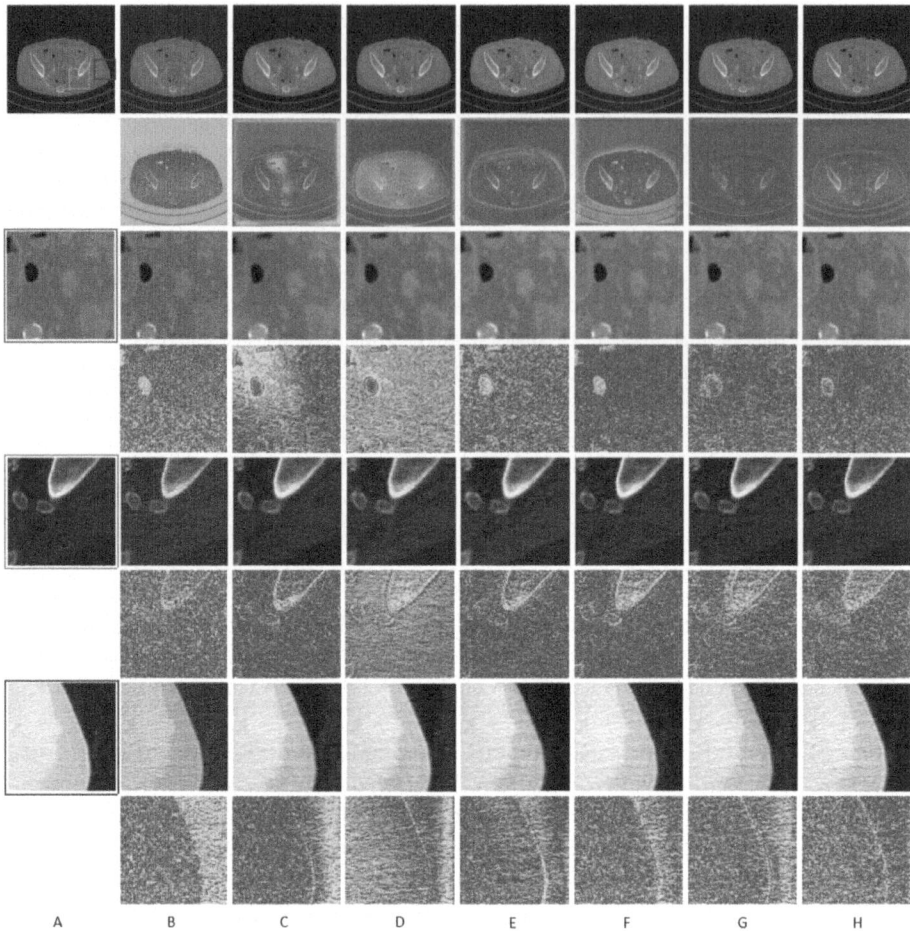

A   B   C   D   E   F   G   H

Fig. 3. The visual comparison of denoising results for each model is presented as follows: Rows 1–2 show the CT images and the residual maps between the images and the noise-free images. Rows 3–4, 5–6, and 7–8 display the images for three selected ROI (Regions of Interest). Column A represents the NDCT images, column B represents the LDCT images, and columns C-H illustrate the denoising results using different models as encoders, C: UNet; D: UNet+SE; E: UNet+ECA; F: UNet+SE+ECA; G: UNet+ASPP; H: Our proposed MANetUNet, which combines UNet with all the aforementioned modules.

Ablation experiments demonstrate that using a mixed loss function composed of perceptual loss and L1 loss as the identity mapping loss during network training can achieve better denoising results. To further investigate the impact of the mixed loss function on network performance, we used two parameters, α and β, to adjust the ratio of perceptual loss to L1 loss, as shown in Eq. 15. Based on this, we conducted two sets of comparative experiments: i) setting $\beta = 1$ and gradually increasing α from 0 to 1 in increments of 0.1; ii) setting $\alpha = 1$ and gradually increasing β from 0 to 1 in increments of 0.1. We trained the denoising network using different combinations of the identity mapping loss function and evaluated the network performance. The experimental results are shown in Fig. 4.

We observed that using both perceptual loss and ontology mapping loss simultaneously for network training yields better denoising results compared to using either one alone. The denoising performance is optimal when $\alpha = 0.8$ and $\beta = 1$. The trend of the curves in the figure indicates that the L1 loss plays a dominant role during training, so changing the proportion of L1 loss alone leads to more unstable network performance. However, adding an appropriate amount of perceptual loss improves the denoising performance.

$$L_{Identity} = \alpha L_{Perceptual}(G) + \beta L_{L1}(G) \tag{15}$$

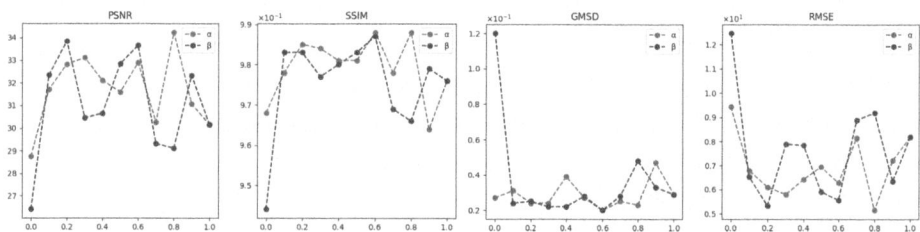

Fig. 4. Analyze the impact of the proportion of perceptual loss and L1 loss in the change of the identity mapping loss function on network performance. The red and blue curves represent the effects of gradually increasing α with a fixed $\beta = 1$ and gradually increasing β with a fixed $\alpha = 1$, respectively, on denoising performance. (Color figure online)

Additionally, we compared our proposed MANet-CycleGAN denoising framework with six advanced LDCT denoising methods, including two conventional CNN-based algorithms: UNet and RED-CNN, three GAN-based methods: WGAN, WGAN-VGG [11] and the original CycleGAN network, and a Diffusion-based method: Dn-Dp [10]. In this comparison, UNet, RED-CNN, and the two WGAN-based methods utilized their original network structures and employed paired data during training. The CycleGAN generator first extracted features using 9 residual blocks and then upsampled the images through transposed convolutions. The discriminator used the standard CycleGAN discriminator network and operated by unpaired dataset. Dn-Dp utilize two interconnected diffusion models: one for denoising low-resolution images and the other for converting low-resolution images to high-resolution images, The training can be accomplished using only NDCT images.

The results are shown in Table 2. Our proposed unpaired data denoising method achieved optimal results in PSNR, SSIM, and RMSE, even outperforming some algorithms trained with paired data. The improvement compared to the original CycleGAN algorithm, which also used unpaired data, was particularly significant, demonstrating the effectiveness of our proposed solution.

Table 2. Comparison of Various Denoising Methods

Model	PSNR	SSIM	GMSD	RMSE
LDCT	26.932	0.967	0.026	12.169
UNet	29.857	0.978	0.025	8.721
RED-CNN	32.332	0.985	**0.021**	6.532
WGAN	30.339	0.973	0.033	7.924
WGAN-VGG	31.244	0.976	0.024	7.083
CycleGAN	28.551	0.967	0.043	9.956
Dn-Dp	28.582	0.916	0.047	11.421
Ours	**34.239**	**0.988**	0.023	**5.137**

To further validate the model's generalization ability, we added more test data and conducted experiments on multiple different test sets. We tested each model using the first 200 and the last 200 pairs of NDCT and LDCT images, which were not included in the training data, as test sets. The results are shown in Table 3 and Table 4. Overall, the supervised method training by paired data outperforms the method training by unpaired data. Our approach achieves the best results across different test sets and demonstrates relatively stable performance.

Table 3. Comparison of Various Denoising Methods (The first 200 pairs of images)

Model	PSNR	SSIM	GMSD	RMSE
LDCT	26.358	0.964	0.030	13.199
UNet	29.123	0.974	0.026	9.798
RED-CNN	31.452	0.983	0.024	7.493
WGAN	27.477	0.961	0.047	11.732
WGAN-VGG	30.417	0.976	0.031	8.342
CycleGAN	27.477	0.961	0.047	11.732
Dn-Dp	28.311	0.955	**0.021**	10.191
Ours	**32.798**	**0.985**	0.027	**6.470**

Table 4. Comparison of Various Denoising Methods (The last 200 pairs of images)

Model	PSNR	SSIM	GMSD	RMSE
LDCT	27.725	0.964	0.024	11.367
UNet	30.292	0.975	0.026	8.415
RED-CNN	33.047	0.983	**0.019**	6.109
WGAN	32.150	0.970	0.027	6.523
WGAN-VGG	34.203	0.981	0.027	5.139
CycleGAN	29.384	0.954	0.045	9.012
Dn-Dp	29.644	0.917	0.042	10.478
Ours	**34.584**	**0.983**	0.024	**4.931**

5   Conclusion

This study proposes an improved framework, MANet-CycleGAN, to address the denoising problem of low-dose CT (LDCT) images, successfully tackling the issue of training with unpaired data. We selected UNet as the backbone network for the GAN generator and enhanced it using a channel attention mechanism and an ASPP module that employs convolutional kernels of varying sizes for multi-scale feature extraction, thereby improving denoising performance.

For the GAN discriminator, inspired by PatchGAN, we calculated the loss function using image patches rather than mapping the entire image to a single value. Additionally, we employed a mixed loss function that combines perceptual loss from a pre-trained VGG network and L1 loss for training the network. Through ablation studies and comparative experiments, we demonstrated the effectiveness of our approach.

We found that even without paired data, satisfactory denoising results can be achieved, which is significant for scenarios where paired data is difficult to obtain. Training the model directly on unpaired real data, instead of relying on simulated paired data, enhances the model's denoising performance in practical applications. Our future work will continue to explore image denoising methods based on unpaired data to further improve model performance and training stability.

Author Contributions. J. Tian, and L. Shen. designed this study. J. Tian, T. Zhao, L. Shen, and Q. Pu. analyzed and drafted the manuscript. J. Tian, T. Zhao, and L. Shen. completed numerical experiments. T. Zhao, Z. Fan, J. Wang, and J. Wei. revised the manuscript. All authors were involved in explaining the concept and results of the data. All authors have reviewed and approved the final version of the manuscript.

Resource Availability. Further information and requests for resources and reagents should be directed to and will be fulfilled by the lead contact Qiumei Pu (puqiumei@muc.edu.cn). All data reported in this paper will be shared by the lead contact upon request. The source code of our work can be found in: https://github.com/JinglingTian/CycleGAN_LDCT_Denoising.

Disclosure of Interests. All authors declare no competing interests.

References

1. Arjovsky, M., Chintala, S., Bottou, L.: Wasserstein GAN, December 2017. arXiv preprint arXiv:1701.07875 (2017)
2. Chen, H., et al.: Low-dose CT with a residual encoder-decoder convolutional neural network. IEEE Trans. Med. Imaging **36**(12), 2524–2535 (2017)
3. Dabov, K., Foi, A., Katkovnik, V., Egiazarian, K.: Image denoising by sparse 3-D transform-domain collaborative filtering. IEEE Trans. Image Process. **16**(8), 2080–2095 (2007)
4. Fan, C.M., Liu, T.J., Liu, K.H.: SUNet: Swin transformer UNet for image denoising. In: 2022 IEEE International Symposium on Circuits and Systems (ISCAS), pp. 2333–2337. IEEE (2022)
5. Goodfellow, I., et al.: Generative adversarial networks. Commun. ACM **63**(11), 139–144 (2020)
6. Herbreteau, S., Kervrann, C.: DCT2net: an interpretable shallow CNN for image denoising. IEEE Trans. Image Process. **31**, 4292–4305 (2022)
7. Li, P., Liang, J., Zhang, M., Fan, W., Yu, G.: Joint image denoising with gradient direction and edge-preserving regularization. Pattern Recogn. **125**, 108506 (2022)
8. Liu, G., Dang, M., Liu, J., Xiang, R., Tian, Y., Luo, N.: True wide convolutional neural network for image denoising. Inf. Sci. **610**, 171–184 (2022)
9. Liu, J., et al.: Deep iterative reconstruction estimation (DIRE): approximate iterative reconstruction estimation for low dose CT imaging. Phys. Med. Biol. **64**(13), 135007 (2019)
10. Liu, X., et al.: Diffusion probabilistic priors for zero-shot low-dose CT image denoising. Med. Phys. **52**(1), 329–345 (2025)
11. Ma, Y., Wei, B., Feng, P., He, P., Guo, X., Wang, G.: Low-dose CT image denoising using a generative adversarial network with a hybrid loss function for noise learning. IEEE Access **8**, 67519–67529 (2020)
12. Mastora, I., Remy-Jardin, M., Suess, C., Scherf, C., Guillot, J.P., Remy, J.: Dose reduction in spiral CT angiography of thoracic outlet syndrome by anatomically adapted tube current modulation. Eur. Radiol. **11**, 590–596 (2001)
13. McCollough, C.: TU-FG-207A-04: overview of the low dose CT grand challenge. Med. Phys. **43**(6Part35), 3759–3760 (2016)
14. Mcdonnell, M., et al.: Effects of gastro-oesophageal reflux and pulmonary micro-aspiration in bronchiectasis (2018)
15. Mehta, D., Padalia, D., Vora, K., Mehendale, N.: MRI image denoising using U-Net and image processing techniques. In: 2022 5th International Conference on Advances in Science and Technology (ICAST), pp. 306–313. IEEE (2022)
16. Naidich, D.P., Marshall, C.H., Gribbin, C., Arams, R.S., McCauley, D.I.: Low-dose CT of the lungs: preliminary observations. Radiology **175**(3), 729–731 (1990)

17. Pu, Q., Shen, L., Tian, J., Wei, J.: Overview of deep learning-based denoising methods for low-dose CT images. Chin. J. Stereology Image Anal. **004**, 028 (2023)
18. Qinghua, Z., Yaguang, F., Youlin, Q., Guozhen, Z., Yan, S.: Guidelines for low-dose CT screening of lung cancer in china (2023 edition). Chin. J. Lung Cancer **26**(1), 1–9 (2023)
19. Rabbani, H.: Image denoising in steerable pyramid domain based on a local Laplace prior. Pattern Recogn. **42**(9), 2181–2193 (2009)
20. Ronneberger, O., Fischer, P., Brox, T.: U-Net: convolutional networks for biomedical image segmentation. In: Proceedings of the 18th International Conference on Medical Image Computing and Computer-Assisted Intervention, MICCAI 2015, part III 18, Munich, Germany, 5–9 October 2015, pp. 234–241. Springer (2015)
21. Sagheer, S., George, S.N.: A review on medical image denoising algorithms. Biomed. Sig. Process. Control **61**, 102036 (2020)
22. Tian, C., Fei, L., Zheng, W., Xu, Y., Zuo, W., Lin, C.W.: Deep learning on image denoising: an overview. Neural Netw. **131**, 251–275 (2020)
23. Wang, T., et al.: Deep learning-based image quality improvement for low-dose computed tomography simulation in radiation therapy. J. Med. Imaging **6**(4), 043504–043504 (2019)
24. Wang, Z., Bovik, A.C., Sheikh, H.R., Simoncelli, E.P.: Image quality assessment: from error visibility to structural similarity. IEEE Trans. Image Process. **13**(4), 600–612 (2004)
25. Wang, Z., Zhang, D.: Progressive switching median filter for the removal of impulse noise from highly corrupted images. IEEE Trans. Circ. Syst. II Analog Digit. Sig. Process. **46**(1), 78–80 (1999)
26. Wu, S., Dong, C., Qiao, Y.: Blind image restoration based on cycle-consistent network. IEEE Trans. Multimedia **25**, 1111–1124 (2022)
27. Wu, W., Lv, G., Liao, S., Zhang, Y.: FEUNet: a flexible and effective u-shaped network for image denoising. SIViP **17**(5), 2545–2553 (2023)
28. Xue, W., Zhang, L., Mou, X., Bovik, A.C.: Gradient magnitude similarity deviation: a highly efficient perceptual image quality index. IEEE Trans. Image Process. **23**(2), 684–695 (2013)
29. Yin, Z., Xia, K., Wang, S., He, Z., Zhang, J., Zu, B.: Unpaired low-dose CT denoising via an improved cycle-consistent adversarial network with attention ensemble. Vis. Comput. **39**(10), 4423–4444 (2023)
30. You, C., et al.: CT super-resolution GAN constrained by the identical, residual, and cycle learning ensemble (GAN-circle). IEEE Trans. Med. Imaging **39**(1), 188–203 (2019)
31. Zhang, H., Lian, Q., Zhao, J., Wang, Y., Yang, Y., Feng, S.: RatUNet: residual U-Net based on attention mechanism for image denoising. PeerJ Comput. Sci. **8**, e970 (2022)
32. Zhang, J., Niu, Y., Shangguan, Z., Gong, W., Cheng, Y.: A novel denoising method for CT images based on U-Net and multi-attention. Comput. Biol. Med. **152**, 106387 (2023)
33. Zhang, K., et al.: Practical blind image denoising via Swin-Conv-UNet and data synthesis. Mach. Intell. Res. **20**(6), 822–836 (2023)
34. Zhang, K., Zuo, W., Chen, Y., Meng, D., Zhang, L.: Beyond a gaussian denoiser: residual learning of deep CNN for image denoising. IEEE Trans. Image Process. **26**(7), 3142–3155 (2017)
35. Zhang, Q., Xiao, J., Tian, C., Chun-Wei Lin, J., Zhang, S.: A robust deformed convolutional neural network (CNN) for image denoising. CAAI Trans. Intell. Technol. **8**(2), 331–342 (2023)

36. Zhang, Y., Yang, J., Yi, B.: Improved residual autoencoder network for low-dose CT image denoising. J. Shanghai Jiaotong Univ. (Chin. Ed.) **53**(8), 7 (2019)
37. Zhou, S., Yang, J., Konduri, K., Huang, J., Yu, L., Jin, M.: Spatiotemporal denoising of low-dose cardiac CT image sequences using RecycleGAN. Biomed. Phys. Eng. Exp. **9**(6), 065006 (2023)
38. Zhu, J.Y., Park, T., Isola, P., Efros, A.A.: Unpaired image-to-image translation using cycle-consistent adversarial networks. In: Proceedings of the IEEE International Conference on Computer Vision, pp. 2223–2232 (2017)

M^3: Manipulation Mask Manufacturer for Arbitrary-Scale Super-Resolution Mask

Xinyu Yang[1], Xiaochen Ma[1], Xuekang Zhu[1], Bo Du[1], Lei Su[1], Bingkui Tong[1],

Zeyu Lei[1,2], and Jizhe Zhou[1,3(✉)]

[1] College of Computer Science, Sichuan University, Chengdu, China
2021141460237@stu.scu.edu.cn
[2] Department of Computer and Information Science, University of Macao, Macao SAR, China
[3] Engineering Research Center of Machine Learning and Industry Intelligence, MOE,
Sichuan University, Chengdu, China
jzzhou@scu.edu.cn

Abstract. In the field of image manipulation localization (IML), the small quantity and poor quality of existing datasets have always been major issues. A dataset containing various types of manipulations will greatly help improve the accuracy of IML models. Images found on public forums, such as those in online image modification communities, are often manipulated using various techniques. Creating a dataset from these images can significantly enhance the diversity of manipulation types in our data. However, due to resolution and clarity issues, images obtained from the internet often contain noises, making it difficult to obtain clean masks by simply subtracting the manipulated image from the original. These noises are difficult to remove, rendering the masks unusable for IML models. Inspired by the field of change detection, we treat the original and manipulated images as changes over time for the same image and view the data generation task as a change detection task. Due to clarity issues between images, conventional change detection models perform poorly. Therefore, we introduced a super-resolution module and proposed the Manipulation Mask Manufacturer (MMM) framework, which enhances the resolution of both original and tampered images to improve comparison. Simultaneously, the framework converts the original and tampered images into feature embeddings and concatenates them, effectively modeling the context. Additionally, we used our MMM framework to create the Manipulation Mask Manufacturer Dataset (MMMD), which covers a wide range of manipulation techniques. We aim to contribute to the fields of image forensics and manipulation detection by providing more realistic manipulation data through MMM and MMMD. Detailed information about MMMD and the download link can be found at: https://github.com/ndyysheep/MMMD.

Keywords: Content security of visual media · image manipulation localization(IML) · Datasets of visual media · Datasets Generation · Arbitrary-Scale Super-Resolution

1 Introduction

Advances in digital image processing [5] have made software like Adobe Photoshop [42] and GIMP [18] more powerful, facilitating widespread image manipulation.

© The Author(s), under exclusive license to Springer Nature Singapore Pte Ltd. 2025
P. Didyk and J. Hou (Eds.): CVM 2025, LNCS 15663, pp. 295–308, 2025.
https://doi.org/10.1007/978-981-96-5809-1_16

Increasingly, there are examples of false information, retouched photographs, or edited video being released on social media. In many cases, this information goes "viral" in just days, even hours [17]. This proliferation of false information and manipulated images threatens public knowledge, trust, and safety. Thus, image manipulation localization has emerged, and in some literature, it is also referred to as "forgery detection [16]" or "tamper detection [45]." Its purpose is to discern whether an input image is manipulated or authentic and to depict the exact manipulated parts of an image through a mask [40]. These parts are semantically different from the original content (the original image before manipulation). It does not include purely generated images (e.g., images generated from pure text) or the introduction of noise or other non-semantic changes through image processing techniques that do not alter the underlying meaning of the image. Standard tampered images and their masks are shown in Fig. 1.

Fig. 1. Tampered images and their corresponding masks for the image manipulation localization task.

However, a common benchmarking image dataset for algorithm evaluation and fair comparison is still lagging behind [10]. Most existing datasets are manually created and annotated by researchers [49], with limited tampering types and techniques, and the volume of datasets is also restricted. This leads to models with poor generalization and robustness. Therefore, we thought of creating datasets by sourcing a large number of original and manipulated images from the internet. But we found that images and videos from the internet suffer from compression and clarity issues [4], and simply subtracting the original and manipulated images results in noisy images, as shown in the third row of Fig. 2, that traditional methods struggle to clean up.

Change detection [30, 37] involves identifying differences at the same location over different times, which is similar to our task of detecting differences between the original and manipulated images. Inspired by this, we treat the original and manipulated images as changes over time for the same picture, viewing the dataset generation task as a change detection task. However, due to the clarity disparity [41] between the two images in our task, directly using change detection models is not ideal. Therefore, we introduced a super-resolution processing module to enhance the details of the two images before generating the mask. This is the main idea behind our proposed Manipulation Mask Manufacturer (MMM) framework. Some of the masks we generated and their corresponding original images and tampered images are shown in Fig. 2.

The framework pipeline inputs the original and tampered images into a Fully Convolutional Network (FCN) [28] to extract high-level features. These features are aligned

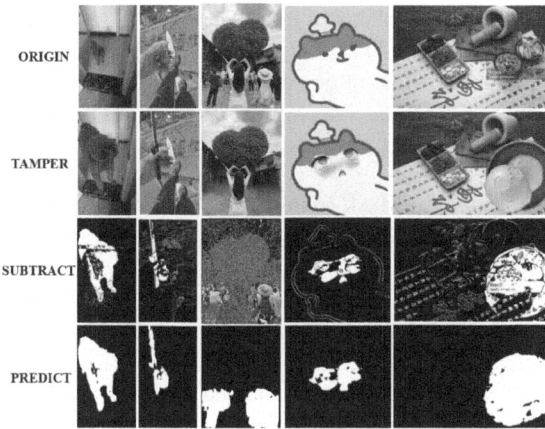

Fig. 2. MMM framework generated result images. From highest to lowest, the sequence is as follows: original image, tampered image, image obtained by directly subtracting the two images and binarizing with a threshold of 30, and MMM predicted image.

using Maximum Mean Discrepancies (MMD) [29,38] and concatenated. They are then processed through a Cross-scale Local Attention Block (CSLAB) [7] and a Local Frequency Encoding Block (LFEB) [7] to enhance resolution and detail. Finally, the features are split, decoded, subtracted, and a mask is obtained.

Table 1. The primary datasets in the field of image manipulation localization. Most of these datasets suffer from issues such as limited quantity, single type of tampering, and inability to grow further, and they are all tampered with by the issuers of the datasets themselves.

Dataset	Tampered Images	Image Sources		Dataset Growth		Type	
		Self	Others	Scalable	Non-scalable	Traditional	AI-manipulated
Columbia	180	✓	–	–	✓	✓	–
CASIAv1	920	✓	–	–	✓	✓	–
CASIAv2	5,063	✓	–	–	✓	✓	–
Coverage	100	✓	–	–	✓	✓	–
NIST16	564	✓	–	–	✓	✓	–
DEFACTO	149,587	✓	–	–	✓	✓	–
IMD20	2,010	✓	–	–	✓	✓	✓
MMMD(Ours)	11,069	–	✓	✓	–	✓	✓

Our framework has achieved excellent annotation results on the IMD2020 [35], NIST16 [21], and CASIAv2 [13] datasets. Additionally, we created the Manipulation Mask Manufacturer Dataset (MMMD), containing 11,069 original images, tampered images, and masks, with potential for continuous growth. The dataset includes various resolutions and manipulation types, such as copy-move [1,8], splicing [23], transformation [36], Deepfake [34], Image Inpainting [14], Image Morphing [47], Reconstruction [11], and Image Style Transfer [24]. It features diverse images like cartoons, portraits, landscapes, interiors, food, and accessories. The main parameters of our dataset compared to existing datasets are shown in Table 1. We used MMMD to train and test MVSS-Net [12] and IML-ViT [31]. Other 10 models pre-trained on CASIAv2 [13] struggled to achieve high metrics on our dataset, while models trained on our dataset demonstrated better generalization. This highlights the limitations of existing datasets.

In summary, our contributions are as follows:

– We propose a Manipulation Mask Manufacturer (MMM) framework that can accurately annotate the differences between original and tampered images even when there is a significant disparity in their clarity.
– We generated a large and diverse Manipulation Mask Manufacturer Dataset (MMMD) using the MMM framework to address the shortage of datasets in the field of image manipulation detection.
– Models pre-trained with our MMMD achieved higher F1 scores and demonstrated better generalization. Other pre-trained models struggled to perform well on our dataset, highlighting the limitations of existing tampering detection datasets. Our dataset better reflects real-world tampering scenarios.

2   Related Work

2.1   Existing Dataset Generation Methods

Current methods for generating image manipulation detection datasets include manual manipulation, which involves editing images by hand using tools like Adobe Photoshop [42], a time-consuming and expertise-demanding process [43]. Automatic manipulation employs software tools and scripts to rapidly produce large volumes of data, though these images may look unnatural or have obvious manipulation traces. Image synthesis combines elements from different images to create new visual scenes, enhancing dataset diversity but requiring complex techniques and substantial processing time [46]. The improved Total Variation Denoising Method [49] automatically subtracts a tampered image from the original to obtain a noisy mask, which is then denoised, but this method often fails to convert many types of tampered images due to diverse noise and low generalization capability of traditional methods.

2.2   Existing Change Detection Methods

In recent years, change detection methods based on deep learning have rapidly developed. Hao Chen et al. proposed the Bitemporal Image Transformer (BIT) [6], which converts input images into a small number of semantic tokens, uses a transformer encoder to model contextual information within the compact token space-time domain, and then projects the context-rich tokens back into the pixel space through a decoder to enhance the original features. The final change detection results are generated through feature difference images. ChangeFormer [3] uses a transformer-based Siamese network architecture for change detection from a pair of co-registered remote sensing images. This method combines a hierarchical transformer encoder and a multi-layer perceptron (MLP) decoder, effectively extracting multi-scale long-range feature differences. This is similar to image manipulation localization, and multi-scale techniques are also commonly used in decoders [51]. In SNUNet-CD [15], ChangeFormer extracts multi-scale features of bitemporal images through a hierarchical transformer encoder and generates change detection maps by fusing these feature differences using a lightweight MLP decoder. However, since the change detection considers the same image at different times with consistent clarity, it does not need to account for image degradation. Therefore, existing change detection models are not effective for our data generation tasks.

2.3 Existing Tampered Datasets

The development of datasets in the field of image manipulation detection has been relatively slow. Currently, widely recognized and used datasets are still those from four or five years ago, or even from over a decade ago.

Datasets for Traditional Tampering Techniques. Almost all datasets include traditional tampering methods like splicing [23], copy-move [1,8], removal, and various image enhancements to produce "fake" or "forged" images. Columbia [39] uses cropping and splicing [23], embedding parts from other images into a single image. CASIAv1 [13] employs Adobe Photoshop [42] for cutting and pasting, including geometric transformations [36] like scaling [2] and rotation [19]. CASIAv2 [13] adds more post-processing and has a richer variety of images, divided into eight categories: scenes, animals, buildings, people, plants, objects, nature, and textures. COVERAGE [46] consists of real images taken with an iPhone 6 front camera, processed with Photoshop CS4 using methods like translation, scaling, rotation, free transformation [36], lighting changes, and combinations thereof. NIST [21] uses local pixel modification, compression, noise addition, blurring, and geometric transformations [36]. DEFACTO [33], based on the MSCOCO [26] database, aims to produce semantically meaningful forged images, including splicing [23], copy-move [1,8], object removal [9], and warping [20].

Deep Learning-Based Tampering Datasets. Modern image tampering techniques have achieved unprecedented realism through artificial intelligence and deep learning, particularly with Generative Adversarial Networks (GANs). These techniques include deepfakes [34], which can perform facial replacement, expression synthesis, and generate images of non-existent people, making image and video tampering very realistic [52]. Deep learning also excels in image restoration and enhancement by denoising, filling in missing parts, and improving resolution, thus making damaged images look new and low-resolution images appear clear and detailed. Tools and frameworks such as TensorFlow, PyTorch, Keras, and OpenCV have greatly simplified the implementation and application of these techniques. In IMD2020 [35], GANs were used to generate tampered regions of images, and inpainting techniques [14] were employed to fill in missing or damaged parts of images, making them appear natural and coherent. This also presents greater challenges for image manipulation detection. Current models are increasingly in need of diverse data that better reflects real-world scenarios.

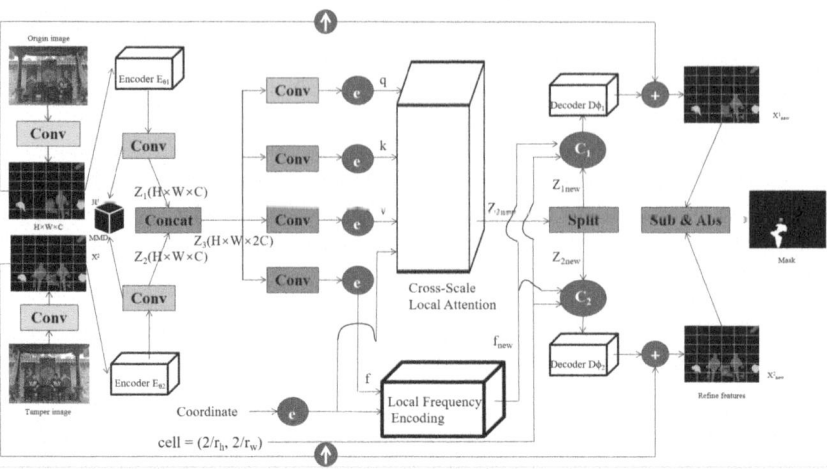

Fig. 3. The proposed MMM framework. The local sampling operation samples input embeddings based on a grid of coordinates.

3 Proposed Method

3.1 The Pipeline of the Entire Framework

The entire MMM framework is divided into three modules: feature extraction and concatenation, super-resolution processing, and feature separation mask generation. We obtain the original images and a large number of tampered images from the network, keeping only the images of the same size as our original data. After obtaining the original and tampered images, we input them into our Manipulation Mask Manufacturer (MMM) framework. The MMM framework extracts high-level features from the original and tampered images using a Fully Convolutional Network (FCN) [28]. These features are aligned with Maximum Mean Discrepancies (MMD) [29, 38] and concatenated. The idea of concatenating high-level features is inspired by the Bitemporal Image Transformer (BIT) [6]. During super-resolution, the concatenated features are processed by the Cross-scale Local Attention Block (CSLAB) [7] and the Local Frequency Encoding Block (LFEB) [7] to enhance the resolution and detail representation of the images. The framework then separates these embeddings, uses decoders to generate residual images, and combines them with the original images. The final mask is produced by computing the absolute difference between the high-resolution features of the original and tampered images. The entire MMM structure is shown in Fig. 3.

3.2 Specific Processing Algorithm

Extraction and Concatenation of Image Features. First, we use a Fully Convolutional Network (FCN) [28] to extract high-level features from the original image and the tampered image, respectively. Then, these features are input into encoder $E_{\theta 1}$ and encoder $E_{\theta 2}$, resulting in the feature embeddings $Z_1 \in \mathbb{R}^{H \times W \times C}$ and $Z_2 \in \mathbb{R}^{H \times W \times C}$. Z_1 and

Z_2 are subjected to Maximum Mean Discrepancies (MMD) [29,38] calculation to eliminate the differences in data distribution, allowing the model to focus more on the differences in content. Simultaneously, Z_1 and Z_2 are concatenated into $Z_3 \in \mathbb{R}^{H \times W \times 2C}$.

Arbitrary-Scale Super-Resolution. Z_3 will be projected by four separate convolutional layers to obtain four latent embeddings, corresponding to query q, key k, value v, and frequency f. Since the sizes of the two images are the same, we use the coordinates and cell of the original image. The original image and the tampered image will generate 2D high-resolution coordinates based on an arbitrary upsampling scale $\mathbf{r} = \{r_h, r_w\}$ in 2D low-resolution coordinates. Next, the 2D coordinates, along with q, k, and v, will be input into the Cross-Scale Local Attention Block (CSLAB) [7] to estimate a local latent embedding $Z_{3new} \in \mathbb{R}^{G_h G_w \times 2C}$. f and the 2D coordinates will also be input into the Local Frequency Encoding Block (LFEB) [7] to estimate a local frequency embedding $f_{new} \in \mathbb{R}^{G_h G_w \times 2C}$. Specifically, G_h and G_w represent the height and width of the local grids used for performing local coordinate sampling. CSLAB [7] and LFEB [7] estimate Z_{3new} and f_{new} as follows:

$$Z_{3new} = CSLAB(\delta x, q, k, v) \tag{1}$$

$$f_{new} = \text{LFEB}(\delta x, f) \tag{2}$$

$$\delta \mathbf{x} = \left\{ x_q - x^{(i,j)} \right\}_{i \in \{1,2,...,G_h\}, j \in \{1,2,...,G_w\}} \tag{3}$$

CSLAB and LFEB draw on the work of Chen et al. [7], with specific structures shown in Fig. 4. The primary function of the Cross-scale Local Attention Block (CSLAB) is to aggregate cross-scale local feature information, utilizing query, key, and value features to enhance the model's ability to capture fine-grained details, thereby improving the accuracy of image manipulation detection. The Local Frequency Encoding Block (LFEB) is responsible for performing local frequency encoding on the input frequency features, enhancing the model's sensitivity to edge and texture information by capturing local frequency variations.

Separate Image Features and Generate a Mask. Z_{1new} and Z_{2new} are derived from splitting Z_{3new}. Decoder $D\phi_1$ and Decoder $D\phi_2$ respectively utilize these embeddings along with the provided cell to generate residual images. Then, the original and tampered images are upsampled and added element-wise to their corresponding residual images. This results in the high-resolution high-level features of the original and tampered images. We subtract these two high-resolution high-level features and take the absolute value to obtain the final mask.

Loss Function. The loss function of the model is defined as follows:

$$L = \frac{1}{H_p \times W_p} \sum_{h=1}^{H} \sum_{w=1}^{W} l\left(P_{hw}, M_{hw}\right) \tag{4}$$

Here, $H_p \times W_p$ is the total number of pixels in the image, P_{hw} is the probability distribution of the model at (h, w), and M_{hw} is the mask label at position (h, w). $l(P_{hw}, M_{hw})$ is the cross-entropy, which is calculated as:

$$l(P_{hw}, M_{hw}) = -\sum_c M_{hw}^{(c)} \log(P_{hw}^{(c)}) \tag{5}$$

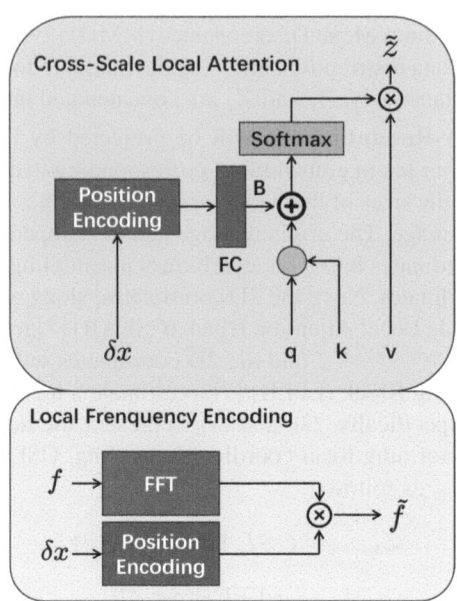

Fig. 4. The framework of CSLAB and LFEB.

where c indexes the classes, $M_{hw}^{(c)}$ is a binary indicator (0 or 1) if class label c is the correct classification for position (h, w), and $P_{hw}^{(c)}$ is the predicted probability of class c at position (h, w). The cross-entropy measures the dissimilarity between the true label distribution and the predicted probability distribution, and it is used to optimize the model parameters by minimizing this dissimilarity.

4   Experimental Results and Analysis

4.1   Creation of Manipulation Mask Manufacturer Dataset (MMMD)

We crawled images from websites containing tampered images on the internet, such as Baidu PS Bar. It is an ideal source for both original and tampered images [49]. Most users request others to help modify the pictures they provide. As a result, there are often numerous tampered images under their posts. We save the original and tampered images from different posts, allowing us to collect a large amount of data in a short period. We take the first image of each post as the original image, like the first row in Fig. 2, and consider all other images of the same size in that post as tampered images, like the second row in Fig. 2.

We then subtract the grayscale images of the original and tampered images to obtain a mask image containing a significant amount of noise. This is because images undergo irreversible compression and quality degradation during transmission over the internet, and they also experience compression when opened with image editing software like

Photoshop. The original and tampered images contain noise differences that are imperceptible to the human eye, making the directly subtracted mask image unsuitable for use as training data. The images in the NIST16 dataset are multi-scale, so we used it to pre-train the MMM framework. Therefore, we input the original and corresponding tampered images as pairs into our MMM framework, which consists of three steps: feature extraction and concatenation, super-resolution processing, and feature separation mask generation. This process ultimately produces the predicted mask image shown in the last row of Fig. 2. The predicted image has significantly reduced noise and can be used for tamper detection models. Since the first image from the PS forum is assumed to be original and subsequent ones tampered, but this isn't always true, it leads to noisy, mostly white masks. Special tampering techniques also cause noisy masks. Therefore, masks with more than 70% or less than 1% white area are deemed invalid and removed.

The entire MMMD is divided into three groups: original images, tampered images, and predicted masks, each containing 11,069 images. Each tampered image has a corresponding original image and mask in the other two groups. The dataset contains images with different resolutions and various manipulation types, including copy-move [1,8], transformation [36], Deepfake [34], image inpainting [14], morphing [47], reconstruction [11], and style transfer. It encompasses a wide range of image categories, such as cartoons, portraits, landscapes, interiors, food, and accessories.

4.2   Accuracy of the Model on Existing Datasets

Our innovative use of deep learning for annotating image manipulation detection datasets has no existing comparable methods. Thus, we train and validate our model on the NIST16 [21], IMD2020 [35], and CASIAV2.0 [13] datasets to demonstrate its effectiveness in distinguishing between original and tampered images. The experimental results are shown in Table 2. The model performs exceptionally well on all three datasets, with high levels across all metrics (F1, Precision, Recall, IoU, and Accuracy). It demonstrates strong generalization capability on image manipulation detection datasets, particularly on datasets involving traditional tampering methods. The performance is slightly lower on the IMD2020 [35], which uses deep learning techniques such as GANs and inpainting [14], but overall, the model exhibits good adaptability and performance across various datasets.

Table 2. Performance of Our Model on Different Datasets.

Dataset	F1	Precision	Recall	IoU	Accuracy
IMD2020	0.88	0.90	0.87	0.81	0.97
NIST16	0.94	0.95	0.92	0.89	0.98
CASIAv2	0.95	0.96	0.95	0.91	0.98

Implementation Details. Our models are implemented on PyTorch. Our training is set with a learning rate of 0.01 and a maximum of 100 epochs. The learning rate decay iterations are set to 100. Validation is performed after each training epoch, and the model that performs best on the validation set is used for evaluation on the test set.

Evaluation Metrics. We use the F1-score to evaluate the performance of our model. It balances between tamper detection (recall) and avoiding false positives (precision), preventing the bias that comes from solely pursuing high recall or high precision. The formula for F1-score is as follows:

$$F1\text{-score} = 2 \times \left(\frac{\text{Precision} \times \text{Receall}}{\text{Precision} + \text{Recall}} \right) \tag{6}$$

Precision and Recall are expressed using the four metrics: True Positive (TP), False Positive (FP), False Negative (FN), and True Negative (TN). Additionally, we use IoU (Intersection over Union) to represent the model's localization accuracy and Accuracy to evaluate the overall performance of the model. The formula of IoU is $\text{IoU} = \text{TP}/(\text{TP} + \text{FN} + \text{FP})$ and The formula of Accuracy is $\text{Accuracy} = (\text{TP} + \text{TN})/(\text{TP} + \text{TN} + \text{FN} + \text{FP})$.

4.3   Effect of the Generated Dataset on Existing Models

IMDL-BenCo [32] reproduces mainstream IML models, and our model experiments are based on this framework.

Table 3. The F1 scores of various models pre-trained on MMMD across different datasets. Left: Pre-trained with CASIAv2, Right: Pre-trained with MMMD (ours).

Model	Dataset			
	COVERAGE	Columbia	NIST16	IMD2020
MVSS-Net	0.26/**0.34**	0.39/**0.49**	0.25/**0.28**	0.28/**0.32**
IML-ViT	0.43/0.29	0.78/**0.81**	0.33/**0.34**	0.33/**0.37**

We used our MMMD to train two major models, MVSS-Net [12], and IML-ViT [31], and validated their generalization. The results are shown in Table 3.

As shown in the table, MVSS-Net and IML-ViT trained using MMMD achieved higher metrics across various datasets compared to models pre-trained on CASIAv2. They exhibit higher generalization and robustness on MMMD. Since MMMD is much larger than commonly used datasets and covers a wider variety of manipulation types and scenarios, it helps improve the generalization ability of existing manipulation detection models. Models pre-trained on MMMD are expected to achieve better performance on other datasets, which is consistent with our experimental results.

We used MMMD to validate image manipulation detection models Mantra-Net [48], MVSS-Net [12], CAT-Net [25], ObjectFormer [44], NCL-IML [50], TruFor [22], IML-ViT [31] and PSCC-Net [27], pre-trained on CASIAv2 [13] and discovered the shortcomings of existing datasets compared to our MMMD. The results are shown in Table 4.

Table 4. The F1 scores of various models pre-trained on CASIAv2 across different datasets.

Model	Dataset			
	COVERAGE	Columbia	CASIAv1	MMMD(Ours)
Mantra-Net	0.08	0.46	0.12	**0.09**
MVSS-Net	0.26	0.39	0.53	**0.26**
CAT-Net	0.30	0.58	0.58	**0.30**
ObjectFormer	0.29	0.34	0.43	**0.32**
NCL-IML	0.22	0.45	0.50	**0.26**
TruFor	0.42	0.86	0.72	**0.30**
IML-ViT	0.43	0.78	0.72	**0.24**
PSCC-Net	0.23	0.60	0.38	**0.32**

As shown in the table, various models pre-trained on CASIAv2 [13] struggled to achieve high metrics on MMMD. CASIAv2 is one of the larger datasets in recent years for manipulation detection, covering a wide range of manipulation types and commonly used as a pre-training dataset for models. However, models pre-trained on CASIAv2 exhibited lower metrics on our MMMD compared to other datasets, highlighting the limitations of traditional datasets. In contrast to our MMMD, these datasets are smaller in size, cover fewer manipulation types, and are still somewhat distant from real-world manipulated images. As a result, models trained on these datasets struggle to perform well on real-life manipulated images.

Evaluation Metrics. We also use the F1-score to measure the accuracy of the model's detection, with the calculation formula given in Eq. 6.

Effect Without Using Super-Resolution. When processing images directly without using the super-resolution module, for certain severely degraded images, we still obtain noisy images without super-resolution. These images are not suitable for use as training data for manipulation detection models.

5   Conclusion

In this paper, we creatively propose a Manipulation Mask Manufacturer (MMM) framework for generating image manipulation detection datasets. It addresses the issues of small dataset size, poor quality, and limited types of tampering detection in the field of image manipulation detection. It concatenates image feature embeddings, performs context modeling, and captures long-range relationships between pixels. It uses MMD to eliminate the differences in data distribution. Extensive experiments have validated the effectiveness of our method. We demonstrated the strong performance of the MMM framework on existing datasets. The MMMD dataset we proposed better aligns with the real-world tampering scenarios that manipulation detection models must face. This will help these models improve their generalization and robustness in practical applications. We also demonstrated that MMMD outperforms other datasets in training effectiveness.

References

1. Amerini, I., Ballan, L., Caldelli, R., Del Bimbo, A., Serra, G.: A sift-based forensic method for copy-move attack detection and transformation recovery. IEEE Trans. Inf. Forensics Secur. **6**(3), 1099–1110 (2011)
2. Andreadis, I., Amanatiadis, A.: Digital image scaling. In: 2005 IEEE Instrumentation and Measurement Technology Conference Proceedings, vol. 3, pp. 2028–2032. IEEE (2005)
3. Bandara, W.G.C., Patel, V.M.: A transformer-based SIAMESE network for change detection. In: IGARSS 2022 - 2022 IEEE International Geoscience and Remote Sensing Symposium, pp. 207–210 (2022)
4. Boudier, T., Shotton, D.M.: Video on the internet: an introduction to the digital encoding, compression, and transmission of moving image data. J. Struct. Biol. **125**(2–3), 133–155 (1999)
5. Castleman, K.R.: Digital Image Processing. Prentice Hall Press (1996)
6. Chen, H., Qi, Z., Shi, Z.: Remote sensing image change detection with transformers. IEEE Trans. Geosci. Remote Sens. **60**, 1–14 (2021)
7. Chen, H.-W., Xu, Y.-S., Hong, M.-F., Tsai, Y.-M., Kuo, H.-K., Lee, C.-Y.: Cascaded local implicit transformer for arbitrary-scale super-resolution. In: Proceedings of the IEEE/CVF Conference on Computer Vision and Pattern Recognition, pp. 18257–18267 (2023)
8. Christlein, V., Riess, C., Jordan, J., Riess, C., Angelopoulou, E.: An evaluation of popular copy-move forgery detection approaches. IEEE Trans. Inf. Forensics Secur. **7**(6), 1841–1854 (2012)
9. Criminisi, A., Pérez, P., Toyama, K.: Region filling and object removal by exemplar-based image inpainting. IEEE Trans. Image Process. **13**(9), 1200–1212 (2004)
10. Dang-Nguyen, D.-T., Pasquini, C., Conotter, V., Boato, G.: Raise: a raw images dataset for digital image forensics. In: Proceedings of the 6th ACM Multimedia Systems Conference, pp. 219–224 (2015)
11. Demoment, G.: Image reconstruction and restoration: overview of common estimation structures and problems. IEEE Trans. Acoust. Speech Signal Process. **37**(12), 2024–2036 (1989)
12. Dong, C., Chen, X., Ruohan, H., Cao, J., Li, X.: MVSS-Net: multi-view multi-scale supervised networks for image manipulation detection. IEEE Trans. Pattern Anal. Mach. Intell. **45**(3), 3539–3553 (2022)
13. Dong, J., Wang, W., Tan, T.: CASIA image tampering detection evaluation database. In: 2013 IEEE China Summit and International Conference on Signal and Information Processing, pp. 422–426. IEEE (2013)
14. Elharrouss, O., Almaadeed, N., Al-Maadeed, S., Akbari, Y.: Image inpainting: a review. Neural Process. Lett. **51**, 2007–2028 (2020)
15. Fang, S., Li, K., Shao, J., Li, Z.: SNUNET-CD: A densely connected SIAMESE network for change detection of VHR images. IEEE Geosci. Remote Sens. Lett. **19**, 1–5 (2022)
16. Farid, H.: Image forgery detection. IEEE Signal Process. Mag. **26**(2), 16–25 (2009)
17. Fitzpatrick, N.: Media manipulation 2.0: the impact of social media on news, competition, and accuracy (2018)
18. GIMP GIMP. Gimp. Página Principal. Disponível em, 6 (2013)
19. Ginsberg, R.H.: Image rotation. Appl. Opt. **33**(34), 8105_1–8108 (1994)
20. Glasbey, C.A., Mardia, K.V.: A review of image-warping methods. J. Appl. Stat. **25**(2), 155–171 (1998)
21. Guan, H., et al.: MFC datasets: large-scale benchmark datasets for media forensic challenge evaluation. In: 2019 IEEE Winter Applications of Computer Vision Workshops (WACVW), pp. 63–72. IEEE (2019)

22. Guillaro, F., Cozzolino, D., Sud, A., Dufour, N., Verdoliva, L.: Trufor: leveraging all-round clues for trustworthy image forgery detection and localization. In: Proceedings of the IEEE/CVF Conference on Computer Vision and Pattern Recognition, pp. 20606–20615 (2023)
23. Hsu, Y.-F., Chang, S.-F.: Detecting image splicing using geometry invariants and camera characteristics consistency. In: 2006 IEEE International Conference on Multimedia and Expo, pp. 549–552. IEEE (2006)
24. Jing, Y., Yang, Y., Feng, Z., Ye, J., Yizhou, Yu., Song, M.: Neural style transfer: a review. IEEE Trans. Visual Comput. Graphics **26**(11), 3365–3385 (2019)
25. Kwon, M.-J., Nam, S.-H., In-Jae, Yu., Lee, H.-K., Kim, C.: Learning jpeg compression artifacts for image manipulation detection and localization. Int. J. Comput. Vision **130**(8), 1875–1895 (2022)
26. Lin, T.-Y., et al.: Microsoft COCO: common objects in context. In: Fleet, D., Pajdla, T., Schiele, B., Tuytelaars, T. (eds.) ECCV 2014. LNCS, vol. 8693, pp. 740–755. Springer, Cham (2014). https://doi.org/10.1007/978-3-319-10602-1_48
27. Liu, X., Liu, Y., Chen, J., Liu, X.: PSCC-net: progressive SPATIO-channel correlation network for image manipulation detection and localization. IEEE Trans. Circuits Syst. Video Technol. **32**(11), 7505–7517 (2022)
28. Long, J., Shelhamer, E., Darrell, T.: Fully convolutional networks for semantic segmentation. In: Proceedings of the IEEE Conference on Computer Vision and Pattern Recognition, pp. 3431–3440 (2015)
29. Long, M., Cao, Y., Wang, J., Jordan, M.: Learning transferable features with deep adaptation networks. In: International Conference on Machine Learning, pp. 97–105. PMLR (2015)
30. Dengsheng, L., Mausel, P., Brondizio, E., Moran, E.: Change detection techniques. Int. J. Remote Sens. **25**(12), 2365–2401 (2004)
31. Ma, X., Du, B., Liu, X., Al Hammadi, A.Y., Zhou, J.: IML-VIT: image manipulation localization by vision transformer. arXiv preprint arXiv:2307.14863 (2023)
32. Ma, X., et al.: IMDL-BENCO: a comprehensive benchmark and codebase for image manipulation detection & localization. arXiv preprint arXiv:2406.10580 (2024)
33. Mahfoudi, G., Tajini, B., Retraint, F., Morain-Nicolier, F., Dugelay, J.L., PIC Marc: Defacto: image and face manipulation dataset. In: 2019 27Th European Signal Processing Conference (EUSIPCO), pp. 1–5. IEEE (2019)
34. Mirsky, Y., Lee, W.: The creation and detection of deepfakes: a survey. ACM Comput. Surv. (CSUR) **54**(1), 1–41 (2021)
35. Novozamsky, A., Mahdian, B., Saic, S.: Imd2020: a large-scale annotated dataset tailored for detecting manipulated images. In: Proceedings of the IEEE/CVF Winter Conference on Applications of Computer Vision Workshops, pp. 71–80 (2020)
36. Petrou, M.M.P., Petrou, C.: Image Processing: The Fundamentals. Wiley (2010)
37. Rensink, R.A.: Change detection. Ann. Rev. Psychol. **53**(1), 245–277 (2002)
38. Sejdinovic, D., Sriperumbudur, B., Gretton, A., Fukumizu, K.: Equivalence of distance-based and RKHS-based statistics in hypothesis testing. Ann. Stat. 2263–2291 (2013)
39. Shi, J., Malik, J.: Normalized cuts and image segmentation. IEEE Trans. Pattern Anal. Mach. Intell. **22**(8), 888–905 (2000)
40. Su, L., Ma, X., Zhu, X., Niu, C., Lei, Z., Zhou, J.-Z.: Can we get rid of handcrafted feature extractors? sparsevit: nonsemantics-centered, parameter-efficient image manipulation localization through spare-coding transformer. arXiv preprint arXiv:2412.14598 (2024)
41. Tan, Y., et al.: CrossNet++: cross-scale large-parallax warping for reference-based super-resolution. IEEE Trans. Pattern Anal. Mach. Intell. **43**(12), 4291–4305 (2020)
42. Adobe Creative Team, Gyncild, B.: Adobe Photoshop CC. Pearson Education (2013)
43. Thakur, R., Rohilla, R.: Recent advances in digital image manipulation detection techniques: a brief review. Forensic Sci. Int. **312**, 110311 (2020)

44. Wang, J., et al.: Objectformer for image manipulation detection and localization. In: Proceedings of the IEEE/CVF Conference on Computer Vision and Pattern Recognition, pp. 2364–2373 (2022)
45. Wang, W., Dong, J., Tan, T.: A survey of passive image tampering detection. In: Ho, A.T.S., Shi, Y.Q., Kim, H.J., Barni, M. (eds.) Digital Watermarking, pp. 308–322. Springer, Heidelberg (2009)
46. Wen, B., Zhu, Y., Subramanian, R., Ng, T.-T., Shen, X., Winkler, S.: Coverage-a novel database for copy-move forgery detection. In: 2016 IEEE International Conference on Image Processing (ICIP), pp. 161–165. IEEE (2016)
47. Wolberg, G.: Image morphing: a survey. Vis. Comput. **14**(8–9), 360–372 (1998)
48. Wu, Y., AbdAlmageed, W., Natarajan, P.: Mantra-net: manipulation tracing network for detection and localization of image forgeries with anomalous features. In: Proceedings of the IEEE/CVF Conference on Computer Vision and Pattern Recognition, pp. 9543–9552 (2019)
49. Yang, X., Zhou, J.: Manipulation mask generator: high-quality image manipulation mask generation method based on modified total variation noise reduction. In: 2023 IEEE 4th International Conference on Pattern Recognition and Machine Learning (PRML), pp. 218–223. IEEE (2023)
50. Zhou, J., Ma, X., Du, X., Alhammadi, A.Y., Feng, W.: Pre-training-free image manipulation localization through non-mutually exclusive contrastive learning. In: Proceedings of the IEEE/CVF International Conference on Computer Vision, pp. 22346–22356 (2023)
51. Zhu, X., et al.: Mesoscopic insights: orchestrating multi-scale & hybrid architecture for image manipulation localization. arXiv preprint arXiv:2412.13753 (2024)
52. Zhuang, P., Li, H., Tan, S., Li, B., Huang, J.: Image tampering localization using a dense fully convolutional network. IEEE Trans. Inf. Forensics Secur. **16**, 2986–2999 (2021)

Agent-Conditioned Multi-contrast MRI Super-Resolution for Cross-Subject

Xinrong Hu[1,2(✉)], Chao Fang[1,2], Yu Chen[1,2], Kai Yang[1,2], Chun-Mei Feng[3(✉)], and Ping Li[4]

[1] School of Computer Science and Artificial Intelligence, Wuhan Textile University, Wuhan 430200, Hubei, China
{hxr,kyang}@wtu.edu.cn, 2215063028@mail.wtu.edu.cn
[2] Engineering Research Center of Hubei Province for Clothing Information, Wuhan Textile University, Wuhan 430200, Hubei, China
[3] Institute of High Performance Computing (IHPC), Agency for Science, Technology and Research (A*STAR), Singapore 138632, Republic of Singapore
strawberry.feng0304@gmail.com
[4] Department of Computing, School of Design, and Research Institute for Sports Science and Technology, The Hong Kong Polytechnic University, Hong Kong, China
p.li@polyu.edu.hk

Abstract. Multi-contrast MRI super-resolution (SR) techniques require the simultaneous acquisition of multiple contrasts from the same subject, which is often challenging in real-world clinical settings. In this paper, we propose a novel agent-conditioned multi-contrast MRI SR with cross-subject adaptation, termed AgentMRI. AgentMRI is the first attempt to improve the quality of target contrast images using external auxiliary contrasts from different subjects. It expands the traditional attention mechanism from a triplet to a quadruplet format (Query, Agent, Key, Value), where the agent can be trained to capture commonalities from the auxiliary contrast. These commonalities represent foundational anatomical and tissue structure features that are shareable, rather than details specific to a particular contrast. By interacting the agent with the target contrast, AgentMRI dynamically adjusts the model adapting the agent's knowledge to the target contrast image. This adapting process assists in identifying inherent connections between the auxiliary and target contrasts, even when they are not directly paired. Our extensive testing on fastMRI and clinical datasets demonstrates that our AgentMRI sets a new benchmark, surpassing state-of-the-art methods across various evaluation metrics.

Keywords: Magnetic resonance imaging · super-resolution · agent attention

1 Introduction

Magnetic Resonance Imaging (MRI) is a non-invasive technique that generates images of the human body's internal tissues using strong magnetic fields and radiofrequency

© The Author(s), under exclusive license to Springer Nature Singapore Pte Ltd. 2025
P. Didyk and J. Hou (Eds.): CVM 2025, LNCS 15663, pp. 309–327, 2025.
https://doi.org/10.1007/978-981-96-5809-1_17

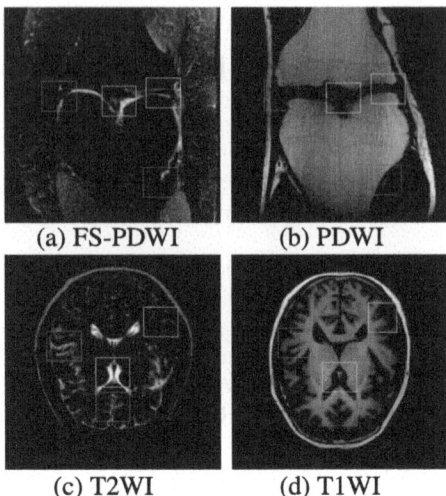

(a) FS-PDWI   (b) PDWI

(c) T2WI   (d) T1WI

Fig. 1. Examples of four different imaging modalities. Images (a) and (b) show fat-suppressed proton density-weighted imaging (FS-PDWI) and proton density-weighted imaging (PDWI) from different subjects in the fastMRI dataset. Images (c) and (d) represent T2-weighted imaging (T2WI) and T1-weighted imaging (T1WI) from different subjects in a real-world clinical dataset. Despite their differences (marked by the red boxes), these different modalities from different subjects share fundamental anatomical and tissue structure features (marked by the green, blue-gray, and orange boxes). (Color figure online)

pulses [11]. Compared to other medical imaging technologies, such as Computed Tomography (CT) and Positron Emission Tomography (PET), MRI offers several advantages, including superior soft tissue contrast, absence of ionizing radiation, and the ability to acquire functional and metabolic information. This makes MRI particularly useful in neurological, musculoskeletal, cardiovascular, and oncological imaging. However, MRI also has limitations that impact its clinical utility. One primary limitation is its longer imaging times, which can lead to patient discomfort, increased susceptibility to motion artifacts, and higher costs due to prolonged use of the MRI system [32]. Another limitation is the lower signal-to-noise ratio (SNR) in MRI compared to CT and PET. Factors like magnetic field strength, coil quality, and imaging parameters affect SNR. Lower SNR can result in grainier images, obscuring fine anatomical details crucial for accurate diagnosis and treatment [41]. Therefore, accelerating MR imaging and improving its SNR have become prominent research topics.

In clinical settings, MR scanners sequentially acquire images in different modalities following specific imaging protocols tailored to diagnostic needs. For the same subject, each imaging modality often provides consistent data across multi-contrast and modality-specific anatomical and physiological information. The multi-contrast attributes of MRI have inspired researchers to exploit the complementary information among modalities that share analogous anatomical structures [6,8,30], where T1-weighted images (T1WIs) and T2-weighted images (T2WIs), as well as proton density and fat-suppressed proton density-weighted images (PDWIs and FS-PDWIs), provide complementary structural perspectives. Due to the inherent physical properties of MRI, T1WI is generally easier to acquire than T2WI because it requires shorter repetition times (TR) and echo times (TE). Specifically, within the same imaging sequence, the acquisition time for T2WI tends to exceed that for T1WI due to the longer TR requirements of T2, as seen with T2SE acquisition times being longer than those for T1SE. This multi-modal imaging strategy utilizes faster-acquired modalities as auxiliary contrast images to guide and accelerate the imaging of target modalities with slower acquisition speeds, which has been verified by previous study [23,25,31]. For example, bicubic interpolation, Lanczos resampling, sparse representation, dictionary learning, and patch-based methods have been extensively applied in multi-modal MR imaging SR tasks. Qu et al. [35] integrated nonlocal means filtering with parallel imaging for MRI SR. Wang et al. [44] utilized Laplacian pyramids and adaptive sparse representation for multi-modal medical image fusion to achieve MRI SR work. Recently, the focus has shifted towards leveraging the capabilities of deep learning to address the challenges inherent in MRI SR. For example, Feng et al. [6] designed a multi-stage integration network that explores the dependencies among hierarchical stages in multi-contrast images. Li et al. [25] used transformer attributes to transfer the contextual information from auxiliary contrast to target contrast features across different scales, which significantly enhances the super-resolution quality of images. Li et al. [28] introduced a novel diffusion model for multi-contrast MRI SR which fully utilizes the prior knowledge from the diffusion model (DM) to ensure that the reconstructed MR images remain undistorted.

Despite significant advancements in processing multi-contrast MRI data, practical applications still face challenges in acquiring complete datasets of all contrasts for each patient due to regional development disparities and acquisition time and cost constraints [10]. Indeed, we observe that unpaired multi-contrast data still share commonalities, such as fundamental anatomical structure features (e.g., joint spaces, cartilage areas, cerebral cortex regions, and ventricular systems) present in the images. As shown in Fig. 1, (a) and (b) are a pair of FS-PDW and PDW knee MR images from different subjects in the fastMRI dataset, and (c) and (d) are a pair of T2W and T1W brain MRI images from different subjects in a real-world clinical dataset. Although these MR images are from different individuals, certain consistent anatomical and tissue structural features are present across different modalities and subjects. These common features offer constructive guidance for the SR of target images. Moreover, learning specific knowledge between contrasts, such as the capability of T1WI to describe morphological and structural information, can effectively complement the generation of T2WI [1,7,27,51]. This complementarity of multi-contrast information encourages us to explore multi-contrast features in MRI SR tasks, thereby enhancing image quality and diagnostic precision. Importantly, the vast online resources of medical images remain underutilized, motivating us to explore the correlations between different contrasts as well as subjects and repurpose extensive publicly available medical image data to generate high-quality target images from unpaired data [2].

To tackle this challenge, we introduce AgentMRI, an agent-conditioned technique for multi-contrast MRI SR that embraces cross-subject adaptability. This approach is designed to uncover both the *commonalities* and *distinctiveness* present in data across subjects, ultimately enhancing the target contrast. Different from previous methods that rely on paired images, despite the absence of paired images, AgentMRI expands the traditional attention mechanism from a triplet to a quadruplet format (Query, *Agent*, Key, Value) to extract and capture *shareable foundational anatomical and tissue structure features* from auxiliary contrast. The interaction between the agent and the target contrast guides the model to focus on task-specific features, adapting auxiliary contrasts in the cross-subject to the target image. This adaptation process helps to identify the intrinsic connections between auxiliary and target contrasts, even when they are not directly paired.

For clarity, the main contributions of our work are summarized as follows:

– AgentMRI is the *first* to achieve SR of target contrasts using cross-subject auxiliary contrast images. Clinically, AgentMRI enables cost-effective multi-contrast MRI using public datasets for auxiliary contrast without requiring pairing with target images.
– We develop an *agent-conditioned* multi-contrast MRI SR approach that employs agent vectors to enable the model to transfer knowledge across *different contrasts and subjects*. This method adapts cross-subject auxiliary contrast data through an agent-conditioned mechanism, infusing beneficial features into the target image, e.g., foundational anatomical structures, and supplementary information.
– We conducted extensive experiments on the fastMRI and clinical medical image datasets, demonstrating that AgentMRI yields superior results over the state-of-the-art.

2   Related Work

2.1   MR Imaging

In clinical practice, magnetic resonance imaging (MRI) provides excellent soft-tissue contrast for clinical diagnosis and research. Image SR and reconstruction significantly improve the quality and speed of MRI imaging. Traditional MR image SR methods, such as bicubic interpolation [4], iterative deblurring algorithms [16,39], and compressed sensing (CS) [12], have made significant strides in multi-frame MR image SR tasks. However, these methods offer limited information when processing individual images and usually rely on prior data information. In recent years, deep learning-based SR methods have demonstrated superior performance due to their ability to fully exploit the inherent attributes of images contained in extensive training datasets. For instance, Qui et al. [34] applied convolutional neural networks (CNNs) for knee MR image SR, and Lyu et al. [30] used ensemble learning for brain MR image SR. Jin et al. [20] employed UNet to capture spatial information for addressing inverse problems in MRI. More recently, generative adversarial networks (GANs) have been applied to MR images SR. For example, Jiang et al. [18] proposed a fused attentive generative adversarial networks framework to generate SR MR images from low-resolution (LR) MR images. Li et al. [26] incorporated attention mechanisms and cyclic loss within GANs for pelvic image SR. To learn essential regional feature representations from single MR images, Zhang et al. [49] introduced the squeezed and inspired inference attention network, demonstrating its effectiveness. Qui et al. [33] developed a gradual back-projection residual attention network to reconstruct MR images SR. Feng et al. [9] proposed an end-to-end task transformer network that integrates MRI reconstruction and SR into a single framework. Salvetti et al. [37] introduced a residual attention model using 3D convolutions and nested residual connections for multi-image super-resolution in remote sensing. However, the above methods usually focus only on single-contrast images, such as T1WI or T2WI, ignoring the multi-contrast information in MRI data.

2.2   Multi-modal Representation Learning

Multi-modal representation learning [19] extracts shared features from diverse data modalities such as text, images, and speech. For example, Kwon et al. [22] used the inherent properties of image-text paired data to implicitly learn the cross-modal alignment between language tokens and image patches for reconstructing the masked signal of one modality using another. Liu et al. [29] proposed an autoencoder-based multi-view missing data completion framework to learn a general representation of Alzheimer's diagnosis. Given the strong capability of multi-modal technology in representation learning [47], it has recently been widely applied in medical images. For instance, Tsai et al. [40] proposed a multi-modal transformer for unaligned multi-modal MRI sequences, demonstrating the effective integration of heterogeneous MRI data. Zhang et al. [48] utilized graph neural networks to fuse PET and MRI data, enhancing tumor segmentation and treatment planning by using spatial and functional information from both modalities. In contrast to the multi-contrast MR image segmentation task, the super-resolution (SR) task divides images into auxiliary and target contrasts. Given its shorter acquisition time, the auxiliary contrast can guide the restoration of the target contrast. For example, Lyu et al. [30] demonstrated that fusing multi-contrast information in high-level feature spaces yields superior results compared to low-level pixel-based combinations. Li et al. [25] pioneered hierarchical transformer networks for joint multi-contrast MRI reconstruction and SR. Feng et al. [6] proposed a multi-stage feature fusion mechanism where features from previous stages guide the learning of subsequent target features in multi-contrast SR tasks. Li et al. [25] pioneered the application of transformers in multi-contrast MRI SR, introducing a transformer-empowered multi-scale contextual matching and aggregation network. Li et al. [27] later enhanced this approach by integrating wavelet transforms with a cross-attention mechanism, further improving performance. However, existing multi-modal representation learning for MR images SR generally integrates data from different modalities acquired simultaneously from the same subject. In contrast, our method implicitly learns commonalities among multi-contrasts from different subjects.

2.3   Vision Transformer

Transformer was originally proposed as a sequence-to-sequence model in natural language processing (NLP) for tasks such as machine translation [24]. Due to its powerful and flexible modeling capabilities, researchers began exploring its application to computer vision tasks. For example, Dosovitskiy et al. [5] first proposed the Vision Transformer (ViT), which splits an image into multiple fixed-size patches and processes these patches as sequences. Following this, various variants and improvements of the transformer framework emerged [15]. ViT's powerful learning capability benefits from the self-attention mechanism. However, it faces challenges due to the quadratic complexity of Softmax attention. To reduce computational costs, several variants have been proposed, such as the sparse global attention of PVT [42], the convolution-like attention of NAT [17], and the deformable attention of DAT [45]. These methods, however, inherently limit the global receptive field of self-attention. On the other hand, linear attention addresses this issue by reducing the complexity to $\mathcal{O}(N)$ [21]. For instance, FLatten Transformer [13] introduced a focused function and adopted depthwise convolution to maintain feature diversity. Efficient Attention [38] applied the Softmax function to both Q and K. While these methods are effective, the expressive power of linear attention remains limited.

In this work, we propose a high expressiveness and efficient cross-modal agent transformer, where the agent is trained to capture commonalities from the auxiliary contrast and guide the target contrast to dynamically adjust and learn these commonalities, thus achieving SR tasks between unpaired MR data.

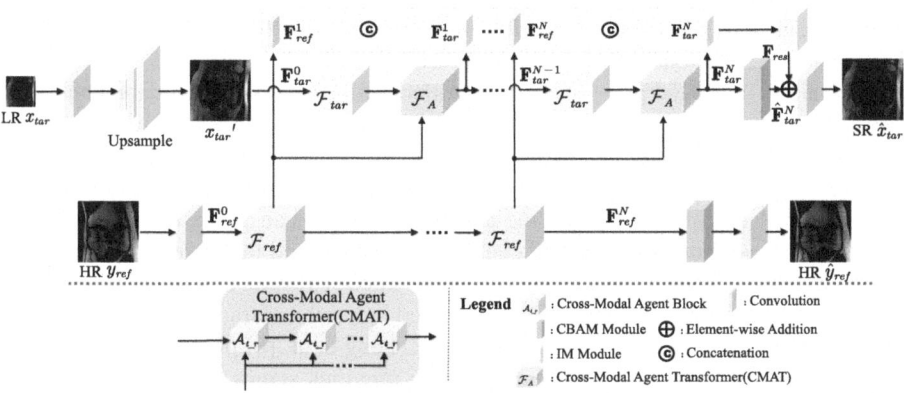

Fig. 2. Architecture of the proposed agent-conditioned multi-contrast MRI SR network and cross-modal agent transformer. 'CBAM' and 'IM' refer to the channel-spatial attention module and the layer attention module, respectively, and have the same design as in [6].

3   Methodology

3.1   Overall Architecture

Our approach adopts a novel perspective, allowing the use of an HR reference image $y_{ref} \in \mathbb{R}^{H \times W}$ from different subjects to guide the SR reconstruction of the target image $x_{tar} \in \mathbb{R}^{h \times w}$. Specifically, for a $2\times$ enlargement scale, the HR reference image y_{ref} has dimensions $H = W = 320$, while the target image x_{tar} has input dimensions $h = w = 160$. As illustrated in Fig. 2, our proposed network can accept HR reference images from any patient as an auxiliary input. We explore the commonalities and distinctiveness of the same stage features from the two branches. Subsequently, we capture agent commonalities that are not specific to any contrast. We then broadcast these commonalities back to each target feature, allowing them to interact with the target contrast. This process dynamically adjusts and learns to adapt to the commonalities of the target contrast. This approach better transfers knowledge between unpaired data and provides beneficial features for unpaired target images and subjects.

Feature Iterative Extraction. To explore commonalities and distinctiveness from auxiliary contrast images of different subjects, we use a cascaded residual layer [50] to extract multi-stage features. First, we apply separate 3×3 convolutional layers to extract the initial LR and HR representations. Specifically, this operation converts the single-channel input to a 64-channel feature representation, where the HR reference representation is denoted as $\mathbf{F}^0_{ref} \in \mathbb{R}^{64 \times 320 \times 320}$. Here, we rescale the LR target representation of size $64 \times 160 \times 160$, according to the scaling factor of the SR task to match the spatial dimensions of $\mathbf{F}^0_{ref}$. The feature representation of each branch at any stage is as follows:

$$\mathbf{F}^{n+1}_{tar} = \mathcal{F}_A(\mathbf{F}^n_{tar}, \mathbf{F}^n_{ref}), \quad \mathbf{F}^n_{ref} = \mathcal{F}^n_{ref}(\mathbf{F}^{n-1}_{ref}). \tag{1}$$

Here, n and N ($n \in N$) represent the index of the current residual group and the total number of residual groups across all branches, respectively. $\mathcal{F}_A$ denotes the cross-modal agent transformer (CMAT) module, and $\mathcal{F}^n_{ref}$ is the residual group at the nth stage. Throughout the entire process, both residual features $\mathbf{F}^n_{tar}$ and $\mathbf{F}^n_{ref}$ maintain a consistent feature dimensionality of $64 \times 320 \times 320$, ensuring spatial alignment across all residual groups and promoting effective knowledge transfer across different contrasts and subjects.

Agent-Conditioned Feature Learning. Inspired by [14], we designed the CMAT module to identify the inherent connections between reference and target contrasts, even in the absence of direct pairing. Specifically, we use agent tokens as intermediaries for transferring key knowledge across contrasts and between subjects. By expanding the traditional attention mechanism from a simple triplet (Query, Key, Value) to a quadruplet that includes an ***Agent*** component, the agent token A can capture commonalities and specific knowledge. As shown in Fig. 2, the shallow features $\mathbf{F}_{tar} \in \mathbb{R}^{64 \times 320 \times 320}$ and $\mathbf{F}_{ref} \in \mathbb{R}^{64 \times 320 \times 320}$ are fed into the CMAT module to extract and capture shareable foundational anatomical and tissue structure features from auxiliary contrasts. Our specifically designed agent tokens A originate from reference contrast data to guide the model to concentrate on task-specific features. To further facilitate the interaction between the agent and the target contrast, our designed query vector Q originates from the target branch. Formally, we have the following definitions:

$$(Q, A, K, V) = (\mathtt{w}\mathbf{F}_{tar}, \mathtt{avgpool}(\mathtt{w}\mathbf{F}_{ref}), \\ \mathtt{w}\mathbf{F}_{ref}, \mathtt{w}\mathbf{F}_{ref}), \tag{2}$$

where W denotes the matrix for generating tokens, and avgpool is an average pooling operation. The query vector Q formulated as $Q \in \mathbb{R}^{H \times L \times d}$, where $H = 8$ is the number of attention heads, $L = 102400$ is the number of tokens, and $d = 8$ is the per-head embedding dimension. Similarly, the key vector K and value vector V have the same shape as Q, i.e., $K, V \in \mathbb{R}^{H \times L \times d}$. The agent tokens A are defined as $A \in \mathbb{R}^{H \times L_a \times d}$, where $L_a = 49$ is the number of agent tokens.

Through this agent-conditioned mechanism, knowledge transfer across different contrasts and subjects is achieved. These agent tokens not only learn commonalities but also effectively broadcast this information back to the query tokens Q of the target contrast, thereby dynamically adjusting cross-subject reference contrast data and supplementing beneficial features. The above process is formulated as follows:

$$
\begin{aligned}
\mathbf{F}_{tar}^{n+1} = &\texttt{Reshape}(\texttt{Softmax}(Q, A, \texttt{Softmax}(A, K, V)) \\
&+ \texttt{DWC}(V)) + \mathbf{F}_{tar}^n,
\end{aligned}
\tag{3}
$$

where Softmax denotes Softmax attention, and DWC denotes a 3×3 depthwise convolutional operation. It is worth noting that our designed CMAT contains multiple cross-modal agent blocks. In these blocks, the tokens for K and V are computed from the feature $\mathbf{F}_{ref}$, while the tokens for Q are computed from the output of the previous block. This design allows the agent tokens to continuously transfer knowledge of commonalities and distinctiveness in data across subjects, enabling the target branch can absorb foundational anatomical details.

Image Reconstruction. Finally, inspired by [6], we employ a CBAM and an IM module to reveal responses from all dimensions of the feature map. The output of the final CMAT, $\mathbf{F}_{tar}^N \in \mathbb{R}^{64 \times 320 \times 320}$, is fed into the CBAM module to obtain the $\mathbf{F}_{tar}^{\hat{N}} \in \mathbb{R}^{64 \times 320 \times 320}$. Furthermore, our model stores the intermediate features at each stage. To maintain feature diversity, these features are activated through the linear layer IM module to obtain the enriched representation $\mathbf{F}_{res} \in \mathbb{R}^{64 \times 320 \times 320}$. After that, a 1×1 convolutional layer is used to obtain the final reconstructed target SR image $\hat{x}_{tar} \in \mathbb{R}^{1 \times 320 \times 320}$, which can be written as:

$$
\hat{x}_{tar} = \texttt{Conv}(\mathbf{F}_{res} \oplus \mathbf{F}_{tar}^{\hat{N}} \oplus \mathbf{F}_{tar}^0),
\tag{4}
$$

where $\oplus$ means element-wise summation.

Loss Function. The L_1 loss is used to evaluate the SR results of the target image:

$$
\mathcal{L} = \lambda_{tar} \|\hat{x}_{tar} - x_{tar'}\|_1 + \lambda_{ref} \|\hat{y}_{ref} - y_{ref}\|_1,
\tag{5}
$$

where λ_{tar} and λ_{ref} weigh the trade-off between the target image and reference image reconstruction.

3.2 Cross-Modal Agent Block

As shown in Fig. 3, the agent tokens $A \in \mathbb{R}^{H \times L_a \times d}$ act as intermediaries for $Q \in \mathbb{R}^{H \times L \times d}$ and $K \in \mathbb{R}^{H \times L \times d}$, collecting commonalities knowledge from the reference

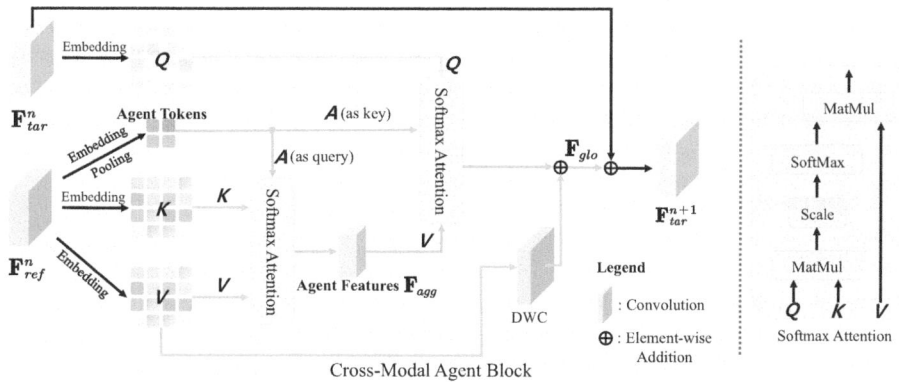

Fig. 3. Architecture of the proposed Cross-Modal Agent Block, where the right side of the dashed line represents the computation process of Softmax attention.

branch and then broadcasting these commonalities back to the target branch. Recall that Eq. 2 provides an overview of the representations of query, key, value, and agent tokens. Agent tokens A, serving as a commonalities feature query agent, capture commonalities from reference contrasts during training. These commonalities reflect shareable foundational anatomical and tissue structure features rather than specific details of a particular contrast. Therefore, the agent features we capture $\mathbf{F}_{agg} \in \mathbb{R}^{H \times L_a \times d}$ are characterized by foundational anatomical commonalities. Furthermore, the introduced agent bias helps maintain spatial consistency in the model. The features of agent commonalities $\mathbf{F}_{agg}$ can be represented as:

$$\mathbf{F}_{agg} = \mathtt{Softmax}\left(\frac{A(K)^\top}{\sqrt{d_k}} + \mathbf{B}_1\right)V, \tag{6}$$

where $\mathbf{B}_1 \in \mathbb{R}^{H \times L_a \times L}$ is the agent bias for the commonalities calculation, $d_k = 8$ represents the channel dimension of K, and the calculation methods for A, K, Q and V refer to Eq. 2. After that, we use A as the key (differently from the first instance) and the features of agent commonalities $\mathbf{F}_{agg}$ as the value, while employing the original query matrix Q for a second round of global attention calculation. This process enables the precise allocation and broadcasting of the features of agent commonalities onto the query tokens of the target contrast. Consequently, this approach guides the target contrast to focus on learning commonalities while enhancing its understanding of the distinctiveness of different anatomical structures. This method delves deeper into the intrinsic connections between the auxiliary and target contrasts, even though they are unpaired. To augment the diversity of target features, a depthwise convolution is employed at the end to preserve the feature diversity of the reference branch, and can be expressed as:

$$\mathbf{F}_{glo} = \mathtt{Softmax}\left(\frac{Q(A)^\top}{\sqrt{d_k}} + \mathbf{B}_2\right)\mathbf{F}_{agg}^V + \mathtt{DWC}(V), \tag{7}$$

where $\mathbf{B}_2 \in \mathbb{R}^{H \times L \times L_a}$ serves as the agent bias for the second attention calculation, and $\mathbf{F}_{agg}^V \in \mathbb{R}^{H \times L_a \times d}$ represents the value in the second attention calculation is directly computed from features of agent commonalities $\mathbf{F}_{agg}$. Finally, we derive the output of the cross-modal agent block, denoted as $\mathbf{F}_{glo} \in \mathbb{R}^{1 \times 102400 \times 64}$.

4   Experiments

4.1   Datasets

We evaluated the performance of our proposed network on three datasets, including two in-house brain datasets: **SMS** and **uMR**, and one public multi-contrast MRI dataset: **fastMRI** [46]. For **fastMRI**, the largest open-access raw MR image dataset, we use the unpaired PDWI contrast to guide the SR of FS-PDWI contrast, randomly filter out 200 and 40 PDWI and FS-PDWI brain volumes for training and validation, respectively, as unpaired experimental configurations. The **SMS** dataset was acquired with fully k-space sampling using a clinical 3T Siemens Magnetom Skyra scanner on 155 subjects, where each MR scanning parameter was as follows: T1WI with TR = 2001 ms, TE = 10.72 ms; T2WI with TR = 4511 ms, TE = 112.86 ms. Both sequences had a slice thickness of 5 mm, a matrix size of $320 \times 320 \times 20$, and a field of view of $230 \times 200 \, \text{mm}^2$. The **uMR** brain dataset was acquired using a 3T whole-body scanner on 50 subjects, where each MR scanning parameter was as follows: T1WI with TR = 2001 ms, TE = 10.72 ms; T2WI with TR = 4511 ms, TE = 112.86 ms. Both sequences had a slice thickness of 4 mm, a matrix size of $320 \times 320 \times 20$, and a field of view of $220 \times 250 \, \text{mm}^2$. The **SMS** and **uMR** datasets are randomly matched subjects-wise with a ratio of 7:1:2 for the training, validation, and test sets as unpaired experimental configurations.

4.2   Baselines

We compared our AgentMRI with various recent state-of-the-art methods to demonstrate its effectiveness, including two single-contrast SR methods: (1) Unet [36], a widely used convolutional network for biomedical image tasks; (2) UnetSN [43], an SR algorithm that restores low-resolution images with unknown and complex degradation using spectral normalization; (3) HAT [3], an SR algorithm that uses hybrid attention to fully exploit the potential of transformers in image restoration tasks, and two multi-contrast methods: (4) McMRSR [25], an MRI SR algorithm that matches and aggregates multi-scale context between contrasts to model long-range dependencies in both reference and target images; (5) MINet [6], an MRI SR algorithm that integrates multi-stage representations between the reference and target contrasts. For a fair comparison, all baselines were retrained with their predefined parameter configurations.

4.3   Implementation Details

Our model is implemented in PyTorch and runs on a single NVIDIA RTX 3090 GPU with 24 GB of memory. We use the Adam optimizer with a learning rate of 1e-3 and a mini-batch size of 8 for network training over 35 epochs, with the first-moment and second-moment coefficients set to 0.9 and 0.999, respectively. The hyperparameters

Table 1. Quantitative metrics results on three datasets with 2× enlargement scales. The best quantitative metrics results are marked in red.

Dataset	fastMRI [46]			SMS			uMR		
Metrics	SSIM↑	PSNR↑	NMSE↓	SSIM↑	PSNR↑	NMSE↓	SSIM↑	PSNR↑	NMSE↓
Unet [36]	0.2287	22.5696	0.2246	0.7678	34.8329	0.0111	0.6515	33.8070	0.0264
UnetSN [43]	0.5034	25.1499	0.1252	0.9754	39.4558	0.0038	0.9813	39.6306	0.0067
McMRSR [25]	0.6767	30.0768	0.0449	0.8969	38.8810	0.0044	0.9709	39.8956	0.0063
MINet [6]	0.6941	31.0488	0.0377	0.9832	41.8756	0.0022	0.9867	42.0970	0.0038
HAT [3]	0.7000	31.4128	0.0356	0.9850	41.7250	0.0023	0.9855	41.3772	0.0045
AgentMRI	0.7007	31.5696	0.0348	0.9867	42.3221	0.0020	0.9904	42.2374	0.0037

Table 2. Quantitative metrics results on three datasets with 4× enlargement scale. The best quantitative metrics results are marked in red.

Dataset	fastMRI [46]			SMS			uMR		
Metrics	SSIM↑	PSNR↑	NMSE↓	SSIM↑	PSNR↑	NMSE↓	SSIM↑	PSNR↑	NMSE↓
Unet [36]	0.0015	12.8584	2.2429	0.5459	27.9188	0.0552	0.4310	27.0451	0.1281
UnetSN [43]	0.0065	14.2090	1.5879	0.8683	31.3687	0.0248	0.8192	32.0166	0.0394
McMRSR [25]	0.5513	27.2725	0.0810	0.4674	31.0003	0.0269	0.8533	33.6797	0.0264
MINet [6]	0.5837	28.4560	0.0633	0.8719	32.8143	0.0175	0.8393	34.2608	0.0230
HAT [3]	0.6004	29.4626	0.0516	0.9198	33.4658	0.0151	0.9413	34.5221	0.0217
AgentMRI	0.6008	29.5927	0.0507	0.9045	33.5515	0.0148	0.9401	34.8800	0.0200

λ_{tar} and λ_{ref} are set to 0.7 and 0.3, respectively, and N is set to 6. The cross-modal agent attention head number is set to 8, and the patch size is 1×1. Following [14], the number of agent tokens is 49.

4.4   Quantitative Results

We evaluated our SR results by computing the SSIM, PSNR, and NMSE between the super-resolved image and the fully sampled ground truth image. Tables 1 and 2 present the quantitative comparison between our proposed method and various baselines under 2× and 4× enlargement using unpaired configurations, respectively. As shown, our method yields the best results in terms of PSNR and NMSE metrics, demonstrating that AgentMRI can effectively explore the intrinsic connection between the reference contrast and the target contrast, even when they are not directly paired. We note that single-contrast methods are far less effective than multi-contrast models. Furthermore, multi-contrast SR models are less effective than our method because they struggle to capture foundational anatomical features from unpaired data. These models are unable to achieve effective interaction between reference and target contrasts, resulting in the inability of the captured commonalities and distinctiveness knowledge to adapt to target contrast images effectively. More importantly, even though reconstructing SR images at 4× enlargement, our method can still outperform previous methods, which can be attributed to providing beneficial information supplements for target contrast

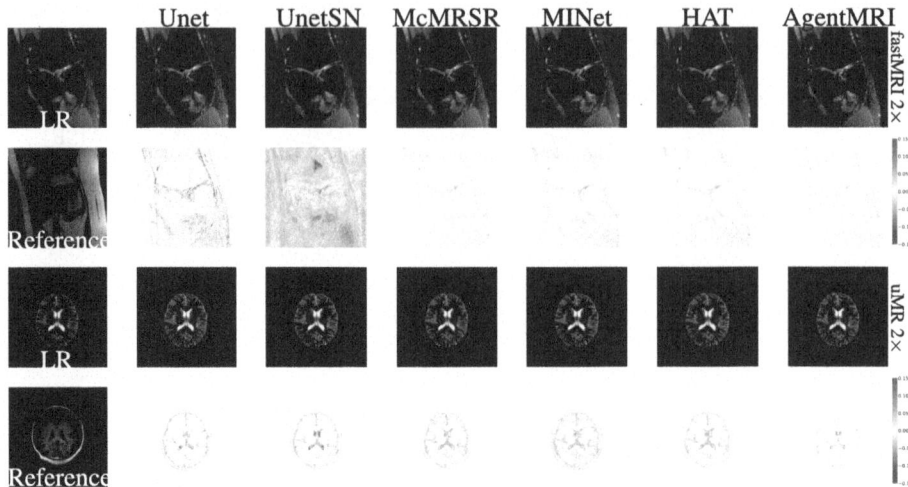

Fig. 4. Visual SR results and error maps of different methods on the **fastMRI** and **uMR** datasets with 2× enlargement scale.

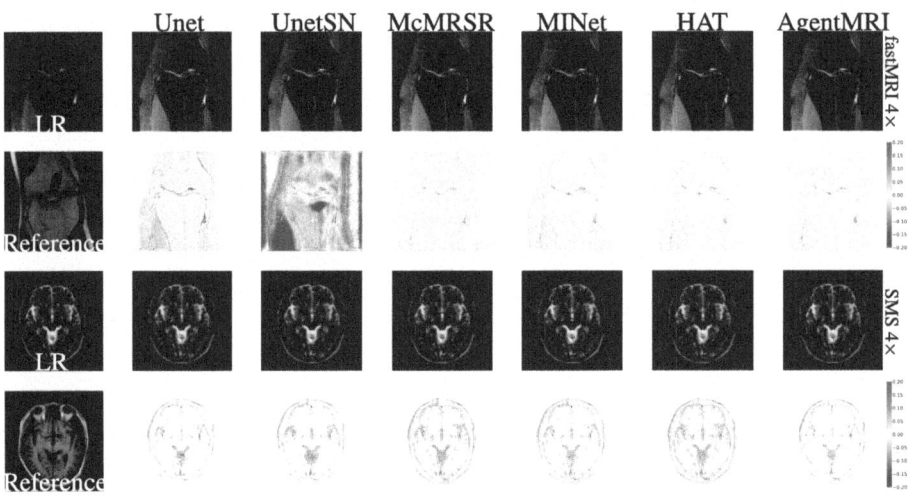

Fig. 5. Visual SR results and error maps of different methods on the **fastMRI** and **SMS** datasets with 4× enlargement scale.

data across subjects through an agent-conditioned mechanism. Although SSIM did not significantly outperform existing methods in some experiments, we attribute this to the sensitivity of SSIM to noise in the dataset. In contrast, the improvements in PSNR and NMSE more objectively reflect the robustness of the model. Our AgentMRI achieves 31.5696 dB and 29.5927 dB in PSNR on the **fastMRI** dataset, 42.3221 dB and 33.5515 dB on the **SMS** dataset, as well as 42.2374 dB and 34.8800 dB on the **uMR** dataset.

Table 3. Ablation study on different variants under three datasets with a 2× enlargement scale. The best quantitative metrics results are marked in red.

Dataset	fastMRI [46]			SMS			uMR		
Metrics	SSIM↑	PSNR↑	NMSE↓	SSIM↑	PSNR↑	NMSE↓	SSIM↑	PSNR↑	NMSE↓
w/o $\mathbf{B_1}$	0.6925	30.9664	0.0384	0.9729	41.9054	0.0022	0.9666	41.8241	0.0041
w/o $\mathbf{B_2}$	0.6843	30.6074	0.2246	0.9726	42.2453	0.0020	0.9395	40.8532	0.0051
w/o DWC	0.6906	30.8367	0.0388	0.9779	41.2401	0.0025	0.9664	41.7416	0.0041
w Cross-Vanilla Att.	0.6862	30.7800	0.0395	0.9768	41.0214	0.0027	0.9871	42.0681	0.0038
w $\mathbf{B_1}$	0.6973	31.2315	0.0362	0.9851	42.0130	0.0027	0.9833	42.0570	0.0038
w $\mathbf{B_2}$	0.6937	30.9651	0.0381	0.9841	42.1152	0.0021	0.9738	41.9699	0.0039
w DWC	0.6980	31.3462	0.0358	0.9860	42.1825	0.0020	0.9835	42.2111	0.0037
AgentMRI	0.7007	31.5696	0.0348	0.9867	42.3221	0.0020	0.9904	42.2374	0.0037

Table 4. Ablation study on different variants under three datasets with a 4× enlargement scale. The best quantitative metrics results are marked in red.

Dataset	fastMRI [46]			SMS			uMR		
Metrics	SSIM↑	PSNR↑	NMSE↓	SSIM↑	PSNR↑	NMSE↓	SSIM↑	PSNR↑	NMSE↓
w/o $\mathbf{B_1}$	0.4604	25.3290	0.1307	0.8324	33.0821	0.0165	0.8494	33.6912	0.0268
w/o $\mathbf{B_2}$	0.5323	26.7480	0.0924	0.7589	33.0083	0.0168	0.7789	33.4524	0.0285
w/o DWC	0.5356	26.7596	0.0940	0.8439	33.2791	0.0157	0.8196	32.7649	0.0338
w Cross-Vanilla Att.	0.5485	27.3697	0.0815	0.7949	30.4481	0.0315	0.9158	34.3611	0.0226
w $\mathbf{B_1}$	0.5768	27.7572	0.0726	0.9015	33.3044	0.0157	0.9090	34.5627	0.0215
w $\mathbf{B_2}$	0.5430	26.813	0.0907	0.8277	32.7762	0.0180	0.8323	32.6149	0.0354
w DWC	0.5873	28.6027	0.0600	0.9019	33.3554	0.0155	0.9029	34.6077	0.0212
AgentMRI	0.6008	29.5927	0.0507	0.9045	33.5515	0.0148	0.9401	34.8800	0.0200

4.5 Qualitative Evaluation

To further evaluate the robustness of our method, we conducted a quantitative analysis of the performance of AgentMRI. Figures 4 and 5 show SR results and error maps for unpaired **fastMRI**, **SMS**, and **uMR** at both 2× and 4× enlargements. The SR images indicate that single-contrast methods can restore the basic structure of the MR image. However, multi-contrast SR methods improve the results, with fewer structural losses. Specifically, our AgentMRI produces high-quality images with clear details, minimal checkerboard effects, and less structural loss, effectively restoring the entire structure of the knee or brain. This is attributed to the proposed agent-conditioned mechanism, which has excellent learning abilities in both commonalities and distinctiveness. More importantly, the error maps for different enlargement scales demonstrate that our method yields the smallest errors across various datasets.

4.6 Ablation Study

Component Analysis. Here, we investigate the importance of each key component of AgentMRI. To verify whether the agent-conditioned multi-contrast MRI SR possesses cross-subject adaptability, we designed seven different variants, i.e., w/o $\mathbf{B_1}$, which

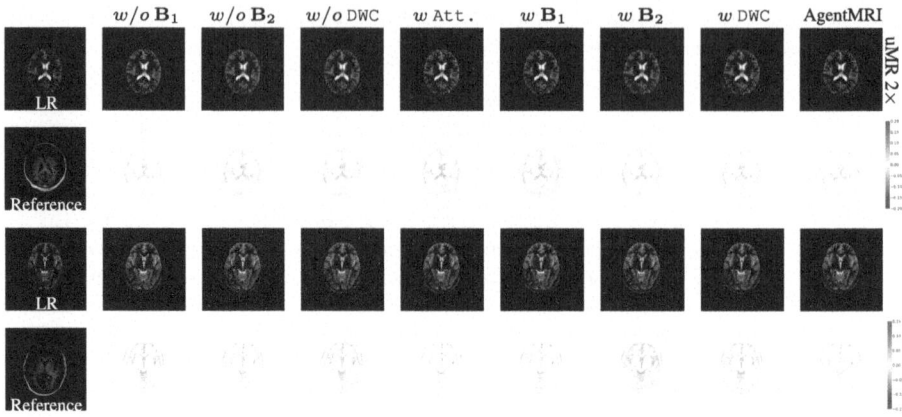

Fig. 6. Ablation study of the key components in our method, where w/o $\mathbf{B}_1$, w/o $\mathbf{B}_2$, w/o DWC, w Att., w $\mathbf{B}_1$, w $\mathbf{B}_2$, and w DWC represent seven variations of our model. Here, w Att. refers to w Cross-Vanilla Att.. Visual SR results and error maps of different variations on the **uMR** dataset with $2\times$ enlargement scale.

uses cross-modal Softmax attention calculation [40] without capturing the spatial information of agent commonalities through agent bias; w/o $\mathbf{B}_2$, which directly employ agent feature $\mathbf{F}_{agg}$ for the second Softmax attention calculation to evaluate whether agent bias can direct focus to task-specific features by sharing agent commonalities with the target branch; w/o DWC, which uses agent attention without a depthwise convolution (DWC) module to evaluate whether the knowledge of commonalities and distinctiveness from the unpaired reference and target contrast can inject diversity features into the target image; w $\mathbf{B}_1$, which performs only Softmax attention calculation between the agent bias $\mathbf{B}_1$ and agent tokens A; w $\mathbf{B}_2$, which performs only Softmax attention calculation between the agent features $\mathbf{F}_{agg}$ and agent tokens A; w DWC, which only uses a depthwise convolution (DWC) module without agent attention. We conducted additional ablation studies by restoring and comparing the vanilla attention with our CMAT, referred to as w Cross-Vanilla Att.. The vanilla attention follows the traditional Query-Key-Value triplet, where the query vector is generated from target image features, and the key and value vectors are derived from the reference contrast data. Unlike our CMAT, vanilla attention does not use agent features to extract cross-subject shared information, relying instead on reference contrast data for feature fusion. The quantitative metrics for each variant model across three datasets at the $2\times$ enlargement scale and the $4\times$ enlargement scale are presented in Tables 3 and 4, respectively. The qualitative results are also presented in Fig. 6. It can be observed that all variant models perform worse than our AgentMRI. This indicates that removing these key components leads to a performance decline, thereby verifying their importance in AgentMRI. Specifically, w/o $\mathbf{B}_1$ has the lowest performance, supporting our initial hypothesis that even unpaired multi-contrast data have commonalities that can guide the SR of the target contrast. w/o $\mathbf{B}_2$ outperforms w/o $\mathbf{B}_1$ because the agent bias can better guide the reference contrast to adapt to the target image. Similarly, the performance of w/o

Table 5. Ablation study on different parameter settings under **uMR** with a $2\times$ enlargement scale. The best quantitative metrics results are marked in red.

Hyperparameter	SSIM↑	PSNR↑	NMSE↓
λ_{tar}=0.5, λ_{ref}=0.5	0.9861	42.2273	0.0037
λ_{tar}=0.3, λ_{ref}=0.7	0.9680	41.3301	0.0046
λ_{tar}=0.8, λ_{ref}=0.2	0.9681	41.8269	0.0040
λ_{tar}=0.2, λ_{ref}=0.8	0.9621	40.8509	0.0051
λ_{tar}=0.5, λ_{ref}=1	0.9836	42.2365	0.0037
λ_{tar}=1, λ_{ref}=0.5	0.9847	42.1555	0.0037
λ_{tar}=**0.7**, λ_{ref}=**0.3**	0.9904	42.2374	0.0037

DWC also shows a decline, as the depthwise convolution module helps to inject diversity features. Furthermore, the experimental results show that when only $\mathbf{B}_1$, $\mathbf{B}_2$, and DWC are used, the performance is inferior to that of the complete AgentMRI model. w Cross-Vanilla Att. underperforms compared to AgentMRI because the model fails to integrate cross-subject auxiliary contrast data into the target image without agent tokens, as evidenced by the lower PSNR and SSIM metrics, and the higher NMSE metric. In summary, AgentMRI outperforms other models, demonstrating its robust ability to maximize the use of commonalities in unpaired data.

Hyperparameter Analysis. We conducted a hyperparameter ablation analysis on the **uMR** dataset to evaluate the impact of different parameter settings for the weights λ_{tar} and λ_{ref}. As shown in Table 5, the results indicate that the trade-off between the values of λ_{tar} and λ_{ref} is important for optimal model performance. Specifically, when the weights are equal, the model shows the second-best performance. However, when the model relies too heavily on reference contrast, performance significantly declines, suggesting that reference data alone cannot adequately restore the fine details of the target image. Similarly, an overemphasis on target contrast does not result in performance improvements, demonstrating the indispensable role of unpaired reference contrast in providing task-specific information and supplementary details. The best performance was observed when the weights slightly favored the target contrast, indicating that prioritizing the target data helps enhance SR quality, while the unpaired reference data still provides beneficial features. Based on the results of the ablation study, we find that setting λ_{tar} to 0.7 and λ_{ref} to 0.3 yields the best performance.

5 Conclusion

In this work, we focus on exploring the commonalities and distinctiveness between unpaired MR images to enhance MRI with target contrast. For this purpose, we introduce agent-conditioned multi-contrast MRI SR with cross-subject adaptation, which can achieve SR of target images under the guidance of any HR reference contrast. Specifically, AgentMRI mines commonalities independent of the target contrast through a trained agent and then interacts with the target contrast to guide the model to focus on task-specific features. In the future, we will explore repurposing the abundant yet untapped medical image resources to further investigate the potential relationships between unpaired data.

Acknowledgments. This work was supported in part by the CCF-ZhiPu Large Model Fund Project (202212), in part by the Textile's Light Applied Basic Research Project (J202209), in part by The Hong Kong Polytechnic University (PolyU) under Grant P0042740, and in part by the PolyU Research Institute for Sports Science and Technology under Grant P0044571.

Disclosure of Interests. The authors have no competing interests to declare that are relevant to the content of this article.

References

1. Akçakaya, M., Moeller, S., Weingärtner, S., Uğurbil, K.: Scan-specific robust artificial-neural-networks for k-space interpolation (RAKI) reconstruction: database-free deep learning for fast imaging. Magn. Reson. Med. **81**(1), 439–453 (2019)
2. Bhinder, B., Gilvary, C., Madhukar, N.S., Elemento, O.: Artificial intelligence in cancer research and precision medicine. Cancer Discov. **11**(4), 900–915 (2021)
3. Chen, X., et al.: Hat: hybrid attention transformer for image restoration. arXiv preprint arXiv:2309.05239 (2023)
4. Dong, C., Loy, C.C., He, K., Tang, X.: Image super-resolution using deep convolutional networks. IEEE Trans. Pattern Anal. Mach. Intell. **38**(2), 295–307 (2015)
5. Dosovitskiy, A.: An image is worth 16x16 words: transformers for image recognition at scale. arXiv preprint arXiv:2010.11929 (2020)
6. Feng, C.-M., Fu, H., Yuan, S., Xu, Y.: Multi-contrast MRI super-resolution via a multi-stage integration network. In: de Bruijne, M., et al. (eds.) MICCAI 2021. LNCS, vol. 12906, pp. 140–149. Springer, Cham (2021). https://doi.org/10.1007/978-3-030-87231-1_14
7. Feng, C.M., Li, B., Xu, X., Liu, Y., Fu, H., Zuo, W.: Learning federated visual prompt in null space for MRI reconstruction. In: Proceedings of the IEEE/CVF Conference on Computer Vision and Pattern Recognition (CVPR), pp. 8064–8073 (2023)
8. Feng, C.M., et al.: Multimodal transformer for accelerated MR imaging. IEEE Trans. Med. Imaging **42**(10), 2804–2816 (2023)
9. Feng, C.-M., Yan, Y., Fu, H., Chen, L., Xu, Y.: Task transformer network for joint MRI reconstruction and super-resolution. In: de Bruijne, M., et al. (eds.) MICCAI 2021. LNCS, vol. 12906, pp. 307–317. Springer, Cham (2021). https://doi.org/10.1007/978-3-030-87231-1_30
10. Gentry, S.E., et al.: The impact of redistricting proposals on health care expenditures for liver transplant candidates and recipients. Am. J. Transplant. **16**(2), 583–593 (2016)
11. Glover, G.H.: Overview of functional magnetic resonance imaging. Neurosurgery Clin. **22**(2), 133–139 (2011)
12. Haldar, J.P., Hernando, D., Liang, Z.P.: Compressed-sensing MRI with random encoding. IEEE Trans. Med. Imaging **30**(4), 893–903 (2010)
13. Han, D., Pan, X., Han, Y., Song, S., Huang, G.: Flatten transformer: vision transformer using focused linear attention. In: Proceedings of the IEEE/CVF International Conference on Computer Vision (ICCV), pp. 5961–5971 (2023)
14. Han, D., Ye, T., Han, Y., Xia, Z., Song, S., Huang, G.: Agent attention: on the integration of softmax and linear attention. arXiv preprint arXiv:2312.08874 (2023)

15. Han, K., et al.: A survey on vision transformer. IEEE Trans. Pattern Anal. Mach. Intell. **45**(1), 87–110 (2022)
16. Hardie, R.: A fast image super-resolution algorithm using an adaptive wiener filter. IEEE Trans. Image Process. **16**(12), 2953–2964 (2007)
17. Hassani, A., Walton, S., Li, J., Li, S., Shi, H.: Neighborhood attention transformer. In: Proceedings of the IEEE/CVF Conference on Computer Vision and Pattern Recognition (CVPR), pp. 6185–6194 (2023)
18. Jiang, M., et al.: Fa-GAN: fused attentive generative adversarial networks for MRI image super-resolution. Comput. Med. Imaging Graph. **92**, 101969 (2021)
19. Jiang, Q., et al.: Understanding and constructing latent modality structures in multi-modal representation learning. In: Proceedings of the IEEE/CVF Conference on Computer Vision and Pattern Recognition (CVPR), pp. 7661–7671 (2023)
20. Jin, K.H., McCann, M.T., Froustey, E., Unser, M.: Deep convolutional neural network for inverse problems in imaging. IEEE Trans. Image Process. **26**(9), 4509–4522 (2017)
21. Katharopoulos, A., Vyas, A., Pappas, N., Fleuret, F.: Transformers are RNNs: fast autoregressive transformers with linear attention. In: International Conference on Machine Learning, pp. 5156–5165. PMLR (2020)
22. Kwon, G., Cai, Z., Ravichandran, A., Bas, E., Bhotika, R., Soatto, S.: Masked vision and language modeling for multi-modal representation learning. arXiv preprint arXiv:2208.02131 (2022)
23. Lei, P., Fang, F., Zhang, G., Zeng, T.: Decomposition-based variational network for multi-contrast MRI super-resolution and reconstruction. In: Proceedings of the IEEE/CVF International Conference on Computer Vision (ICCV), pp. 21296–21306 (2023)
24. Lewis, M.: Bart: Denoising sequence-to-sequence pre-training for natural language generation, translation, and comprehension. arXiv preprint arXiv:1910.13461 (2019)
25. Li, G., et al.: Transformer-empowered multi-scale contextual matching and aggregation for multi-contrast MRI super-resolution. In: Proceedings of the IEEE/CVF Conference on Computer Vision and Pattern Recognition (CVPR), pp. 20636–20645 (2022)
26. Li, G., Lv, J., Tong, X., Wang, C., Yang, G.: High-resolution pelvic MRI reconstruction using a generative adversarial network with attention and cyclic loss. IEEE Access **9**, 105951–105964 (2021)
27. Li, G., Lyu, J., Wang, C., Dou, Q., Qin, J.: Wavtrans: synergizing wavelet and cross-attention transformer for multi-contrast MRI super-resolution. In: International Conference on Medical Image Computing and Computer-Assisted Intervention, pp. 463–473. Springer (2022)
28. Li, G., Rao, C., Mo, J., Zhang, Z., Xing, W., Zhao, L.: Rethinking diffusion model for multi-contrast MRI super-resolution. In: Proceedings of the IEEE/CVF Conference on Computer Vision and Pattern Recognition (CVPR), pp. 11365–11374 (2024)
29. Liu, Y., et al.: Incomplete multi-modal representation learning for Alzheimer's disease diagnosis. Med. Image Anal. **69**, 101953 (2021)
30. Lyu, Q., et al.: Multi-contrast super-resolution MRI through a progressive network. IEEE Trans. Med. Imaging **39**(9), 2738–2749 (2020)
31. McGinnis, J., et al.: Single-subject multi-contrast MRI super-resolution via implicit neural representations. In: International Conference on Medical Image Computing and Computer-Assisted Intervention, pp. 173–183. Springer (2023)
32. Plenge, E., et al.: Super-resolution methods in MRI: can they improve the trade-off between resolution, signal-to-noise ratio, and acquisition time? Magn. Reson. Med. **68**(6), 1983–1993 (2012)
33. Qiu, D., Cheng, Y., Wang, X.: Gradual back-projection residual attention network for magnetic resonance image super-resolution. Comput. Methods Programs Biomed. **208**, 106252 (2021)

34. Qiu, D., Zhang, S., Liu, Y., Zhu, J., Zheng, L.: Super-resolution reconstruction of knee magnetic resonance imaging based on deep learning. Comput. Methods Programs Biomed. **187**, 105059 (2020)

35. Qu, X., Hou, Y., Lam, F., Guo, D., Zhong, J., Chen, Z.: Magnetic resonance image reconstruction from undersampled measurements using a patch-based nonlocal operator. Med. Image Anal. **18**(6), 843–856 (2014)

36. Ronneberger, O., Fischer, P., Brox, T.: U-Net: convolutional networks for biomedical image segmentation. In: Navab, N., Hornegger, J., Wells, W.M., Frangi, A.F. (eds.) MICCAI 2015. LNCS, vol. 9351, pp. 234–241. Springer, Cham (2015). https://doi.org/10.1007/978-3-319-24574-4_28

37. Salvetti, F., Mazzia, V., Khaliq, A., Chiaberge, M.: Multi-image super resolution of remotely sensed images using residual attention deep neural networks. Remote Sensing **12**(14), 2207 (2020)

38. Shen, Z., Zhang, M., Zhao, H., Yi, S., Li, H.: Efficient attention: attention with linear complexities. In: Proceedings of the IEEE/CVF Winter Conference on Applications of Computer Vision (WACV), pp. 3531–3539 (2021)

39. Tourbier, S., Bresson, X., Hagmann, P., Thiran, J.P., Meuli, R., Cuadra, M.B.: An efficient total variation algorithm for super-resolution in fetal brain MRI with adaptive regularization. Neuroimage **118**, 584–597 (2015)

40. Tsai, Y.H.H., Bai, S., Liang, P.P., Kolter, J.Z., Morency, L.P., Salakhutdinov, R.: Multimodal transformer for unaligned multimodal language sequences. In: Proceedings of the conference. Association for computational linguistics. Meeting. vol. 2019, p. 6558. NIH Public Access (2019)

41. Van Reeth, E., Tham, I.W., Tan, C.H., Poh, C.L.: Super-resolution in magnetic resonance imaging: a review. Concepts Magnetic Resonance Part A **40**(6), 306–325 (2012)

42. Wang, W., et al.: Pyramid vision transformer: a versatile backbone for dense prediction without convolutions. In: Proceedings of the IEEE/CVF International Conference on Computer Vision (ICCV), pp. 568–578 (2021)

43. Wang, X., Xie, L., Dong, C., Shan, Y.: Real-esrgan: training real-world blind super-resolution with pure synthetic data. In: Proceedings of the IEEE/CVF International Conference on Computer Vision (ICCV) Workshops, pp. 1905–1914 (2021)

44. Wang, Z., Cui, Z., Zhu, Y.: Multi-modal medical image fusion by Laplacian pyramid and adaptive sparse representation. Comput. Biol. Med. **123**, 103823 (2020)

45. Xia, Z., Pan, X., Song, S., Li, L.E., Huang, G.: Vision transformer with deformable attention. In: Proceedings of the IEEE/CVF Conference on Computer Vision and Pattern Recognition (CVPR), pp. 4794–4803 (2022)

46. Zbontar, J., et al.: FastMRI: an open dataset and benchmarks for accelerated MRI. arXiv preprint arXiv:1811.08839 (2018)

47. Zhang, C., Yang, Z., He, X., Deng, L.: Multimodal intelligence: representation learning, information fusion, and applications. IEEE J. Sel. Top. Signal Process. **14**(3), 478–493 (2020)

48. Zhang, Y., He, X., Chan, Y.H., Teng, Q., Rajapakse, J.C.: Multi-modal graph neural network for early diagnosis of Alzheimer's disease from SMRI and pet scans. Comput. Biol. Med. **164**, 107328 (2023)

49. Zhang, Y., Li, K., Li, K., Fu, Y.: MR image super-resolution with squeeze and excitation reasoning attention network. In: Proceedings of the IEEE/CVF Conference on Computer Vision and Pattern Recognition (CVPR), pp. 13425–13434 (2021)

50. Zhang, Y., Li, K., Li, K., Wang, L., Zhong, B., Fu, Y.: Image super-resolution using very deep residual channel attention networks. In: Proceedings of the European Conference on Computer Vision (ECCV) (2018)
51. Zhou, B., Zhou, S.K.: DudorNet: learning a dual-domain recurrent network for fast MRI reconstruction with deep t1 prior. In: Proceedings of the IEEE/CVF Conference on Computer Vision and Pattern Recognition (CVPR) (2020)

Vision Modeling in Complex Scenarios

SEA-Net: A Severity-Aware Network with Visual Prompt Tuning for Underwater Semantic Segmentation

Jiayong Zhu[1] and Tao Zhang[2]([✉])

[1] Jiangnan University, Wuxi, Jiangsu, China
6223112046@stu.jiangnan.edu.cn
[2] Central South University, Changsha, Hunan, China
taozhang@csu.edu.cn

Abstract. Underwater image semantic segmentation is widely used in the recognition and navigation of vision-guided underwater robots. However, due to issues such as insufficient underwater scene illumination and turbidity of the water, the contrast between targets and backgrounds is low. Existing underwater semantic segmentation methods ignore the recognition differences between underwater images, making it challenging for models to extract sufficiently robust visual features from noisy underwater images. To address this problem, we propose SEA-Net, which incorporates a SEA-Adapter and Visual Prompt Tuning. In the framework, we use a severity metric to address various complex noise problems in underwater images. The severity metric classifies all underwater images into High and Low-severity images and combines the Visual Prompt Tuning of two-branch alternating training, this allows the model to learn more robust visual features from different perspectives. On both the SUIM and DeepFish benchmarks, our proposed SEA-Net outperforms state-of-the-art methods in underwater image semantic segmentation tasks.

Keywords: Underwater semantic segmentation · visual prompt tuning · adapter

1 Introduction

Underwater semantic segmentation is closely related to industrial information and has wide applications in marine engineering, resource development, and ocean monitoring. Accurately identifying underwater objects and environments enhances operational efficiency, optimizes resource exploration and development processes, and improves environmental monitoring and protection in marine industries. This technology offers precise underwater scene understanding, providing crucial information to support decision-making and operations. More and more researchers are increasingly focusing on the field of underwater vision tasks [21], which includes underwater image target detection [50], underwater image enhancement [1], underwater image semantic segmentation [38]. Underwater image semantic segmentation provides powerful support for underwater

P. Didyk and J. Hou (Eds.): CVM 2025, LNCS 15663, pp. 331–348, 2025.
https://doi.org/10.1007/978-981-96-5809-1_18

robots to explore and exploit resources, and underwater image semantic segmentation models can provide the corresponding semantic information to better help underwater robots identify marine targets.

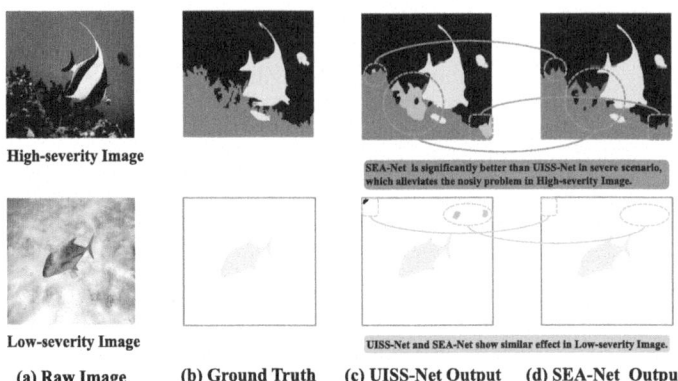

Fig. 1. Qualitative results of underwater image semantic segmentation on the SUIM benchmark. For High and Low-severity images, we show the corresponding ground-truth map and the results of UISS-Net and our proposed SEA-Net method. We highlight some improved predictions with white dashed circles. It is evident that the performance of UISS-Net and SEA-Net is similar when processing Low-severity images. However, when processing High-severity images, the SEA-Net outperforms UISS-Net.

However, the quality of underwater images is often unstable due to light absorption and scattering in the water, resulting in an overall blue-green color tone in underwater images. Decreased image quality leads to low contrast between targets and backgrounds, color deviations, blurry edges, and details of objects, as well as uneven brightness [35], which restricts the application of underwater robots in real scenes.

Existing underwater image semantic segmentation methods, such as those proposed by Islam et al. [19], Liu et al. [29], and He et al. [16] ignore the difference in recognition difficulty between various underwater images, resulting in models struggle to extract sufficiently robust visual features from underwater images with noises such as low-lighting complexity and lack of generalization to images in the presence of other underwater noises. Inspired by Gong et al. [12,13,23], we propose SEA-Net to address this problem, which consists of a SEA-Adapter and Visual Prompt Tuning. In the framework of SEA-Net, we provide a novel solution for the underwater image semantic segmentation task, e.g.we use the severity metric to unify the various complex noise problems of underwater images and direct the model to focus on the severity of the image recognition difficulty. The severity metric classifies all underwater images into High and Low-severity images and combines Visual Prompt Tuning with two-branch alternating training, which enables the model to learn more robust visual features from different perspectives. Visual Prompt Tuning, a learnable component within the SEA-Net, activates visual prompts to enhance High and Low-severity images. This mechanism ensures the two branches progressively highlight different severity levels, directing the model's focus toward the severity rather than specific underwater noises of the image. As shown in Fig. 1, the SEA-Net outperforms UISS-Net when processing High-severity images. We also design a SEA-Adapter specifically for underwater scenarios, which consists of a Down-Projection, a ReLU Activation Function, an Up-Projection, a 3×3 Convolution, and a Residual Connection sequentially to optimize the low-level features.

Our contributions are summarized as follows:

- We provide a new perspective on underwater image semantic segmentation tasks by proposing a novel Severity-Aware Network called SEA-Net. The framework employs a severity metric to unify the High-severity and Low-severity images and guides the model to focus on the severity of the recognition difficulty of the underwater images.
- SEA-Net consists of a SEA-Adapter and Visual Prompt Tuning. The SEA-Adapter is designed to be more compatible for underwater scenarios, where both the visual prompts and the SEA-Adapter can automatically update during training, without the need to adjust these hyperparameters manually.
- SEA-Net achieves a 3.8% higher mean Intersection over Union (mIoU) compared to the state-of-the-art on the SUIM benchmark for underwater semantic segmentation, with an improvement of 1.1% mIoU in paper. This demonstrates the effectiveness of the proposed method in learning robust features from noisy underwater images, aiding underwater robots in better recognizing marine life.

2   Related Work

2.1   Underwater Image Semantic Segmentation

In recent years, semantic segmentation models based on deep learning methods have made great progress, such as FCN [28], VGG [37], and ResNet [16]. He et al. propose ResNet, which extracts features hierarchically and upsamples the low-dimensional features through a decoder network to generate the final semantic labels. Ronneberger et al. [34] propose U-Net architecture, which significantly improves performance by reusing the output of each encoder layer. Badrinarayanan et al. [2] use the pixel indexes in the encoder that performs maxpool for unpooling, thus eliminating the need for upsampling. Chen et al. [4] propose DeepLabv1, which uses atrous convolution to keep the receptive field consistent based on VGG. Chen et al. [5] introduce ASPP to add multi-scale training and larger receptive fields. Chen et al. [6] improve ASPP and propose both cascade and parallel architectures.

All of the above methods have achieved better results on natural images. However, the quality of underwater images is highly unstable, primarily due to light absorption by water. Therefore, directly transferring the aforementioned semantic segmentation methods to underwater images would be ineffective [41].

In recent years, researchers are committed to presenting underwater segmentation datasets and processing underwater images, Lian et al. [26] have proposed the first underwater image instance segmentation dataset UIIS to facilitate the training and evaluation of underwater instance segmentation models, which provides an in-depth discussion of instance segmentation of underwater scenes. Islam et al. [19] propose the first large-scale semantic segmentation dataset for underwater images, which provides a new benchmark for future research on semantic segmentation of underwater images. Wang et al. [39] use image enhancement based on multi-space transform to improve the quality of the original image. Liu et al. [29] introduce an unsupervised color correction method (UCM) module into the encoder structure of the framework to improve the quality of the images. He et al. [17] use a lightweight network to assist the backbone model and enhance the robustness of the model to better adapt to the images of the underwater scene. SAM, which is the vision foundation model, has achieved excellent results in many application scenarios such as Zhang et al. [47], Li et al. [24], Zhang et al. [48]. Very recently, Xu et al. [42] apply SAM to the underwater foreground segmentation task, achieving better performance on underwater foreground segmentation. O'Byrne et al. [32] propose to use realistic synthetic images to train models.

2.2   Visual Prompt Tuning

Prompt-based learning [20] is initially proposed in Natural Language Processing (NLP), it involves only a few parameters in the input space to fine-tune large pre-trained models for downstream tasks. Subsequently, prompt tuning has tended to be investigated in the field of computer vision (CV). Many approaches [22, 33,43,51] conduct some attempts to prompt visual language models (VLMs) in the form of text, and Jia et al. [20] first introduce the concept of "visual prompt" as a learnable vector. Bahng et al. [3] treat prompts as continuous task-specific vectors and individual image perturbations (e.g. soft prompts) are learned by backpropagation with frozen model parameters to demonstrate that prompts are feasible in the CV domain. Gong et al. [12,13,23] propose to classify images into High and Low-severity images in the unsupervised domain adaptation semantic segmentation task (UDASS), instructing the model to learn domain-invariant features, but ignoring scene-specific features.

2.3   Adapter

The concept of Adapter is first introduced in NLP [18], which acts as a compact and scalable module for fine-tuning large pre-trained models to each downstream task [7]. In the field of computer vision, Adapters have been recently used in the vision foundation model and vision-language foundation model, such as Li et al. [25] suggest fine-tuning ViT [11] for target detection with minimal modifications. Zhang et al. [46] propose Tip-Adapter, which trains Adapters without any backpropagation, instead of creating weights through a key-value caching model constructed from a small number of training sets, through this non-parametric approach, performance-optimized adapter weights can be obtained without any training. Chen et al. [8] propose ViT-Adapter, which utilizes adapters to enable ordinary ViTs to perform a variety of downstream tasks. Chen et al. [7] propose SAM-Adapter, which is the first method to apply Adapters to the pretrained segmentation foundation model SAM for camouflage target detection and shadow detection. In this work, we propose the SEA-Adapter based on a vanilla adapter [18], which is designed to adapt to underwater scenes and optimize low-level features.

3 Method

3.1 Architecture

Inspired by U-Net, the overall architecture of our SEA-Net adopts a U-shape structure, using ResNet50 [16] as the backbone, we also follow [17], which uses an auxiliary network [15] for feature extraction in the encoder part to extract richer semantic information. The SEA-Net mainly consists of a SEA-Adapter and Visual Prompt Tuning. Severity-Aware Network uses a severity metric to unify various complex noise problems of underwater images, then all underwater images will be classified into High-severity and Low-severity images based on the severity metric. Visual Prompt Tuning is a learnable component based on the Severity-Aware Network. When the Severity-Aware Network determines the image as a High-severity image, the visual prompts are activated and added to the High-severity images to enhance the High-severity images. Similarly, when

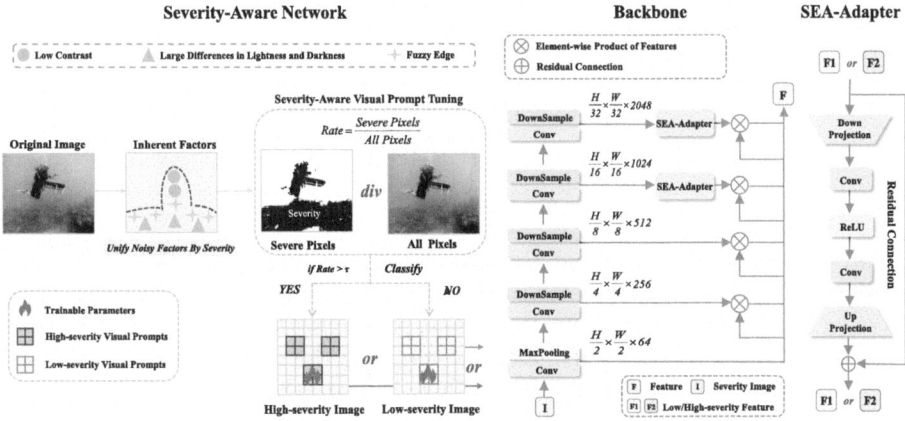

Fig. 2. Overview of our proposed SEA-Net framework. It consists of three parts: Visual Prompt Tuning, Backbone, and SEA-Adapter. Blue arrows indicate the flow for data pre-processing, green arrows indicate the flow for Low-severity images, red arrows represent the flow for High-severity images, and gray arrows represent the flow for forward propagation. Given original images, we first pass them through severity metric and Visual Prompt Tuning to obtain High and Low-severity images, then we pass them to Backbone to obtain the final features. (Color figure online)

the Severity-Aware Network determines the image as a Low-severity image, the visual prompts are activated and added to the Low-severity images to enhance the Low-severity images. By training the dual branches alternately in this way, the model learns more robust visual features from different perspectives. SEA-Adapter, which absorbs prompt information from the visual prompts and optimizes the model's low-level features. The overall structure of SEA-Net is shown in Fig. 2.

3.2   Severity-Aware Network

Severity-Aware Network is primarily designed to classify input images into High-severity and Low-severity images with a severity metric. Visual Prompt Tuning is a learnable component, which is built on top of the Severity-Aware Network to enhance the High and Low-severity images by adding visual prompts.

Severity Metric. Severity-Aware Network utilizes a severity metric to address various noise issues in underwater images, treating all noisy pixels in underwater images as severity pixels. Firstly, the input image $\boldsymbol{X} \in \mathbb{R}^{H \times W \times C}$ is converted to a grayscale image $\boldsymbol{X}_g \in \mathbb{R}^{H \times W}$, where H, W, and C denote the height, width, and number of channels of the image respectively. Then, the noisy pixels in the grayscale image with grayscale values lower than the grayscale threshold α are considered as High-severity pixels. As grayscale values between 0 and 50, the image is very dark and details may be difficult to discern, we set the grayscale threshold α to 40. We then calculate the ratio of High-severity pixels in all pixels of the original image. If this ratio is higher than the severity threshold τ, the image is classified as a High-severity image. Otherwise, it is classified as a Low-severity image. As is shown in Fig. 3(b), the darker regions in the image represent High-severity pixels, while the brighter regions represent Low-severity pixels.

$$\text{severity metric} = \begin{cases} \text{High, if } \frac{X_g < \alpha}{H \times W} > \tau \\ \text{Low, else} \end{cases} \tag{1}$$

Visual Prompt. We represent the visual prompts as $VPT \in \mathbb{R}^{H_{vpt} \times W_{vpt} \times C}$, the number of visual prompts for each image is 3, $H_{vpt} = W_{vpt} = 64$. To avoid excessive masking the image by the visual prompts, the three visual prompts are added at the top two corners and the center of the image respectively. As is shown in Fig. 3(c), the equations for adding the visual prompts to an image are as follows:

$$X^H = X^h + 3 \cdot VPT^h \tag{2}$$

$$X^L = X^l + 3 \cdot VPT^l \tag{3}$$

$$\hat{X} = X^H \cup X^L \tag{4}$$

where X^h, X^l denotes a High-severity image and a Low-severity image respectively. VPT^h, VPT^l denotes a High-severity visual prompt and a Low-severity

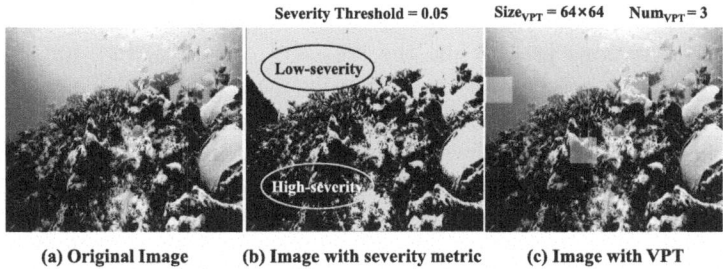

Severity Threshold = 0.05   Size$_{VPT}$ = 64×64   Num$_{VPT}$ = 3

Low-severity

High-severity

(a) Original Image   (b) Image with severity metric   (c) Image with VPT

Fig. 3. Visualizations of High and Low-severity pixels and visual prompts on a single image from the SUIM dataset. We set the severity threshold to 0.05 and set the size of visual prompts to 64, and the number of visual prompts to 3.

visual prompt respectively. X^H, X^L denotes the High-severity images and Low-severity images after adding the visual prompts, respectively. $\hat{X}$ denotes the enhanced images.

3.3 SEA-Adapter

We design a SEA-Adapter for underwater scenarios, which is based on the vanilla adapter. It consists of Down-projection, RELU Activation Function, Up-projection, 3×3 Convolution, and a Residual Connection.

This SEA-Adapter optimizes the low-level features F_1, F_2 among the five features $[F_1, F_2, F_3, F_4, F_5]$ output from Backbone. In this process, the SEA-Adapter aims to leverage beneficial prompts from visual prompts to better optimize the latent features of the model. The pipeline equation of SEA-Adapter is as follows:

$$F_1^{\hat{H}/L} = F_1^{H/L} + \text{Adapter}\left(F_1^{H/L}\right) \tag{5}$$

$$F_2^{\hat{H}/L} = F_2^{H/L} + \text{Adapter}\left(F_2^{H/L}\right) \tag{6}$$

where $F_1^{\hat{H}/L}, F_2^{\hat{H}/L}$ represent the feature maps for High and Low-severity features respectively.

3.4 Overall Training Flow

The whole training flow is shown in Fig 2. The Severity-Aware Network classifies input images into High-severity images and Low-severity images based on a severity metric. Visual prompts are explicitly added to both types of images to generate enhanced High and Low-severity images. These images are then fed into a Backbone Network to obtain five features at different levels. The SEA-Adapter is used to further optimize two of the lower-level features. Finally, the features from all five layers are upsampled, multiplied, and concatenated to form the final feature map. The entire training process is supervised by the loss function L_{final} . SEA-Net utilizes both the binary cross-entropy loss [27] and the dice loss functions [31]. While the cross-entropy (CE) loss function excels in multi-classification scenarios by effectively measuring the disparity between model predictions and actual labels, it also promotes faster convergence and enhanced performance. Nonetheless, it demands strong model stability and can be sensitive to uneven sample distributions. On the other hand, the dice loss function is skilled at handling significant imbalances in sample classes, prioritizing foreground region extraction during training. To address dataset irregularities and expedite model convergence, we combine both loss functions. The loss function is concerned with both the model's accurate prediction of segmentation boundaries (Dice Loss) and the model's accurate classification of foreground and background (BCE). The equations for the cross-entropy loss function and dice edge segmentation loss function are as follows:

$$L_{BCE} = -\sum_{i=0}^{N} y_i ln\left(p\left(x_i\right)\right) \tag{7}$$

$$\text{Dice coefficent} = \frac{2TP}{2TP + FP + FN} \tag{8}$$

$$L_{\text{Dice loss}} = 1 - \text{Dice coefficent} \tag{9}$$

where N is the number of samples, y_i is the label of the sample, and $p\left(x_i\right)$ is the foreground probability of predicting the sample x_i.

$$L_1 = L_{BCE}(GT, \text{predict}\left(x\right)) \tag{10}$$

Table 1. Comparison between SEA-Net and current mainstream models on the SUIM benchmark. We present the per-class and mean IoU (mIoU). We highlight the best and second-best results in each column in bold and italics, respectively

Model	IoU (%)								mIoU (%)
	BW	HD	PF	WR	RO	RI	FV	SR	
U-Net [34]	79.46	32.25	21.85	33.94	23.65	50.28	38.16	42.16	39.85
U-Net (ResNet)	**90.14**	72.53	2.37	62.65	59.19	69.93	73.13	**69.31**	62.41
U-Net (VGG)	90.03	79.81	4.25	62.23	51.43	*71.23*	74.11	68.27	62.73
SegNet [2]	80.63	45.67	17.45	32.24	55.72	47.62	43.92	51.51	46.85
SUIM-Net [19]	80.64	63.45	23.27	41.25	60.89	53.12	46.02	57.12	53.22
PSPNet [49]	82.51	65.04	28.54	46.56	62.88	55.8	46.78	55.98	55.51
DeepLab [4]	81.82	50.26	17.05	43.33	63.6	57.18	43.56	55.35	51.52
LEDNet [40]	82.96	58.47	18.02	42.86	50.96	58.13	46.13	54.99	51.36
BiseNetv2 [44]	83.67	59.29	18.27	39.58	56.54	58.16	47.33	56.93	52.47
UISS-Net [17]	87.18	**87.03**	*29.48*	**71.27**	**84.11**	70.7	**79.44**	67.54	*72.09*
UISS-Net (test)	89.11	80.88	24.37	68.54	79.22	69.78	76.95	65.96	69.35 (+0.00)
SEA-Net (ours)	*89.75*	*84.69*	**38.45**	*71.11*	*80.49*	**72.68**	79.11	*68.92*	**73.15** (+3.80)

$$L_2 = L_{\text{Dice loss}} \ (GT_{\text{seg}} \ , \text{predict} \ (x_{\text{seg}} \ )) \tag{11}$$

Where L_1 is the main network loss function, GT is the exact semantic labels, predict(x) is the obtained segmentation result, L_{BCE} is the computation process of cross-entropy loss. L_2 is the edge loss, GT_{seg} is the edge label obtained from the real semantic label of the real semantic label, predict (x_{seg}) is extracted from the edge extracted from the segmentation result, $L_{\text{Dice loss}}$ is the calculation process of the dice loss. The loss function of SEA-Net is as follows:

$$L_{\text{final}} \ = L_1 + L_2 \tag{12}$$

4   Experiments

4.1   Datasets and Training Setup

SUIM proposed by Islam et al. [19] is a large-scale dataset for underwater image semantic segmentation benchmark. It contains annotations for eight object classes, including Fish and Vertebrates (FV), Coral Reefs and Invertebrates (RI), Aquatic Plants and Sea-grasses (PF), Wrecks or Ruins (WR), Human Divers (HD), Robots (RO), Sea-floor and Rocks (SR), and Background (Waterbody) (BW). 1525 RGB images are used for training and validation, while 110 images are used for benchmark evaluation of the model. The images in SUIM have different resolutions including $1906 \times 1080, 1280 \times 720, 640 \times 480, 256 \times 256$. DeepFish proposed by Saleh et al. [36] consists of approximately 40,000 underwater images collected from 20 Australian tropical marine environment habitats. The dataset initially contained only classification labels, and 300 fish semantic segmentation labels were added later. In this paper, the training and test sets are divided according to the ratio of 9:1. The images in both datasets are preprocessed and resized to 512×512. The proposed method is trained for 100 epochs on NVIDIA RTX 3090 GPU with Pytorch version 1.13.0. In addition, we follow the UISS-Net [17], with the initial learning rate set to 0.0004, weight decay set to 0.0001, and momentum set to 0.5.

4.2   Evaluation Criteria

In order to thoroughly assess the model's performance, we have chosen mean Intersection over Union (mIoU), mean Pixel Accuracy (mPA), and Precision (Accuracy) as the evaluation metrics. mIoU is the average of the ratio between the intersection and union of predicted results and ground truth for all classes. mPA is the average ratio of correctly classified pixels for each class. Accuracy is the ratio of pixels that are correctly classified into their respective categories out of the total number of pixels, assuming that $P_i, (i \in N)$ is the accuracy for each class at pixel i, mIoU, mPA, and Accuracy are defined as:

$$mIoU = \frac{1}{N} \times \sum \left(\frac{TP}{TP + FP + FN} \right) \tag{13}$$

$$Accuracy = \frac{TP + TN}{FP + TP + FN + TN} \qquad (14)$$

$$mPA = \frac{1}{N} \times \sum (P_i) \qquad (15)$$

where N denotes the number of categories, TP denotes the number of pixels correctly predicted by the model as positive samples, FP denotes the number of pixels that the model correctly predicts as positive samples, TN denotes the number of pixels that the model correctly predicts as negative samples, and FN the number of pixels that the model incorrectly predicts as negative samples.

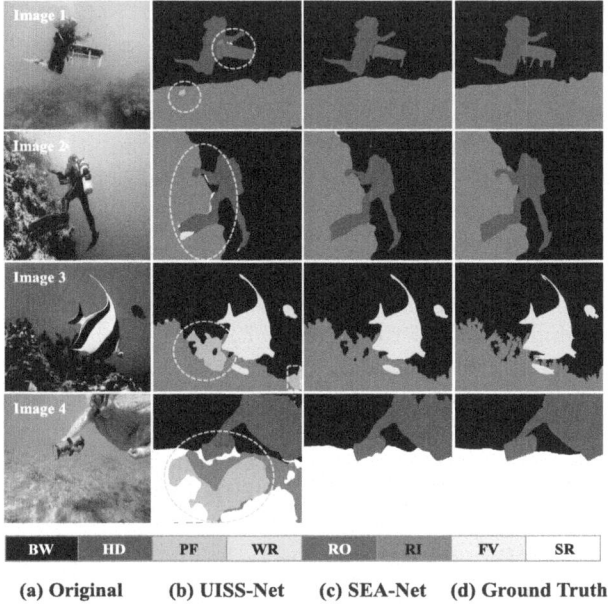

(a) Original   (b) UISS-Net   (c) SEA-Net   (d) Ground Truth

Fig. 4. Quantitative experiments between UISS-Net and SEA-Net on the SUIM dataset. For each target image, we show the corresponding ground truth map and the results of UISS-Net and our proposed SEA-Net. We highlight some improved predictions with blue dashed circles. (Color figure online)

4.3   State-of-the-Art Performance Comparison

Table 1 and Table 2 summarize the performance of our method SEA-Net compared with state-of-the-art methods on the SUIM and DeepFish benchmark respectively. Table 1 shows that our proposed SEA-Net method performs much better on average than all state-of-the-art methods on the SUIM benchmark. This advantage is derived from improvements over several classes such as aquatic plants and seaweed (PF), coral reefs, and invertebrates (RI), we achieved the best or second-best performances for all classes. We also present visual comparisons of the proposed SEA-Net with UISS-Net on the SUIM dataset in Fig. 4. Table 2 shows that our proposed SEA-Net method performs much better on average than all state-of-the-art methods on the DeepFish dataset and Fig. 5 presents visual comparisons of the proposed SEA-Net with UISS-Net on the DeepFish dataset. It is evident that, compared with the other methods, our method can not only provide sharper edges of classes in Low-severity images, such as aquatic plants and seaweed, but also improve the detection of classes in High-severity images, such as signs and lights. This demonstrates the effectiveness of the proposed SEA-Net on underwater images.

Table 2. Comparison between SEA-Net and current mainstream models on the Deep-Fish benchmark. We present the per-class and mean IoU (mIoU). We highlight the best and second-best results in each column in bold and italics, respectively

Model	IoU (%)		mIoU (%)
	Background	Foreground	
SUIM-Net [19]	99.03	78.4	88.71
SegNet [2]	98.89	68.94	83.91
PSPNet [49]	99.11	71.35	85.23
FCN [28]	99.15	72.61	85.88
DeepLabv3 [6]	99.21	66.3	82.75
HANet [10]	99.25	81.37	90.31
DGCNet [45]	99.21	81.42	90.32
MFAS-Net [14]	99.15	84.86	92.01
DPANet [9]	99.31	82.56	85.88
UISS-Net [17]	*99.55*	*90.55*	*95.05*
UISS-Net (test)	99.49	89.03	94.26 (+0.00)
SEA-Net (ours)	**99.57**	**90.73**	**95.15 (+0.89)**

4.4   Ablation Study Analysis

Ablation Study on Different Components. To better understand the impact of each component of our SEA-Net, we conducted an ablation study by selectively deactivating each component and measuring the effect on the performance of the underwater semantic segmentation task. Specifically, we defined five nested subset models:

(1) VPT: Using the basic architecture from U-Net with visual prompts in Sect. 3.2 and BCE loss (Eq. (10) and Dice loss (Eq. (11)). We set the number of visual prompts to 3 without severity metric and severity threshold to 0.05.
(2) SM: We set the number of visual prompts to 3 with the severity metric and severity threshold to 0.05.

(3) SEA-Adapter: Using the basic architecture from U-Net with SEA-Adapter in Sect. 3.3.
(4) VPT+SEA-Adapter: Further adding the SEA-Adapter based on VPT.
(5) SM+SEA-Adapter: Further adding the SEA-Adapter based on SM.

The results are presented in Table 3 showing that our overall SEA-Net resulted in a performance gain of 3.8% over the basic architecture in mIoU. The VPT (Visual Prompt Tuning) alone is responsible for a 0.87% improvement, the SM (Visual Prompt Tuning with severity metric produces an additional 1.23% improvement, and the SEA-Adapter provides a 1.52% improvement. This verifies the importance of the Visual Prompt Tuning, severity metric, and SEA-Adapter components of our SEA-Net.

Table 3. Ablation study of SEA-Net components on the SUIM Dataset. VPT means SEA-Net without the severity metric. SM means SEA-Net with the severity metric. We highlight the best and second-best results in each column in bold and italics, respectively

Input Size	VPT	SM	SEA-Adapter	mIoU (%)	mPA (%)	Accuracy (%)
512 × 512				69.35 (+0.00)	78.26	86.98
512 × 512	✓			70.22 (+0.87)	78.95	87.20
512 × 512		✓	✓	*71.77* (+2.42)	*80.34*	*88.23*
512 × 512		✓		70.87 (+1.52)	79.62	87.23
512 × 512	✓			71.45 (+2.10)	79.90	87.56
512 × 512		✓	✓	**73.15** (+3.80)	**81.52**	**88.01**

Ablation Study of Visual Prompt Tuning. The size, number, and position of the visual prompts may impact the learning process. To verify this, we set different sizes of visual prompts during training, such as 8×8, 16×16, 32×32, and 64×64. As shown in Table 4, the performance of visual prompts with the size of 64×64 is better than the other sizes of visual prompts, which achieves 71.45% mIoU. However, the performance of visual prompts with the size 8×8 and 16×16 are relatively lower compared to the others. The reason for this could be smaller mask areas constrain the model's representational capacity for specific tasks, preventing it from adequately capturing the features of the images, which causes models to learn worse.

Meanwhile, we also set different numbers of visual prompts such as 1, 3, 4, 5. As shown in Fig. 6(b), the performance of visual prompts with the number 5 is better than other numbers of visual prompts, which achieves 72.13% mIoU. However, the performance of visual prompts with the number 1 is relatively lower compared to the others. The reason for this could be few mask blocks introduce more diverse conditions, which causes models to learn worse.

UISS-Net crops images by placing gray bars on the input image to prevent distortion. However, if visual prompts are placed on the gray bars, the model might

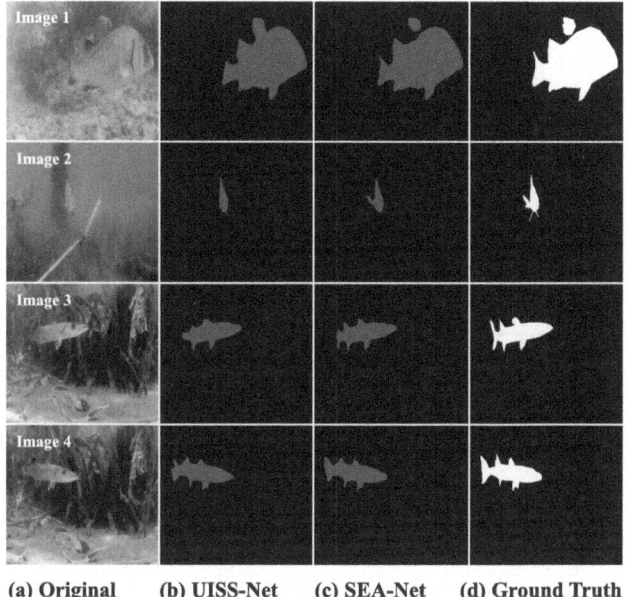

(a) Original   (b) UISS-Net   (c) SEA-Net   (d) Ground Truth

Fig. 5. Quantitative experiments between UISS-Net and SEA-Net on the DeepFish dataset. For each target image, we show the corresponding ground truth map and the results of UISS-Net and our proposed SEA-Net.

learn unrelated features. Therefore, we have also examined how the position of the visual prompts affects performance. Based on the three visual prompts, we arranged them with different starting positions. The first set has center positions at 200 and corner positions at 320. The second set is centered at 200, with corner positions at 400. The third set has a center position of 200 and corner positions at 448. The fourth set has a center position of 200 and corner positions at 496. As shown in Table 5, the visual prompts with center positions at 200, and two corner positions at 400 perform better than the visual prompts with other positions, which achieves 71.05% mIoU.

Table 4. Sensitivity analysis of Visual Prompt Size on the SUIM dataset. We highlight the best results in each column in bold

Visual Prompt Size	8×8	16×16	32×32	64×64
mIoU	69.30	68.53	70.10	**71.45**
mPA	78.40	77.85	79.13	**79.90**
Accuracy	86.28	84.45	87.17	**87.56**

Ablation Study of Severity Threshold. We apply the severity threshold in our method: τ. The setting of the severity threshold also has an effect on

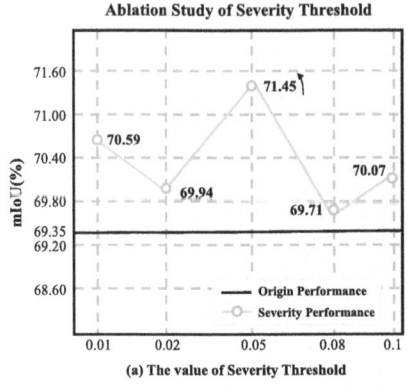
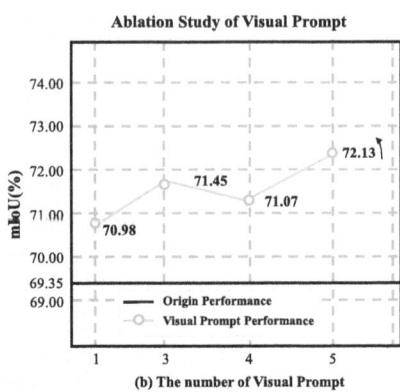

Fig. 6. Ablation study of the severity threshold and visual prompt on the SUIM dataset by line graph visualization. The results show that the selection of severity threshold and visual prompt can significantly impact the performance of the model.

Table 5. Sensitivity analysis of Visual Prompt Position on the SUIM dataset. We highlight the best results in each column in bold

Visual Prompt Position	320	400	448
mIoU	**71.45**	71.12	70.31
mPA	**79.90**	79.84	79.37
Accuracy	**87.56**	87.05	86.97

the model's performance as well. In order to verify this, we set different severity thresholds during training, such as 0.01, 0.02, 0.05, 0.08, 0.1. As shown in Fig. 6(a), the model performs best at $\tau = 0.05$, which achieves 71.45% mIoU.

Ablation Study of SEA-Adapter. We apply the SEA-Adapter in our method. The position of the SEA-Adapter also have an effect on the model's performance as well. In order to verify this, we set different positions of SEA-Adapter by adding SEA-Adapter after each of the five features $[F_1, F_2, F_3, F_4, F_5]$ output from Backbone. As shown in Table 6, the model performs best when adding SEA-Adapter after F_1, F_2, which achieves 71.77% mIoU.

4.5   Limitations and Future Work

As illustrated by the previous experimental results (Figs. 4 and 5), the proposed SEA-Net performs well in most situations. However, it still has some limitations, for example, it may fail to detect some underwater fish clusters with very

Table 6. Sensitivity analysis of SEA-Adapter Position on the SUIM dataset. We highlight the best results in each column in bold

SEA-Adapter Position	mIoU	mPA	Accuracy
$[F_1]$	70.87	79.62	87.23
$[F_2]$	70.62	79.20	88.15
$[\mathbf{F_1, F_2}]$	**71.77**	**80.34**	**88.23**
$[F_1, F_2, F_3]$	70.01	78.89	85.99
$[F_1, F_2, F_3, F_4]$	66.15	75.50	84.71
$[F_1, F_2, F_3, F_4, F_5]$	69.10	77.50	86.11

small sizes. Therefore, in future work, we will investigate how to improve the performance by training our model with the help of boundary detection. For example, boundary detection [30] can be helpful for learning a clearer contour for each object. Despite this, differences in biological species and water quality in various marine regions can cause models to perform differently. As a result, future efforts may involve creating specific datasets for different sea areas and utilizing unsupervised domain adaptation techniques for semantic segmentation to enhance the model's generalization across diverse underwater environments.

5   Conclusions

In this paper, we propose a new approach that uses a severity metric to unify various complex noise problems in underwater images. The proposed SEA-Net consists of a SEA-Adapter and Visual Prompt Tuning. The Severity-Aware Network addresses all the noise problems in underwater images through a severity metric, and Visual Prompt Tuning is a learnable component built on the Severity-Aware Network. This approach achieves state-of-the-art performance on both underwater semantic segmentation datasets SUIM and DeepFish, offering new insights for future research. Nonetheless, variations in biological species and water quality across different marine regions may lead to divergent model performance. Thus, future endeavors may entail the creation of specialized datasets for distinct sea areas and the application of unsupervised domain adaptive semantic segmentation methods to enhance model generalization across diverse underwater environments.

References

1. Anwar, S., Li, C.: Diving deeper into underwater image enhancement: a survey. Sig. Process. Image Commun. **89**, 115978 (2020)
2. Badrinarayanan, V., Kendall, A., Cipolla, R.: SegNet: a deep convolutional encoder-decoder architecture for image segmentation. IEEE Trans. Pattern Anal. Mach. Intell. **39**(12), 2481–2495 (2017)

3. Bahng, H., Jahanian, A., Sankaranarayanan, S., Isola, P.: Exploring visual prompts for adapting large-scale models. arXiv preprint arXiv:2203.17274 (2022)

4. Chen, L.C., Papandreou, G., Kokkinos, I., Murphy, K., Yuille, A.L.: Semantic image segmentation with deep convolutional nets and fully connected CRFs. arXiv preprint arXiv:1412.7062 (2014)

5. Chen, L.C., Papandreou, G., Kokkinos, I., Murphy, K., Yuille, A.L.: DeepLab: semantic image segmentation with deep convolutional nets, atrous convolution, and fully connected CRFs. IEEE Trans. Pattern Anal. Mach. Intell. **40**(4), 834–848 (2017)

6. Chen, L.C., Papandreou, G., Schroff, F., Adam, H.: Rethinking atrous convolution for semantic image segmentation. arXiv preprint arXiv:1706.05587 (2017)

7. Chen, T., et al.: SAM fails to segment anything?–SAM-adapter: adapting SAM in underperformed scenes: camouflage, shadow, and more. arXiv preprint arXiv:2304.09148, **1**(2) 5 (2023)

8. Chen, Z., et al.: Vision transformer adapter for dense predictions. arXiv preprint arXiv:2205.08534 (2022)

9. Chen, Z., Cong, R., Xu, Q., Huang, Q.: DPANet: depth potentiality-aware gated attention network for RGB-D salient object detection. IEEE Trans. Image Process. **30**, 7012–7024 (2020)

10. Choi, S., Kim, J.T., Choo, J.: Cars can't fly up in the sky: improving urban-scene segmentation via height-driven attention networks. In: Proceedings of the IEEE/CVF Conference on Computer Vision and Pattern Recognition, pp. 9373–9383 (2020)

11. Dosovitskiy, A.: An image is worth 16x16 words: transformers for image recognition at scale. arXiv preprint arXiv:2010.11929 (2020)

12. Gong, Z., Li, F., Deng, Y., Bhattacharjee, D., Zhu, X., Ji, Z.: CoDA: instructive chain-of-domain adaptation with severity-aware visual prompt tuning. arXiv preprint arXiv:2403.17369 (2024)

13. Gong, Z., et al.: Train one, generalize to all: generalizable semantic segmentation from single-scene to all adverse scenes. In: Proceedings of the 31st ACM International Conference on Multimedia, pp. 2275–2284 (2023)

14. Haider, A., Arsalan, M., Choi, J., Sultan, H., Park, K.R.: Robust segmentation of underwater fish based on multi-level feature accumulation. Front. Mar. Sci. **9**, 1010565 (2022)

15. Han, K., Wang, Y., Tian, Q., Guo, J., Xu, C., Xu, C.: GhostNet: more features from cheap operations. In: Proceedings of the IEEE/CVF Conference on Computer Vision and Pattern Recognition, pp. 1580–1589 (2020)

16. He, K., Zhang, X., Ren, S., Sun, J.: Deep residual learning for image recognition. In: Proceedings of the IEEE Conference on Computer Vision and Pattern Recognition, pp. 770–778 (2016)

17. He, Z., et al.: UISS-Net: underwater image semantic segmentation network for improving boundary segmentation accuracy of underwater images. Aquac. Int. **32**, 5625–5638 (2024)

18. Houlsby, N., et al.: Parameter-efficient transfer learning for NLP. In: International Conference on Machine Learning, pp. 2790–2799. PMLR (2019)

19. Islam, M.J., et al.: Semantic segmentation of underwater imagery: dataset and benchmark. In: 2020 IEEE/RSJ International Conference on Intelligent Robots and Systems (IROS), pp. 1769–1776. IEEE (2020)

20. Jia, M., et al.: Visual prompt tuning. In: European Conference on Computer Vision, pp. 709–727. Springer (2022)

21. Jian, M., Liu, X., Luo, H., Lu, X., Yu, H., Dong, J.: Underwater image processing and analysis: a review. Sig. Process. Image Commun. **91**, 116088 (2021)
22. Ju, C., Han, T., Zheng, K., Zhang, Y., Xie, W.: Prompting visual-language models for efficient video understanding. In: European Conference on Computer Vision, pp. 105–124. Springer (2022)
23. Li, F., et al.: Parsing all adverse scenes: severity-aware semantic segmentation with mask-enhanced cross-domain consistency. In: Proceedings of the AAAI Conference on Artificial Intelligence, vol. 38, pp. 13483–13491 (2024)
24. Li, S., Cao, J., Ye, P., Ding, Y., Tu, C., Chen, T.: ClipSAM: CLIP and SAM collaboration for zero-shot anomaly segmentation. arXiv preprint arXiv:2401.12665 (2024)
25. Li, Y., Mao, H., Girshick, R., He, K.: Exploring plain vision transformer backbones for object detection. In: European Conference on Computer Vision, pp. 280–296. Springer (2022)
26. Lian, S., Li, H., Cong, R., Li, S., Zhang, W., Kwong, S.: WaterMask: instance segmentation for underwater imagery. In: Proceedings of the IEEE/CVF International Conference on Computer Vision, pp. 1305–1315 (2023)
27. Lin, T.: Focal loss for dense object detection. arXiv preprint arXiv:1708.02002 (2017)
28. Lin, T.Y., Dollár, P., Girshick, R., He, K., Hariharan, B., Belongie, S.: Feature pyramid networks for object detection. In: Proceedings of the IEEE Conference on Computer Vision and Pattern Recognition, pp. 2117–2125 (2017)
29. Liu, F., Fang, M.: Semantic segmentation of underwater images based on improved DeepLab. J. Mar. Sci. Eng. **8**(3), 188 (2020)
30. Marmanis, D., Schindler, K., Wegner, J.D., Galliani, S., Datcu, M., Stilla, U.: Classification with an edge: improving semantic image segmentation with boundary detection. ISPRS J. Photogramm. Remote. Sens. **135**, 158–172 (2018)
31. Milletari, F., Navab, N., Ahmadi, S.A.: V-Net: fully convolutional neural networks for volumetric medical image segmentation. In: 2016 Fourth International Conference on 3D Vision (3DV), pp. 565–571. IEEE (2016)
32. O'Byrne, M., Pakrashi, V., Schoefs, F., Ghosh, B.: Semantic segmentation of underwater imagery using deep networks trained on synthetic imagery. J. Marine Sci. Eng. **6**(3), 93 (2018)
33. Radford, A., et al.: Learning transferable visual models from natural language supervision. In: International Conference on Machine Learning, pp. 8748–8763. PMLR (2021)
34. Ronneberger, O., Fischer, P., Brox, T.: U-Net: convolutional networks for biomedical image segmentation. In: Navab, N., Hornegger, J., Wells, W.M., Frangi, A.F. (eds.) MICCAI 2015. LNCS, vol. 9351, pp. 234–241. Springer, Cham (2015). https://doi.org/10.1007/978-3-319-24574-4_28
35. Rout, D.K., Subudhi, B.N., Veerakumar, T., Chaudhury, S.: Walsh-Hadamard-Kernel-based features in particle filter framework for underwater object tracking. IEEE Trans. Industr. Inf. **16**(9), 5712–5722 (2019)
36. Saleh, A., Laradji, I.H., Konovalov, D.A., Bradley, M., Vazquez, D., Sheaves, M.: A realistic fish-habitat dataset to evaluate algorithms for underwater visual analysis. Sci. Rep. **10**(1), 14671 (2020)
37. Simonyan, K., Zisserman, A.: Very deep convolutional networks for large-scale image recognition. arXiv preprint arXiv:1409.1556 (2014)
38. Vohra, R., et al.: Detecting underwater discrete scatterers in echograms with deep learning-based semantic segmentation. In: Proceedings of the IEEE/CVF Conference on Computer Vision and Pattern Recognition, pp. 375–384 (2023)

39. Wang, J., He, X., Shao, F., Lu, G., Hu, R., Jiang, Q.: Semantic segmentation method of underwater images based on encoder-decoder architecture. PLoS ONE **17**(8), e0272666 (2022)
40. Wang, Y., et al.: LEDNet: a lightweight encoder-decoder network for real-time semantic segmentation. In: 2019 IEEE International Conference on Image Processing (ICIP), pp. 1860–1864. IEEE (2019)
41. Waszak, M., Cardaillac, A., Elvesæter, B., Rødølen, F., Ludvigsen, M.: Semantic segmentation in underwater ship inspections: benchmark and data set. IEEE J. Oceanic Eng. **48**(2), 462–473 (2022)
42. Xu, M., Su, J., Liu, Y.: AquaSAM: underwater image foreground segmentation. arXiv preprint arXiv:2308.04218 (2023)
43. Yao, Y., Zhang, A., Zhang, Z., Liu, Z., Chua, T.S., Sun, M.: CPT: colorful prompt tuning for pre-trained vision-language models. AI Open **5**, 30–38 (2024)
44. Yu, C., Wang, J., Peng, C., Gao, C., Yu, G., Sang, N.: BiSeNet: bilateral segmentation network for real-time semantic segmentation. In: Proceedings of the European Conference on Computer Vision (ECCV), pp. 325–341 (2018)
45. Zhang, L., Li, X., Arnab, A., Yang, K., Tong, Y., Torr, P.H.: Dual graph convolutional network for semantic segmentation. arXiv preprint arXiv:1909.06121 (2019)
46. Zhang, R., et al.: Tip-Adapter: training-free CLIP-adapter for better vision-language modeling. arXiv preprint arXiv:2111.03930 (2021)
47. Zhang, X., Liu, Y., Lin, Y., Liao, Q., Li, Y.: UV-SAM: adapting segment anything model for urban village identification. In: Proceedings of the AAAI Conference on Artificial Intelligence, vol. 38, pp. 22520–22528 (2024)
48. Zhang, Y., Shen, Z., Jiao, R.: Segment anything model for medical image segmentation: current applications and future directions. Comput. Biol. Med. **171**, 108238 (2024)
49. Zhao, H., Shi, J., Qi, X., Wang, X., Jia, J.: Pyramid scene parsing network. In: Proceedings of the IEEE Conference on Computer Vision and Pattern Recognition, pp. 2881–2890 (2017)
50. Zhou, J., Pang, L., Zhang, D., Zhang, W.: Underwater image enhancement method via multi-interval subhistogram perspective equalization. IEEE J. Oceanic Eng. (2023)
51. Zhou, K., Yang, J., Loy, C.C., Liu, Z.: Learning to prompt for vision-language models. Int. J. Comput. Vis. **130**(9), 2337–2348 (2022)

LAGNet: A Location-Aware Guidance Network for Weak and Strip Defect Detection

Lisha Cui⬤, Helong Jiao⬤, Tengyue Liu⬤, Chunyan Niu$^{(\boxtimes)}$⬤, Ming Ma⬤, Xiaoheng Jiang⬤, and Mingliang Xu⬤

Zhengzhou University, Zhengzhou 450001, Henan, China
ielscui@zzu.edu.cn

Abstract. Automatically surface defect detection plays a crucial role during the industrial production process. Unfortunately, some special defects, such as weak and strip-like defects, are relatively difficult to classify and localize accurately. In this paper, we propose a novel Location-Aware Guidance Network for weak and strip defect detection, termed as LAGNet. To enhance the feature representation of weak defects, we introduce the Location Activation Map (LAM) by visualizing the confidence score map that indicates the probability of the existence of an object in each region. The LAM and RGB images are fed into the network in a parallel manner for feature extraction, and then we fuse these two branches via a Location Guidance Block (LGB) that inherently encodes comprehensive and complementary information for detection. Additionally, a Strip Convolution Enhancement Module (SCEM) is presented using the depthwise strip convolutions with long but narrow kernels and attention mechanism and plugged into the detection neck to model the long-range dependencies along both horizontal and vertical spatial directions, thus improving the detection performance of anisotropic defects with banded structures. Notably, LAGNet achieves the top-ranking results on two popular steel benchmarks and significantly outperforms the baseline network YOLOv5: **85.5%** mAP (*vs.* 76.2%) on NEU-DET and **76.6%** mAP (*vs.* 66.0%) on GC10-DET.

Keywords: Defect detection · Weak defect · Location activation maps · Strip convolution · Attention mechanism

1 Introduction

With the continuous evolution of industrial production, steel, as a key structural material, is widely utilized in various types of infrastructure and engineering projects. However, diverse surface defects accidentally occur during the manufacturing and processing of steel, which seriously jeopardizes the quality and service life. Therefore, rapid and accurate detection of these defects has become a key assurance of product quality and safety.

Traditional manual defect inspection is not only time-consuming and labor-intensive but also susceptible to subjective factors that lead to high false and missed detection rates. Classic automatic defect detectors [1–4] rely on hand-crafted features,

© The Author(s), under exclusive license to Springer Nature Singapore Pte Ltd. 2025
P. Didyk and J. Hou (Eds.): CVM 2025, LNCS 15663, pp. 349–368, 2025.
https://doi.org/10.1007/978-981-96-5809-1_19

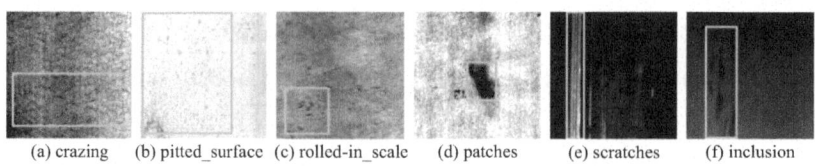

(a) crazing　(b) pitted_surface　(c) rolled-in_scale　(d) patches　(e) scratches　(f) inclusion

Fig. 1. Examples of steel surface defects in NEU-DET dataset.

which fail to deal with the diversity of defects and have high requirements for image quality as well. Recent advances based on deep learning techniques, especially Convolutional Neural Networks (CNN), have achieved remarkable performances and occupied a dominant position in the field of defect detection [5–7]. Such detectors have been proven to have stronger generalization ability and adaptability.

Although defect detectors based on CNN have shown significant advantages, the performance is still less than satisfactory due to the complexity of defect images. Compared with general object detection, defect detection usually has the following challenges: (1) The subtle texture difference between defective and defect-free areas in RGB images. Due to the randomness in the production process and objective factors in the data acquisition process, such as lighting conditions, certain defects exhibit weak features, low contrast, and indistinct boundaries, as shown in Fig. 1(a), (b), and (c). This makes it more challenging to accurately classify and localize defects, resulting in a higher rate of false positives and false negatives. (2) The extremely large aspect ratios of the defects with banded structures. Unlike the objects in Pascal VOC [8], some of the defects are in long and thin shapes, such as *scratches* and *inclusion* shown in Fig. 1(e) and (f). It is difficult for the detectors to deal with the defects with arbitrary aspect ratios.

To cope with the first issue, it makes very logical sense for the network to encode and enhance the location information of weak defects in RGB images. Consequently, we purposely introduce the location activation maps by visualizing the importance of different regions for the localization task in the form of color-coded heat maps. The brighter color on the maps indicates the stronger response and greater contribution of each point to the localization task. The RGB image and its corresponding activation map are fed into the network in a parallel fashion to encode respective features. Besides, a location guidance block is proposed to integrate the outputs of the two branches in the middle and late stages and guide the network to capture comprehensive and complementary features, especially strengthening the location information and improving the recall of weak defects in RGB images.

For the strip objects in defective images, the standard square kernel fails to model their long-range spatial dependencies, and may also incorporate irrelevant contaminating information from the background. Based on this observation, we propose a strip convolution enhancement module based on strip convolutions and attention mechanisms to improve the modeling ability of CNN for long-distance spatial information. The strip convolutions, such as 1×5 or 5×1, enable the network to capture long-range context along the horizontal or vertical directions. Moreover, following the strip convolutions, we introduce channel and spatial attention to further strengthen the feature representation of weak defects.

The strip convolution enhancement module performs finer and more comprehensive feature extraction for elongated defective regions in both horizontal and vertical directions, thus improving defect detection performance, especially the weak and slender defects. Also notably, the module is lightweight and flexible to be plugged into any network.

In summary, the main contributions of this work can be summarized as follows:

- We innovatively introduce the Location Activation Map (LAM) as the auxiliary data to compensate for the poor location information in RGB images. Meanwhile, the Location Guidance Block (LGB) is tailored exclusively for effectively integrating the parallel RGB and LAM branches, guiding the network to encode more comprehensive and discriminative features for weak defect detection.
- We propose a computation-friendly Strip Convolution Enhancement Module (SCEM) based on the long but narrow kernel and attention mechanisms, modeling the long-range dependencies along horizontal and vertical directions while focusing on local details of defects.
- We present a novel Location-Aware Guidance Network for weak and strip defect detection, abbreviated as LAGNet. LAGNet consistently produces competitive results on the widely used defect benchmarks NEU-DET (85.5% mAP) and GC10-DET (76.6% mAP). Most notably, the small version of LAGNet achieves 84.9% mAP and reaches 73.6 FPS on NEU-DET with only 8.9M parameters.

2 Related Work

2.1 General Object Detection

Deep learning has achieved great success in the field of computer vision, especially with the emergence of CNNs which have greatly improved the performance of general object detection. Currently, object detectors based on deep learning can be roughly divided into two- and one-stage object detection.

The R-CNN [9–11] family is the classical two-stage object detector. R-CNN [9] applies a region proposal network (RPN) to generate candidate object regions, then extracts the features of each region by CNN, and finally adopts a classifier and regressor to classify and localize the object. Instead of generating candidate regions first, one-stage object detectors accomplish object localization and classification directly in a single neural network, as represented by the SSD [12] and YOLO [13–18] series. SSD adopts multi-scale feature maps to predict objects with different scales, and directly predict the confidence scores and box offsets through convolutions. The YOLO series divides the image into fixed-size grid cells and predicts bounding boxes and category probabilities in each cell. YOLOv4 [16] is an efficient object detection model that combines multiple optimization techniques to improve detection accuracy while maintaining real-time speed. YOLOv5 [17] further improves the training strategies and optimized loss functions, making it an ideal choice for real-time applications. YOLOv7

[18] introduces model reparameterization, label assignment strategies, extended efficient layer aggregation networks (ELAN), and auxiliary head training techniques.

Although these classic general object detectors have achieved excellent results on routine tasks, they have difficulty in accurately detecting defects with faint features, low contrast, and arbitrary aspect ratios.

2.2 Defect Detection

The successful application of CNN in the field of image classification and object detection provides a brand new direction for defect detection. Therefore, defect detection algorithms based on CNN have become a hot research topic for industrial quality inspection at present.

Zhao et al. [19] innovatively design a double feature pyramid network (DFPN) based on Res2Net [20] to increase the semantic information. Liu et al. [21] propose a parallel architecture of dilated convolution (PADC) with different dilation rates to capture multi-scale contextual information and a feature enhancement and selection module (FESM) to enhance single-scale features. On the basis of CenterNet [22], Tian et al. [23] propose an anchor-free framework, DCC-CenterNet, for steel surface defect detection by introducing the dilated feature enhancement model (DFEM) and the centerness function center-weight (CW). In addition, to cope with the problem of visual defect detection in complex images, Yu et al. [24] propose a progressively refined redistribution pyramid network.

Although the aforementioned algorithms have improved the overall accuracy of defect detection, their performance is still unsatisfactory when facing weak defects with low contrast. To overcome this challenge, we employ the location activation maps as a localization guide to motivate the network to focus on the weak defective areas.

2.3 Strip Convolution

Beyond the regular convolutional kernel with a square shape of $k \times k$, strip convolutions apply long but narrow kernels, such as $1 \times k$ or $k \times 1$, to efficiently model long-range dependencies. ACNet [25] introduces strip convolution blocks, replacing the common 3×3, 5×5, and 7×7 square kernels, to effectively support the extraction of certain asymmetric image features. Strip Pooling [26] captures long-range relationships in isolated regions by performing pooling operations along the horizontal or vertical dimension.

In InceptionNeXt [27], the large-kernel depth convolution is decomposed into four parallel branches, including small square kernels, two strip convolution kernels, and a unit map, to achieve more flexible feature extraction. SegNeXt [28] employs two depth strip convolutions to approximate standard depth convolutions with large kernels. Depth strip convolution is lightweight and only requires a pair of $k \times 1$ and $1 \times k$ convolutions to imitate a standard convolution with a square kernel size of $k \times k$.

Based on the above findings, in this paper, we present a strip convolution enhancement module to capture long-range context and focus on local details, thus improving the detection performance of strip defects.

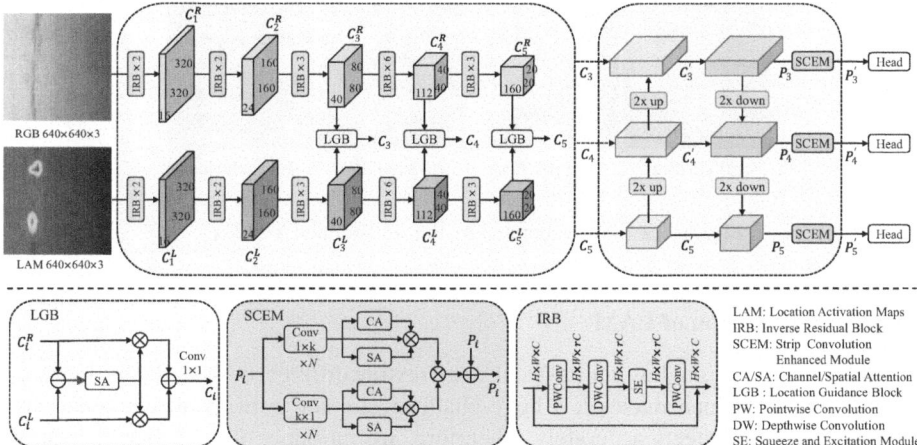

Fig. 2. The overall structure of proposed LAGNet, which consists of the dual-branch backbone, the feature pyramid neck, and a multi-scale detection head. The LAM could provide RGB auxiliary rich location information and guide the network to focus on the discriminative defective areas through LGB. The SCEM deployed in the detection neck adopts the strip convolutions and attention mechanism to model the long-range spatial dependencies of strip defects.

3 Proposed Method

In this section, we first introduce the overall pipeline of proposed LAGNet and the generation of LAM. Subsequently, we describe the backbone network with two parallel branches of RGB and LAM in detail, as well as the fusion module LGB. Finally, we elaborate on the structure of SCEM.

3.1 Overall Structure

Figure 2 illustrates the overall framework of the proposed LAGNet, which mainly consists of three parts: a two-pathway backbone, a feature pyramid neck, and a multi-scale detection head.

The backbone network is composed of two parallel branches, each with RGB images and LAM as input respectively. Considering the edge end employment in embedded devices, we choose the lightweight MobileNetV3 [29] to extract features from both RGB images and LAM simultaneously. The corresponding output feature maps of each branch in the middle and late stages undergo the LGB and integrate together to learn complementary signals, producing location-enhanced feature maps C_3, C_4, and C_5. Subsequently, these feature maps are fed into a top-down and bottom-up bidirectional pathway to build high-level and strong semantic features P_3, P_4, and P_5. Notice that the proposed SCEM is placed after the multiple hierarchical features to efficiently model long-range dependencies and produce P_3', P_4', and P_5'. Finally, the predictions are made on these multi-scale feature maps to deal with large variants of defect sizes.

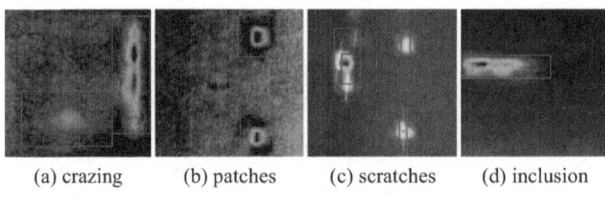

(a) crazing   (b) patches   (c) scratches   (d) inclusion

Fig. 3. The LAM generated by the well-trained YOLOv5.

3.2   The Generation of LAM

The faint defects present low contrast and small texture differences from the background in RGB images, which makes it a huge challenge for the network to recognize and localize the weak defects accurately. Therefore, we introduce the location activation maps.

Specifically, we first fine-tune a popular detector (such as YOLOv5) on the defect benchmarks and achieve the well-trained models. For each input image, the well-trained model predicts the box coordinates, classes, and confidence scores of defects. The confidence score map (CSM) indicates the probability of the existence of an object in each region, where the higher the value, the greater the possibility that an object exists. We first normalize the CSM output by three YOLOv5 detection heads to [0, 1] using the sigmoid activation function, and then multiply them by 255. Then a location information map is obtained by selecting the maximum value among the processed three CSMs with different scales. Finally, the color-coded LAM is produced by fusing the location information map with its corresponding image in a ratio of 1:1, as shown in Fig. 3. Mathematically, the generative process can be formulated as follows:

$$LAM = \alpha(RGB) \oplus \beta(255 \otimes sigmoid(CSM)) \tag{1}$$

where RGB and CSM represent the input RGB image and corresponding confidence score map, respectively. α and β refer to the proportional coefficients when fusing RGB and CSM, and both are set to 0.5 after experimental trials. $\oplus$ and $\otimes$ refer to element-wise summation and multiplication, respectively. As illustrated in Fig. 3, the higher brightness on LAM indicates that this region contributes more to the localization task. Therefore, the LAM could highlight the defect area and compensate for the location information of weak defects in RGB images.

3.3   The Dual-Branch Backbone

RGB images are rich in texture, color, and shape information, whereas susceptible to interference from background noise, light, *etc.*. Conversely, the LAM could highlight the defective areas and enhance the contrast with the background. Fully utilizing the complementary information of both RGB images and LAM is beneficial for improving defect detection performance, especially the weak defects.

Based on the above considerations, we propose the LAGNet for weak defect detection with a dual-branch backbone, *i.e.* RGB and LAM branches. As illustrated in Fig. 2,

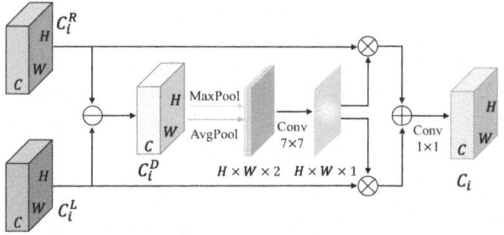

Fig. 4. Illustration of the proposed LGB.

the RGB images and corresponding LAM are fed forward into the network to encode features of input data separately. Then we specially design the LGB that fuses the output features of both branches in the middle and late stages to enhance the location details and construct more comprehensive feature maps. Figure 4 depicts the structure of the proposed LGB.

Specifically, imagine C_i^R, $C_i^L \in \mathbb{R}^{H \times W \times C}$ are the feature maps output by RGB and LAM branches in stage i, where H, W, and C denote the height, width, and number of channels, respectively. First, let C_i^R and C_i^L perform subtraction to enhance the visible features and produce the differential-modality feature maps C_i^D $(i = 3, 4, 5)$. Subsequently, the spatial attention module is applied to further enhance the defect feature representation, and the attention map is then multiplied by C_i^R and C_i^L, respectively. Finally, the dual branches are integrated together by element-wise summation and pass through a 1×1 convolution layer to refine the fusion features, producing $C_i \in \mathbb{R}^{H \times W \times C}$. The process can be described as follows:

$$C_i^D = C_i^R \ominus C_i^L, i = 3, 4, 5 \tag{2}$$

$$C_i = Conv_{1 \times 1}((C_i^R \otimes SA(C_i^D)) \oplus (C_i^L \otimes SA(C_i^D))) \tag{3}$$

where $\ominus$ refers to element-wise subtraction. SA stands for the spatial attention module.

The LGB could guide the network to pay more attention to defective areas, and thus produce more informative and representative feature pyramids C_3, C_4, and C_5. Considering the dual-branch backbone in LAGNet inevitably introduces extra parameters and computational complexity, we choose the efficient and lightweight MobileNetV3 as the backbone for feature extraction. MobileNetV3 is based on Inverse Residual Block (IRB) shown in Fig. 2, whose feature space remains constant at the input and output while internally expanding to a higher dimension. Additionally, IRB replaces the traditional convolution layers with depthwise separable convolutions to efficiently trade off between latency and accuracy.

3.4 Strip Convolution Enhancement Module

The box regression of strip defects, such as *scratches* and *inclusion*, is a challenging task compared with nearly square-shaped defects. The standard convolution with a regular shape of $k \times k$ (such as commonly used 3×3) fails to capture long-range contextual information. A larger kernel (such as 7×7) is able to encode more comprehensive

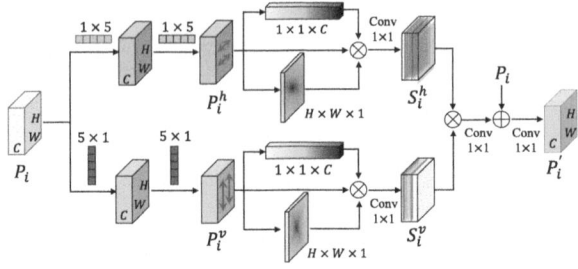

Fig. 5. Illustration of SCEM. The upper and lower branches aim to model the spatial relations along the horizontal and vertical directions, respectively.

information, but may introduce contaminating information from irrelevant background, as well as additional parameters.

Regarding this problem, we devise the SCEM based on the depth-separable strip convolution with long but narrow kernels and plug it into the detection neck to model the long-range dependencies, as demonstrated in Fig. 5. Specifically, the feature hierarchies C_3, C_4, and C_5 generated by LGB first undergo a top-down and bottom-up pipeline to encode high-level semantic features, producing P_3, P_4, and P_5, respectively.

$$C_5' = Conv_{1 \times 1}(C_5), C_i' = Up(C_{i+1}') \oplus C_i, i = 3, 4 \tag{4}$$

$$P_3 = Conv_{1 \times 1}(C_3'), P_i = Down(P_{i-1}) \oplus C_i', i = 4, 5 \tag{5}$$

P_3, P_4, and P_5 are then fed into SCEM to capture long-range relations of local regions. More concretely, taking $P_i \in \mathbb{R}^{H \times W \times C}$ $(i = 3, 4, 5)$ as input, SCEM consists of two parallel pathways as shown in Fig. 5. The upper branch first deploys n stacked depthwise strip convolutions with the size of $1 \times k$ to encode global context along the horizontal spatial dimension. Similarly, the lower branch is to capture global vertical information using n consecutive $k \times 1$ convolutions. By conducting ablation experiments in Sect. 4.5, we set $n = 2$ and $k = 5$ in this study. The intermediate output feature maps of the upper and lower branches in this step are P_i^h and P_i^v respectively, which can be described as:

$$P_i^h = DWConv_{1 \times k}(DWConv_{1 \times k}(P_i)), i = 3, 4, 5 \tag{6}$$

$$P_i^v = DWConv_{k \times 1}(DWConv_{k \times 1}(P_i)), i = 3, 4, 5 \tag{7}$$

where $DWConv$ denotes the depthwise strip convolution and P_i is the input feature map.

To further enhance the feature representation for weak defects, P_i^h and P_i^v go through the attention mechanism in both the channel and spatial dimensions. The channel tensor $1 \times 1 \times C$ predicts the importance of each channel and pays attention to what is in the image, while the spatial map $H \times W \times 1$ indicates the significance of each location and focuses on where is the defect. The channel and spatial attention module are arranged in a parallel fashion, and then multiplied by P_i^h and P_i^v, respectively.

As usual, a pointwise convolution $1 \times 1 \times C$ is followed to compute the linear combination of the output from preceding layers, fully mixing inter-channel information and producing S_i^h and S_i^v which can be formulated as:

$$S_i^h = PWConv_{1 \times 1}(P_i^h \otimes CA(P_i^h) \otimes SA(P_i^h)) \tag{8}$$

$$S_i^v = PWConv_{1 \times 1}(P_i^v \otimes CA(P_i^v) \otimes SA(P_i^v)) \tag{9}$$

where $PWConv$ represents the pointwise convolution. CA and SA are the channel and spatial attention, respectively.

Finally, we perform an element-wise multiplication of S_i^h and S_i^v, and then introduce a residual connection with P_i by element-wise summation. Both of these fusion operations are followed by one $1 \times 1 \times C$ convolution to refine the features, generating the more comprehensive P_i'. Mathematically, P_i' can be written as:

$$P_i' = Conv_{1 \times 1}(P_i \oplus Conv_{1 \times 1}(S_i^h \otimes S_i^v)), i = 3, 4, 5 \tag{10}$$

SCEM considers the long but narrow spatial dependencies along both horizontal and vertical directions over the whole scene, thus improving the capability of modeling long-range information for strip defects. Simultaneously, the depth-separable convolutions considerably reduce the computational complexity and module size, making SCEM lightweight and easily plugged into any architecture.

The output feature maps of SCEM, P_i' ($i = 3, 4, 5$), inherently encode long-range spatial dependencies and discriminative features, which are then utilized to predict multi-scale defects.

3.5 Training Objective

The training objective of LAGNet is the weighted sum of the box regression loss, confidence loss, and classification loss. The box loss (L_{box}) is the CIoU loss:

$$L_{box} = L_{CIoU} = 1 - IoU + \frac{\rho^2(b, b^{gt})}{c^2} + \alpha v \tag{11}$$

$$IoU = \frac{|b \cap b^{gt}|}{|b \cup b^{gt}|} \tag{12}$$

$$v = \frac{4}{\pi^2}\left(\arctan\frac{w}{h} - \arctan\frac{w^{gt}}{h^{gt}}\right)^2 \tag{13}$$

where b and b^{gt} represent the predicted and ground-truth boxes, respectively. ρ refers to the distance between the center points of the two bounding boxes, and c is the diagonal length of the smallest outer rectangle of the two boxes. α is the weight coefficient and is usually set to 0.5. w and h denote the width and height of the predicted box, while w^{gt} and h^{gt} are the width and height of the ground-truth box.

The confidence loss (L_{obj}) and classification loss (L_{cls}) are Binary Cross-Entropy (BCE) Loss. The total loss function L is the weighted sum of these three parts:

$$L = \lambda_{box}L_{box} + \lambda_{obj}L_{obj} + \lambda_{cls}L_{cls} \tag{14}$$

where λ_{box}, λ_{obj}, and λ_{cls} are the weight coefficients and set to 0.05, 1, and 0.5, respectively.

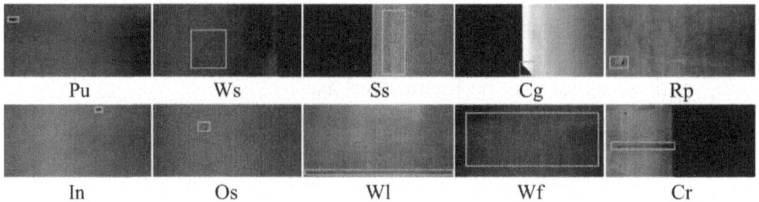

Fig. 6. Examples of defects in the GC10-DET dataset.

4   Experiments

In this section, we first elaborate the implementation details and evaluation metrics of the experiments and introduce the defect datasets employed in this paper. Subsequently, we present comprehensive comparisons of results regarding LAGNet and the current SOTA methods. Finally, we analyze and validate the effectiveness of each component in LAGNet through extensive ablation studies.

4.1   Implementation Details

The proposed LAGNet and other comparison algorithms are carried on the PyTorch framework. We implement all the experiments on a computing platform equipped with an NVIDIA GeForce RTX4090 GPU. The stochastic gradient descent (SGD) algorithm is utilized to optimize the model parameters, where the momentum and weight decay are set to 0.937 and 0.0005, respectively. The initial learning rate is set to 0.01, and a warm-up strategy and cosine annealing learning rate strategy are introduced with a total training epoch of 500. The batch size is uniformly set to 16. During the training process, we apply data augmentation techniques such as Mosaic and Mixup for both RGB images and LAM to improve the generalization ability of the models. Moreover, LAGNet is based on the MobileNetV3-Large as the backbone for feature extraction, while a small version is created by adopting MobileNetV3-Small to meet industrial demands, namely LAGNet-s.

4.2   Datasets

We validate the proposed LAGNet and LAGNet-s on two publicly available defect detection datasets (NEU-DET [30] and GC10-DET [31]) and one self-constructed dataset (GB-DET). **NEU-DET** (Fig. 1) contains 6 classes of common steel surface defects: *patches*, *crazing*, *rolled-in_scale*, *pitted_surface*, *inclusion*, and *scratches*. Each category comprises 300 images, making a grand total of 1800 defect images, each with a size of 200×200. The whole dataset is randomly partitioned into the training and test set with a ratio of 7:3 in [30], namely 1260 images for training and 540 images for testing. **GC10-DET** shown in Fig. 6 contains 10 types of defects: *punching (Pu)*, *welding line (Wl)*, *crescent gap (Cg)*, *water spot (Ws)*, *oil spot (Os)*, *silk spot (Ss)*, *inclusion (In)*, *rolled pit (Rp)*, *crease (Cr)*, and *waist folding (Wf)*. There are 2294 images in total, each

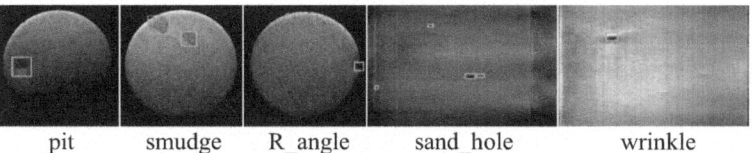

pit   smudge   R_angle   sand_hole   wrinkle

Fig. 7. Examples of defects in the GB-DET dataset.

with the size of 2048×1000 pixels. Following other algorithms, we randomly divide the whole dataset into the training and test set with a ratio of 9:1 [32], namely 2064 images for training and 230 images for testing. The images in both datasets are scaled to 640×640 as input during training and testing. Among these 10 types of defects, *Ss*, *Wl*, and *Cr* are typically strip-like defects. **GB-DET** is a self-constructed dataset for surface defect detection of renewable energy batteries, which contains 5 types of defects: *pit*, *smudge*, *R_angle*, *sand_hole*, and *wrinkle*. As shown in Fig. 7, the images containing circular bottom shells have a resolution of 320×320, whereas the images containing rectangular side shells have a resolution of 800×512. There are 6368 images in total, and we randomly divide them into the training and test set with a ratio of 7:3, namely 4458 images for training and 1910 images for testing.

4.3   Evaluation Metrics

We utilize the average precision (AP), mean average precision (mAP), number of model parameters (Params), and frame per second (FPS) to evaluate the performance of different algorithms on NEU-DET and GC10-DET. The AP denotes the average accuracy of the model about a certain class, which is measured by the area under the precision-recall curve. The mAP represents the mean accuracy of the model for all classes, which is calculated by the average value of all APs. AP and mAP are defined as follows:

$$P = \frac{TP}{TP + FP}, R = \frac{TP}{TP + FN} \tag{15}$$

$$AP = \int_{0}^{1} P(R)dR \tag{16}$$

$$mAP = \frac{1}{N} \sum_{i=1}^{n} AP_i \tag{17}$$

where P and R represent the precision and recall. TP, FP, and FN refer to true positives, false positives, and false negatives, respectively. The Params and FPS are to evaluate the model size and inference speed, respectively. The threshold of intersection over union (IoU) is set to 0.5. Besides, we also draw the Precision-Recall (PR) curves to evaluate the classification performance across different threshold settings. These metrics help to fully and comprehensively evaluate the performance of different methods.

Table 1. Detection results of state-of-the-art methods on NEU-DET.

Method	Backbone	FPS	Params	mAP (%)	crazing	inclusion	rolled-in_scale	scratches	patches	pitted_surface
Object detectors										
Faster R-CNN [11]	ResNet50	22.3	28.4M	77.9	52.5	76.5	74.4	90.3	89.0	84.7
SSD512 [12]	VGG16	64.9	27.0M	72.1	39.9	79.6	61.9	84.4	86.7	79.8
YOLOv5 [17]	CSPDarkNet	109.3	46.1M	76.2	38.4	82.0	64.5	94.0	**94.8**	83.3
YOLOv7 [18]	-	62.5	36.5M	75.9	42.0	83.9	63.0	89.1	94.3	83.0
YOLOX [33]	CSPDarkNet	53.7	54.2M	76.8	47.6	81.7	60.9	94.4	92.9	83.3
YOLOv10 [34]	CSPDarkNet	161.1	24.4 M	75.9	40.6	87.1	67.4	91.5	84.2	84.5
Defect detectors										
DIN [35]	-	-	-	80.5	61.4	85.6	64.6	88.3	93.0	90.3
RDN [36]	ResNet18	-	-	80.0	53.7	84.9	64.4	95.9	93.8	87.0
DDN [30]	ResNet50	-	-	82.3	62.4	84.7	76.3	90.1	90.7	89.7
EFD-YOLOv4 [37]	CSPDarkNet	-	-	79.9	45.7	85.4	72.7	93.6	97.0	85.0
Zhang's [38]	CSPDarkNet	-	-	78.2	40.6	**90.3**	60.7	**96.1**	94.4	86.9
Multi-branch detectors										
CFT [39]	CSPDarkNet	23.8	206.2M	83.1	60.5	83.8	**82.5**	93.1	92.7	86.2
ICAFusion [40]	CSPDarkNet	24.5	120.3M	83.0	62.3	81.8	79.7	94.3	91.9	88.2
SuperYOLO [41]	CSPDarkNet	99.1	9.9M	78.9	54.9	80.1	72.1	86.9	91.4	87.2
Ghost [42]	CSPDarkNet	54.1	7.7M	72.0	46.5	72.2	72.3	71.7	89.3	80.9
LAGNet (Ours)	MobileNetV3	45.1	31.9M	**85.5**	**64.2**	86.4	82.4	**96.1**	94.4	89.2
LAGNet-s (Ours)	MobileNetV3	73.6	8.9M	84.9	63.6	85.3	80.5	95.5	94.4	**90.9**

4.4   Comparisons with the SOTA Detectors

To demonstrate the effectiveness of the proposed method, we compare it with state-of-the-art detectors, including general object detectors, defect detectors, and multi-branch object detectors on both NEU-DET and GC10-DET datasets.

Results on NEU-DET. Quantitative Results. Table 1 shows the extensive results of the proposed LAGNet and other state-of-the-art detectors on NEU-DET. It is observed that LAGNet achieves the highest 85.5% mAP, with an increment of 9.3% over the baseline YOLOv5 (76.2%). Compared with other RGB-only detectors, such as classic YOLOX (76.8%) and defect detector DDN (82.3%), LAGNet still has significant performance improvements. Although the multi-branch RGB- and LAM-based detectors, such as CFT (83.1%) and ICAFusion (83.0%), are of relatively higher accuracy, they have too many parameters to be deployed and applied. Fortunately, the proposed LAGNet can still exceed such detectors over 2 points with fewer parameters.

Notably, LAGNet-s substantially reduces the model size from 31.9M to 8.9M compared with LAGNet, which can be deployed on a computationally limited platform. Although the mAP of LAGNet-s (84.9%) has decreased slightly in comparison with LAGNet (85.5%), it can still outperform the lightweight SuperYOLO (78.9%) and Ghost (72.0%) by large margins with approximate model size. Additionally, LAGNet and LAGNet-s consistently achieve better results in terms of the AP. Especially for weak defect *crazing*, the AP of LAGNet is significantly improved to 64.2%, which lies in the enhanced location information from the LAM branch. Similarly, for *scratches* that have long and thin shapes, LAGNet encodes the long-range spatial dependencies by SCEM and further elevates the AP to 96.1%. The experimental results demonstrate the effectiveness of LAGNet for defect detection, especially the weak and strip defects.

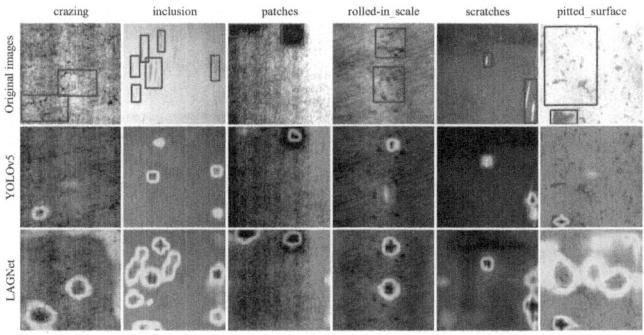

Fig. 8. Comparison of activation maps generated by YOLOv5 and LAGNet on NEU-DET.

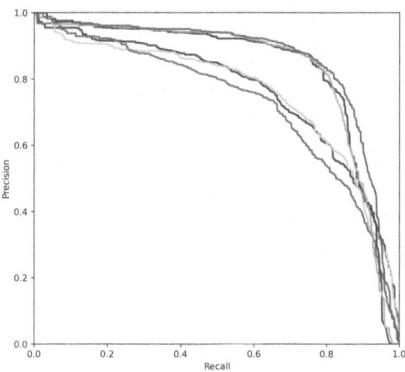

Fig. 9. Comparison of PR curves for different models on NEU-DET.

We also evaluate the inference speed and time efficiency of different algorithms on NEU-DET, as shown in the third column of Table 1. LAGNet introduces an additional LAM branch and extra parameters, so it inevitably impairs the model efficiency compared with the baseline network (109.3 FPS). Even so, LAGNet and LAGNet-s could still achieve 45.1 and 73.6 FPS, respectively. Especially, LAGNet-s could achieve the best trade-off among the detection accuracy, model size, and time efficiency in comparison with prevailing detectors.

Qualitative Results. To visually demonstrate the localization ability of the models, we draw the activation maps using the well-trained YOLOv5 and LAGNet on NEU-DET, as shown in Fig. 8. The topmost row is the defect images of 6 classes with ground-truth boxes. By contrast, it is observed that the proposed LAGNet could highlight the defective areas more completely and comprehensively compared with YOLOv5. We believe that the LGB enables the network to effectively focus on and enhance the representations of weak defects by supplementing location information, thus considerably improving the localization performance of the model. Figure 9 presents the comparison of the PR curves for different detectors. It is observed that the proposed LAGNet

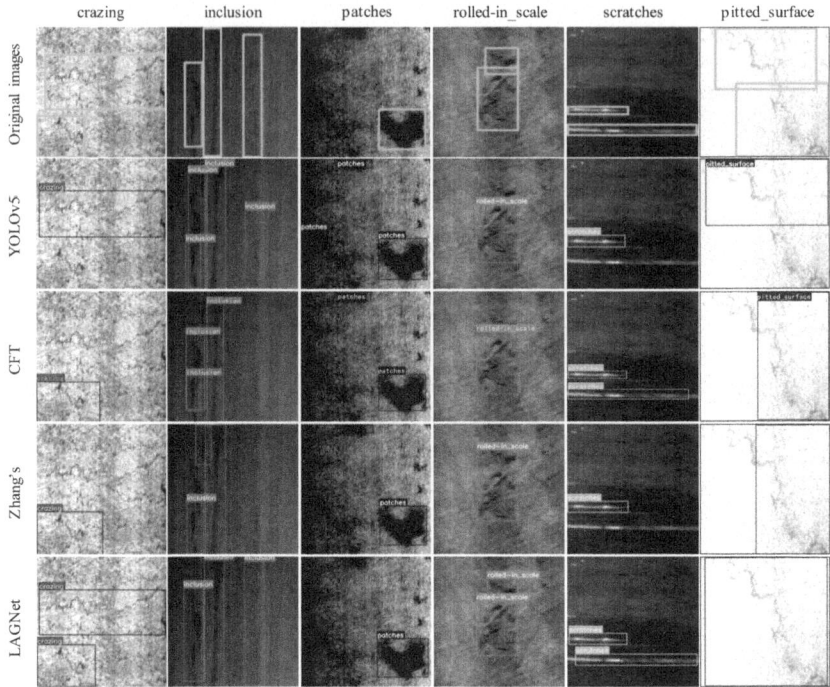

Fig. 10. The visualization results of different models on NEU-DET. The green boxes in the first row indicate the ground-truth boxes. (Color figure online)

achieves a better trade-off between precision and recall, demonstrating superior classification performance compared with other algorithms.

Furthermore, we display the visualization detection results of LAGNet compared with YOLOv5 (general detector), CFT (multi-branch detector), and Zhang's (defect detector) on NEU-DET in Fig. 10. The prediction boxes of different classes are distinguished by different colors. It can be visualized that LAGNet can accurately locate the weak defects in the low contrast background, such as *crazing* in the first column. Likewise, our method can also predict the strip defects in the fifth column more precisely than other detectors, demonstrating the effectiveness of SCEM in capturing long-range spatial dependencies.

Results on GC10-DET. To further verify the effectiveness and robustness of LAGNet, we also conduct experiments on GC10-DET, and the comparison results are illustrated in Table 2. LAGNet and LAGNet-s achieve 76.6% and 75.4% mAP, boosting the baseline YOLOv5 (66.0%) by 10.6 and 9.4 points, respectively. For general object detectors, YOLOv7 yields a desirable result with a mAP of 72.4%, which is the best result among YOLO families. For defect detectors, Zhang's obtains the excellent mAP of 71.9% using CSPDarkNet as the backbone. For multi-branch detectors, although CFT gets the impressive 74.4% mAP, it is under the guidance of the Transformer

Table 2. Detection results of state-of-the-art methods on GC10-DET.

Method	Backbone	Params	mAP (%)	Pu	Wl	Cg	Ws	Os	Ss	In	Rp	Cr	Wf
Object detectors													
Faster R-CNN [11]	ResNet50	28.4M	59.6	91.0	38.9	87.9	**79.7**	59.9	60.1	31.3	40.5	49.3	57.5
SSD512 [12]	VGG16	27.0M	60.6	95.7	91.7	**96.7**	66.6	60.8	45.7	16.1	22.1	26.1	**84.6**
YOLOv5 [17]	CSPDarkNet	46.1M	66.0	82.9	75.4	93.1	75.9	66.5	73.2	45.4	26.0	44.2	77.5
YOLOv7 [18]	-	36.5M	72.4	91.0	97.1	93.0	79.0	70.0	74.0	46.0	31.0	67.0	74.0
YOLOX [33]	CSPDarkNet	54.2M	71.0	84.2	96.1	93.4	78.0	64.7	69.9	42.2	28.0	**80.0**	73.8
YOLOv10 [34]	CSPDarkNet	24.4M	62.6	93.5	79.1	86.8	72.4	64.8	60.2	22.4	33.9	28.6	84.2
Defect detectors													
MSC-DNet [21]	ResNet50	34.1M	69.1	**97.7**	95.2	92.5	75.2	67.0	61.1	37.6	48.8	31.2	84.5
MSC-DNet [21]	ResNet101	-	71.6	95.5	96.1	94.9	76.5	66.5	65.8	34.1	53.4	48.5	84.0
EFD-YOLOv4 [37]	CSPDarkNet	-	54.7	96.3	**98.0**	85.3	75.0	53.3	43.2	18.2	50.0	27.3	0
DCC-CenterNet [23]	ResNet50	32.8M	61.9	84.1	85.5	96.2	77.3	50.9	54.8	30.2	13.9	49.9	76.6
Zhang's [38]	CSPDarkNet	-	71.9	97.8	88.9	96.2	79.1	67.3	53.2	33.2	43.7	75.8	83.6
Multi-branch detectors													
CFT [39]	CSPDarkNet	206.2M	74.4	96.0	78.5	90.1	76.5	68.4	67.9	49.8	**66.5**	72.8	77.1
ICAFusion [40]	CSPDarkNet	120.3M	72.5	91.8	81.6	90.9	72.2	65.1	72.0	54.8	54.1	65.5	77.6
SuperYOLO [41]	CSPDarkNet	9.9M	69.1	85.9	76.8	87.1	70.6	66.6	62.4	56.8	63.1	49.5	72.5
Ghost [42]	CSPDarkNet	7.7M	64.5	89.9	59.9	82.1	65.4	63.4	68.8	35.4	51.0	62.0	67.4
LAGNet (Ours)	MobileNetV3	31.9M	**76.6**	93.7	85.3	95.1	77.7	66.5	**75.0**	56.8	59.1	79.5	77.1
LAGNet-s (Ours)	MobileNetV3	8.9M	75.4	94.8	85.1	91.9	77.2	**70.5**	74.7	**60.1**	65.3	56.2	78.4

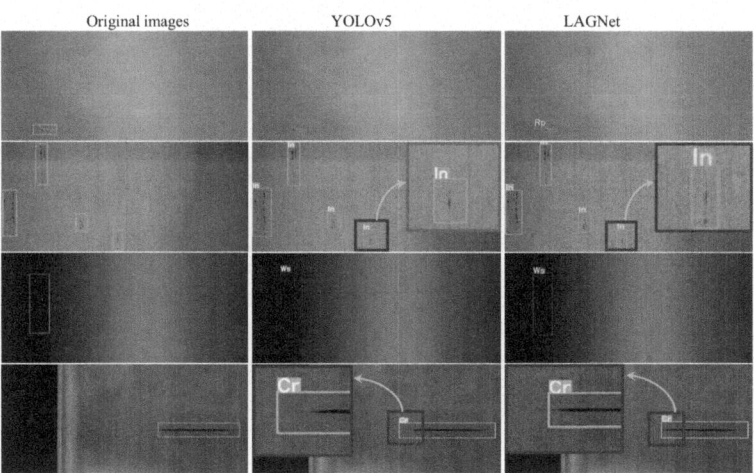

Fig. 11. The visualization results of LAGNet on GC10-DET, where different colors represent different defect classes.

[43] scheme with a large model size (206.2M). Fortunately, LAGNet and LAGNet-s could outperform these different types of detection algorithms with acceptable parameter quantity.

Table 3. Detection results of state-of-the-art methods on GB-DET.

Method	mAP (%)	R_angle	pit	sand_hole	smudge	wrinkle
Faster R-CNN [11]	43.2	90.1	72	3.9	50.2	0
Cascade R-CNN [44]	53.1	92.4	83.1	23.9	66.2	0
SSD512 [12]	64.0	91.6	78.1	34.6	55.3	60.4
RetinaNet [45]	72.1	83.2	66.2	62.9	63.2	84.9
YOLOv3 [15]	79.8	92.1	82.8	77.6	67.5	79.0
YOLOv5 [17]	90.6	94.6	91.5	91.8	78.1	97
YOLOX [33]	79.7	**96.2**	92.2	75.0	75.2	59.2
YOLOv7 [18]	88.8	94.9	90.2	90.6	73.8	94.7
SuperYOLO [41]	89.6	93.6	90.1	92.3	78.0	94.1
YOLOv10 [34]	89.3	93.7	94.8	92.2	78.0	87.6
LAGNet (Ours)	**93.2**	95.1	**96.1**	**95.9**	**81.8**	**97.1**

Table 4. Ablation studies of LAM and SCEM on NEU-DET.

Method	Backbone	Params	mAP(%)
YOLOv5	CSPDarkNet	46.1M	76.5
YOLOv5+LAM	CSPDarkNet	86.8M	82.3
YOLOv5+SCEM	CSPDarkNet	53.0M	78.6
YOLOv5+LAM+SCEM	CSPDarkNet	93.7M	84.6
YOLOv5+LAM	MobileNetV3	25.7M	83.6
YOLOv5+SCEM	MobileNetV3	28.6M	77.8
YOLOv5+LAM+SCEM	MobileNetV3	32.2M	**85.5**

It is noticeable that the APs of other methods vary greatly within a wide range, which may result from the imbalance of data distribution in GC10-DET. Despite that, LAGNet has yielded relatively stable APs for all defect classes. Additionally, Fig. 11 depicts the visualization results of LAGNet on GC10-DET, where the weak defect *Rp* and slender defect *Cr* could be successfully predicted. Notably, LAGNet produces more accurate and compact bounding boxes than YOLOv5, which indicates that our model is more sensitive to the location of defects due to the introduction of LAM.

Results on GB-DET. We further evaluate LAGNet on our own dataset GB-DET with more defective images. The results are shown in Table 3. LAGNet achieves 93.2% mAP, which is superior to other algorithms. Two-stage detectors such as Faster R-CNN (43.2%) and CascadeR-CNN (53.1%) do not perform well, mainly because they adopt a single-scale detection strategy and are not friendly to detect small defects in GB-DET. Especially, LAGNet also ranks the first AP in terms of 4 types of defects: *pit* (96.1%), *sand hole* (95.9%), *smudge* (81.8%), and *wrinkle* (97.1%). The results further validate the robustness and effectiveness of LAGNet.

Table 5. Ablation studies of kernel size and number in SCEM.

Dataset	mAP\k / n	1×3 / 3×1	1×5 / 5×1	1×7 / 7×1	1×9 / 9×1
NEU-DET	1	83.9	84.4	84.8	85.0
	2	84.0	**85.5**	84.5	83.8
	3	84.6	83.8	83.5	82.9
GC10-DET	1	71.3	74.1	73.4	**76.3**
	2	74.4	**76.6**	75.8	74.8
	2	74.3	70.7	70.2	68.0

4.5 Ablation Studies

Impact of Each Module. We first validate the effects of the separate LAM branch and SCEM, as shown in Table 4. By incorporating the LAM branch into the baseline network using CSPDarkNet as the backbone, the mAP is dramatically improved from 76.5% to 82.3%. The significant performance gain results from the improvement of network localization capability, that is, the LAM could provide the RGB branch with more complementary location information. Meanwhile, integrating SCEM separately brings a 2.1-point performance gain as well. When both the LAM and SCEM are introduced, the mAP further goes up to 84.6%.

Considering the significant parameter increase when integrating both LAM and SCEM, we replace the backbone with the lightweight MobileNetV3. Surprisingly, not only the number of parameters drastically decreases to 32.2M from 93.7M, but the mAP also achieves an improvement of 0.9%. We argue that this may be attributed to the squeeze-and-excite bottleneck in MobileNetV3, which is beneficial for extracting features of weak defects. Additionally, the lightweight backbone's suitability for training defect datasets with fewer images may also contribute to this outcome.

Kernel Size and Number in SCEM. We conduct comparison experiments to validate the optimal kernel size (k) and number (n) of strip convolutions utilized in SCEM. As demonstrated in Table 5, the best results (85.5% mAP on NEU-DET and 76.6% mAP on GC10-DET) are achieved when applying two 1×5 and 5×1 strip convolutions in horizontal and vertical directions, respectively. It is found that the performance can be first improved and then dropped as the kernel size and number increase. We believe that appropriately increasing the kernel size and number of strip convolutions helps enlarge the receptive field of neurons, but excessively large and many kernels may introduce irrelevant background interference information, thus hampering the detection accuracy. In conclusion, we set the kernel size $k = 5$ and number $n = 2$ in SCEM.

5 Conclusion

In this paper, we present a novel LAGNet for weak and strip surface defect detection. The LAM is introduced to focus on the discriminative areas and enhance the subtle visual differences between defective and defect-free areas. Meanwhile, the LGB inherently guides the RGB branch to pay more attention to the spatial features, thus improving the localization ability for weak defects in images. Furthermore, SCEM is delicately designed using depth strip convolutions, tailored for encoding the long-range spatial relations of strip defects efficiently. The experimental results demonstrate the effectiveness and efficiency of LAGNet. To further achieve efficient model deployment on industrial production lines, it is worth simplifying the network by getting rid of the auxiliary LAM branch in the inference stage in our future work.

Acknowledgments. This study was supported in part by the China Postdoctoral Science Foundation (Grant 2021TQ0301), and in part by the National Natural Science Foundation of China (Grant 62106232, Grant 62172371, Grant 62036010, and Grant U21B2037).

References

1. Wang, J., Li, Q., Gan, J., Yu, H., Yang, X.: Surface defect detection via entity sparsity pursuit with intrinsic priors. IEEE Trans. Industr. Inf. **16**(1), 141–150 (2019)
2. Wang, H., Zhang, J., Tian, Y., Chen, H., Sun, H., Liu, K.: A simple guidance template-based defect detection method for strip steel surfaces. IEEE Trans. Industr. Inf. **15**(5), 2798–2809 (2018)
3. Zhou, A., Zheng, H., Li, M., Shao, W.: Defect inspection algorithm of metal surface based on machine vision. In: Proceedings of the IEEE International Conference on Measuring Technology and Mechatronics Automation (ICMTMA), pp. 45–49 (2020)
4. Israni, S., Jain, S.: Edge detection of license plate using Sobel operator. In: Proceedings of the IEEE International Conference on Electrical, Electronics, and Optimization Techniques (ICEEOT), pp. 3561–3563 (2016)
5. Zhou, Q., Wang, H.: CABF-YOLO: a precise and efficient deep learning method for defect detection on strip steel surface. Pattern Anal. Appl. **27**(2), 36 (2024)
6. Yang, K., Liu, Y., Zhang, S., Cao, J.: Surface defect detection of heat sink based on lightweight fully convolutional network. IEEE Trans. Instrum. Meas. **71**, 1–12 (2022)
7. Gong, Y., Liu, M., Wang, X., Liu, C., Hu, J.: Few-shot defect detection using feature enhancement and image generation for manufacturing quality inspection. Appl. Intell. **54**, 375–397 (2024)
8. Everingham, M., Van Gool, L., Williams, C., Winn, J., Zisserman, A.: The pascal visual object classes (VOC) challenge. Int. J. Comput. Vis. **88**(2), 303–338 (2010)
9. Girshick, R., Donahue, J., Darrell, T., Malik, J.: Rich feature hierarchies for accurate object detection and semantic segmentation. In: Proceedings of the IEEE Conference on Computer Vision and Pattern Recognition (CVPR), pp. 580–587 (2014)
10. Girshick, R.: Fast R-CNN. In: Proceedings of the IEEE International Conference on Computer Vision (ICCV), pp. 1440–1448 (2015)
11. Ren, S., He, K., Girshick, R., Sun, J.: Faster R-CNN: towards real-time object detection with region proposal networks. Adv. Neural Inf. Process. Syst. **28** (2015)
12. Liu, W., et al.: SSD: single shot multibox detector. In: Proceedings of the IEEE European Conference on Computer Vision (ECCV), pp. 21–37 (2016)
13. Redmon, J., Divvala, S., Girshick, R., Farhadi, A.: You only look once: unified, real-time object detection. In: Proceedings of the IEEE Conference on Computer Vision and Pattern Recognition (CVPR), pp. 779–788 (2016)
14. Redmon, J., Farhadi, A.: YOLO9000: better, faster, stronger. In: Proceedings of the IEEE Conference on Computer Vision and Pattern Recognition (CVPR), pp. 7263–7271 (2017)

15. Redmon, J., Farhadi, A.: YOLOv3: an incremental improvement. arXiv preprint arXiv:1804.02767 (2018)
16. Bochkovskiy, A., Wang, C.Y., Liao, H.Y.M.: YOLOv4: optimal speed and accuracy of object detection. arXiv preprint arXiv:2004.10934 (2020)
17. Jocher, G.: YOLOv5 by Ultralytics, May 2020. https://github.com/ultralytics/yolov5. https://doi.org/10.5281/zenodo.3908559
18. Wang, C.Y., Bochkovskiy, A., Liao, H.Y.M.: YOLOv7: trainable bag-of-freebies sets new state-of-the-art for real- time object detectors. In: Proceedings of the IEEE/CVF Conference on Computer Vision and Pattern Recognition (CVPR), pp. 7464–7475 (2023)
19. Zhao, C., Shu, X., Yan, X., Zuo, X., Zhu, F.: RDD-YOLO: a modified YOLO for detection of steel surface defects. Measurement **214**, 112776 (2023)
20. Gao, S.H., Cheng, M.M., Zhao, K., Zhang, X.Y., Yang, M.H., Torr, P.: Res2Net: a new multi-scale backbone architecture. IEEE Trans. Pattern Anal. Mach. Intell. **43**(2), 652–662 (2019)
21. Liu, R., Huang, M., Gao, Z., Cao, Z., Cao, P.: MSC-DNet: an efficient detector with multi-scale context for defect detection on strip steel surface. Measurement **209**, 112467 (2023)
22. Duan, K., Bai, S., Xie, L., Qi, H., Huang, Q., Tian, Q.: CenterNet: keypoint triplets for object detection. In: Proceedings of the IEEE/CVF International Conference on Computer Vision (ICCV), pp. 6569–6578 (2019)
23. Tian, R., Jia, M.: DCC-CenterNet: a rapid detection method for steel surface defects. Measurement **187**, 110211 (2022)
24. Yu, X., Lyu, W., Wang, C., Guo, Q., Zhou, D., Xu, W.: Progressive refined redistribution pyramid network for defect detection in complex scenarios. Knowl. Based Syst. **260**, 110176 (2023)
25. Ding, X., Guo, Y., Ding, G., Han, J.: ACNet: strengthening the kernel skeletons for powerful CNN via asymmetric convolution blocks. In: Proceedings of the IEEE/CVF International Conference on Computer Vision (ICCV), pp. 1911–1920 (2019)
26. Hou, Q., Zhang, L., Cheng, M.M., Feng, J.: Strip pooling: rethinking spatial pooling for scene parsing. In: Proceedings of the IEEE/CVF Conference on Computer Vision and Pattern Recognition (CVPR), pp. 4003–4012 (2020)
27. Yu, W., Zhou, P., Yan, S., Wang, X.: InceptionNeXt: when inception meets ConvNeXt. arXiv preprint arXiv:2303.16900 (2023)
28. Guo, M.H., Lu, C.Z., Hou, Q., Liu, Z., Cheng, M.M., Hu, S.M.: SegNeXt: rethinking convolutional attention design for semantic segmentation. Adv. Neural. Inf. Process. Syst. **35**, 1140–1156 (2022)
29. Howard, A., et al.: Searching for MobileNetV3. In: Proceedings of the IEEE/CVF International Conference on Computer Vision (ICCV), pp. 1314–1324 (2019)
30. He, Y., Song, K., Meng, Q., Yan, Y.: An end-to-end steel surface defect detection approach via fusing multiple hierarchical features. IEEE Trans. Instrum. Meas. **69**(4), 1493–1504 (2019)
31. Lv, X., Duan, F., Jiang, J., Fu, X., Gan, L.: Deep metallic surface defect detection: the new benchmark and detection network. Sensors **20**(6), 1562 (2020)
32. Kou, X., Liu, S., Cheng, K., Qian, Y.: Development of a YOLO-V3-based model for detecting defects on steel strip surface. Measurement **182**, 109454 (2021)
33. Ge, Z., Liu, S., Wang, F., Li, Z., Sun, J.: YOLOX: exceeding yolo series in 2021. arXiv preprint arXiv:2107.08430 (2021)
34. Wang, A., et al.: YOLOv10: real-time end-to-end object detection (2024). https://arxiv.org/abs/2405.14458
35. Hao, R., Lu, B., Cheng, Y., Li, X., Huang, B.: A steel surface defect inspection approach towards smart industrial monitoring. J. Intell. Manuf. **32**, 1833–1843 (2021)
36. Wang, L., Liu, X., Ma, J., Su, W., Li, H.: Real-time steel surface defect detection with improved multi-scale YOLO-v5. Processes **11**(5), 1357 (2023)

37. Li, S., Kong, F., Wang, R., Luo, T., Shi, Z.: EFD-YOLOv4: a steel surface defect detection network with encoder-decoder residual block and feature alignment module. Measurement **220**, 113359 (2023)
38. Zhang, L., Fu, Z., Guo, H., Sun, Y., Li, X., Xu, M.: Multiscale local and global feature fusion for the detection of steel surface defects. Electronics **12**(14), 3090 (2023)
39. Fang, Q., Han, D., Wang, Z.: Cross-modality fusion transformer for multispectral object detection. Available at SSRN 4227745 (2022)
40. Shen, J., Chen, Y., Liu, Y., Zuo, X., Fan, H., Yang, W.: ICAFusion: iterative cross-attention guided feature fusion for multispectral object detection. Pattern Recogn. **145**, 109913 (2024)
41. Zhang, J., Lei, J., Xie, W., Fang, Z., Li, Y., Du, Q.: SuperYOLO: super resolution assisted object detection in multimodal remote sensing imagery. IEEE Trans. Geosci. Remote Sens. **61**, 1–15 (2023)
42. Zhang, J., Lei, J., Xie, W., Li, Y., Yang, G., Jia, X.: Guided hybrid quantization for object detection in remote sensing imagery via one-to-one self-teaching. IEEE Trans. Geosci. Remote Sens. **61** (2023)
43. Vaswani, A., et al.: Attention is all you need. Adv. Neural Inf. Process. Syst. **30** (2017)
44. Cai, Z., Vasconcelos, N.: Cascade R-CNN: delving into high quality object detection. In: 2018 IEEE/CVF Conference on Computer Vision and Pattern Recognition, pp. 6154–6162 (2018). https://doi.org/10.1109/CVPR.2018.00644
45. Lin, T.Y., Goyal, P., Girshick, R., He, K., Dollár, P.: Focal loss for dense object detection. In: 2017 IEEE International Conference on Computer Vision (ICCV), pp. 2999–3007 (2017). https://doi.org/10.1109/ICCV.2017.324

Weighted Spatiotemporal Feature and Multi-task Learning for Masked Facial Expression Recognition

Shiwei He, Yingjuan Jia, Hanpu Wang, Xinyu Liu, Jianmeng Zhou, Huijie Gu, Mengyan Li, and Tong Chen$^{(\boxtimes)}$

Southwest University, Chongqing, China
c_tong@swu.edu.cn

Abstract. Human facial expressions are a vital form of non-verbal communication that convey significant emotional information. Occasionally, individuals exhibit facial expressions that do not correspond to their genuine emotions, which are termed masked facial expressions (MFEs). Automatic recognition of MFEs can reveal individuals' real feelings. However, the complexity inherent in MFEs, resulting from various factors, poses a significant challenge for extracting discriminative representations from MFE videos. In this study, we innovatively designed a multi-task learning network to decompose the challenging task of mixed expression recognition task into two simpler sub-tasks, thereby alleviating the learning burden on the network. Furthermore, we propose a method called spatiotemporal feature modulation (STFM), which comprises a spatiotemporal feature extractor (STFE) and feature weighting module (FWM), aiming to enable the network to focus on features that are beneficial for classification. Additionally, we developed an adaptive spatial attention module (ASAM) to eliminate redundant data in videos and enhance model efficiency by leveraging the action information embedded in dynamic images. The experimental results demonstrate that our method excels in most challenging 36-class task, achieving an accuracy improvement of 4.75% and 0.77% on the 36-class task and 6E task respectively compared to the current state-of-the-art methods.

Keywords: Masked facial expression · Emotion recognition · Multi-task learning · Dynamic image · Transformer

1 Introduction

Humans have the remarkable ability to convey a wide range of emotions through complex facial muscle movements, which are commonly known as facial expressions [2,10,18]. Studies have indicated that 55% of human emotional information is communicated through facial expressions [15]. Facial expressions provide a direct insight into an individual's internal emotional state. Occasionally, facial expressions are consistent with genuine emotions, but in certain situations, individuals may disguise their real feelings by employing specific facial expressions due to social strategies, cultural habits, or personal defense mechanisms. For instance, during a negotiation, even if someone feels angry at the other

© The Author(s), under exclusive license to Springer Nature Singapore Pte Ltd. 2025
P. Didyk and J. Hou (Eds.): CVM 2025, LNCS 15663, pp. 369–393, 2025.
https://doi.org/10.1007/978-981-96-5809-1_20

party's provocation, they may choose to smile instead of showing anger in order to avoid revealing their vulnerability [4]. These inconsistent expressions, which arise from conscious control of facial muscles that do not reflect genuine emotions, are termed masked facial expressions (MFEs) [8]. Research suggests that MFEs occur quite frequently in human daily life [20]. Even children are capable of distinguishing between real emotions and those deliberately expressed [7]. In MFEs, individuals are unable to fully suppress the leakage of their real emotions [21]. Consequently, by accurately identifying and interpreting individuals' MFEs, it is possible to infer their current emotional state. This technology has a multitude of applications, including medical diagnosis, business negotiation, judicial interrogation, and human-computer interaction.

In recent years, the rapid advancement of computer vision technology has significantly propelled the field of automatic expression recognition. In addition to the traditional automatic expression recognition, novel research areas such as micro-expression recognition have also emerged [12,19,26]. As a new challenge in this field, the progress of research on MFEs has historically been constrained by the lack of dataset resources. It was not until 2021 that the Institute of Psychology of the Chinese Academy of Sciences established the first masked facial expression dataset (MFED) [16], effectively addressing this shortage. In the dataset, participants would first be induced with the experienced emotion through an emotional video. Then they would be asked to immediately complete some required expressions. The required expression may or may not be consistent with the experienced emotion. The combination of 6 experienced emotions and 6 required expressions gives a total of 36 mixed expressions. Among these, when the experienced emotion is consistent with the required expression, they form ordinary macro-expressions, totaling of six. The remaining 30 expressions, where the experienced emotion does not match the required expression, are categorized as masked facial expressions. The MFED uses video clips from the moment participants received an emotional cue (onset) to the moment their expression ended (offset). For each sequence of MFEs, for example, "sad to happy" indicates that the experienced emotion is sad and the required expression is happy. Figure 1 shows a segment of the "sad to happy" sequence for subject 18 from the MFED and the apex frame marking the moment when the required expression reaches its highest intensity.

After the publication of MFED, Zhou et al. [32] firstly conducted a further study and found that the onset frames do not necessarily contain the leakage of the experienced emotion, while the apex frames are more likely to contain the features of the required expressions. Therefore it is difficult to accurately identify MFEs by simply using the onset and apex frames. Subsequently, through statistical testing of LBP-TOP features, Zhou et al. demonstrated that even when the required expression is the same, there are significant differences in the facial action units (AUs) movement patterns when participants use a different expression to mask their experienced emotions. In the task of recognizing masked expressions, the key lies in how to extract discriminative features from

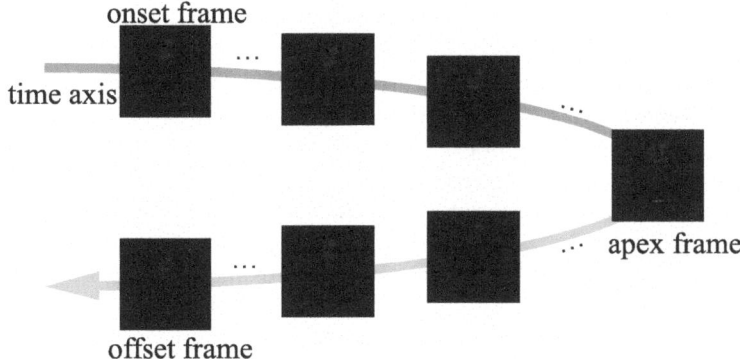

onset frame

time axis

apex frame

offset frame

Fig. 1. A segment of the "sad to happy" sequence for subject 18

expression sequences. This process should make full use of the AU movement pattern characteristics of different masked expressions.

Traditional facial expression recognition tasks typically involve classifying the basic six categories of facial expressions [22], including happiness, sadness, anger, surprise, disgust, and fear. Despite the intricate nature of facial muscle movements, the six expressions exhibit recognizable patterns of facial muscle activity [3]. However, in contrast to typical facial expressions, masked facial expressions (MFEs), as illustrated in Fig. 2, are often dominated by the required expression's spatial features. This dominance results in more similar spatial characteristics among mixed expressions when the required expression is the same, thereby making them more challenging to differentiate. Moreover, the required expression and the experienced emotion are deeply coupled. Throughout the sequences of MFEs, the leakage of the experienced emotion can happen at any moment and appear in various forms. For instance, it might only influence the display of AUs related to the required expression, whereas in other cases, it could also show AUs that consistent with the experienced emotion. Although CNN-based methods have achieved good recognition performance in macro-expressions and micro-expressions, they can not effectively capture long-range dependencies and lack the ability to address deep coupling issues.

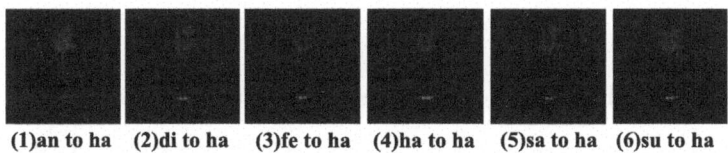

(1)an to ha   (2)di to ha   (3)fe to ha   (4)ha to ha   (5)sa to ha   (6)su to ha

Fig. 2. The onset frames of the six mixed expressions for subject 18 when required expression is happy, where (1)–(6) represent the experienced emotions of anger, disgust, fear, happiness, sadness, and surprise, respectively.

In this study, we propose a transformer-based multi-task spatial-temporal weighting network (MTSTWN) for recognizing MFEs. To address the issue of spatial feature similarity in MFEs under the same required expression, MTSTWN introduces the spatiotemporal feature modulation(STFM) method. In the STFM, the spatiotemporal feature extractor (STFE) explores the spatiotemporal features within the feature maps, enabling the network to fully leverage temporal information. Subsequently, the feature weighting module (FWM) applies spatiotemporal feature weights to the extracted features, aiming to enable the network to focus on learning critical features while ignoring irrelevant ones. To solve the challenge of deep coupling between genuine emotions and posed expressions, MTSTWN applies a multi-task learning framework to MFEs recognition task. This framework simplifies the complex task of 36 mixed expressions classification into two simpler sub-tasks: 6 experienced emotions classification and 6 required expressions classification. This approach not only significantly reduces the difficulty of classification but also effectively separates the two types of expression features, thereby enhancing the robustness of the features learned by the model. Furthermore, by utilizing the Transformer architecture, MTSTWN can efficiently capture long-range dependencies, enabling more accurate extraction of cues related to the experienced emotion from the overall features. MTSTWN also includes an adaptive spatial attention module (ASAM) based on dynamic images. It generates dynamic images from sequential data and uses a lightweight network to learn a mask, which is applied to the feature map. This ensures that the extracted features focus on the regions where actions occur, reducing redundant information in the video.

The contributions of this paper are summarized as follows:

1. The STFM module is proposed to enhance the model's ability of learning spatiotemporal features while suppressing the impact of inter-class similar features in the spatial domain.
2. A multi-task learning framework is innovatively introduced into the field of masked facial expression recognition. It enables the network to more effectively learn the disentangled features of two types of expressions.
3. We propose the ASAM module, which directs the network to focus on expression-related regions while minimizing the impact of irrelevant areas, thereby further improving the model's attention to key features.

2   Related Work

2.1   Automatic Recognition of Masked Facial Expression

When emotions arise, people can adopt different strategies to conceal their true feelings. If they choose to maintain a neutral expression, micro-expressions will appear when the suppression of genuine emotions fails. If they use another expression to replace the one that corresponds to their genuine emotions, this is referred to as a masked expression [32]. After the release of MFED, Zhou et al. [32] conducted further research. Using statistical testing methods, it was demonstrated that the AU movement pattern of different masked expressions exhibit distinct differences. Based on this, they proposed a special spatiotemporal handcrafted feature called dynamic AU intensity feature (DAIF). This feature captures the intensity of different AUs in each frame of the masked expression sequence and uses a weighting module to amplify the pattern differences between various expressions. The DAIF is then fed into a network with a visual transformer architecture to perform the classification task, achieving a significant improvement in recognition accuracy compared to the baseline. In addition, there are other works that further contribute to this field. Zhang et al. [29] employ CNNs (VGGNet, GoogLeNet, ResNet, MobileNet) along with data augmentation and regularization techniques, achieving a notable improvement in recognition performance compared to traditional methods. Similarly, Liu et al. [13] introduce a transfer learning approach using pre-trained ResNet18, combined with data augmentation, to enhance the model's generalization ability.

2.2   Multi-task Learning

Multi-task Learning (MTL) is a paradigm in machine learning. Unlike the traditional approach where tasks are executed independently, MTL simultaneously optimizes multiple related tasks, uncovering and leveraging the common features required by these tasks. This encourages the model to learn shared representations that can generalize across tasks, thereby improving the model's learning efficiency and generalization ability [30]. In MTL, the total loss is a combination of the losses from various related tasks. For each task, the other related tasks can be viewed as constraints on that task, which effectively narrows the hypothesis space of the MTL model by handling multiple tasks at once, thereby reducing the risk of over-fitting [27]. Multi-task Learning is also widely applied in expression recognition. For example, Li et al. [11] introduced the poker face vision transformer (PF-ViT) in facial expression recognition, simultaneously performing emotion recognition and generating emotionless faces, integrating multi-task learning to achieve disentanglement between emotion-related and emotion-irrelevant features. Hu et al. [9] designed a new sparse multi-task learning framework that combines handcrafted features and deep features to achieve micro-expression recognition. Zheng et al. [31] proposed DDMTL, which utilizes deep multi-task learning to integrate category label information and sample space distribution information for recognizing facial expressions, demonstrating superior performance even with less training data. Savchenko [23] researched the application of multi-task learning in facial recognition and attribute classification (including age, gender, and ethnicity), achieving excellent emotion classification performance on the AffectNet dataset. Nie et al. [17] introduced the GEME network, which treats gender recognition as an auxiliary task to assist the main task of micro-expression recognition, thereby improving the accuracy of micro-expression recognition.

2.3   Dynamic Image

Obtaining precise representations of videos is a core challenge in the field of video understanding. Fernando et al. [6] argue that if a function can accurately order the frames of a video in time based on the video's appearance, then this function can effectively capture the evolution of appearance within the video. By learning such an ordering function, the parameters of these functions can be used as a new representation of the video. Based on this idea, Bilen et al. [1] proposed the concept of dynamic image, where the temporal average features of each frame in the video are treated as vectors to be ordered. They learn to find a target vector (i.e. the dynamic image) such that the inner product between this target vector and the average feature vectors at each time point reflects the temporal order of the video frames. Since the target vector has the same dimensions as the frames, it can be represented as a standard RGB image, namely the dynamic image. The dynamic image not only succinctly captures the main visual content of the video but also retains important temporal information. The advantage of this method lies in its ability to compress the spatiotemporal information of the video into a single image, allowing traditional image processing techniques to be directly applied to video analysis tasks. For example, Verma et al. [24, 25] introduced the dynamic image into the field of micro-expression recognition. They employed convolutional neural networks to process the dynamic images generated by micro-expression sequences, extracting multi-scale features that contain both temporal and spatial information, thereby significantly improving the accuracy of micro-expression recognition.

3   Method

3.1   Overview

In the task of masked facial expressions (MFEs) recognition, it is crucial to accurately classify two distinct types of facial expressions. One is the individual's genuine inner emotions, also known as the experienced emotion. The other is the false expressions that individuals deliberately present to conceal their true feelings, referred to as the required expression. The framework of the proposed MTSTWN is shown in Fig. 3. Specifically, this study utilizes a multi-task learning framework that combines knowledge learned from two recognition tasks: required expressions and experienced emotions, to classify 36 types of mixed expressions. As shown in Fig. 3, after image preprocessing, the video sequences are normalized to 30 frames. Next, a fast dynamic image algorithm [1] is utilized to compute the dynamic image for each sequence (see Sect. 3.3). Subsequently, the dynamic images are input into a lightweight network to generate the attention mask. Meanwhile, the sequence data is converted into grayscale images and sent to the CNN network, where 3D convolution is used to extract primary features. The attention mask is then applied to the obtained feature map, and the results are sent into the multi-task learning framework for further feature extraction and classification. For the multi-task learning framework, this study adopts a hard parameter sharing strategy. The input data first passes through layers with shared parameters to extract features common to both tasks. Within the shared layers, a spatiotemporal feature modulation mechanism is incorporated (see Sect. 3.5). This mechanism is composed of two components. The first is the spatiotemporal feature extractor (STFE), which is capable of comprehensively extracting the spatiotemporal features hidden within the video sequences. The second component is the spatiotemporal feature weighting module (FWM). This module enables the model to focus on the features that are conducive to classification. At the output stage, task-specific methods are applied to extract task-relevant features and complete the classification. The model is optimized by combining the weighted losses from both tasks.

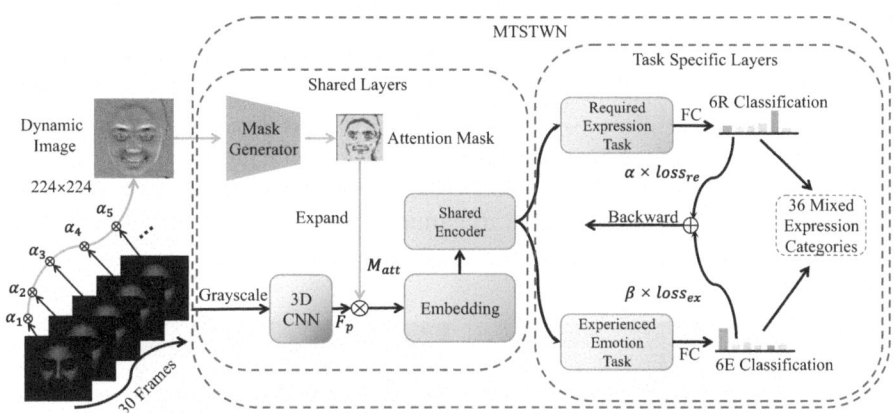

Fig. 3. Structure diagram of the multi-task spatial-temporal weighting network (MTSTWN)

3.2 Preprocessing

Before feeding the video frame data into the network, this study applies a series of preprocessing strategies aimed at ensuring the network focuses on facial information while removing background and other irrelevant features. First, the MTCNN algorithm [28] is used to detect faces in each video frame and crop them to a uniform size, effectively eliminating background and unrelated content. Next, three landmarks of a standard facial model are selected as references to construct an affine transformation matrix, aligning the faces to mitigate issues caused by inconsistent facial angles or head movements during the experiments. Following that, the temporal interpolation model (TIM) [33] is applied to interpolate the data, standardizing all video sequences to the optimal 30 frames [16]. Finally, the preprocessed data is structured into dimensions of $3 \times 30 \times 224 \times 224$ to serve as the input for the network.

3.3   Adaptive Spatial Attention Module (ASAM)

Unlike image classification tasks, video understanding involves a significant amount of redundant information. In the case of MFEs sequences, preprocessing video frames can help eliminate background clutter, allowing the model to focus more on facial muscle movement features. Even within the facial region, some features, like those around the tip of the nose, may not contribute much to expression classification. Thus, for the task of recognizing MFEs, the network needs to concentrate on areas where significant motion changes occur. To achieve this, this study introduces an adaptive spatial attention module based on dynamic images. This module guides the network in identifying which facial features are most relevant for classifying MFEs, ultimately enhancing recognition performance.

Dyanmic Image. Dynamic image, a concept first introduced by Bilen et al. [1] for action recognition, serve as an effective representation of video frame sequences. They encapsulate the features of actions, including the spatial features of the areas where those actions occur. Compared to using onset frames to predict action location information, dynamic images can capture more relevant action information.

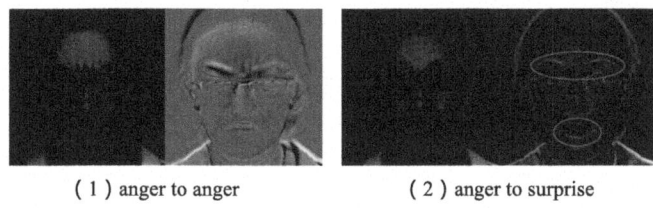

(1) anger to anger   (2) anger to surprise

Fig. 4. Illustration of dynamic images. The experienced emotion and required expression for (1) are both anger, (2) has a experienced emotion of anger and required expression is surprise. For both (1) and (2), the left side shows the sequence onset frame, and the right side displays the dynamic image.

Figure 4 illustrates a comparison between the onset frame of a sequence sample and the dynamic image generated from that sequence. In Fig. 4(1), movement occurs in the eyebrow and mouth regions, which is also reflected in the dynamic image. Conversely, for pixels where no movement occurs, the dynamic image tends to average out the information. Moreover, in Fig. 4, when observing the mouth region in (1) and (2), it is evident that the greater and more intense the movement, the more pronounced the relevant areas appear in the dynamic image. Therefore, we can utilize the dynamic image to localize facial action regions.

Given a video data $V = \{I_1, I_2, \ldots, I_n\}$ with n frames, where i is the index of the i-th frame in the video, the dynamic image can be computed using a fast algorithm. The process is as follows:

$$DI(V) = \sum_{t=1}^{n} \alpha_t I_t \qquad (1)$$

Where α_t is computed using the following formula:

$$\alpha_t = 2(n - t + 1) - (n + 1)(H_n - H_{t-1}) \qquad (2)$$

Here, $H_t = \sum_{j=1}^{t} 1/j$ is the j-th harmonic number, with $H_0 = 0$. After obtaining the dynamic image, we further attempt to learn the spatial attention mask for each sequence's dynamic image.

Mask Generator. To learn which parts of the facial area deserve more attention, we first extract the dynamic image for each sequence. Then, we use a mask generator to create a mask for the feature map and apply it to the feature map. This study employs a lightweight network design, specifically a 2D convolutional layer, as the mask generator to avoid introducing excessive additional parameters. The specific process is as follows:

$$M_{att} = Expand(2DConv(DI)) \qquad (3)$$

Here, M_{att} is the generated attention mask. Applying the attention mask to the feature map F_p can be expressed as:

$$\widehat{F}_p = M_{att} \times F_p \qquad (4)$$

Here, $\widehat{F}_p$ is the feature map after applying the attention mask.

3.4 Multi-task Learning Framework

In MFEs, experienced emotions and required expressions are deeply coupled, and this coupling manifests in various ways. For example, the leakage of genuine expression may occur or not occur in the first frame of the sequence. Furthermore, the extent to which experienced emotions influence required expressions varies throughout the entire frame sequence, making it challenging to directly extract features from the 36 types of mixed expressions. To address this challenge, this study employs a multi-task learning framework with hard parameter sharing, dividing the network structure into shared layers and task-specific layers. The shared layers extract common emotional features from the frame sequences, while the two task-specific layers focus on mining effective features from the outputs of the shared layers, allowing for a certain level of decoupling between required expressions and experienced emotions. This approach reduces the complexity of classification.

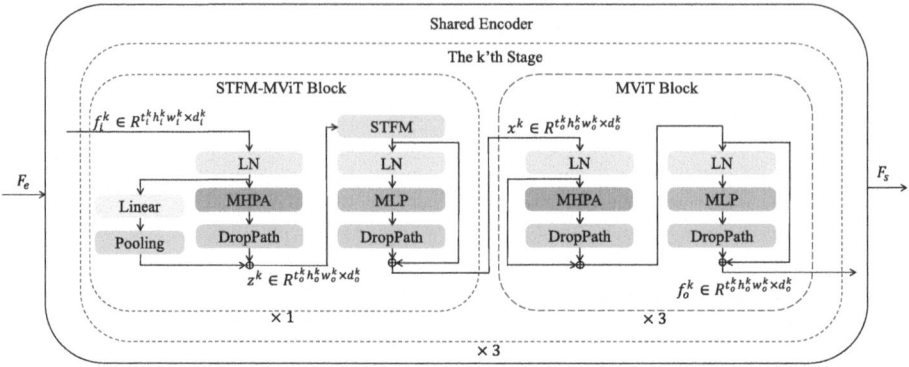

Fig. 5. Structure diagram of the shared encoder

Shared Layers. The shared layers are divided into two parts, as shown in Fig. 3. The first part consists of the 3D convolutional neural network (CNN) and the mask generator, while the second part is the shared encoder. Given a video sequence, after preprocessing and grayscale conversion we obtain a video $V \in R^{1 \times 30 \times 224 \times 224}$ that is sent to the 3D CNN to extract primary features from the frame V while reducing the scale of the feature map in both spatial and temporal dimensions. The feature map $F_p \in R^{C \times T \times H \times W}$ is derived from the CNN, where C is the number of channels in the feature map after CNN, T is the size in the temporal dimension, and H and W are the height and width of the feature map. After applying the attention mask to the feature map, the results are fed into the patch embedding module to obtain $F_e \in R^{THW \times D}$, where D is the dimension of the embedding vector. Finally, F_e serves as the input to the shared encoder.

The structure of the shared encoder is shown in Fig. 5. The shared encoder is responsible for extracting the shared features of experienced emotions and required expressions from the frame sequences while eliminating emotion-irrelevant features from the data. Considering that the characteristics of genuine emotions are embedded within the entire sequence, the network must possess strong long-range modeling capabilities. To balance model performance with computational complexity, this study employs multiscale vision transformers (MViT) [5] as the backbone. The shared encoder consists of three stages, with the first block of each stage being an MViT block that includes the spatiotemporal feature modulation module, called the STFM-MViT block. Each block includes a multi-head pooling attention (MHPA) module, which differs from the traditional multi-head attention module. Before performing the multi-head attention calculations, the MHPA module first pools the query, key, and value. The output length of the MHPA is determined solely by the length of the query. Moreover, if the length of the query decreases, the channel dimension of the output features will increase. The computation process of the self-attention mechanism in the MHPA module of the first block of the k-th stage is summarized as follows: Firstly, the input is passed through a linear transformation, which can be represented by the following formula:

$$\widehat{Q} = LN(f_i^k)W_Q, \ \widehat{K} = LN(f_i^k)W_K, \ \widehat{V} = LN(f_i^k)W_V. \tag{5}$$

where, As shown in Fig. 5, f_i^k represents the input feature of the k-th stage, and LN stands for the layer-normalization, $W_Q, W_K, W_V \in R^{d_i^k \times d_o^k}$ (d_i^k is the input feature dimension of the k-th stage) are all embedding matrices. Then, the input is processed through a pooling layer and performs self-attention calculations, which can be represented by the following formula:

$$Q = P(\widehat{Q}; \Theta_Q), \ K = P(\widehat{K}; \Theta_K), \ V = P(\widehat{V}; \Theta_V) \tag{6}$$

$$Attention(Q, K, V) = Softmax\left(QK^T/\sqrt{d_o^k}\right)V \tag{7}$$

where The operator $P(\cdot; \Theta)$ performs a pooling kernel computation on the input tensor along each of the dimensions. Θ represents the parameters of the pooling operation and consists of three parts: the pooling kernel k, the stride s, and the padding p. As shown in Fig. 5, for the first Block of each stage in MHPA, the pooling stride of the Query is set higher than 1, which reduces the input feature dimensions from $t_i^k h_i^k w_i^k \times d_i^k$ to $t_o^k h_o^k w_o^k \times d_o^k$, To keep the feature sizes consistent in the residual connections, linear and pooling layers are applied to adjust the feature dimensions accordingly. For the last three blocks of each stage, the query's pooling stride is 1, so the input dimensions remain unchanged. Additionally, the first block includes an STFM module to further capture spatiotemporal features and enhance classification performance (see Sect. 3.5). Overall, as shown in Fig. 5, the computation process for the kth stage is as follows:

$$z^k = DropPath(MHPA(LN(f_i^k))) + Pooling(Linear(LN(f_i^k))) \tag{8}$$

$$x^k = DropPath(MLP(LN(STFM(z^k)))) + STFM(z^k) \tag{9}$$

$$f_o^k = MViTBlock^n(x^k), \ n = 3 \tag{10}$$

Here, $DropPath(\cdot)$ is a commonly used regularization technique in transformers, $Linear(\cdot)$ is a linear transformation layer used to change the feature dimension from d_i^k to d_o^k, and $Pooling(\cdot)$ is a pooling layer used to reduce the feature length from $t_i^k h_i^k w_i^k$ to $t_o^k h_o^k w_o^k$. And z^k represents the output of the MHPA module in the first block of the k-th stage, and x^k represents the output of the first block in the k-th stage. $MViTBlock^n(\cdot)$ refers to a sequence of n consecutive MViT blocks. Finally, F_e is processed by the shared encoder to produce F_s which is then passed to the subsequent task-specific layers.

Task-Specific Layers. As shown in Fig. 3, the data passes through the shared layers to generate a shared representation F_s for both the required expression and experienced emotion. In traditional single-task learning, F_s would go through global average pooling and a classification head. However, with 36 types of mixed expressions, identifying discriminative features is challenging because the leak-age way of genuine expressions are different across samples. MFEs are already encoded by the human brain as a blend of required expressions and genuine expression, which can be seen as prior knowledge for the network. This helps the network analyze MFEs from both perspectives, making classification easier. Additionally, neural networks are prone to over-fitting, which reduces the test accuracy. Studies show that multi-task learning can effectively reduce the risk of over-fitting [27].

To effectively extract useful features from the shared representation F_s, which comes from a transformer-based network, both task-specific layers utilize the original transformer encoder structure, with parameters that are independent of each other. The computation process can be expressed as follows:

$$F_{ex} = MHA(F_e) \tag{11}$$

$$F_{re} = MHA(F_e) \tag{12}$$

Here, $MHA(\cdot)$ stands for multi-head attention mechanism. F_{ex} and F_{re} represent the features output from the experienced emotion branch and the required expression branch, respectively. Each feature is processed through a global aver-age pooling layer and a fully connected (FC) layer to obtain the classification results p_{ex} and p_{re} for 6 categories. To obtain the classification results for 36 cate-gories, this study defines a matrix $M = \{m_{ij}|0 \leq i \leq 5, 0 \leq j \leq 5, m_{ij} \in \mathbb{R}\}$, and let $m_{p_{ex}p_{re}} = p_{36}$. Meaning that the predicted results p_{ex} and p_{re} are mapped to the corresponding 36-category prediction result.

Both tasks are classification tasks, and this study employs the cross-entropy loss function to calculate the loss for each task individually. The two losses are then combined using a weighted sum to obtain the final loss. The calculation process can be expressed as follows:

First, the cross-entropy loss function is defined as:

$$CELoss = -\frac{1}{N} \sum_{j=1}^{N} \sum_{i=1}^{K} y_{ji} \log(\hat{y}_{ji}) \tag{13}$$

Here, N is the number of samples, K is the number of expression types, the labels are represented as $Y = \{y_{ji}\}$, and the predicted results are denoted as $\hat{Y} = \{\hat{y}_{ji}\}$, where $j = 1, 2, \cdots, N, i = 1, 2, \cdots, K$. Then, by applying the cross-entropy loss function, we can obtain $Loss_{ex}$ and $Loss_{re}$, and calculate the final loss as follows:

$$Loss = \beta \times Loss_{ex} + \alpha \times Loss_{re} \tag{14}$$

Where β and α are the weights used to adjust the contributions of the experi-enced emotion task and the required expression task, respectively.

3.5   Spatiotemporal Feature Modulation (STFM)

Another factor that hinders the improvement of the recognition rate for 36 types of mixed expressions is the inter-class similarity of these expressions under the same required expression. And this similarity is primarily concentrated in the spatial features. For example, in Fig. 2, when the required expression is happiness, AU12 is activated across all instances. This similarity makes it challenging for the network to effectively extract distinguishing features for each category. Zhou et al. [32] conducted a comparative study by extracting the intensity of action units (AUs) from video frames and found that when the required expression is happy, AU12 is activated, but the degree of activation varies. For instance, when the real emotion is sad, the activation level of AU12 is significantly lower than when the real emotion is happy. To learn these features more effectively, this study proposes a spatiotemporal feature modulation module comprising a spatiotemporal feature extractor (STFE) and a feature weighting module (FWM). The feature extractor is responsible for further extracting spatiotemporal features, while the feature weighting module focuses on identifying which features are most beneficial for recognizing mixed expressions.

Spatiotemporal Feature Extractor (STFE). To extract spatiotemporal features more effectively from sequential data, this study introduces a dedicated temporal and spatial feature extraction module. This module splits the input data into three parts along the channel dimension, with one part for extracting temporal features, another for extracting spatial features, and the remaining the left part unchanged. Finally, the three outputs are concatenated in their original order to create the module's final output. Figure 6 illustrates the structure of the STFE.

In the STFM-MViT Block, the output of the first residual structure $z^k \in R^{t_o^k h_o^k w_o^k \times d_o^k}$ (where k indicates the stage in the shared encoder) will serve as the input to the STFE. First, to enable operations along the temporal and spatial dimensions, z^k needs to be reshaped into $\hat{z}^k$, changing the data dimensions from $t_o^k h_o^k w_o^k \times d_o^k$ to $d_o^k \times t_o^k \times h_o^k \times w_o^k$. Next, $\hat{z}^k$ is split into three parts along the channel dimension, a process that can be expressed as:

$$\hat{z}_1^k = S(\hat{z}^k; 0, \frac{1}{3}d_o^k) \tag{15}$$

$$\hat{z}_2^k = S(\hat{z}^k; \frac{1}{3}d_o^k, \frac{2}{3}d_o^k) \tag{16}$$

$$\hat{z}_3^k = S(\hat{z}^k; \frac{2}{3}d_o^k, d_o^k) \tag{17}$$

Where $S(x; start, end)$ denotes slicing x along the channel dimension, starting from $start$ and ending at $end - 1$. $\hat{z}_1^k$ is directed to the temporal feature extractor to extract temporal features. $\hat{z}_2^k$ is sent to the spatial feature extractor to extract spatial features. $\hat{z}_3^k$ is retained as a part of output.

The cues for experienced emotions are distributed along the entire sequence, requiring a focus on global temporal features. Although traditional convolutional neural network can extract temporal features, their limited receptive fields may prevent them from fully capturing these global features, impacting the performance. Inspired by DTF [14], this study replaces one-dimensional time domain

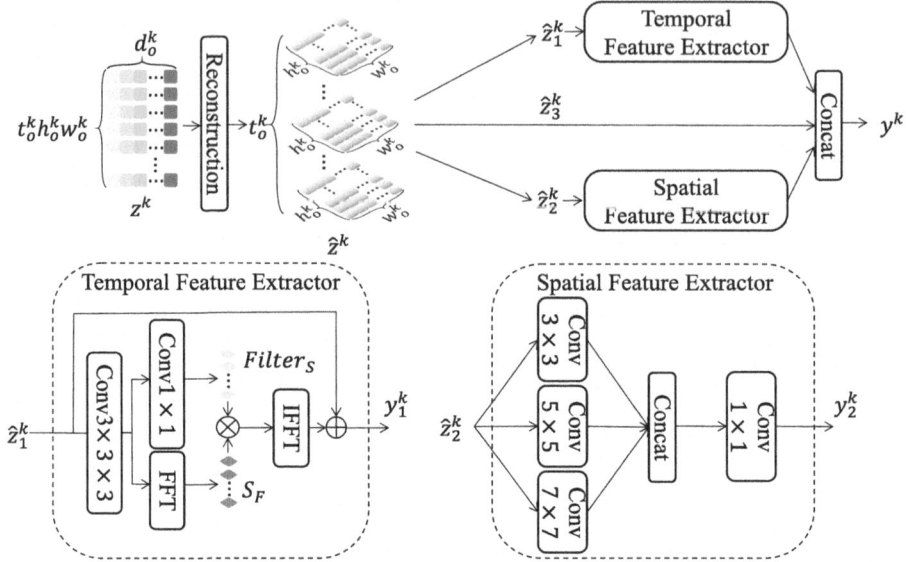

Fig. 6. Structure diagram of spatiotemporal feature extractor (STFE)

convolution with frequency domain modulation for temporal feature extraction. This approach is based on the principle that time domain convolution is equivalent to multiplication in the frequency domain. Specifically, the method involves learning the frequency domain filters from the time domain data, multiplying it with the result obtained from applying the fast fourier transform (FFT), and then using the inverse fast fourier transform (IFFT) to return to the time domain. The detailed process for extracting temporal features is as follows:

As shown in Fig. 6, in temporal feature extractor, before applying the FFT on the time axis of the feature map, a 3D convolution with a kernel size of 3 is used to aggregate local spatiotemporal features at each spatial location, enabling the extraction of richer temporal features at every spatial position. Then, the FFT is applied to the time domain data, which can be expressed as follows:

$$S_F = FFT(3DConv(\hat{z}_1^k)), \ S_F \in C^{c \times m \times h_o^k \times w_o^k} \tag{18}$$

Here, S_F is the feature transformed into the frequency domain and $c = d_o^k/3$ represents the number of channels in $\hat{z}_1^k$, and $m = \lfloor t_o^k/2 \rfloor + 1$ denotes the number of frequency domain filters' point number after applying the FFT to the time domain data. Additionally, the time domain data is processed through a convolution layer to learn parameters with dimensions $d_o^k \times m \times h_o^k \times w_o^k \times 2$, which are ultimately combined to form $Filter_S \in C^{d_o^k \times m \times h_o^k \times w_o^k}$. The frequency domain modulation is then performed, followed by the IFFT to obtain the processed time domain data, expressed as follows:

$$y_1^k = IFFT(S_F \times Filter_S) + \hat{z}_1^k \tag{19}$$

where y_1^k is the output of the temporal feature extractor.

In MFEs recognition, spatial features are equally important, requiring the network to capture subtle differences in spatial information. To achieve this, this study employs a multi-scale convolution approach to further extract effective spatial features from the feature maps. Specifically, the input data will merge the time dimension and the batch size dimension before being fed into convolutional layers with kernel sizes of $3 \times 3, 5 \times 5, 7 \times 7$ to extract multi-scale spatial features. The outputs from these layers are then concatenated along the channel dimension. Finally, to maintain consistency between the input and output dimensions, a 1×1 convolution is used for downsampling along the channel dimension. The above process can be summarized as follows:

$$y_2^k = Conv_{1\times1}\{Concat[Conv_{3\times3}(\hat{z}_2^k), Conv_{5\times5}(\hat{z}_2^k), Conv_{7\times7}(\hat{z}_2^k)]\} \tag{20}$$

Here, y_2^k represents the output of the spatial feature extractor. Finally, the outputs from the three parts are concatenated to obtain the output of the STFE module, expressed as follows:

$$y^k = Concat(y_1^k, y_2^k, \hat{z}_3^k) \tag{21}$$

Here, y^k represents the output of the STFE.

Feature Weighting Module (FWM). After passing through the STFE module, the features produce the output y^k. Next, the FWM module learns which parts of the features are more beneficial for classification. The structure of the FWM is illustrated in Fig. 7.

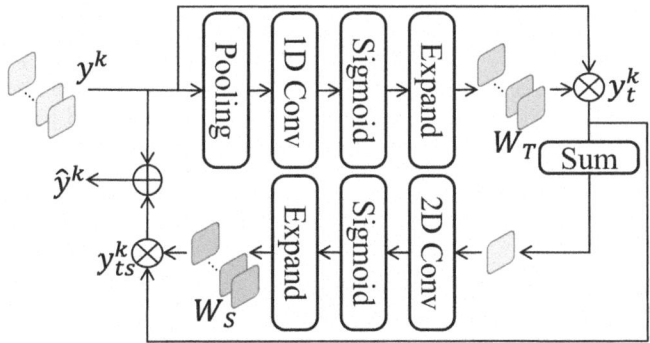

Fig. 7. Structure diagram of feature weighting module (FWM)

The FWM consists of two stages. The first stage focuses on learning the weights for each time point in the feature map, while the second stage learns the weights for each spatial location. Specifically, the FWM takes $y^k \in R^{d_o^k \times t_o^k \times h_o^k \times w_o^k}$ as input. It first applies average pooling to compress the spatial information, resulting in a data dimension of $d_o^k \times t_o^k \times 1 \times 1$ This data is then fed into a one-dimensional convolution to learn the weights for each time point, followed by a sigmoid activation function to obtain the final weights. Once the weights are acquired, they are broadcasted across the spatial dimension to yield $W_T \in R^{d_o^k \times t_o^k \times h_o^k \times w_o^k}$. Finally, the weights W_T are applied to y^k, a process that can be expressed as:

$$y_t^k = W_T \times y^k \tag{22}$$

Here, y_t^k is the output of y^k after applying temporal weighting. Similarly, y_t^k undergoes spatial weight learning. First, the temporal dimension information is compressed by summing along the time dimension, resulting in data with dimensions $d_o^k \times h_o^k \times w_o^k$. This data is then passed through a 2D convolution to learn spatial weights, followed by sigmoid function to obtain the spatial weights. After broadcasting, the final weight W_s is obtained, and this weight is applied to y_t^k. This process can be expressed as:

$$y_{ts}^k = W_S \times y_t^k \tag{23}$$

Here, y_{ts}^k is the result of applying both temporal and spatial weighting to y^k. Finally, a residual connection is added to obtain the final output y^k.

4   Experiments

4.1   MFED

The Masked Facial Expression Database (MFED) consists of 778 masked facial expression sequences contributed by 22 participants (including 10 males and 12 females). Each video sequence in this dataset has a resolution of 1280×720 pixels and is recorded at a frame rate of 25 frames per second. There are four classification tasks within this dataset: one for classifying 36 types of mixed expressions, one for classifying 6 types of experienced emotions (referred to as 6E), one for classifying 6 types of required expressions (referred to as 6R), and a binary classification task to distinguish whether facial expressions are disguised.

4.2   Experimental Setup

All experiments in this study were conducted using the leave one-subject-out (LOSO) strategy for validation. The 36-class classification task served as the primary task for module ablation experiments. Model performance was evaluated using accuracy, F1 score, and recall as metrics. During the training phase, random rotation was employed for data augmentation, and the SGD optimizer was chosen. The learning rate of the SGD optimizer is set to 0.0001, the momentum is set to 0.9, and the weight decay is set to 0.0005.

4.3   Ablation Experiment

Ablation of MTL. As shown in Table 1, firstly, we conducted baseline experiments using a traditional single-task learning approach based on MViT. The results showed an accuracy of 19.28%, an F1 score of 18.70%, and a recall of 19.18%. These results indicate that relying solely on a single-task expression recognition approach is insufficient to effectively capture the complexity of MFEs. To improve the model's performance, we introduced a multi-task learning (MTL) strategy, dividing the original 36-class mixed expression classification task into two subtasks: requested expression recognition and experienced emotion recognition. With MTL, the model's accuracy increased to 21.08%, the F1 score reached 20.32%, and the recall rose to 21.03%. Compared to single-task learning, multi-task learning improved accuracy, F1, and recall by 1.8%, 1.62%, and 1.85%, respectively. This significant improvement demonstrates that MTL helps the model better understand MFEs from multiple perspectives and enhances its ability to distinguish complex expressions. Building on this, we further incorporated the spatiotemporal feature modulation (STFM) module and the adaptive spatial attention module (ASAM) to improve model performance and conducted an ablation study with MTL. The results showed that, with the integration of both two modules and MTL, the model's accuracy improved to 26.86%, the F1 score increased to 26.25%, and recall rose to 26.85%. Compared to the results without MTL, accuracy, F1, and recall improved by 2.57%, 3.09%, and 2.59%, respectively. These results indicate that our model achieved state-of-the-art (SOTA) performance in the most challenging 36-class classification task.

Table 1. Ablation experiments of Multi-task learning.

Task	Methods	Accuracy	F1	Recall
36 Mixed Expression	Baseline	19.28%	18.70%	19.18%
	MTL	21.08%	20.32%	21.03%
	ASAM+STFM	24.29%	23.16%	24.26%
	ASAM+STFM+MTL	**26.86%**	**26.25%**	**26.85%**

To directly demonstrate the performance of our method on the 36-classification task, Fig. 8 shows the confusion matrix of the experimental results using multi-task learning along with the ASAM and STFM modules, from which it can be intuitively seen that our method performs best in the "sad to happy" category.

To further validate the effectiveness of multi-task learning, we conducted ablation studies on both task 6E and task 6R using MTL. The experimental results are detailed in Table 2. Notably, when performing task 6E, the loss function weight for the 6R task branch was set to 0.1, similarly, when handling task 6R, the loss function weight for the 6E task branch was also set to 0.1. This

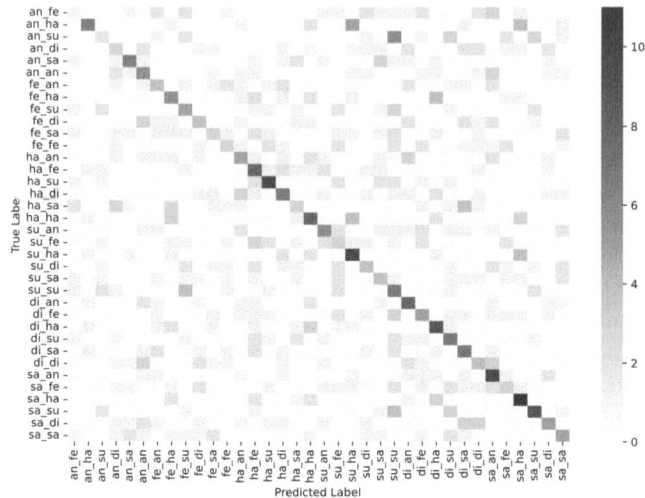

Fig. 8. Confusion matrix of the mixed expression recognition

Table 2. Comparison of single-task learning and multi-task learning for 6E and 6R

Task	Methods	Accuracy	F1	Recall
6E	ASAM+STFM	39.08%	38.53%	38.99%
	ASAM+STFM+MTL	**42.93%**	**42.78%**	**42.88%**
6R	ASAM+STFM	58.94%	58.42%	58.94%
	ASAM+STFM+MTL	**62.34%**	**61.88%**	**62.39%**

design is intended to prevent the auxiliary task from overly influencing the main task.

In the first group, the experimental results of the network on the 6E task are presented. When using the ASAM and STFM modules with multi-task learning, the accuracy, F1 score, and recall achieved improvements of 3.85%, 4.34%, and 3.89%, respectively. This indicates that for the 6E task, introducing a task branch for required expressions helps the network learn the features of the genuine expressions hidden under the required expressions. In the second group, the experimental results of the network on the 6R task are presented. The results show that when employing multi-task learning, the accuracy, F1 score, and recall improved by 3.40%, 3.46%, and 3.45%, respectively. This also demonstrates that introducing auxiliary branches with appropriate weights benefits the classification of required expressions. By incorporating multi-task learning, the risk of over-fitting in the neural network can be reduced, which is also an important reason for the improvement in recognition accuracy.

To investigate the contribution of different tasks to the overall recognition rate, we conducted a series of experiments to examine the impact of varying loss weights on the performance of the 36-class classification. The experiments did not employ any additional modules but instead introduced multi-task learning based on MViT. The results are shown in Table 3.

Table 3. Experiment on the values of β and α

β/α	Accuracy	F1	Recall
0.8/1.2	19.54%	18.87%	19.55%
0.9/1.1	18.38%	17.75%	18.35%
1.0/1.0	**21.08%**	**20.32%**	**21.03%**
1.1/0.9	20.44%	19.93%	20.37%
1.2/0.8	19.67%	19.17%	19.65%

when the loss weights of the two tasks are equal, the overall recognition accuracy reached its highest point at 21.08%. Furthermore, the results shows that when the weight of experienced emotions is set to 1.1 and 1.2, the recognition performance is better than when the same weights are applied to required expressions. This suggests that when the weights of experienced emotions and required expressions are not equal, increasing the weight of experienced emotions is more beneficial for improving the classification accuracy of 36 types of mixed expressions, compared to increasing the weight of required expressions. Moreover, to balance the two tasks, setting their loss weights to be equal is a more reasonable choice.

Ablation of STFM. In this section, we explore the impact of the STFM module on the 36-class classification task. First, we conducted a series of ablation experiments to verify the effectiveness of the STFM module. The results are shown in Table 4.

Table 4. Ablation of the STFM module

Task	Methods	Accuracy	F1	Recall
36 Mixed Expression	Baseline	19.28%	18.70%	19.18%
	STFM	22.11%	21.35%	22.07%
	ASAM+MTL	22.50%	22.10%	22.55%
	ASAM+STFM+MTL	**26.86%**	**26.25%**	**26.85%**

As shown in Table 4, The results show that, compared to MViT without any methods, introducing the STFM module improves the accuracy, F1 score, and recall by 2.83%, 2.65%, and 2.89% respectively in the 36-class classification task. When combined with ASAM and multi-task learning (MTL), adding the STFM module further boosts accuracy, F1 score, and recall by 4.36%, 4.15%,

Table 5. Analysis of the different structures of the STFM module

Task	Methods	Accuracy	F1	Recall
36 Mixed Expression	Only Temporal Feature	21.08%	19.93%	21.04%
	Only Spatial Feature	20.82%	20.07%	20.93%
	Only STFE	21.21%	20.50%	21.26%
	Only FWM	20.44%	20.06%	20.48%
	STFM	**22.11%**	**21.35%**	**22.07%**

and 4.30%, respectively. This demonstrates that using the STFM module for temporal feature extraction significantly enhances the model's performance.

Next, we evaluated the impact of different structure of STFM. The results are shown in Table 5. The results indicate that when only use temporal features yields an accuracy of 21.08%, while relying solely on spatial features results in a slight decline in performance. These findings indicate that a single feature type is insufficient and that temporal features play a more critical role. After implementing the spatiotemporal feature extractor (STFE), the model's accuracy improves to 21.21%. Moreover, compared to using only the FWM or STFE module, simultaneously employing both (STFM) leads to a more significant improvement, with the recognition accuracy reaching 22.11%. This suggests that integrating temporal feature extraction with feature weighting techniques can significantly improve the model's performance. By leveraging the strengths of both approaches, the model can better capture essential patterns and dynamics in the data, leading to more accurate predictions and enhanced overall effectiveness.

Ablation of ASAM. In this section, we will investigate the impact of the ASAM module on model performance. First, we conducted a series of ablation experiments, and the results are presented in Table 6.

Table 6. Ablation of ASAM

Task	Methods	Accuracy	F1	Recall
36 Mixed Expression	Baseline	19.28%	18.70%	19.18%
	ASAM	20.18%	19.95%	20.13%
	STFM+MTL	25.45%	24.99%	25.41%
	ASAM+STFM+MTL	**26.86%**	**26.25%**	**26.85%**

In the Table 6, After introducing the ASAM module into MViT, the model's accuracy, F1 score, and recall improved by 0.9%, 1.25%, and 0.95%, respectively. When combined with MTL and STFM, the introduction of the ASAM module further enhanced the accuracy, F1 score, and recall, with increases of 1.41%, 1.26%, and 1.44%, respectively. These results indicate that the spatial attention mechanism of the ASAM module enables the network to focus more on the critical regions where expression actions occur, effectively reducing the negative impact of redundant information in the video on the model's performance.

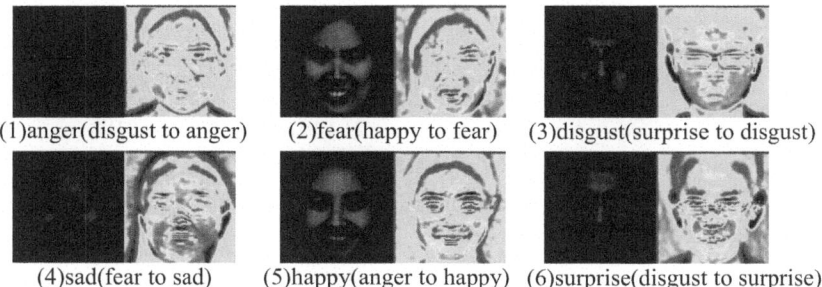

| (1)anger(disgust to anger) | (2)fear(happy to fear) | (3)disgust(surprise to disgust) |
| (4)sad(fear to sad) | (5)happy(anger to happy) | (6)surprise(disgust to surprise) |

Fig. 9. Visualization results of the ASAM module attention mask

To visually demonstrate the effect of ASAM, we selected several samples of the spatial attention masks for visualization, and the results are shown in Fig. 9. As shown in the picture, The apex frames of different samples under six different required expressions are displayed, along with their corresponding visualized attention masks. Redder colors indicate higher attention levels, while bluer colors signify lower attention from the model in that area. As shown in Fig. 9(1), when the required expression is anger, AU4 is activated in the apex frame, and the corresponding mask indicates that more attention is focused on the eyebrow area of the face. Similarly, as shown in Fig. 9(5), when the required expression is happiness, AU12 is activated in the apex frame, resulting in increased attention on the mouth area of the face in the mask. This indicates that ASAM, through dynamic images and a lightweight network, enables the model to operate more effectively.

4.4   Comparison with Other State-of-the-Art Methods

In this section, we compare our method with other state-of-the-art methods. The results are shown in Table 7

In Table 7, we conducted a comparative analysis of the recognition performance in the 36 mixed expression task, as well as the 6 expressions of experienced emotions (6E). The results highlight the performance differences between our method and other existing approaches. To compare the performance differences between image-based methods and video-based methods, we have listed a series of image-based methods. Among them, ResNet34, the methods proposed by Zhang et al. [29] and Liu et al. [13] are image-based methods. Specifically, Zhang et al. achieved the best results by leveraging GoogLeNet in combination with data augmentation techniques. Liu et al., on the other hand, adopted transfer learning methods in an attempt to enhance the model performance. When conducting the 6E task and the 36-mixed expression classification task, the

Table 7. Comparison with state-of-the-art methods

Task	Methods	Accuracy	F1	Recall
36 Mixed Expression	Ours	**26.86%**	**26.25%**	**26.85%**
	MFED [16]	11.25%	-	-
	ResNet34 [29]	20.82%	19.96%	20.82%
	Zhang [29]	22.11%	21.15%	22.11%
	Liu [13]	21.21%	19.83%	21.21%
	3DCNN [32]	10.95%	10.94%	10.94%
	Zhou [32]	21.20%	21.12%	21.03%
6E	Ours	**42.93%**	42.78%	**42.88%**
	MFED [16]	26.83%	-	-
	ResNet34 [29]	37.66%	35.38%	37.66%
	Zhang [29]	39.97%	38.93%	39.97%
	Liu [13]	42.16%	41.47%	42.16%
	3DCNN [32]	25.19%	25.38%	25.60%
	Zhou [32]	42.08%	**43.13%**	42.37%

image-based methods use the apex frame at which the expression reaches its maximum intensity as the input to the network. The remaining methods are video-based methods. Among them, 3DCNN is a common method for extracting spatio-temporal features. Zhou et al. [32], in view of the characteristics of MEFs, proposed a dynamic AU intensity feature and achieved very good results.

In the 36 mixed expression task, our method achieved the best performance, with an accuracy of 26.86%, an F1 score of 26.25%, and a recall of 26.85%. Compared to the method of Zhang et al., which was previously the best approach, our method achieves improvements of 4.75%, 5.10%, and 4.74% in accuracy, F1 score, and recall, respectively, for the 36-class classification task. This indicates that the apex frames can hardly fully contain all the information of MEFs. Using video sequences as input and employing multi-task learning in conjunction with the ASAM and STFM modules can more effectively extract discriminative features, significantly enhancing recognition accuracy. In the 6E task, our method also demonstrated exceptional performance, achieving an accuracy of 42.93%, an F1 score of 42.78%, and a recall of 42.88%. Compared to the previous best result, our model achieves an improvement of 0.77% in accuracy.

In summary, across the various tasks compared in the tables, our method consistently performed well in recognizing 36 mixed expressions, 6 experienced emotions. It particularly excelled in mixed emotion classification tasks, highlighting the effectiveness and potential of the models we employed in the field of MFEs recognition.

5   Conclusion

In this study, we propose a multi-task spatiotemporal feature weighting network based on the multiscale vision transformer, designed for masked facial expression recognition. By using a multi-task learning strategy, we simplify the complex 36-class classification task into two more direct tasks: required expression recognition and experienced emotion recognition. This approach allows the network to learn from both perspectives, capturing more robust features. Additionally, the two tasks act as mutual regularizers, reducing over-fitting. We also introduce a spatiotemporal feature modulation (STFM) module, consisting of a spatiotemporal feature extractor (STFE) and a feature weighting module (FWM). STFE efficiently extracts spatiotemporal features, addressing spatial similarity among mixed expressions with the same required expression, while FWM emphasizes features that aid classification and suppresses irrelevant ones. Moreover, An adaptive spatial attention module (ASAM) enhances the network's focus on regions with significant expression changes, further reducing the impact of irrelevant information. Experimental results demonstrate that our method outperforms existing approaches, improving accuracy by 4.75% on the 36-class task and 0.77% on the 6E task. However, recognizing masked facial expressions remains challenging due to their complexity, suggesting a need for further research. Future research can explore the use of targeted feature extraction methods for different tasks within a multi-task framework, in order to fully leverage the advantages of multi-task learning.

References

1. Bilen, H., Fernando, B., Gavves, E., Vedaldi, A., Gould, S.: Dynamic image networks for action recognition. In: Proceedings of the IEEE Conference on Computer Vision and Pattern Recognition, pp. 3034–3042 (2016)
2. Ekman, P.: Universals and cultural differences in facial expressions of emotion. In: Nebraska Symposium on Motivation. University of Nebraska Press (1971)
3. Ekman, P., Friesen, W.V.: Facial action coding system. In: Environmental Psychology & Nonverbal Behavior (1978)
4. Ekman, P., Friesen, W.V.: Felt, false, and miserable smiles. J. Nonverbal Behav. 6(4), 238–252 (1982)
5. Fan, H., et al.: Multiscale vision transformers. In: Proceedings of the IEEE/CVF International Conference on Computer Vision, pp. 6824–6835 (2021)
6. Fernando, B., Gavves, E., Oramas, J.M., Ghodrati, A., Tuytelaars, T.: Modeling video evolution for action recognition. In: Proceedings of the IEEE Conference on Computer Vision and Pattern Recognition, pp. 5378–5387 (2015)
7. Harris, P.L., Donnelly, K., Guz, G.R., Pitt-Watson, R.: Children's understanding of the distinction between real and apparent emotion. Child Dev., 895–909 (1986)
8. Hess, U., Kleck, R.E.: Differentiating emotion elicited and deliberate emotional facial expressions. Eur. J. Soc. Psychol. 20(5), 369–385 (1990)
9. Hu, C., Jiang, D., Zou, H., Zuo, X., Shu, Y.: Multi-task micro-expression recognition combining deep and handcrafted features. In: 2018 24th International Conference on Pattern Recognition (ICPR), pp. 946–951. IEEE (2018)

10. Izard, C.E.: Facial expressions and the regulation of emotions. J. Pers. Soc. Psychol. **58**(3), 487 (1990)
11. Li, J., Nie, J., Guo, D., Hong, R., Wang, M.: Emotion separation and recognition from a facial expression by generating the poker face with vision transformers. IEEE Trans. Comput. Soc. Syst. (2024)
12. Li, J., et al.: CAS(ME)3: a third generation facial spontaneous micro-expression database with depth information and high ecological validity. IEEE Trans. Pattern Anal. Mach. Intell. **45**(3), 2782–2800 (2022)
13. Liu, Y., Zhao, K., Fu, X.: Recognition of masked facial expressions based on transfer learning and data augmentation. In: 2023 International Annual Conference on Complex Systems and Intelligent Science (CSIS-IAC), pp. 80–86. IEEE (2023)
14. Long, F., Qiu, Z., Pan, Y., Yao, T., Ngo, C.W., Mei, T.: Dynamic temporal filtering in video models. In: European Conference on Computer Vision, pp. 475–492. Springer (2022)
15. Mehrabian, A.: An Approach to Environmental Psychology. Massachusetts Institute of Technology (1974)
16. Mo, F., Zhang, Z., Chen, T., Zhao, K., Fu, X.: MFED: a database for masked facial expression. IEEE Access **9**, 96279–96287 (2021)
17. Nie, X., Takalkar, M.A., Duan, M., Zhang, H., Xu, M.: GEME: dual-stream multi-task GEnder-based micro-expression recognition. Neurocomputing **427**, 13–28 (2021)
18. Pantic, M., Rothkrantz, L.: Automatic analysis of facial expressions: the state of the art. IEEE Trans. Pattern Anal. Mach. Intell. **22**(12), 1424–1445 (2000)
19. Peng, M., Wang, C., Bi, T., Shi, Y., Zhou, X., Chen, T.: A novel apex-time network for cross-dataset micro-expression recognition. In: 2019 8th International Conference on Affective Computing and Intelligent Interaction (ACII), pp. 1–6. IEEE (2019)
20. Porter, S., Ten Brinke, L.: Reading between the lies: identifying concealed and falsified emotions in universal facial expressions. Psychol. Sci. **19**(5), 508–514 (2008)
21. Porter, S., Ten Brinke, L., Wallace, B.: Secrets and lies: involuntary leakage in deceptive facial expressions as a function of emotional intensity. J. Nonverbal Behav. **36**, 23–37 (2012)
22. Russell, J.A.: Core affect and the psychological construction of emotion. Psychol. Rev. **110**(1), 145 (2003)
23. Savchenko, A.V.: Facial expression and attributes recognition based on multi-task learning of lightweight neural networks. In: 2021 IEEE 19th International Symposium on Intelligent Systems and Informatics (SISY), pp. 119–124. IEEE (2021)
24. Verma, M., Vipparthi, S.K., Singh, G.: AffectiveNet: affective-motion feature learning for microexpression recognition. IEEE Multimedia **28**(1), 17–27 (2020)
25. Verma, M., Vipparthi, S.K., Singh, G., Murala, S.: LEARNet: dynamic imaging network for micro expression recognition. IEEE Trans. Image Process. **29**, 1618–1627 (2019)
26. Wang, C., Peng, M., Bi, T., Chen, T.: Micro-attention for micro-expression recognition. Neurocomputing **410**, 354–362 (2020)
27. Yu, J., et al.: Unleashing the power of multi-task learning: a comprehensive survey spanning traditional, deep, and pretrained foundation model eras. arXiv preprint arXiv:2404.18961 (2024)
28. Zhang, K., Zhang, Z., Li, Z., Qiao, Y.: Joint face detection and alignment using multitask cascaded convolutional networks. IEEE Sig. Process. Lett. **23**(10), 1499–1503 (2016)

29. Zhang, X., Liu, Y., Zhao, K., Fu, X.: Recognition of masked facial expressions based on convolutional neural networks and data augmentation. In: 2023 International Annual Conference on Complex Systems and Intelligent Science (CSIS-IAC), pp. 351–357. IEEE (2023)

30. Zhang, Y., Yang, Q.: A survey on multi-task learning. IEEE Trans. Knowl. Data Eng. **34**(12), 5586–5609 (2021)

31. Zheng, H., et al.: Discriminative deep multi-task learning for facial expression recognition. Inf. Sci. **533**, 60–71 (2020)

32. Zhou, J., et al.: Seeing through the mask: recognition of genuine emotion through masked facial expression. IEEE Trans. Comput. Soc. Syst. (2024)

33. Zhou, Z., Zhao, G., Pietikäinen, M.: Towards a practical lipreading system. In: CVPR 2011, pp. 137–144. IEEE (2011)

MBGNet: Mamba-Based Boundary-Guided Multimodal Medical Image Segmentation Network

Ke Xu[1], Min Li[2], Guangjian Liu[1], Chen Chen[1], Cheng Chen[1], Enguang Zuo[3], and Xiaoyi Lv[1(✉)]

[1] College of Software, Xinjiang University, Urumqi, China
liuguangjian@stu.xju.edu.cn, xjuwawj01@163.com
[2] School of Computer Science and Technology, Xinjiang University, Urumqi, China
[3] College of Intelligent Science and Technology (Future Technology),
Xinjiang University, Urumqi, China
zeg@xju.edu.cn

Abstract. Multimodal medical image segmentation plays an important role in fields such as medical image diagnosis and biomedical research. Although Mamba performs well in medical image feature extraction, it still faces challenges in capturing fine boundaries in lesions. Therefore, in this paper, a Mamba-based boundary-guided multimodal medical image segmentation network (MBGNet) is proposed. To address Mamba's deficiency in capturing boundary information, we designed a Boundary Information Encoding Module (BIEM). This module employs multiple boundary extraction strategies to capture boundary information across different modalities and uses an external attention mechanism to enhance the interaction and understanding of boundary relationships. Additionally, we designed an Information Guidance Module (IGM) to address information loss during boundary and content fusion. This module uses the boundary segmentation map as a guideline, integrating local features and global context for content segmentation, effectively overcoming information loss. Finally, experimental results on the BraTS2019 and BraTS2020 glioma tumor datasets show that MBGNet achieves DICE coefficients of 88.17% and 88.12%, and Hausdorff 95 distances of 5.21 and 5.08, respectively. These results confirm the superior performance of MBGNet in the segmentation of complex lesion regions, providing a more accurate and reliable method for multimodal medical image analysis.

Keywords: Multimodal medical image segmentation · Mamba · Feature extraction · Boundary information guidance

1 Introduction

Image segmentation is pivotal in medical image analysis, aiming to accurately distinguish between lesions and background [29]. To accomplish this, multimodal

P. Didyk and J. Hou (Eds.): CVM 2025, LNCS 15663, pp. 394–411, 2025.
https://doi.org/10.1007/978-981-96-5809-1_21

medical image segmentation techniques have been developed, providing comprehensive insights into tissue and pathological states by integrating information from diverse imaging modalities. Nonetheless, the multimodal glioma medical image segmentation used in this study faces challenges due to inter-modal inconsistencies, such as variations in imaging parameters, resolution, and contrast, which can degrade segmentation performance [30]. The Mamba methodology addresses these issues by employing dynamic weights to adapt across different modalities, thus enhancing segmentation accuracy [27]. Despite its efficacy with multimodal data, Mamba may lack sensitivity in capturing subtle boundary details. To remedy this, integrating Mamba with boundary information is proposed to precisely delineate the fine boundaries of tissues and lesions, thereby improving the accuracy and reliability of segmentation outcomes.

Currently, mainstream methods in medical image segmentation primarily include those based on Convolutional neural networks (CNNs) and Transformers [16]. CNNs effectively recognize local features through convolutional operations. However, they are limited in capturing global contextual information, which affects the overall segmentation performance. In contrast, Transformers have shown significant advantages in modeling global information due to their unique self-attention mechanism. Despite this, the high computational complexity of self-attention poses challenges for efficient segmentation. Recently, the Mamba approach has garnered attention in the image domain [11]. Mamba allows each element in a sequence to interact with previously scanned samples via a unique compressed hidden state, effectively reducing computational complexity from quadratic to linear [28].

Although Mamba offers significant advantages in terms of reduced parametric and computational costs and efficient extraction of image feature information, it struggles with capturing the edge information of lesion regions due to the inherent quality issues in multimodal medical images. This limitation prevents various segmentation models from achieving optimal performance in multimodal image segmentation. Boundary information is crucial not only for the positional localization of lesion regions but also for determining the accuracy of image segmentation. Therefore, ensuring the accurate extraction of edge information while maintaining the efficient segmentation performance of Mamba has become the central focus of this research.

In summary, this study makes the following core contributions:

- In this study, we propose a Mamba-based boundary-guided multimodal medical image segmentation network, named MBGNet. This model retains the global information modeling efficiency inherent in Mamba while incorporating a boundary extraction module to enhance the identification of fine boundaries. This integration significantly improves the segmentation accuracy for small and complex structures in medical images.
- In this study, we construct a Boundary Information Encoding Module (BIEM). This module extracts boundary data from different modalities and facilitates interaction through an external attention mechanism. By effectively fusing

multiple boundary information sources, the BIEM enhances the accuracy and reliability of boundary segmentation.

- In this study, we designed an Information Guidance Module (IGM). This module utilizes a complete boundary segmentation map as an external auxiliary input, integrating boundary contours with lesion area features to achieve precise segmentation of lesions.

2   Related Work

2.1   Mamba's Application in Image Segmentation

With the introduction of Mamba into the visual domain, an increasing number of researchers have begun to explore its methods and applications in image segmentation. In 2D image segmentation, Ruan et al. [21] proposed a model employing a U-shaped architecture using SSM (VM-UNet). This model addresses challenges in long-range modeling and computational complexity in medical image segmentation by incorporating Visual State Space (VSS) blocks to capture extensive contextual information. In 3D image segmentation, Xing et al. [24] introduced a 3D medical image segmentation model (SegMamba), which leverages Mamba to capture long-range dependencies within full-volume features at each scale, thereby tackling computational challenges associated with high-dimensional medical images. Compared to transformers, Mamba exhibits lower complexity, prompting researchers to explore more lightweight segmentation models. For instance, Liao et al. [14] proposed a lightweight medical image segmentation model (LightM-UNet) aimed at addressing computational resource limitations of existing UNet models in mobile healthcare applications. In the domain of multimodal image segmentation, Mamba has also demonstrated exceptional performance. Wan et al. [23] introduced a network for multimodal semantic segmentation (Sigma), which employs a Siamese encoder and an innovative Mamba fusion mechanism to efficiently select and segment key information from different modalities, such as RGB, thermal imaging, and depth information, enhancing the model's robustness and reliability under adverse conditions. Given the complexity of multimodal medical image data, current Mamba models have not fully exploited their potential. Therefore, this paper proposes a Mamba-based method and utilizes glioma datasets to address the challenges of multimodal medical image segmentation. This method not only selects specific feature extraction schemes based on the characteristic differences of multimodal glioma data but also compensates for detail loss in image segmentation through guided segmentation.

2.2   Boundary Segmentation Techniques in Image Segmentation

Boundary segmentation techniques are vital in the field of image segmentation, particularly for tasks requiring fine-grained segmentation. These methods aim to accurately identify and extract boundary information of objects within an image, overcoming challenges such as complex backgrounds, similar regions, and blurred edges. In recent years, extensive research has explored the application of boundary segmentation techniques. For example, Gab Allah et al. [1] proposed the Edge U-Net model, which achieves precise segmentation of brain tumor MRI images by integrating multi-scale boundary-related information and adjacent contextual data during the decoding phase. Similarly, Yang et al. [25] developed a novel 3D network for automatic CT image segmentation, focusing on spatial context modeling and explicit edge segmentation priors, significantly enhancing the accuracy and robustness of abdominal organ segmentation. Bui et al. [4] introduced a multi-scale edge-guided attention network (MEGANet) that addresses challenges in polyp segmentation within colonoscopy images by combining classical edge detection techniques with attention mechanisms. Chen et al. [7] proposed an edge-enhanced semantic segmentation network, which improves the extraction of edge information by sharing parameters between backbone networks and employing specialized loss functions. Despite these advancements, the aforementioned models face limitations when addressing edge blurring in multimodal image data. Different modalities possess distinct feature distributions and noise characteristics, potentially reducing segmentation accuracy. Therefore, this paper proposes the use of different edge detection operators to separately extract boundary information from multimodal data while employing an external attention mechanism for fusion. This method clarifies the complementarity between the interior and boundary of lesions, enhancing segmentation performance.

3   Method

3.1   Preliminaries for Mamba

State Space Models. State Space Models (SSMs) are employed for sequence-to-sequence modeling and are characterized by their dynamic properties, which remain constant over time [12]. Due to their linear complexity, SSMs can implicitly map sequences to a latent state space, effectively capturing the inherent dynamics of the system. Formally, an SSM is defined by the following equations:

$$h'(t) = \boldsymbol{A}h(t) + \boldsymbol{B}x(t) \tag{1}$$

$$y(t) = \boldsymbol{C}h(t) \tag{2}$$

Here, x(t), h(t), and y(t) represent the input, hidden state, and output, respectively, while h'(t) denotes the time derivative of h(t). A is the state matrix, and B and C are projection parameters.

Models based on SSMs are typically continuous-time models and require discretization when integrated into deep learning algorithms [19]. SSMs achieve this by introducing a time scale parameter Δ and employing the Zero-Order Hold (ZOH) rule to transform A and B into discrete parameters $\overline{\mathrm{A}}$ and $\overline{\mathrm{B}}$. The equations are as follows:

$$\overline{\mathbf{A}} = e^{\Delta \mathbf{A}} \tag{3}$$

$$\overline{\mathbf{B}} = \Delta \mathbf{A}^{-1}(e^{\Delta \mathbf{A}} - \mathbf{I}) \cdot \Delta \mathbf{B} \tag{4}$$

$$\bar{\mathbf{C}} = \mathbf{C} \tag{5}$$

$$h_t = \overline{\mathbf{A}}h_{t-1} + \overline{\mathbf{B}}x_t \tag{6}$$

$$y_t = \bar{\mathbf{C}}h_t \tag{7}$$

Finally, the model computes the output y through global convolution operations within a structured convolution kernel $\overline{\mathbf{K}}$:

$$\overline{\mathbf{K}} = (\mathbf{CB}, \mathbf{CAB}, \mathbf{CA}^2\overline{\mathbf{B}}, \dots, \mathbf{CA}^{L-1}\overline{\mathbf{B}}) \tag{8}$$

$$y = \overline{\mathbf{K}} \otimes y_t \tag{9}$$

2D Selective Scan Mechanism. To address the incompatibility between the original one-dimensional input sequence in SSMs and the two-dimensional data in the visual domain, researchers have introduced the 2D Selective Scan (SS2D) mechanism [18]. Figure 1 illustrates the functioning of SS2D. SS2D constructs four independent sequences by scanning image patches in the 2D visual data across four different directions. This four-directional scanning approach ensures that each element in the feature map can incorporate information from all other positions in every direction. Subsequently, each feature sequence is processed using the Selective Scanning State Space Model (S6) [8]. Finally, the processed feature sequences are aggregated to reconstruct the 2D feature map.

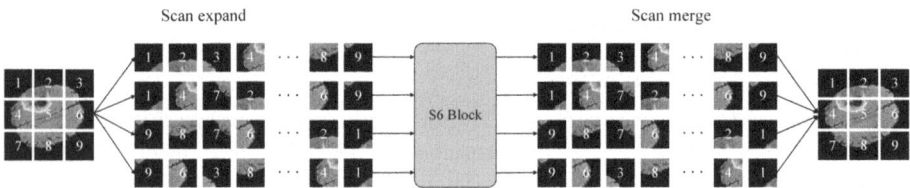

Fig. 1. Overview of the 2D Selective Scan mechanism.

3.2   Overview of the Model Architecture

Figure 2 illustrates the architecture of the proposed model. To extract boundary and content information, we divided the four modalities of glioma MRI data (FLAIR, T1ce, T1, and T2) into two groups: one consisting of FLAIR and T1ce, and the other including all four modalities, as shown in the orange and blue boxes on the left side of Fig. 2. For boundary information extraction, we prioritized the FLAIR and T1ce modalities because these modalities more clearly depict the boundary contours of the lesion areas. For content information extraction, multimodal image data can compensate for the lack of rich features in

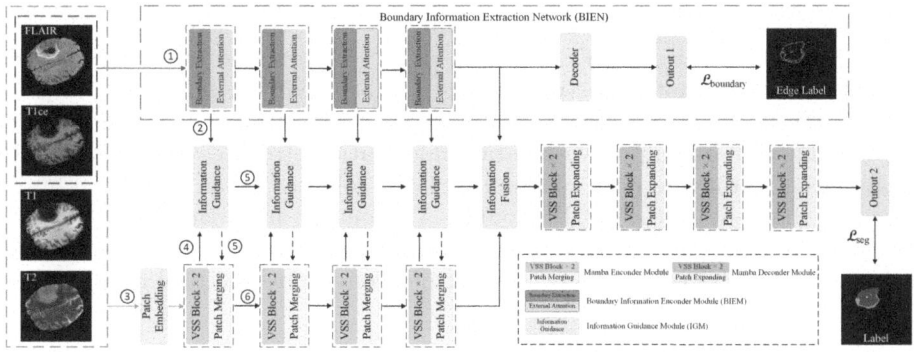

Fig. 2. Overview of the MBGNet Model Framework.

single-modality images. Therefore, all four modalities were used as input data for content segmentation.

In the proposed architecture, the model operates in two stages. The first stage involves the extraction of boundary information. Initially, the data is fed into the Boundary Information Encoding Module (BIEM), after which the image dimensions are restored through the decoder. Subsequently, the output is compared with the boundary labels to train an efficient Boundary Information Extraction Network (BIEN). Through iterative training, this network is progressively optimized to effectively extract the boundaries of smaller and more challenging segmentation content, ultimately generating a boundary segmentation map that can serve as a guiding map, as illustrated in Output1 of Fig. 2. Once the boundary information accurately reflects the contours of the lesion areas, the model proceeds to the second stage: boundary-guided content segmentation. In this stage, the parameters of the BIEN remain unchanged. Based on the existing boundary segmentation results, the Mamba encoding module is utilized to extract content information, which is then fed into the Information Guidance Module (IGM) to achieve boundary-guided content segmentation. The segmentation result is shown as Output2 in Fig. 2. The flow of this stage follows the numerical order illustrated in Fig. 2.

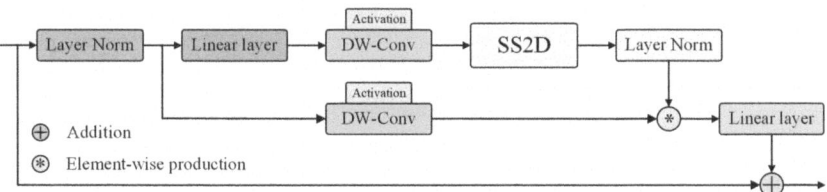

Fig. 3. Overview of the 2D Selective Scan mechanism.

As illustrated in Fig. 2, both the Mamba encoding module and the Mamba decoding module utilize the Visual State Space (VSS) as the backbone for feature extraction. The internal structure of the VSS module is depicted in Fig. 3. Initially, the input data is processed through an initial linear embedding layer and subsequently split into two separate information streams. One information stream passes through a deep convolution layer, followed by an activation function, and then enters the SS2D module. The output from the SS2D module undergoes layer normalization and is then combined with the output from the other information stream. The merged output constitutes the final result of the VSS block.

3.3   Boundary Information Encoding Module

In multimodal medical image segmentation, boundary information segmentation faces numerous challenges. Firstly, the contrast differences across various modality images may lead to blurred boundaries, complicating accurate identification. Additionally, imaging noise and artifacts can interfere with boundary information extraction, thereby increasing segmentation uncertainty. Collectively, these issues limit the accuracy and reliability of segmentation. To address these challenges, we propose a BIEM designed to extract boundary information from medical images. This module consists of a Boundary Extraction Module and an External Attention Mechanism, as illustrated in Figs. 4 and 5, respectively.

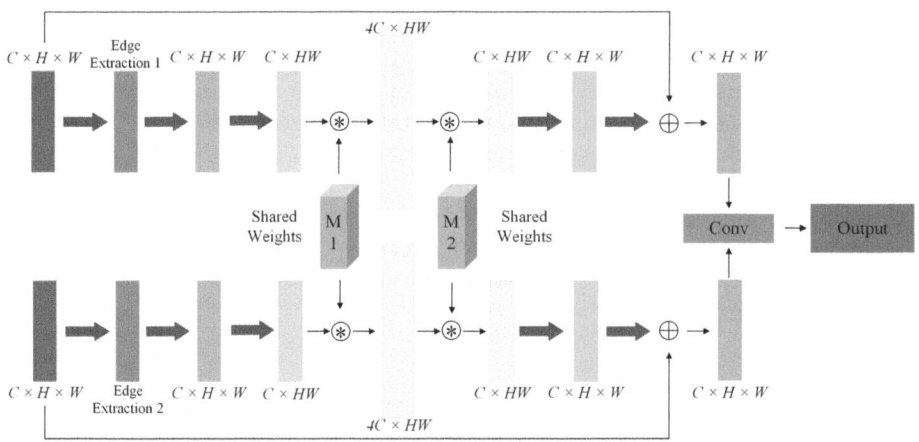

Fig. 4. Overview of the Boundary Extraction Module.

The internal structure of the Boundary Extraction Module is illustrated in Fig. 4. The model employs both Sobel and Canny edge detection operators to perform edge detection on the images. The Sobel operator calculates the gradient of the image intensity to effectively identify coarse contours of the edges, while the Canny operator, with its multi-stage processing, provides more precise edge

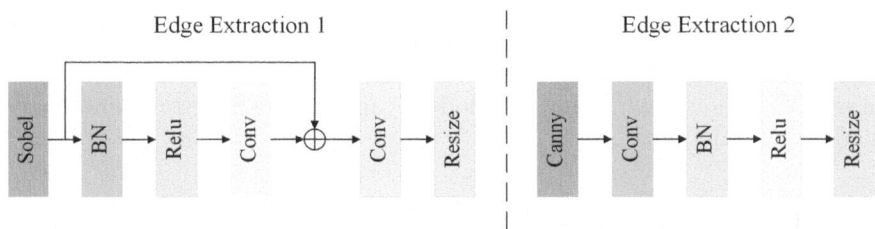

Fig. 5. Overview of the External Attention Mechanism.

detection results. By combining the strengths of both operators, we can capture richer and more accurate edge information.

In implementing the external attention mechanism, this study draws inspiration from the work of Ruan et al. [9, 10, 22]. Their research implicitly considers potential associations between different samples to capture global features within the dataset, thereby enhancing both the quality of feature representations and the model's generalization ability. This concept aligns closely with the objective of enhancing inter-modal interactions in multimodal image processing. Thus, we extend this approach to the field of multimodal medical image processing, aiming to improve model performance and robustness by strengthening inter-modal interactions.

As shown in Fig. 5, the data from the two modalities, X_1 and X_2, are fed into two separate branches as inputs. Both X_1 and X_2 belong to $\mathbb{R}^{C \times H \times W}$. First, the boundary extraction module processes these inputs, yielding boundary features that integrate information from different modalities. Subsequently, convolution operations reshape the inputs into $X \in \mathbb{R}^{C \times HW}$. The memory unit M1 then expands the feature map to $X \in \mathbb{R}^{4C \times HW}$, followed by memory unit M2 restoring it to $X \in \mathbb{R}^{C \times HW}$.

$$X_1' = M2(M_1(Conv(Sobel(X_1)))) \tag{10}$$

$$X_2' = M2(M_1(Conv(Sobel(X_2)))) \tag{11}$$

In this context, Conv denotes a 1×1 convolution, and the memory units M_1 and M_2 share parameters. These units are designed to map input features to a higher-dimensional space, facilitating the learning of global feature representations. The shared parameters allow the external attention mechanism to compute and apply correlations between images, achieving bidirectional enhancement and fusion of features, thereby improving the model's performance in processing multimodal information. After these operations, the feature map is restored to the original image dimensions and is connected with the original image through residual connections. Finally, convolution operations are applied to fuse the concatenated information.

$$X_1'' = X_1 + Conv(X_1') \tag{12}$$

$$X_2'' = X_2 + Conv(X_2') \tag{13}$$

$$Output = Conv(Concat(X_1', X_2')) \tag{14}$$

In this manner, the BIEM effectively integrates features from diverse information sources, thereby enhancing the model's capacity to understand and analyze boundary information.

3.4 Information Guidance Module

In multimodal medical image processing, content segmentation often suffers from decreased accuracy due to the complex shapes of target regions and blurred boundary information, which consequently impacts diagnostic precision. Therefore, effectively utilizing boundary information is crucial for improving segmentation accuracy and diagnostic reliability. Boundary information provides structural cues that assist the model in accurately localizing target regions. Based on this, we propose a boundary Information Guidance Module (IGM).

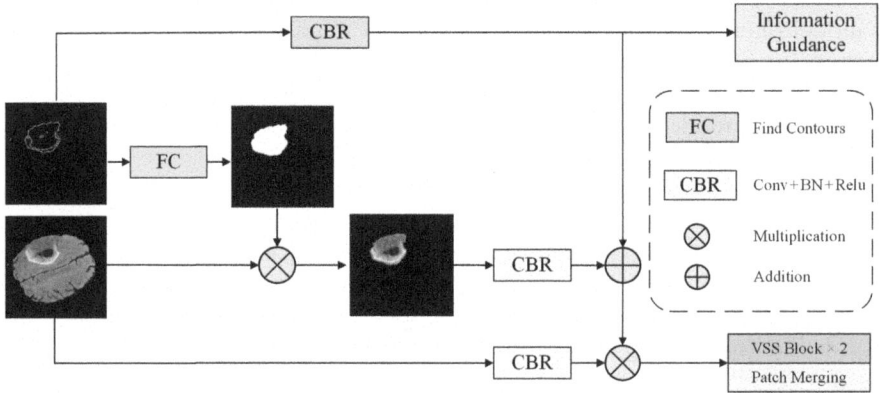

Fig. 6. Overview of the Information Guidance Module.

The working principle of the IGM is illustrated in Fig. 6. We collectively refer to convolution, batch normalization, and ReLU activation as the CBR module. Initially, the boundary map Y is processed through the CBR module to generate Output1, which is then passed to the subsequent Information Guidance Module:

$$Output_1 = \text{CBR}(Y) \tag{15}$$

Simultaneously, the Find Contours operation is employed to extract contour information from the image, resulting in a lesion region contour map Y' composed of 0 and 1. This contour map can be viewed as an attention map, aiding the model in focusing on critical regions:

$$Y' = FC(Y) \tag{16}$$

Next, the contour map Y' is element-wise multiplied with the original image Z to produce an image Y'', where non-lesion regions are set to 0. This enhances the segmentation effect of the lesion regions.

$$Y'' = Y' * Z \tag{17}$$

Then, the CBR operation is applied to this image, and the result is added to Output1. Finally, the summed result is element-wise multiplied with the CBR processed original image to obtain the information-guided output $Output_2$, which is then fed back into the Mamba encoding module:

$$I = Output_1 + CBR(Y'') \tag{18}$$

$$I' = I + CBR(Z) \tag{19}$$

$$Output_2 = I * I' \tag{20}$$

Through this process, the module effectively utilizes boundary information to guide the model's focus on lesion areas, thereby enhancing the accuracy of segmentation and responsiveness to critical regions.

3.5   Loss Function

This study incorporates two loss functions. The first, termed $L_{boundary}$, is designed to extract boundary information by combining binary cross-entropy with Dice loss. The second, termed L_{seg}, integrates cross-entropy and Dice loss to regularize content segmentation.

$$L_{boundary} = -\frac{1}{N} \sum_{i=1}^{N} [y_i \log (\hat{y}_i) + (1 - y_i) \log (1 - \hat{y}_i)] + \left(1 - \frac{2|y \cap \hat{y}|}{|y| + |\hat{y}|}\right) \tag{21}$$

$$L_{seg} = -\frac{1}{N} \sum_{i=1}^{N} \sum_{c=1}^{C} y_{i,c} \log(\hat{y}_{i,c}) + \left(1 - \frac{2|y \cap \hat{y}|}{|y| + |\hat{y}|}\right) \tag{22}$$

In $L_{boundary}$, N represents the number of samples, y_i denotes the ground truth label of the i-th sample, and $\hat{y}_i$ is the predicted label. Both of these values are binary, indicating whether the sample is a boundary. On the other hand, L_{seg} addresses a multi-class classification problem, where C represents the total number of categories. For the i-th sample, $y_{i,c}$ denotes its ground truth label for the C-th category, while $\hat{y}_{i,c}$ is the corresponding predicted label.

4   Experimental Details

4.1   Datasets and Evaluation Metrics

In this study, we utilized the BraTS 2019 and BraTS 2020 glioma tumor MRI datasets [2,3,17] to evaluate the performance of our model. Each sample includes

MRI images from the FLAIR, T1, T1 contrast-enhanced, and T2. The label information covers four main regions: healthy tissue, necrotic and non-enhancing tumor regions, edema regions, and enhancing tumor regions. Specifically, the whole tumor (WT) region encompasses all tumor areas, including necrotic non-enhancing tumor, edema, and enhancing tumor. Conversely, the tumor core (TC) region comprises the necrotic parts of the non-enhancing tumor and the enhancing tumor (ET) region.

In this study, we employed the Dice Similarity Coefficient (DSC) and Hausdorff Distance 95 (HD95) to evaluate the segmentation performance of the model on the WT, ET, and TC regions. The DSC is used to measure the overlap between the segmentation result P1 and the ground truth T1. The calculation formula is as follows:

$$DSC(P1, T1) = \frac{2|P1 \cap T1|}{|P1| + |T1|} \tag{23}$$

Here, P1 represents the predicted segmentation result, while T1 denotes the ground truth. The Hausdorff Distance between two surfaces, A and B, can be computed as follows:

$$H(A, B) = \max(d(A, B), d(B, A)) \tag{24}$$

The calculation formulas for d(A,B) and d(B,A) are as follows:

$$d(A, B) = \min(||a - b||) \tag{25}$$

$$d(B, A) = \min(||b - a||) \tag{26}$$

Here, d(A, B) and d(B, A) represent the one-way Hausdorff distance from set A to set B, and from set B to set A, respectively. $||X - Y||$ denotes the Euclidean distance between point sets X and Y.

4.2 Comparative Experiment

To validate the efficacy of our model, we compared the experimental results with various mainstream medical image segmentation models, including U-Net and its variants (U-Net [20], ResUNet++ [13], TransUNet [6], Swin-Unet [5]), as well as Mamba-based segmentation models (VM-UNet [21], Swin-UMamba [15], LightM-UNet [14], VM-UNET-V2 [26]).

Table 1 illustrates the performance of our model on the BraTS 2019 and 2020 datasets, while Figs. 7 and 8 provide a visual representation of the segmentation results for various models. As shown in Table 1 for the BraTS 2020 dataset, the proposed segmentation model demonstrates superior performance in terms of the Dice and HD95 metrics. Notably, the model achieves the best performance in tumor regions WT, TC, and ET, with improvements of 5.29%, 0.79%, and 0.28%, respectively, over the second-best competitor. This indicates that our model effectively aligns predicted results with ground-truth segmentation labels. Additionally, in terms of the HD95 metric, our model shows outstanding performance in the three lesion regions, with improvements of 0.31, 0.42,

Table 1. Performance Metrics of Various Models on the BraTS 2019/2020 Dataset.

Datasets	Models	DICE				HD95			
		WT	TC	ET	Average	WT	TC	ET	Average
BraTS2019	Unet	80.94	77.13	67.56	75.21	8.87	9.77	5.63	8.09
	ResUNet++	80.51	79.48	71.19	77.06	7.91	7.01	6.56	7.16
	TransUnet	79.76	79.05	69.94	76.25	8.57	7.83	6.07	7.49
	Swin-Unet	85.09	80.59	72.40	79.36	8.03	7.06	6.12	7.07
	VM-UNet	85.27	86.34	80.45	84.02	5.95	6.15	5.01	5.70
	Swin-UMamba	85.67	86.56	80.89	84.37	5.78	5.84	4.92	5.51
	LightM-UNet	83.45	85.90	79.67	82.99	5.89	6.07	5.14	5.70
	VM-UNET-V2	87.89	86.78	81.23	85.30	5.76	5.93	5.08	5.59
	MBGNet	**90.57**	**89.23**	**84.72**	**88.17**	**5.50**	**5.67**	**4.48**	**5.21**
BraTS2020	Unet	81.73	77.31	68.02	75.69	8.03	9.76	5.50	7.76
	ResUNet++	81.27	80.51	71.20	77.66	8.01	7.53	6.62	7.39
	TransUnet	80.13	79.76	69.94	76.61	8.42	7.64	5.91	7.32
	Swin-Unet	85.19	80.74	73.01	79.65	8.00	7.09	5.94	7.01
	VM-UNet	82.58	88.17	81.81	84.18	5.92	6.14	4.57	5.54
	Swin-UMamba	85.93	86.09	83.19	85.07	5.65	5.98	4.97	5.53
	LightM-UNet	83.14	86.17	83.76	84.35	6.02	6.54	5.03	5.86
	VM-UNET-V2	86.09	85.73	83.48	85.10	5.87	6.32	5.14	5.77
	MBGNet	**91.38**	**88.96**	**84.04**	**88.12**	**5.34**	**5.65**	**4.25**	**5.08**

and 0.32, respectively, compared to the second-best model. This success can be attributed to the boundary-guided segmentation approach we proposed, which enhances the model's focus on edge information in lesion areas, thereby improving the HD95 metric.

Figures 7 and 8 present the comparative segmentation results of MBGNet and other segmentation models across different scenarios, intuitively demonstrating the performance superiority of MBGNet. To more clearly highlight the differences in segmentation performance, regions with significant discrepancies are enlarged and marked with red boxes. In Fig. 7, we compare the segmentation results of MBGNet with the traditional U-Net and its derived versions. From Sample 1 and Sample 2, it can be observed that MBGNet exhibits high sensitivity to small lesion areas, accurately capturing these regions while maintaining consistency with the ground truth labels. In Sample 3 and Sample 4, MBGNet showcases its remarkable capability to analyze the shapes and boundaries of complex lesion structures, delivering clear delineation of individual lesion regions while ensuring both integrity and precision.

Figure 8 illustrates the performance comparison between MBGNet and segmentation models based on the Mamba architecture in other scenarios. As observed in Sample 1 and Sample 2, MBGNet demonstrates an excellent ability to model boundary details, accurately capturing intricate boundary features and achieving a high degree of consistency with the ground truth lesion labels.

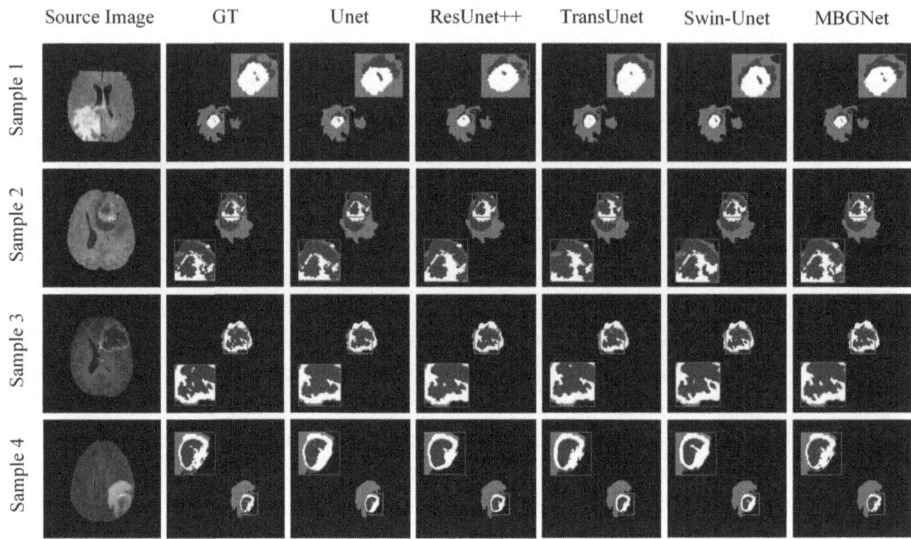

Fig. 7. Visual Results of Various Segmentation Models on the BraTS2019 Dataset.

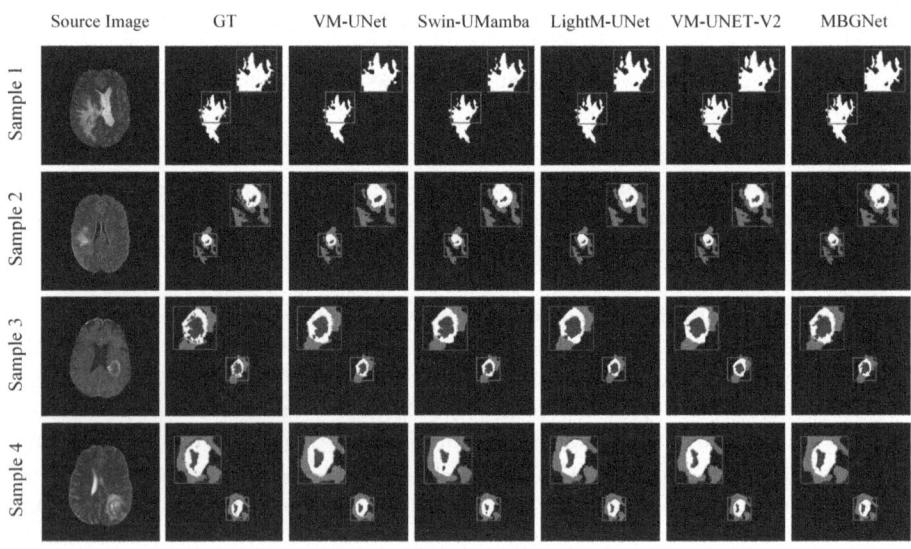

Fig. 8. Visual Results of Various Segmentation Models on the BraTS2020 Dataset.

In Sample 3 and Sample 4, even in cases where certain lesion regions in the original images are difficult to discern, MBGNet is still able to accurately segment these areas and clearly distinguish between different lesions. This highlights its robust capability to extract lesion features from low-quality images. These results indicate that MBGNet exhibits strong robustness and reliability when processing various types of lesions. Furthermore, its adaptability enables it to meet the demands of segmentation tasks in diverse and complex scenarios.

4.3   Ablation Study

To validate the efficacy of the proposed boundary-guided segmentation app-roach, this section conducts detailed ablation studies on each individual mod-ule. By analyzing the performance of these modules one by one, we can assess their impact on the overall model performance, thereby gaining a deeper under-standing of the advantages of the boundary-guided segmentation method. The comparisons in this subsection include the entire Boundary Information Extrac-tion Network (BIEN) from the first phase, the Boundary Information Encoding Module (BIEM), and the Information Guidance Module (IGM).

Table 2. Performance Metrics of Various Models on the BraTS 2019/2020 Dataset.

Datasets	Modules				DICE				HD95			
	BIEN	BIEM	IGM	Mamba	WT	TC	E	Average	WT	TC	ET	Average
BraTS2019	✗	✗	✗	✗	84.47	85.23	80.04	83.24	6.17	6.54	5.23	5.98
	✓	✗	✗	✗	86.61	86.18	83.06	85.28	5.68	5.78	4.59	5.35
	✗	✓	✗	✗	86.32	86.91	83.45	85.56	5.95	5.91	4.76	5.54
	✗	✗	✓	✗	88.14	87.44	82.70	86.09	6.03	6.12	4.82	5.65
	✗	✗	✗	✓	87.09	87.17	82.95	85.73	5.84	5.88	4.73	5.48
	✓	✓	✓	✓	**90.57**	**89.23**	**84.72**	**88.17**	**5.50**	**5.67**	**4.48**	**5.21**
BraTS2020	✗	✗	✗	✗	85.23	86.14	80.95	84.10	6.01	6.25	5.09	5.78
	✓	✗	✗	✗	85.23	86.34	83.23	84.93	5.47	5.76	4.36	5.19
	✗	✓	✗	✗	88.67	88.59	82.45	86.57	5.58	5.89	4.57	5.34
	✗	✗	✓	✗	89.98	87.78	83.67	87.14	5.62	5.93	4.72	5.42
	✗	✗	✗	✓	89.81	88.16	83.42	87.13	5.53	5.87	4.40	5.26
	✓	✓	✓	✓	**91.38**	**88.96**	**84.04**	**88.12**	**5.34**	**5.65**	**4.25**	**5.08**

As indicated in Table 2, the model performance decreases on both datasets when all modules are removed, as well as when only BIEN, BIEM, or IGM is retained. The specific reasons are as follows: Firstly, the absence of BIEN impairs the model's ability to locate and distinguish complex structures, dimin-ishing its robustness against morphological variations and irregular boundaries, ultimately affecting the overall segmentation quality. Secondly, the lack of BIEM results in the loss of boundary information extraction and interaction between multi-modal boundary information. This challenge hampers the model's ability to identify clear segmentation boundaries and weakens the correlation between different modalities. Lastly, when IGM is removed, content segmentation lacks the guidance of boundary information, potentially leading to the omission of subtle lesion features, resulting in less precise segmentation of the lesion areas. In summary, these modules play a crucial role in the overall performance of the model, and their absence significantly negatively impacts the segmentation outcomes.

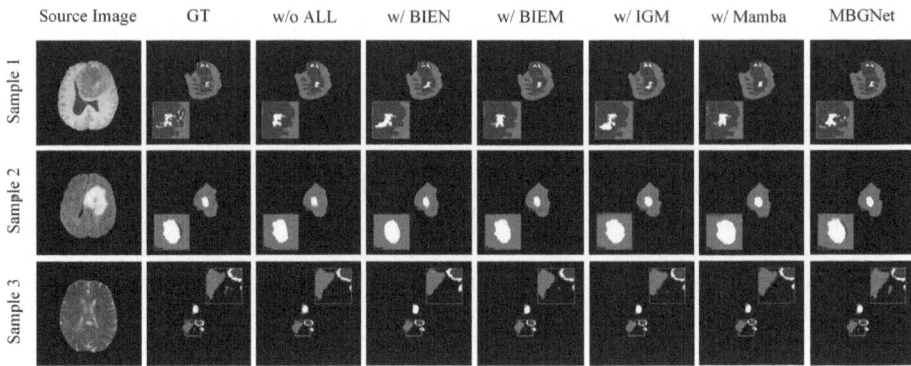

Fig. 9. The ablation study results for the modules on the BraTS2019 dataset.

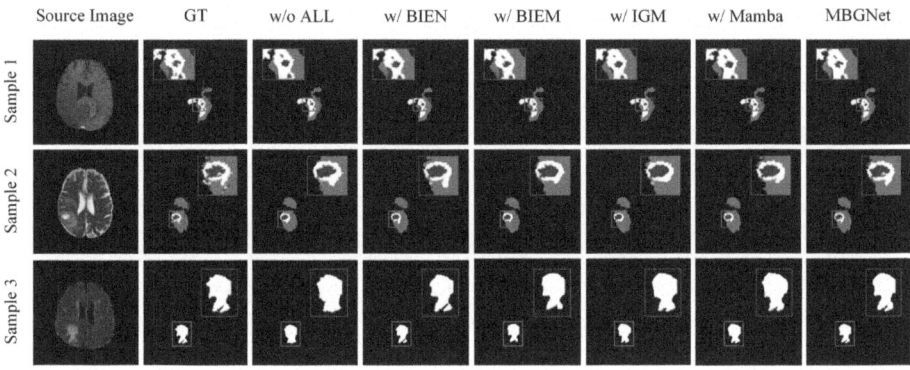

Fig. 10. The ablation study results for the modules on the BraTS2020 dataset.

Figures 9 and 10 present the visualized results of ablation experiments conducted on different datasets using MBGNet. To more intuitively highlight the differences in segmentation performance, regions with significant discrepancies are enlarged and marked with red boxes. From the comparative results shown in Figs. 9 and 10, it can be observed that when all modules are removed, the segmentation performance of the model declines significantly, barely maintaining a rudimentary segmentation framework with noticeably reduced accuracy. Upon the introduction of the BIEN module, the model's boundary capture capabilities are substantially enhanced, enabling clear delineation of lesion boundaries and avoiding boundary ambiguity or confusion between different lesion types. When the BIEM module is incorporated, the model's ability to segment poorly expressed lesion areas in the original images is significantly improved. This improvement is attributed to the multi-modal interaction mechanism within the BIEM, which effectively enhances the model's understanding and grasp of global segmentation regions. With the addition of the IGM module, the model further improves its segmentation performance in complex regions. This improvement is due to the guidance provided by the boundary segmentation map within IGM, which enables the model to focus more effectively on critical regions requiring segmentation while accurately distinguishing between different lesion areas. Finally, when all modules are integrated, the model demonstrates significant improvements in boundary information extraction, content segmentation, and regional delineation. This indicates that the modules exhibit strong synergistic effects, with each module contributing significantly to the overall performance enhancement. These findings validate the effectiveness of the module designs and underscore the superiority of the overall architecture.

5   Conclusion

In this study, we aim to enhance the accuracy and boundary identification capability in multimodal glioma image segmentation. To address these objectives, we focus on two pivotal issues: the precise extraction of boundary information and the prevention of information loss during content segmentation. Inaccurate boundary extraction can lead to blurred segmentation boundaries, while information loss affects the integrity of the segmented regions. To tackle these challenges, we employed Mamba as the backbone for feature extraction of multi-modal information and integrated a boundary extraction module to enhance the precision of boundary information. Additionally, we designed a BIEM that fuses multiple boundary information through an external attention mechanism, enabling the model to focus more intently on key boundary details within the image. Concurrently, to combat the problem of content information loss, we developed an IGM. This module uses the complete boundary segmentation map as a guidance map in content segmentation and, by integrating existing multi-modal information, effectively compensates for information that might be lost during the segmentation process. Our approach was systematically evaluated on the BraTS2019 and BraTS2020 datasets. The results demonstrate that, compared to current medical image segmentation models, our method exhibits superior performance in both boundary identification and overall segmentation accuracy.

In future research, we plan to further expand the application scope of the segmentation model MBGNet, with a particular focus on exploring its performance and applicability across various multimodal medical imaging datasets. Specifically, we aim to investigate the potential of MBGNet in handling more complex multimodal data scenarios, in order to validate its robustness and effectiveness in different types of medical imaging and disease diagnosis tasks.

Acknowledgement. This work was supported by the "Tianshan Innovation Team Program" of the Autonomous Region (Grant No. 20231103582) and the Research Project of the Fundamental Research Funds for Universities in Xinjiang Uygur Autonomous Region (Grant No. XJEDU2023P012).

References

1. Allah, A., Sarhan, A.M., Elshennawy, N.M.: Edge U-Net: brain tumor segmentation using MRI based on deep u-net model with boundary information. Exp. Syst. Appl. **213**, 118833 (2023)
2. Bakas, S., et al.: Advancing the cancer genome atlas glioma MRI collections with expert segmentation labels and radiomic features. Sci. Data **4**(1), 1–13 (2017)
3. Bakas, S., et al.: Identifying the best machine learning algorithms for brain tumor segmentation, progression assessment, and overall survival prediction in the brats challenge. arXiv preprint arXiv:1811.02629 (2018)
4. Bui, N.T., Hoang, D.H., Nguyen, Q.T., Tran, M.T., Le, N.: MEGANet: multiscale edge-guided attention network for weak boundary polyp segmentation. In: Proceedings of the IEEE/CVF Winter Conference on Applications of Computer Vision, pp. 7985–7994 (2024)
5. Cao, H., et al.: Swin-Unet: Unet-like pure transformer for medical image segmentation. In: European Conference on Computer Vision, pp. 205–218. Springer (2022)
6. Chen, J., et al.: TransUNet: transformers make strong encoders for medical image segmentation. arXiv preprint arXiv:2102.04306 (2021)
7. Chen, L., Qu, Z., Zhang, Y., Liu, J., Wang, R., Zhang, D.: Edge enhanced GCIFFNet: a multiclass semantic segmentation network based on edge enhancement and multiscale attention mechanism. IEEE J. Sel. Top. Appl. Earth Observ. Remote Sens. (2024)
8. Dong, W., et al.: Fusion-Mamba for cross-modality object detection. arXiv preprint arXiv:2404.09146 (2024)
9. Guo, M.H., Liu, Z.N., Mu, T.J., Hu, S.M.: Beyond self-attention: external attention using two linear layers for visual tasks. IEEE Trans. Pattern Anal. Mach. Intell. **45**(5), 5436–5447 (2022)
10. Hu, B., et al.: LeaNet: lightweight U-shaped architecture for high-performance skin cancer image segmentation. Comput. Biol. Med. **169**, 107919 (2024)
11. Huang, J., et al.: MambaMIR: an arbitrary-masked mamba for joint medical image reconstruction and uncertainty estimation. arXiv preprint arXiv:2402.18451 (2024)
12. Huang, T., Pei, X., You, S., Wang, F., Qian, C., Xu, C.: LocalMamba: visual state space model with windowed selective scan. arXiv preprint arXiv:2403.09338 (2024)
13. Jha, D., et al.: ResUNet++: an advanced architecture for medical image segmentation. In: 2019 IEEE International Symposium on Multimedia (ISM), pp. 225–2255. IEEE (2019)
14. Liao, W., Zhu, Y., Wang, X., Pan, C., Wang, Y., Ma, L.: LightM-UNet: Mamba assists in lightweight UNet for medical image segmentation. arXiv preprint arXiv:2403.05246 (2024)
15. Liu, J., et al.: Swin-UMamba: Mamba-based UNet with ImageNet-based pretraining. In: International Conference on Medical Image Computing and Computer-Assisted Intervention, pp. 615–625. Springer (2024)
16. Ma, J., Li, F., Wang, B.: U-Mamba: enhancing long-range dependency for biomedical image segmentation. arXiv preprint arXiv:2401.04722 (2024)
17. Menze, B.H., et al.: The multimodal brain tumor image segmentation benchmark (BRATS). IEEE Trans. Med. Imaging **34**(10), 1993–2024 (2014)
18. Pei, X., Huang, T., Xu, C.: EfficientVMamba: atrous selective scan for light weight visual Mamba. arXiv preprint arXiv:2403.09977 (2024)
19. Qiao, Y., et al.: VL-Mamba: exploring state space models for multimodal learning. arXiv preprint arXiv:2403.13600 (2024)

20. Ronneberger, O., Fischer, P., Brox, T.: U-Net: convolutional networks for biomedical image segmentation. In: Navab, N., Hornegger, J., Wells, W.M., Frangi, A.F. (eds.) MICCAI 2015. LNCS, vol. 9351, pp. 234–241. Springer, Cham (2015). https://doi.org/10.1007/978-3-319-24574-4_28

21. Ruan, J., Xiang, S.: VM-UNet: vision Mamba UNet for medical image segmentation. arXiv preprint arXiv:2402.02491 (2024)

22. Ruan, J., Xiang, S., Xie, M., Liu, T., Fu, Y.: MALUNet: a multi-attention and lightweight UNet for skin lesion segmentation. In: 2022 IEEE International Conference on Bioinformatics and Biomedicine (BIBM), pp. 1150–1156. IEEE (2022)

23. Wan, Z., et al.: Sigma: Siamese Mamba network for multi-modal semantic segmentation. arXiv preprint arXiv:2404.04256 (2024)

24. Xing, Z., Ye, T., Yang, Y., Liu, G., Zhu, L.: SegMamba: long-range sequential modeling mamba for 3D medical image segmentation. In: International Conference on Medical Image Computing and Computer-Assisted Intervention, pp. 578–588. Springer (2024)

25. Yang, Z., Lin, D., Ni, D., Wang, Y.: Recurrent feature propagation and edge skip-connections for automatic abdominal organ segmentation. Exp. Syst. Appl. **249**, 123856 (2024)

26. Zhang, M., Yu, Y., Jin, S., Gu, L., Ling, T., Tao, X.: VM-UNET-V2: rethinking vision mamba UNet for medical image segmentation. In: International Symposium on Bioinformatics Research and Applications, pp. 335–346. Springer (2024)

27. Zhu, L., Liao, B., Zhang, Q., Wang, X., Liu, W., Wang, X.: Vision Mamba: efficient visual representation learning with bidirectional state space model. arXiv preprint arXiv:2401.09417 (2024)

28. Zhu, Q., et al.: Samba: semantic segmentation of remotely sensed images with state space model. Heliyon **10**, e38495 (2024)

29. Zhu, Z., et al.: Boosting knowledge diversity, accuracy, and stability via tri-enhanced distillation for domain continual medical image segmentation. Med. Image Anal. **94**, 103112 (2024)

30. Zhu, Z., He, X., Qi, G., Li, Y., Cong, B., Liu, Y.: Brain tumor segmentation based on the fusion of deep semantics and edge information in multimodal MRI. Inf. Fus. **91**, 376–387 (2023)

MSD: Mask-Guided and Semantic-Guided Diffusion-Based Framework for Stone Surface Defect Detection

Longtao Chen[1]([✉]) [ID], Jinjie Zheng[1] [ID], Fenglei Xu[2] [ID], Jing Lou[3] [ID],
and Huanqiang Zeng[1,4] [ID]

[1] Engineering College, Huaqiao University, Quanzhou 362021, Fujian, China
`longtaochen@hqu.edu.cn`
[2] Suzhou University of Science and Technology, Suzhou 215000, Jiangsu, China
[3] Changzhou Vocational Institute of Mechatronic Technology, Changzhou 213000, Jiangsu, China
[4] Quanzhou Digital Institute, Quanzhou 362021, Fujian, China

Abstract. Stone surface defect detection plays a critical role in industrial quality control. Traditional Few-Shot Anomaly Detection (FSAD) methods exhibit limitations in reconstruction fidelity and segmentation accuracy, thereby restricting their broader applications in stone surface inspection. Moreover, the scarcity of high-quality stone surface defect datasets poses significant challenges for research advancement in this domain. To address these issues, we propose Mask-Guided and Semantic-Guided Diffusion-based (MSD) framework, a novel system leveraging multiple representation spaces and advanced guidance mechanisms for precise and efficient detection of stone surface defects. The framework integrates pixel-space, feature-space and latent-space representations, enhanced by two meticulously designed modules: a Mask-Guided Knowledge Distillation network (MGKD) focusing on anomalous regions to improve reconstruction accuracy, and a Semantic-Guided Enhancement Network (SGEN) for preserving semantic fidelity during reconstruction. Additionally, we introduce Stone Defect Dataset (StoneDD), to the best of our knowledge, the first few-shot stone surface defect dataset specifically designed for vision-based defect detection and segmentation. In this study, comprehensive experiments are conducted to evaluate MSD against traditional detection methods. The experimental results demonstrate that MSD achieves superior performance, underlining its potential for future deployment in industrial quality inspection applications.

Keywords: Few-shot anomaly detection · Diffusion-based framework · Stone surface defect detection

1 Introduction

Stone surface defects, resulting from manufacturing faults and material imperfections, can significantly compromise the aesthetic integrity and functional performance of stone products, posing critical challenges across applications such as architectural

P. Didyk and J. Hou (Eds.): CVM 2025, LNCS 15663, pp. 412–427, 2025.
https://doi.org/10.1007/978-981-96-5809-1_22

cladding and interior decoration. The detection process faces significant challenges due to the complex nature of stone surfaces and their defects. These challenges include: (1) intricate surface textures that make anomaly identification difficult, (2) theoretically infinite variety of potential defects, and (3) limited availability of defective samples for dataset construction. While many manufacturers still rely on manual inspection methods, this approach has proven to be both inefficient and subjective, necessitating the development of automated detection solutions.

Various studies have attempted to develop automatic detection methods utilizing synthesis-based and embedding-based approaches [6,29]. However, these conventional methods struggle with multiple challenges, particularly in managing diverse negative sample categories and addressing the long-tail phenomenon [31]. Recent advances in diffusion-based methods [10,27,30] have shown promise in overcoming these limitations through their superior capability in image reconstruction and complex distribution modeling.

Several notable diffusion-based frameworks have been proposed for anomaly detection. The Diffusion-based framework for multi-class Anomaly Detection (DiAD) [10] employs diffusion models to synthesize anomalies while fine-tuning pre-trained feature extractors. Similarly, Denoising Diffusion Anomaly Detection (DDAD) [19] leverages score-based diffusion models for normal sample generation and enhances domain transfer through pre-trained feature extractors. However, when applied to stone surface defect detection, these methods often misclassify background textures as defects during the denoising process, resulting in elevated false detection rates and suboptimal reconstruction quality, as illustrated in Fig. 1. To tackle the aforementioned challenges in stone surface defect detection, we propose Mask–Guided and Semantic-Guided Diffusion-based framework (MSD), which incorporates two novel strategies: (1) A Mask-Guided Knowledge Distillation network (MGKD) that focuses on anomalous regions while suppressing background interference, and (2) A Semantic-Guided Enhancement Network (SGEN) that leverages multi-scale features for precise anomaly detection and localization.

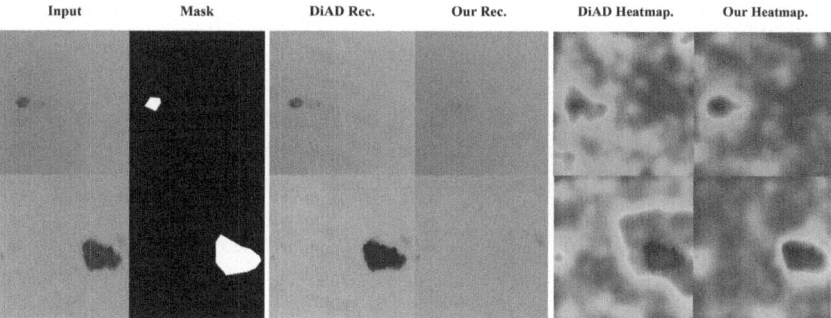

Fig. 1. Comparison of results of different methods. (a) DiAD exhibits poor reconstruction quality and insufficient heatmap convergence. (b) Our proposed approach demonstrates superior defect detection capability and improved image reconstruction quality.

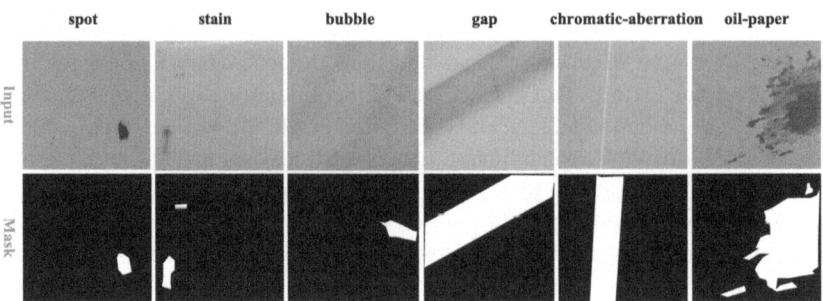

Fig. 2. Samples from StoneDD.

Besides, to address the limitations in existing stone surface defect detection research, particularly the lack of publicly available datasets, we introduce StoneDD, a comprehensive dataset specifically designed for this domain. As shown in Fig. 2, this dataset presents various challenges and possesses the following distinctive characteristics:

- **Defect types:** spot, stain, bubble, gap, chromatic-aberration, and oil-paper (paper sticks to the stone).
- **Data volume:** 1,290 images with corresponding masks, representing the first dedicated dataset for stone surface defects
- **Multi-resolution:** images available in both 900×900 and 256×256 resolutions to support comprehensive experimentation
- **Diversity:** features richly textured stone slabs with subtle variations in local color, presenting realistic challenges in distinguishing natural textures from actual defects

Our key contributions can be summarized as follows:

- We develop the MGKD network that effectively differentiates between anomalous regions and background areas through weighted allocation, leading to enhanced reconstruction precision.
- We introduce the SGEN network, designed to integrate multi-scale features and improve both anomaly detection and localization accuracy, effectively reducing false detection rates.
- We present StoneDD, the first few-shot Stone Surface Defect dataset, and demonstrate the effectiveness of our MSD framework through extensive experimentation, achieving outstanding localization and detection scores of 95.8/67.3 and 99.1/97.6 (AUROC/AP), respectively.

2   Related Work

2.1   Stone Surface Detection

Stone surface detection is an essential task across various industries, including construction, archaeology, and quality control in stone manufacturing. Over the years, numerous methodologies [2, 9, 13–15, 19, 22] have been proposed to enhance the precision and efficiency of detecting anomalies and features on stone surfaces.

Traditional approaches often relied on manual inspection, a process that is not only time-consuming but also susceptible to human error. With advancements in computer vision and machine learning, automated detection techniques have increasingly taken center stage. For example, P. Kapsalas et al. [14] utilized optical detection techniques to quantify surface decay in stone materials, while J. Lee et al. [15] explored robust and efficient automatic methods for detecting tool defect in polished stone. Additionally, A. Borel et al. [2] discussed optimization methods for wear detection and characterization on stone tool surfaces.

Recently, many studies have begun to use deep learning methods to detect surface defects in stone surface. M. Guerrieri et al. [9] used deep learning with inexpensive detection equipment to identify and measure damage on flexible and rocky road surfaces. H. Kabir et al. [13] employed Mask R-CNN for stone detection and segmentation in underground pipeline inspection robots. M. Smith et al. [22] discussed using machine vision technology for inspecting polished stone materials in manufacturing processes. Additionally, A. Mousakhan et al. [19] utilized a score-based pre-trained diffusion model to generate normal samples and fine-tuned feature extractors for domain transfer, enhancing detection across various stone surfaces.

Despite these advancements, challenges remain due to the variability and complexity of stone surface textures. Future research should focus on developing more robust and adaptable models, which can use weakly supervised anomaly detection methods to detect various abnormal defects on stone surfaces.

2.2 Anomaly Detection

Traditional stone surface detection methods often struggle with issues such as out-of-distribution detection for unseen samples during training. Anomaly detection techniques, however, can mitigate these challenges. Anomaly detection [8, 16, 23] can be categorized into three primary approaches:

1) **Synthesis-based methods** generate anomalies from normal image samples. During training, both normal and artificially generated abnormal images are fed into the network, helping in anomaly detection and localization. Zavrtanik et al. [29] proposed the Discriminatively Trained Reconstruction Anomaly Embedding Model (DRAEM), an end-to-end network combining a reconstruction component with a discriminative sub-network for synthesizing and generating out-of-distribution anomalies. However, synthesizing all possible anomaly variations remains challenging due to the diverse and unpredictable nature of anomalies in real-world scenarios.

2) **Embedding-based methods** map the original image's three-dimensional information into a high-dimensional feature space [21]. Several approaches [11, 17, 24, 25] utilize networks pre-trained on ImageNet [7] for feature extraction. Deng et al. [6] proposed the Reverse Distillation paradigm For Anomaly Detection (RD4AD), using Wide Residual Networks (WideResNet50) as a teacher model for feature extraction and a reverse network as a student model to compute anomaly scores based on cosine similarity. Defard et al. [5] introduced Patch Distribution Modeling (PaDiM), leveraging

pretrained CNNs for patch embedding and multivariate Gaussian distributions to probabilistically represent the normal class.

You et al. [28] developed the Unified model for multi-class Anomaly Detection (UniAD), which enhances reconstruction networks with layer-wise query decoders, neighbor-masked attention modules, and feature jittering. However, discrepancies between industrial images and ImageNet's data distribution may limit these features' applicability for industrial anomaly detection [3, 21, 26].

3) **Diffusion-based methods** train models on anomaly-free data to identify patterns in normal data. The diffusion model [27] has garnered significant attention due to its impressive reconstruction capabilities. It has shown exceptional performance in various tasks, including image generation [30], video generation [12], object detection [4], and image segmentation [1]. Blattmann et al. [20] proposed High-Resolution Image Synthesis with Latent Diffusion Models (LDM), which introduces conditioning via cross-attention to control the generation process. However, accurately preserving the original semantic content in reconstructed images remains a challenge. Wyatt et al. [27] introduced Anomaly Detection with Denoising Diffusion Probabilistic Models (AnoD-DPM), the first application of a diffusion model for medical anomaly detection. He et al. [10] developed a Diffusion-based framework for multi-class Anomaly Detection (DiAD), utilizing a diffusion model to generate synthetic anomalies while fine-tuning a pre-trained feature extractor for improved detection across various anomaly classes.

However, the reconstruction results of these methods often exhibit limitations, such as susceptibility to background noise, which can lead to normal features being misclassified as anomalies. To overcome these issues, this paper proposes a mask-guided and enhanced semantic-guided diffusion-based framework for marble slab surface anomaly detection, improving the quality of reconstructed images and enhancing the pixel-level localization of anomalies.

To overcome these challenges, we propose a mask-guided and semantic-enhanced diffusion-based framework for stone surface anomaly detection, which effectively refines the quality of reconstructed images and significantly enhances the precision of pixel-level anomaly localization.

3   Method

During training $(S_1, \{P_1, P_2, P_3\}, S_2, S_3)$. S_1: Encoding the input image x as the latent-space representation; $\{P_1, P_2, P_3\}$: $\{P_1$: Forward diffusion, adding noise to the latent-space representation; P_2: Enter the latent-space representation into SGEN for a more definitive location of the defect edge P_3: The latent-space representation is overlaid with masks and then into MGKD for precise defect ranges$\}$; S_2: Integrating Mask-Guided and Semantic-Guided representation to facilitate the reverse denoising process and obtain reconstructed representation; S_3: Decoding the reconstructed representation as the reconstructed image $\hat{x}_0$ (i.e. flawless image/ Repaired image).

During testing (S_4). x and $\hat{x}_0$ are inputted into the same pre-trained feature extraction network to obtain feature maps $\{f_1, f_2, f_3\}$ of different scales, and calculate their anomaly scores S by cosine similarity.

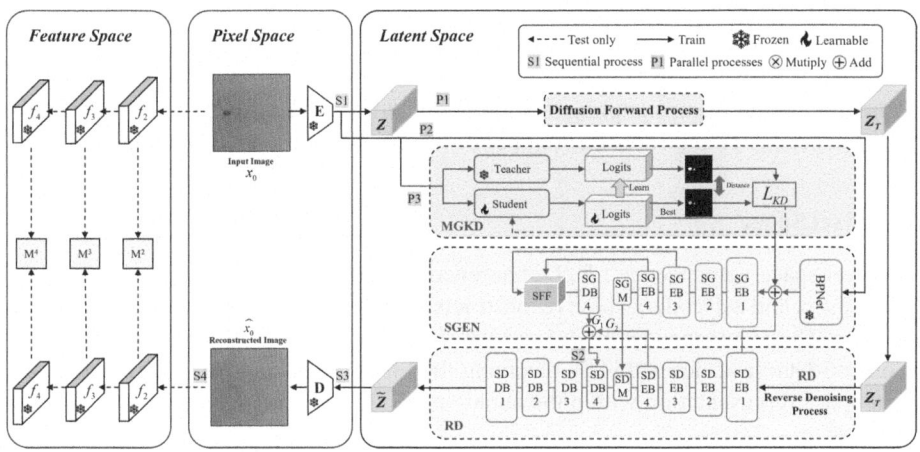

Fig. 3. Framework of the proposed MSD. During training $(S_1, \{P_1, P_2, P_3\}, S_2, S_3)$, the input image x_0 is processed in parallel by $\{P_1, P_2, P_3\}$, Then reverse denoising Process RD to get the reconstructed image $\hat{x}_0$. During testing (S_4), x_0 and $\hat{x}_0$ are inputted into the feature space to generate feature maps and calculate anomaly scores S.

How it Work. When the input image passes through the latent space on the right, a defect-free reconstructed image is generated. Both the input and the reconstructed images are then passed to the left to compute the cosine distance. The greater the pixel-level difference, the more pronounced the corresponding anomaly in the heatmap. In simple terms, by comparing the differences between the two images, the regions of discrepancy are displayed in red. Therefore, the accuracy of the heatmap largely depends on the quality and level of detail in the reconstructed image. To address this issue, we employed semantic and mask guidance to optimize the reconstruction process, resulting in more precise reconstructions and achieving heatmap convergence.

The proposed MSD pipeline, depicted in Fig. 3, comprises three components: 1) Feature Space, 2) Pixel Space, 3) Latent Space.

3.1 Feature Space

For defect localization and detection, we utilize the same pre-trained ResNet50 feature extraction network Ψ to extract features from both the input image x and the reconstructed image $\hat{x}_0$. We then calculate the anomaly map on different scale feature maps M_n using cosine similarity:

$$\mathcal{M}^n(x_0, \hat{x_0}) = 1 - \frac{(\Psi^n(x_0, \hat{x_0}))^T \cdot \Psi^n(x_0, \hat{x_0})}{\|\Psi^n(x_0, \hat{x_0})\| \|\Psi^n(x_0, \hat{x_0})\|}, \tag{1}$$

Where n denotes the n-th feature layer f_n, and the anomaly score S for an input-pair of anomaly localization is:

$$\mathcal{S} = \sum_{n \in N} \sigma_n \mathcal{M}^n \left(x_0, \hat{x_0} \right), \tag{2}$$

Where σ_n denotes the upsampling factor to maintain the original dimension of the pixel space image, and N indicates the number of feature layers used during inference.

3.2   Pixel Space

The pixel space autoencoder $\{E, D\}$: an encoder, which maps the input image to the latent-space, and a decoder, which reconstructs the latent-space representation back into an image. These autoencoder module is tasked with learning low-dimensional representations of data. It achieves this by receiving the input image and encoding them as the latent-space representation within the latent-space.

3.3   Latent Space

The latent-space primarily encompasses three components: latent diffusion model (LDM), Mask-Guided Knowledge Distillation network (MGKD), and Semantic-Guided Enhancement Network (SGEN). We will elaborate on each of these three modules below:

Latent Diffusion Model. Latent Diffusion Model (LDM) focuses on the low-dimensional latent space with conditioning mechanisms. The network compresses images using an encoder, conducts diffusion and denoising operations in the latent representation space, and subsequently reconstructs the images back to the original pixel space using a decoder. The training optimization objective is:

$$\mathcal{L}_{LDM} = \mathbb{E}_{z_0,t,c,\epsilon \sim \mathcal{N}(0,1)} \left[\| \epsilon - \epsilon_\theta \left(Z_t, t, c \right) \|_2^2 \right], \tag{3}$$

where c represents the conditioning mechanisms which can consist of multimodal types such as text or image, connected to the model through a cross-attention mechanism. Z_t represents the full-noise representation,

The LDM [27] comprises two processes: diffusion forward process and reverse denoising process, just as Fig. 4.

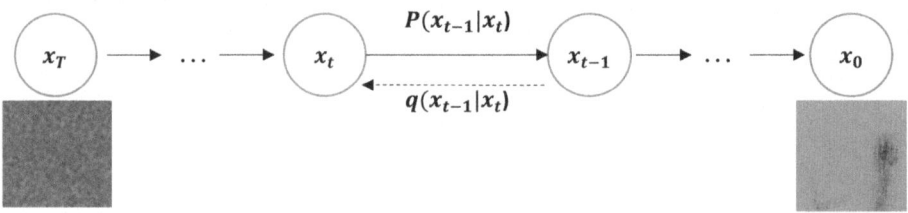

Fig. 4. Denoising diffusion probabilistic model.

In the diffusion forward process, a noisy sample x_t is generated through a Markov chain that gradually introduces Gaussian-distributed noise to an initial data sample x_0 as Eq. (4).

$$x_t = \sqrt{\bar{\alpha}_t} x_0 + \sqrt{1 - \bar{\alpha}_t} \epsilon_t, \epsilon_t \sim \mathcal{N}(\mathbf{0}, \mathbf{I}), \tag{4}$$

Where $\alpha_t = 1 - \beta_t$, $\bar{\alpha}_t = \prod_{i=1}^{T} \alpha_i = \prod_{i=1}^{T}(1 - \beta_i)$, and β_i represents the noise schedule regulating the amount of noise added at each timestep.

In the reverse denoising process, x_t is sampled from Eq. (4), and x_{t-1} is reconstructed using x_t and the model prediction $\epsilon_\theta(x_t, t)$ as Eq. (5).

$$x_{t-1} = \frac{1}{\sqrt{\alpha_t}} \left(x_t - \frac{1 - \alpha_t}{\sqrt{1 - \bar{\alpha}_t}} \epsilon_\theta(x_t, t) \right) + \sigma_t z, \tag{5}$$

Where $z \sim \mathcal{N}(0, I)$, σ_t is a fixed constant related to the variance schedule, and θ represents the learnable parameters.

Mask-Guided Knowledge Distillation Network. Mask-Guided Knowledge Distillation network (MGKD) focus on more precise and larger possible areas of defects. Specifically, the latent-space representation and grid are overlaid by dot product to obtain the mask representation, then the mask teacher model and student model are passed in synchronously, the mask weights are used as a benchmark to correct the student model, simultaneously the student model is allowed to learn from the teacher through L_{KD}, as Eq. (1). The gap between them is continuously reduced in n rounds of iteration, and finally the best weights optimize the Semantic-Guided network, which assists in the reverse denoising process so that it is bound to be effective in the flawed region search.

The network consists of a pre-trained teacher encoder E, sourced from Automatic-Mask-Generation, and a trainable student decoder D. During training, the student decoder learns to mimic the teacher encoder's behavior by minimizing the similarity loss L_{KD}. The best logits are generated based on this learning process, which are then used to further optimize the SGEN model.

$$\mathcal{L}_{\text{MSE}} = \text{Dist}(z_S, z_T) == \frac{1}{n} \sum_{i=1}^{n} \left(z_T^{(i)} - z_S^{(i)} \right)^2 \tag{6}$$

Where $\text{Dist}(\cdot)$ denotes the Euclidean distance and n denotes the number of categories, Z_T and Z_s denote the outputs of the mask teacher model and student model;

$$\mathcal{L}_{\text{KL}} = \frac{1}{n} \sum_{i=1}^{n} \sigma(z_T^{(i)}/\tau) \cdot \log \left(\frac{\sigma(z_T^{(i)}/\tau)}{\sigma(z_S^{(i)}/\tau)} \right) \tag{7}$$

where L_{KL} denotes the Kullback-Leibler scattering loss function, and σ denotes the Softmax function, τ denotes the temperature parameter, which is used to adjust the degree of "softening" of Softmax;

$$\mathcal{L}_{\text{KD}} = \alpha \cdot \mathcal{L}_{\text{MSE}} + \beta \cdot \mathcal{L}_{\text{KL}} \tag{8}$$

where L_{KD} denotes the overall loss function of the knowledge distillation network, α and β denote the weighting coefficients, which can be manually adjusted to achieve the optimal distillation effect.

Semantic-Guided Enhancement Network. Semantic-Guided Enhancement Network (SGEN) focuses on accurately locating the edges and contours of defects. Specifically, the pre-trained BPNet first extracts multi-level features and integrates them to obtain semantic representations. Through a series of semantic modules that progressively refine the defective edges, the Spatial-aware Feature Fusion (SFF) block then combines the fused features with the original features, which collaboratively optimizes the reverse denoising process and this will surely be able to find the defective edges for subsequent heat map visualization.

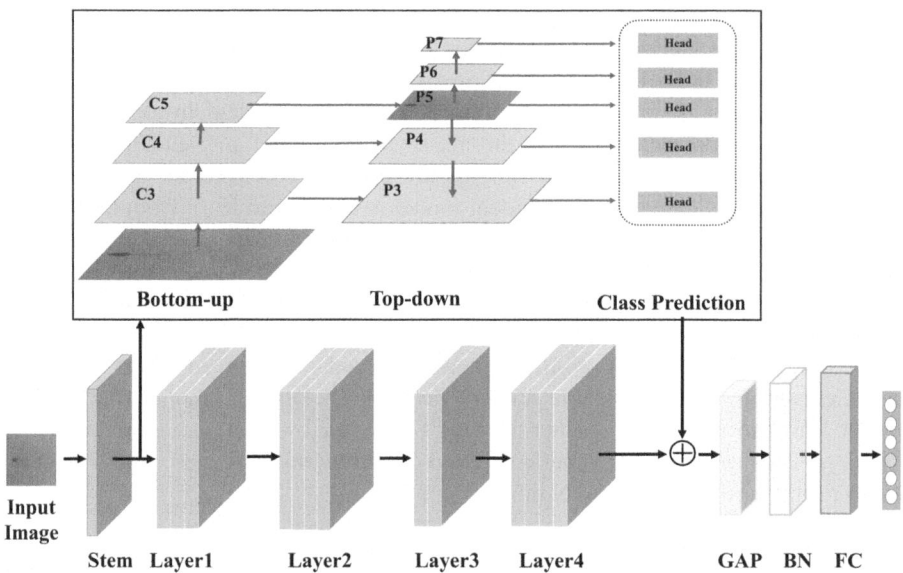

Fig. 5. The structure of the BPNet.

BPNet, as shown in Fig. 5, combines bottom-up and top-down modules to enhance low-resolution feature maps by fusing them with high-resolution ones, thereby enriching semantic information. SGEN reconstructs anomaly areas while retaining the original image's semantics, leveraging multi-scale features for precise localization and classification. The model focuses on identifying anomalies while minimizing attention to irrelevant background elements.

SGEN is designed to tackle the specific challenges faced by LDMs in multi-class defect detection tasks. To address the limitations associated with LDMs, particularly in effectively reconstructing anomalies while retaining the semantic information of the input image, we introduce the SGEN as a solution to enhance performance in multi-class scenarios.

Given an input image $x_0 \in \mathbb{R}^{3 \times H \times W}$ in pixel space, the pre-trained encoder $\mathcal{E}$ encodes x_0 into a latent-space representation $z \in \mathbb{R}^{c \times h \times w}$, where $z = \mathcal{E}(x_0)$. Now, the forward diffusion process can be characterized as follows: $z = \mathcal{E}(x_0)$. Now, the forward diffusion process can be characterized as follows:

$$z_t = \sqrt{\bar{\alpha}_t} z_0 + \sqrt{1 - \bar{\alpha}_t} \epsilon_t, \epsilon_t \sim \mathcal{N}(\mathbf{0}, \mathbf{I}). \tag{9}$$

The perturbed representation z_T and input X are simultaneously fed into the RD and SGEN network, respectively. After T steps of the reverse denoising process, the final variable $\hat{z}$ is restored to the reconstructed image $\tilde{X}$ from the pre-trained decoder $\mathcal{D}$ giving $\hat{X} = \mathcal{D}(\hat{z})$. The training objective of MSD is:

$$\mathcal{L}_{MSD} = \mathbb{E}_{z_0, t, c_i, \epsilon \sim \mathcal{N}(0,1)} \left[\left\| \epsilon - \epsilon_\theta \left(z_t, t, c_i \right) \right\|_2^2 \right] + \lambda L_{\text{KD}}. \tag{10}$$

Table 1. Comparison with other detection methods on StoneDD dataset.

Metrics	Non-Diffusion Methods				Diffusion-based Methods		
	PaDiM	DRAEM	RD4AD	UniAD	AnoDDPM	DiAD	**MSD**
	21'ICPR	21'ICCV	22'CVPR	22'NeurIPS	22'CVPR	24'AAAI	**Ours**
AUROCseg	88.7	91.5	93.7	94.8	89.3	93.8	**95.8**
APseg	-	18.3	23.9	43.1	47.1	47.0	**56.8**
F1maxseg	-	17.3	26.3	49.5	11.2	**55.1**	49.7
AUROCcls	86.9	60.9	79.1	96.5	67.9	98.7	**99.1**
APcls	-	84.6	95.2	97.9	78.1	**99.5**	97.6
F1maxcls	-	88.7	90.3	95.7	88.7	99.2	**99.2**

Table 2. Ablation studies of different feature extraction backbones.

Metrics	VGG19	ResNet50	WideResNet101
AUROCseg	92.5	95.8	**96.4**
AUROCcls	91.3	**99.1**	95.6

4 Experiment

4.1 Stone Defect Dataset

In the field of stone surface defect detection, to the best of our knowledge, we are the first team to propose the few-shot Stone Defect Dataset (StoneDD). We hope that the

Table 3. Ablation studies of different feature layers.

f1	f2	f3	f4	f5	AUROCseg	AUROCcls
✓	✓	✓	✓	✓	94.1	93.9
	✓	✓	✓		95.4	97.0
		✓	✓	✓	**95.8**	97.2
✓	✓	✓			**95.8**	**99.1**

StoneDD will provide effective support for subsequent researchers to advance the stone surface defect detection technology, thus helping the stone industry to move away from traditional manual inspection methods to automated and intelligent defect detection. We aim to provide a small-scale muti-resolution Stone Defect Dataset (StoneDD) with comprehensive annotations that can expose the challenges of stone surface defect detection and segmentation. The specific process of dataset construction is shown in the Fig. 6.

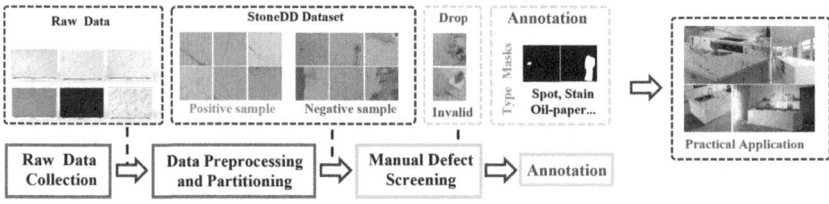

Fig. 6. The generation pipeline of StoneDD, which includes raw data collection, data preprocessing and partitioning, manual defect screening, and annotation.

Raw Data Collection. We manually photographed and collected original stone images and selectively collected complete, high-resolution images of the stone surface. Because these images contained many types of defects that were difficult to recognize, we manually selected the six most obvious and distinguishable types of defects, resulting in 1,045 original images (defect types: spot, stain, bubble, gap, chromatic-aberration, and oil-paper).

Data Preprocessing and Partitioning. We preprocess the collected raw data through cropping, segmentation, and normalization. The dataset is then organized into positive samples (without defects) and negative samples (with defects) using the COCO format to facilitate subsequent experiments.

Manual Defect Screening. We perform manual screening, primarily removing stone images that contain arrow labels and artificially drawn lines. Subsequently, we select high-quality images to ensure both the quality and quantity of The StoneDD.

Annotation. We use the Labelme tool for annotation, which consists of two main steps: first, labeling the defective regions and generating masks; and second, categorizing each defect and recording its type. This detailed annotation process is crucial for subsequent model training and evaluation. As shown on the right side of Fig. 6, the thoroughness of this approach ensures high-quality annotations that significantly contribute to the model's performance.

The StoneDD dataset supports a range of downstream tasks, such as target detection and instance segmentation. It is characterized by small sample sizes, a wide variety of defects, and similar background textures, making it particularly suited for few-shot anomaly detection.

We hope that the presentation of this dataset will provide a solid foundation for subsequent researchers in the field of few-shot anomaly detection, thereby promoting technological advances, fostering research innovations, and enhancing practical applications in this field.

4.2 Evaluation Metrics

Building on prior research, this study employs AUROC, AP, and F1max metrics to assess both defect localization and detection tasks. Specifically, 'seg' refers to pixel-level defect localization, while 'cls' denotes image-level defect detection.

Among these metrics, AUROC is the most representative. However, since this study focuses on detecting defect edges for localization, we place greater emphasis on the segmentation metric (i.e., AUROCseg is considered the most important and representative metric), subsequent experiments will primarily be evaluated based on the AUROC metric.

4.3 Implementation Details

This design adopts ResNet50 as the feature extraction network and chooses $n \in \{2, 3, 4\}$ as the feature layers used in calculating the anomaly localization. We train on a single NVIDIA Ampere A40 GPU for 1000 epochs on 48 GB, with a batch size of 12. The learning rate is set to 1×10^{-5} for the Adam optimizer [18].

4.4 Comparison with Other Anomaly Detection Methods

Quantitative Experiment. We employ recent state-of-the-art (SOTA) methods as benchmark comparisons. As illustrated in Table 1, our proposed MSD method achieves significantly superior performance in both pixel-level defect segmentation and image-level localization.

Qualitative Experiment. To better illustrate the experimental effects, we present heatmaps for transparent visualization. This allows for a clearer observation of our refined experimental outcomes, demonstrating that our method is more suitable for stone surface defect detection, as shown in Figs. 7 and 8. Where Rec. represents reconstructed images, GT represents ground truth for the anomaly location, and Loc. represents heatmap images.

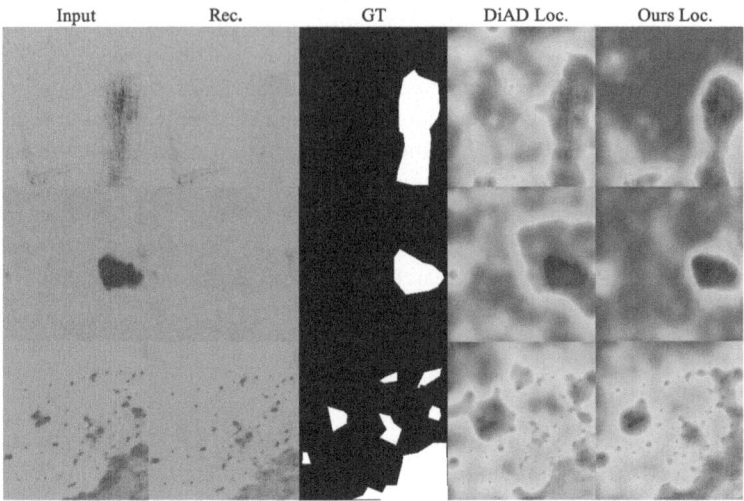

Fig. 7. Qualitative comparison results of anomaly localization (256 * 256).

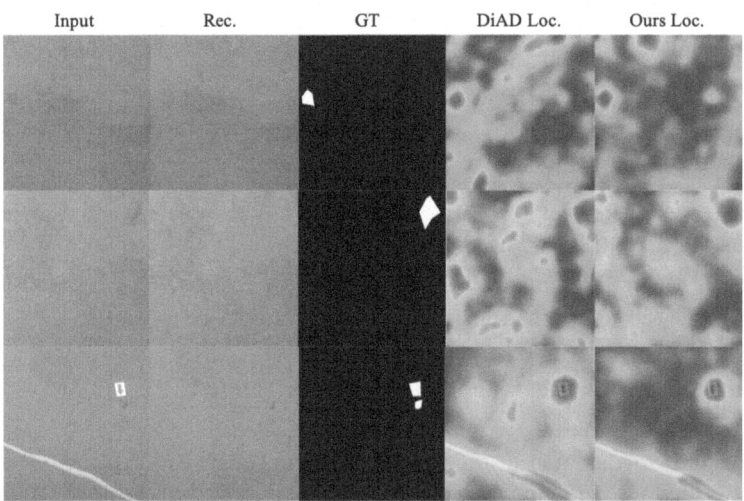

Fig. 8. Qualitative comparison results of anomaly localization (900 * 900).

4.5 Ablation Studies

Effect of Pre-trained Feature Extractors. Table 2 shows the use of different pre-trained backbone networks for quantitative comparison of feature extraction networks. We use ResNet50 as the pre-trained feature extraction network.

Effect of Different Feature Layers Used in Anomaly Score Calculating. The specific data is presented in Table 3. After obtaining the feature maps at various degrees, we extract features at five different scales using a pre-trained backbone. The anomaly score is then calculated by determining the cosine similarity between the feature maps of different layers.

The Architecture Design of MSD. The method of this design achieves 99.1/97.6/99.2 and pixel-level accuracy, respectively. The AUROC/AP/F1max index of 95.8/56.8/49.7. We conducted ablation experiments on the architecture design of MSD to verify the effectiveness of SGEN and MGKD networks. The specific data is shown in Table 4.

Table 4. Ablation studies on the design of MSD(%).

SD	SGEN	MGKD	$AUROC_{seg}$	$AUROC_{cls}$
✓			93.8	98.7
✓	✓		95.7	93.1
✓		✓	94.6	98.6
✓	✓	✓	**95.8**	**99.1**

5 Conclusion

This paper presents a Mask-Guided and Enhanced Semantic-Guided Diffusion-based framework (MSD) for Stone Surface Anomaly Detection, addressing the challenges of poor reconstruction quality and high false positive rates in diffusion-based methods. The Mask-Guided Knowledge Distillation Network (MGKD) emphasizes anomalous regions to enhance image reconstruction precision, while the Semantic-Guided Enhancement Network (SGEN) integrates multi-scale features to improve anomaly detection accuracy and reduce false detection rates.

We also introduce StoneDD, the first to include diverse stone surface defects at varying resolutions. Our MSD approach achieves impressive localization and detection AUROC/AP scores on StoneDD. Despite its high performance, there is potential for further improvement in pixel-level localization and detection. Future work will focus on expanding The StoneDD and utilizing larger models to enhance reconstruction performance.

References

1. Amit, T., Shaharbany, T., Nachmani, E., Wolf, L.: SegDiff: image segmentation with diffusion probabilistic models. arXiv preprint arXiv:2112.00390 (2021)
2. Borel, A., Deltombe, R., Moreau, P., Ingicco, T., Bigerelle, M., Marteau, J.: Optimization of use-wear detection and characterization on stone tool surfaces. Sci. Rep. **11**(1), 24197 (2021)
3. Chen, R., et al.: EasyNet: an easy network for 3D industrial anomaly detection. In: Proceedings of the 31st ACM International Conference on Multimedia, pp. 7038–7046 (2023)

4. Chen, S., Sun, P., Song, Y., Luo, P.: DiffusionDet: diffusion model for object detection. In: Proceedings of the IEEE/CVF International Conference on Computer Vision, pp. 19830–19843 (2023)

5. Defard, T., Setkov, A., Loesch, A., Audigier, R.: PaDiM: a patch distribution modeling framework for anomaly detection and localization. In: International Conference on Pattern Recognition, pp. 475–489. Springer (2021)

6. Deng, H., Li, X.: Anomaly detection via reverse distillation from one-class embedding. In: Proceedings of the IEEE/CVF Conference on Computer Vision and Pattern Recognition, pp. 9737–9746 (2022)

7. Deng, J., Dong, W., Socher, R., Li, L.J., Li, K., Fei-Fei, L.: ImageNet: a large-scale hierarchical image database. In: 2009 IEEE Conference on Computer Vision and Pattern Recognition, pp. 248–255. IEEE (2009)

8. Ding, C., Pang, G., Shen, C.: Catching both gray and black swans: open-set supervised anomaly detection. In: Proceedings of the IEEE/CVF Conference on Computer Vision and Pattern Recognition, pp. 7388–7398 (2022)

9. Guerrieri, M., Parla, G.: Flexible and stone pavements distress detection and measurement by deep learning and low-cost detection devices. Eng. Fail. Anal. **141**, 106714 (2022)

10. He, H., et al.: A diffusion-based framework for multi-class anomaly detection. In: Proceedings of the AAAI Conference on Artificial Intelligence, vol. 38, pp. 8472–8480 (2024)

11. He, K., Zhang, X., Ren, S., Sun, J.: Deep residual learning for image recognition. In: Proceedings of the IEEE Conference on Computer Vision and Pattern Recognition, pp. 770–778 (2016)

12. Ho, J., et al.: Imagen video: high definition video generation with diffusion models. arXiv preprint arXiv:2210.02303 (2022)

13. Kabir, H., Lee, H.S.: Mask R-CNN-based stone detection and segmentation for underground pipeline exploration robots. Appl. Sci. **14**(9), 3752 (2024)

14. Kapsalas, P., Maravelaki-Kalaitzaki, P., Zervakis, M., Delegou, E., Moropoulou, A.: Optical inspection for quantification of decay on stone surfaces. NDT & E Int. **40**(1), 2–11 (2007)

15. Lee, J., Smith, M.L., Smith, L.N., Midha, P.S.: Robust and efficient automated detection of tooling defects in polished stone. Comput. Ind. **56**(8–9), 787–801 (2005)

16. Li, C.L., Sohn, K., Yoon, J., Pfister, T.: CutPaste: self-supervised learning for anomaly detection and localization. In: Proceedings of the IEEE/CVF Conference on Computer Vision and Pattern Recognition, pp. 9664–9674 (2021)

17. Liang, Y., Zhang, J., Zhao, S., Wu, R., Liu, Y., Pan, S.: Omni-frequency channel-selection representations for unsupervised anomaly detection. IEEE Trans. Image Process. (2023)

18. Loshchilov, I., Hutter, F.: Decoupled weight decay regularization. arXiv preprint arXiv:1711.05101 (2017)

19. Mousakhan, A., Brox, T., Tayyub, J.: Anomaly detection with conditioned denoising diffusion models. arXiv preprint arXiv:2305.15956 (2023)

20. Rombach, R., Blattmann, A., Lorenz, D., Esser, P., Ommer, B.: High-resolution image synthesis with latent diffusion models. In: Proceedings of the IEEE/CVF Conference on Computer Vision and Pattern Recognition, pp. 10684–10695 (2022)

21. Roth, K., Pemula, L., Zepeda, J., Schölkopf, B., Brox, T., Gehler, P.: Towards total recall in industrial anomaly detection. In: Proceedings of the IEEE/CVF Conference on Computer Vision and Pattern Recognition, pp. 14318–14328 (2022)

22. Smith, M., Smith, L.: Machine vision inspection for polished stone manufacture. Key Eng. Mater. **250**, 131–137 (2003)

23. Tan, D.S., Chen, Y.C., Chen, T.P.C., Chen, W.C.: TrustMAE: a noise-resilient defect classification framework using memory-augmented auto-encoders with trust regions. In: Proceedings of the IEEE/CVF Winter Conference on Applications of Computer Vision, pp. 276–285 (2021)

24. Tan, M., Le, Q.: EfficientNet: rethinking model scaling for convolutional neural networks. In: International Conference on Machine Learning, pp. 6105–6114. PMLR (2019)
25. Tao, X., Gong, X., Zhang, X., Yan, S., Adak, C.: Deep learning for unsupervised anomaly localization in industrial images: a survey. IEEE Trans. Instrum. Meas. **71**, 1–21 (2022)
26. Wang, Y., Peng, J., Zhang, J., Yi, R., Wang, Y., Wang, C.: Multimodal industrial anomaly detection via hybrid fusion. In: Proceedings of the IEEE/CVF Conference on Computer Vision and Pattern Recognition, pp. 8032–8041 (2023)
27. Wyatt, J., Leach, A., Schmon, S.M., Willcocks, C.G.: AnoDDPM: anomaly detection with denoising diffusion probabilistic models using simplex noise. In: Proceedings of the IEEE/CVF Conference on Computer Vision and Pattern Recognition, pp. 650–656 (2022)
28. You, Z., et al.: A unified model for multi-class anomaly detection. Adv. Neural. Inf. Process. Syst. **35**, 4571–4584 (2022)
29. Zavrtanik, V., Kristan, M., Skočaj, D.: DRAEM - a discriminatively trained reconstruction embedding for surface anomaly detection. In: Proceedings of the IEEE/CVF International Conference on Computer Vision, pp. 8330–8339 (2021)
30. Zhang, L., Rao, A., Agrawala, M.: Adding conditional control to text-to-image diffusion models. In: Proceedings of the IEEE/CVF International Conference on Computer Vision, pp. 3836–3847 (2023)
31. Zhou, B., Cui, Q., Wei, X.S., Chen, Z.M.: BBN: bilateral-branch network with cumulative learning for long-tailed visual recognition. In: Proceedings of the IEEE/CVF Conference on Computer Vision and Pattern Recognition, pp. 9719–9728 (2020)

A New Heterogeneous Mixture of Experts Model for Deepfake Detection

Qichang Wang[1] and Ruixia Liu[2](✉)

[1] School of Mathematics and Statistics, Qilu University of Technology
(Shandong Academy of Sciences), Jinan, China
[2] Shandong Artificial Intelligence Institute, Qilu University of Technology
(Shandong Academy of Sciences), Jinan, China
liurx@sdas.org

Abstract. Deepfake detection remains a challenging task due to the diversity of forgery techniques and the distributional shifts between training and testing data. Existing methods, often framed as binary classification tasks, struggle with generalization, particularly in real-world scenarios involving unknown forgery types. To address this challenge, we propose DFMoE, a novel deepfake detection framework based on a Heterogeneous Mixture of Experts (HMoE) model. Our approach incorporates dynamic gating networks that adaptively select expert networks of varying capacities and scales according to the input characteristics, enabling precise identification of different types of forgeries. Leveraging a pre-trained face recognition model for multi-scale feature extraction, DFMoE combines expert specialization with adaptive data augmentation to enhance the detection of both known and unknown deepfake types. Experimental results show that our method significantly improves detection accuracy and robustness, offering a highly effective solution for deepfake detection across diverse scenarios.

Keywords: Deepfakes · Forgery Detection · Mixture of Experts · Gating network · Robustness · Data augmentation

1 Introduction

With the rapid advancement of deepfake technology, AI-generated highly realistic visual content has garnered widespread attention. Although Generative Adversarial Networks (GANs) have brought significant economic and entertainment value to the field of computer vision, their misuse poses serious concerns, such as violations of personal privacy, manipulation of public opinion, and threats to public safety. To address these challenges, developing deepfake detection methods with broad applicability has become a pressing need.

Initially, most detection methods treated deepfake detection as a simple binary classification task. While these methods perform well in detecting specific types of forgeries, their generalization ability in real-world scenarios is limited. In real-life applications, the training and test data often come from different distributions, and the feature distributions of various types of forgeries differ,

P. Didyk and J. Hou (Eds.): CVM 2025, LNCS 15663, pp. 428–449, 2025.
https://doi.org/10.1007/978-981-96-5809-1_23

causing these methods to exhibit significant performance drops in practical use, limiting their wide applicability.

In recent years, some methods have attempted to enhance generalization capabilities through pre-trained models, data augmentation, and more efficient model designs. Although these methods have made some progress in cross-domain detection, they often overfit certain forgery types. Moreover, many methods rely on a single encoder to parse different types of forgery data, but in real-world scenarios, numerous complex and unknown forgery types exist. The limitations of a single model make it difficult to effectively handle these complexities. Although some studies have designed multiple networks to handle different forgery types using strategies like knowledge distillation, these methods fail to dynamically select the most suitable network based on the differences in forgery types.

Another line of research has used data augmentation to generate more diverse and representative forgery samples, training more generalizable detectors. For example, some studies have generated new fake faces through pixel-level mixing, increasing the diversity of training samples and enhancing the robustness of detection models. Other studies have proposed semantic-based data augmentation strategies, manipulating semantic content such as lighting, facial expressions, and angles to generate forgery samples. Compared to simple pixel operations, semantic-level augmentation methods better simulate complex forgery scenarios.

While data augmentation methods show good potential for improving model generalization, their limitations are becoming apparent. Since current data augmentation methods mainly rely on combinations and transformations of existing forgery types, they cannot fully cover all possible unknown forgery types.

To address the aforementioned issues, this paper proposes a deepfake detection method based on a Heterogeneous Mixture of Experts (HMoE) [36] model–DFMoE. Our design allows the system to adaptively select the most appropriate expert network based on the scale of different forgery features, thus improving detection accuracy and generalization capability.

Inspired by prior work, we also introduced a gating network based on a pre-trained face recognition model to capture rich facial features in real-world scenarios. Through the gating network, our method can adaptively select different expert networks for processing based on the characteristics of the forgery types.

In addition, we made innovations in data augmentation strategies. Existing forgery data features typically exhibit a discrete distribution in latent space, which fails to effectively cover the features of unknown forgery types. This shortcoming severely affects the model's ability to generalize in real-world applications. To overcome this problem, we enhance the features extracted by expert networks through data augmentation, enabling these enhanced features to better cover the feature domain of unknown forgery types. Specifically, we introduced latent space-based feature interpolation and expansion methods, generating more diverse feature representations by mixing and perturbing the features of known forgery types. These feature augmentation strategies significantly improve the classifier's generalization ability, enabling it to accurately handle previously unseen forgery types.

In summary, our method addresses the limitations of traditional deepfake detection approaches in terms of generalization by introducing the HMoE model and advanced data augmentation techniques. By adaptively selecting expert networks of different scales to handle forgery types, our method can not only cope with known forgery types but also possesses strong capabilities in handling unknown forgery types, achieving better performance with fewer activated parameters. Our research provides a novel approach and technical pathway for the field of deepfake detection, with broad application prospects. The contributions of our work are as follows:

1. We propose a deep false detection method based on the Heterogeneous Mixture of Experts model, named DFMoE, which incorporates a dynamic gating network that adaptively selects an appropriately sized expert network based on the characteristics of the input false samples.
2. Our method adaptively selects expert networks of different scales based on the differences in forgery characteristics, breaking the limitations of relying on a single network structure and enhancing the model's flexibility and adaptability.
3. We introduce adaptive data augmentation operations, where expert networks adaptively select appropriate augmentation methods, significantly improving detection accuracy and generalization capability.
4. Through extensive experimental validation, our method outperforms existing methods on multiple datasets, demonstrating significant improvements.

2   Related Work

In this section, we briefly review deepfake detection methods, which are predominantly categorized into two areas: image spatial domain-based detection methods and image frequency domain-based detection methods.

Image Spatial Domain-Based Detection Methods. Some early studies have achieved relatively good results in the field of binary classification, and some backbones have been proposed with good results, such as Xception [7] and Efficient-Net [33]. However, these backbones are not specifically designed for forgery detection tasks. When the model detects false images synthesized by unknown forgery methods, the accuracy of the detection decreases rapidly, and the robustness is insufficient when facing common perturbation methods such as image compression. Zhao [41] believed that the difference between real and fake faces mainly exists in subtle local areas, so he proposed a new multi-attention Deepfake detection Network, which enhances the texture information extracted by the model in the shallow network and fully excavates the subtle texture artifacts. However, the above methods often overfit and produce artifacts of specific forgery methods. In order to avoid overfitting specific forgery methods, Li [20] proposed the Face X-ray model to make judgments by detecting the edge splicing area between the forged face and the background. Relying on the detection of artifact traces of specific forgery methods, it has good generalization ability across data sets. Unlike Face X-Ray, which needs to rely on other faces with similar key points to generate fake faces, Shiohara [32] learned feature-representations with stronger generalization capabilities, and propose self-blended images (SBI) as synthetic fake images. It only transforms the key points of the face image itself, and at the same time cooperates with the data augmentation method to generate realistic Fake face images. These methods do not depend on using fake faces from a specific forgery technique to train the network. As a result, they exhibit strong generalization abilities when confronted with synthetic images generated by unknown forgery methods. However, due to their reliance on the self-forgery process, these approaches prove ineffective in dealing with fake images synthesized through unknown forgery methods. It performs poorly on fake images synthesized by whole face synthesis methods. In addition, Cao [5] proposed a RECCE framework for face forgery detection, which uses reconstruction classification to mine common features of real faces, and proposed a reconstruction-guided attention module that uses the difference between the reconstructed image and the original image as an attention map for Guide the model toward areas more likely to be tampered with. There is also some work on the interpretability of detection models. For example, Dong [11] assumed that the detection model determines the authenticity of an image by detecting information unrelated to the person's identity in the image. Therefore, the face identity is used as an auxiliary label to design a source feature encoder and The target encoder performs the identity recognition task, and the FST-Matching deep fake detection model is proposed to decouple the feature representations in the image that are relevant and irrelevant to the person identity recognition task, and improve the fake detection performance of compressed videos.

2.1   Image Frequency Domain-Based Detection Methods

Detection methods based on the image frequency domain mainly focus on mining high-frequency signals, phase spectrum, etc. in the image frequency signal, and use frequency domain features or fusion features of the frequency domain and spatial domain to detect deep facial forgery videos. For example, Qian [27] found that the artifact details caused by forgery methods can be well mined in the frequency domain; in order to obtain comprehensive frequency domain information, a frequency domain perceptual decomposition module was designed to adaptively capture the artifacts in the image. Forgery clues, since detection relies on frequency domain information, this method still maintains excellent detection performance in the face of highly compressed forgery images. Liu [23] found that cumulative upsampling will lead to significant changes in the frequency domain, especially the phase spectrum, so they proposed a new spatial-phase shallow learning (SPSL) method, which combines spatial images and phase spectrum to capture the upsampling artifacts of face forgery to improve transferability for face forgery detection. In order to more comprehensively capture artifacts in the frequency domain, Li [23] proposed an adaptive frequency feature generation module to extract differential features from different frequency bands in a learnable manner. At the same time, considering the different feature distributions of different forgery methods, single center loss (SCL) is proposed to improve the intra-class compactness of real faces and increase the inter-class difference between real faces and fake faces.

The above methods mainly use image frequency domain features for deep fake video detection, but ignore the pixel features of the original spatial domain features. Therefore, combining frequency domain and spatial domain features can effectively make up for the shortcomings of both. Therefore, Gu [14] proposed a progressive reinforcement learning framework to utilize RGB and fine-grained frequency cues to perform fine-grained decomposition of RGB images to completely decouple real and false trajectories in frequency space. Wang [38] proposed a multi-modal approach that combines frequency domain and spatial domain to mine robust forgery traces in images that do not change due to different forgery techniques. Chen [6] divided the original image/video frame into several areas. Taking into account the small difference between real areas and the large gap between real areas and fake areas, based on dividing the original image into several areas, The difference between two areas is calculated from both frequency domain features and spatial domain features to determine the authenticity of the video. Recently, Yan [39] proposed a simple yet effective detector to expand the forgery space by constructing and modeling the variations within and between forged features in the latent space, thus achieving a generalizable deepfake detector.

2.2   Mixture of Experts (MoE)

The core concept of the MoE [16] method lies in the introduction of multiple expert networks, enhancing the flexibility and adaptability of the model. Each expert network is specifically trained for a particular forgery type and possesses unique feature extraction capabilities. Through a gating mechanism, the model dynamically selects the most suitable expert network based on the characteristics of the input samples, significantly improving detection accuracy and generalization ability. The concept of MoE was first introduced in natural language processing [4,18,30]and computer vision [24,25,28,31]. Jacobs [16] initially proposed this supervised learning process, in which a system contains multiple independent networks, each processing a subset of all training samples. Shazeer [30] later discovered that not all expert networks are used-only a few experts participate in inference-thus greatly increasing model scalability with minimal computational overhead. Lepikhin [18] extended MoE to Transformers, and Fedus [13] simplified MoE routing algorithms, designing a more intuitive model improvement scheme that reduces communication and computation costs. Recently, Wang [36]proposed the Heterogeneous Mixture of Experts (HMoE) model, where experts are of different scales. This heterogeneity allows more specialized experts to effectively handle complex features. In our work, we draw inspiration from the concept of HMoE, incorporating a gating network to intelligently and adaptively select expert networks of different scales based on the differences in forgery features, thus achieving efficient deepfake detection.

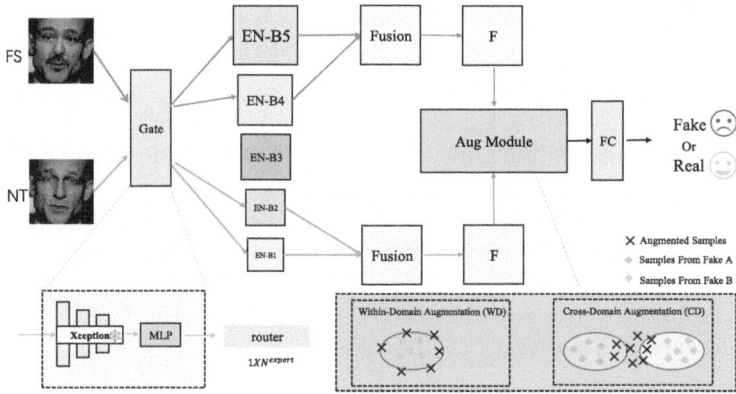

Fig. 1. The overall pipeline of our proposed method (two fake types are considered as an example). (1) Multi-scale feature extraction is performed using a pre-trained Xception network, with the early layers of the network frozen. (2) Expert networks of different scales are adaptively selected for training. (3) For the learning of the forgery feature, we apply the within-domain(WD) and cross-domain (CD) augmentation.

3   Method

We propose a novel architecture, DFMoE, based on Heterogeneous Mixture of Experts, which significantly differs from traditional training architectures. DFMoE consists of several key components: a fusion gating network, expert networks, and a data augmentation module. We design a multi-scale feature extraction and dynamic expert selection mechanism based on the MoE model, combined with both within-domain and cross-domain data augmentation strategies, to enhance the detection performance of both known and unknown types of forgeries.

3.1   Overall Architecture

Figure 1 illustrates the overall architecture of the proposed DFMoE model. The input images are processed through a pre-trained Xception network to extract features, serving as a shared feature extractor responsible for generating high-dimensional facial representations. These features are then embedded into an N-dimensional expert space via a multi-layer perceptron (MLP). Following this, the gating network dynamically selects the most suitable combination of expert networks (EfficientNet sub-networks), each learning forgery-specific features at different scales. Finally, after passing through a fusion module and a data augmentation module, the features are fed into a fully connected (FC) layer for binary classification of real vs. fake.

3.2   Gating Network

The gating network is the core mechanism of DFMoE, responsible for dynamically assigning expert networks based on the input sample's features. The gating network consists of two main parts: multi-scale feature selection and dynamic expert assignment. These components ensure that the system efficiently captures different types of deepfake features.

Multi-scale Feature Selection. To capture multi-scale features from forgery samples, we use the pre-trained Xception network to extract features from various scales. These features are processed by the MLP to generate a weight matrix W, which guides the gating network in weighting and selecting features from different scales.

Given an input image i, we define the feature extractor $f_{\text{Xception}}(I)$, which produces feature maps at N_{scales} different scales:

$$\mathbf{F}_i = f_{\text{Xception}}(\mathbf{I})_i, i = 1, \ldots, N_{\text{scales}} \tag{1}$$

These feature maps represent the input image's representations across different scales. Next, the MLP generates a corresponding weight vector W for each feature map:

$$\mathbf{w}_i = MLP(\mathbf{F}_i), i = 1, \ldots, N_{scales} \tag{2}$$

These weights measure the importance of each scale's features, determining which features are routed to the expert networks.

Dynamic Expert Assignment. We adopt a top-K routing strategy to select the most relevant expert networks, where K is a hyperparameter controlling the number of experts selected by the gating network at each time. Through experimentation, we found that setting $K = 2$ provided the best performance, leading us to use a top-2 routing strategy.

For each input sample, the gating network selects the top K most important features based on the weight matrix w and assigns the sample to the corresponding expert networks. Specifically, the gating network sorts the weights and selects the top-K features with the highest weights, then routes the corresponding features to the appropriate expert networks for processing.

Assuming that the gating network outputs a feature weight matrix $w = [w_1, w_2, \ldots, w_{N_{\text{experts}}}]$, we select the top K experts with the highest weights.

$$\text{Top} - \text{Kexperts} = \text{argmax}_K(\mathbf{w}) \tag{3}$$

In this study, the value of K is set to 2 based on experimental results, meaning each sample is assigned to two expert networks, which constitutes our top-2 routing strategy.

3.3   Expert Networks

Expert networks are the core modules in our DFMoE model, designed to handle different types and scales of forgery features. Based on the characteristics of the input sample, these expert networks are dynamically assigned, allowing them to process various types of counterfeit, thus improving detection accuracy and generalization ability.

Heterogeneous Expert Network Architecture. In the DFMoE model, we use the EfficientNet series (EN-B1 to EN-B5) as the heterogeneous expert network architecture. Each expert network processes the selected features from the gating network and extracts deep-level forgery-related features. These expert networks are specifically optimized for different forgery types and feature scales, forming a heterogeneous expert system. Specifically, given the input features $\mathbf{F}_{\text{selected}}$, chosen by the gating network, each expert network E_i extracts its corresponding high-dimensional feature representation:

$$\mathbf{z}_i = E_i(\mathbf{F}_{\text{selected}}), i = 1, \ldots, N_{\text{experts}} \tag{4}$$

where $\mathbf{z}_i$ represents the output feature vector of the i-th expert network.

Fusion of Expert Networks. To effectively integrate the outputs from multiple expert networks, we introduce a feature fusion module. By performing weighted summation or concatenation of the output features from the experts, we obtain a more representative global feature representation, thereby improving the overall performance of forgery detection. We adopt a weighted feature fusion strategy, combining the output feature vectors from the selected experts. Suppose the outputs from the top-K experts selected by the gating network are $z_1, z_2, \ldots, \mathbf{z_K}$, then the fused feature is defined as:

$$\mathbf{F}_{\text{fused}} = \sum_{i=1}^{K} \alpha_i \mathbf{z}_i \tag{5}$$

where α_i is the weight assigned to each expert network, calculated from the feature weight matrix W output by the gating network. This fusion approach leverages the expertise of each expert, combining the diversity of forgery features to effectively enhance the robustness and accuracy of forgery detection.

3.4 Adaptive Augmentation Module

In this study, we propose an adaptive augmentation module that dynamically determines the applicability of augmentation strategies based on the feature entropy of the expert network outputs and the network selection mechanism. For within-domain (WD) and cross-domain (CD) augmentation, we define three main augmentation strategies:

Feature Stretching Augmentation (FSA): This strategy expands the distances between features to generate more challenging samples. Specifically, the operation is as follows:

$$z_{aug} = z + \omega_j \cdot \alpha \cdot (z - \mu_i) \tag{6}$$

where α is a random coefficient, μ_i represents the center of the i-th forgery domain, and ω_j is the adaptive weight.

Feature Perturbation Augmentation (FPA): This strategy adds noise perturbations in feature space to improve robustness. It can be achieved by adding Gaussian noise:

$$z_{aug} = z + \omega_i \cdot \beta \cdot \mathcal{N}(0, \sigma^2) \tag{7}$$

where β is a scaling factor, and $\mathcal{N}$ is Gaussian noise.

Cross-Expert Feature Fusion (CFF): This strategy generates cross-expert augmented samples by performing linear interpolation between features from different experts. Let $f_i(x)$ and $f_j(x)$ represent the feature outputs of two different experts, the linear interpolation is computed as:

$$z_{aug} = \lambda f_i(x) + (1 - \lambda) f_j(x) \tag{8}$$

where λ is a randomly selected weight between 0 and 1. During the augmentation process, for each input sample, we first compute its feature output through the expert network f_i, and based on the gating network's selection and the feature entropy, we compute the adaptive weight w. The selection of the augmentation strategy no longer solely depends on feature entropy but is complemented by the output of the gating network, ensuring that the augmentation strategy and expert network selection mechanism work in tandem. The final augmented sample can be represented as:

$$z_{aug} = \text{AdaptiveAug}(f_i(x), \omega_i) \tag{9}$$

where AdaptiveAug represents a combination of the aforementioned three augmentation strategies, dynamically chosen and applied based on the adaptive weight ω_i.

3.5   Loss Function

To optimize the overall performance of the deepfake detection model, we designed a comprehensive loss function. This loss function consists of three components: binary classification loss $\mathcal{L}_{BCE}$, feature entropy-based expert assignment constraint loss $\mathcal{L}_{entropy}$, and augmentation consistency loss $\mathcal{L}_{consistency}$.

Parameter Penalty Loss. To prevent the model from excessively relying on large-scale experts during the expert selection process, which could lead to underutilization of smaller-scale experts, we introduce a parameter penalty loss. This loss is applied based on the hidden state size of the experts, ensuring that smaller-scale experts are activated for appropriate tasks, thereby avoiding resource waste. The specific loss is defined as follows:

$$\mathcal{L}_{P-Penalty} = \frac{1}{T} \sum_{i=1}^{N} M_i \cdot \widehat{P}_i \tag{10}$$

where $\mathcal{M}_i$ represents the average hidden state dimension of expert i, and i is the activation probability of that expert. By penalizing the use of experts with larger hidden dimensions, the model is encouraged to more efficiently utilize smaller-scale experts.

Expert Assignment Constraint Loss. To optimize the expert network selection and reduce redundancy among expert networks, we introduce an expert assignment constraint loss based on feature entropy. Feature entropy measures the uncertainty or complexity of the features, where high entropy indicates more challenging classification, and low entropy suggests simpler classification. By minimizing feature entropy, the model is encouraged to assign experts appropriately based on the complexity of the input sample. This loss increases the entropy of the expert selection process to prevent the model from over-relying on a particular set of experts. The entropy loss is defined as:

$$\mathcal{L}_{entropy} = -\frac{1}{N} \sum_{i=1}^{N} P_i \cdot \log(P_i) \tag{11}$$

where P_i is the selection probability of expert. By minimizing low entropy cases in the expert selection process, the model can more evenly distribute tasks among multiple experts, thereby improving generalization capability.

Augmentation Consistency Loss. To ensure consistency in the feature space between the original and augmented samples generated by expert networks, we propose an augmentation consistency loss $\mathcal{L}_{consistency}$. This loss is designed to constrain the augmented samples to retain the characteristics of the original features. Specifically, the consistency loss is calculated by comparing the Euclidean distance between the original sample features and the augmented sample features:

$$\mathcal{L}_{consistency} = \frac{1}{N} \sum_{i=1}^{N} \| f(x_i) - f(z_{aug}) \|_2^2 \tag{12}$$

where $f(x_i)$ denotes the feature representation of the original sample, and $f(z_{aug})$ represents the feature representation of the augmented sample. By minimizing this loss, we ensure that the augmented samples do not deviate from the original feature distribution, thereby enhancing the effectiveness of the augmentation strategies in the model.

Total Loss. Finally, the total loss function of the model is composed of the weighted sum of the above loss terms:

$$\mathcal{L}_{total} = \mathcal{L}_{BCE} + \lambda_1 \mathcal{L}_{P-Penalty} + \lambda_2 \mathcal{L}_{entropy} + \lambda_3 \mathcal{L}_{consistency} \tag{13}$$

where λ_1, λ_2 and λ_3 are hyperparameters that control the weights of each loss term. By adjusting these weights, the contributions of each loss to the total loss can be balanced, allowing for flexible control over expert assignment, diversity, and augmentation consistency during the optimization process.

4   Experiments

4.1   Settings

Dataset. To evaluate the generalization ability of our proposed framework, we conducted experiments on several commonly used deepfake datasets, including: Faceforensics++ (FF++) [29], Celeb-DF-v1 (CDFv1) [22], Celeb-DF-v2 (CDFv2) [22], Faceshifter (Fsh) [19], DeepfakeDetection (DFD) [12], Deepfake Detection Challenge (DFDC) [9] and its preview version (DFDCP) [10], and UADFV [21]. The FF++ dataset comprises 4,000 fake videos and 1,000 real videos, with the fake images generated using four facial forgery algorithms: Deep-Fakes (DF) [1], Face2Face (F2F) [35], FaceSwap (FS) [2], and NeuralTexture (NT) [34]. FF++ provides three versions with different compression rates: raw, high quality (c23), and low quality (c40). We selected the high-quality version (c23) for training and testing to ensure that the data's visual quality closely aligns with real-world application scenarios. The CDFv1 dataset contains 795 fake videos and 408 real videos generated from celebrity interview footage using DeepFake technology. CDFv2 is an upgraded version that adds 590 original videos and 5,639 corresponding fake videos sourced from YouTube, covering diverse ages, races, and genders. CDFv2 is currently one of the most challenging datasets for deepfake detection, with its fake videos being visually more difficult to distinguish. The Fsh dataset consists of 1,000 fake videos generated from real videos in FF++. The DFD dataset includes 363 real videos and 3,068 fake videos, employing various generation techniques that exhibit high data quality and diverse scenes. The DFDC dataset contains over 100,000 fake videos and 20,000 real videos, encompassing a wide range of forgery techniques and different contexts, significantly increasing the generalization requirements for models in real-world applications. DFDCP is an early version of the DFDC challenge, which, although smaller in size, still contains videos generated by multiple forgery techniques. The UADFV dataset consists of 49 real videos and 49 fake videos, sourced from YouTube, and is one of the earlier research datasets in the field of deepfake detection.

Evaluation Metrics. By default, we adopted the area under the ROC curve (AUC) and equal error rate (EER) as evaluation metrics. AUC measures the area under the Receiver Operating Characteristic (ROC) curve, while EER represents the false positive rate (FPR), equal to the true positive rate (TPR).

Implementation Details. We employed a pre-trained Xception model as the feature extraction network for the gating mechanism, while using an Efficient system network as the expert network. During the data preprocessing stage, Dlib [17] was utilized for face detection, cropping, and alignment. All face images were resized to 256×256. For both training and testing phases, we used the Adam optimizer with a learning rate of 0.0002. The batch size was set to 32, and each video was sampled with 32 frames for training and testing purposes. We set β in Eq. 7 as 0.2. In the loss function formulation, the hyperparameters λ_1, λ_2, and λ_3 were set to 0.1, 0.1, and 0.05 in Eq. 13, respectively. All models were implemented using the PyTorch framework and were trained on NVIDIA Tesla A100 GPUs.

4.2 Performance Evaluation

Within-Domain Evaluations. To further assess the performance of our proposed DFMoE model within the same dataset, we conducted within-domain evaluation experiments. The model was trained and tested on different forgery types within the FF++ (c23) dataset, covering four forgery methods: FF-DF, FF-F2F, FF-FS, and FF-NT. The experimental results are presented in Table 1, with AUC as the evaluation metric.

Table 1. Comparison of within-domain experimental results with state-of-the-art methods regarding the AUC (%) metric. Bold and underlined values correspond to the best and the second-best values

Method	Backbone	FF++ (c23)	FF-DF	FF-F2F	FF-FS	FF-NT
Meso4 [3]	MesoNet	62.69	75.06	62.10	58.64	57.91
Capsule [26]	Capsule	68.14	74.82	69.99	65.67	68.81
Resnet34 [15]	Resnet	97.80	99.02	98.87	99.16	96.19
Xception [7]	Xception	98.23	99.15	99.14	99.33	96.77
EfficientB4 [33]	Efficient	97.62	98.68	98.67	99.24	96.08
Face X-ray [20]	HRNet	95.26	97.98	99.04	99.15	95.59
FFD [8]	Xception	98.24	99.01	98.94	99.29	96.79
Recce [5]	Xception	97.98	99.08	99.05	99.34	96.13
RFM [37]	Xception	97.57	98.89	98.44	99.18	96.03
UCF [40]	Xception	98.50	99.29	<u>99.18</u>	99.40	96.67
LSDA [39]	Efficient	<u>99.05</u>	<u>99.37</u>	99.17	<u>99.47</u>	<u>97.41</u>
Ours	Efficient	**99.15**	**99.56**	**99.23**	**99.51**	**97.62**

In Table 1, our method demonstrates outstanding performance across various subtasks of the FF++ (c23) dataset. Specifically, DFMoE achieved AUC values of 99.56%, 99.23%, 99.51%, and 97.62% for FF-DF, FF-F2F, FF-FS, and FF-NT, respectively, surpassing all baseline models. In contrast, traditional models like Meso4 and Capsule performed poorly, with AUC values below 70% in all tasks. More mature models such as Resnet34 and Xception performed well but still showed some gap compared to our DFMoE model. This indicates that DFMoE, through its dynamic expert selection and adaptive enhancement strategies, can more accurately detect different types of forgery videos, demonstrating higher generalization ability and robustness. Overall, our method exhibits a clear advantage in handling complex forgery types, especially in the FF-DF and FF-FS tasks, where AUC exceeded 99.5%, validating the superior performance of DFMoE in deepfake detection tasks.

Cross-Domain Evaluations. To verify the model's generalization capability across datasets, we conducted cross-domain evaluation experiments. All models were trained on the FF++ (c23) dataset and tested on multiple public deepfake detection datasets, including CDFv1, CDFv2, Fsh, DFD, DFDC, DFDCP,

Table 2. Comparison of cross-domain experimental results with state-of-the-art methods regarding the AUC (%) metric. Bold and underlined values correspond to the best and the second-best values.

Method	Backbone	CDFv1	CDFv2	Fsh	DFD	DFDC	DFDCP	UADFV
Meso4 [3]	MesoNet	65.67	64.33	58.62	54.59	56.51	57.98	71.50
Capsule [26]	Capsule	65.59	67.48	63.06	65.65	63.89	64.89	91.60
Resnet34 [15]	Resnet	78.59	76.17	61.47	72.65	71.53	72.97	90.05
Xception [7]	Xception	74.36	74.93	66.73	_81.77_	70.46	75.32	95.30
EfficientB4 [33]	Efficient	81.03	77.60	67.56	69.54	63.51	71.01	_95.37_
Face X-ray [20]	HRNet	71.62	68.32	67.98	76.65	61.87	69.81	90.11
FFD [8]	Xception	78.49	77.70	65.88	80.12	69.45	76.55	94.32
Recce [5]	Xception	79.78	75.25	66.36	80.15	71.18	73.53	93.65
RFM [37]	Xception	78.79	75.17	61.62	78.55	68.16	72.71	93.70
UCF [40]	Xception	74.51	76.42	71.11	80.22	73.16	77.86	95.22
LSDA [39]	Efficient	_82.13_	_78.04_	_72.17_	81.75	_73.74_	_78.17_	95.17
Ours	Efficient	**83.25**	**79.32**	**73.10**	**81.92**	**73.95**	**78.51**	**95.58**

and UADFV. The evaluation metric was AUC, which measures the model's classification performance across different datasets. The results are shown in Table 2.

Table 2 presents the cross-domain evaluation results of different methods across various datasets. It is evident that performance varies significantly across datasets for different methods. Early models such as MesoNet and Capsule performed poorly in cross-domain tests, with AUC values generally below 70%, indicating that these models struggle to adapt to different types of deepfake data. Resnet34 and Xception, as stronger baseline models, performed reasonably well on several datasets, particularly on DFD and DFDC, with AUC of 72.65% and 81.77%, respectively. EfficientB4 performed notably well on datasets outside of FF++, achieving an AUC of 95.27% on the UADFV dataset, indicating good generalization capability for handling deepfakes from different domains. Among all tested methods, our model demonstrated strong generalization ability across most datasets, especially on CDFv1, CDFv2, DFD, and UADFV, where our method achieved AUC values of 83.25%, 79.32%, 81.92%, and 95.18%, respectively, significantly outperforming other comparison methods. Compared to other models, our DFMoE method is better at handling various types of deepfake data, mainly due to the proposed dynamic expert selection mechanism and adaptive enhancement strategies.

Robustness Experiments. In the robustness experiments, the aim was to evaluate the model's performance under different image perturbation conditions, especially when the input images are subjected to various common attacks or transformations (e.g., Gaussian blur, block perturbation, contrast change, saturation change, and JPEG compression). The results demonstrate how the model's performance changes across these scenarios. As shown in the Fig. 2,

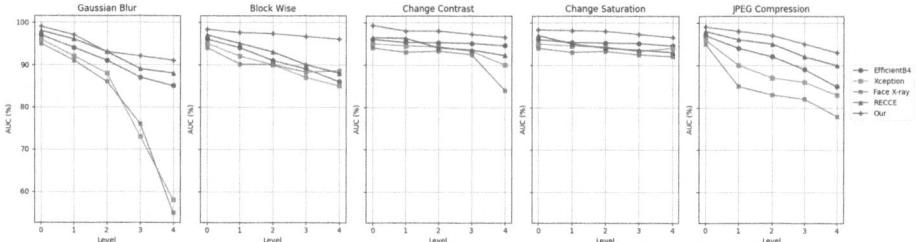

Fig. 2. Robustness against unseen perturbations: We report the video-level AUC (%) across five specific types of perturbations at five different degradation levels, comparing our results with four prior methods to demonstrate our robustness.

our proposed method demonstrates remarkable robustness compared to baseline models such as EfficientB4, Xception, Face X-ray, and RECCE.

Gaussian Blur: Even under severe blur levels (Level 3 and Level 4), our model maintains high AUC values, outperforming all baselines.

Block-Wise Perturbations: Our method experiences minimal performance degradation compared to others.

Contrast and Saturation Changes: The model remains consistently resilient across all levels of these perturbations, maintaining stable AUC values.

JPEG Compression: While most baseline methods show significant performance drops at Level 4, our model achieves the highest robustness, effectively addressing real-world compression artifacts.

Thanks to our multi-scale feature selection mechanism and data augmentation strategies, our model exhibits superior robustness under all types and intensities of perturbations, particularly under high-level perturbations. This demonstrates the strong adaptability of our model in real-world scenarios where image quality may degrade.

4.3 Ablation Studies

In this section, we discuss various techniques and methods to evaluate the performance and effectiveness of the proposed detection model. Through both quantitative and qualitative assessments, we delve into the underlying mechanisms of the model, focusing on the impact of different loss functions and network architectures on model performance.

Effect of Different Loss Functions. Our proposed method incorporates several key loss functions: parameter penalty loss, expert assignment constraint loss, and data augmentation consistency loss. To verify the impact of each loss, we first construct a baseline model A, which only utilizes the extracted features for detection through a classification head, without any additional loss terms.

Then, we develop several variant models to explore the impact of different combinations of loss functions on model performance: (1) Model B: includes only the parameter penalty loss; (2) Model C: includes both the parameter penalty loss and the expert assignment constraint loss; (3) Model D: includes the parameter penalty loss, expert assignment constraint loss, and data augmentation consistency loss. All models are trained on the FF++ (c23) dataset and tested on the FF++ (c23), CDFv1, and CDFv2 datasets. We use AUC (%) as the evaluation metric, and the results are shown in Table 3.

As shown in Table 3, the baseline model A achieves an AUC of 98.66% on the FF++ dataset, but its performance in cross-domain testing (DFDCP and CDFv2) is relatively poor. After incorporating the parameter penalty loss in model B, the performance on FF++ improves slightly, with a significant improvement in cross-domain performance. Model C, which further incorporates the expert assignment constraint loss, shows additional improvements in cross-domain generalization. Finally, Model D, which combines all losses, achieves the best performance across all datasets, especially in cross-domain tasks. The results indicate that introducing the parameter penalty loss, expert assignment constraint loss, and data augmentation consistency loss is crucial for enhancing the model's cross-domain robustness, particularly on the CDFv2 and DFDCP datasets. The combination of these three losses significantly improves the model's generalization ability.

Table 3. We trained various baseline models on the FF++ (c23) dataset and tested them on the FF++, DFDCP, and CDFv2 datasets, with the AUC (%) metric.

Model	$\mathcal{L}_{P-Penalty}$	$\mathcal{L}_{entropy}$	$\mathcal{L}_{consistency}$	FF++	DFDCP	CDFv2
A				98.66	76.58	72.49
B	✓			98.95	77.25	75.62
C	✓	✓		99.06	77.61	78.46
D	✓	✓	✓	**99.15**	**78.51**	**79.32**

Exploring Different Backbones in Gate Network.   To further enhance the feature extraction capabilities of our model, we explore the impact of different backbones on model performance. We selected ResNet34, EfficientNet-B4 (EN-b4), and Xception models, trained them on the FF++ (c23) dataset, and evaluated them on both in-domain and cross-domain datasets. The evaluation metrics are AUC (%) and EER (%), and the results are shown in Table 4. The experimental results demonstrate that Xception achieves the best performance in both in-domain and cross-domain tests, particularly excelling in cross-domain generalization. This indicates that using more complex feature extraction networks, such as Xception, can better capture subtle features in deepfake data, thereby enhancing cross-domain detection robustness.

Table 4. Exploring different backbones in Gate Network. All models are evaluated on the in-domain FF ++ (c23) dataset and cross-domain CDFv2, DFDCP, and DFD datasets regarding AUC (%) and EER (%).

Backbone	FF++		CDFv2		DFDCP		DFD	
	AUC (%)	EER (%)	AUC (%)	EER (%)	AUC (%)	EER (%)	AUC (%)	EER (%)
ResNet34	98.32	3.45	74.54	34.81	74.29	32.62	77.54	28.49
EN-b4	99.02	3.28	76.62	31.95	77.15	28.22	80.49	24.63
Xception	**99.15**	**2.56**	**79.32**	**26.56**	**78.51**	**26.46**	**81.92**	**23.55**

The Impact of the K Hyperparameter. To verify the role of the K value in expert network selection, we designed a series of experiments to assess the impact of different K values on model performance. We trained models on the FF++ (c23) dataset and tested them on the CDFv2 dataset, using AUC, AP, and EER as evaluation metrics. All experiments were conducted within the same DFMoE framework, keeping the model architecture and training parameters consistent. The results are shown in Table 5. As shown in Table 5, the model's performance varies with changes in the K value. When K = 2, the model achieves the best AUC, AP, and EER across both in-domain and cross-domain tasks, indicating that expert network selection is most effective with K = 2, allowing the model to better handle diverse feature distributions. When K becomes too large (e.g., K = 4 or K = 5), model performance declines slightly, likely due to an increase in model complexity, leading to overfitting. Moreover, in in-domain evaluations, performance fluctuations across different K values are minor, suggesting that the K value has less impact on relatively simple in-domain tasks. However, in cross-domain tasks, the influence of K is more significant, highlighting the importance of selecting the appropriate number of expert networks in cross-domain tasks. Considering both model performance and computational cost, we ultimately select K = 2 as the hyperparameter for expert network selection.

Table 5. Performance Metrics for Different K Values

K Value	FF++ (c23)			CDFv2		
	AUC (%)	AP (%)	EER (%)	AUC (%)	AP (%)	EER (%)
1	98.45	99.23	2.67	77.59	86.62	27.62
2	**99.15**	**99.52**	**2.56**	**79.32**	**88.41**	**26.56**
3	99.04	99.46	2.95	78.62	88.16	27.49
4	98.89	99.30	3.15	78.15	87.26	28.10
5	98.40	98.85	3.16	77.34	86.14	28.12

Impact of the Total Number of Experts On performance and Computational Cost. We further systematically analyze the impact of the total number of experts on performance and computational cost. We train on the FF++ dataset and test on the CDFv1 dataset. The evaluation indicators are AUC, ACC, inference time (ms), and FLOPs (GFLOPs) when increasing or decreasing the total number of experts.

Table 6. Analyze the impact of the total number of experts on performance and computational cost. Evaluation metric are AUC (%), ACC (%), inference time (ms) and FLOPs (GFLOPs).

Number of Experts	AUC (%)	ACC (%)	Inference Time (ms)	FLOPs (GFLOPs)
2	79.85	77.51	15.06	35.10
3	81.64	78.28	17.15	60.21
4	82.15	78.72	20.41	91.02
5	83.25	80.02	25.06	129.57
6	83.51	80.49	31.84	172.02

As can be seen from Table 6, AUC and accuracy improve with the increase in the number of experts, indicating that more experts can better capture complex forgery features, and the corresponding inference time and computational cost are also increasing. However, it is worth noting that when the number of experts exceeds 5, the performance improvement gradually slows down, so when we set the total number of experts to 5, it may be the best compromise between performance and computational efficiency, especially in resource-constrained environments.

In addition, in order to analyze the feasibility of deploying the model in a resource-constrained environment, we conducted a comparative experiment. Compared with the baseline, our method increased FLOPs by 14 GFLOPs, and the inference time increased by 20(%) accordingly. Despite the increase in computational overhead, the experimental results show that our proposed method can still maintain good performance in a resource-constrained environment, especially under reasonable optimization. In addition, we also discussed possible optimization directions, such as using lightweight expert networks or model pruning techniques to reduce computational costs. We expect that further optimization of these parts can effectively reduce computational overhead while ensuring performance and adapt to more resource-constrained scenarios.

Impact of Different Expert Network Fusion strategies on Performance.
In order to further analyze the impact of different expert network fusion strategies on the experimental results, we used three fusion methods for comparison, including weighted feature fusion, maximum fusion and average fusion. We chose to train and test on the FF++ dataset.

Table 7. Three fusion methods were used for comparison, including weighted feature fusion, maximum fusion and average fusion, and trained and tested on the FF++ dataset. Evaluation metric are AUC (%), ACC (%)

Fusion method	AUC (%)	ACC (%)
Weighted feature fusion	99.15	96.87
Maximum Fusion	99.02	96.24
Average Fusion	98.57	95.75

The results are shown in Table 7. The weighted feature fusion method achieved the best performance, the maximum fusion method had a slight decrease in performance, and the AUC reached 99.02(%), while the average fusion method had the worst effect, only achieving 98.57(%) AUC. To further explore the reasons for the performance differences, we analyzed the feature distribution and model decision mechanism under different fusion strategies. Weighted feature fusion can dynamically adjust the weights according to the output contributions of different expert models, so as to more effectively aggregate information of different scales and different feature spaces, so it performs best in a variety of forgery detection tasks. Although the maximum fusion strategy can capture some significant features, it is easy to ignore some critical information with small contributions, resulting in a slight decrease in performance. The average fusion strategy gives the same weight to all expert model outputs, which cannot fully reflect the heterogeneity advantages of different expert networks, so it performs the worst.

The Impact of Different Modules Within the Framework on Performance. To further verify the contribution of the enhancement module and the expert network to the model performance, we designed three sets of comparative experiments, including three configurations: "enhancement module + expert network", "enhancement module only" and "expert network only", and trained and tested them on the FF++ dataset.

The results are shown in Table 8. As can be seen from the results, the combination of the enhancement module and the expert network can achieve the best detection performance, with an AUC of 99.15(%) and an ACC of 96.87(%). This configuration fully utilizes the adaptive optimization capability of the enhancement module for the feature space and the accurate capture capability of the expert network for different scales and feature patterns. The configuration using only the enhancement module can improve the feature expression capability of the model, but due to the lack of diversity support of the heterogeneous expert network, the performance is reduced, with the AUC and ACC reduced to 96.21(%) and 92.65(%) respectively. The configuration using only the expert network performs slightly better than the case of only the enhancement module, with an AUC of 97.54(%) and an ACC of 94.56(%). This shows that the het-

Table 8. Three sets of comparative experiments, including "enhancement module + expert network", "enhancement module only" and "expert network only", were trained and tested on the FF++ dataset. Evaluation metric are AUC (%), ACC (%)

Module composition	AUC (%)	ACC (%)
Enhancement Module	96.21	92.65
Expert Network Module	97.54	94.56
Enhancement + Expert Network	99.15	96.87

Fake   Expert1(B1)   Expert2(B2)   Expert3(B3)   Expert4(B4)   Expert5(B5)

Fig. 3. Different expert networks capture different forgery features. Here we use networks B1 to B5 as five different expert networks.

erogeneity and multi-scale feature extraction capabilities of the expert network play an important role in improving the performance of the model.

Visualizations of the Captured Artifacts. We further use GradCAM to locate which regions are activated when detecting forgeries. The visualization results shown in Fig. 3 show that when using different expert networks to locate forged regions for the same forged image, experts 3 and 4 can accurately locate the forged regions, while other experts capture limited forged regions. Therefore, the gating network can help select experts 3 and 4 well, thereby capturing accurate forged regions to distinguish between true and false. This visualization further shows that our gating network estimates that the expert network captures more general forgery features.

5   Conclusion

In this paper, we introduced DFMoE, a framework for deepfake detection that integrates a Heterogeneous Mixture of Experts model and adaptive feature enhancement strategies to boost generalizability and robustness. DFMoE dynamically selects experts based on input features, enabling effective handling of diverse deepfake attacks. Compared to existing methods, our approach excels in detecting both known and unknown forgery types. The model leverages multi-scale feature extraction and applies in-domain and cross-domain augmentations to improve robustness. Our optimization strategy balances expert selection through parameter penalty and entropy loss, preventing over-reliance on large experts. Experimental results show DFMoE's superior performance across multiple datasets, particularly in detecting unknown forgery samples. Future work will focus on scaling the model, optimizing expert networks, and developing new augmentation techniques to keep pace with evolving forgery methods.

Acknowledgements. This work is supported by the Natural Science Foundation Innovation and Development Joint Fund Project of Shandong Province under Grant NO. ZR2023LZH009.

References

1. Deepfakes (2020). www.github.com/deepfakes/faceswap. Accessed 02 Sept 2020
2. Faceswap (2021). www.github.com/MarekKowalski/FaceSwap. Accessed 03 Sept 2020
3. Afchar, D., Nozick, V., Yamagishi, J., Echizen, I.: MesoNet: a compact facial video forgery detection network. In: 2018 IEEE International Workshop on Information Forensics and Security (WIFS), pp. 1–7. IEEE (2018)
4. Artetxe, M., et al.: Efficient large scale language modeling with mixtures of experts. arXiv preprint arXiv:2112.10684 (2021)
5. Cao, J., Ma, C., Yao, T., Chen, S., Ding, S., Yang, X.: End-to-end reconstruction-classification learning for face forgery detection. In: Proceedings of the IEEE/CVF Conference on Computer Vision and Pattern Recognition, pp. 4113–4122 (2022)
6. Chen, S., Yao, T., Chen, Y., Ding, S., Li, J., Ji, R.: Local relation learning for face forgery detection. In: Proceedings of the AAAI Conference on Artificial Intelligence, vol. 35, pp. 1081–1088 (2021)
7. Chollet, F.: Xception: deep learning with depthwise separable convolutions. In: Proceedings of the IEEE Conference on Computer Vision and Pattern Recognition, pp. 1251–1258 (2017)
8. Dang, H., Liu, F., Stehouwer, J., Liu, X., Jain, A.K.: On the detection of digital face manipulation. In: Proceedings of the IEEE/CVF Conference on Computer Vision and Pattern Recognition, pp. 5781–5790 (2020)
9. Dolhansky, B., et al.: The DeepFake detection challenge (DFDC) dataset. arXiv preprint arXiv:2006.07397 (2020)
10. Dolhansky, B., Howes, R., Pflaum, B., Baram, N., Ferrer, C.C.: The DeepFake detection challenge (DFDC) preview dataset. arXiv preprint arXiv:1910.08854 (2019)
11. Dong, S., Wang, J., Liang, J., Fan, H., Ji, R.: Explaining DeepFake detection by analysing image matching. In: European Conference on Computer Vision, pp. 18–35. Springer (2022)
12. Dufour, N., Gully, A.: Contributing data to DeepFake detection research (2019). https://ai.googleblog.com/2019/09/contributing-data-to-deepfake-detection.html. Accessed 24 Sept 2019
13. Fedus, W., Zoph, B., Shazeer, N.: Switch transformers: scaling to trillion parameter models with simple and efficient sparsity. J. Mach. Learn. Res. **23**(120), 1–39 (2022)
14. Gu, Q., Chen, S., Yao, T., Chen, Y., Ding, S., Yi, R.: Exploiting fine-grained face forgery clues via progressive enhancement learning. In: Proceedings of the AAAI Conference on Artificial Intelligence, vol. 36, pp. 735–743 (2022)

15. He, K., Zhang, X., Ren, S., Sun, J.: Deep residual learning for image recognition. In: Proceedings of the IEEE Conference on Computer Vision and Pattern Recognition, pp. 770–778 (2016)
16. Jacobs, R.A., Jordan, M.I., Nowlan, S.J., Hinton, G.E.: Adaptive mixtures of local experts. Neural Comput. **3**(1), 79–87 (1991)
17. King, D.E.: Dlib-ml: a machine learning toolkit. J. Mach. Learn. Res. **10**, 1755–1758 (2009)
18. Lepikhin, D., et al.: GShard: scaling giant models with conditional computation and automatic sharding. arXiv preprint arXiv:2006.16668 (2020)
19. Li, L., Bao, J., Yang, H., Chen, D., Wen, F.: Advancing high fidelity identity swapping for forgery detection. In: Proceedings of the IEEE/CVF Conference on Computer Vision and Pattern Recognition, pp. 5074–5083 (2020)
20. Li, L., et al.: Face X-ray for more general face forgery detection. In: Proceedings of the IEEE/CVF Conference on Computer Vision and Pattern Recognition, pp. 5001–5010 (2020)
21. Li, Y., Chang, M.C., Lyu, S.: In Ictu Oculi: exposing AI generated fake face videos by detecting eye blinking. In: IEEE International Workshop on Information Forensics and Security (WIFS) (2018)
22. Li, Y., Yang, X., Sun, P., Qi, H., Lyu, S.: Celeb-DF: a new dataset for DeepFake forensics. In: Proceedings of the IEEE/CVF Conference on Computer Vision and Pattern Recognition, pp. 1–6 (2020)
23. Liu, H., et al.: Spatial-phase shallow learning: rethinking face forgery detection in frequency domain. In: Proceedings of the IEEE/CVF Conference on Computer Vision and Pattern Recognition, pp. 772–781 (2021)
24. Lou, Y., Xue, F., Zheng, Z., You, Y.: Cross-token modeling with conditional computation. arXiv preprint arXiv:2109.02008 (2021)
25. Mustafa, B., Riquelme, C., Puigcerver, J., Jenatton, R., Houlsby, N.: Multimodal contrastive learning with LIMoE: the language-image mixture of experts. In: Advances in Neural Information Processing Systems, vol. 35, pp. 9564–9576 (2022)
26. Nguyen, H.H., Yamagishi, J., Echizen, I.: Capsule-forensics: using capsule networks to detect forged images and videos. In: 2019 IEEE International Conference on Acoustics, Speech and Signal Processing (ICASSP), ICASSP 2019, pp. 2307–2311. IEEE (2019)
27. Qian, Y., Yin, G., Sheng, L., Chen, Z., Shao, J.: Thinking in frequency: face forgery detection by mining frequency-aware clues. In: European Conference on Computer Vision, pp. 86–103. Springer (2020)
28. Riquelme, C., et al.: Scaling vision with sparse mixture of experts. Adv. Neural. Inf. Process. Syst. **34**, 8583–8595 (2021)
29. Rossler, A., Cozzolino, D., Verdoliva, L., Riess, C., Thies, J., Nießner, M.: FaceForensics++: learning to detect manipulated facial images. In: Proceedings of the IEEE/CVF International Conference on Computer Vision, pp. 1–11 (2019)
30. Shazeer, N., et al.: Outrageously large neural networks: the sparsely-gated mixture-of-experts layer. arXiv preprint arXiv:1701.06538 (2017)
31. Shen, S., Yao, Z., Li, C., Darrell, T., Keutzer, K., He, Y.: Scaling vision-language models with sparse mixture of experts. arXiv preprint arXiv:2303.07226 (2023)
32. Shiohara, K., Yamasaki, T.: Detecting deepfakes with self-blended images. In: Proceedings of the IEEE/CVF Conference on Computer Vision and Pattern Recognition, pp. 18720–18729 (2022)
33. Tan, M., Le, Q.: EfficientNet: rethinking model scaling for convolutional neural networks. In: International Conference on Machine Learning, pp. 6105–6114. PMLR (2019)

34. Thies, J., Zollhöfer, M., Nießner, M.: Deferred neural rendering: image synthesis using neural textures. ACM Trans. Graph. (TOG) **38**(4), 1–12 (2019)
35. Thies, J., Zollhofer, M., Stamminger, M., Theobalt, C., Nießner, M.: Face2Face: real-time face capture and reenactment of RGB videos. In: Proceedings of the IEEE Conference on Computer Vision and Pattern Recognition, pp. 2387–2395 (2016)
36. Wang, A., et al.: HMoE: heterogeneous mixture of experts for language modeling. arXiv preprint arXiv:2408.10681 (2024)
37. Wang, C., Deng, W.: Representative forgery mining for fake face detection. In: Proceedings of the IEEE/CVF Conference on Computer Vision and Pattern Recognition, pp. 14923–14932 (2021)
38. Wang, J., et al.: M2TR: Multi-modal multi-scale transformers for DeepFake detection. In: Proceedings of the 2022 International Conference on Multimedia Retrieval, pp. 615–623 (2022)
39. Yan, Z., Luo, Y., Lyu, S., Liu, Q., Wu, B.: Transcending forgery specificity with latent space augmentation for generalizable DeepFake detection. In: Proceedings of the IEEE/CVF Conference on Computer Vision and Pattern Recognition, pp. 8984–8994 (2024)
40. Yan, Z., Zhang, Y., Fan, Y., Wu, B.: UCF: uncovering common features for generalizable DeepFake detection. In: Proceedings of the IEEE/CVF International Conference on Computer Vision, pp. 22412–22423 (2023)
41. Zhao, H., Zhou, W., Chen, D., Wei, T., Zhang, W., Yu, N.: Multi-attentional DeepFake detection. In: Proceedings of the IEEE/CVF Conference on Computer Vision and Pattern Recognition, pp. 2185–2194 (2021)

Author Index

© The Editor(s) (if applicable) and The Author(s), under exclusive license
to Springer Nature Singapore Pte Ltd. 2025
P. Didyk and J. Hou (Eds.): CVM 2025, LNCS 15663, pp. 451–454, 2025.
https://doi.org/10.1007/978-981-96-5809-1

The manufacturer's authorised representative in the EU is Springer
Nature Customer Service Centre GmbH, Europaplatz 3, 69115 Heidelberg,
Germany. If you have any concerns regarding our products, please
contact ProductSafety@springernature.com

Printed and bound by CPI Group (UK) Ltd, Croydon, CR0 4YY
27/04/2026
02097586-0017